SOUTH AFRICA: A MODERN HISTORY

SOUTH AFRICA

A Modern History

FOURTH EDITION
UPDATED AND EXTENSIVELY REVISED

T. R. H. DAVENPORT

University of Toronto Press
Toronto and Buffalo

First edition 1977
Second edition 1978
Reprinted 1979, 1980, 1981, 1984
Third edition 1987
Reprinted 1989
Fourth edition 1991

Published in Great Britain by
MACMILLAN ACADEMIC AND PROFESSIONAL LTD
Houndmills, Basingstoke, Hampshire RG21 2XS
and London
Companies and representatives
throughout the world

First published in Canada and the United States by
UNIVERSITY OF TORONTO PRESS
Toronto and Buffalo

ISBN 0–8020–5940–6 (cloth)
ISBN 0–8020–6880–4 (paper)

Printed in Hong Kong

Canadian Cataloguing in Publication Data
Davenport, T. R. H.
South Africa: a modern history
4th ed.
Includes bibliographical references and index.
ISBN 0–8020–5940–6 (bound)   ISBN 0–8020–6880–4 (pbk.)
1. South Africa—History.   I. Title.
DT766.D38   1991   968   C91–093156–9

For Marian, Tony and Catherine
and in memory of Eric Stokes

Contents

Contents

SECTION II CHIEFDOMS, REPUBLICS AND COLONIES IN THE NINETEENTH CENTURY

Contents

List of Illustrations

List of Maps

List of Tables

Preface to the First Edition

The study of South African history, so dependent in the early part of this century on the work of George McCall Theal, has undergone two significant changes in the twentieth century and is now involved in the beginnings of a third.

The first resulted from the work of what may be termed the 'Macmillan School' after its pioneer W. M. Macmillan, who began to question the validity of the received version, above all in its presumption in favour of the 'colonial' as against the 'missionary' point of view in the inter-racial controversies of the early nineteenth century. Macmillan's followers have also been referred to as the 'liberal' school.

The second major change was a consequence of the revolution in the study of African history after the Second World War, with its new emphasis on the indigenous peoples of Africa, rather than on Africa as a focus for the study of the European imperial overflow. The history of Africa was 'decolonised'. The philosophical basis of this 'Africanist' school was indistinguishable from the liberal. It was largely a product of the discovery that the history of the peoples of Africa could be written in greater depth by a reflective correlation, in the writings of historians, of the findings of anthropologists, archaeologists and linguists.

This does not mean, however, that the whole of South African history has been twice rewritten, as the Soviet *Short Course* is said to have been rewritten after the elimination of the 'cult of personality' in the Khruschev era. South African historians, unlike their Russian counterparts, have not reached a series of changing unanimities in their interpretations of what happened. The traditional nineteenth-century version still has its adherents, still dominates large areas of the textbook world as if the Macmillan and the Africanist schools had never existed. Indeed, a picture emerges of conflicting schools which pursue their courses in isolation from each other. The Macmillan revision was largely ignored by the traditionalists, just as the Afrikaner nationalist rewriting of the conflict between Boer and Briton was largely ignored by English-speaking historians concerned with this imperial issue.

Yet there are some signs of change. The *Oxford History of South Africa*, the pioneer 'Africanist' interpretation, of which the first volume appeared in 1969, was noticed by traditionalists as well as by the Africanists for whom it catered. Few important reviews were neutral. It started a debate among historians, the keenness of which stemmed from the fact that the rival interpretations of historians seemed to touch directly on the live

xvii

public issues of the day. That remains the position in South Africa.

But the assumptions of the liberal Africanist school have also come under attack from Marxist historians who have criticised the liberals for what they term an inadequate conceptual framework, a reluctance to interpret the South African story in terms of defined categories of class conflict, or as a classic illustration of how rival power groups rationalise their actions in the light of fixed, immutable, utterly dominant economic interests.

It is impossible for the historian to escape the impact of this debate because conflicting *a priori* versions of the historical story have been pressed into the service of rival political power-groups at a moment of major confrontation in the country's history. On the one hand, the dogmatism of a white establishment assumes the perpetuation of racial difference to be part of a divine plan, or at any rate as a fixed point from which all policy calculations start. At the other extreme, a predominantly expatriate element see as inevitable the revolutionary overthrow of the existing order, on the ground that the inherent logic of the situation rules out the possibility of a peaceful transition to an acceptable social system.

If this book is to be labelled as the product of a school of thought, the author would hope to be classified as sharing the basic premises of the liberal Africanists, while admitting to inadequacy in one important respect: an inability to handle the vernacular source material which is rightly coming to be regarded as an essential tool for the historian of Africa. For this reason, above all, the best he can claim for the book is that it is an interim report, an attempt to present the current state of knowledge about a society in rapid transition. The book contains no optimistic assertion that economic growth and industrialisation are any kind of trumpet to flatten the walls of apartheid's Jericho, nor any assumption that major change will be effected through the medium of the existing political system, nor any suggestion that the opposites will happen either. Its function is not to predict, or to justify, but to look at the past in the light of tested standards, in the belief that the maintenance of such standards holds out the best hope for any society of any complexion in any age. These include adherence to the rule of law, which is not necessarily the same thing as the rule of laws, and is a very different thing from rule by decree. The rule of law is related to distributive justice, for a fair deal implies the power to pay for justice as well as the right of access to it. On the issue of political democracy versus pluralism the book takes a neutral stance. Dissimilar cultures have frequently failed to maintain harmony when grouped together in a single state; but when territorial partition has been introduced as a solvent, the solution – on the evidence of India, Ireland and Israel in our own times – is not necessarily rendered less volatile. Nor does this book recommend the overthrow of an avowedly unjust and violent society by even greater physical violence. Revolutions set a premium on power, whereas civilised government demands the taming of power. There are too many lions and foxes in the political world, but not enough people of compassion.

Grahamstown   T. R. H. D.
September 1976

Preface to the Second Edition

Candid critics have kindly drawn my attention to errors of fact and clumsiness of style. I have sought to correct these, and to bring the narrative up to date.

Grahamstown   T. R. H. D.
January 1978

Preface to the Third Edition

This is an extensive revision of the original work. Every chapter has been rewritten in the light of research completed or published since 1977.

Readers of the first chapter should notice a somewhat clearer appreciation of the work of archaeologists and historians into the origin of Khoisan and the Bantu-speaking peoples of the region, as well as echoes of some ingeniously persuasive writing on the great unrest of the early nineteenth century, known as the Mfecane.

Richard Elphick and Hermann Giliomee's *Shaping of South African Society* has, I hope, left its mark on Chapter 2, as on the estimate of the Dutch East India Company and Cape Calvinism in Chapter 3. That chapter also picks up new work in the 1820 settlement and the emancipation of the Khoikhoi.

The comparative study of African Chiefdoms in Chapter 4 has been turned round so as to present broad statements at the end rather than the beginning, to facilitate comparison with the Boer Republican and the Colonial societies in the next two chapters. The appearance of half a dozen excellent monographs on the history of particular African societies has made some rewriting necessary, though less here than in Chapter 7. Critics of the first edition sometimes argued, justly, that whereas the chapter on African Chiefdoms had been conceived largely as a structural study, that on the Boer Republics contained too little structure and too much narrative. Now, with more structural material on the South African Republic to draw upon, it has been possible to rectify the balance in part. I saw no reason to cut the narrative, however, since a story told in so much detail in Afrikaans histories has not been so fully told in English, while the politics of regional and religious conflict themselves have structural implications. Chapter 5 also picks up some recent work on the Transvaal background to the Anglo-Boer War.

Chapter 6, like Chapter 4, has been turned round, to place the comparison between the Cape and Natal at the end, not the beginning, and to finish rather than start with the debate over the meaning of Cape liberalism. The growth of diamond-mining in Kimberley, which was insufficiently noticed in earlier editions, also comes more into its own, thanks to the appearance of some informative new writing. The early history of African politics in the Cape Colony has recently come alive, largely through the work of André Odendaal, to whom I owe much. Norman Etherington's revival of the notion of Natal imperialism (previously highlighted by Edgar Brookes) may stand as representative of the new movement in that area.

In the section handling confrontation themes, Chapter 7 (on Black–White relations) has been considerably enlarged. Nearly every chiefdom worth notice in a general text now has its own specialist historian. Many of them emanated from the University of London, whose contribution to this and to other aspects of South African historiography in recent years has been exceptional. The chapter also seeks to present, rather more fully, the role of the missionaries in context, and to chart significant changes in the history of land ownership.

The leading developments which necessitated a re-think about Chapter 8 have been those relating to the history of the gold mines in the international economy, on which J. J. van Helten and Peter Richardson have usefully applied the ideas of monetary historians. I have also been able to draw upon new insights into the Anglo-Boer War, provided by the recent publication of several diaries left by participants of different kinds, and by the research of such scholars as Albert Grundlingh, Burridge Spies, Malvern van Wyk Smith and Peter Warwick.

Chapter 9, which presents the background to unification, had of necessity to focus on the revived debate about the success or failure of Milnerism, in the light of perceptive studies by Denoon, Marks and Trapido, Jeeves, Kubicek, and others already mentioned. In recent years we have also seen a much fuller presentation of the activities of black political movements prior to Union.

Work on the emergence of segregation has increasingly come to pinpoint the period 1910–24 (Chapter 10) as an important formative moment, whether that be in relation to land policy – and Colin Bundy's book appeared after the first edition of this *History* – or urban history, in which Maynard Swanson's work has a special place, or in the industrial field, where David Yudelman's treatment of the nexus between the Chamber of Mines and the young South African State could not fail to leave an impact on a mind baffled by the complexities of 'fractionalism'. Marian Lacey's insights into the relationship between farming and mining, with their conflicting labour demands, have also given food for much thought, especially in relation to the Hertzog era, 1924–39 (covered by Chapters 11 and 12). In the debate about the meaning of Afrikaner nationalism in the 1930s, and the rival claims for neo-Calvinist, neo-Fichtean and petty bourgeois origins, I have profited from the ideas of Irving Hexham, Dunbar Moodie, André du Toit and Dan O'Meara, and feel rather more warmth towards Hexham's approach than has been expressed in some recent writings.

The chapter on the Second World War (Chapter 13) retains most of its original shape and content, but draws on J. A. Basson's very detailed study of Transvaal Afrikaner politics and (as is the case with other chapters) I have drawn on several new doctoral theses relating to the history of South Africa's Indians.

The early chapters on Nationalist rule since 1948 have not been altered greatly; but more attention has been paid to black politics generally, for this was made possible by the completion of the Karis and Carter volumes, Gail Gerhart's study of Black Power, and the superb telling of the black political story since 1945 by Tom Lodge, to say nothing of the monographs which have now appeared on the Soweto violence of 1976.

On such topics as Homeland development, including the relocation (resettlement) of peoples, the creation of 'independent' states, and the various attempts to relocate the Coloured and Indian populations politically, the earlier edition of this book had little to say. An attempt is now made to look at these through the years of P. W. Botha's ministry to 1985 (Chapter 17). In Chapter 18, new questions tackled under the heading of foreign relations include the questions of boycott, sanctions, the status of the Cape sea route, the 'constellation' dream and the Nkomati accords.

In the concluding section of the book, now re-titled 'The Political Economy of South Africa', I have tried as in earlier editions to provide a cross-weave, by looking at individual themes in time depth. The treatment is now rather fuller, and – as an olive branch to colleagues in the Marxist camp – I have handled 'base' before 'superstructure'. It no longer seemed necessary or desirable to highlight the confrontation between liberal and Marxist approaches. That confrontation has already produced such stimulating debate that it seems better to look at it reflectively in the context of particular historical crises, than to set it out, as it were, in battle array.

Grahamstown   T. R. H. D.
January 1986

Preface to the Fourth Edition

During the four years which have elapsed since the last preface was written, South Africa has undergone a great deal of turbulence, and these words are being written at a moment when considerable uncertainty exists as to the direction in which the country is moving.

It seemed wise, therefore, to call a halt at two events which appear likely to become identifiable milestones: the release of Nelson Mandela from prison on 11 February, and the achievement of independence by Namibia on 21 March 1990. Beyond that, the promisé of a rational, negotiated devolution of power, and the threat of a reversion to jungle law, are too evenly poised for comfort. On the one hand, one is reminded of Machiavelli's frightening prediction that, when faced with a crucial political choice, humankind invariably chooses the least sensible course, which also seems to be the most heroic; but one is encouraged to think, on the other hand, that enlightened self-interest, linked to the social concern which a strong minority of informed South Africans, irrespective of race, still possess, may pull the Beloved Country through to better times.

Most of the changes made in this edition relate to the beginning and the end of the story, and are to be found in Chapters 1, 17, 18, 19 and 20.

The first chapter has been rewritten to take into account the new insights into palaeolithic rock art achieved by David Lewis-Williams and his team, and the imaginative though necessarily far more hesitant approach to the archaeological past reflected in the work of Martin Hall and others, as the discovery of new evidence threatens the coherence of earlier hypotheses. It has also become less easy to dismiss the unrest of the early nineteenth century, commonly known as the *mfecane*, as a self-contained outbreak of black on black violence. Earlier theories have once again come under attack through new emphasis on slaving and enserfment activities; but this needs to be correlated with a recent restatement of the case for an underlying ecological catastrophe, and it is not yet clear beyond reasonable doubt that traditional hypotheses have been dislodged.

For the rest, the chapters covering the central portion of South African history have not been significantly changed, though I have taken note of new work on the Kimberley story, in association with several new studies of Rhodes. Iain Smith's current work on late nineteenth-century politics, may also have filtered through via some helpful conversations on the background to the war of 1899–1902, and on the surprisingly modest contribution which the banking houses now appear to have made to the imperialist drive.

xxiii

There is now much more people's history to read, of which Paul Maylam's history of the African people, and Gavin Lewis's book on the politics of the coloured community are the most general works. This is an area in which historians working in South Africa have more than caught up with the initiatives from London lauded in the previous edition, and it has been a privilege to be able to draw on work of such quality as Jeff Peires's study of the Xhosa Cattle-killing, Helen Bradford's investigation of the rural I.C.U., Tim Keegan's descriptive and analytical presentations of rural black workers and peasants, and Josette Cole's monograph on Crossroads.

Of necessity most of the focus of this edition has fallen on the rapidly changing socio-economic and political scene since the mid-term crisis of P. W. Botha's Government. A sizeable flood of new writing is only partly picked up in the greatly extended bibliographical guide to this period. Scholarly exercises in contemporary South African history are few, perhaps necessarily so on account of the embargo placed on the free reporting of contemporary events; but this is counter-balanced by a revived interest – with good reason – in the study of constitutional law. A sophisticated debate has started, on the basis of empirical experience, about the effectiveness of economic pressure on the Republic. There has also been a good deal of new writing about black political leaders, as reflected in several works about Chief Buthelezi and the recent appearance of two lives of Nelson Mandela – which suggests that white public opinion is taking African leaders seriously for the first time in living memory.

Grahamstown   T. R. H. D.
April 1990

Acknowledgements

This *History* was first started when I was granted a Visiting Smuts Fellowship at the University of Cambridge, and enjoyed the hospitality of Magdalene College. As a volume in the Cambridge Commonwealth Series, its publication was entrusted to Macmillan, London, in association with Macmillan South Africa, who were subsequently for several years incorporated in Southern Books, and with the University of Toronto Press. I want to express my appreciation for the helpfulness of the editorial staff in all these publishing houses.

The Council of Rhodes University granted me leave to study abroad on three occasions so that I could work on the successive editions of this book, and subsidised my overseas travel on a fourth, for all of which I am very grateful.

On the academic side, my first acknowledgement is to the late Professor Eric Stokes, then General Editor of the Cambridge Commonwealth Series. The extent of my debt to other scholars, which is very considerable, is best picked up in the bibliographical references, though for help on particular points in this new edition I wish to mention John Coleman, Tony Cubbin, David Everatt, Janet Farquharson, Pierre Hugo, David Lewis-Williams, Rob Shell and Iain Smith.

Colleagues at Rhodes University in the Department of History and the Institute for Social and Economic Research, as well as my own research students, have provided helpful support, as have Michael Berning and Sandy Rowoldt and their staff in the Cory Library.

Thomas A. Dowson of the Rock Art Research Unit, University of the Witwatersrand, provided the drawings of Bushman paintings, and Oakley West of the Rhodes University Geography Department has revised and added to the maps.

To Betty, once again, my warm thanks for her critical and very supportive candour.

T. R. H. D.

Part One
The Prelude to White Domination

Section I
The Setting of the Human Problem

1 From the Dawn of History to the Time of Troubles

1.1 THE EARLIEST SOUTH AFRICANS

South Africa has provided a home for human settlement since very early times. The presence of homo sapiens goes back perhaps 125,000 years (Tobias). These 'first South Africans', as Inskeep calls them, were followed much later by hand–tool makers of the Middle Stone Age, probably 40,000 years ago. For the Late Stone Age, dating back to about 20,000 years before the present, some six hundred sites assigned by archaeologists to the so-called Wilton–Smithfield cultural system have been uncovered. They are characterised by small flake tools and weapons, and a few pottery finds, though they have so far thrown little light on the daily lives of their occupants.

But the once obscure linkage between these Late Stone Age people and the earliest distinctively negroid inhabitants, who may have arrived as early as 8,000 years ago, is no longer entirely dependent on guesswork, for three reasons. One is the growing certainty of physical anthropologists that the Khoisan (that is Bushman-Hottentot) and Negroid peoples emerge from common gene pools. The second is that before stock-raising and agriculture had arrived, people had always been reduced to gathering edible roots and hunting game to stay alive.

The third clue is provided by the remarkable evidence of rock art, which may go back some 26,000 years, according to Lewis-Williams, and which was still being produced in the nineteenth century. It has opened a way into the minds of the artists which would hardly have been thought possible even two decades ago. Drawing upon the observations of the German ethnologist, W. H. Bleek, and his daughter Dorothea, supplemented by help from living Bushmen, Lewis-Williams has established that many of the rock paintings must be associated with shamanistic beliefs, involving the ecstatic transformation of medicine-men and -women (who were and still are relatively numerous in Bushman society) into the body of an eland or other beast, on account of the relationship which was seen to exist between them in their shared experiences of life, and reflected above all in rites associated with hunting, rain-making, puberty, sickness and death.

These discoveries about the rock paintings have bridged the gap between the cultures of the Stone and Iron Ages, and helped to produce new perspectives for the archaeologists of southern Africa, which are of

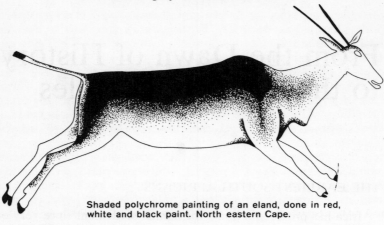

Shaded polychrome painting of an eland, done in red, white and black paint. North eastern Cape.

Seated hunter with bow and sectioned arrows. Shamans of the game wore eared caps. Natal Drakensberg.

Shaman partially transformed into an eland. Note eland horns and hoofs. North eastern Cape.

Transformed shaman. Note spirit line from head and nasal blood.

Copies by
Thomas A Dowson,
Rock Art Research Unit,
University of the Witwatersrand.

1   The rock art of the hunter-gatherers

considerable importance for the study of history as well. It is now necessary to adopt a much less dogmatic, culture-bound approach to the demographic, economic and cultural changes which overtook the region during the Iron Age, and stereotypes of earlier generations have had to be discarded as unhelpful. The hope, cherished until the 1980s, that it would be possible to work out a coherent 'Iron Age package' (Hall), in which the evidence of physical anthropology, linguistics, ceramics, farming practices and metallurgy would disclose the broad features of datable human migrations from north to south, in accordance with commonly held assumptions, has largely been abandoned.

There is a growing consensus that earlier racial distinctions – for example between Khoisan and Negroid peoples – must give place to the concept of 'breeding populations' out of which distinctive 'gene pools' emerged under different environmental influences. Scholars prefer to talk about 'traditions' rather than 'cultures' in the classification of research finds, so as to allow for more flexibility of interpretation where the divisions between cultural systems are not clear. Thus earlier attempts to trace a pattern of human migration on the evidence of pottery types linked to language affinities have broken down on account of the difficulty of correlating ceramic evidence with that from linguistics. The manner and the dating of language diffusion are particularly difficult to measure even if, as Ehret found, significant contact between human groups can be traced through the spread of 'loan words' which have cultural or economic significance. Nor is it legitimate to assume that mass migration of peoples from the north happened at all, in view of the possibility that farming practices, vocabularies, pottery and metallurgical skills, can as easily be borrowed as imposed by conquest. But this is not to say that there was no movement, for, as will be shown, movement of people across the continent with new techniques often provides the most convincing explanation for the changes which took place.

It is also becoming clear that the explanation of the spread of technology, without which human movement cannot be seen in context, requires an overview of changes in the continent of Africa as a whole. Thus the spread of pastoralism in Africa may well have resulted from the desiccation of the Sahara (once a region in which crops were habitually grown) after about 6000 BC. Compelling arguments have proposed its movement southwards into the west and east African savannahs, and it is very likely that stock-holding nomads, moving from the desiccated regions of the north, took with them techniques of metallurgy which seem to have been acquired through contact with the Mediterranean world, but could have been developed in the Saharan region, not only for the manufacture of weapons, but – more significantly – for the cutting of crops. The iron blade made the reaping of the tough stems of sorghum possible, and this in turn facilitated the emergence of agriculture.

1.2   THE KHOISAN PEOPLES

San hunter-gatherers, likely descendants of the Late Stone Age peoples described above, may never have exceeded 20,000 in number. They lived in small, loosely-knit patrilineal bands of twenty to two hundred persons. They were highly mobile on account of their dependence on game, and for the same reason widely dispersed territorially. Their political organisation was very rudimentary. Chiefs, about whom little is known, commonly seem to have had ritual importance in rain-making and in various other ways, and they seem to have been respected as leaders of kin-groups, but to have had almost no institutionalised authority at all. San languages have been classified by Westphal in three main groups, located respectively today in south-eastern Angola, between the upper reaches of the Zambesi and the Limpopo, and on the Botswana–Namibian border in the northern Kalahari [see Map 1].

The similarity between the main surviving Khoikhoi language, Nama, and those of the middle Bushman group (Tshu-Khwe) has led writers such as Elphick, the historian, and Robertshaw, the archaeologist, to accept that in origin the Khoi were hunter-gatherers speaking Tshu-Khwe dialects, who obtained cattle from some outside source further north about 2,000 years ago, and in consequence acquired a self-sufficiency which enabled them to migrate in search of new pastures. Linguistic arguments are advanced by Ehret to suggest that Khoikhoi words for cow, goat, ram and milk-ewe derived from Central Sudanic, not Bantu, languages. Although some, notably Cooke and Robertshaw, argued from ceramic evidence that the Khoikhoi migrated westwards from northern 'Botswana' into Namibia, then southwards into the western Cape and beyond, Elphick has suggested a southward route east of the Kalahari to the Orange–Vaal confluence, at which point some continued southwards to the coast and then moved either east or west, while others travelled down the Orange to become the Nama people. Elphick's argument seems the stronger on linguistic grounds, for similarity between the languages of the Nama and the Kora (on the middle Orange), and dissimilarity between those of the Nama and the Cape Khoi, suggests that the latter had not migrated south from Namaqualand.

The Khoikhoi, numbering at most 100,000 people when the Dutch arrived, according to Elphick's calculation (which is half Monica Wilson's estimate), lived mainly along the Orange and on the coastal belt stretching from Namibia to the trans-Kei. The Umzimvubu river is sometimes taken as the limit of their settlement; but there is some speculation, based on the influence of Khoi clicks on the Zulu as well as the Xhosa languages, that they may have penetrated Natal. They had a more elaborate social organisation than the San, and were distributed in patrilineal tribes of up to 2,500 members, and occasionally more. They possessed fat-tailed sheep of Persian origin, and cattle – generally the long-horned strain from which the modern 'Afrikanders' emerged, rather than the lighter Sanga strain possessed by the Nguni. It seems that before the white man's arrival they conducted a trade with their Bantu-speaking neighbours in cattle and

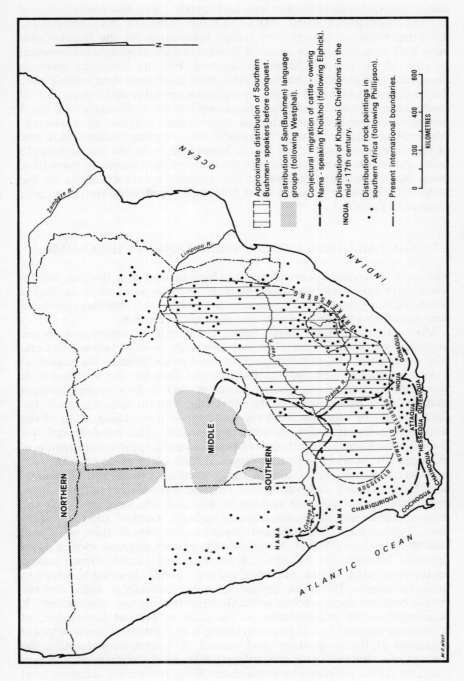

Map 1 Bushman and Khoikhoi settlements in pre-colonial times

dagga, and to a small extent in iron and copper. They also interacted, and to some extent intermarried, with Cape Nguni, Tlhaping and other groups. After the white settlement they traded their cattle for the Dutch Company's tobacco, and began to act as brokers in a developing trade between the Europeans and the Xhosa to the east. But the European advance eventually cost the Khoikhoi their land, their stock, and their trading role. Twice defeated in battle in the seventeenth century, and decimated by smallpox in 1713 and 1755, they ultimately lost their identity as a distinct group. Most were driven into the white man's service, as herdsmen, labourers or militiamen in the Colonial forces, or gained admission to one of the mission stations set up by the Europeans from the late eighteenth century onwards. Some withdrew to the valley of the Orange, to leave their mark on the turbulent frontier of the nineteenth century, those on the lower Orange being referred to as Nama[qua] and those on the middle Orange as Kora[na].

1.3   THE EMERGENCE OF BANTU-SPEAKING CHIEFDOMS

The myth, once held in innocence and long propagated, that the Bantu-speaking peoples arrived as immigrants on the highveld of the trans-Vaal at about the same time as the Europeans first settled in Table Bay, has been demolished as a consequence of archaeological research.

Most writers until the 1980s linked the spread of language with the migration of people. Thus Phillipson originally posited two routes, one (the eastern stream) crossing north of the Congo basin to the region of Lake Victoria between 200 and 100 BC, and then moving southwards in about the second to the fourth centuries AD in two prongs towards 'Zambia' and 'Mozambique'. The other (the western stream), fed in the third century by migrants from the eastern group travelling south of the tropical forest, moved directly south into 'Angola'. This was followed by a second subsequent concentration of peoples in the approximate region of 'Katanga', from which a further dispersal took place at about 1000 AD, northwards into 'Uganda' and 'Kenya', south-eastwards into 'Tanzania' and 'Mozambique', and southwards into the trans-Vaal. Huffman, however, proposed a different pattern of advance. He suggested that the western stream moved south-eastwards through 'Zambia' and the eastern trans-Vaal to the 'Zululand' and 'Natal' coasts, where they were well established before 500 AD. Meanwhile the eastern migrants moved down the coast between 250 and 350 AD, while a third, central stream moved southwards into southern 'Mashonaland' by 550 AD. In order to adjust to further evidence, Phillipson revised his thesis radically in 1985. But the debate between these scholars is mainly important for two reasons: first, it demonstrated the impossibility, in the state of present knowledge, of reconciling ceramic and linguistic evidence with a theory of the southward migration of Bantu-speakers; and second, it helped to undermine the concept of a short 400-year chronology for Bantu-speaking migration into southern Africa proposed by Schofield in 1935, and widely accepted until the 1960s. That chronology was subsequently demolished, with the help of carbon-14 dating techniques, by the investigation of Iron Age sites in the trans-Vaal and along the south-east coast (Hall), for Silver Leaves near Tzaneen, Broederstroom west of Johannesburg, and Enkwazini and Mzonjani in Natal, have yielded carbon dates from the third to the fifth centuries AD.

The southward penetration of pastoralists, as already noted, brought Khoikhoi stock farmers to the western Cape, where sheep can be traced to the early Christian era, and cattle to about the end of the first millennium AD. But for the beginning of agriculture it is necessary to look to the east. The growing of bullrush millet, associated with the very early settlements, and (from about 1700) of maize, which required much higher rainfall, limited the main areas of settlement to the summer rainfall regions. There a pattern of mixed farming developed, as settlers acquired livestock and lived as a rule in small villages within range of the sweetveld pastures up to 1,000 metres above sea level.

The evidence points to major cultural changes at the start of the late Iron Age, though as Inskeep has observed, all the elements of the later Iron Age were already present in the earlier. Livestock increased, so did the population. The villages tended to grow in size, and settlement on the highveld spread. Forms of social and political organisation now became more complex, pottery styles became more localised, stone buildings began to appear, and metal production became linked with trading activities beyond the settlement itself. Indeed, the distribution of communities on the highveld came to depend largely on the location of minerals – gold, copper, and above all iron ore – and on the directions followed by new trade routes between Mozambique and the highveld. Phalaborwa and Great Zimbabwe were important centres for this trade; but it now seems that the settlements at Mapungubwe and Bambandyanalo in the Limpopo valley, which were once thought to be tributary to Great Zimbabwe, existed in their own right as trading centres before Great Zimbabwe came into its own.

The works of Garlake, Huffman and Beach leave little doubt that the visible remains of this impressive settlement represent a late Iron-Age cattle-raising community of over 10,000 people which reached the height of its prosperity in the twelfth to the fifteenth centuries as an assertive military power able, thanks to its geographical position, to control trade between the gold-producing areas of 'Matabeleland' and the coast. The buildings were unquestionably the work of Bantu-speakers, even if the possibility of coastal influence on their decoration cannot be discounted. Great Zimbabwe's external trade links have been demonstrated by the discovery of Persian pottery and Islamic glass on site, together with quantities of Ming glazed stoneware; but there is virtually no blue and white Chinese porcelain which had replaced stoneware on the coast by about 1500. The commercial decline of the settlement was linked with that of Kilwa. The collapse of Great Zimbabwe dates from the sixteenth century mainly as a result of economic exhaustion. This probably induced a migration westwards to Khami (near the present Bulawayo), not northwards to establish an 'empire' of Mwene Mutapa, as has often been supposed. Another Shona state, Torwa, now emerged, based on Khami, and it was here that a domestic revolution in the late seventeenth century saw the emergence of a new ruler, the Changamire, whose followers were collectively known as Rozvi. They developed a strong government sustained by the organised collection of tribute from client chiefdoms on their periphery, and by asserting control over the succession to subordinate chiefdoms. They held off both the Mwene Mutapa (a petty ruler south of the Zambesi who had none of the imperial authority vested in him by tradition), and also the Portuguese. That Rozvi rule had an unsettling effect on their neighbours can hardly be doubted, for both the Venda and the Lovedu south of the Limpopo have traditions of flight from the Changamire in the north, though in Beach's view the Changamire's power has been exaggerated.

Four main groups are normally distinguished among the Bantu-speakers south of the Limpopo. These were the Venda themselves, the Sotho-Tswana, the Nguni and the Tsonga. The distinction is essentially linguistic, and the evidence points to the likelihood that at some stage there were several distinct southern Bantu cultures which subsisted for a considerable period, either north or south of the Limpopo, in isolation from each other.

The Venda of the Soutpansberg, though speaking a language akin to Shona, have cultural associations with the Sotho, and nurtured the distinctive craft traditions of the subordinate Lemba, who may have had earlier Arab associations, in metalwork, pottery and weaving. Venda traditions remain largely unexplored, but they began to flourish as a people with the southward shift of east coast trading activity during the eighteenth century, when Inhambane and Delagoa Bay began to eclipse Sofala, and iron- and copper-working spread in the trans-Vaal.

The original Sotho-speakers are not easy to identify. The area of Sotho dominance between the Drakensberg, the Kalahari and the Limpopo was apparently occupied by three settler waves: first, the Fokeng; then, the Rolong and the Tlhaping, who possessed similar cultures, and with whom it seems possible to associate the beginnings of iron-smelting; and subsequently those chiefdoms – the Hurutshe, Kwena, Kgatla, Ngwato, Ngwaketse, Pedi and others – which looked back to a founder named Mangope (as distinct from Morolong of the Fokeng) and which survived into the twentieth century as separate political entities.

Though Van Warmelo remains cautious, Legassick has posited a further distinction between the Kgatla and the Kwena clusters, arguing that they acquired traditions of a common ancestry only at a late stage in their development. The Kwena, following this line of argument, dispersed during the sixteenth century from a centre in the western trans-Vaal, and spread westwards towards the Kalahari and south-eastwards to the upper Caledon valley. One sub-group, the Hurutshe, who without question developed iron-smelting on a considerable scale, moved to the headwaters of the Marico river, driving the Rolong southwards. Another group of Kwena moved to the region of Swartkoppies on the Crocodile river. A third group, who have a tradition of having legitimised their occupation by intermarriage with the Fokeng, crossed the Vaal river and entered the districts of present-day Frankfort and Vrede, where they were established by the end of the eighteenth century. Meanwhile the Kgatla, who fissioned in about 1500, at about the same time as the Kwena, spread over the eastern trans-Vaal. They gave rise to chiefdoms such as the Phuting, the Kgoloko (which would later become identified with the southern Sotho) and the Pedi, who moved to the Leolu mountains in the eastern trans-Vaal in the mid-seventeenth century, incorporated a large population in the eighteenth, and may well have anticipated the northern Nguni in the development of efficient state-building techniques. The Tlokwa and Lovedu were also sub-groups of the Kgatla, as were the Karanga (Kgalaka) north of the Limpopo.

At the time when the Kgatla and Kwena were spreading across the trans-Vaal, the Nguni were well established in the coastal regions of Natal and the trans-Kei. Portuguese travellers shipwrecked off the southern African coast came across Bantu-speaking peoples in the coastal regions in the sixteenth and seventeenth centuries, and received the impression of a considerably larger settlement of people on the sweetveld pastures set back from the coast – a people they described on one occasion (1554) as 'very black in colour, with woolly hair', and on another (1593) as herdsmen and cultivators of millet, living in small villages in huts made of reed mats, practising circumcision (which was not a Khoikhoi custom), obeying chiefs called 'ancosses' (*nkosi*, an Nguni term), and being prepared to barter cattle for iron and copper.

The argument for a very early settlement of the Natal and trans-Keian coastal region by the Nguni peoples derives strength from further considerations. The Xhosa have a tradition of an ancestral home in the upper Umzimvubu valley. Some Nguni groups living in the trans-Vaal, notably the Ndzundza, or Transvaal Ndebele, who now speak Sotho, have a tradition of having arrived there very early from the south-east. On the negative side, Theal's identification of the 'Mumbos', whose southward crossing of the Zambesi is recorded in the Portuguese documents, with the Mbo of later history, was a guess, while the arguments of A. T. Bryant, the most articulate theorist of an Nguni migration from the north, have been shown to be inaccurate in important details. Van Warmelo, the pioneer of South African ethnography, was and remains sceptical of all theories about Nguni origins. The most that can be said, perhaps, is that migration of Nguni-speaking peoples from the north at some early date is likely, and that – as Marks and Gray have shown with reference to various lesser chiefdoms among the northern Nguni, and the Xhosa, Mpondo and Mpondomise among the southern – the main axis of Nguni migration prior to the Shakan wars was fairly consistently in a south-westerly direction.

The Tsonga, occupying the coastal area from the Save river in Mozambique as far south as St Lucia Bay, spoke a language very different from Zulu. They differed culturally from the Zulu in some respects – by being fish-eaters, for example, whereas the Nguni in general had fish taboos. Their control of the hinterland of Delagoa Bay gave them a special role in the promotion of trade during the eighteenth century, with iron and

copper, ivory and slaves, as the main commodities. Tsonga trading activities ranged inland, along routes which reached the iron-smelting regions of
the western trans-Vaal, involving the Pedi as middlemen. North and south
along the coast, they sought ivory and introduced European ware – cloth,
beads, brassware and, later on, guns. Some of the ivory exported through
Delagoa Bay came from Natal, and Natal received substantial imports.
Trade goods landed at Delagoa Bay were seen on the Umzimvubu, and
Tsonga traders from Delagoa Bay were encountered at Ngqika's kraal in
the eastern Cape. At first it was the Tsonga Tembe who dominated the
trade from their base on the shores of Delagoa Bay, but in the course of the
eighteenth century control passed from them to an offshoot chiefdom, the
Mabudu, who established themselves on the Makatini Flats south of the
Bay at the latest by 1794.

1.4   THE UPHEAVALS OF THE EARLY NINETEENTH
        CENTURY

By this time the European settlement had not only taken root in the
western Cape [see pp. 19ff], but the vanguard of its frontiersmen had
already made contact with the Bantu-speaking communities east of the
Gamtoos river and north along the valley of the Gariep (Orange). In the
early years of the nineteenth century, not long after this initial contact, a
major dislocation took place among the Bantu-speaking chiefdoms, the
causes of which, like the problem of Bantu origins, have become a matter
of contention. The troubles have been referred to as the *Mfecane*, a Xhosa
term perhaps derived from *ukufaca* ('to be weak, emaciated from hunger').
The Sotho equivalent, *Lifaqane* (pronounced *Difaqane*) conveys the notion of forced removal. It seems likely that these terms each throw
significant light on the crisis.

The broad picture of a massive human tragedy stands out; but as soon as
one begins to ask why the events were significant, differences of perspective, which have tainted the historical awareness of later generations, begin
to emerge. One such, by ascribing the responsibility for the troubles to the
evil genius of Shaka Zulu, or Mzilikazi of the Ndebele, or the Tlokwa
queen MmaNthatisi, has diverted attention away from the structural aspect
of the troubles and helped to foster a damaging caricature of some black
communities, with possible long-term implications (Cobbing, Hamilton).
Another assumption has been that the highveld was effectively cleared of
black occupation as a result of actions for which blacks themselves were
entirely responsible, thus leaving the way clear for the Voortrekkers a
decade later. This distorted the vision of later generations with regard to
the vital issues of white ownership and black access to the land (Davenport
and Hunt).

The crucial question on which clarity is needed, and which has not yet
been adequately resolved, is the extent to which the widespread violence,
which undoubtedly took place, was a product of developments internal to
African society, and the extent to which it was precipitated by pressures on

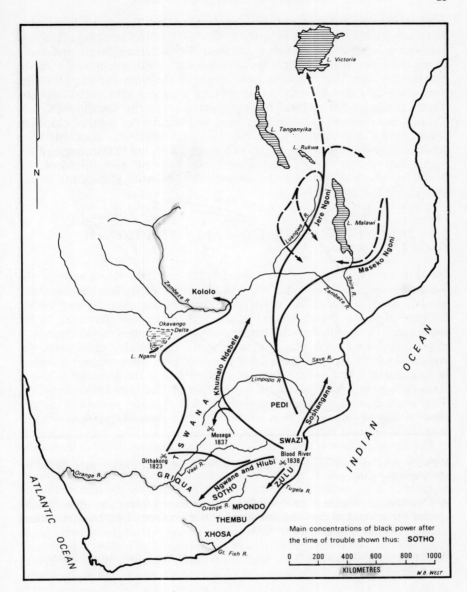

The following labels appear on the map:

L. Victoria

L. Tanganyika

L. Rukwa

Luangwa R.

Jere Ngoni

L. Malawi

Maseko Ngoni

Shire R.

Zambeze R.

Kololo

Zambeze R.

Okavango Delta

L. Ngami

Save R.

Khumalo Ndebele

Limpopo R.

PEDI

Soshangane

T S W A N A

SWAZI

Mosega 1837

Blood River ✗ 1838

INDIAN OCEAN

Dithakong 1823

Vaal R.

GRIQUA

Ngwane and Hlubi

SOTHO

ZULU

Orange R.

Orange R.

MPONDO

Tugela R.

THEMBU

XHOSA

Gt. Fish R.

ATLANTIC OCEAN

N

Main concentrations of black power after
the time of trouble shown thus: **SOTHO**

0   200   400   600   800   1000

KILOMETRES

W.O. WEST

The problem of the Mfecane

Map 2A, based on J.D. Omer-Cooper's *Zulu Aftermath*, shows a reconstruction of
the unrest of the 1820s as a violent outward movement of peoples from the
northern Nguni-speaking heartland. For this a political explosion resulting from
endemic drought, and/or external trade links, have been proposed, with a focus on
Zulu power.

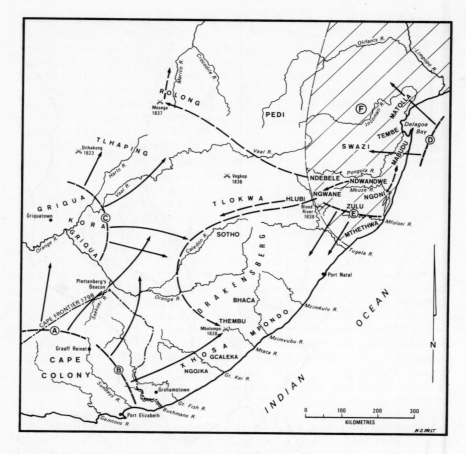

Map 2B picks up new emphases, and the reformulation of earlier ones, based on the following pointers:

A   Northward advance of trekboers in search of grazing, game and labour following the opening of the Cape northern frontier from the 1770s. Mission stations set up in the Orange River valley.

B   European–Xhosa conflict from the 1770s opens the Cape eastern frontier for settler expansion.

C   Griqua and Kora labour raids in regions north of the Orange River, presented as the explanation of the battle of Dithakong, 1823. In association with the white advance they destabilise the highveld and the Caledon Valley (Cobbing).

D   Trading from Delagoa Bay, mainly in ivory, as occasion for coalescence of Nguni-speaking chiefdoms (Wilson, Smith, Hedges). Slave-trading proposed as the main cause of the destabilisation (Cobbing), but only as a consequence (Harries).

that society from outside, and if so, of what kind and by whom.

Ingenious speculations have been predicated on the assumption that the *Mfecane* was essentially an event determined by internal stresses. Thus Gluckman argued in 1960 that 'by the end of the eighteenth century Zululand was becoming overcrowded in terms of current methods of land use'. Guy interpreted this to mean that the population had outstripped its resources, on account of the ease with which the patrilineal segmentary lineage system of the northern Nguni could expand production in times of plenty, as household heads acquired more wives through the possession of more cattle and each wife's homestead became a unit of production, to such an extent that this made survival difficult in times of drought. This ingenious linkage of production mode and economic crisis may be hard to substantiate; but it cannot be shrugged off in the light of Newitt's fresh evidence on the severity of the droughts which affected the whole region between 'Natal' and 'Malawi' in 1794–1802 and 1817–31. This evidence suggests reasons for a great deal of 'emaciation and hunger'.

Wilson and Smith both argued that the rise of powerful chiefdoms in south-east Africa, which preceded the *Mfecane* and gave it an intelligible setting, was itself a consequence of the impact of new forms of external trade. This thesis has been developed by Hedges's work on the ivory trade from Delagoa Bay, which reached a peak in the second half of the eighteenth century. But while ivory-trading could generate competition among the indigenous communities, and thus promote state-formation, as it assuredly did, it seems necessary to look for a more traumatic development if we are to account for the massive human misery which is often suggested by contemporary accounts. Cobbing has suggested that this can be found in the evidence which exists of a widespread and often brutal search for labour.

Work by Liesegang has provided a picture of slave exports mainly from northern Mozambique rising from 47,000 in the decade 1800–9 to 129,000 in the decade 1820–9. Harries, while refraining from suggesting any causal connection with the *Mfecane*, has noted the ease with which slaves could be exported from Inhambane and Lourenco Marques once the slave traders had begun to converge on these ports 'when the first ripples of the *Mfecane* were being felt in southern Mozambique'. Harries has also drawn attention to the extremely low price a slave commanded at first purchase on shore during the mid-1820s, when compared to the prices paid by the shipper on purchase and realised on delivery at Rio de Janeiro. This suggests over-supply at source – the work of over-enthusiastic raiders taking advantage of a buyers' market itself created perhaps by the desperate self-commendation of the famished.

E   Zulu raids into southern Nguni-speaking regions, with Shaka seen in a reactive role (Cobbing) rather than a proactive one.

F   Area of severe famine, 1794–1802 and 1817–31 (Newitt), modifying but confirming earlier attempts to advance ecological arguments as background to unrest by Daniel, Hall, Guy and others.

Enough is known about the convulsions in south-east Africa to enable us to locate the start of the disturbances in about 1817, two years after Britain recognised the right of the Portuguese to take captives between Cape Delgado and Delagoa Bay (Jackson-Haight). During the late eighteenth century, the Tsonga Tembe chiefdom, whose power was increasingly eroded by the Mabudu living east of the Pongola river, controlled access to the southern shores of the Bay, while the Matolla and Mpafumo, who were in conflict with each other during the 1790s, controlled the northern and western. At about the same time the Mabudu concluded an alliance with Dingiswayo's Mthethwa, lying to their south, thus fulfilling Dingiswayo's wish to gain access to trading in the Bay. The alliance effectively excluded the Ndwandwe, who lived inland, from access to the coast, and may have inspired the attack of their ruler, Zwide, on both chiefdoms in 1817. He won the fight, killed Dingiswayo, and in so doing, in Harries's words, 'initiated the *Mfecane*'.

On Dingiswayo's death Shaka, illegitimate son of the Zulu chief Senzangakhona, who had been a client of Dingiswayo, seized power over the Mthethwa, whose armies he commanded. He continued the war against the Ndwandwe, and by exploiting the art of close in-fighting by his well-disciplined soldiers, he beat Zwide's armies in 1819 at Gqokoli Hill and on the Mhlatuze river. The Ndwandwe leaders fled – Zwide to the west, the Ngoni under Nxaba and Zwangendaba, and the Gaza under Soshangane northwards to the Bay area, where they became involved in conflict with the Matolla and other peoples, entering into arrangements of various kinds with the Portuguese for the supply of ivory, slaves and other wares. Despite the assumption of mainstream anthropologists and historians that enslavement of people was alien to northern Nguni tradition, it seems quite clear that most chiefdoms of the area, including the Zulu, became involved, either as raiders or as hunted or as both, in the anarchical situation which developed, even if the 'epicentre of violence' (Cobbing) needs to be sought in the immediate hinterland of Delagoa Bay rather than further south in the heart of Zulu country on the Mfolosi. Cobbing suggests a series of shock waves spreading outward from the Bay region, as 'whole peoples fled up the Limpopo and Olifants river systems into the eastern Transvaal', as well as up the Pongola, to be absorbed by chiefdoms of the interior, notably the Sotho, the Pedi and, for a short while, the Ndebele.

In 1821, which was the year in which the Ngoni began to move northwards, the Khumalo Ndebele (Matabele) under Mzilikazi, who was Zwide's son-in-law, fled into the eastern trans-Vaal, where they seem to have tried to set up a new territorial base until conflict with the Pedi, followed by Kora and Griqua attacks, induced them to move west to the Marico region. There, defeat by the Boers at Mosega (1837) eventually forced them to move away north of the Limpopo, to establish a new base at Bulawayo near the Matopo hills, in 1837. The traditional view of the Ndebele as an aggressor nation seeking to establish their power over the entire trans-Vaal is in the process of revision [see pp. 61, 159].

The Zulu are commonly portrayed as having advanced not only north to Delagoa Bay, which Shaka attacked shortly before his murder in 1828, but also south into the trans-Kei, setting the Mpondo, Bhaca and Thembu against each other, and driving refugees into the arms of the Gcaleka Xhosa further south, till their advance was halted by Shaka's murder at the hands of Zulus anxious to arrest his 'reign of terror'. Cobbing's contrasting picture presents the southward movement of the Zulu as a flight of refugees (though he notes that they too were slave-raiders), and attributes both the raiding into the trans-Kei and the murder of Shaka to white adventurism.

A necessary background to the *Difaqane* on the highveld was the spread of Kora settlements on the middle Orange, mingled with colonies of Bantu-speaking Sotho-Tswana, dating from the eighteenth century. Heedless of ethnic background, all these groups either ran stock, raised crops or traded their ivory and other wares, often through intermediaries, as far afield as the east coast. According to Legassick, a shift in the power balance seems to have occurred before the end of the century. The dominant Tswana-speaking Rolong met trading competition from the Ngwaketse in the north, while their Tlhaping clients, who occupied a large area including much of the later Griqualand West, entered into closer trading relations with the Kora. Meanwhile white frontier settlement began to spread north from the eastern Cape as the Bushmen retreated before the musket, while the Bastaards (soon to be known as Griqua), a mixed-blood community of frontiersmen who professed adherence to Christianity and possessed guns, moved upstream from the lower Orange [see p. 29].

After setting up their capital at Klaarwater (the later Griquatown) in 1804–5, with the help of the London Missionary Society, the Griqua began to assert control over the northern frontier region. Aided by their superior weaponry, they took over large areas occupied by the Sotho-Tswana. Despite the poor reporting of their activities, it is clear that the Griqua became involved in raids on the peoples fleeing from the Delagoa Bay area down the Caledon valley and in the trans-Vaal during the 1820s, attacking and often taking fugitives captive. These fugitives acquired the name 'Mantatees', perhaps from a mistaken association with the Tlokwa queen MmaNthatisi (to whom extraordinary legends attached), who was supposed to have led an army of destitute refugees against the Tlhaping capital of Dithakong in 1823; but it has also been suggested that 'Mantatee' could equally derive from a mishearing of the name 'Matabele'. A later suggestion by How that it was the victims of Tlokwa wrath, the Kololo, Hlakwana and Phuting, who conducted the assault on Dithakong needs to be matched against Cobbing's suggestion that the event, far from being an attack by a huge army of starving, yet cattle-driving, vagrants on a defenceless settlement, as is described in the accounts of Melvill (in Thompson) and Moffat, was a Griqua raid for cattle and slaves, in which the 'attackers' were in reality the victims.

A suggestion that 'Mantatee' was a euphemism for captive labour derives some support from its linkage to the needs of the eastern Cape, where labour was a scarce commodity during the early years of the 1820 Settlement. This is reflected in a comment of the 1820 settler, Thomas

Philipps, in 1825, that the Government had 'brought down a great many people belonging to the more distant nations, who have been driven on by the more hostile tribes beyond them again', and distributed them on five- to seven-year apprenticeship terms at the rate of one family per non-slave-owning household. The Cape Ordinance 49 of 1828, which for the first time permitted the movement of Xhosa into the Colony as labourers, was also designed to ease a continuing problem among the settlers, who were barred from possessing slaves.

The experience of Matiwane's Ngwane, who had been beaten by Zwide in 1817, and then crossed the Drakensberg, reinforces this picture. They ran the gauntlet of Griqua hostility during their eventful flight down the Caledon valley, coming into conflict with Moshweshwe – and perhaps, with the latter's provocation, even with the Zulu (Sanders). They then crossed the Orange, perhaps settled among and certainly raided the Thembu, by whom they were described as *fetcani*, or marauders. The Cape authorities, whose forces then attacked them at Mbholompo, on the Mthatha river in 1828, supposedly believed them to be a Zulu force sent by Shaka [see p. 116], perhaps as a result of disinformation by the diarist, Henry Fynn (Cobbing). Bird's *Annals* contain the further observation that 'the prisoners captured on that occasion became the first Kafir labourers who entered the service of the Old Colony'.

To conclude, therefore, it appears likely: first, that the jostling of northern Nguni chiefdoms for position as a result of new trading opportunities was a necessary precondition for the *Mfecane* to take place; second, that much of the emphasis needs to be taken off the Zulu and the Ndebele, even if their actions can hardly be dismissed as simply reactive, especially as some rulers – notably Moshweshwe, Sekwati of the Pedi, and perhaps Mzilikazi himself – seem to have tried to halt the anarchy by trying to set up new centres of order and power; and third, that the search for labour, whether as slaves from Delagoa Bay destined mainly for the South American and Indian Ocean markets, or as the broken remnants of people fleeing across the highveld inviting seizure by armed horsemen for enserfment in the Cape, is at least an important contributory explanation of the disturbances. This seems to make better sense than any explanation based simply on human brutality or the unadaptability of production methods in Nguni society, provided that the reality of two massive droughts is seen as an indispensable backdrop.

2 The Birth of a Plural Society

2.1 THE EARLY YEARS OF EUROPEAN SETTLEMENT

European association with southern Africa began with the Portuguese circumnavigation of the Cape of Good Hope at the end of the fifteenth century. With rare exceptions, however, the Portuguese did not land there, preferring to frequent Saint Helena and east coast havens rather than put in at the 'Cape of Storms'. Although the English, French and Dutch East India Companies all considered establishing a base during the seventeenth century, only the Dutch did so. On 6 April 1652, Jan van Riebeeck arrived with three ships to settle in Table Bay. The high sickness and mortality rates among sailors reflected in the Cape *Journal* of the *Vereenigde Oostindische Compagnie* (V.O.C.) show what chiefly lay behind the decision, for the worst cases on record were very severe. Three vessels which arrived on 18 February 1726 had lost between them 251 men out of a total of 557 on board; another two which arrived on 15 February 1732 had lost 370 out of 439; and Moodie records that in 1771 twelve ships lost between them 1,034 men – approximately half their crews – chiefly from scurvy. The continuing need for a vegetable garden and a hospital, which van Riebeeck was instructed to establish, is not hard to understand.

The V.O.C. did not intend in the first instance to establish a full-fledged colony, but it committed itself to such a policy when it decided in 1657 to allow nine Company servants their freedom to establish private farms at the Rondebosch, below the eastern slopes of Table Mountain. In 1679, when Simon van der Stel arrived as governor, a further twenty settlers were granted land beyond the dunes of the Cape Flats in what became the district of Stellenbosch. The granting of farms to private citizens encouraged the immigration of white women, though for many decades after the settlement the proportion of men to women among the settlers remained very high. The V.O.C. drew on large areas of the European hinterland for a very high proportion of its servants, its seamen and – by extension – its settlers. Thus in 1689 it brought in some 180 Huguenot refugees who had fled from France, and settled them mainly in the Stellenbosch district near what became Franschhoek. Successful resistance by the free burghers to the rule of Governor Willem Adriaen van der Stel in 1705, however, lowered official enthusiasm for the immigration of free settlers from

Europe, of which there was very little during the first half of the eighteenth century. After 1750 the directors tried to encourage it again, in the belief that a larger population would reinvigorate a struggling economy; but even then the settlement attracted far fewer newcomers than the colonies of settlement in America. When the rule of the V.O.C. came to an end in 1795, there were only about 15,000 free burghers in the Colony.

The Huguenots might have developed into a distinct community, but Simon van der Stel settled them along the Berg river among Dutch settlers, requiring them so far as possible to learn, worship, and communicate with the authorities through the Dutch language. French therefore gradually died out, while German never became established because although more German- than Dutch-speakers arrived during the eighteenth century, they generally married Dutch, and in a number of cases free black women, and their children were brought up to speak Dutch (Hoge). An originally diverse European settler population was thus coaxed into cultural uniformity, with the language of the Netherlands and the religion of the Reformed Church for cement. The Afrikaner people, an amalgam of nationalities, came gradually into being during the century after Hendrik Bibault described himself as an 'Africaander' in 1707.

A small settlement of expatriate Europeans, many of them of humble origin, could hardly have been expected to develop rapidly into a cultural outpost of sophisticated Europe, and it did not. Education was mainly limited during the Company period to the catechism (for all teachers were licensed by the Church as well as by the State) and the three Rs. At the seaport, several primary schools were established during the eighteenth century, attended in all cases by the children of the white settlers and their slaves; but, apart from an abortive attempt in 1714, there was no move for secondary education until the campaign of Serrurier and Fleck in the 1790s. Yet there was a noteworthy quickening of cultural life from the time of Ryk Tulbagh's governorship (1751–71). The colonial wars of the latter part of the eighteenth century brought periodic prosperity to the Cape, especially in the years 1756–63 and 1780–3. This was reflected in the architectural revival starting under Tulbagh, which flowered in the late eighteenth century under the stimulus of Thibault and reached its climax in the 1830s and 1840s, when money was easier to come by. With the discovery of a new architectural idiom should be grouped the baroque decorative art of Anton Anreith, and the rococo Cape furniture, European in style, though sometimes the work of Malay craftsmen.

2.2 THE KHOIKHOI AND THE DUTCH

Even before the Dutch settlement, the Cape was a place where different races met. Khoikhoi regularly supplied Dutch and English crews with fresh meat from the 1590s, in return for tobacco, copper and iron, though the Dutch banned the sale of iron after 1652 because of its usefulness in weapon manufacture. After they had planted a colony, the Dutch found sufficient supplies of meat increasingly hard to get, as the Khoikhoi, who were at first prepared to barter cattle at the fort, began to demand higher prices, and tried to conserve their limited cattle resources by offering only sheep or inferior beasts. The Company therefore sent expeditions inland to get livestock, Commandant Zacharias Wagenaar leading an expedition himself in 1663. Company officials, even in Van Riebeeck's day, came under the strong temptation to enslave the peninsular Khoikhoi as part of a strategy to seize their cattle, but the directors prohibited such action, though it allowed the expeditions to the interior to extend the settlement's trading relationship with more distant chiefdoms.

Trading, however, soon brought friction between the Company officials and the free burghers, and between both and the Khoikhoi. Thus in June 1663 the *Journal* deplored the fact that 'the trade has now for some time been spoilt by the freemen', who were giving more tobacco for an animal than the Company offered, but also supplying the natives with rice and brandy. Proclamations were issued to keep the free burghers out of the market. Meanwhile relations with the Khoikhoi were embittered by an increase in thefts of livestock and property (by no means always by Khoikhoi on whites). Open conflict broke out in 1659, as a result of which the Khoikhoi agreed that the Company was in some sense sovereign over the lands of the free burghers, but they kept their booty intact.

In the longer term, though, the dice were loaded against the Khoikhoi. The Company launched a military campaign against them in 1673–7, aiming to punish the Cochoqua chief Gonnema, whom it accused of responsibility for assaults on white settlers and hunters. After four punitive expeditions, in which the V.O.C. enlisted the support of the Cochoquas' rivals and managed to capture a substantial haul of cattle – 800 beasts on the first occasion – Gonnema accepted tributary status and agreed to pay thirty cattle annually 'upon the arrival of the return fleet'. The Khoikhoi chiefs gradually came to acknowledge the Company's right to adjudicate disputes between them; and from the early eighteenth century chiefs began to accept the Company's gifts of copper-headed canes 'on which their names were engraved' as symbols of their authority – and of their subservience.

After the encounter with Gonnema, the V.O.C.'s bartering expeditions into the interior increased. Dorha ('Klaas') of the Chainoqua became a useful middle man, accepting consignments of Company goods which he exchanged for livestock with other chiefs on the Company's behalf, keeping the calves as commission. But the alliance with Klaas collapsed in 1693, after a change of policy by Simon van der Stel for reasons which are obscure. Klaas, whose position as a Company client had been weakened by opposition, was disowned, captured, and imprisoned on Robben Island. Thereafter the Company dealt directly with individual Khoikhoi chiefdoms.

It might have had little success, though, if it had not been able to move into the political vacuum which the divisions among the Khoikhoi had already started to create. But the Company had already moved. As early as 1671, it began to exercise jurisdiction over individual Khoikhoi by passing sentence on them in its courts, especially in cases involving theft or violence between Khoikhoi and the Company's own subjects. Even more significantly, the cumulative effects of their loss of livestock and land forced Khoikhoi into the life of the Colony as labourers. It is quite clear that the decline in their resources of cattle and sheep was substantial, especially during the early years of the eighteenth century, when the herds of the free burghers more than doubled in size, and their flocks multiplied over six-fold. Very soon afterwards an inland movement of pastoral *trekboers* beyond the Hottentots Holland mountains began to gain momentum. According to Guelke and Shell, who have overturned a common assumption that life was very hard for the small farmers at the turn of the eighteenth century, the white free burghers were beginning from the 1680s to employ Khoikhoi as labourers and herdsmen because they were cheaper than *knechts* (white company servants released for service with the settlers) and slaves. Khoikhoi were thus involved in the lower echelons of Colonial society before their numbers were drastically reduced by a sequence of smallpox epidemics during the eighteenth century, of which the 1713 epidemic was the most severe. If they had been cultivators of the soil, the Khoikhoi might have been harder to drive from their lands and their fountains. As mere pastoralists, they were especially defenceless. Those who were not incorporated were often forced to revert to hunting and raiding for survival, and were soon picked up in the official records as 'so-called Bushmen' and 'Bushmen-Hottentots' whose resistance the white colonists encountered at the beginning of the eighteenth century in the region beyond present-day Paarl [see pp. 27–9].

2.3 CAPE SLAVERY

Before the free burghers had discovered the value of Khoikhoi labour, the Company had already allowed the importation of slaves into the Cape settlement for its own and for private possession. Two substantial shipments arrived in 1658–9, one from Dahomey, and the other as a result of the capture of a Portuguese slaver *en route* from Angola to Brazil. Thereafter, the importation of slaves was continuous, though their sources varied, until well after the first British occupation of the Cape in 1795. Two thirds of the slaves brought in by expeditions sent from the Cape derived from Madagascar. A small but constant trickle were collected, from 1680 onwards, from the many parts of Asia touched by V.O.C. activities, on ships returning to Europe. From 1767, however, the Batavian intake was reduced from a fear that such people were prone to crimes of violence and to 'running amok'. For a short spell in 1724 to 1732 the Company maintained a post at Delagoa Bay, and traded slaves from there, while in 1776–86 it sought supplies from Zanzibar and Mozambique. Thereafter it organised no more slaving voyages, and left the supply to foreign traders.

Company slaves, who were housed in the slave lodge at the top end of the Heerengracht in Cape Town, seldom topped the 600 mark. Privately-owned slaves rose from 16,839 in 1795 to 25,754 in 1798, after a steady increase from the 1770s. The annual growth of the slave population closely matched that of free burghers. This reflects a fairly even distribution and the absence of large-scale plantation slavery such as existed in the West Indies and the Southern States. Very few owners possessed as many as fifty. Most who had slaves had less than five, and many had none at all. Adult males were relatively more numerous among the slaves than among the white settlers. Throughout the eighteenth century slave women gave birth, on average, to less than half the number of children produced by whites – a spectacular difference which helps to explain why the slave community was not self-reproducing, even though the children of extra-marital intercourse between slave and slave, and between white male and slave female, retained the unfree status of their mothers.

In 1717, at a time when there were barely 2,000 slaves at the Cape, the directors of the Company in Amsterdam debated the principle of slave labour, and invited the Cape authorities to state 'whether European farm hands and agriculturalists would be less expensive than slaves'. They saw it as an economic rather than as a moral problem. Only one member of the Council of Policy, Dominique de Chavonnes, in reply proposed South Africa's first 'white labour policy', urging an end to slave importation on the ground that white labourers were more productive, would add more to the general prosperity of the Colony, increase its security and make possible a more concentrated land settlement. Other members of the Council thought differently. White labourers, they urged, would be less controllable as well as more expensive, and they could not be expected to do 'slaves' work'. The continued importation of slaves was therefore allowed, and so Cape society developed along caste lines, an almost unbridgeable legal and social divide separating the free men who possessed civil rights – the right to marry, to own property, to provide for their children, to bring or defend an action in court – and the slaves who, as the Roman Law enforced by the statutes of Batavia and local Cape *placaaten* made clear, possessed only the natural rights consistent with remaining alive: the right to eat and sleep, and to cohabit, and not to be deprived of life without sufficient cause. Baron van Imhoff strongly condemned the demoralising effects of such a system on the Europeans when he reported on his visit to the Cape in 1743.

Cape slavery, it is often urged, was essentially benign. This commonly held view owes much to the known absence of large-scale plantation slavery, and rests on the assumption that because few slaves were unknown personally to their masters, and many were brought within the intimacies of the white family home as domestics, or as wet-nurses, then it followed that their treatment was necessarily humane. Mentzel was enthusiastic about the happy lot of the slave on a well-run farm. Victor de Kock has shown, from a number of examples, how domestic slaves in Cape Town often became artisans, the craftsmen who built the houses, the carpenters who made the furniture, the boatbuilders and the fishermen. Skilled slaves could hire themselves out and earn money to buy their freedom, and even own slaves themselves. In individual instances, these illustrations are true, but statistically they are insignificant, and recent researches have over-turned a number of stereotypes of this kind. One is that conversion to Christianity generally led to manumission. While it is true that Christian owners commonly manumitted their slaves by testamentary bequest, investigations have shown that in the eighteenth century there was very little correlation between the baptism of slaves and their manumission, even though a statute of Batavia in 1770 required masters to emancipate baptised slaves should they relinquish ownership for any reason. As the eighteenth century advanced, the Company repeatedly raised the charge on a slave owner for manumitting a slave, until by 1783 he had to pay 50 rixdollars and guarantee that the ex-slave would not be a burden to the state for twenty years. For Muslim slaves, of whom there were considerable numbers, the route to freedom via baptism was in any case closed. Similarly, whereas in other societies European fathers commonly manumitted their offspring by slave mothers, this seldom happened at the Cape. Finally, the overall rate of manumission was fractionally lower at the Cape than in Brazil and Peru (under two per thousand of the total slave force per annum, as against one in a hundred in these other societies), with the result that, although a Free Black population did emerge at the Cape, it never acquired sufficient numerical strength to constitute a political or social factor of much significance, even though Free Blacks were legally entitled to marry whites, to run their own businesses and own their own slaves (all of which they also commonly did). Elphick and Shell conclude, on the basis of all the evidence, that the Cape in the eighteenth century was 'one of the most closed and rigid slave societies so far analysed by historians'.

Slavery was controlled under a tough penal system which aimed, as the Council of Justice explained to the British authorities in 1796, 'to aggravate the severity of capital punishments in order to diminish the frequency of crimes'. At a time when the courts of Europe were still inclined to hand down barbarous sentences for crimes of a socially sensitive nature, the Cape records gave evidence of a similar persuasion. Thus the murder or rape of a white person by a black was commonly punished by breaking on the wheel and the amputation of a limb, though offences by whites were much more leniently treated. The normal penalty for desertion – the easiest escape route for the slave – consisted in a mixture of scourging, branding on the cheek, amputation of the ears, nose or other members, and manacling, followed by restoration of the fugitive to the owner. Desertion was a real threat to the slave order. Rebellion was not, because the slaves lacked the opportunity to organise, and a sufficient concentration of numbers in any one area. Thus, although minor mutinies took place from time to time, the only rebellions of any size occurred after the British occupation, in 1808 and 1825, and both failed.

2.4   THE V.O.C. AND THE CAPE STATION

The V.O.C. was governed on federal lines by a board of directors, the Heren Zeventien, which met in Amsterdam. The directors were frequently regents of their respective towns, and this ensured that they were able to head off most political opposition which might arise from within the States General, the supreme political body in the United Netherlands. Its charter, granted in 1602, gave it sovereign authority from the Cape of Good Hope eastwards, and the right to make treaties, to govern, to administer justice, and to trade in any territory where it might conclude such arrangements. As the largest trading organisation in the Netherlands, and an enterprise in which large numbers of Netherlanders were small shareholders, it commanded wide support.

The Cape was an outstation (*buitencomptoir*) of the V.O.C.'s eastern empire based on Batavia, in Java. Until 1732, when it was brought fully under the control of Amsterdam, it was ruled both directly by the Seventeen and by the Governor-General of the Indies. Dutch Commissioners-General would often call at the Cape on their outward or homeward voyages. From 1672 (regularly only from 1691) it had a governor of its own, who presided over the Council of Policy (*Politieke Raad*), consisting originally of eight senior merchants, which issued regulations (*placaten*) and, when enlarged by one or more burghers in place of the Governor, acted as a court of justice. The free burghers also had representation on the Matrimonial Court and the Orphan Chamber, which were offshoots of the High Court of Justice. This governmental structure remained essentially unaltered throughout the period of Company rule, but was added to from time to time. Thus a petty court for minor civil disputes, and a decentralised system of local government under official *landdrosts* and burgher *heemraden* were set up in 1682 during the governorship of Simon van der Stel. A special watchdog over the administration of finance and justice, the Independent Fiscal, was first appointed in 1689. This unpopular officer would help to ensure that the Company kept effective control over the station, in the interest of maximum service to Company shipping at minimum expense to the shareholders.

The main object of the V.O.C. was to make trading profits, and this fact has commonly led to the Company being presented in an unfavourable light, to the advantage of the free settlers. From the very nature of its role as a trading body holding political power, it was likely to clash from time to time with the free burghers, who had been released from service primarily for business reasons: to grow food at minimal cost to the Company, which in any case reserved the right of first access to visiting ships for the sale of its own produce. It commandeered cattle, corn and wine from the burghers, at prices which it had itself laid down, and it limited retail activities in the port by a system of monopolies (acquired by Dutch auction) for the sale of liquor, tobacco, bread, meat and other commodities. It kept a salt monopoly for itself. There was not enough wheat for export until 1684. Thereafter, fluctuations in the size of the wheat harvest, or in the quality of the vintage, or in Batavia's arbitrary decisions as to how much Cape produce it would buy, played havoc with the burghers' calculations. From the middle of the eighteenth century, however, until the Anglo–Dutch War of 1780–4, Cape wheat had an assured market in the Asian colonies.

But, as Schutte has urged, it would be wrong to indict the V.O.C. of economic heartlessness without taking into account the presuppositions of the time and the circumstances under which it had to operate. It did try, from a distance, to rule the Cape responsibly, to control the excesses of officials without unduly inhibiting their use of patronage; to rule subject peoples, as the Khoikhoi became, by indirect means through their chiefs; and to discourage uncontrolled expansion of the settlement by intervening 'unobtrusively and correctively' – but with perhaps as little chance of satisfying the ambitions of the settlers as Britain had of satisfying the frontiersmen in her mainland American colonies during the same era.

For much of the early period, conditions for the free burghers of Cape Town and its environs were not tough. According to Guelke and Shell, it was possible for even the small farmer to realise 20 per cent on his capital at the beginning of the eighteenth century. It was, indeed, because the market was so lucrative that the Van der Stels, father and son, and their top officials, moved into farming on a large scale, much to the indignation of a wealthy burgher group led by Henning Husing and Adam Tas. If Willem Adriaen van der Stel exceeded the bounds of official propriety, his opponents seem to have been as much motivated by a sense of business rivalry as by a desire to maintain a public principle. Van der Stel's difficulty, in broad terms, was that he had encouraged the expansion of crop production, particularly of vines, to meet a real shortage, only to find that the Company was unable to provide sufficient market outlets. He was recalled in 1705, but not disgraced.

2.5   THE EMERGENCE OF THE TREKBOER

By that date, when the *akkerboere* (crop farmers), of the Cape Peninsula and Stellenbosch were running into real difficulties for want of capital and labour, the trekboer was beginning to emerge as the Cape's first white frontiersman. The advance of stockfarmers eastwards across the Hottentots Holland mountains into the Overberg region, and northwards to the Land of Waveren (later Tulbagh) began at the start of the century, and can be explained in various ways. The interior attracted the adventurous, whether for hunting or for the acquisition of land and stock from the Khoikhoi, by purchase or violent seizure. In a settler community which had unusually large families, land was itself becoming scarce, while the Roman–Dutch law of succession, which required equal division among the heirs, meant that the son who bought out his brothers to retain the family farm often lacked the capital to develop it. Mentzel's picture of the younger son, who had sought out and found 'a decent place to settle, if possible next to a Hottentot Kraal', built a house and found a willing wife, and received from his father 'a wagon and a span of six, eight or ten oxen, a bull (rather than cows) and a few sheep, represents the trekboer stereotype.

Under the loan farm system which grew out of grazing permits, the trekboer could lay claim to a 2,000 morgen (4,500 acre) farm, provided it was not too close to another man's homestead, and keep it indefinitely on payment of an annual fee in 'recognition' of the Company's dominium. If he neglected to pay the fee, he was most unlikely to be evicted; and he could in practice bequeath, alienate or subdivide, though the law forbade these things. The loan farm system discouraged soil conservation and encouraged in the Boer a taste for the ownership of wide open spaces, and a style of stock farming based on the practice of transhumance, or the seasonal trek with his livestock to different regions for summer and winter grazing.

The extent to which the trekboer, as he set off into the interior, was motivated by business principles, has generated a debate. At first, it was generally assumed that he was concerned with no more than subsistence. Neumark suggested that there was a probable correlation between the timing of applications for loan farms and an increase in the number of ships which called at the Cape, arguing that the trekboer was motivated by market instincts since he needed to sell his meat in order to buy his gunpowder and other necessaries of life, which was the case. But Guelke has shown that the greatest demand for loan farms occurred in the 1760s, a full decade before the late eighteenth-century increase in shipping visits began, thus refuting one of Neumark's novel ideas on chronological grounds. We are left, therefore, with an open question best answered by the observation that the trekboer did develop a remarkable degree of independence. He used the fat tail of his Hottentot sheep for candle- and soap-making. He shot game for the pot, and for the making of karosses so as to preserve his own livestock. He returned periodically to the Cape to sell hides, ostrich eggs, tallow, meat and other surplus products in order to be able to procure necessary supplies. Ross notes evidence of regional market specialisations. But poor roads and long distances precluded the possibility of significant profits as is now generally recognised.

The quest for water and pasture, the ease with which informal title could be acquired, and the ease with which the indigenous inhabitants could be forced to retreat or to enter service with their stock, ensured that the spread of the settlement was rapid. The Berg and Breede rivers had been crossed by 1720. The Little Karoo had been entered by the 1740s, while by mid-century the settlers had moved into the plains below the Roggeveld and Nuweveld mountains of the Great Karoo [see Map 4, p. 89]. By the 1770s they were in the Camdeboo and had penetrated northwards beyond the Sneeuberg and eastwards to Bruintjes Hoogte. *Drostdies* (magistracies) set up by the authorities at Swellendam in 1743 (when the eastern frontier was fixed at the Great Brak river), at Graaff-Reinet in 1785 (after Governor van Plettenberg had proclaimed a frontier along the upper Fish and Bushman's rivers) and at Uitenhage in 1803 registered the effort of officialdom to retain some control over the advancing frontier; but control was of the lightest in a land without roads or towns, save where resistance from two new kinds of enemy was stiff. These were the strong groups of San in the mountains of the Great Karoo, to the northern side of the trekker advance, and the Bantu-speaking Nguni in the east.

2.6 CONFLICT BETWEEN TREKBOERS AND KHOISAN, WHO EITHER ACCEPT INCORPORATION OR RETREAT

In the Nuweveld range of the central Karoo, north of the present Beaufort West, the path of the trekboers was obstructed by San hunters who began to attack their flocks. These do not seem to have been the same kinds of people as the Cape frontiersmen had encountered at the beginning of the century in the regions north of Paarl, but more skilled adversaries whose tactics frustrated the trekboers, who had no answer to them. The San for their part resented alien intruders who shot the game on their hunting grounds. Moodie gives evidence of their widespread raiding for cattle and sheep, often accompanied by the killing of Khoikhoi herdsmen. Their archers directed covering fire on Boer homesteads to prevent the occupants emerging to recover their stock. Commandos of whites and Khoikhoi bearing arms were organised in retaliation, sometimes on a large scale, as when three separate units of about 250 men under the overall leadership of Commandant G. R. Opperman set out in 1774. Together they accounted for 500 Bushmen killed and half as many taken prisoner, in a sweep which was intended to remove the danger once and for all. But its object was not achieved. San raids continued unabated till the end of the decade. Farms were frequently abandoned by their Boer occupants, whose appeals for help often carried a note of real anguish. Rumours reached one frontier officer in 1779 that the farmers of the Camdeboo had bought immunity from the San in return for an undertaking not to interfere with the passage of stolen livestock on its way out of the Colony past their homesteads. The growing desperation of the white frontiersmen and of the authorities can be seen in the change of emphasis between Opperman's instructions of 1774 and those given to the 'Commandant of the Eastern Country' in 1780. Opperman was told 'to employ every possible means to enter into an amicable negotiation [with the Bushmen] . . . presenting them [with] tobacco and other bagatelles and trinkets, together with a promise of some farms to reside upon'. But his successor in 1780 was told to distinguish between the 'Kafirs', with whom a treaty could reasonably be concluded, and the Bushmen, who 'by their predatory proceedings, ceaselessly annoy the inhabitants and render their property insecure, and with whom we can entertain no hope of a tenable peace'. For this reason he was authorised to wage total war upon them, though – rather incongruously – without shedding innocent blood.

Meanwhile many Khoi pastoralists, who had lost their access to land, and also evaded incorporation in the white Colony as labour, had moved out of the Colonial orbit and begun to set themselves up outside the borders of white settlement. Those who moved north to the lower Orange during the eighteenth century were commonly referred to as Nama, while those who settled on the middle Orange in the region of its confluence with the Vaal were known as Kora (Korana). But one should not think of these frontier communities as racially distinguishable in any precise sense. An admixture of adventurous whites, runaway slaves, and offspring of mixed unions of various kinds – in short, any who had wanted or needed to escape from the Colony – moved into the area and came to be known collectively as *Bastaards*. They were a gun-owning assortment of frontiersmen who retained some traces of their earlier links with the Colony, like an interest in owning property and perhaps a link with the Christian religion.

By the second half of the eighteenth century, the Bastaards were becoming the dominant element in these frontier communities. They included groups led by a succession of Adam Koks, the first of whom was an ex-slave from Piketberg turned landowner, who had left the Colony after a conflict with a rival, Klaas Afrikaner. Klaas himself led out the 'Oorlam' Khoi (this was a Malay term which reflected their skill in handling horses and firearms – Du Bruyn). He and his successors Jager (who died in 1823) and Jonker (who died in 1861) maintained a shifting relationship with the white settlers and the Khoisan outside the Colonial borders, helping the former to drive out the latter in return for arms and ammunition, and helping their Khoisan kinsmen to resist white encroachment on their hunting grounds when this seemed safe or possible. In the longer term they built up a position of dominance not only over the frontier region south of the Orange river, but also over the Herero and other peoples of present-day Namibia.

As already noted, these elements played a leading role in the unsettling of the highveld during the 1820s, at the time of the *Mfecane*.

The Bastaards owed much to the London Missionary Society, whose first missionaries reached the Cape in 1799. It was the missionaries who persuaded them to change their name to *Griqua*, in recognition of the Grigriqua (Khoikhoi) element in their make-up. To the missionaries they also owed the founding of their capital, Griquatown, in 1804–5, and their governmental system. When Lichtenstein encountered them in 1805, he found them to be a well-organised community, though it contained less stable elements, who were set in motion in 1819 when a group of young rebels known as the Hartenaars chose Andries Waterboer, a Griquatown schoolmaster, as their leader and drove out the existing chiefs, Adam Kok II and Barend Barends. These groups included the 'Bergenaars', who moved north and terrorised the inhabitants of the Langeberg mountains, and Kora, whose thrust was rather towards the east [see p. 128]. What gave these elements particular significance was that in the period of the *Mfecane* they moved into the areas of black dislocation, achieved military successes against the Sotho-Tswana peoples of the northern 'Orange Free State' and Vaal–Harts area with the help of their horses and firearms, and occupied much of their territory.

By the middle of the nineteenth century, therefore, the separate identity of the Khoikhoi had begun to disappear through admixture with other elements, both within the Colony and on the frontiers. The Griqua on the borders would eventually be reincorporated in the Colony and given territorial bases in Griqualand East and Griqualand West, which in the long term proved much less secure than was originally intended [see p. 130–4, and Map 6]. The Cape Khoi, for their part, came to be linked with the surviving community of Free Blacks and the ex-slaves after the emancipation legislation of 1828–33 [see pp. 41–4], and given an identity – at first informal but after 1948 forbiddingly formal, and incorporating the Griqua as well – as the Cape Coloured People.

2.7 THE CREATION OF A STRATIFIED SOCIETY

In this chapter we have noted the coming together, under V.O.C. auspices, of several human groups which formed the nucleus of settlement at the

Cape. To the indigenous Khoikhoi were added, first, a community of white settlers from the Netherlands and other parts of continental Europe who later identified themselves as Afrikaners; and second, slaves from various parts of Africa and the east. Within a few decades, the European community was dominant, and all others had been relegated to, or confirmed in, a position of legal and political inferiority.

As Elphick and Giliomee have very clearly shown, the reasons for this development are more straightforward and considerably less mystical than has sometimes been supposed. It was once commonly accepted that the European ascendancy was a product of race attitudes which grew up on the frontier, and involved a transference of ideas by Calvinist Dutchmen, who were used to seeing themselves as part of the Christian 'elect' in opposition to the heathen 'damned' and not only began to identify 'Christian' with 'white' and the 'damned' with 'black', but managed to transform the legal basis of Cape society in conformity with this new perspective. Evidence that the small number of Reformed clergy at the Cape in the eighteenth century took any kind of initiative in building up a theology of this kind and then imposing it on the authorities has never been demonstrated, and it seems that the nearest one can approach to such a theology is to imagine that a sufficient number of trekboers who read their bibles (which by no means all of them did) sensed that their position on the frontier was similar to that of the Children of Israel as they fought their way through Sinai to the Promised Land.

As an alternative interpretation, Elphick and Giliomee offer the much more straightforward suggestion that the stabilisation of Cape society under white dominance resulted rather from the establishment of clearly defined legal status groups as a direct result of V.O.C. policy. According to their analysis,

> Only Company servants and freeburghers could hold land or gain political power in the official hierarchy of the colony. But since the Company recruited its servants and free immigrants in Europe and brought few Asian or Eurasian employees and settlers to the Cape, it created the precedent of a political and economic elite which was almost exclusively European. By importing slaves, none of whom were European, it intensified the correlation between legal status and race. And by regarding Khoikhoi initially as aliens and later as subjects who were not freeburghers, it effectively precluded them from political and economic advancement in colonial society (p. 365).

Things might conceivably have worked out differently. Suggestions by Van Riebeeck and by Simon van der Stel that agriculture might be turned over to Free Blacks, as was the case in the V.O.C.'s eastern possessions, could have built that community into the kind of force which it never became. A decision might have been taken in 1717 not to continue the importation of slaves, which could have led to the introduction of a European labouring class at a time when slave numbers were still insignificant, and thus have blurred the emergence of a class colour bar; but if that had happened, the Cape would have followed a course diametrically opposed to those of the American colonies, north and south. A noteworthy feature of the Swellengrebel petition signed by Cape colonists in 1784 [see p. 34], was that by that date it was unreasonable to expect young white men to enter service on an equal footing with Hottentots and slaves. The V.O.C. therefore continued to rely on white entrepreneurs to supply its needs, and those entrepreneurs built up their farms and businesses on a basis of unfree and servile labour. The process was consolidated when the trekboers established their dominance over the Khoikhoi of the interior. And the various subordinate communities – the Khoikhoi, the San, the slaves, the Free Blacks, and the Bastaards – were never able to unite to resist the assertion of white domination.

3 The Enlightenment and the Great Trek

3.1 THE EIGHTEENTH-CENTURY REVOLUTION AND CAPE COLONIAL 'CALVINISM'

Between 1776 and 1833 the settlement at the Cape, which had by that time developed into a plural, stratified, slave-owning society, was exposed to the tremors of an ideological earthquake far less painful than, but in stark contrast to the brutalities of the Mfecane to which the black peoples were being subjected. The change may be summarised as an onslaught by the values of the Enlightenment on white colonials whose presuppositions were already moulded by a defensive desire to keep their caste, labour-repressive society in being. The fact that this was also a period in which British rule superseded Dutch immensely complicated the situation by dividing the loyalties of the dominant but essentially insecure minority.

Cape society was nominally Calvinist, and held baptism to be an important symbol of status for at any rate its white inhabitants. The Company paid the salaries of clergy nominated by the Amsterdam *classis* (convocation), and the first of these arrived in 1665. After the building of churches in the outlying districts of Stellenbosch, Drakenstein, Roodezand (Tulbagh) and Zwartland (Malmesbury), the Company authorised a combined assembly in 1746, and appointed its own political commissioner to watch its activities. But the intensity of Cape Calvinism must be a matter for conjecture, and should not be rated high simply on the evidence of nominal adherence or the strict discouragement of other sects. Evidence cited by Elphick and Giliomee tends to the conclusion that its hold was slight, though Spoelstra has argued for the existence of a frontier Calvinism which preserved its identity in the isolation of the interior during the eighteenth century, remote from the liberal challenge of the 1770s.

The ideological revolution which erupted on the opposite sides of the Atlantic in 1776 and 1789 was essentially a movement of the human spirit which embraced in its area of concern a variety of under-dogs: the victims of French religious persecution and the English-owned slaves, the Russian serfs and the inmates of Italian prisons, as well as others. Its inspiration derived partly from the non-dogmatic rationalism of the *philosophes*, partly from the humanitarianism of the evangelicals, partly from a new democratic enthusiasm among disciples of Locke and Rousseau.

The point has been well made by Du Toit and Giliomee, that the

32

protests of the Willem Adriaen van der Stel era [see p. 26] amounted to little more than a defence of group interests by a small number of wealthy burghers and were devoid of articulate political ideology.

It is also possible to observe, as the eighteenth century advanced, the growth of a somewhat crude attitude towards the 'lesser breeds', which suggests linkages between the slave-owning mentality of the more settled districts and the emergent lawlessness of the border ruffian. Both *akker-boere* and frontiersmen sometimes assumed a liberty to deal as they liked with their own servants or with Khoikhoi beyond the frontiers, without fear of consequences. When, in 1739, a party of settlers and Khoikhoi from Piketberg who were defying a Company ban on stock-bartering, set upon a group of Nama near the Orange river mouth, killed several, and stole some cattle, the landdrost of Stellenbosch ordered the members of the expedition to appear before him. Though subsequently ordered to Cape Town to stand trial, the men refused and went into rebellion on the urging of Etienne Barbier, a military deserter who had escaped from prison after making allegations against an officer, and now accused the Acting Governor, D. van den Henghel, of 'favouring Hottentots and Chinese above white men'. The rising was put down, and Barbier executed, the first important martyr for the cause of unequal justice. His stand is of interest mainly because of the support which he clearly enjoyed among the local population, in consequence of which the authorities meted out to his followers a punishment which was so lenient as to be hardly exemplary (Schutte).

Such attitudes could not have been expected to disappear with the initial impact of the liberal revolution, which reached the Cape during the 1780s, when the *Kaapse Patriotte* first made their appearance at the time of Carel Buytendag's arrest in 1779. This was a good example of how a local grievance arising out of the customary relationship between master and servant in a largely slave-owning society could express itself in the universal language of European and American liberalism, yet retain the essential ethos of the world the slave-owners made. Buytendag, who was allegedly a brutal employer of his coloured labourers, was banished without trial to Batavia, after being arrested by armed slaves on the order of the Independent Fiscal, W. C. Boers. His arrest provided the occasion for a petition to the Directors, signed by a group of *Kaapse Patriotten*, mainly citizens of Cape Town and immediate environs, men from the business and official world who sent their spokesmen B. J. Artoys, N. G. Heyns, T. Roos and J. van Reenen to the Netherlands, where they presented their case to the Seventeen and made contact with liberal, anti-Orangist political circles.

Beyers argued that the *Patriotten* had substantially assimilated the liberal doctrines of their European mentors, while Idenburg and Schutte have emphasised their links with Hollanders of the stature of Joan Derk van der Capellen and Elie Luzac, one of whose earlier pamphlets was published at the Cape in abbreviated form, and without acknowledgment, as *De Magt en Vrijheden eener Burgerlijke Maatschappij* (The Power and Liberties of a Citizen Society). But recent historians are sceptical of the idea that there was much ideological assimilation between the Dutch and the Cape

Patriots, even if, as Schutte suggests, a 'good deal' of Dutch literature reached the Cape. In particular, Du Toit and Giliomee have noted that the documents of the period which most clearly represent Cape thinking – notably a pamphlet of 1778 addressed to 'fellow citizens of the Cape of Good Hope', the Burgher Petition of 1779, a pamphlet of 1783 entitled *Nederlandsch Afrika*, and a petition drafted in Holland by Hendrik Swellengrebel, son of the Cape Governor, and sent to the Cape for signature in 1784 – differed from the new European liberalism in their lack of interest in universal rights, popular sovereignty, or independence. The Burgher Petition, for example, was divided into three sections all related to local issues. The first centred on economic grievances, suggesting that a number of the complaints of 1705 still needed attention. The second enlarged on the improper conduct of officials, in particular the Fiscal, whose behaviour was said to be in conflict with 'the lawful and natural rights and freedoms of the burgher'. The final section contained thirty-seven demands, including better access to justice, greater certainty over the laws they were supposed to obey, and proper representation on the Council of Policy. Blending these political demands with a strong desire to protect their immediate self-interest, they also insisted that in future white men should not be arrested by 'caffers' (slaves who served as auxiliary police), that burghers should be allowed to punish their own slaves without tyrannising over them, that Englishmen and Frenchmen should be denied residential rights, and that Chinese, Javanese and convicts should not be allowed to live among the burghers and run businesses in competition with theirs. *Nederlandsch Afrika*, the fullest statement of their ideas in the view of Du Toit and Giliomee, looked back on the Van Riebeeck era as a golden age, and took continuing political ties with the Netherlands entirely for granted. The Swellengrebel petition, written at a time when the Cape was enjoying boom conditions as a consequence of the visit of a French fleet during the war of American independence, was a tightly argued document which urged the establishment of a free market economy, and accepted its slave labour basis in a mood of mild resignation.

The Heren XVII rejected the Petition of 1779, but after a long delay, in 1883, the Cape community derived some minor rewards for persistence during the relatively prosperous governorships of Van Plettenberg and Van der Graaff. Thus the Company allowed them to trade with foreign ships after its own interests had been served in 1783, authorised the consolidation of the law in a general *placaat*, which was in due course carried out (Davenport), and gave them equal representation on the Council of Justice and a measure of self-government in a body later known as the Burgher Senate.

The 1790s, however, were a period of extreme economic crisis as the V.O.C. drifted steadily into bankruptcy and the settlers at the Cape began to experience the inflationary effects of an over-printing of paper money since its introduction in 1782. The visit of two special commissioners, S. C. Nederburgh and S. H. Frijkenius in 1792, in a vain attempt to bring about severe cutbacks in expenditure, did not relieve the plight of the Cape merchant and farming classes, as Muller's study of J. F. Kirsten reveals only too clearly, so that when the British occupation of the Cape took place in 1795 the opposition was somewhat muted by the experience of distress.

There was more opposition on the frontier than in the agricultural districts, but this stemmed in the first instance from frontier circumstances some five years before the British arrived. The trekboers, engaged in conflict with the 'Bushmen' on the northern border in the Karoo [see p. 113], were also beginning to make contact with Nguni settlements in the region between the Gamtoos and Fish rivers [see p. 115]. Giliomee presents the frontier crisis of the 1790s as a conflict between the farmers on the northern frontier and those of the eastern for control of policy-making with regard to the peoples beyond the border, with the easterners now preferring a more forceful use of commandos than the northerners saw the necessity for. In the district of Graaff-Reinet, established as a separate *drostdy* in 1785, public attention came to focus on the activities of M. H. O. Woeke and H. C. D. Maynier, the first two landdrosts, whose difficult task it was to reconcile the demands of the frontier Boers with their own views on the proper exercise of their authority. Maynier, the more contentious of the two figures, was landdrost from 1792 to 1801. He was denounced not only for unsuccessfully leading a commando against the Xhosa, but for insisting on the release of captured women and children whom the burghers coveted for labour service, and for claiming that white frontiersmen were exaggerating the rumours of Xhosa raids in order to provoke a conflict with a view to seizing Xhosa stock. His accusers, who indicted him with excessive concern for the noble savage, themselves used language clothed in revolutionary slogans, greeting each other as 'Citizen [*Burger*] So-and-So', denouncing 'aristocrats', sporting tricolour cockades, and standing for the 'Voice of the people' (*Volksstem*) against that of authority. The attitude of these frontier 'republicans', if such they were, for they were the self-proclaimed spokesmen of the farmers on the south-eastern frontier and never laid claim to the sovereignty of the *Volksstem* as such, resembled that of the Patriot movement in that they availed themselves of whatever slogans of opposition were ready to hand without real grasp of their original significance. How far their revolutionary language implied support for the Patriotten of the Netherlands, in opposition to the House of Orange, which had returned to power with the help of Prussian arms in 1787, and which enjoyed the support of the Heren XVII, it seems impossible to say. Such loyalties might help to explain their resistance to British rule after 1795, but opposition to British rule can be explained equally well on grounds of an unpopular frontier policy.

3.2   THE FIRST BRITISH OCCUPATION, 1795

The transfer of the Cape Colony from Company to British control took place in stages. After the French invasion of the Netherlands in 1795, a British force was dispatched to the Cape and landed successfully on the shores of False Bay, and the Colonial troops under Commissioner Sluysken failed to repel it at Muizenberg. The invasion had been undertaken by arrangement with the exiled House of Orange, which continued to oppose the French, and it was justified by the exigencies of war. An administration was set up under Earl Macartney as governor in 1796. Wine, wheat and livestock production increased and prices rose. Business recovered, though British importers fared better than established Dutch firms. The British authorities trod carefully, anxious not to alienate more people than they had to. They retained the Dutch officials in their posts, but on a salaried basis, and banned fees. They guaranteed property and the Roman–Dutch legal system, and put an end to torture and monopolies. They also tried to buy the elite with entertainment at the castle. But they could not prevent minor rifts developing between 'Jacobijnen' and 'Anglomannen'.

It was, above all, on the frontier that they found problems. The Graaff-Reinetters may not have responded to Sluysken's plea for aid; but among the 'Volksstem' were at least some committed supporters of the new Batavian Republic, who defied General Craig. They only gave in when the prospect of a reoccupation of the Colony by the Dutch receded with the capture by the British of Admiral Lucas's fleet in August 1796. Their opposition came alive again in 1799 when Adriaan van Jaarsveld, who had led the opposition to Maynier, was arrested on a charge of forgery. Rebels, led by Marthinus Prinsloo, released Van Jaarsveld by force, at the same time demanding permission to cross the Fish to graze cattle and apprehend runaway servants. General Vandeleur, using dragoons and Khoikhoi levies, managed to put down the rebellion.

The following year a more serious Xhosa invasion followed by a Khoikhoi rising took place. Under these circumstances, the British authorities treated the Boers as leniently as they dared. Van Jaarsveld and Prinsloo, with fifteen others, were tried in Cape Town, and the first two sentenced to death. But the Acting Governor, General Dundas, on his own authority commuted the sentences to imprisonment. Though Van Jaarsveld died in jail, the rest were subsequently released by the Batavian regime.

Unrest among the Khoikhoi labourers in the east was matched during the first British period by the official encouragement of missionary work among them. The Moravian Missionary Society, which enjoyed a brief spell of work among the Khoikhoi in 1737–44 until their leader Georg Schmidt was expelled, had returned to the Cape in 1792 and resumed work at Baviaanskloof (later known as Genadendal). They were joined by the London Missionary Society when Dr J. T. van der Kemp, himself a Hollander, arrived to establish Bethelsdorp (near Uitenhage) in 1799. The Moravians were not free from the criticism of white landowners, who often regarded the mission stations as undesirable refuges for potential workers, but on the whole they devoted their efforts to building up religious communities rather than to the expression of social criticism. Through Van der Kemp and his equally well-known colleague, Dr John Philip, the L.M.S. would soon begin to challenge the assumptions of Cape society from an evangelical humanitarian standpoint, which for the Cape was something new [see p. 42].

3.3   BATAVIAN RULE, 1803–6

In February 1803, under the terms of the Treaty of Amiens, the Cape was made over to the Batavian Republic (as the United Netherlands had become known), and the British authorities withdrew. The Batavians, as heirs of the V.O.C., arrived expecting to stay, even if they had doubts about the long-term value of the Cape as a colony. In Governor Janssens, and above all in Commissioner-General J. A. de Mist, who had cleared his own thoughts before arrival in the Colony by the compilation of a lucid *Memorandum* as a blueprint for policy, the Cape experienced two rulers who were representative of the best in Revolutionary thought. They were tolerant and allowed all but the senior Orange officials to retain their posts. They again made Dutch the sole official language. They also set about the overhaul of central and local governmental institutions with conviction, turned the Council of Policy (which the British had suspended) from a board of commercial management into a more compact and regularly constituted instrument of government, changed the system of accounting, and for the time being got rid of the Fiscal. They gave the Burgher Senate a more democratic basis and renamed it the *Raad der Gemeente* (Community Council). They brought the frontier farmers closer to the administration of local government by promoting some of their number to the rank of field cornet (*veld kornet*) and entrusting them with minor administrative and judicial responsibilities. They revised the educational system with a view to training civil servants for posts of responsibility, and decentralised local government still further by establishing new *drostdies* in the troublesome frontier districts of Tulbagh and Uitenhage. If the Batavian rulers alienated Cape opinion, it was not because they could not govern or because they were seen as intruders, but because in their ideology, above all in their tolerant view of creeds other than the Reformed, in their preparedness to secularise marriage and public education, and in their liberal humanitarianism, they were innovators of a kind the colonials had been taught to view with extreme suspicion. Their reputation remained high, however, because in fact they had time to change very little.

3.4   THE RETURN OF THE BRITISH, 1806

With the resumption of hostilities in Europe by Napoleon in 1805, the Amiens treaty fell into abeyance, and the Cape again lay open to seizure, as a strategic base of value to any power which needed to secure its access to the East. The British Government was quick to act, and in January 1806 it landed a force of 6,700 troops at Blouberg on Table Bay. They defeated the small contingent sent against them by Governor Janssens, who surrendered ten days later after first retreating to the Hottentots Holland mountains. This time, even if it was to be another nine years before the fact was confirmed beyond doubt, British authority had come to stay, though it had come, as Harlow wrote, 'to occupy a fortress' and not, like the Batavians, 'to inaugurate a social revolution'.

The Instructions given to the first governor, the Earl of Caledon, restored an autocracy even narrower than that of the V.O.C., subjecting him to no local control at all. He governed by proclamation, legislated by proclamation even on important matters, and held supreme authority over all branches of government, though he took advice in practice from men with official experience at the Cape.

Of necessity the life of the Colony had to go on, whatever its eventual destiny was to be, and the early years of British rule saw several normative changes. Examples were the abolition of the slave trade and the laying down of rules to govern Khoikhoi vagrancy. To make governmental control more effective still, Sir John Cradock, Caledon's successor, introduced circuit courts in 1811 in order to bring justice nearer to the frontier plaintiff. The results of this policy were positive, as the 'Black Circuit' of 1812 would confirm, even if it led by a chain reaction to the so-called Slagters Nek rebellion of 1815 [see p. 42]. Cradock also promoted a revolution in land tenure with the introduction of perpetual quitrent title in 1813, with the object of restricting expansion and ensuring better revenues from the sale of leases, though Duly has shown how ineffective early British land policy at the Cape was in practice. Where the Colonial economy was concerned, the British authorities hoped to make the Cape an entrepôt to which the traders of all nations in the West might come to buy goods supplied by the English East India Company from its trading bases in the East (Arkin). The E.E.I.C. was not disposed to accept this arrangement, however, though in 1813 the British Parliament deprived it of its monopoly over all commodities produced in the East save tea, and the entrepôt scheme did not get off the ground. On the other hand, Cape wine producers, in particular, were favoured by a protected market in Britain throughout the Napoleonic wars and for many years afterwards.

Britain's legal acquisition of the Cape took place during the general pacification of 1815, when a treaty between Britain and the Netherlands transferred the Colony to Britain in return for a British acceptance of responsibility for financial commitments of £6 million incurred by the Dutch Government towards other European powers (Harlow).

Even before they were secured in possession, the British authorities at the Cape, under the rule of Lord Charles Somerset from April 1814, took deliberate steps to ensure the Colony's British character. They therefore promoted British settlement, not only in Cape Town itself, to which a considerable number of British merchants had already begun to move, but on the eastern Cape frontier as well.

3.5 THE ALBANY SETTLEMENT OF 1820 AND ITS CULTURAL IMPACT

In the mind of Lord Charles Somerset, the primary aim of British settlement in the eastern Cape was to provide a defence for the Colony in the Suurveld, which had recently been forcefully cleared of its indigenous occupants by Colonel John Graham, the frontier commandant. To support the military blockhouses which had then been set up between the two new centres of Graham's Town and Cradock, Somerset envisaged a scattering of small settler villages behind the line of the Fish river. The Colonial Office was at first slow to react; but by 1819 a select committee of the House of Commons on the poor laws was ready with a plan for assisted emigration prompted (though perhaps for the wrong reasons) by the increase in social distress and public violence in Britain in that year. The Xhosa prophet Makanda's attack on Graham's Town in the same year gave the Cape authorities a stronger sense of urgency, and it was an indication of the heavy demand for passages that – in spite of the awesome nature of Cruickshank's contemporary cartoons – some 90,000 people applied to emigrate to the Cape from many parts of the British Isles. Almost the first of a series of attempts in the early nineteenth century to people the Empire with British subjects, the scheme to settle the new district of Albany brought some 4,000 people to the Colony during the first half of 1820. Some arrived in parties under wealthy leaders, who received special privileges for recruiting ten or more adult males. Bailie's party, for example, consisted of 84 adult men, 47 adult women and 91 children (Nash). Other settlers were recruited as individuals. Most adult males were either farmers or tradesmen, the two groups being roughly equal in Bailie's party, which also contained a sprinkling of professional men. Soldiers, teachers and clergy were in a small minority. Nash's comment that 'none of the settlers of 1820 is known to have owned land in Britain', even if some party leaders came from the land-owning classes, shows the extent to which this frontier farming settlement was a 'leap in the dark'.

As their surviving diaries and published works reveal, they were a literate community, and their role in the struggle for press freedom was of the utmost significance for the development of independent thought and, later, of self-government for the colony. Thomas Pringle and John Fairbairn fought their political battles in the polemical language of Regency Britain, and after a few years won them, despite the resistance of the Governor, Lord Charles Somerset. A Commission of Inquiry appointed by the Imperial Government in 1823 supported their main demands. It recommended to the Secretary of State the appointment of an advisory council which the Governor should be obliged to consult. Such a council was formed in 1825 (Donaldson). This was the first step in a process which would lead to the creation of Executive and Legislative Councils in 1834, and to representative government in 1853 [see pp. 90–1].

Oppressed in the early years by natural disasters, and by periodic Xhosa cattle raids, the 1820 Settlers became acclimatised to their new surroundings as the frontier Boers had done before them, developing the physical and moral toughness and the harder race attitudes common to the inhabitants of turbulent frontier districts, yet helping to bridge the gap between Colonial and African society, which warfare had tended to widen, and unobtrusively to weaken the bonds of African society through trade, missionary activities, and, increasingly, the employment of Africans as labourers within the settlement. The settlers were not permitted to keep slaves, but there was evasion of the rule.

Though marriage outside the settler community did occur, and the settlers' relationship with the Afrikaner frontiersmen remained harmonious, the 1820 Settlers retained a self-awareness which the Huguenots had largely lost. This they were able to do because the Somerset regime sought to replace Dutch by English in all spheres of public life. Afrikaner scholars have commonly laid the later development of Afrikaner nationalism at the door of Somerset's anglicisation policy, and there can be no doubt that, in intention, British policy was to adjust the cultural life of Colonial society to the legal realities of British rule. English, stated the proclamation of 1822, was to be exclusively used in the courts after five years. Special incentives were given to teachers who taught through English. In due course, English would also become the sole language of the legislature. Somerset also introduced a team of Scots clergy to fill the vacant pulpits of the Nederduits Gereformeerde Kerk. Yet before convicting the regime of oppression, it is desirable to distinguish between its intentions and the manner of their execution. Where the clergy were concerned, for example, the Scotsmen were only appointed after an attempt to obtain Dutchmen had failed. They were sent to the Netherlands to learn Dutch before going to the Cape. Their descendants tended in practice to become absorbed in the Afrikaner community which they had come to serve, and in no sense became agents of cultural conquest. Nor did they constitute any kind of liberal wing in the N. G. synod. In the case of the schools, by contrast, it is clear that Dutch education suffered, both in the short and the longer term, and this fact, coming so soon after the Batavian regime had taken the trouble to place it on a sound footing, did cause resentment. Yet Dutch-medium instruction survived in the country districts at the primary level in sufficient strength to be able to underpin a successful Dutch revival in the 1870s, even though the literary Dutch of the Bible and the classroom differed from the spoken language of everyday use, which at that time had no literature of its own. In the case of the courts, it must be stressed that the Boer who had no English was always entitled to an interpreter (though he might resent betraying intimate secrets to an interpreter who was a Coloured man). His real objection concerned the abolition in 1827 of the traditional courts of *landdrost* and *heemraden*, and the removal of the judicial powers of the farmers' friends the field cornets in the interest of the better enforcement of the rule of law. These officers were replaced by resident magistrates and civil commissioners. Their titles did not necessarily mean that they had English names, but until the introduction of elected municipal councils after 1836, divisional road boards in 1843, and elected divisional councils in 1867, such local democracy as had existed now went into eclipse. The law and its enforcement were the concern of higher, generally alien authorities, who legislated in English, but gazetted the law in Dutch as well.

British institutions made inroads into the commercial as well as the political and cultural life of the Colony. Commerce had revived at the Cape during the Batavian period, when the first chamber of commerce was set up. But the scale developed markedly after the second British occupation, under the stimulus of imperial preference, and it was for the most part the

British immigrants who captured the market. They also began to penetrate the interior, where the Boer needed to buy his gunpowder, coffee, and other basic domestic comforts. It was generally English-speakers or aliens who set up as shopkeepers at the centres where the Boers repaired for the quarterly celebration of the Lord's Supper (*Nagmaal*), which became the first towns of the interior. After the Great Trek, the inland towns became outposts of British culture even in the Boer republics; and Afrikaner propagandists had come to caricature English culture by the 1870s as that of 'soakers, robbers and reds' – that is, of canteen-keepers, shopkeepers and redcoats. But it was a culture which produced missionaries and humanitarians as well.

3.6 THE EMANCIPATION OF THE SLAVES AND THE CAPE COLOURED PEOPLE

The humanitarians attacked and eventually destroyed Cape slavery, but the process was not as effective as most of the literature implies. Although the British Parliament made the slave trade illegal throughout the British Empire in 1807, the number of slaves at the Cape continued to rise largely on account of clandestine imports, legal evasion, and surreptitious enserfment of local people to meet the demands of a growing economy. This demand was reflected in a doubling of the average price of slaves in twenty years from £75 to £150, a demand for the abolition of the Hottentot Corps in order to release workers for the market, and signs of an attempt to switch from slave to Khoikhoi labour in both the western and the eastern districts. Meanwhile the abolition of the trade was not seen as sufficient by the anti-slavery campaigners, because discretionary manumission on which they had hoped to rely did not keep up with the natural increase of the slaves, especially as there was no tradition of regular manumission to build upon. The automatic manumission of all children born to slave parents, which was seriously considered, would have taken much longer than the reformers were prepared to wait. Nor did a policy of amelioration by means of tighter control measures, such as the introduction of a slave registry in 1816, the laying down of minimum standards for food, clothing, hours of work and maximum punishments in 1823, and the compulsory recording and limitation of punishments in 1826, achieve the end desired, because these measures were treated by slave-owners as an inconvenient intrusion into their privacy and often ignored.

It was therefore against a background of slave-owners' protests that the slaves throughout the Empire were set free under a law of December 1833. This Act allowed for a period of four years' apprenticeship for domestic slaves and six for plantation slaves, before they were free to leave their masters' service, in the hope that this would cushion the shock. But there was intense resentment at the Cape, and some active opposition. The Act had been drawn up with West Indian conditions chiefly in mind, and Cape owners felt themselves not only undercompensated for the value of their slaves, but unable in many cases to draw the compensation money, which was payable only in London. Further, when emancipation did take effect in 1838–40, dislocation was considerable.

The emancipation of the Khoikhoi who, along with Free Blacks in general, were coming to be known as the Cape Coloured people, was the work of pressure groups within the Colony rather than in London, in particular that of the London Missionary Society, which had built a network of stations inside the Colony and beyond its northern border by the end of the first British occupation in 1803. Some of its leaders, though by no means all, were conspicuous for their willingness to confront farmers, or the Government, or both, over the treatment of the free Coloured people, or over frontier policy. The saintly Van der Kemp, founder of Bethelsdorp and friend of the well-known frontiersman Coenraad de Buys, defied labour-hungry farmers who sought to grab his neophytes, but his mission was badly run. James Read, who took up the case of Coloured servants who had alleged maltreatment by their employers in the celebrated 'Black Circuit' of 1812, secured some convictions but made many enemies for himself and the Society through the mere act of laying charges.

It was as a consequence of the Black Circuit that in 1815 Frederick Bezuidenhout defied an order to appear in court to answer charges of maltreating a Coloured servant. After his death at the hands of Khoikhoi soldiers while resisting arrest, his brother raised a rebellion on the frontier, appealing to Ngqika, the Rharhabe chief, to help him to overthrow the Colonial Government. This was in turn suppressed, and its leaders executed; but the collapse of the gallows at the place of execution, named Slagters Nek, followed by the re-hanging of the convicts, left a bitter memory in the minds of the witnesses, and gave the racialism of the Bezuidenhouts more favourable publicity than their actions warranted.

John Philip, who arrived in 1819 and remained superintendent of the London missions till his death in 1851, became the most controversial figure of all. He was capable of making wrong allegations as well as right ones in fluent prose, lost one libel action as a result of this, and became the *bête noire* of white settlers for the damning criticism of their labour relations in his *Researches in South Africa* (1828). His effectiveness is in dispute. Historians with as divergent views as Theal and Macmillan considered him to have been highly influential, though Henry Cloete, the earliest historian of the Great Trek, largely ignored him in his lecture on the origins of the Trek, as did S. J. du Toit, the first Afrikaner historian. Galbraith is more inclined than Macmillan to see the hand of the Treasury rather than that of the missionary lobby behind Cape frontier policy in the 1830s; but the intervention of the missionaries was resented by frontiersmen and farmers with very positive ideas of their rights, both with regard to the emancipation of Coloured people and in the matter of frontier policy. In both areas the roles of Philip and of the administrator, Andries Stockenstrom, were undoubtedly influential.

The evolution of Cape policy towards free persons of colour reached its most important stage during the early nineteenth century, when, outside the mission stations, Coloured landlessness was as good as complete. Very few efforts had been made to work out a policy for the Coloured people before the Earl of Caledon promulgated new regulations in 1809. These were intended not only to prevent vagrancy by requiring the Coloured people to carry passes and to compel the unemployed to accept work, but also to protect labourers from debt servitude, truck payments and other forms of exploitation, by means of written contracts recorded at the drostdy. Further proclamations in 1812, 1819, and 1823, governing the apprenticeship of Coloured children and related issues, brought into being a code of protective discipline for the Coloured people which, as Reyburn argued, gave them 'only a lowly status in society . . . but defended them in it'. Philip and others attacked this code on the ground that it discriminated against the Coloured people as a class, and in 1828 the Governor-in-Council promulgated an Ordinance (Number 50), which freed Coloured people from having to carry passes, made it clear that they could legally own land, and stressed their employers' continued obligation to give them service contracts – if written, for up to a year's duration, if oral for not more than a month. Whether Philip, who was in England when the Ordinance was received, helped to secure an Order-in-Council prohibiting its repeal without the authority of the British Government is by no means clear. But he did help to bring about the subsequent rejection of a Cape Vagrancy Ordinance introduced in 1834, which might have destroyed its effectiveness as an emancipatory measure. Newton-King has stressed the linkage in official policy between Ordinance 50 and Ordinance 49 of the same year, under which Africans were permitted to enter the Colony as labourers under safeguards. Her argument that Ordinance 50 had, as one of its objectives, the creation of proper incentives to Coloured labourers, so that they could accumulate their earnings and sell their labour on the best market, makes sense in the light of the need to promote a contented labour force at a time when labour was in short supply, but this is to reinforce the commonly accepted view that Ordinance 50 was a protective device rather than to undermine it. The best evidence as to the limits of Ordinance 50 as a protective device comes from Duly. By concerning himself less with the problem of motivation and more with that of implementation, Duly is able to demonstrate that, whatever its intentions, Ordinance 50 was to a large extent 'inoperable' under the conditions of the frontier, largely on account of distances. He also shows that oral rather than written contracts became the norm, with the encouragement of the magistrates whose job it was to enforce the law, and that the Supreme Court presided over by Judges Wylde and Menzies did little to encourage the notion that before the law black and white should be treated equally. He suggests further that, if Ordinance 50 had not been passed, the Khoikhoi would have stood a better chance of profiting from the emancipation of the slaves because of the mistaken assumption of contemporaries that Ordinance 50 had resolved their problems.

The main defect of Ordinance 50, from this white farmers' point of view, was the removal of any control over vagrancy. Andries Stockenstrom, a member of the Council and also Commissioner-General of the Eastern Cape from 1826, busied himself with the expulsion of Maqoma from his Kat river lands in 1827 [see p. 117], and seems to have anticipated that this would help to throw his subjects on to the labour market in the Colony. He also set up the Kat River Settlement on those lands in 1829, so that Coloured people who left the missions or their employment could set themselves up as smallholders and thus cease to trouble the white farmers. But Kat River was on a military frontier, the quality of its administration deteriorated, and when rebellion broke out among the inhabitants during the war of 1850–3, the experiment collapsed.

3.7   THE START OF THE GREAT TREK

Government frontier policy remained a bone of contention under British rule, largely on account of the resentment of white frontiersmen at the political influence, real or imagined, of the missionary lobby. Though it is clear from studies made since Macmillan's work on Philip that Treasury influences behind British policy were at least as important, the efforts of Philip and Stockenstrom to influence policy were easy to observe, and the achievements of these two men, who had lost much of their credibility among Dutch and British settlers through their candid testimony before the Aborigines Committee of 1836, were branded as inimical to the interests of white colonials. Philip's main achievement was to lobby successfully against the expulsion of blacks from the Queen Adelaide Province which Governor D'Urban sought to annex in May 1836, though it is not clear that he was behind Lord Glenelg's instruction to cancel the annexation itself. Stockenstrom found himself in the invidious position in the same year of being appointed Lieutenant-Governor of the Eastern Province with the assigned task of reversing D'Urban's annexation of the territory, which was popular among white settlers, while D'Urban remained in office, and introducing the treaty system with the Xhosa chiefs which he and Philip favoured, and which the Boers in particular mistrusted (Muller). These policy decisions seem to have had a very direct influence on the decision of some Cape Afrikaners to pull up their roots and leave the colony permanently for the interior.

Plans for a large-scale Boer exodus from the Colony were made a good eighteen months before the reversal of D'Urban's frontier policy. After Dr Andrew Smith had reported favourably on his journey to Port Natal in 1832, an overland *kommissie-trek* under Piet Uys set off in September 1834 to examine the possibility of a settlement there together with the prospects for hunting and for trading with the Africans, while other parties explored the Soutpansberg and south-west Africa. Small trekker parties left for the northern and eastern trans-Vaal under Louis Tregardt of Somerset East and Hans van Rensburg from Graaff-Reinet. Another, under Hendrik Potgieter of Tarka, set off late in 1835 or early 1836, and another under Gerrit Maritz of Graaff-Reinet in September of the latter year, after he had travelled extensively in the Colony to concert plans with other would-be

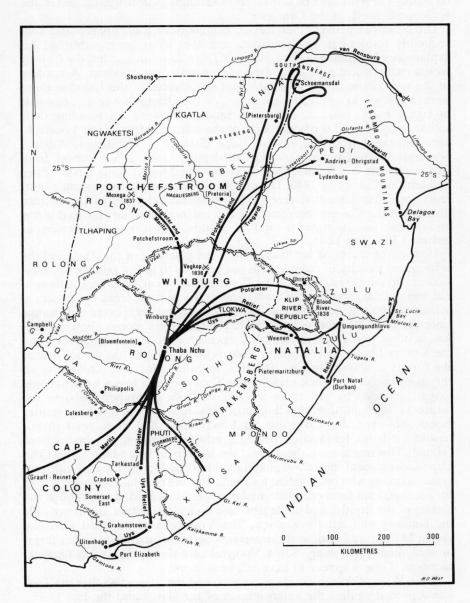

Map 3 The Great Trek: the main Voortrekker routes

emigrants. The Voortrekkers decided to concentrate in the Thaba'Nchu–Vet river area of central trans-Orangia, leapfrogging the Griqua settlements north of the Orange.

On 2 February 1837, Piet Retief, originally of Stellenbosch and subsequently resident in Grahamstown and the Winterberg, published his explanatory Manifesto in the *Graham's Town Journal*, and left the Colony with a party of just over a hundred men, women and children. According to the same issue of the *Journal*, 'near the sources of the Caledon there were, a few weeks ago, 230 wagons . . . on the Orange River . . . upwards of eighty more, and . . . numerous small cavalcades, all wending their solitary way beyond the boundaries of the colony.' Most of the Voortrekkers emanated from the eastern Cape districts of Uitenhage, Albany, Somerset East, Cradock and Graafff-Reinet, with a few others from Beaufort West and Swellendam. According to Muller, some 6,000 whites had left the Colony by 1840. Duvenage, whose calculations rest on admittedly imperfect statistical records of population changes in the eastern districts of the Colony, corrected by the balance between reported births and deaths, has estimated a total emigration of just over 15,000 persons between 1834 and 1840.

Because of the need for discretion in the planning of the Trek and the consequent paucity of records, it is not possible to give a reliable explanation of why, in detail, most of the Voortrekkers went. The Trek followed, but was not the same kind of movement as the periodic treks by farmers in search of labour or seasonal grazing, who had regularly crossed the Orange since the 1820s and always intended to return to the Colony. The *Voortrekker*, in other words, was not simply a *trekboer*, even if some trekboers, like the Kruger family, later became Voortrekkers. Muller has demonstrated the variety of ways in which a frontier Boer might feel insecure, above all through exposure to stock raids by the Xhosa, even if losses were to some extent recouped by victory in the war of 1835. Apprehension over the future security of their landholdings may have worried some frontier Boers, however, for Governor Sir Lowry Cole had threatened to put unsold lands up for auction in 1832, misunderstanding his instructions (Hunt). This might have threatened the holders of some loan farms. The Cape Government, moreover, had failed to expedite the issue of quit-rent grants to many who had applied for them. But the land had not been put up for auction, loan farm occupiers had not been disturbed, and although the closing of the frontier had made new land difficult to obtain, it was not only the landless who left the Colony. The Voortrekkers included men like Gerrit Maritz, well-endowed property-owners who abandoned their farms or sold them for a song. Some Voortrekkers clearly made big financial sacrifices. Others appear to have left as debtors.

Some Voortrekkers were slave-owners, and the suggestion that the Trek was a protest against the emancipation of the slaves and the free blacks gained some currency. Newton-King has argued that about one-fifth of the slaves at the Cape in 1828 were to be found in the eastern districts, even if most slave-owners who suffered losses lived in the western Cape, and did not trek. Slave emancipation did not become effective until the end of 1838, after the Voortrekkers had already gone, though it is clear that in the transitional years of apprenticeships ex-slave-owners suffered marginal inconvenience. Further, if Khoikhoi vagrancy after 1828 and their movement to the mission stations and the Kat River Settlement made some farmers short of labour in the early 1830s (at a time when African labour had been made easier to obtain), it seems that a good many ex-slaves and free blacks left the Colony with the Voortrekkers, and continued in their service though no longer technically living in bondage. The attractions of the veld, Walker's *lekker lewe*, including the excitements and emoluments of the chase, obviously played some part in the Voortrekkers' decision to go. But Germanic wanderlust in itself, selected as 'first cause' of the Trek by Henry Cloete and after him by S. J. du Toit, has rightly been rejected by Muller. For him the Trek was 'no spontaneous folk migration', but 'the best solution which a group of Afrikaner frontier leaders could devise . . . to withdraw from a situation which had become intolerable'.

The 'intolerable' conditions referred to may, as suggested, have included economic hardship or the fear of economic hardship. But it is difficult to avoid the conclusion that the Trek was, at bottom, inspired by a desire to escape from distant authorities which seemed to be both wrongly motivated and at the same time more effective than any that the frontiersmen had previously known. Peires attaches special importance to the work of the Commission of Eastern inquiry in alienating frontier sentiments [see p. 88]. The burden of argument in Retief's Manifesto and in his niece Anna Steenkamp's diary (published by Preller) was that the authorities had abandoned the proper way of handling white–black, master–servant relations, and offended the law of God as well as human susceptibilities in doing so, all at the behest of 'interested and dishonest persons' acting 'under the cloak of religion'. Slurs cast against Boers for their treatment of slaves or Khoikhoi servants bit deep because they could not be shrugged off. The memory of the Black Circuit rankled, even if the executions at Slagters Nek seemed less important after the passage of a few years that they had done at the time. Yet, as Fredrickson has noted, for all their white supremacism, the Voortrekkers did not take a stand on the right of the slave-owner to keep his slaves as slaves.

There is a tradition in Afrikaner historiography which has represented the Trek as a milestone in the development of conscious Afrikaner nationalism, portraying the Voortrekkers as 'nationally aware Afrikaners' linking the Age of the Patriotten with the age of Paul Kruger. However undemonstrable, in the strict sense, this proposition may be, its existence became of great significance historically in helping to build up the Trek as perhaps the central event in the evolution of an Afrikaner mystique [see p. 70]. But any suggestion that the Trek was a demonstration against alien government because it was alien needs to be qualified. The burden of anglicisation was, as noted above, lighter than some subsequent commentators have argued. Furthermore, if the Trek was a demonstration about Government policy, it was a demonstration in support of some aspects of it, and against others. D'Urban was the Trekkers' hero; Glenelg, and those who testified on behalf of the Xhosa to the Aborigines Committee in London, their villains. In this, they enjoyed the support of frontier British opinion on the whole, as the formal presentation of a Bible by W. R. Thompson to Jacobus Uys, on the eve of his departure, was meant to symbolise.

Section II
Chiefdoms, Republics and Colonies in the Nineteenth Century

4 African Chiefdoms

In this chapter an attempt is made to set out the main characteristics of African political communities in southern Africa as they existed in the mid-nineteenth century, after the Mfecane and before their incorporation into the white political systems. The chiefdoms are handled regionally, mainly in terms of the Sotho-Nguni cultural divide, with the Sotho-Tswana element considered first – the Tswana chiefdoms of the Kalahari borderlands, the Pedi and groups with which they came into contact in the northern and eastern Transvaal, and the southern Sotho. Brief accounts then follow of the main southern Nguni peoples (the Xhosa, Thembu, Mfengu and Mpondo) and of the northern Nguni and their offshoots (the Zulu, Swazi, Ngoni and Ndebele). The list is not exhaustive, partly because sufficient work has not been done on the history of some chiefdoms to make even a brief treatment appropriate.

At the end of the chapter generalisations are made about the structures of African societies, where these seem relevant, for the sake of comparison with the British colonial and Boer republican systems with which they came into contact.

4.1 TSWANA CHIEFDOMS OF THE KALAHARI BORDERLAND

The Tswana people of the Kalahari border fell into three main groups: a southern group consisting of the Tlharo, Tshidi-Rolong, Tlhaping, Hurutshe, Ngwaketse, Kwena, Kgatla (Mmanaana) and some Kgalagadi; a northern group which included the Ngwato, Tawana and the bulk of the Kgalagadi; and an eastern group to which the Lete, Tlokwa (unrelated to the Tlokwa of Sekonyela), and Kgatla (Kgafela) belonged. These clusters also included a good many incorporated aliens, who constituted a substantial numerical majority in the Ngwato federation. The Tswana social structure consisted of nobles (*dikgoshana*), commoner-vassals (*batlanka, bashimane, bagaladi*) and servants (*malata*). Unlike the Nguni, they retained not only a memory of earlier political association between chiefdoms, but some rituals in which the memories of earlier paramountcies received practical expression. Thus the Kwena, Ngwaketse and Ngwato accepted an original Hurutshe paramountcy, which was reflected in the precedence given to members of the Hurutshe tribe present at their

51

first-fruits ceremonies, and the holding of that ceremony only after the Hurutshe chief had given permission.

Sansom has drawn a broad distinction between 'western' (Sotho Tswana) and 'eastern' (Nguni) political systems based on the different economic systems to be found in each kind of chiefdom. Characteristic of Tswana society, he argues, was the 'tribal estate', that is, the organisation of the whole territory of the tribe into three clearly defined areas: one for residence, where the large closely settled town of perhaps 25,000 people known as the *metse* was the characteristic feature; one for growing of crops; and one for grazing the hunting. The main functions of government in this kind of society were partly to regulate land use, making sure that the right kind of activities took place in the three regions, partly to settle the claims of rival headmen on behalf of their kin groups for access to particular areas of land, and partly to prevent the movement of townsmen away from the nuclear area of settlement and control. If residential settlements developed at the cattle posts or in the agricultural districts, perhaps twenty miles from the *metse*, then the authority of the chief might collapse, as it did among the Tlhaping of Taung when Molala succeeded Mankurwane in the 1890s. Furthermore, the defensive strategy of the tribe, which was based on the town as the strong point, would also be in jeopardy. To obviate these dangers, the regular meeting of the tribal *pitso* was necessary, so that rival interests could be harmonised and the rules of the settlement reaffirmed. 'Rulers of tribal estates were manipulators of bounds and grants,' Sansom writes, and this activity became the 'basis of political life'. The chiefdom, under such circumstances, exercised its authority behind a protective barrier of formal discussion and consultation, at the same time deriving an income from a variety of sources, of which Schapera stresses the *sehuba* (tribute of various kinds – one tusk of every elephant slain, the skin of every lion, the breast of game slaughtered), the *dikgafela* (a basket of corn from each female member of the tribe after a good harvest), the produce of public fields for which the chief had provided the seed, and so on. The chief also possessed, in his *batlanka*, an army of commoners who performed some kind of service on his behalf, such as caring for his cattle on the royal cattle posts, or repairing his homestead, in return for the right to milk those cattle, or use his wagons, and such gifts as he might shower upon them; and being dependent on the chief for their income, they were at his beck and call.

4.2   CHIEFDOMS OF THE EASTERN TRANSVAAL: PEDI, LOVEDU, VENDA AND NDZUNDZA

The Pedi belonged, with the Tswana, to Sansom's 'western' group of chiefdoms, but differed from them in that, living in an area of higher rainfall, their 'unit of exploitation', that is 'the largest area over which members of a given population would wish to range in furthering their productive activities', tended to be smaller [see pp. 141–5]. Under these circumstances, state-building among the Pedi involved the chief in the amalgamation of a number of separate 'tribal estates'. The Pedi thought in terms of a hierarchical social structure, headed by the royal lineage (*bakgomana*), with commoners (*balata*), incorporated aliens (*bafaladi*) and slaves or captives (*mathupya*) as the lowest grades. The success of Sekwati (1824–60) and his heirs in absorbing other elements turned them into paramount chiefs over more than a hundred small units. Sekwati, who had survived the onslaughts of the Ndwandwe (not the Ndebele, according to Delius) and skirmishing with Potgieter's Boers, played a political role among the northern Sotho not unlike that of Moshweshwe among the southern. He restored order among his people, and rooted out cannibalism, the evidence for which may, in Delius's view, have been exaggerated in the reports of the missionaries. He bought Mpande's friendship with a gift of ostrich feathers and animal pelts after repelling a Zulu attack. He established a political relationship with Boer and Colonial governments, as a result of which Pedi migrants, among the first Africans to do so, began to seek employment in the outside world, some forty years before conquest, and ahead of any imposition of white control, taxation, or economic disasters (Delius). The Pedi 'empire', writes Mönnig, 'cannot be described as a nation or as a state, or as a single tribe', but as a federation built 'by force and by marriage', that is, by conquest and diplomacy. By force, Sekwati had extended his bounds from the edge of the Soutpansberg to the Vaal river, even though he never felt able to wrest the control of the age regiments from the hands of incorporated rulers. But the Pedi rulers were also able to 'establish themselves as wife-givers to all subordinate chiefs' (Sansom), thus exploiting the value of their womenfolk not merely in the productive process (the acquisition of female labour power through polygyny), but in the political process as well. Sekwati refused to confirm in office any chief who did not marry into the royal house. He thus achieved by dynastic diplomacy the kind of extension of the paramount's influence which Shaka had achieved by the distribution of his regiments, and which the Swazi achieved by the ritual transmission of the King's medicated blood. What was more, the Pedi contrived, through the ritual of fire-lighting, to combine the assertion of paramountcy with the recognition of local autonomy among subordinate peoples. On arrival of a royal bride, for whom the tribe had given a substantial brideprice in cattle, all fires in the village were extinguished. They were subsequently relit from the fire kindled in her new homestead, thus establishing a symbolic relationship, through her, with the Pedi chiefdom itself. The tribe, says Mönnig, was then given the right to 'feed' the sons of the tribal wife, or in other words, to pay tribute to their local chief and not to the Pedi, the tribute owing to the Pedi paramount chief being limited to an annual gift of food, the *maduna*, made after the harvest.

The other eastern trans-Vaal chiefdoms, whose traditions have already been noted [see pp. 10–11] still await full ethno-historical treatment. The matrilineal Lovedu, located north of the Olifants river, claimed a Kgatla origin which distinguished them from the Pedi, and also from the Venda of the Soutpansberg who were culturally linked with the Shona. The Sotho-speaking Ndzundza, or Transvaal Ndebele, are similarly to be distinguished from the early nineteenth-century Ndebele intruders under Mzilikazi [see p. 145], who also claim to have arrived in the Transvaal from the south-east, but at a much earlier date.

4.3   THE SOUTHERN SOTHO

Moshweshwe built a political community in the Caledon river valley in the course of the Difaqane, out of elements which were partly Sotho and partly Nguni in composition, but mainly the former. The village, rather than the kinship clan, was the unit of Sotho society, even before the Difaqane. Indeed, had society been structured more pronouncedly on kinship lines, it would have been difficult for Moshweshwe, the head of the Mokotedi, a very junior branch of the Kwena, either to establish his rule over the southern Sotho in the first place, or to build up so distinctive a dynasty of his own. The creation of the Sotho state, both the achievement itself and the manner of it, testify to the statesmanship of this remarkable man [see also pp. 134–9].

Although the Sotho were among the first to possess the age-regiment system under which Moshweshwe was himself brought up, Moshweshwe did not perpetuate it as a control device, partly because the acquisition of horses and firearms gave his people an alternative military system to that devised by the Zulus, and partly because the adoption of Shaka's methods would probably have doomed Moshweshwe's efforts to extend his influence in the crucial early years: it was sufficient that, in time of war, all his chiefs should immediately mobilise his regiments, however independently they acted at other times.

The creation of the southern Sotho state resulted from Moshweshwe's ingenuity to an unusual degree. Appeasing the strong on the one hand by strategic gifts of cattle, Matiwane, Shaka and Mzilikazi all coming in for their share, he was able on the other hand to recoup his losses by successful raids on the Thembu, Tlokwa and others, build up a livestock bank, protect it on his mountain of Thaba Bosiu, and then distribute it as occasion arose – either as brideprice on behalf of impoverished wards, his *bahlanka*, which bought their affection and tied them to him, or as *mafisa*-stock, that is, livestock taken from a defeated enemy or rebellious subordinate, which were returned to him in trust, on condition of his continued good behaviour. Moshweshwe welcomed adherents of all types, reformed cannibals included – even, to their surprise, the band under RaKotswane who had killed and eaten his grandfather. Moroka's Rolong were allowed to settle with the Wesleyans at Thaba'Nchu in 1833. Like Sekwati, but unlike Sekwati's son Sekhukhune, Moshweshwe admitted missionaries, in his case the Paris Evangelicals, and found in Arbousset and Casalis two dedicated advisers who brought heavy pressure on him to adopt Christianity. Moshweshwe was immensely impressed by the European way of life, of which Christian values seemed to him to form an important element. His problem, as it was the problem of Sekhukhune, Setshele, Kgama and others, was to reconcile the commands of the

Church, in particular Christian monogamy, with those customs of his society which held it together. For Moshweshwe's state was not an autocracy, but a loose confederation held together by two kinds of bond, the maintenance of family ties within a large ruling house, and the consent of subordinate chiefs. To disown wives, as in fact Moshweshwe did in a small measure, was both to undermine the respect of large sections of his followers, and also perhaps to undermine the extension of his own authority, and it may have been as much for this reason as any that Moshweshwe put off his baptism until in the end death came first. In general, Moshweshwe controlled his sons and his leading subordinates – the two eldest sons, Letsie and Molapo in particular – by giving them their head as much as possible, and balancing their influence in the tribal *khotla* with that of his councillors, some of whom were his own Christian younger sons.

4.4   THE SOUTHERN NGUNI PEOPLES: XHOSA, THEMBU, MPONDO

Sansom's characterisation of Nguni polities as being by definition of small size, fairly evenly distributed over the land, each village a self-contained economic unit, where agricultural plots and pastures were interspersed and locally controlled by headmen, makes more sense of the southern Nguni socio-political structures than of the northern, as Hall has suggested. Among the southern Nguni, competition between villages for good land, where room for expansion was limited, could be very keen. For survival, villages needed land containing varieties of soil and climate so as to ensure year-round grazing for stock. These were conditions which led more easily to political friction, especially as cattle, on which both the economy and the social system were highly dependent, were a temptation to would-be predators. In this kind of society, the chief could control the relationship between villages, and establish his authority over them for military and fiscal purposes, only by giving constant and visible reminders of his presence. He made progresses through his domain, exercising a right to hospitality, and he levied a tribute of skins, pads and tusks of royal game, as well as receiving proceeds from the sale of privileges and justice. But the effort involved necessarily limited the area of his effective control, unless extreme forms of intimidation were used to compel obedience over a wide area such as some of the northern Nguni chiefs were prepared to indulge in. The insecure economic position of the southern Nguni chief was well-illustrated by the experience of the Mpondo paramountcy, which, as Beinart has shown, was well placed after the Mfecane, during which it lost very large numbers of cattle, to establish close control over the productive activities of the people as they clustered round the great place and began to switch to crop production. But a gradual rebuilding of the depleted herds as a consequence of successful trading led by the 1880s to a decline in the economic power of the paramount ruler, as individual peasants began to acquire livestock of their own, and to sell beasts and produce for good prices to traders from Natal and the eastern Cape.

The political systems of the southern Nguni, by contrast with those of the Zulu and Zulu successor states, were very loosely structured. Though they possessed a common language and culture, they belonged politically to distinct 'tribal clusters', of which the Xhosa, Thembu, Mpondo, Mpondomise and Bomvana, all of which had occupied the area between Natal and the eastern Cape since at least the sixteenth century, were the most important.

The southern Nguni never seem to have formed a single cohesive political unit. The coherence of chiefdoms was in turn affected by a tendency to segmentation or fission, the former term implying the emergence of divisions within a common polity, the latter an actual break-up of the chiefdom into politically separate units. This tendency has been directly linked by Hammond-Tooke and others with the marriage customs of Nguni society, in particular the distinction drawn between the chief's great and his right-hand wife. There is plenty of evidence that the heir of the right-hand wife, who, by custom, lived at some distance from the royal kraal, could set himself up as an independent chief – perhaps as compensation for loss of seniority – and, on irregular occasions in the history of the Xhosa, Thembu, Bhaca, Mpondomise, Mpondo and Xesibe clusters, actually did so. The split between the Rharhabe and Gcaleka in about 1740 was a classic example. Secession of the right-hand house was by no means the only kind of fission to occur, however. The sons of minor wives could also move out. Sons of chiefs, in general, were enabled to build up their own entourages on the occasion of their initiation, when they also received gifts of land and stock on achieving manhood. This was an encouragement to segment, but not necessarily to break right away. Secession normally followed a dispute; and it was sometimes accompanied or preceded by violence. The ease with which it could happen militated against the rise of despotism. When secession occured, the ability of the paramount chief to assert control of any kind over the breakaway segment, for example the right to receive tribute or military aid, could only depend on the availability of agents to use force on his behalf. If he had exceptional personal authority, a paramount might intervene in disputes between units which had passed beyond his control, but he had no recognised machinery for doing this. On the other hand, the formal precedence of the Gcaleka paramount over all Xhosa chiefs did entitle him, as head of the Tshawe (royal) clan, to expressions of allegiance at the annual firstfruits ceremony, and to an overriding power to initiate or to veto military campaigns. Only Ngqika of the Rharhabe ever challenged this authority. Subordinate chiefs in general had little reason for rejecting his paramountcy, for as Peires states, 'absolute domination was no part of the Xhosa political ethic.'

Political divisions among the Cape Nguni in the face of Settler pressure from the Cape were particularly marked between the Ndlambe and Ngqika Xhosa at the beginning of the nineteenth century, between the Gcaleka and the Rharhabe Xhosa during the wars of the mid-nineteenth century, and between the Xhosa, the Thembu and the Mpondo during the 1870s. Divided, they eventually fell in 1878–94. United, they would either have survived, or – perhaps more probably – fallen faster [see pp. 113–28].

The Thembu, though speaking the same language as the Xhosa, have traditions which give them priority of settlement over all other Nguni peoples in the trans-Keian regions; but as Wagenaar has emphasised they are hard to classify, save in terms of a loyalty to the ruling Hala dynasty even less intense than that of the Xhosa to the Tshawe. They incorporated peoples of diverse origins, including Sotho and Mfengu, who never lost their distinctive identities. When they first moved to the region of the Mbashe river, supposedly about 1600, they appear to have had plenty of elbow room. Segmentation was easy and there was little need for central control. It was only under Ngubencuka (c. 1810–30) that they began to coalesce, by which time they had come under attacks by Bhaca and others, and they looked chiefly to Hintsa's Gcaleka and – with advice from their Methodist missionaries – to the Colony for support. After Ngubencuka's death, at a moment of turmoil on the Cape eastern frontier, the Tshatshu sub-chiefdom under Maphasa broke away and moved over the Kei towards the Colonial border. Settling in the district now known as Whittlesea, where he allowed the Moravian missionaries to set up their station of Shiloh, Maphasa remained neutral in the frontier war of 1834–5, but accepted custody of cattle stolen from the Colony, and therefore had to come to terms with the Colony when the war was over. He agreed to come in under Stockenstrom's treaty system [see p. 119]. But when Governor Maitland instituted a second round of treaties in 1844, it was Mtirara, heir to Ngubencuka, whom he approached to sign on behalf of all the Thembu. The Thembu were thus engaged as clients of the Colony by peaceful means, and despite the traumatic experience of the cattle-killing of 1857, in which they were marginally involved [see p. 123], they remained in control of two geographically distinct areas: their heartland on the Mbashe river, which passed under the control of Mtirara's brother Joyi, and the 'Tambookie Location' west of the Indwe river, later known as Glen Grey, over which Nonesi, Mtirara's mother, was recognised as queen-regent until her son Ngangelizwe came of age in 1863. These territories were linked by the occupation of Emigrant Thembuland in the 1860s. Rivalries connected with this, and with the trans-Keian crisis of the 1870s [see pp. 124–6] continued to make Thembu unity an idle dream, yet the Thembu were to achieve something that eluded nearly all African chiefdoms during the conquest era: survival, with minimal loss of land, and without any major conflict with the colonising power, by the date of their incorporation under British rule in 1876.

The Mpondo, who stayed out of the wars with the Cape altogether, were divided into an eastern and a western branch. This happened when Faku tried to avoid a conflict between Ndamase, his right hand son and commander of his armies, and the heir of his great wife, Mqikela. He sent the former west across the Umzimvubu and allowed him considerable independence. The split lasted because Mqikela was unable, owing to the opposition of other chiefs, to restore the unity of the chiefdom round his own great place at Qaukeni (Beinart). Like the southern Nguni in general, the Mpondo rulers had no age regiments to help them in such a task.

4.5   THE MFENGU (FINGO) PEOPLE

In the history of this region the Mfengu have a special place. Their name derived, apparently, from the Xhosa verb *ukumfenguza* (to seek service), though the missionary Ayliff noted that the name was soon anglicised to 'Fingo'. The name implied status rather than ethnic affiliation, for they were apparently remnants of various broken chiefdoms – the Bhaca, whom Faku had subjected to Mpondo rule; the Bhele, Zizi and Hlubi from 'Natal', who had suffered in conflict with the Ngwane; as well as the Ngwane themselves, after their defeat at Mbholompo in 1828, at the hands of Colonel Somerset [see p. 116]. After this defeat the Thembu and Gcaleka rulers distributed these suppliants as labourers among their own people. Hintsa called them his 'dogs' without apparently implying servility, and they used their survival skills to build up considerable cattle stocks by purchase and by looting before they were taken west across the Fish from Gcalekaland by British forces in May 1835. In view of the labour shortage in the eastern Cape [see p. 43], the suggestion that the Mfengu were being removed to servitude in the Colony must be considered, especially as Ayliff noticed that 'hundreds' of the 16,000 who crossed the Fish into the Colony were engaged as farm servants; but they entered with 20,000 cattle, which may or may not have been included in the 60,000 taken by British troops. The Cape Governor intended to settle them on the Fish river frontier, until the reversal of his policy by the British Government made this impossible [see pp. 117–18]. Thereafter they were given locations in various parts of the eastern Cape and found favour with the authorities as soldiers fighting in the Colonial interest, as peasant farmers and townsmen holding European title, as successful scholars and religious converts, as hard-bargaining traders, and in due course as parliamentary voters, for all of which literal enslavement in the Colony would have been a somewhat surprising starting-point.

4.6   THE NORTHERN NGUNI PEOPLES: ZULU, GAZA, NGONI, AND SWAZI

The Zulu and Zulu successor states made rather more progress than the southern Nguni in building and maintaining a strong, centralised chieftainship, but at a costly price [see pp. 149–54]. Those chiefs survived best who devised techniques for extending their control over their weaker neighbours without alienating them or creating seedbeds of disaffection which they could not smother. Here the development of the age-regiment system which was practised in one form or another by all the Zulu successor states, including the Swazi, and by most of the Tswana and Sotho peoples as well, met the situation. Dingiswayo and Shaka deliberately allowed the traditional circumcision rituals to fall into disuse, perhaps because they could be used to encourage separatist dreams among ambitious princes of the blood. Instead, they drafted the youth of both sexes into separate regiments, which were located in a series of large barracks at places scattered through the kingdom. Here, till their regiments were disbanded and they were granted permission to marry, the young men worked, hunted, raided and fought for their king. The emphasis may well have lain primarily on working rather than on fighting (Cobbing, Guy) or, as Peires has put it, on providing a means whereby 'human labour could be diverted out of the homestead between the ages of puberty and marriage, and channelled into the service of the state'. Not only could the king thus control and appropriate the produce of labour, but by maintaining control over the age of marriage he could provide himself with a highly efficient device for the maintenance of public order. The sons of conquered peoples were also drafted into the regiments, and the regiments were placed under the command of the king's loyal *indunas*. Meanwhile the chiefs of defeated enemies and subordinate clans were, as a general rule, allowed to remain in office and exercise territorial jurisdiction; but they had no control over the regiments. Shaka's experience with Mzilikazi may have taught him the danger of leaving territorial armies under the command of their own local leaders.

The Zulu system was not broken after the death of Shaka or even that of Dingane; but under Mpande, who owed his territorial security in some measure to the good offices of the Boers and the British colonial regime in Natal, it changed in some of its externals. Mpande was not the effete, sex-ridden slug of popular legend. He wisely avoided direct confrontation with white power, but this is not to say that he allowed the Zulu military system to fall into decay. He enrolled at least thirteen new age-regiments during his reign, and probably commanded larger armies than ever Shaka had done, though like the 'Sergeant King' of Prussia he hardly ever sent them on expeditions (his attacks on the Swazi and the Pedi between 1847 and 1852 being important exceptions). He murdered rivals in his own family, notably his brother Gqugqu in 1843; he took vigorous measures to discourage the emigration of refugees, especially after Gqugqu's murder had resulted in a wholesale migration from south-east Zululand into Natal. He relaxed the externals of his predecessor's despotism, however, choosing to take the advice of a council for much of the time, as was normally the Zulu practice. But this compromise position proved, in the long run, hard to hold. Perhaps through lack of vigilance he allowed opposition factions to develop in the provinces, led by Ngqengelele in the north, Maphita and his son Zibhebhu among the Mandlakazi, and Hamu the levirate son of his own dead brother's wife as well as some others. This might not in itself have mattered, but for his neglect, deliberate or otherwise, to select a great wife, and perhaps even his encouragement of rivalry between his two sons. These were Cetshwayo, head of the Usuthu faction, and Mbuyazi of the Gqoza, whom Mpande forced to live apart on the argument that two bulls ought not to live in the same kraal. Civil war broke out between the factions in 1856. Cetshwayo, with larger armies, beat his opponent and slaughtered his dependants without mercy, achieving such an ascendancy in the kingdom as a result that he became the effective ruler and left Mpande little more than titular office, before succeeding to the kingship on his father's death in 1872. The inner strength of the Zulu political system, despite the periodic succession conflicts and intergenerational feuding which disturbed it, is well described by Guy, whose account of the kingdom in the days of Cetshwayo lays emphasis on the economic strength of the system of production based on the spread of segmenting homesteads and the passage of cattle as bridewealth into the hands of homestead leaders, the *umnumzana*, and from them as tribute to the king, who could therefore put an army of 30,000 men into the field. Not only did the traditional chiefs of pre-Shakan days participate in the great council, or *ibandla* (which also contained other notables as occasion demanded), but their territorial principalities kept their identities in such a way that Sir Garnet Wolseley could use them as a basis for his fragmented Zulu state in 1879 [see p. 152]. Alongside these local seats of potential resistance, however, were the homesteads of the numerous Zulu royal lineage, who could act as *vassi dominici*, the eyes and ears of the king. After his dethronement Cetshwayo later gave the Barry Commission a relaxed account of Zulu government as he saw it – a system in which the king never made laws or gave judgement without taking the advice, not of the people, but of their leaders; but he expected his pronouncements to carry unquestioning obedience when he uttered them for precisely this reason, and because there was 'nobody in Zululand who does not know the law' as promulgated by word of mouth through the regiments on the great feast days.

The Swazi had settled in the region west of the Lebombo mountains and north of the Pongola river. They incorporated Sotho-speaking peoples in the area and appear to have picked up from them the custom of cross-cousin marriage (as distinct from the exogamous practice of the Nguni), and, in the *libandla*, a form of government by conference comparable with the *pitso* of the Sotho [see p. 65]. Like Sekwati and Moshweshwe of the Sotho, Sobhuza I was, in Bonner's words, 'one of the Mfecane's great survivors', perhaps because he and his 'conquering aristocracy' showed a capacity for adapting to the customs of their new subjects. During the reign of Mswati (1839–65), the Swazi state took shape under the inspiration of the Queen Mother, Thandile, who not only saw to the build-up of a system of age regiments, but also developed the annual *incwala* (first fruits) ceremonies into an occasion for the ritual upliftment of the royal office. Mswati moved his capital to the Hhohho region north of the Komati river, partly as a consequence of his growing involvement with the Boers of the eastern Transvaal, partly to distance himself from the Zulu. From this northern base he expanded his control southward through the build-up of marriage alliances, Sotho-fashion, and the imposition of tribute on the subordinate chiefdoms, linked with a small amount of predatory slave-raiding in the lowveld. This created an altogether misleading impression of security in view of the troubles which were later to descend upon the kingdom [see p. 148].

Of the Ndwandwe chiefdoms which migrated northwards after their defeat at the hands of Shaka, the Gaza under Soshangane made the easiest adjustment to their new circumstances – for a time. The followers of Soshangane were a privileged cattle-raising community who dominated the Tsonga, Ndau and other peoples of the region south of the Save river.

They maintained an age-regiment system less tightly controlled than that of the Zulu, and dominated their subject peoples under an elaborate hierarchical structure of status groups graded by lineages, in which the Ndwandwe royal lineage had precedence over their Tsonga, Ndau and Tonga subjects. In order to govern more effectively, the ruling lineage devised a system of territorial apanages under royal siblings, which increased steadily and were redivided after a civil conflict on the death of Soshangane in 1858, when Mzila beat his brother Mawewe for the succession. From 1860, however, the Gaza state went into decline, as its prosperity from ivory and slave sales fell with the shooting out of the elephants and the growing dependence of the society on the proceeds of migrant labour to Natal, Kimberley and the Transvaal goldfields. It was involvement in the economy of the white-controlled states that eventually destroyed the Gaza kingdom in the 1890s.

Zwangendaba's Ngoni preserved their aristocratic identity among numerous subject peoples, even though they were constantly on the move. Matrimonial liaisons of the ruling dynasty were kept within the Ngoni group. As new villages were established, the arrangement of the huts was in strict accordance with the status of the householders within the clan, just as the territorial distribution of the clan-heads in relation to the king was regulated by a fixed rule. The age regiments did not live in separate military towns, as with the Zulu, but were based on the households of the king or his relatives, though only the king could initiate major campaigns. The system enhanced the status of the king, but also lent itself to centrifugal tendencies. When they settled among the Tumbuka to the north-east of lake Malawi, after conquering them, they made a number of mistakes more commonly associated with white colonialism (Vail). They overworked the land and impoverished the soil. They first discouraged, but subsequently promoted, the slave trade, and in the end they faced rebellion by a people who had been deprived of their status without losing their capacity to fight back when hard pressed.

4.7   THE KHUMALO NDEBELE

Mzilikazi's Ndebele advanced into the trans-Vaal as an army as well as a people, but Cobbing argues that the military character of their state has been exaggerated. The king was as much ruler as general, and like other settled chiefs he was at the centre of the religious and economic life of the tribe, he 'tried hard to make rain', and he was the chief dispenser of justice. The military towns (*amabutho*) became, through maturation, the centres of a civil administration from which villages of settlement (*imizi*) proliferated. They were not massive Tswana-style towns but small settlements under an *induna* of commoner origin, who built up his power through the incorporation of war captives and – contrary to common belief – the increase of his own cattle herds, for not all the cattle belonged to the king. When the Ndebele moved north of the Limpopo, the *Zansi* (that is, those who came from south of the Vaal) came to live in close association with the *Enhla* (the Sotho-Tswana elements from north of the Vaal), in proximity to the Great Place at Bulawayo. They formed the nucleus of a state, sixty per cent of whose population may have been natives of the region who accepted tributary status. Some of these spoke Sindebele and pierced their ears as a sign of allegiance, whereas others – generally those who lived at a distance from the capital – were reluctant taxpayers at best, and subject to periodic raids [see also pp. 157–60].

4.8   THE BONDS OF AFRICAN SOCIETY IN THE NINETEENTH CENTURY

Taking African societies as a whole during their period of consolidation between the Mfecane and the imposition of white rule, one can detect the influence of forces old and new. If in some societies the authority of the chief was endowed with increased ritual significance, as among the Swazi, the Venda and the Lovedu, in others strength was discovered in new forms of military organisation – either the horses and firearms of the Sotho and Pedi, or the age-sets which so many chiefdoms adopted and used as a device for holding down conquered territory or incorporating conquered people. Less assertive devices for extending political authority were the techniques of bride-giving developed by the Lovedu and the Pedi, and the distribution of *mafisa* cattle practised by Moshweshwe. Finally, there were the beginnings of a bureaucratic breakthrough, commonly initiated by the missionaries, whose influence paved the way for a takeover by the magistrates; and this, in the case of families like the Ayliffs, Brownlees and Shepstones, meant literally a transfer of responsibility from fathers to their sons.

The articulation of government in these African societies bore little resemblance in detail to that in the white-controlled states, whether British or Boer; but comparisons are instructive because all were concerned with the organisation and control of power, the rationalisation of decision-making in the interest of group survival, and issues of distributive and natural justice.

Size could vary markedly in black polities, as in white. Commentators have written of 'empires' like the Zulu, or 'kingdoms' like the Swazi, and where the degree of cohesion was in doubt, of 'chiefdoms' (tribes) and 'tribal clusters', as among the Cape Nguni. There was a big difference in the size of the rambling Ngwato federation on the one hand and the minute Lovedu principality in the northern trans-Vaal on the other.

Kinship ties helped to regulate social relations and cultural obligations in African society, but their supposed connection with government or the production of food or merchandise is less emphasised now than it used to be. A person belonged first to his family, and beyond that to a clan sharing a common 'praise name' in Nguni society, or totem group in Sotho. Totems in Sotho-Tswana society, usually some sacred animal like the porcupine of the Pedi, or the crocodile of the Kwena, or perhaps the iron (*tshipi*) of the Rolong, may have had some original connection with the economic activities of the tribe, notably hunting or iron-smelting, and most were once associated with food taboos; but in historic times they seem to have had social rather than ritual significance. To share a totem or a 'praise name' gave a person access to the fraternity of others across a number of chiefdoms who bore it. But whereas Sotho were encouraged to marry a partner from the same totem group, it was forbidden for the Nguni to marry within the clan. One advantage of endogamous marriage was that it led to tighter control over the distribution of cattle given as bridewealth.

In most societies by the nineteenth century the kinship ties had been superseded for most political purposes by territorial. The organisation of local government was by districts and wards under sub-chiefs and head-men. In the Sotho-Tswana chiefdoms, the large towns in which the people congregated were commonly divided into patrilineal wards, while Nguni village headmen were normally hereditary. But there is evidence that during the late nineteenth century the concentration of particular lineages in the town wards was beginning to disappear, and the ward headman selected from among his own people was being replaced by a new official, the district headman, increasingly drawn from the royal lineage. Pauw, in his study of the Tlhaping of Taung, noted that this development started to take place at about the time of Chief Mankurwane's death in 1892, and linked it with an attempt to check the declining authority of the chief when pressure on the land was becoming critical.

This trend is an important pointer to what was happening in the chief-dom itself, the keystone of the African political arch. Some scholars view the office of chief as rooted in the idea of authority over persons, ruling through hereditary headmen and ward heads. Others see it as the headship of a defined territorial unit subdivided into districts and wards. It seems that there was a tendency for territorial lordship to grow, and for the office to become increasingly formalised as a result of European influences and the growth of literacy among the chief's advisers. But the coherence of African society always depended on the chief himself. He was the distribu-tor of land and controller of its use, the regulator of labour, the ritual rain-maker and the organiser of the hunt. As a Zulu proverb expressed it, he was the 'breast of the nation', the universal provider in times of need from the royal herds, which were largely composed of beasts levied as fines or tribute. He could also be the judge of the most serious misdemeanours, the lawgiver, and the war leader.

From the use by historians and anthropologists of the terms 'king' and 'chief' it seems fair to state that the distinction between them is largely a matter of the degree of authority and power. 'Kingdom' is a name com-monly ascribed to amalgamations of chiefdoms (Thompson), and this is the general line followed here, the terms 'king' and 'paramount chief' being regarded as equivalent. The Zulu, Swazi and Sotho rulers are generally referred to by their historians as kings, the Pedi rulers not. Where the southern Nguni are concerned Peires uses the terms interchangeably; Monica Wilson regarded the distinction as essentially 'fuzzy'.

So important a figure was the chief, that rituals for strengthening the monarchy, usually connected with the first-fruits ceremonies, were common to most societies. The Zulu *Umkhosi* ceremony, like the *Incwala* ceremony of the Swazi, and the *Ingxwala* of the Mpondo, had its parallels in Bhaca, Mpondomise and Xhosa rituals. Hilda Kuper describes the *Incwala* as more than a first-fruits festival, more than an historical pageant, and above all a 'ritualisation of the king', a device for protecting the tribe by allaying the evil forces which might harm their ruler, and consolidating the political nation around him. Among the Venda, according to Lestrade, the chief acquired an exceptionally elevated status, and could confer divinity on himself towards the end of his life. Mönnig ascribes similar attributes to the Pedi paramount, who was referred to as 'God of the Earth.'

The chief had his own councillors and officers of state. These were not in the first instance the learned clerks of a medieval European kingdom with its passion for keeping records; but the Sotho, the Mpondo and some other chiefdoms did make use of missionaries for this purpose, and by the late nineteenth century some chiefs – notably Dinuzulu, Kgama and Mbandzeni – employed literate African clerks. Councillors, however, were not so much bureaucrats as, in Sansom's words, 'leaders of followings'. From the chief's side, running government involved plying the men he valued with the plums of office – headmanships, district governorships, military leaderships, and wealth in wives and cattle – and at the same time depriving those he wished to edge out. There was, however, some evidence of specialisation in the Great Place. Behind the chief generally stood the great *induna*, with a combination of viceregal and judicial authority like that of a medieval justiciar. He can be found in both Tswana and Nguni societies. Control over economic affairs was also vested in a variety of high-ranking officers, such as the *isandla senkosi* (chief's hand) of the Bhaca, the *mofa-masemo* (economic supervisor) of the Pedi, and the *modisa* (controller of pastures) of the Tswana.

In their appointment of councillors, tribal rulers might prefer either their kinsmen or commoners, sometimes a mixture of both. The proliferation of offices held in Basutoland by the sons of Moshweshwe, often at the cost of displacing other people, and almost to the exclusion of commoners, brought real danger to public peace. Swazi convention graded its aristocracy strictly in accordance with their proximity to the ruling Dlamini line, but kings avoided giving too much power to male kinsmen and reserved some key posts for leading commoners. In the Pedi and Tswana societies, chiefs tended to consult close relatives, but felt free to invite anybody whose advice could be useful to their councils, commoners included.

The councils on which the chief depended were of various kinds, formal and informal. All societies, even the Zulu in normal times, laid stress on the principle of government by discussion and consent. The *pitso* of the Sotho, the *imbito* (*imbizo*) of Nguni chiefdoms, the *libandla* of the Swazi, like the folkmoot of the Anglo-Saxons, provided a sounding-board for the ruler as he tried to determine the big issues of state. Thus Ashton describes the *pitsos* of Moshweshwe:

> Discussion, according to contemporary observers, was keen, great free-
> dom of speech allowed, and great weight attached to the opinion and

attitude of the people. The people, as often as not, followed the line they judged the chief was taking, but if, for some reason, they opposed him, and he expected their opposition to be firm, he would not often risk forcing the issue. Moshesh himself constantly asserted that he could do nothing without consulting and gaining the consent of his sons and other chiefs, and in his announcements and proclamations he usually used such phrases as 'Given with the advice and concurrence of our tribe,' or, as in his proclamation against witchcraft, 'This word is assented to by Letsie, by all my brothers and by all men of the tribe who spit on the lie of witchcraft and cover its face with their spittle.' (p. 216).

One of the most elaborate conciliar systems was to be found among the Pedi, who had a kind of inner cabinet (the *lekgotla la teng la kgosi*), a larger 'privy council' for important but confidential business (the *lekgotla la thopa*), various special councils within particular tribes which made up the kingdom, and two types of assembly for important public business – a general assembly of adult males meeting voluntarily (the *lekgotla la banna*), and the *pitso*, at which attendance was as obligatory as attendance at a feudal great council. Similar varieties of council were to be found among the Tswana.

The decisions of a council would normally be promulgated in the name of the chief, whose task it was to ascertain the consensus of the meeting. If he ignored the advice or made a bad decision, the headmen in the wards might simply neglect to carry out his will. If he flew in the face of public opinion, he might face a political breakaway by large sections of the tribe. He had, however, certain advantages. In theory he could do no wrong. To take an extreme case, if the Queen of the Lovedu failed to make rain, it was the court official responsible for the ritual who shouldered the blame. The chief was also entitled to expect faithful service from his subjects (*khonza* in Xhosa, *khonta* in Swazi). But he could not count on continued acceptance of his authority unless he was able to exert it effectively in particular situations, and he could be tried before a tribal court for misconduct.

The councillors might sit either as a court or as a law-making body, but they were not likely to get these functions mixed up. Legislation, as distinct from the affirmation or adaptation of custom, was rare, though it did happen, especially when a king committed his tribe to the adoption of Christianity, and sought as a consequence of missionary pressure to abolish payment of brideprice, or initiation ceremonies, or the brewing of strong drink among his people. Though himself unbaptised, Moshweshwe promised the French missionaries that his own offspring would not be initiated. Kgama, Setshele and Lentswe, all Christians, introduced far-reaching changes in the above customs, but as Dachs suggests, they found enforcement very difficult.

Succession to the chieftainship was another matter on which a good deal of uniformity prevailed. It normally passed to the eldest son of the great wife – that is, of a wife selected at a late stage in the chief's life, certainly after his accession to the chieftainship, and who was generally a member of the royalty of another tribe. The Xhosa paramount, for example, habitually married a Thembu princess, the Swazi an Ndwandwe. The chief's council nevertheless had to register its approval of the chosen heir, and the councils among the Swazi, Venda and northern Sotho could pass over an unsuitable heir reasonably easily (as the witan of Wessex had repeatedly been able to do), so long as they picked a member of the ruling house. Among the southern Sotho, it was a council of the sons of Moshweshwe who made the choice, and gave impressive backing, for example, to Lerothodi in 1891 and Letsie II in 1905. Female succession, except among the Lovedu from the time of Modjadji I, was generally ruled out; but queen-regents were not unknown, MmaNthatisi of the Tlokwa being a notable example, while the Swazi Ndlovukazi (queen-mother, literally 'she-elephant') had an important function, as the one through whom public authority was transmitted, in helping to select the heir to the chiefdom. Her role was not unlike that in which Bagehot cast Queen Victoria, for her powers included the right to be consulted, and the right to rebuke her son. Bonner's description of Thandile, the mother of Mswati, highlights the 'remarkable' political role of this Ndlovukazi in particular.

One of the main problems of chiefly government was the instability which stemmed from a number of causes inherent in the system. Assassination of chiefs sometimes occurred, generally as a consequence, not of social revolution or of ideological disagreement, but of a succession dispute. The mothers of a chief's sons, watchful over their offspring's claims, were quick to jump on irregularities which might keep them out of the running. Schapera notes that among some Tswana and Tsonga chiefdoms the succession was so frequently contested that the installation ceremony contained a public challenge to rivals to come forward and fight, which was 'not always an empty gesture'. Regents in the saddle were sometimes reluctant to vacate office when their wards reached manhood – a significant cause of unrest, for the fact that an Nguni chief married his great wife late in life frequently meant that his heir was a minor on accession, and what was more, surrounded by elder half-brothers from among whom his regent was likely to have been selected. Some rulers tried to make their positions secure by the murder of potential rivals – a practice in which the Zulu excelled, for Shaka and Dingane killed all their sons at birth, Dingane all his brothers.

4.9   NEW CONCENTRATIONS OF POWER AFTER THE MFECANE

The Mfecane, followed by the Great Trek and the penetration of white settlement into the highveld and Natal, radically redistributed power among the Bantu-speaking chiefdoms, and for a time promoted its aggregation into fewer, stronger hands. Thus Moshweshwe of the southern Sotho, who died in 1870, achieved spectacular success in building up a kingdom east of the Caledon river out of the residue of various Sotho and Nguni peoples. Most of the Tswana chiefdoms on the edge of the Kalahari succumbed to white pressure, but Kgama's Ngwato were an important exception. Like Moshweshwe, and with just enough support from the British Government, Kgama played his cards skilfully and was able to preserve the greater part of his lands from white settlement. Together with Mswati and his successors in Swaziland, who were far less successful in resisting white encroachment, they laid the foundations of the High Commission Territories of the twentieth century, which became independent states as Lesotho, Botswana and Swaziland in the 1960s.

Some chiefdoms were successful for a time, but later succumbed. Notable among these was the Zulu state, which survived the military overthrow of Dingane in 1838–9. His successor, Mpande, refrained from risking another military confrontation before his death in 1872; but he conserved the military system for use once more against the whites by his successor Cetshwayo (1872–9), under whom it suffered destruction [see pp. 149–53]. Other chiefdoms which fell after resisting the spread of white settlement were the Pedi of Sekhukhune in the eastern trans-Vaal, who were overthrown between 1876 and 1879 [see pp. 141–5], the Ndebele of Mzilikazi and Lobengula, whose collapse resulted from the conflicts of 1893 and 1896–7 [see pp. 157–60], and on the eastern Cape frontier the Nguni chiefdoms of the Xhosa, Thembu, Mpondo and their associates, whose failure to combine, save on rare occasions, ensured their piecemeal absorption by the Cape Colony over a prolonged period [see pp. 113–28].

5 Boer Republics

5.1 VOORTREKKER TRIBULATIONS

The Voortrekkers set out in their tented wagons as groups of families with their retainers and their cattle, their horses and their guns, intending to preserve those features of life on the frontier which they had learnt to enjoy in the Colony [see pp. 44–8]. These included easy access to land on which to run their cattle; the right to make use of available indigenous labour without having to answer to external authority in the matter of its treatment; and the right to make their own accommodation with the peoples with whom they came into contact, and to take such action as might be necessary to preserve the safety of their communities in the face of external threats.

They thought, apparently, that they were moving into empty land, or at any rate land where they would be able to reach an understanding with those already living there. They found very quickly that their own occupancy was contested, sometimes because they insisted on ownership rather than mere occupation, and the resultant conflicts forced them into a tighter group coherence than had ever been necessary for the trekboer graziers who had previously ventured north of the Orange. The *laager* of wagons and thornbushes became their emergency fortress, the mounted rifleman their main resource for attack, as they attempted to settle on thinly populated stretches of veld where water resources were relatively scarce, and where the demand for land was determined by the unreliability of rainfall and the need to hunt game as a vital rather than a supplementary activity.

Almost the first task which Hendrik Potgieter's men faced after leaving the trekker rendezvous at Thaba 'Nchu, west of the Caledon river and crossing the Vaal was the repulse of the Ndebele, who attacked his men thinking they were aggressive Griqua. Potgieter's party was organised on traditional commando lines, and controlled by a *krygsraad* (war council). Their task of subduing the Ndebele only half completed, they returned to Thaba 'Nchu in November 1836, shortly after Maritz had arrived there from the south. The trekkers then held an open meeting on 2 December, and by ballot chose a *Burgerraad* (citizen council) of seven, electing Maritz as its president and Potgieter as their *legerkommandant* (army commander). The *Raad*, whose members were called *regters* (judges) was envisaged as a combined lawmaking, law-enforcing and policy-making body, though it may not have made any laws.

Personal animosity, fired by policy disagreements between Maritz and Potgieter, split this Burgerraad. Potgieter thought that the best line of advance lay northwards, with control of the highveld and access to the sea through Mozambique as the proper objectives, while Maritz saw Natal as the promised land. After the N. G. Kerk of the Cape had explicitly refused to supply a pastor for the trekkers, Potgieter and his associates proposed the Methodist Archbell, head of the Thaba 'Nchu mission. Maritz doubted the suitability of his own brother-in-law, the elderly and rather prickly Erasmus Smit; but Smit was nevertheless supported strongly by Maritz's colleague, Piet Retief.

Maritz courted Retief's favour when the latter reached the Voortrekker base from the Colony in April 1837. In a fresh election to the Burgerraad, Retief was elected 'Governor' and Maritz 'Judge President of the Council of Policy' and 'Governor's Deputy'. Retief also took over the role of commandant from Potgieter, who, though the victor over Mzilikazi, did not gain a seat on the Raad. This was unfortunate for Voortrekker unity. Potgieter's defeat was further reflected in the Nine Articles adopted at Winburg on 6 June 1837, which purported to set up a 'Free Province of New Holland in South East Africa', and made Retief 'Overseer of our United Company [*Maatschappij*] in this camp'. Its reformed members were required to dissociate from the English missionaries (a reference to Archbell and the Methodists) on penalty of expulsion from the community. Retief sought to lay down guidelines for this emergent polity in his Instructions to Commandants and Field Cornets issued in July. Field cornets were made responsible, under threat of punishment, for drawing up militia lists. Failure to turn out on commando service was made a serious offence. Care of the veld, control over hunting, and supervision of subject people were placed in the hands of these semi-military officials, who were to bring to trial before *landdrost* and *heemraden* not only those who maltreated servants, but those who 'booked in' the children of Bushmen or other aboriginals for service. Good relations with the surrounding chiefdoms were essential, and in October Retief made a treaty with Moroka of Thaba 'Nchu and his Rolong.

Differences between the leaders induced them, before long, to go their separate ways. Potgieter went north to finish his fight with the Ndebele and make the trans-Vaal safe for Boer settlement. Retief, with the backing of Maritz, who followed him after an interval, moved over the Drakensberg into 'Natalia', reaching Port Natal on 19 October, 'not having met a soul on the way', and receiving a cordial welcome from the British settlers and traders already established at the port. Retief immediately wrote to Dingane, asking for the cession of territory which Shaka and Dingane between them had granted to white applicants on three previous occasions (Davenport and Hunt), and on 27 October set out for Dingane's capital of Umgungundlovu.

As the Voortrekkers had recently smashed the power of Mzilikazi, Dingane could not fail to be impressed by Boer strength. When, in the following January, Retief successfully recaptured cattle taken from the Zulu by Sekonyela, the Tlokwa chief, that impression could only have been strengthened. Retief failed to read Dingane's mind, rather presumptuously lectured him on the defeat of Mzilikazi as a sign of divine disapproval, yet walked into Dingane's prepared trap on 6 February 1838 without taking the sort of precautions which other Voortrekker leaders clearly thought necessary. After first signing a paper which granted the land between the Tugela, the Umzimvubu and the Drakensberg to the Boers, Dingane had Retief and his party murdered on the same day, and followed this up with attacks on the other Boer settlements, all but destroying the Voortrekker presence in Natal in a series of engagements on the Bloukrans and Bushman's rivers, at Italeni and on the Buffalo, between February and August, during which some 500 Voortrekkers, of whom nearly 300 were white (Muller) lost their lives, and many livestock were captured. Not till November could effective relief be organised, by which time Maritz had also died. But then Andries Pretorius, who had already scouted for the Voortrekkers on several fronts on the highveld and in Natal, arrived from Graaff-Reinet with a commando of 470 men, to win a sensational victory over Dingane in what came to be known as the battle of Blood River on 16 December 1838. Boer fire power from a defensive laager on the bend of the river accounted, it is said, for 3,000 Zulu dead at the cost of only three minor casualties among the defenders. Whether the victory be attributed to Boer marksmanship or to God – a matter on which there has been some difference of opinion among the experts, as Liebenberg and Van Jaarsveld have testified – it is not difficult to understand why the battle should have become revered as a sacred moment in Afrikaner history. Sarel Cilliers, tHe Voortrekker leader whose biographer was reminded of the battles of Tours and Plassey (thus perhaps underrating the aspect of revenge), recorded in his memoirs that before the battle the Boers had made a vow to treat the occasion as holy if victory should come their way. The Church of the Vow was accordingly built in Pietermaritzburg, the new capital named after Retief and Maritz for the Republic of Natalia, which now came into being.

5.2   THE REPUBLIC NATALIA

The Republic of Natalia, bordered by the Black Umfolosi, the Drakensberg and the Umzimvubu, was the first Boer state properly so called, and became for five years after Blood River the main territorial base for the Trek as a whole. Its constitution of March 1839 featured the principle of representative democracy, ruled by a *Raad van Representanten van het Volk*, a body of twenty-four men aged between twenty-four and sixty, elected annually in open ballot by white male adult suffrage. This insistence on an ethnically restricted suffrage, so pronounced a feature of all subsequent trekker constitutions, was not even a debating point among a self-contained *volk* living in isolated pockets on their widely scattered farms, coming together perhaps only at quarterly intervals for the *Nagmaal*, and ruling over a territory from which non-members of the *volk* had not been physically excluded. It was a natural precaution, on which group survival depended, at a time when frontiers were still improvised and the institutions of state had not yet settled down. So unthinkable did the enlargement of the franchise seem to be, that an alteration of the rules so as to include out-groups – non-Reformed, Uitlander, non-European – became almost impossible to envisage later on, even when regular government had become established. But although the principle of representation was adopted, and the Raad was given authority to decide on matters of war and peace, the allocation of land, the protection of the established Dutch Reformed Church, and so on, controversial issues were still to be reserved for public debate, enabling a majority of the electors at a public meeting to tie the hands of the Raad. There was a profound suspicion of uncontrolled authority running through the constitution, in marked contrast to the Winburg Articles, which had made Retief a permanent head of state.

Provision was made for a vacation executive of five, to take decisions when the Raad was not engaged in its regular quarterly sessions in January, April, July and October; but all its decisions required subsequent ratification. The Raad elected a new president at each sitting, but with no executive authority independent of his chairmanship of the Raad. The Commandant-General presided over a *krygsraad* of commandants, who, with the help of field cornets, controlled military operations. But with the example of Retief before them, the Raad majority fought hard to prevent Andries Pretorius, who became Commandant-General in May 1839, from wielding independent authority, save in the actual conduct of campaigns. As a sop, Pretorius was admitted to sessions of the Raad as a non-voting adviser on 4 October 1839; but so strong was the feeling of the Raad that its own members should not hold public office, that when Pretorius went in his military capacity to demand cattle from Dingane in January 1840, he had to postpone his swearing-in as a Raad member until he was in a position to resign his military office on his return. The Raad decided in March 1840 to appoint chief commandants only on a temporary basis, though Pretorius was eventually recalled as Commandant-General to handle the conflict with the British in June 1842 [see pp. 98–9].

Natalia admitted to its Volksraad representatives of the highveld communities, and to cater for the needs of Voortrekkers elsewhere the Republic gradually took on a federal complexion. Potgieter had governed his Voortrekker communities on the Mooi River across the Vaal and at Winburg from November 1838 with the help of a *krygsraad*, but Pretorius began to work for amalgamation when he visited the Mooi River settlement in February 1839. Two years later, after a visit by Potgieter to Pietermaritzburg, an *Adjunkt Raad* was set up on the Mooi River, where Potchefstroom was being built, to consist of Volksraad members living on the highveld. It was not to be a separate body, but rather a committee of the Raad proper, and it was supposed to report to the Raad twice yearly, though there is no evidence that it either did so or ever accepted a subordinate role. This Adjunkt Raad became important, and a growth point in trekker constitutionalism, for the reason that after the capitulation of the Natal Volksraad to the British on 15 July 1842 – though it carried on in the shadows until October 1845 – Potchefstroom became the first successor state.

5.3   POTGIETER AND PRETORIUS ON THE HIGHVELD

The Potchefstroom Adjunkt Raad broke away from the Natal Volksraad on 7 August 1843, rejected Natalia's submission to the British, and established a new Voortrekker republic north of the Vaal in April 1844. It adopted a set of Thirty-Three Articles apparently intended as a series of supplementary judicial rules, to be taken in conjunction with the regulations of the Natal Volksraad, under which the northern Voortrekkers continued to live until the drawing-up of new fundamental laws by the Ohrigstad Volksraad in 1846. These articles were tailored for a society in which territorial government was still in the process of being created. The emphasis placed on litigation procedures and the punishment of particular misdemeanours – fraud, physical injury to persons, refusal to go on commando, encroachment on a neighbour's land, disrespect to women – reflect a community with special problems of order and security. The references to the illegal seizure of black children, which may not belong to the original document, reveal a humane if authoritarian approach to racialist temptations in frontier society, where 'bastards . . . down to the tenth degree' were excluded from membership of the Raad.

Between 1845 and 1848 the importance of Potchefstroom was eclipsed by Potgieter's decision to move to the eastern trans-Vaal. The selection of Andries Ohrigstad, named after the head of a Dutch trading company, was prompted by Potgieter's desire to establish independent commercial outlets. He also wanted to keep off territory claimed by the Portuguese, and remove beyond the reach of British authority under the Cape of Good Hope Punishment Act of 1836. The tsetse-fly, however, together with Portuguese and African opposition, killed the prospects of trade and reduced Ohrigstad to a mood of disillusionment, out of which contention sprang. Potgieter took to Ohrigstad his preference for military government, and had the title of *Hoofdkommandant* wished upon him by his supporters. This was not to the liking of J. J. ('Kootje') Burger and his associates, ex-members of the Natal Volksraad, who had migrated to Ohrigstad after the cession of Natal, and were strong in their opposition to autocracy but had the reputation of being 'sell-outs'. They wanted a Natal-style Volksraad and disliked a strong executive, and in spite of their failure in Natal they stood their ground against Potgieter, who moved off with a small following in 1848 to found a new settlement in the Soutpansberg, leaving them in possession of the field.

The eclipse of Potgieter brought Andries Pretorius back to a position of influence in the Voortrekker community and he returned from Natal, where he had lived quietly under the British rule, to lead Boer resistance to Sir Harry Smith's sudden decision early in 1848 to annex trans-Orangia to the British Crown. One group of Boers, led by Michael Oberholzer, had no strong desire to escape from British rule, and had reached an accommodation with the Griqua Chief Adam Kok in 1840, recognising the latter's sovereignty over their lands. Further north, however, in the region of the Modder and Vet rivers, lived a remnant of the original Voortrek, based on their laager at Winburg, whose numbers were swollen by a group of Voortrekkers from Natal led by J. C. Mocke. This group made a brief but ineffective bid to help the Natal Voortrekkers against the British in January 1843; but it was their attempt to oppose Smith's annexation of trans-Orangia in 1848, culminating in defeat at Boomplaats, that undermined their influence and that of Pretorius himself [see p. 169].

The Volksraad party therefore came back into the ascendant, but the government of a Voortrekker community without a strong executive proved hardly easier in practice. At Hekpoort in the Magaliesberg on 9 February 1849, the Potchefstroom and Soutpansberg groups decided to set up a united Volksraad with supreme authority and not to accept British rule. This United Volksraad met at Derde Poort on 23 May, the Ohrigstaders also being present, and agreed to meet regularly three times a year at different centres; but they would not support the appointment of a single head commandant, and eventually decided in January 1851 to divide that office into four – for Mooi River and the Magaliesberg (Pretorius), for the Soutpansberg (Potgieter), for Lydenburg, where the Ohrigstaders had now established their capital (W. F. Joubert), and for Marico (J. A. Enslin), all of them to be subject to the United Volksraad. But when Pretorius tried to convene a Volksraad in September 1851, and again in December, to obtain authority to mediate between Moshweshwe and the Sovereignty in such a way as to secure British recognition of the independence of the Transvaalers, on both occasions there was no quorum. Pretorius therefore had to fall back on his Krygsraad when, in January 1852, he negotiated the Convention of Sand River [see p. 170]. The most eminent of the chief commandants thus pulled off a respectable diplomatic coup without Volksraad support. Ironically, this achievement of the military executive was followed in March by a decision that every burgher could decide to which of the military leaders he would attach himself. Some Potchfestroomers actually elected to serve under Potgieter in the Soutpansberg at the opposite end of the state. This kind of attachment to personal leaders was a characteristic of Afrikaner society, born of the commando system and the experience of the Trek. It became an important bond of cohesion in later history, notably during the Anglo-Boer War, during the 1914 rebellion, and perhaps also in the political associations of later years; but occurring in 1850s, it showed how tenuous the bonds of society had become once the immediate dangers of the Trek were past.

Meanwhile Pretorius found himself increasingly involved in business outside the sphere of defence and diplomacy. He was consulted on questions of public religion, stock theft, the purchase of coffee beans for planting purposes, the reform of the constitution. In short, as Van Heerden has demonstrated, in the years immediately before the drafting of the

Rustenburg Constitution of 1858, Pretorius, though only one of four commandant-generals, was being required to act more and more as a head of state, and appeared to like things that way.

5.4   THE ORANGE FREE STATE REPUBLIC

Firm guidelines were set for Boer constitutionalism when the Orange Free Staters sat down to work out a form of government after getting their independence back under the Bloemfontein Convention of February 1854 [see p. 171]. They based their decisions on Cape Dutch and Voortrekker experience, but also on American and European precedents. Typically, the Free State constitution restricted the vote to male citizens of eighteen years and over, and limited citizenship to whites; but it did not include a confessional test. It provided for a unicameral Volksraad, all members being returned from single-member constituencies, as in Natalia. Executive government was placed in the hands of a State President, chosen for a five-year term, by direct public vote, from a list drawn up by the Volksraad, and re-eligible. He was given an executive council (*Uitvoerende Raad*) of officials and unofficials appointed by the Volksraad, and he was required to report annually to the Volksraad, in which he could initiate legislation but not vote. The Volksraad was to ratify his appointments to public office and confirm or reject his decisions over war and peace and external relations. He was expected to tour his republic annually like a Prussian king, so as to maintain contact with his people. The American influence, introduced mainly through the contributions of J. G. Groenendal, the State Secretary, and J. M. Orpen, Volksraad member for Harrismith, was seen, above all, in the preference given for a rigid constitution, amendment being by a three-quarters majority in three (later reduced to two) successive sessions, with the testing right as a safeguard. Judges held office during good behaviour, and could and did use the testing right when necessary. Until the establishment of a High Court in 1867 and of an Appeal Court in 1874, jurisdiction was shared between the Executive Council and a Circuit Court of United Landdrosts (1856–74). The constitution also contained within it the rudiments of a bill of rights, with its insistence on equality before the law, press freedom, and so on. Local government in the Free State, as in other Boer republics, was conducted by landdrosts in charge of districts, which were subdivided into wards under field cornets.

The state for which this constitution was drawn up became, and remained, a country controlled by white farmers among whom entrepreneurial initiative was largely lacking until the challenge of the Witwatersrand after the Anglo-Boer war created new incentives. The Griqua were cleared from the Philippolis lands, which were bought up by whites, in 1861 [see pp. 130–1]. The Rolong title-holders of Thaba'Nchu sold their farms to whites during the middle 1880s [see p. 140]. This produced as near a white monopoly of land ownership as existed anywhere in southern Africa. Labour for the farms was provided mainly by blacks who lived on the land at the time of the white settlement. The sale of wool provided periodic profits to the landowners, and transport-riding a somewhat steadier income, together with an incentive for resisting the introduction of railways until the late 1880s.

A Free State parliamentarian claimed with apparent conviction in 1930 that his 'pure white country' had brought no problems with it into the Union. Geographically in the middle, the Free State acquired the reputation of being ideologically in the middle, especially during the long presidency of J. H. Brand (1864–88), where relations between Boer and Briton were concerned. It contained many moderate Afrikaners as well as strong anti-Imperialists. English-speakers were welcome, and those who chose to identify themselves with the Republic, of whom J. M. Orpen and J. G. Fraser were good examples, could expect to reach the top in public life. English was commonly spoken in town and business life, even if Dutch alone was permitted in the Volksraad. Though all six Free State presidents were Afrikaners, the last three had strong English cultural ties: Brand had an English legal training and accepted an Engish knighthood, while Reitz had W. P. Schreiner as a brother-in-law, and Steyn normally wrote to his wife in English. Nor do later manifestations of apparent Afrikaner extremism – the 'bitter-end' resistence at the end of the Anglo-Boer War, and the Free Staters' role in the 1914 rebellion – necessarily diminish this image. The Free State nevertheless retained an essentially Afrikaner character because it never acquired a large Uitlander element (though it might easily have done had Brand managed to gain control over Griqualand West in 1871). Without the challenge of a dominant alien culture to disturb their complacency, Free Staters found that they could preserve the political values of the frontier with remarkable ease. It may, as Van Aswegen has shown, have been the English-speaking traders who objected most strongly to the admission of Indian traders to the Republic in the 1880s, but it was the Volksraad, an Afrikaner body in essence, which first restricted their trading rights in 1885 and then banned their admission as residents in 1890. Similarly, the Free State was the only part of South Africa where it became legally impossible for a black person to become a landowner in his own right in the period before Union. The myth of the white nation with an exclusive claim to rights survived remarkably in the Free State, where at any given moment the black population was at least double the white in size.

5.5 THE SOUTH AFRICAN REPUBLIC, THE CIVIL WAR, AND THE RISE OF PAUL KRUGER

There was a chance during the 1850s that the Orange Free State and the Transvaal might have amalgamated into a single republic. When M. W. Pretorius succeeded his father as head commandant in 1853, he kept up a steady pressure to this end, with the aid of allies south of the Vaal, but encountered strong opposition from the supporters of Presidents Hoffman and Boshoff. He eventually gained the presidency of both republics in

February 1860, but the opposition on both sides of the Vaal proved insuperable.

The study of the socio-economic structure of the South African Republic has been largely ignored for the period 1850 to 1900, but the researches of Trapido, Cornwell and others, have begun to fill the void.

The Transvaal was acquired through conquest in a series of conflicts extending over sixty years [see Chapter 7]. Its white population grew from very small beginnings to about 300,000 at the end of the nineteenth century, while its black population was estimated at 945,408 by the Lagden Commission in 1905. White citizens were allowed two farms, supposedly of up to 3,000 morgen, as of right. Blacks, by contrast, were precluded by Volksraad resolution from owning land at all, though in some instances missionary societies took title on their behalf. By the end of the century a mere 860,000 morgen had been set aside as treaty areas for occupation by black chiefdoms or as government locations, out of a total area of 71,000,000 for the Republic as a whole.

Land was the Republic's chief capital asset before the discovery of gold, and for the white citizen it was at first easy to acquire. A man merely found unoccupied land and registered his claim at the landdrost's office, obtaining an extract from the register describing its locality in terms of natural landmarks (perhaps a tree or an anthill). In due course an inspection would be held, objections called for, and a small fee charged. From that date quitrent would become due, but it was not payable until the issue of title. It was therefore in the interest of claimants to delay registration as long as possible, since this delayed the obligation to pay rent. Agar-Hamilton and Cornwell have shown how, under these conditions, the scramble for land among the white settlers was so keen, and the registration of title so imprecise, that confusion often resulted. The issue of burgher land rights had to be suspended in 1866 to 'restore the credit of the state'.

The land steadily appreciated in value. One farm acquired in the Wakkerstroom district in 1860 for £3 15s changed hands on the day of purchase for £112 10s, and had increased in value to £300 by 1869 (Cornwell). Officials, especially landdrosts and field cornets, were particularly well placed to profit from speculation in land. Leading politicians, including both Paul Kruger and Piet Joubert, who had risen via the field cornetcy to positions of authority in the state, became owners of farms on a large scale. From the time of the first British occupation in 1877–81, land companies also entered the speculative game on a very much larger scale, and this helped to create an artificial shortage of land within a few decades.

The state assumed dominium over all unsold lands, including those under tribal occupation, and used them as a capital asset against which to issue non-negotiable interest-bearing certificates (*mandaten*); but these, like the *assignats* of the French Revolution, were superseded by a paper currency, which was also issued against government farms, and the over-issue of these notes caused a crisis of confidence in the late 1860s, not only in the South African Republic but in the Orange Free State as well.

It is also noteworthy that, despite the large amount of speculation in land values, there was relatively little capitalised farming in the South African

Republic in the nineteenth century. Landlords tended rather to use their land as a rent-producing asset through the exaction of cash or labour services from the resident black population. It was only after the Anglo-Boer war, under the stimulus of gold production and the new perspectives of the Milner regime, that Transvaal farming became significantly oriented towards the market.

Transvaal politics, to a greater extent than those of the Free State, were always hampered by the antagonisms of small trekker communities separated from each other by great distances. The United Volksraad found time and again that, for pressing reasons such as farming or military emergencies, it was impossible to raise a quorum for its quarterly sessions. There was no session, for example, between June 1854 and June 1855. They began therefore to take short cuts, and to place increased reliance on the device of a *kommissieraad*, which meant the members of the Raad who lived within range of the place selected for the meeting. On two occasions a kommissieraad declared itself to be a full Volksraad (and therefore competent to take binding decisions) in respect of matters which concerned the locality where it met, but merely a *kommissie* (whose decisions required ratification) in respect of matters dealing with other regions. A reduction of the number of Volksraad sessions to one a year was contemplated, but the plan eventually followed in 1855 was to abandon the peripatetic Volksraad in favour of its location in a central capital, for which the ground was prepared by the purchase of two farms on the Aapies river from which Pretoria was soon to arise.

The controversy which had divided Potgieter from the Volksraad party in Ohrigstad developed after the establishment of the United Volksraad into a regional conflict between Lydenburg, where opinion was led by the survivors of the old Volksraad party, notably H. T. Bührmann and J. A. Smellekamp, and the western Transvalers under M. W. Pretorius. The issue on which conflict flared up was not that of strong versus popular government which had divided Retief from Maritz, and Potgieter from J. J. Burger, but an ecclesiastical one. Although the *Nederduitse Gereformeerde Kerk* (N.G.K.) of the Cape had refrained from giving official support to the Great Trek, from a reluctance to support what the authorities regarded as rebellion, it had nevertheless built churches at Potchefstroom, Rustenburg, Lydenburg and Schoemansdal between 1842 and 1852. But in 1853 a demand for an independent Voortrekker church led to the appointment of Ds. Dirk van der Hoff as minister of the Church in the Transvaal, with the endorsement of the United Volksraad. As if to emphasise the break with the Cape, the name *Nederduitsch Hervormde Kerk* (N.H.K.) was subsequently made definitive through its incorporation in the republican constitution. The Lydenburgers, who were not represented at the Volksraad in question, rejected Van der Hoff. Later, on receiving assurances that they would not be bound by British laws, or a British oath of allegiance, or any obligation to ban racial segregation in worship, they resolved to place themselves under the Cape Synod. This was anathema to the Volksraad, which punished Lydenburg by excluding its Volksraad members. The Lydenburgers decided to go their own way, and received strong backing from the Soutpansbergers at Schoemansdal, whose leader, Stephanus Schoeman, had married Potgieter's widow. Another Boer settlement at Utrecht, on the Buffalo river between Natal and Zululand, whose landdrost A. T. Spies was one of the Lydenburgers whom the Volksraad had decided to punish, also came out in support of Lydenburg.

These eastern Transvaal communities resented Volksraad pushfulness. When it tried to plant a constitution on the other centres, and set in motion a presidential election, which Pretorius won against W. F. Joubert in a very low poll, the Lydenburgers decided to elect their own independent Volksraad, and did so with the encouragement of President Boshoff of the Free State, who was paying Pretorius back in his own coin. Schoeman actually declared war on Pretorius in April 1857. Lydenburg and Soutpansberg resolved to set up a combined Volksraad in September.

Collision was averted at this point by the tact of Paul Kruger, who, though a follower of Pretorius, maintained contact with Schoeman through his brother, Douw Kruger, and brought the two together. Early in 1858 Pretorius offered a joint inquiry to revise the controversial constitution. This was accepted, and the result was the Rustenburg Grondwet of 1858, which proved acceptable to both parties. On 12 September 1859, therefore, the Volksraad of the South African Republic met in Pretoria for the first time, and on 4 December the Lydenburg and Utrecht Volksraads were incorporated in the Republic.

The Rustenburg Grondwet was largely the work of a Hollander, Jacobus Stuart. It was an untidy, rambling document, and like the Thirty-Three Articles, contained much that did not properly belong to a constitution at all. The framework of government was similar to that of the Free State. A popularly elected President, presiding over an Executive Council, was to lead government business in a unicameral Volksraad elected by white burghers. So concerned were the Rustenburg law-makers to preserve the authority of the *volkswil* that they insisted on a three-quarters majority for every law passed, and a minimum period of three months between the first tabling of a measure and its enactment, so as to ensure that the public had plenty of time to react. This hurdle proved too stiff, and led to the short-cut practice of making laws by *besluit* (resolution) of a simple Volksraad majority. This undermined the authority of the constitution, and led eventually to the 'judges crisis' of 1897, when Chief Justice J. G. Kotze refused to recognise legislation made by *besluit*, but chose his ground badly and was dismissed from office by President Kruger [see p. 87]. The Grondwet was more explicitly Calvinist than its Free State counterpart. It affirmed the allegiance of the Republic to the doctrines of the Nederuits Hervormde Kerk and restricted membership of the Volksraad to Hervormdes. By putting the Commandant-General on the Executive Council and establishing that office, at last, as a permanent institution, the Rustenburg Grondwet also brought about a polarisation of power which could not develop in the Orange Free State, whose military commander was never more than an *ad hoc* military appointee without political status. In the unified Transvaal, the Commandant-Generalship became the focus of rival power during the civil war of 1860–4, and again later during the presidencies of T. F. Burgers and Paul Kruger.

Had it not been for his decision to accept the Free State presidency, M. W. Pretorius might well have enjoyed a peaceful reign in the South African Republic. But his acceptance of the double role in 1860, in face of warnings by Sir George Grey that such a union of offices would be treated by Britain as a violation of the Conventions of 1852 and 1854, led the Transvaal Volksraad to suspend him, not as an act of no confidence, but as an act of caution. Instead of appointing Schoeman as Acting President, however, which as the senior member of the Volksraad he should have become in terms of the constitution, the Raad gave the office to J. H. Grobler, who resigned when he found that he did not have popular support. Schoeman was in a strong position, having effectively united the Krygsraad under his own control, even though Lydenburg had been given the right to its own Commandant-General when it joined the Republic in 1860. At first he bided his time; but when signs of support began to appear, he chose the moment of Grobler's resignation to force the Executive Council, in the presence of 150 armed men, to declare himself Acting President and make W. C. Janse van Rensburg his Commandant-General.

It was around Paul Kruger, a member of the Krygsraad whose star was clearly rising, that opposition to the Schoeman coup began to gather. Encouraged by Kruger's stand, the Volksraad censured Schoeman in April 1862, and defied him by choosing Van Rensburg as Acting President and (after some difficulty) T. J. Snyman as Commandant-General. Snyman had martial law proclaimed when Schoeman refused to submit. Schoeman dug in at Potchefstroom, but was dug out by Snyman and fled to the Free State. Returning in November, however, he reoccupied Potchefstroom, and in January 1863 entered Pretoria and drove out the High Court judges who were sitting in judgement on his own misdemeanours. Kruger and his Rustenburgers, however, expelled the Schoemanites and restored the court; and the court – as part of its attempt to restore harmony – ordered new elections for the presidency and the commandant-generalship. After unduly complex proceedings, involving two elections for each office, Van Rensburg emerged above Pretorius as President-elect on a recount, with Kruger overwhelmingly favoured for the military position. The Schoeman party, however, now led by the militant J. H. Viljoen of Marico, made one further bid for power. Kruger therefore had martial law declared for a second time, but even then the supporters of the Government had a hard fight in the Magaliesberg before eventually inducing Viljoen to sue for peace. Negotiations near the Crocodile river in January 1864 then ended the civil war. A fresh presidential election was held, and this time Pretorius turned the tables on Van Rensburg to begin an unbroken period of office which lasted seven years.

5.6 IDEOLOGICAL RIFTS UNDER PRETORIUS AND BURGERS

Pretorius's years as President saw a great deal of conflict with African chiefdoms which opposed attempts to extend the frontiers of the Republic [see pp. 141–5, 173]. The Republic also experienced further religious division in these years. That which occurred in 1859, when the *Gerefor-meerde Kerk* under Ds. Dirk Postma broke away from the Hervormdes, had little political importance. There were some signs in the Rustenburg area during the 1850s of opposition to the use of *Evangelische Gezange* (non-biblical hymns) in public worship, which had been the occasion of troubles in the Colesberg Ring of the Church in 1841; but the establishment of the *Gereformeerde* ('Dopper') *Kerk* resulted not from this but from an offer by the *Afgeskeie* (Separatist) *Gereformeerde Kerk* of the Netherlands to help the Republic to overcome its shortage of clergy. They sent Ds. Postma to the Transvaal and the Rustenburgers took him under their wing. The Ned. Hervormde Kerk decided guardedly to work with Postma, provided that he restricted his work to white people and did not enter the mission field, that he acknowledged the Reformed articles of belief, and refrained from seeking separate recognition of the Afgeskeie Kerk under the Grondwet. These were stiff demands. Postma and his followers, who included Paul Kruger, formed a separate church rather than accept them. In the course of the negotiations, Van der Hoff, for the Hervormdes, skilfully drew attention to the *Gezange* as the main issue of public difference, and thus diverted attention from the exclusive relationship with the State which the Hervormde Kerk continued to enjoy. Yet the Hervormdes and the Gereformeerdes remained, on the whole, on good terms with each other, and the Gereformeerdes threw their weight during the political conflicts of the 1860s behind the reconciliation of the warring groups. Both parties shared a common Transvaal patriotism and a common preference for traditional Dutch forms of religion.

The Schism of 1866, which led to the refounding of a *Nederduits Gereformeerde Kerk* in the Transvaal, was far more serious for the unity of the Republic. It was primarily associated with the activities of Ds. F. Lion Cachet, a mercurial Hollander of French–Jewish descent, who had been educated in Amsterdam, and then served as a minister at Ladysmith, before moving into the Republic to take charge of Utrecht. He then attacked the credentials of the Hervormde Kerk in the Transvaal, objecting to the name 'Hervormde', objecting to the theological liberalism which he claimed to find in its discipline and in its doctrine (at a time when the Cape Church, which had recently tried three of its own clergy for heresy, was particularly sensitive to the need for doctrinal precision), and successfully reopening the rift between the Hervormdes and the Lydenburg congregation which had been repaired by careful negotiation only in 1864. After a tour of the Transvaal settlements in 1865, Cachet convened a general assembly of all malcontents and re-constituted the N.G. Kerk, which failed to gain control of the baptismal registers and funds of the established Church, but managed to take root as a rival body and build up several congregations despite its shortage of clergy.

Cachet's movement was influential for a variety of reasons. It professed loyalty to the N.G. Kerk of the Cape, even after the Cape Supreme Court had declared in Loedolff's Case in 1862 that the Cape Synod had no jurisdiction outside the Colonial frontiers. This kept alive the notion of N.G. congregations north of the Vaal with their own independent government. The Cape Synod had already sent several deputations northwards to discourage the breakaway of the Transvalers. It sent another in 1868, and one of its two members, Ds. J. P. Jooste, remained behind to become a N.G. minister in Potchefstroom in opposition to Ds. van der Hoff of the Hervormdes. He was ordained in the Potchefstroom Methodist Church, whose minister, Ludorf, was described by the historian of the Hervormdes as a 'well-known negrophile'. Concern for the blacks, indeed, became a characteristic of the Transvaal N.G. clergy, whereas the Hervormde Synod at first took a strong line against mission work. N.G. clergy sometimes denounced Transvaal Boer race attitudes. Cachet, for example, attacked Transvaal 'slavery', as did his associate, Ds. P. Huet of Pietermaritzburg, whose *Het Lot der Zwarten in Transvaal*, published in 1869, provided ammunition for external critics of the Republic and attracted the wrath of the authorities for what they claimed to be atrocity-mongering.

The role of the N.G. predikants as 'white ants' of Republican independence was therefore of particular significance, especially during the presidency of T. F. Burgers. Engelbrecht goes so far as to argue that they were a key factor in the fall of the Republic in 1877, suggesting the existence of an alliance between them and unprincipled fortune-seekers on the goldfields at Pilgrim's Rest and in the Transvaal towns. Cachet did argue for the overthrow of the Republic, even if he completely changed his tune in 1882, when his *Worstelstrijd der Transvalers* appeared. Others to advocate British annexation were Jooste and N. J. R. Swart. The latter, who had been trained as a Gereformeerde minister under Postma, switched in 1871 to the Anglican Church and abandoned a clerical career to become Government Secretary, first under Burgers, then under Shepstone, and was considered by some to be Shepstone's informer on Burgers's Executive Council.

The ecclesiastical picture in the Transvaal on the eve of the annexation becomes clearer once it is realised that when T. F. Burgers went to the Transvaal to conduct his presidential campaign in 1872, he was drawn towards the Hervormde Kerk. In his *Schetzen uit de Transvaal* he admitted to having arrived with some prejudice against the Hervormdes, but then noted that they had shown a lack of 'hard-necked and blind dogmatism' of the kind he had experienced in the Cape, and manifested a traditional Dutch outlook untainted by the influences of Scottish Calvinism. To the Transvaal N.G. clergy, on the other hand, Burgers was a convicted heretic. His flamboyant personality and modernist theological views hardly seemed to provide the right formula for electoral success in a Boer republic, even if his acquaintance with Charles Darwin was not generally known; but with Pretorius's diplomatic failure at Bloemhof fresh in the public mind [see p. 175], he won the presidential election of 1872 with only 388 votes cast against him.

Burgers failed more sensationally than any other Transvaal head of state, but his performance needs to be measured against the difficulty of his task, and neither was negligible. It was during his presidency that the first Transvaal gold rush began, with the discovery of alluvial deposits at MacMac and Pilgrim's Rest in the Lydenburg district in 1873. This attracted a group of immigrants, mainly English-speaking and mainly from Natal, whom he would find particularly difficult to control because they settled in a district which was in dispute between the Transvaal and the Pedi [see p. 143]. He capitalised on the gold discoveries by allowing the minting of a gold coinage bearing his own portrait. This offended his straiter subjects. Without intending to divide the people on religious issues, he came in for sharp criticism for his Education Act of 1874, which allowed Biblical studies during school hours but permitted confessional instruction only afterwards. After an arbitration by President Macmahon of France had awarded Lourenço Marques to Portugal rather than Britain in 1875, Burgers did spend unwisely the funds which he raised in Europe the following year to build a railway from the coast. Where the Pretorius Government had faced difficulties with the Venda, Burgers had trouble with the Pedi. Paul Kruger, his Commandant-General, resigned from office in 1873, and for reasons of economy the commandant-generalship was abolished soon after – some said as a calculated bid by Burgers to destroy Kruger's influence. Burgers assumed command in the field, and failed to dislodge the Pedi from strong positions which they defended with firearms. His attempt to raise a special war tax was also widely defied. Yet in February 1877, shortly before Shepstone's annexation, their chief Sekhukhune was persuaded to ask for peace [see p. 144].

Soon after Sir Theophilus Shepstone's arrival in Pretoria to annex the Transvaal in January 1877 [see p. 144], Burgers convened a special session of the Volksraad for 13 February, and warned against the special danger to the State's independence implicit in Shepstone's mission. He submitted the draft of a revised constitution, the chief feature of which was a plan to strengthen the Executive Council by converting it into something like a presidential cabinet, together with proposals for an improved method of raising revenue. The Raad at first rejected Burgers's proposals on the motion of H. T. Bührmann, a Hollander who had arrived at Ohrigstad in 1848 and played a prominent but perhaps irresponsible role in public affairs as a democrat who too easily found signs of executive tyranny in church and state. Before the session ended, Burgers had been granted a new Executive, into which he brought Kruger as Vice-President; but he received no authority to introduce the urgently needed tax reforms. Kruger's role was equivocal. He had not taken part in the campaign against Sekhukhune. Too good a politician and too loyal a Transvaler to allow personal antipathy alone to determine his political conduct, he had initially served under Burgers because he was head of state by popular decision, and therefore, as Kruger saw it, by divine command. But before the end of 1876 he reversed his decision not to stand for president in the election due the following year, and began to build up an organised opposition to Burgers in the early months of 1877. He took no decisive stand in support of Republican independence until after Shepstone's annexation had taken place [see pp. 178–9].

From the angle of Boer politics, the British occupation removed Burgers and his followers from the scene and promoted the political careers of Paul Kruger and Piet Joubert, but effected no more than a brief interruption in the history of the state. That occupation still awaits its historian. De Kiewiet, whose treatment is the fullest, is highly critical of its failure to set right those things which had provided the pretext for annexation, above all the financial weakness which had led the Republic's creditors to start calling in their debt. Not only was Shepstone starved of funds because, as he was told, 'Parliament does not like to have to pay even for what it theoretically approves', but the actual administration of the funds at his disposal was lax and irresponsible.

Paul Kruger's leadership of the Triumvirate, in association with Piet Joubert and M. W. Pretorius, through whom the opposition to British rule was increasingly canalised, gave him a standing in the estimation of his people which he never lost. A son of the Trek, a tough frontiersman to whom tales of valour clung rather as if he was a folk hero straight out of the *Book of Judges*, this natural man of the people was also an intense Calvinist Christian, with a basic integrity not always apparent as he twisted and turned, gave ground or stood firm, to preserve his Republic from Imperial encirclement, from materialist undermining, from English cultural domination, and from insolvency. His record of resistance to British rule gave his eighteen-year presidency an impressive start. First elected in 1883, he won three further contests in 1888, 1893, and 1898, demonstrating on the last occasion that he had an immense backing among his people, two years before his Government was brought down by defeat in the Anglo-Boer War and he left, a forlorn suppliant, for exile in Holland.

5.7   KRUGER'S REPUBLIC AND THE UITLANDER CHALLENGE

Kruger's was not a united republic, however. For a start, the religious divisions among his people persisted. In the afterglow of Majuba [see p. 179], an over-hasty amalgamation of the Hervormde and the N. G. churches, for which the ground had been prepared under British rule, was carried through between 1882 and 1885, without full consultation of the congregations. In the resultant backlash, a number of Hervormde congregations subsequently opted out of the new *Nederduits Hervormde of Gereformeerde Kerk*, or *Verenigde* [United] *Kerk* as the amalgamated body came to be less cumbrously known. There were accompanying legal wrangles as the Verenigde Kerk insisted on its constitutional rights. Kruger tried and failed to restore harmony at a conference over which he presided in August 1891. Engelbrecht has suggested that the anti-Hollander feeling which developed in the Republic in the 1890s was in part an overspill of N. G. opposition to the Hervormdes, generated by the Verenigde Kerk, which was the spiritual home of most of Kruger's Afrikaner opponents. Its Synod attacked the 1891 Education Act of Dr Nicolaas Mansvelt with vigour, as being Dutch rather than Afrikaans in spirit.

Kruger also had to cope with the intrusion of Uitlander gold-seekers in embarrassingly large numbers, whose presence threatened to engulf the impoverished and essentially rural society over which he ruled. The eastern

Transvaal gold discoveries of the 1870s had been followed by further alluvial finds at De Kaap in 1882 and Barberton in 1884. But the most important breakthrough came with the discovery of the Witwatersrand main reef, which was struck at several places by Harrison, the Struben brothers, and other prospectors, in 1886. The rock-embedded gold existed in marketable quantities provided technology could master its extraction without incurring prohibitive costs. In 1887 the coal needed to provide power for the mining process was found nearby. In 1892 the invention of the MacArthur–Forrest cyanide process enormously improved the efficiency of extraction, while the owners, who had set up the Chamber of Mines in 1887 to regulate matters of mutal interest, were eventually able to organise a flow of cheap black contract labourers and keep their wages down to an average of £2 10s by 1896, against the £26 earned monthly by skilled whites. This enabled them to offset the artificially high cost of dynamite, imported under Eduard Lippert's monopoly concession, and thus mine gold at a marginal profit. Kruger tried to milk the wealth of the intruders through the sale of such concessions. He tried to secure his regime by building up vested interests which were loyal, one being the Netherlands South Africa Railway Company, which looked after all railway-building within the Republic. It was the largest of the Dutch concessionaires. This element, on whom Kruger relied for support and service, included Dr W. J. Leyds, his State Secretary and roving diplomat, and Dr Nicolaas Mansvelt, his second Superintendent-General of Education. J. B. Robinson, however, the Langlaagte mining tycoon, whose support Kruger cultivated to provide a counterweight to the Fitzpatricks and Farrars who dominated the Uitlander community, was a son of an 1820 Settler and brother of the William Robinson who had been Kruger's choice for president in 1872.

But a policy of favourites brought enemies. Kruger's concessions became a target, not only for the Uitlander community, which resented the dynamite monopoly in particular, but also for opponents within the Boer community. General Piet Joubert, the Commandant-General, and Ds. S. J. du Toit, the founder of the Afrikaner Bond, who had been Superintendent-General of Education from 1881 to 1890, objected to Kruger's railway policy in the 1880s because they had an interest in the rival firm of Lewis and Marks who planned to build a railway from Kimberley to the Rand (Van der Poel). They mounted an attack on the concession policy across a broad front. Kruger, for his part, had used Joubert and Du Toit as scapegoats for the failure of his attempt in 1884 to incorporate the Republics of Stellaland and Goshen. Because they were chairman and secretary respectively of the Afrikaner Bond in the Transvaal, Kruger's opposition to these two members of his Executive Council was a direct cause of the Bond's failure to establish itself in the Republic. The development of internal Boer opposition to Kruger, which C. T. Gordon has described, grew essentially out of these antecedents. Joubert, who fought Kruger in all four presidential campaigns and came within close reach of him in 1893, headed a 'Progressive' party in the Volksraad which consisted almost entirely of Afrikaners, its nucleus being Schalk Burger, Louis Botha, J. H.

de la Rey, Lukas Meyer, General N. J. Smit (the victor of Majuba), Ewald Esselen and Carl Jeppe. They relied very little on English mining support, and had no tie-up with the Uitlander leaders. They could muster eight to eleven votes out of twenty-four in the First Volksraad in 1893, and perhaps ten out of twenty-seven as late as 1899. They were clear thinkers, generally humane in outlook. They attacked concessions, favours to Hollanders, and corruption. But they had no caucus, no programme, no organisation, and in Joubert a leader who lacked Kruger's steadfastness and consistency. They showed that it was easier to reform Kruger's Government than to remove it, for Kruger did bend to some of their demands, especially by cutting back on favours to Hollanders and by giving the new State Attorney, J. C. Smuts (who may have endorsed the angry sentiments of J. de V. Roos's *Century of Wrong* but only wrote a small part of it – Le Roux and Van Zyl), a free hand to reform the Law Department.

In a homogeneous Afrikaner community the Kruger Government could perhaps have built up a moderate reformist image, but in the shadow of the Uitlander presence this was not an easy reputation to earn. The restored Republic was jealous to preserve its control over its own affairs. This can be seen in the rejection under the London Convention of 1884 of Imperial control over native policy, Imperial direction of the Republic's foreign relations, and the Imperial right to move troops through the Republic at will; and above all, in the decision to restrict Uitlander votes by the imposition of a five-year delay and a high £25 naturalisation fee which immigrants could normally be expected not to want to pay.

Uncertainty over the relative numerical strength of Boer and Uitlander voters added an element of mystery to debates over the franchise, especially as Boers were inclined to exaggerate the number of Uitlanders in order to demonstrate the seriousness of the threat, while Uitlanders inflated their own numbers to demonstrate the injustice of their not being enfranchised. In 1896, according to Marais, there were over 44,000 white aliens in the Transvaal, of whom over 28,000 came from outside south Africa. The Uitlander males probably outnumbered the Transvaal Afrikaner males, and therefore constituted an immediate political threat even if the total Transvaal Afrikaner population was larger, and its capacity for reproducing itself much greater. The extent to which Uitlanders actually wanted the vote became a debating point as well, for many were birds of passage, while enfranchisement involved the duties of citizenship, including commando service. Kruger's Government became alarmed about the Uitlander franchise in 1890, when the flow of immigrants began to increase. It therefore reduced the naturalisation fee to £5, but increased the waiting period before a new immigrant could actually cast a vote to fourteen years from the date of arrival – by most standards an inordinately long delay. The simultaneous creation of a Second Volksraad, elected on a much less rigid franchise, was intended as a sop to Uitlander feelings. This body initiated some useful legislation, but its laws required endorsement by the First Volksraad, so it was seen to be a device of the Government to avoid having to share power with a community which provided the Republic with a very sizeable proportion of its public wealth.

The Uitlanders began to challenge the Boer monopoly of power when Charles Leonard founded his National Union in 1892, from which moment serious Boer–Uitlander tensions bedevilled public life. The abortive Rand rebellion and the Jameson Raid of December 1895 damaged their relationship beyond recall. [see p. 188] By suggesting that this attempted coup was a deliberate bid by deep-level mining interests to overthrow a regime whose policies were the direct cause of their financial losses, Geoffrey Blainey set in motion a debate which has helped to clarify the motivation and tactics of individual Randlords. R. V. Kubicek was able to show that it was not possible to link all the conspirators with deep-level as distinct from outcrop interests, that Wernher Beits were not in such financial straits that they needed to overthrow Kruger, and that some leading Randlords, like J. B. Robinson, who did not take part in the conspiracy, might well have found it a convenient way of alleviating their financial troubles. His observations have been corroborated in important respects by Mendelsohn, who nevertheless concludes that 'the chief difference between firms inside and those outside the conspiracy was that the former were committed by 1895 to long-range mining programmes while the latter were either preoccupied with stock-jobbing or were content with modest holding operations'. The Raid became, for him, 'not the last throw of the despairing but, instead, a bold bid by the audacious'. Its failure led the Kruger Government to impose heavy fines on the ringleaders, after commuting the death sentences imposed by the court. Not surprisingly, as Jeeves has shown, it then set about the undermining of the Randlord class in various ways, resisting its bid to gain rigid control over black labour supplies, and supporting white worker opposition to the mine owners through their newly established propaganda organ, the *Standard and Diggers' News*. This in turn led the Uitlander leaders to place renewed emphasis on the franchise issue because it was the kind of issue that could hold the Uitlander community together, and one on which it was not difficult to appeal for Imperial support.

For the Kruger regime, policy calculations in this atmosphere were difficult to make. Fully effective political concessions would have transformed the character of the Republic. Partial concessions could perhaps have brought about a Progressive–Uitlander coalition and destroyed the basis of Kruger's power, though there was a chance it would also have split the Uitlander front since many of them were not Britishers and would have been content with a revolution which stopped short of a restoration of the Union Jack. The main disadvantage in not treating the Uitlanders fairly was that this gave the Colonial Office a cover behind which to build up its campaign for what it was really after: not so much the extension of Uitlander rights, as the maintenance of paramountcy throughout southern Africa, which was not possible without the political control of its richest area.

The Government did attempt to review its industrial policy in 1897, by setting up an Industrial Commission under Schalk Burger's chairmanship in response to a memorial by Sammy Marks, the resourceful entrepreneur. The Commission's recommendations included the termination of the dynamite concession, a reduction in rail rates, the establishment of an industrial board to control the liquor trade, and the administration of the laws governing passes and gold thefts. But these proposals were turned down in the Volksraad in October 1897, to the great consternation of the British Resident, Greene, who, with the help of Birkenruth of Consolidated Goldfields, FitzPatrick of Ecksteins, and other mining leaders, had worked hard on Smuts to obtain the changes sought. Duminy has shown how negotiations finally broke down between the Chamber and the Government over the publicity given by the former to the issues of the franchise and labour importation. The Volksraad's action threw the Chamber of Mines and its rival, the Association of Mines established by J. B. Robinson, into each other's arms again, and ensured that the magnates would put pressure on the old President again once the new High Commissioner, Sir Alfred Milner, had taken stock of the situation.

A constitutional crisis which occurred simultaneously, though it showed the Republican Government up in a better light than many thought at the time, hardly promoted an atmosphere of calm. It resulted in the dismissal of Chief Justice J. G. Kotzé after his judgment in the case of *Brown* v. *Leyds*, to the effect that Volksraad resolutions (*besluiten*) could not be accorded the force of law – in spite of earlier judgments of a conflicting nature by Kotzé himself, and in spite of long usage in the Republic. The Volksraad itself came up in October 1898 with a new draft constitution which proposed proper amending procedures, but the crisis had given the Government a new authoritarian image which was an embarrassment just at that time.

Kruger's Republic had mellowed considerably from the cluster of warring communities of the period 1837–64. But its administration was fairly corrupt and its burghers in general were poor, relatively unenterprising, and – except for the school-goers of the 1890s – not very well educated. They had little desire to admit to equality men who did not share the Afrikaner's language, his Protestantism, and his interest in the preservation of their group power and security in a land full of potential enemies. The Republic ended by fighting and losing a war to protect itself from such a change. For reasons to be considered later, and which the Kruger Government could not have counted on, its defeated ex-burghers then won the peace and regained access to effective political power.

6 British Colonies

6.1 CAPE POLITICAL AND CONSTITUTIONAL GROWTH, 1820–72, AND THE POLITICS OF SEPARATISM

The progress of the Cape towards self-government took a course similar to that of British colonies of conquest and settlement elsewhere. As in French Canada, a governor with arbitrary power replaced the military rule of the conquest era. As in New South Wales, the Governor was provided in due course with a council of officials (1825), whose advice he could ignore, but not without explanation to the Secretary of State. After the arrival of the 1820 settlers, who carried with them something of the political ferment of post-Napoleonic Britain, the Government at the Cape came under pressure from a small group of radical democrats in both the eastern and the western Cape, who waged a successful campaign for the freedom of the press and for some measure of political representation.

A tradition of journalism was born in the 1820s, as a result of the struggles of Thomas Pringle, John Fairbairn, Abraham Faure and George Greig, to which beleaguered editors in the late twentieth century would often look back. The conflict between these men and Governor Lord Charles Somerset resulted after a four-year struggle in the official acceptance of three key principles: a presumption in favour of the right of individuals to obtain a licence to publish, subject only to the law of libel; their right to engage in political discussion; and their right to report events relating to the government of the Colony without pre-publication censorship. The publication of Fairbairn's *South African Commercial Advertiser* on a regular basis from 1827, after its initial suppression in its year of birth (1824), followed by the appearance of the *Zuid Afrikaan* in 1830 and the *Graham's Town Journal* in 1831, were necessary precursors to political advance.

The British Government bent before the political storm by adding two unofficial nominees to the Council of Advice in 1827. In the view of the Commissioners of Inquiry sent from Britain in 1823 to look into the general administration of the Colony, this body should have possessed more power to control the Governor's acts, for the worst its members could do was to register their individual dissent in the official minutes, in which case the Governor had to justify his policy to the Secretary of State. But a spate of reforms between 1827 and 1836 saw the replacement of the traditional *landdrost* and *heemraden* by resident magistrates, together with the system of jury trials, and the introduction of elective municipal boards in the field

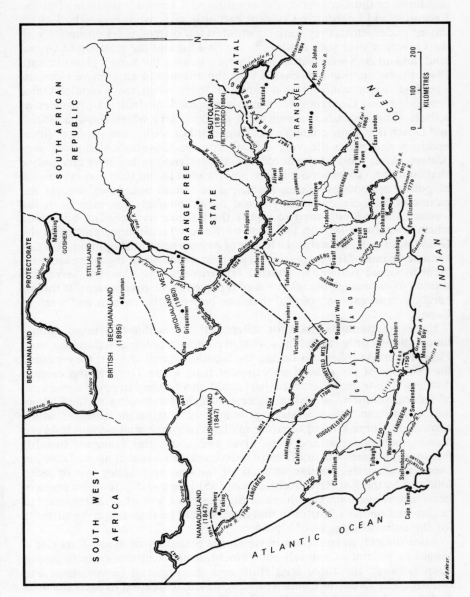

Map 4   The expansion of the Cape Colony, 1652–1895

of local government. The Colony was also granted a decision-making Executive Council in 1834. This body, when enlarged by five to seven nominees of the Governor, also constituted a formal legislature. But the Executive and Legislative Councils had little effective power. The Letters Patent under which they were constituted left discretionary authority with the Governor over such matters as the civil list and the granting of Crown land, and all laws were automatically reserved for the King's pleasure until 1846. Public opinion also chafed over the absence of an elective element. The first major confrontation came in 1849, when the Colonial Office persuaded the Governor to admit a shipload of Irish ex-prisoners as settlers. This unleashed a vehement public outcry which showed British and Dutch that Cape colonials working together could have strong political opinions and make life very difficult for the Government and its supporters. After most of the unofficials had resigned rather than face public chastisement, Governor Sir Harry Smith called for an informal expression of public opinion by asking municipal and road boards to suggest the names of replacements. They voted overwhelmingly for men from the western Cape. Smith tried to rectify the balance by including one name which was lower on the list, that of Robert Godlonton, editor of the *Graham's Town Journal* and a leader of eastern separatist opinion. But this alienated some of the successful majority at a time when the Whig Government in Great Britain, in which Earl Grey was the Colonial Secretary, wanted to encourage the adoption of representative government. It threatened again to expose political divisions between the eastern and western Cape.

Eastern Separatists stood for different things at different times. Sometimes, though only rarely, they wanted complete political separation from Cape Town. At others, as during the frontier war of 1834–5, they wanted the removal of the seat of government from Cape Town to the eastern districts. The term 'separatism' [*sic*] could also be used to cover some kind of federal solution, involving either a straight subdivision of the Colony into an eastern and a western province, or a tripartite division which allowed for some kind of separate midland province which could hold the balance between east and west. Over and above this tendency towards fission on geographical lines, there also developed a real danger of division over colour issues, for the outbreak of the eastern frontier war of 1850, followed by the Kat River Rebellion of 1851 [see p. 120] created a sense of nervousness even among whites of the western Cape which threatened to cut across London's insistence that there should be reasonable opportunity for the enfranchisement of blacks.

After difficult negotiations in which the Secretary of State, Earl Grey, sought to promote Cape self-government, a new constitution was agreed upon between the Cape legislature and the Imperial Government and confirmed by Order-in-Council in March 1853. This tried to cater for both eastern and western interests and at the same time give some political power to indigenous blacks. It made provision for a two-chamber parliament in which the western province received fractionally greater representation in both houses than the eastern. It also laid down relatively low qualifications for the franchise, admitting to the vote males of any race who earned £50 a year or occupied a site and structure together worth £25. The Colonial Office had inclined, on balance, to a lower rather than a higher franchise qualification, which had the support both of English-speaking liberals like John Fairbairn and of Dutch farmers who hoped that they and their Coloured *volk* might together hold the balance against the richer Englishmen of the towns.

Representative government at the Cape had an easy infancy during the governorship of Sir George Grey (1854–61). He was lucky enough to be Governor during the prosperous years of the Namaqualand copper boom and the arrival of the great Imperial banks. He ruled, in Rutherford's words, 'as his own prime minister', taking advice outside as well as inside his Council, and getting away with this at a time when there was no clear-cut party system or serious financial problem. His problems in respect of British Kaffraria and his exercise of the High Commission are discussed below [see pp. 121–3, 171–3].

Sir Philip Wodehouse, who succeeded Grey in 1861, thought, like Lord John Russell in the 1830s, that colonial self-government within the Empire was a contradiction in terms. But he paid more attention to the advice of his executive than Grey had done. He ran into trouble with his legislature, however, proposing big increases of direct and indirect taxation to offset the deficits which hit the Colony from 1864. When he proposed to abolish the upper house as an economy measure, public opposition, suspicious of his political motives, forced him to abandon the plan. Wodehouse's popularity was not increased when the Colonial Office required him to press the annexation of British Kaffraria on the Cape. After its incorporation as the Ciskei in 1865, the Colony became responsible for the cost of its administration and defence.

Resistance by the Colonial Parliament to Wodehouse's policies led the Gladstone Ministry in 1869 to urge the extension of full responsible government to the Colony, if possible as the nucleus for a federated South Africa, incorporating at least Natal, Basutoland (annexed by Wodehouse on behalf of the Imperial Government in 1868), Griqualand West (annexed by Sir Henry Barkly in 1871), and the Boer Republics as well. A federated South Africa, enriched by the revenue accruing from the recent discovery of diamonds, and from a boom in wool exports, would be able to pay for its own defence and administration and relieve the Imperial Government of this burden. Boer republican opposition to British annexations north of the Orange River induced a mood of non-cooperation in the Cape legislature, which was reinforced by a natural reluctance to accept responsibility for the control of new frontiers. But Sir Henry Barkly, who had already introduced responsible government in Jamaica and operated it in the radical Colony of Victoria, was able in 1872, on his second attempt, to persuade the Cape Parliament to accept it by narrow majority. As he had also managed to bring about the incorporation of Basutoland in the Colony in 1871, Barkly went some way towards realising the Gladstonian objectives [see pp. 174–5].

Separatism, however, remained a divisive factor in Cape public life, largely because the formula agreed upon under the constitution of 1853 had not given the easterners the security which they required. A powerful Separation League grew up in Port Elizabeth and Grahamstown in 1860, and used the easterners' indignation over what seemed to be an unfair allocation of public funds for development to press for total political separation of east and west. Easterners had found it impossible during the Wodehouse era to block western schemes, even by the most determined filibusters. The stamina of the resident parliamentarians could always outdistance that of the visitors, and it was only on the occasion of the Grahamstown Parliament of 1864, called by Wodehouse as a sop to the easterners, that the westerners experienced similar treatment in reverse. By that time, however, the lines of division in Cape politics were becoming more complex. The incorporation of the Ciskei in the Colony created a new regional interest less antagonistic to Cape Town than to Port Elizabeth, which was East London's chief rival for the eastern wool trade. When the diamond fields were opened in the 1870s, a new kind of rivalry developed between Grahamstown and Graaff-Reinet, each competing for the possession of the main road and rail routes from Port Elizabeth to the interior. Graaff-Reinet became disenchanted with the easterners' cause, began to cultivate a 'midland' identity, and chose a Capetonian as one of its representatives in Parliament. But because of the new prosperity of the diamond era, when Port Elizabeth obtained a major share of Kimberley's overland trade as well as of the wool export trade, the separatist movement lost much of its drive.

It had its last formal fling in a petition drawn up in Port Elizabeth in 1872. This followed soon after Barkly's appointment of a federation commission which heard a great deal of evidence in favour of dividing the Cape into three provinces, so that the midlands could act as a counterweight to the rival pulls of east and west. Just at this time, when the Colony was in the throes of accepting responsible government, legislative subdivision was found unacceptable. The result was a compromise in 1874. The Cape Parliament carried a Seven Circles Act, which set up seven electoral provinces as constituencies for the upper house, including a midland province, and thus removed the structural reason for suspicion between east and west. A political ghost was thereby exorcised by a minor constitutional change, creating greater flexibility at the seat of power and giving an additional stimulus to country voters, who now discovered that they had a good chance of securing the election of farmers to upper house seats. Farmers' associations with an interest in political questions began to take root in the eastern Cape and the midlands.

But this was not quite the end of the separatist story. The first Cape prime minister, J. C. Molteno (1878–8), represented the midland constituency of Beaufort West, and held the balance until Lord Carnarvon tried to foist on South Africa a federal constitution which appeared to involve the separation of the eastern and the western Cape as distinct units in a larger federal system. Carnarvon's plan was firmly rejected by Molteno's Government, which represented mainly western Cape interests; but Molteno was himself subsequently dismissed from office by Sir Bartle Frere, following a disagreement over the conduct of the frontier war of 1877–8. He was replaced by J. G. Sprigg, whose political base was East London, and whose ministerial colleagues all came from the east and midlands. One of the Sprigg Government's first legislative acts was the imposition of an excise duty on spirits, the incidence of which could be expected to fall far more heavily on the western districts than on the eastern. The formation by Jan Hofmeyr in 1878 of a predominantly western, Dutch-speaking farmers' association, the *Boeren Beschermings Vereeniging*, to resist this tax, showed that the pattern of dominance had for the first time changed. It also marked the moment of transition in Cape politics from a period of regional tension to a period of ethnic Anglo-Boer antagonism.

6.2 THE AFRIKANER REVIVAL AND THE RHODES–HOFMEYR ALLIANCE

The Afrikaner political and cultural revival began in the mid-1870s, at a time when the use of the Dutch language seemed to be in danger of disappearing from public life, and when confrontation between the British and Republican governments over policy in Basutoland and Griqualand West was at the same time beginning to inflame the Afrikaner's national pride. Its focal point was Paarl, where a group of clergy and teachers founded the *Genootskap van Regte Afrikaners* 'to stand for our language our nation and our land'. The Genootskap acquired a printing press, put out the first newspaper in Afrikaans, *Die Afrikaanse Patriot*, and published its own history book, *Die Geskiedenis van ons Land in die Taal van ons Volk*, and a range of school textbooks. In 1879, the *Patriot* began to advocate the formation of a broad Afrikaner organisation to coordinate the activities of the Genootskap, Hofmeyr's B.B.V., the Transvaal *Volkskomité* which was organising resistance to British rule, and other kindred bodies. This was realised with the founding of the first branches of the *Afrikaner Bond* in 1880. The Bond originated in the Cape, but it soon set up branches in the Orange Free State and Transvaal as well, once the Transvaal had regained its independence in 1881. Its prime movers were the brothers S. J. and D. F. du Toit, the former a minister of the N. G. Kerk, the latter a schoolmaster and editor of the *Patriot*. The Bond strongly attacked the spread of British influence at the expense of traditional Afrikaner ways, and adopted the rigorous neo-Calvinism of Dr Abraham Kuyper of the Netherlands as a defence against the culture of 'liquor, lucre and redcoats' which they seized upon as the symbols of British conquest. It was directed more against Imperial rule than against English-speaking colonials, though this distinction was often lost on contemporaries. A United South Africa under its own flag, but with the Imperial navy as the first line of defence, became the Bond's advertised political goal. The tone of its propaganda offended not only Jan Hofmeyr, who saw the Bond as a rival to his own B.B.V., but also President Brand of the Orange Free State, who regarded it as subversive.

Hofmeyr, however, using the Bond's own procedures for branch formation, managed to infiltrate the movement by founding his own branch in Cape Town, and gradually gained control over its parliamentary caucus from 1883, by which time S. J. du Toit had become Superintendent-General of Education in Kruger's South African Republic. The Bond's aims were softened. A united South Africa under its own flag now became the final 'destiny' rather than the final objective; the association of the Bond with neo-Calvinism was broken, especially through the adoption of a moderate Programme of Principles in 1889; and the pan-South African character of the movement gradually disappeared, chiefly because the Bond in the Transvaal, under the leadership of General Piet Joubert and S. J. du Toit, crossed swords with Kruger and lost its fight with him for the support of Transvaal Afrikaners.

After 1883, thanks to the influence of Hofmeyr and to changing political and economic circumstances, the antagonism between the white communities in the Cape gradually lessened. Bondsmen and the members of English-speaking farmers' congresses became increasingly aware of their common concerns as farmers and as citizens of the Cape Colony, especially after the discovery of gold on the Rand in 1886 had given the South African Republic a chance to go its own way economically, threatening to deprive the Cape of railway and customs revenue which close association with the Republic could have produced. Bondsmen, like the Cape merchants, accordingly threw their weight behind attempts to achieve a South African Customs Union; and after a short period of divided counsels, they also came down in favour of the extension of the Cape railway system into the Orange Free State and the South African Republic.

For more than a decade, the Afrikaner Bond was the only organised party in the Cape Parliament, but it did not have a majority in either house. Consequently Hofmeyr, who was its parliamentary leader from 1879 till he resigned his seat in 1895, tried to ensure Bond dominance by entering into alliance with well-disposed politicians, encouraging them to accept office on terms agreeable to the Bond. J. G. Sprigg had been opposed by both the Bond and the B.B.V. during the first ministry (1879–81), but T. C. Scanlen (1881–4) enjoyed the backing of the Bond until it went against his plans to encourage the Imperial Government to take control of the Transkei, Basutoland and Bechuanaland in 1883–4. Sir Thomas Upington (1884–7), who was Hofmeyr's next choice, fought the Bondmen's economic battles prior to the discovery of gold, just as Sprigg did during his second term (1887–90) in the matter of customs and railway policy [see p. 183–4].

Then, in the twelve months after July 1889 Jan Hofmeyr came to a decision of great consequence for the later history of southern Africa by agreeing to pledge the support of the Afrikaner Bond to Cecil Rhodes. The lure was an offer by Rhodes of good prospects for Cape farmers and speculators in central Africa at a time when the South African Republic was standing in the way of such an advance (Davenport).

Rhodes baffled his contemporaries with his strange mixture of mystical credulity in the manifest destiny of the Anglo-Saxon 'race', linked to a contempt for people in general which was implicit in his claim that every man had his price. (Bondsmen, he found, had a weakness for land.) A hard-living, heavy-drinking 'go-getter', who was to die at 49 in 1902, Rhodes believed in the need for growth in a young society, and in the power of money to bring it about. This caused much consternation among his financial backers in the metropolis after he had begun to rely on them from the mid-1880s for the promotion of his activities in Kimberley, Johannesburg and beyond the Limpopo, especially as his methods were commonly secretive. He polarised his contemporaries as he has since done his biographers. Percy FitzPatrick, who first met him at a bazaar in Wynberg in the early 1880s, left a vivid impression of an exceptionally tall, flannel-clad figure with a heavy forehead and dreamy grey-blue eyes, who 'seemed to be superior, and he knew it. And the devil and all was that he did not show it. He was not contemptuous, nor even indifferent, but I froze with hostility on sight'. If things improved for FitzPatrick, Rhodes earned first the awestruck admiration and then the contempt of Olive Schreiner and James Rose Innes, the deep hostility of Paul Kruger, the life-long support of Sir Lewis Michell, his faithful banker, and the infatuation of L. S. Jameson. Jan Hofmeyr experienced the agony of betrayal at his hands, and never forgave him. Africans in general had little reason to like him, for he tended to identify 'civilised' with 'white', and to look upon the black as a potential labourer rather than an object for compassion. His Glen Grey Act of 1894, that 'bill for Africa' over which he took enormous pains, had something to do with the extension of local government to African communities on Cape Colonial lines, but rather more to do with the utilisation of black labour [see p. 164].

The alliance between Rhodes and the Bond was to their mutual advantage. Rhodes was, above all, anxious to establish a strong power base in the Cape Parliament in the year after he had amalgamated the Kimberley diamond interests under his own control, so that he could build up further enterprises beyond the Colonial borders. Amalgamation of the Diamond Fields had not been a simple process. Rhodes, after becoming chairman of the De Beers mine, took advantage of the business strength of this company, which managed its affairs and its labour resources better than its rivals (Newbury), to succeed where others like John X. Merriman had failed. He first bought Jules Porges's French Company with the help of Rothschild money, and amalgamated it with De Beers. He then reached out for the Kimberley Central Company of Barney Barnato, and won its control first by selling the French Company to his rival in return for a stake in Barnato's enterprise, and then bulling the Kimberley Central shares to the point at which Barnato's supporters began to sell for profit, thus enabling Rhodes and his allies to acquire a majority holding.

Although Rhodes had acquired a foothold on the Rand with his founding of Consolidated Goldfields in 1888, he did not obtain as substantial a grip on gold mining as some of his rivals, save perhaps for a brief period in the 1890s. Nor was his enterprise north of the Limpopo [see pp. 157–60] the financial success for which he hoped, though it kept Rhodes and the Afrikaner Bond together, despite a cabinet crisis over ministerial corruption (the Logan affair) in 1893, until the calamitous Jameson Raid of

December 1895. The Bondsmen, in addition to gaining the opportunity of participating as individuals in Rhodes's enterprises, through the acquisition of farms in Charterland or (in the case of some leaders) the acquisition of Chartered shares at par when they were unobtainable even at a great premium on the open market, found their interests as farmers helped in a variety of ways: by the creation of a Ministry of Agriculture, by steps taken to improve the Colony's breeding stock, to establish a fruit export industry, and to bring the farmers closer to their markets in the big towns through the construction of a few important rail links. Rhodes also seems to have subsidised the Bond press (Davenport).

So strong were the ties between Rhodes and the Bond, that although Hofmeyr broke with Rhodes immediately after the Jameson Raid, it was only at its Malmesbury congress in 1897 that the Bond formally followed suit. Even then a small group, led by S. J. du Toit, who had apparently become dependent on Rhodes after returning from the Transvaal in 1890, refused to completely disown him. The Raid created a vacuum in Cape politics. When Sprigg formed his third, caretaker ministry in January 1896, the Bondsmen had had no time to make terms with him. Public opinion quickly polarised in the aftermath of the Raid and they soon withdrew their support. For the first time, something like a two-party system now appeared in Cape politics, with the failure of Du Toit and the reluctance of James Rose Innes to form a moderate centre party. English-speaking elements set up a South African League in the Cape, Transvaal and Natal. By 1898, when the investigations into the Raid in South Africa and in London were over, Rhodes felt free to return to public life, and in the general election of that year he appealed to the voters as the leader of a new Progressive Party, the first political movement with Colony-wide organisation at the constituency level which had ever presumed to challenge the Bond. The events had driven Innes and Merriman apart. The former, after a spell on the cross benches, was eventually drawn back to the Progressives in spite of Rhodes's return, thinking that, evil though Rhodes's actions had been, 'the effect of Transvaal knavery and tyranny upon the rest of South Africa' were worse (see Wright). Merriman's anger, by contrast, had led him to agitate for the confiscation of the British South Africa Company's charter, which did not materialise, and from the time of the 1898 elections he was driven to make common cause with the Bond.

The Council elections of 1898 were close, and the Progressives just pulled ahead. The Assembly elections were even closer, but this time the Bond and its allies won a narrow victory. The new governor, Sir Alfred Milner, asked W. P. Schreiner, who had served as Attorney-General in Rhodes's cabinet, to form a government. The Raid had brought Hofmeyr and Schreiner together, and they worked in close partnership with each other during the critical months prior to the Anglo-Boer War, both seeking to preserve peace between the Imperial Government and the South African Republic, or – if that were impossible – to ensure that the Cape's involvement in the conflict was minimal.

6.3 BLACK POLITICS IN THE NINETEENTH-CENTURY CAPE COLONY

African participation in the political life of the Cape Colony was slow to develop, though many of the thousands who passed through Lovedale and the other mission schools found their way into the professions and the public service. Attempts by Mfengu to register for the vote in large numbers were not very successful in 1866, though Mfengu votes seem to have helped George Wood in the Legislative Council election of 1869. In 1871 the Attorney-General commented on the general failure of Africans to make use of their political rights.

The frontier war of 1877–8 [see p. 124] was so traumatic an experience for Africans that it seriously undermined the confidence which many still retained in the merits of white rule. Not only did it precipitate the Mpondomise rebellion [see p. 125], but it also gave rise to Nehemiah Tile's Thembu Church of 1884 (Saunders), the precursor of many other independent religious movements which revealed a deep desire among Africans to run their own institutions in their own way.

There was also a more restrained reaction among black leaders, very few of whom had gone over to the rebels during the war. This was reflected in the revival by Elijah Makiwane in 1880 of a Native Education Association first founded in 1876. In the same spirit a Mfengu teacher, John Tengo Jabavu, took over the editorship of *Isigidimi SamaXhosa* the vernacular section of Lovedale's *Christian Express*, in 1881.

But it was not long before the moderate black leadership was driven to take a stronger political line, and the particular occasion for this seems to have been the founding of the Afrikaner Bond. *Imbumba yama Nyama*, whose title implied a movement which possessed muscle, was founded by a group of Africans in Port Elizabeth in September 1882, as the 'real' Afrikaner Bond (as distinct from Imbumba Yama Bhulu', the 'Boer Bond' – Odendaal). Like the Afrikaner Bond, it too went for voter registration, with remarkable results in 1882–6 (McCracken, Odendaal). Soon afterwards, a move among whites to disfranchise black voters helped to persuade Jabavu to take a more political stance, as he broke away from his editorial work at Lovedale in 1884 to found an independent Xhosa newspaper *Imvo Zabantsundu*, in time to campaign for a liberal candidate, James Rose Innes, in the Victoria East constituency the same year.

Sprigg's Registration Act of 1887 excluded tribal forms of tenure from the property qualifications for the vote and was seen by blacks as an attempt to 'sew up their mouths' (Odendaal). It provoked them to keep up their political pressure and led Jabavu to convene a conference of Native Vigilance Associations (*Iliso Lomzis*) in King William's Town the same year. But in spite of a continuing drive to keep up their numbers on the voters' rolls, Rhodes's Franchise and Ballot Act of 1892, which raised the property qualifications from £25 to £75, and the clause of the Glen Grey Act (1894) which excluded property ownership altogether as a voting qualification for blacks who held under Glen Grey title, made severe inroads into the black electorate and checked its growth.

Although Odendaal has stressed that African political leaders at the time were 'much closer to their communities than has been realised, and much more interested in traditional matters', Jabavu and his associates felt constrained to moderate their political appeal and to resist the urge to set a mass movement going. Unlike the Afrikaners, who were ready to thrust their language into public life, the African leadership agitated in English. The move into Colonial politics involved, for them, a far bigger cultural leap. Jabavu declined invitations to stand for Parliament. So for that matter did Hofmeyr when it came to the offer of cabinet office. Both men felt the need to promote their people's causes without unnecessary provocation, and this probably helped to produce Jabavu's isolation during the early 1890s.

In 1889–92 a group of Africans led initially by Jonathan Tunyiswa of Mount Coke set about the formation of a Native Congress (*Ingqungqubela*). They disagreed with Jabavu about procedures within the *Imbumba* movement; but it seems likely that there were deeper cross-currents. As Trapido has suggested, the Mfengu–Xhosa rift still existed as a potential line of cleavage. Jabavu was Mfengu, elitist, and enjoyed the authority and control which *Imvo* gave him. In 1895, before the Jameson Raid members of the Native Congress appealed to Rhodes for funding for a newspaper of their own, at a time when Rhodes appears to have been very receptive to such an approach. *Izwi Labantu* was in existence by November 1897, and the Congress for the first time in a position to counter Jabavu's influence. Meanwhile the Raid had shattered the unity of white political life and driven some of the Cape liberals, notably Merriman and Sauer, into the arms of Hofmeyr. Jabavu followed them, after a noteworthy public speech by Hofmeyr before the 1898 general election. An incipient rift in the black community was thus made absolute by a rift in the white, which would cause most blacks to continue to support the English-speaking Progressives, but turn Jabavu into a courageous pro-Boer.

6.4 THE FOUNDING AND SETTLEMENT OF COLONIAL NATAL

A small settlement of traders and hunters established itself at Port Natal in 1824, and by virtue of achieving a working relationship with Shaka it was just able to survive. Shaka welcomed traders like F. G. Farewell, Nathaniel Isaacs and H. F. Fynn. Without apparently appreciating what white people understood by the transactions, he and his successor Dingane ceded to the settlers the major part of what later became the Colony of Natal, even though they had taken under their wing a number of refugees from Zulu rule. The best known of these cessions, that made to the Voortrekker leader, Piet Retief, in February 1838, provided the territorial basis for the Voortrekker Republic of Natalia, whose fundamental law was drawn up in March 1839, on the basis of the Winburg Nine Articles [see p. 69]. But Natalia's history was brief. A British contingent had arrived in December

1838, ostensibly to reestablish order during the confrontation between the
Voortrekkers and the Zulu; but it was withdrawn a year later, when the
accession of Mpande relaxed the tension between the Zulu and the
Trekkers. A second British occupation of Port Natal took place under
Captain T. C. Smith in May 1842, inspired this time apparently by concern
in the Cape over the growth of unrest in Kaffraria as a result of a Boer raid
on Ncaphayi. Smith's presence at Port Natal was resented by the Trekkers,
who seized his cattle. Smith then attacked their base at Congella, failed to
take it, and was himself besieged almost to the point of surrender. He was
relieved by a force sent up from the Cape on information delivered by Dick
King, South Africa's Paul Revere, who had made the five-hundred-mile
overland journey to Grahamstown in ten days. After the siege of Port
Natal had been broken, the Volksraad of Natalia submitted to British
control in July 1842.

The British Government decided to take Natal for a mixture of reasons,
among them a desire to restore a strategic balance upset by the defeat at
Congella. Sir James Stephen, Permanent Under-Secretary in the Colonial
Department, did not want to annex, nor did his political heads with the
exception of Lord John Russell. The suggestions that Natal was taken for
its coal deposits or its cotton potential appear improbable. The Cape
governor, Sir George Napier, announced the extension of British protection over the territory in the Cape Legislative Council on 4 May 1843.
When the Volksraad submitted to the Crown's special Commissioner,
Henry Cloete, on 9 August, it was required to agree that the laws of Natal
should be colour-blind, that raids across the border were not to take place
without governmental sanction, and that slavery was not to be allowed.
But the formal annexation of Natal to the Cape was not proclaimed in
South Africa till August 1845. During the interregnum the Volksraad
continued to meet, though it was powerless to control events, until the first
Lieutenant-Governor, Martin West, reached Natal on 8 December 1845.

The extent to which the region between the Tugela and the Umzimkulu
rivers, which formed the boundaries of Natal, was cleared of population as
a result of the Mfecane, can only be stated in general terms. A list provided
by Lieutenant-Governor Scott in 1864, and published in Bird, and two
maps contributed by Shepstone to the Cape Native Laws Commission of
1883, both name ninety-four tribes which were said to have occupied land
in the region before Shaka's accession. According to Scott's account,
approximately fifty of these were destroyed, or dispersed unrecognisably
among other chiefdoms, approximately twenty fled from their home districts and settled elsewhere in Natal, while the rest either remained in their
home districts or returned to them after being chased out. Shepstone's
maps agree substantially with Scott's account, while that on which he noted
the distribution of chiefdoms after Shaka's wars suggests that when, in
1846, a Government commission of which Shepstone was a member laid
down the boundaries of African locations in Natal, these corresponded
closely with the areas of actual black settlement at the time, though the
possibility of some manipulation should certainly not be discounted.

The regulation of land policy in Natal was a pressing call on West's administration, which had the task of satisfying those Africans who had returned, or were in possession when the wars were over, as well as the white claimants. The Commission rejected the Voortrekker policy of removing all African settlements to the other side of the Tugela and Umzimkulu rivers and recommended a string of locations well within the Colony, amounting to about a tenth of the total surface area, stretching in a horseshoe along the upper and middle Tugela, then turning south parallel to but inland from the coast, with further settlements at Umlazi south of Durban (as Port Natal was now known) and at Swartkops near Pieter-maritzburg.

Definite arrangements with regard to title were not made in the case of the Voortrekkers, whose land claims were very extensive indeed, but generally lacking in precise delimitation. Cloete had found he could not endorse vague Volksraad grants. West's surveyor-general, William Stanger, paid attention to the towns before he looked at the farms, and proceeded so slowly in the latter instance that a number of the trekker families lost patience, withdrew northwards in 1847, and tried to set up an independent republic under Mpande's overlordship in the Klip River district. They were experiencing the kind of delays over the registration of titles which had been common in the Cape only a few years earlier. To make matters worse, a policy of stiffness under Cloete and West was followed by one of chaotic laxity when Sir Harry Smith became governor in 1847. Smith, who came face to face in early 1848 with the Boer leaders of the Klip River insurrection, immediately overrode West's tight land policy and made a provisional alienation of nearly two million acres of land to 360 heads of trekker families, in the hope of persuading them to stay in Natal. Whitehall subsequently disallowed an ordinance abolishing restrictions on land alienation, however, and it was this, apparently, that persuaded most of the remaining trekkers to sell their claims, frequently to speculators at prices of as little as twopence an acre, and emigrate. Perhaps two-fifths of the surface of Natal fell into speculators' hands.

Sir George Grey launched a cheap land scheme linked with military service on his visit to Natal in December 1855, hoping thereby to attract young farmers with a mere £6 a year to pay in quit-rent; but speculation remained Natal's curse, especially when Natal land became a proposition on the London stock exchange, after the founding of the Natal Land and Colonization Company in 1859. By that time fairly systematic settlement of the land, under conditions comparable with the 1820 Settlement, had begun. The Byrne scheme of 1849–50 brought some five thousand English and Scots, many of whom, like their Cape counterparts, found their land allocations far too small, and therefore moved into the towns. Pieter-maritzburg and Durban began under their influence to develop a quicker commercial and cultural life. Politics too became enlivened during the lieutenant-governorship of Benjamin Pine, when the land problem entered its next controversial phase and D. D. Buchanan's *Natal Witness* assumed a role similar to that of Fairbairn's *Commercial Advertiser* at the Cape.

6.5   SHEPSTONE AND AFRICAN ADMINISTRATION IN NATAL

Theophilus Shepstone, the son of a Wesleyan missionary, who had been made diplomatic agent to the tribes of Natal in 1845 after some years of experience in a similar post on the Cape eastern frontier, came in for the wrath of white Natal farmers during the first Lieutenant-governorship of Sir Benjamin Pine on the ground that the locations his commission had set aside were too large, with the result that black workers were not coming forward to work on the farms. Pine, who resented Shepstone as an over-mighty subject, set up a commission composed mainly of land-owning colonials in 1852 to review the decisions of 1846–7. This commission proposed radical changes, criticising the size of the reserves and Shepstone's boosting of the chieftainship; but it was a dead letter because Pine's successor, Scott, supported the view of Shepstone, who, as Secretary for Native Affairs, carried more official weight than he had done earlier as a mere diplomatic agent with the tribes. The storm increased after the achievement of representative government in 1856, when settler representatives in the Legislative Council mounted a sustained attack on the Government's native policy.

Shepstone respected and protected and wielded immense influence over Africans, at any rate in his early years. His movement of large numbers of Africans into the designated reserves was a master-stroke of tact and influence. He would have liked to remove the bulk of Natal's Africans outside the Colony's borders, and thus remove the pressure of black settlement on the Colony. With this end in view he tried to obtain first No-Man's-Land and subsequently Basutoland as annexures to Natal, but was unsuccessful in both instances. Governor Sir George Grey persuaded the Colonial Office to veto the former proposal, and in 1867 Sir Philip Wodehouse headed off the second. It was in the Natal locations, therefore, that his policy of paternal government, one of the earliest variants of 'indirect rule', came to be applied: headmen and chiefs (preferably not traditional rulers but his own appointees) worked alongside white magistrates, who were required if possible to be self-effacing. The chiefs reported to Shepstone himself as the mouthpiece of the Supreme Chief, the Lieutenant-Governor. This designation was conferred on the Lieutenant-Governor by Ordinance 3 of 1849, in a fictitious adaptation of tribal custom. Shepstone won his campaign to keep tribal Africans outside the reach of the Roman–Dutch civil law of the Colony, and subject to their own customs. He was prepared to allow only exceptional individuals to place themselves under Colonial law, and these under very stringent conditions, so that hardly a handful qualified during the whole period of his rule. By 1904, however, some 5,000 had obtained exemption (Odendaal). Shepstone's image as a protector of blacks against exploitation by white landowners has been modified by the work of Etherington, who presents him rather as a promoter of the flow of labour into Natal from Zululand and further north. Although this argument is in need of clarification, it would help to explain Shepstone's failure to develop the reserves themselves. The annual native affairs grant of £5,000 from Colonial revenue, which was guaranteed under the constitution, was ridiculously small, but it has been noted by Welsh and others that even in this fund a surplus of £30,000 had been allowed to accumulate by 1871. Consequently development did not take place; and because it did not, the settlers could argue with at least some plausibility that it was better for Africans to enter the white man's service than to stagnate in the reserves. Many, of course, did work on the farms; many paid rent to speculative land companies for the use of land sold over their heads, but the sugar plantations on the coast, with their requirement of heavy manual labour, were very short of manpower, and the sugar farmers were a growing pressure group. Far fewer Africans found their way to the towns in Shepstone's day. When they did so he was quick to recognise a potential social problem, and came out in 1874 with a schedule of 'togt' (casual labour) regulations, one of the earliest examples of modern influx control.

Shepstone's reputation as Secretary for Native Affairs was damaged in the eyes of posterity by his actions during the crisis over Langalibalele, chief of the Hlubi, in 1873–5. Langalibalele refused either to agree to the registration of firearms which his people had acquired at the Diamond Fields, or to appear personally in Pietermaritzburg to explain his conduct. Instead, he withdrew to Basutoland with his cattle, possibly with the intention of going into rebellion, but he was handed over to the Natal authorities by the Sotho chief Molapo, with whom he had taken refuge. Skirmishes took place between his followers and the Natal Carbineers sent to apprehend him. The troops moved into the Hlubi location, killing over 150 in the subsequent fighting. Langalibalele was deposed, his tribe broken up, his land and cattle confiscated. After that he was put on trial in January 1874 before a special court in Pietermaritzburg, over which Lieutenant-Governor Pine presided as Supreme Chief, sitting with Shepstone, the whole Executive Council, three magistrates and six chiefs. Langalibalele was denied defence counsel with power to cross-examine witnesses. He was found guilty, and sentenced to banishment for life. His appeal to the Executive Council was then dismissed, whereupon a special Act of the Cape Parliament consigned him to Robben Island.

The Imperial Government intervened. Pine had exceeded his authority as both Supreme Chief and Lieutenant-Governor, and was recalled. The Cape Parliament had exceeded its powers by accepting custody of a convicted person from another colony, and was ordered to bring Langalibalele back to the mainland under the British Colonial Prisoners' Removal Act of 1869 which required an address to the Queen by legislatures of both colonies where transportation was proposed. Shepstone had not in any way resisted Pine's proceedings, but may even, in Welsh's words, have 'masterminded the trial arrangements' and worked closely with a Governor who had once been his opponent. Bishop Colenso, who had been a supporter of Shepstone's paternalism until the Langalibalele affair, now turned against him as a despot. He was deprived against his wishes of the judicial authority which had been his by delegation from the Governor, when the Legislative Council created a Native High Court in 1875. But he now began to acquire a reputation in South Africa, as the master-mind behind the

policy of segregation, which was subsequently developed into the distinctive governing principle in the native policies first of Natal and later of the
Union. Yet Shepstone, like Lugard, was a pragmatist rather than an
ideologue, and would probably have disapproved of this trend on account
of its rigidity. Though he was authoritarian to a fault, he was not a maker
of systems, not even a believer in the rigid codification of African law.

6.6 POLITICAL DEVELOPMENTS IN NATAL TO RESPONSIBLE GOVERNMENT, 1893

The political system of Natal, which was in due course adapted to blend
with Shepstone's policy of keeping blacks and whites apart, took its shape
from the Charter granted by Letters Patent in 1856. This gave the Colony a
governor (or lieutenant-governor) who reported direct to London. He was
aided by an executive council composed of five officials and (from 1869)
two unofficials, and an elective legislative council, initially of twelve
members, in which the members of the executive sat and voted. Although
the structure of African administration as devised under Ordinance 3 of
1849, allowed for the government of blacks by special procedures under
their own law, the Charter incorporated the franchise proposals first made
by Pine, theoretically admitting blacks to the vote as well as whites, if they
possessed fixed property worth £50 or paid £10 a year in rent. This
interpretation was challenged, even by the Chief Justice, but supported in
1863 by most members of the Executive Council. It was changed in 1864–5
on account of growing settler concern over the possibility of a widespread
registration of black voters. An Exemption Law now laid down that
Africans desiring to be released from native law had to produce proof of
literacy and take an oath of allegiance, whereupon the Lieutenant-
Governor could admit them to some of the privileges of citizenship at
discretion. A second law, the Native Franchise Act of 1865, laid down that
no more blacks could even petition for inclusion on the electoral roll unless
they had been residents of Natal for twelve years, had held letters of
exemption from native law for seven, and had the approval of three whites
whose word was endorsed by a magistrate; after which the Lieutenant-
Governor could admit them to the roll or exclude them at his discretion
after calling for public objections. The suggestion has been made by
Trapido that the Exemption and Native Franchise laws were the price paid
by Scott to obtain a truce with the legislature in their quarrel with him over
the £5,000 native reserve fund, and over the continued existence of
Shepstone's locations. These the Council agreed to place under the control
of a new Natal Native Trust, consisting of the Governor and Executive
Council, in 1864.

In spite of the tensions of the 1850s and 1860s, it was not until 1870 that
the first exploratory demand for responsible government was made and
withdrawn. Another such demand in 1874, following soon after the Langalibalele affair, and largely inspired by it, was understandably turned down.
Indeed, in 1875 Lord Carnarvon ordered Pine's successor, Sir Garnet

Wolseley, to pack the Legislative Council with almost enough nominees to swamp the elective majority. This 'Jamaican' reform (so called after the curtailing of the constitutional liberty of Jamaica ten years earlier) has generally been regarded partly as a punitive reaction by the Colonial Office to Pine's mismanagement of Langalibalele's trial, and partly as a necessary preliminary for the implementation of Lord Carnarvon's plan to federate south Africa. Etherington has proposed that it should be seen in the context of Shepstone's successful effort in 1874 to persuade Carnarvon of the need to improve the flow of labour from the north to Natal. The federal strategy at least is very clear, though a measure like the Jamaica reform was not the most obvious way to correct a governor's tendency to make judicial mistakes, above all in the light of Shepstone's own questionable role in the Langalibalele trial. But, be that as it may, Wolseley managed the humiliating manoeuvre by drawing heavily on his entertainment allowance, but the demand for responsible government was revived in 1879. Those who did so had not reckoned sufficiently carefully with its implications for defence, or with the Imperial Government's likely demands over native policy. Two general elections fought on the question in 1880 and 1882 showed that the electorate at least was aware of these problems, for the 'responsibles' were well beaten, while a compromise proposal by the Durban lawyer, Harry Escombe, for the appointment of colonials to the Governor's Executive Council was either misunderstood by the Colonial Office, or ignored as unorthodox and unwise. During the late 1880s, John Robinson, editor of the *Natal Mercury*, renewed the campaign for responsible government, having won Escombe over to the cause by 1885 (Lambert). Natal became increasingly locked in economic conflict for the trade of the interior with its self-governing rival, the Cape. This meant that the raising of a loan to extend Natal's railway system to the Transvaal border became a matter of great importance, and it was made clear to the Natal Government that this would be much easier to procure if responsible government were first obtained. Eventually, from a desire to contain the growing strength of the Transvaal, the main political parties in Great Britain began to encourage such a step. Knutsford, for the Conservatives, was prepared to keep a garrison in Natal for five years after the change, though he looked for effective safeguards for black interests, which the Natal politicians were unwilling to provide. In the end, Knutsford sent a draft Bill for submission to the Natal electorate and, if approved in a referendum, for acceptance or rejection by the Legislative Council without amendment. A general election in 1892 resulted in the return of an 'anti-responsible' majority, but the reversal of two results following electoral petitions led Natal to accept responsible government by the same kind of precarious vote as the Cape had done twenty-one years earlier. An upper house of eleven, to be chosen by the Governor-in-Council, and a lower of thirty-seven elected on the existing franchise, constituted the new Parliament. The Colonial Office had receded from its earlier tough stand on the subject of black rights. It had managed to double the native reserve fund to £10,000; it retained the conventional powers of reservation and disallowance with respect to Bills affecting the blacks, and it insisted on the

Governor retaining discretionary powers in the exercise of his authority as Supreme Chief though he was expected to keep his ministers informed.

6.7 THE ARRIVAL OF NATAL'S INDIANS

The Imperial Government might have paid more attention than it did to the safeguarding of black interests, on account of developments where the Indian immigrants to Natal were concerned. Natal's Indian population had arrived for the most part as indentured labourers destined for the sugar plantations, in a succession of shiploads since 1860. They were mainly low-caste Hindus from Madras, and more than a third of those who arrived were women. Among the Zulu, agricultural work was women's work, and the cash incentive for male labourers was still low. The Indians were brought, therefore, to supply an urgent need, on five-year contracts, at agreed low minimum wages, and at the end of their contracts were given the option of serving for another five years, or obtaining their freedom, or returning to India. Those who stayed ten years in service could get free passages home. Recruiting was steady, save for a lull in the depression years 1866–72. When the first Indian repatriates returned home in 1871 and reported on their treatment, the Government of India forbade further recruitment. The Natal legislature therefore took special steps in 1872 to put right the abuses which had been alleged – flogging of workers, and excessive pay deductions for absenteeism, for example – and appointed a Protector of Indian Immigrants. Provision was also made to allocate land to Indians who had completed their contracts, on the ground that such people had skills to contribute to the welfare of the Colony, and should be encouraged to remain. Indian immigration now accelerated, and the population rose from under 10,000 in 1875 to about 100,000 by the end of the century.

From the late 1870s, a new class of 'passenger' Indians reached Natal under their own initiative, Gujerati traders, commonly Muslim in their faith, who set up shops in effective competition with whites in the towns of Natal, the Transvaal and the Orange Free State. White shopkeepers began to agitate against the Indians, alleging unfair competition, while the dangers of the Natal Indian vote became an increasingly common white electoral slogan. This anti-Indian campaign was gathering momentum at the time when Natal achieved responsible government. It resulted, after responsible government, in a legislative programme designed to restrict the political and economic power of the Indian community, and to encourage them to return *en masse* to India. The legislation had three main features. The first was an attempt to disfranchise the Indians, to which the British Government took exception; but, as had happened in the Transvaal in 1885, a new formula which enabled Natal to achieve the same result without appearing to discriminate on racial grounds was not vetoed: under the Franchise Act of 1896, the parliamentary vote was to be denied to people whose countries of origin did not have 'representative institutions founded on the Parliamentary franchise'. The second measure was the introduction of a £3 poll tax on Indians who neither renewed their indentures nor returned to India, to be levied in the first instance on the heads of families, and subsequently on all members of such families, some of which were large. In the third instance, local authorities were empowered to refuse trading licences to Indians without any risk of court actions.

These developments provided the setting for the South African career of a man whose techniques of resistance made him one of the most powerful moral influences of the twentieth-century world. This was Mohandas K. Gandhi, who arrived in Natal in 1893 on a legal assignment to the Muslim traders in Pretoria, very quickly experienced personal slights directed at him on account of his race, and decided to remain in the Colony when he learned that disfranchisement of Indians was intended [see pp. 211, 239–42]. Although the common idea that Gandhi was the initiator of Indian political resistance has been repudiated (Swan), he did take the lead in setting up a Natal Indian Congress and in launching a newspaper, *Indian Opinion*, as vehicles for the merchant pressure group.

6.8 THE CAPE, NATAL, AND THE DEBATE ABOUT LIBERALISM

The institutions of the Cape Colony and Natal were in both cases recognisably British by the middle of the nineteenth century, as was the dominant ethos of both, save for the Cape *platteland* and the northern districts of Natal, where Afrikaans-speaking communities set the tone. Both were colonial societies in the sense that at the level of public expression the black communities had no profile. White settlers owned nearly all the land not designated as Crown land, and the members of other communities either worked as squatter-labourers on white-owned land or farmed by traditional methods on Crown land or on mission reserves. With the exception of the crop-farmers of the Western Cape and the wool farmers of the Karoo there was little commercialised agriculture. The Natal sugar industry still lay in the future. Towns were small, roads almost nonexistent.

The Cape looked back in 1850 to two centuries of cultural contact between indigenous Khoisan and recently freed slaves (now collectively referred to as 'Cape Coloured') and settler Dutch and English, but had had no more than one lifespan in which to relate to its Bantu-speaking neighbours. Natal, as a state, was brand-new like the Cape, not yet self-governing, and with a black population which possessed overwhelming numerical strength in relation to white numbers, but had hardly had time to recover from the severe dislocation of the 1820s and 1830s. Natal's Indian population had not yet arrived.

Under these circumstances, the Cape came to project a liberal image, whereas Natal did not. This has often been crudely summarised in the distinction between the policies of Sir George Grey and Sir Theophilus Shepstone: Grey, the supposedly benign mixer of different cultural traditions so that each could profit from the strengths and support the weaknesses of the other in a great exercise in co-prosperity; Shepstone, the imagined father-figure and segregationist protector of the undeveloped blacks, keen to preserve the distinctions between the different communities until the end of time. The distinction is also made to rest on two further considerations. First, divergent franchise policies gave the vote to all races in the Cape from 1853, but denied it to Africans and Indians in Natal from 1865 and 1896 respectively. Secondly, the Cape Native Laws Commission of 1883 [see p. 126] laid emphasis on the promotion of a uniform legal system, whereas the Natal Native Code of 1891 promoted two parallel systems of law and allowed almost no opportunity for Africans to move from the one to the other.

The Natal system has been seen as essentially static, and Natal white attitudes powerfully reinforced by the impact of the Indian arrival, to produce among Natal whites the kind of naked racism which went berserk at the time of the Zulu rebellion of 1906–7 [see p. 209], and stopped not far short of it during the Indian penetration 'crisis' of 1942–3 [see pp. 317–19]. The Cape, by contrast, is seen as having fought and beaten authoritarianism in the struggle for the freedom of speech in the days of Lord Charles Somerset and the Settlers, and as having liberated – or accepted the liberation of – the slaves and Coloured people, and adopted a legal and political system remarkably free from ethnic restrictions.

To a point, it must be said, the antithesis holds; but as the point of vantage is moved to the twentieth century and the structures are placed under a spotlight, the differences appear to grow smaller. The political aspects of Cape liberalism shrivelled under the pressures of the late nineteenth century: its black franchise was whittled almost out of existence during the registration contests of the 1880s, though the traditional political values were reaffirmed during the Coloured vote crisis of the 1950s [see pp. 332, 342]. Furthermore, as Welsh noted in his discussion of the aftermath of Sigcawu's case in 1895–7, the Cape did not stop far short of giving its governor the authoritarian powers of a supreme chief (though it resisted the full implications of this until 1956). The Cape abolished jobless squatting by blacks ahead of the other colonies (Bundy), and it segregated its public schools in its School Boards Act of 1905.

Trapido has suggested that the most distinctive feature of Cape liberals was a common class base which liberal financiers, administrators, missionaries, lawyers, newspapermen and political opposition leaders are said to have possessed – a base which became eroded with the new capitalist upsurge after the start of the mining revolution of the 1870s. This is true, but it also diverts attention from the problem of what liberalism was really about. The term, then as now, was given a variety of meanings. It was sometimes linked with a brash utilitarian attitude to human relations in the spirit of Sir George Grey, addressing the Kaffir Relief Committee of 1857 (Peires). The intellectual liberalism of the Cape was better manifested in the outlook of William Porter, an Irish Presbyterian who linked his 'New Light' theology with the rule of law, and strove as attorney-general from 1839 to 1872 to administer justice without favour to either white master or Coloured underdog (McCracken). He also worked for a colour-blind political system. The most distinctive feature of nineteenth-century liberalism in the southern African experience was a concern for the rights of other cultural groups or individuals which, being relatively rare, was often seen as suspect, as a 'dishonest masquerade under the cloak of religion', or as an exotic plant which could not be expected to acclimatise. 'Kafferboetie' and 'Pro-Boer' became terms of abuse, though there was something impressive about the efforts of a Saul Solomon or an Olive Schreiner to defend the black underdog, or of a John X. Merriman to stand up for the rights of the Afrikaner. 'Onze Jan' Hofmeyr, Tengo Jabavu, and above all M. K. Gandhi showed a rare capacity for promoting a partisan cause without giving offence to the other side. Liberals were often paternalists, and in the late nineteenth century they found the logic of their position harder to defend: whether, for example, to support or oppose the extension of low franchise qualifications to blacks in the Transkei who had no experience of a Western electoral system, when such an extension might materially affect the political balance in the Colony; or whether to maintain or remove restrictions on the sale of the 'white man's liquor' to Africans, when to retain them was to deny recognition of adulthood. The liberals appear to have been, for the most part, intelligent people who agonised humanely and with integrity about difficult situations.

Section III
The Struggle for Possession

7 White and Black: The Struggle for the Land

7.1 THE TERRITORIAL CONFRONTATION: PRELIMINARY OBSERVATIONS

One view of the territorial changes which took place in the nineteenth century holds that they led to a fair and rational distribution of the land, the black chiefdoms holding on to what was traditionally theirs, the white settlers moving into areas which, though previously used by Khoisan and Bantu-speaking people, had been left empty as a result of the Difaqane. It should be clear from the events recorded in this chapter that such a view has little historical basis, and that outright competition for land – an increasingly scarce commodity – best explains the history of south Africa's nineteenth-century frontiers.

So long as competition for the control of land remained the main issue, the frontier should be seen as 'open'. Stock-farming communities which also depended on hunting for their livelihood faced each other across poorly defined or non-existent boundaries, each acknowledging governments whose ability to control them was minimal, and therefore relying on their own resources for offence and retaliation. A heightened sense of group awareness came to be seen by the thinly-spread white frontiersmen as an important key to survival, though it may be doubted if the more numerous blacks were thus animated to the same extent. At the same time, mutual avidity for trade goods and the generally conciliatory role of Christian missionaries ensured that these were not simply frontiers of conflict, while the desire of white farmers for labour could be an incentive for cooperation. But in a situation where able-bodied workers were scarce in relation to the land available, labour was hard to obtain save under favourable conditions of clientage, or through the indenturing of captives taken in war, adult or juvenile, under what came to be known as the apprenticeship system (*inboekstelsel*).

Frontiers would in due course become 'closed', when – as happened everywhere – the white governments incorporated the black-held areas, substituting the rule of written laws for the authority of persons, and bringing the control of all land and the regulation of labour within their supervision. But the new relationships of the closed frontier are reserved for discussion in Part Two. The present chapter is concerned with the struggle for possession, first on the northern and eastern Cape frontiers,

111

but subsequently on a multiplicity of new frontiers created as a result of the Great Trek. It was, in its essentials, a story of black–white confrontation in which the white man, with his superior weapons and his notion of individual ownership, his theodolite and his title deed, generally gained at the expense of the black. Black chiefdoms seldom became involved in interwhite quarrels, whereas the advancing whites were often able to exploit the divisions in black societies which developed all too frequently as a direct result of their initial loss of land.

7.2   CONFLICTS ON THE SAN FRONTIERS DURING THE EIGHTEENTH AND NINETEENTH CENTURIES

A little-documented frontier of conflict was that between the white settlers and the San, who fought their main rearguard action along the line of Bokkeveld, Hantam, Roggeveld, Nuweveld and Sneeuberg ranges between 1770 and 1800, and at first drove the frontier Boers to exasperation by their raids [see p. 28 and Map 4], as the Boers drove them to desperation by occupying their hunting grounds and shooting out their game.

By 1809, however, Colonel Collins, who toured the eastern districts on behalf of the British authorities, found these Bushmen less intractable, and was able to recommend 'a more liberal line of policy than that which I think necessary to be observed . . . towards the Caffres'. They were no longer a serious danger, though they still raided periodically. He suggested that a more humane policy conducted since the 1790s, and associated initially with Governor Macartney and the first L. M. S. missions, had apparently reduced the tension. Restraints had been imposed upon the commandos. Frontier farmers were winning the confidence of the San in places, by giving them slaughtered game. The Bushmen could therefore be 'more safely introduced into the Colony, collected and instructed in institutions, and dispersed among the inhabitants'. There was need for the civilising influence of missions in particular areas, and Collins singled out for special attention the region of the Riet and Sak rivers, where Kicherer's L. M. S. mission had had to close down in 1806, the region of the Tarka, and the Swartberg, where there were still many Bushmen in the mountains. Collins's reliance on the missions was overoptimistic. Tooverberg, Hephzibah, Philippolis and Bethulie, all opened after 1809 to attract Bushmen, were either closed in a few years or turned over to other communities, largely because white farmers had come to look upon mission stations as hideouts for thieves and the idle. But this reaction itself reflected a changing relationship, for some San were beginning to enter into the service of white farmers. Burchell, travelling through the northeast Cape in 1816, spent some hours with a very friendly San community; but there were still whites who could think of them only as vermin, as his compatriot George Thompson found in 1823, while Griqua were sometimes as enthusiastic exterminators of Bushmen as these whites.

The Great Trek cut a swath through the San-occupied regions of the interior, isolating those of the northern Cape from those whose base of operations remained the Drakensberg mountains to the east. The former either became absorbed in the Colony, intermarrying with Khoikhoi and other groups, or they retreated gradually towards the lower Orange. Periodic friction developed on this little-publicised frontier because no steps were ever taken to provide the Bushmen with a Reserve of their own, though this had been the intention of the Government at the time of the 1774 commando, and of Macartney in 1798, while it remained the main substantive proposal of Louis Anthing when he investigated the troubles of the northern border in 1862 (Marais). Because there was no Reserve, friction continued between the San and the farmers. In 1883, the *Zuid Afrikaan* considered that the troubles north of Victoria West were rather like those of the Ceres district at the end of the previous century.

The Drakensberg San retained greater independence for a time, raiding farms of Natal frequently between 1845 and 1872 along the whole length of the range from Witzieshoek in the north to No-Man's-Land in the south (Wright). Here the anarchy of the Karoo was repeated, though on a smaller scale. The raiders were far fewer – perhaps only a few hundred – but in Natal they were often mounted and therefore harder to apprehend. On the Cape frontier there were some suggestions of collaboration between the San raiders and the Tswana. On the Natal frontier, their collaboration with the Bhaca, the Phuti, the Mpondomise, and other chiefdoms seems to have endured over a long period, though it was a brittle relationship which failed to survive increased white pressure, especially when the Natal Government planted African locations on the access routes into the Colony and thus gave them a vested interest in resisting the San raids – for which purpose they were sometimes supplied with firearms. The Drakensberg San, encircled by white settlements in Natal and the Orange Free State, finally succumbed when their fastnesses in Basutoland were penetrated by the retreating Sotho in the 1860s, and when their base in No-Man's-Land was weakened with the resettlement of the Philippolis Griqua at about the same time. Lacking the cohesion and the power to resist white encroachment, they either stayed put and lost their identity, or retreated northwards in pursuit of the game. By the end of the nineteenth century few San were to be found south of the Orange river. In the mid-twentieth there may have been fifty thousand north of it. By the 1980s those in Namibia were being torn from their traditional way of life through cooptation in the Angolan war.

7.3   THE EASTERN FRONTIER OF THE CAPE COLONY

The beginnings of contact between the Xhosa and the colonists

The saga of the Cape eastern frontier was a story of rivalry, conflict and peaceful contact which lasted from the earliest encounters between the southern Nguni in the eighteenth century to the incorporation of Pondoland in the Cape Colony in 1894. Nine wars were fought between 1778 and 1878. Far more than any other frontier, it was one on which policies were

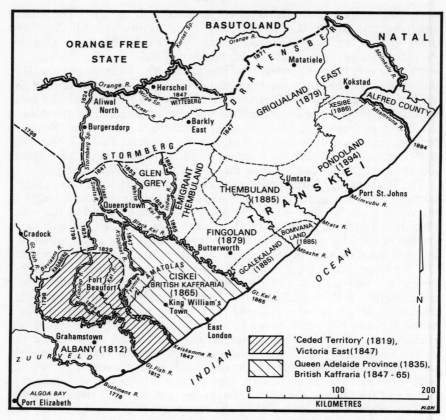

Map 5   The Cape eastern frontier, 1778–1894

thought out and deliberately applied. The blockhouse system and the military village; the buffer strip, the frontier of no outlets and the trading pass; the trade fair, mission station, hospital and school; the spoor law, the treaty system, the government agent, the magistrate – all these were tried in various combinations, in a bid to maintain order and peaceful coexistence at the meeting point of two disparate but competing cultures. Policies were debated, not only at the chief's great place and in Cape Town, but also in London, where permission had to be given before the Colonial borders could be extended. Extension followed a complex double process, with the authority of the Governor (from 1846 the High Commissioner) exercised through Colonial magistrates, frequently preceding annexation to the Colony proper. On the black side of the frontier, as on the white, power was not monolithic but divided. If this made for weakness in the individual chiefdom, it also ensured that conquest would be piecemeal and take much longer to achieve.

The Dutch East India Company tried to contain the frontier by regulating settlement, controlling trade, and imposing limits beyond which trekboers were not to proceed. But it failed in all three respects. The loan farm system did not contain settlement, as Tulbagh found when he tried to prohibit land grants beyond the Gamtoos river in 1770. Control over barter with the Xhosa proved impossible to enforce, because the border could not be effectively patrolled. Van Plettenberg proclaimed a frontier along the line of the Fish river in 1778, with the injunction that it should not be crossed. Macartney softened this policy, in the light of experience, in 1797, when he ordered farmers who had engaged Xhosa servants to discharge them within twelve months; but he also allowed the Landdrost of Graaff-Reinet to issue 'passports' to individuals who wished to cross the border. The Batavian authorities tried to adhere to a rigid frontier policy, in association with Ngqika, chief of the Rharhabe, when De Mist visited the eastern Cape in 1805. They threatened to confiscate the cattle of colonials who crossed the frontier, though they too accepted a passport system to regulate transit.

It was the Rharhabe and the Gqunukwebe who bore the initial impact of the white colonial advance in the late eighteenth century. The latter, a people of mixed Nguni and Khoi attributes, were settled in the Zuurveld between the Sundays river and the Fish. Under their leader, Chungwa, they were hemmed in among the Rharhabe and the Boers, and forced into a relationship of clientage to both. After successfully facing a commando led by Barend Lindeque in 1793, and surviving an attack by a British force in 1799, Chungwa stayed out of a conflict between the Boers and the Xhosa in 1801, but eventually lost his life, and his people their lands, when the Colonial Government had the Zuurveld cleared of black settlement in 1812.

After the second British occupation, the Government for the first time tried to impose a frontier settlement by force. Colonel Collins, sent by the Earl of Caledon to review the problem in 1809, negotiated directly with Hintsa, who had become the chief of the Gcaleka and paramount of all the Xhosa in 1804. Collins recommended that Ndlambe's Rharhabe and the Gqunukwebe should be expelled across the Fish, and that the Zuurveld should be thickly settled by white colonists. Colonel John Graham was sent by Governor Cradock to carry out this policy in 1811–12, and did so with brutal zest (Maclennan). Ndlambe, with his 20,000 subjects, was driven out of Ngqika's territory, their huts and gardens destroyed, and the Fish frontier fortified by a series of strong points between new villages named Grahamstown and Cradock.

It became British policy from 1817 to honour Ngqika as the Rharhabe leader, and hold him responsible on the Xhosa side for the effective recovery of stolen cattle under a modification of the traditional spoor law, which allowed for the pursuit of stolen cattle across the border and the recovery of the beasts (or their equivalent in number or value) by an armed force accompanied by the owner. But hot pursuit could lead to rough justice, and try though Somerset's successors did to modify the system in the light of experience, it proved impossible, as Macmillan has shown, to maintain the rule of law, or indeed stability, by methods such as these. Nor was it sound policy to place such a load on Ngqika, unless the intention was to undermine his power. He was not the Xhosa paramount. He enjoyed an ascendancy over his uncle Ndlambe, but lost it in 1818 after suffering defeat by the combined forces of Ndlambe and Hintsa at Amalinde, during a civil war provoked by Ngqika himself, which could hardly have overtaken the Xhosa people at a less propitious moment. A year later Ndlambe's men, led by the celebrated war doctor Nxele (Makanda), attacked Grahamstown and met with a sharp defeat. The Colonial Government now enlisted a not unwilling Ngqika in an invasion of the lands of Ndlambe and Hintsa, in the course of which some 23,000 cattle were taken. At the same time it required its allies, Ngqika's people, to quit the area east of the Fish as far as the Keiskamma, either so that this should become a neutral belt devoid of human settlement (which Ngqika was led to understand), or so that it could be ceded to the Colony for purposes of white settlement (which Macmillan and Peires declare, with supporting references, to have been Lord Charles Somerset's real intention). What happened in practice was that in Somerset's absence Sir Rufane Donkin, his deputy, allowed a settlement of ex-officers to be sited at Fredericksburg in the ceded territory in 1821, whereupon Maqoma, Ngqika's second son, crossed back from the east to his home in the Kat river basin, and was not prevented from reoccupying it.

By hinting in 1817 that he would allow controlled access by the Xhosa to Grahamstown to hold fairs twice a year, Somerset had relaxed the earlier rigidity of British frontier policy. The arrival of the 1820 Settlers [see pp. 38–9] gave an important boost to trans-frontier trade, for which, as Peires has shown, the Xhosa people had an enormous appetite. During Somerset's absence from the Cape in 1820, Donkin authorised a fair at Fort Willshire on the Fish river, which had become a thrice-weekly occasion by 1824.

As with trade, so with labour. Removal from their lands gave many Xhosa a necessary reason for entering into a relationship, the like of which they had never experienced in their own society, of dependence on employment as contract farm workers. Special provision was made for this in Sir Richard Bourke's Ordinance 49 of 1828, which enabled Xhosa migrants to enter the Colony to seek work.

But in the late 1820s several developments took place to unsettle the frontier. Xhosaland was disturbed by the ripple effect of the Mfecane [see pp. 12–18], with Bhaca invasions in 1823–5, followed in 1828 by the arrival of Ngwane refugees from the north among the Thembu, to the accompaniment of rumours that Shaka's Zulu were on the rampage in the area. Commandant Henry Somerset, concluding that the Ngwane were Zulu, attacked and routed them at Mbholompo in August 1828, with the aid of Xhosa, Thembu and Mpondo regiments. This provided an incentive for the Colonial Government, on the advice of Andries Stockenstrom, Commissioner-General of the Eastern Districts, to tackle the double problem of drought relief and frontier security by establishing a buffer Khoikhoi settlement in the Kat river basin. It was unfortunate for the stability of the frontier that this should have involved the re-expulsion of Maqoma, not least because he was readmitted by Henry Somerset, only to be forthwith expelled again to land without 'a morsel of grass . . . as bare as a parade', even though he had never taken up arms against the Colony.

This 'extermination' of Maqoma has to be seen in the context of growing tensions on the frontier arising from stock thefts, allegations of stock thefts, and corrective action taken by military patrols, if the outbreak of war in 1834 is to be understood. In one such incident in October, Xhoxho, one of Ngqika's younger sons, was shot in the head. To the surprise of the military authorities, who had wrongly advised the Governor, Sir Benjamin D'Urban, that the situation was well in hand, Xhosa regiments swept into the Colony in December, with the express approval of Hintsa, destroying households and seizing cattle in an out-and-out war of revenge clearly initiated by themselves.

The Sixth Frontier War and the treaty system

Macmillan argued that the outbreak of this Sixth Frontier War was largely the fault of Sir Benjamin D'Urban, because he failed to take seriously the advice of Dr John Philip, superintendent of the London missions, who plied him with good advice, begged him not to delay his visit to the frontier, and at the same time urged the chiefs to be patient. Philip's efforts need not be questioned; but Lancaster has demonstrated that D'Urban's failure to visit the frontier until after the war had broken out can be explained by the risks and difficulties attendant upon slave emancipation in the western Cape [see pp. 41–2], linked with the misrepresentations of his military advisers in the east. D'Urban, as Galbraith explains, in fact had a policy for the frontier: it was to restructure relationships through a system of treaties with the chiefs, on lines laid down by the Secretary of State, Earl Stanley, in December 1833, and already carried out on the northern frontier through a treaty concluded with Andries Waterboer early in December 1834, which had also received Philip's encouragement [see p. 132]. D'Urban also wanted the establishment of a border force under carefully selected field cornets for the suppression of stock theft, linked (until Henry Somerset advised against the idea) with a return of the Xhosa to the Ceded Territory on condition of their good behaviour.

Once the invasion had started, D'Urban sent Colonel Harry Smith to repel it, and by May 1835 the Xhosa were back in their own territory. The British troops invaded Hintsa's territory beyond the Kei, and Hintsa was persuaded, on a promise of safe conduct, to enter the British camp to negotiate the return of 50,000 Colonial cattle of which he had taken delivery. He was also prepared to allow the Mfengu refugees to whom he had granted asylum during the Mfecane to move to Fort Peddie with the 22,000 cattle they had acquired under his protection. But he drew the line at ordering Maqoma and his brother Tyhali to surrender, and over the payment of a ransom for his own release. Then, realising that he had been made a hostage, he made a bid for freedom only to be cornered, killed and then mutilated by his pursuers. D'Urban, who had begun to allow a vindictive tone to creep into his dispatches, even over the treatment of Hintsa, proclaimed the annexation of the whole area between the Kei-skamma and the Kei rivers as Queen Adelaide Province, with the require-ment that all the defeated chiefs should remove their followers beyond the Kei. He informed Lord Glenelg, the Secretary of State, of his decision.

But such a settlement was unenforceable because, as Peires and Lancas-ter both stress, the Xhosa had not been beaten militarily, but were driven rather by the attrition of war to agree to peace, and to drive them out was no way to solve their problem. Moreover, the Colonial Government shared with the Xhosa the difficulty of keeping their own forces in the field. D'Urban accordingly imposed a new settlement in September, under which Queen Adelaide Province was to remain open for white settlement; but the Ngqika, Ndlambe and Gqunukwebe chiefdoms were to be allowed to remain there, in locations under paid white resident agents who were to be given responsibility for law and order. This was a radical departure from previous policies, the first plan for the direct administration of the Xhosa, with the double object of breaking the power of the chiefs and converting their communities to European habits and the Christian religion.

Before the September policy could be applied, however, Glenelg reacted to D'Urban's May policy in a dispatch dated 26 December 1835, by demanding good reasons for not ordering the abandonment of Queen Adelaide Province forthwith. He was angered by D'Urban's derogatory references to Xhosa as 'unreclaimable savages', and ordered that no Khoi or whites, other than missionaries, were to be allowed to settle east of the Fish, and announced his intention of appointing a lieutenant-governor for the eastern districts, whose task it would be to enter into treaty relations with chiefs, as sovereign rulers, beyond the border. When news of D'Ur-ban's September policy later reached Glenelg, he dismissed it out of hand as being in conflict with his own decision to disannex.

The Lieutenant-Governor appointed to the Eastern Cape was Andries Stockenstrom, previously Commissioner-General, and since then a key witness before the Aborigines Committee which had sat in London in 1836 to investigate the conditions of black Colonial subjects throughout the Empire. Neither Stockenstrom's awkward personality nor his evidence before that committee endeared him to the whites of the eastern Cape, who felt threatened by his ill-mannered philanthropy. But Stockenstrom was the brains behind the treaty system which Glenelg had appointed him to enforce, and he began to implement it between October 1836 and January 1837, by entering into engagements with the main Rharhabe, Gqunukwebe, Thembu and Mfengu chiefdoms across the border. These treaties defined the boundaries between the Colonial and tribal territories, laid down that customary law would operate in the latter, and provided for the appointment of diplomatic agents near the residences of the chiefs. These agents were given the task of mediating in inter-racial disputes and in all negotiations with chiefs. The actual control of passage across the frontiers remained with the military, who could establish posts in black territory but were not permitted to patrol on the African side of the border.

Stockenstrom's appointment offended D'Urban, not unnaturally, for he had been given no advance notice of the identity of the officer whose task was to dismantle his own policy. Stockenstrom had full control over his own officials in the eastern Cape, but he was dependent on D'Urban's Executive Council (which knew how to drag its heels) for the release of funds, for the ratification of the treaties he concluded, and for all necessary legislation. D'Urban tried to thwart the treaty arrangements from the start, and Glenelg was forced to dismiss him for insubordination in August 1837. But Glenelg was himself displaced in February 1839, and in August Stockenstrom's appointment was terminated, and the scope of the office restricted, by the British Government on account of local opposition to his policies. Stockenstrom's opponents denied that the treaties had worked, and the argument that they were bound to fail served, like the abandonment of Queen Adelaide, to justify the emigration of the Voortrekkers [see pp. 44–8], on the ground that they increased the insecurity of the frontier. A personal quarrel between Stockenstrom and the Voortrekker leader, Piet Retief, helped to highlight the issue, though not necessarily to vindicate the argument. Nearly all the 272 cases recorded in the diary of C. L. Stretch, who as one of Stockenstrom's diplomatic agents, handled almost a third of all cases dealt with in 1837–46 were settled amicably with the chiefs (Crankshaw). Peires found that in so far as the system had flaws, these were rooted mainly in the failure of the authorities, under pressure from land-hungry farmers keen to expand their sheep runs, to hold on to the principle that it was more important to devise ways of preventing thefts than to find a foolproof way of recovering stock once it had been taken. The treaty system failed in the long run because Stockenstrom's successors misinterpreted its spirit – Governor Napier and Lieutenant-Governor Hare by refusing to condone the arming of herdsmen and by allowing aggrieved whites to cross the frontier in search of their own beasts; and Governor Maitland by restoring the patrols associated with the old spoor law, and imposing his decision on the chiefs without consulting them. Maitland's revision contributed directly to the outbreak of the War of the Axe in 1846.

The conflicts of 1846–53

This war resulted from incidents relating to the killing of a white farmer near the Fish river, and a dispute between Ngqika's heir, Sandile, and the Colonial Government over the siting of a Colonial military post at Block Drift in Sandile's territory. Like the war of 1834–5, this one also began with a successful Xhosa invasion of the Colony, with drives towards Graaff-Reinet and Port Elizabeth. Apart from one successful cavalry charge, at Gwanga in May, when the Ndlambe rashly abandoned bush cover, the British forces enjoyed singularly little success; but it was another war of attrition like that of 1835, and the Xhosa surrendered for lack of food.

Earl Grey, who became Secretary of State for war and the Colonies in 1846, favoured a strategy similar to that of D'Urban's policy in September 1835, but with the extension of British rule as far as the Kei river, the Africans thus incorporated becoming British subjects. In choosing Sir

Henry Pottinger to implement this plan, he picked a man of Indian experience, who, when armed with the new title of High Commissioner, would be expected to concern himself personally with the chiefdoms beyond the border and draw them into a kind of Imperial penumbra. Though he agreed with Grey's broad policy, Pottinger had little enthusiasm for a Cape assignment, especially as he found his task on arrival was to end the war rather than build the peace; but Grey had no difficulty in replacing him with the now titled Sir Harry Smith, who had covered himself with glory at the expense of the Sikhs and was more than keen to revive the frontier strategy of his ex-master, D'Urban. Smith arrived in December 1847. After explaining to the assembled chiefs, with dramatic sound effects, that he proposed to get rid of the treaty system, he annexed the Keiskamma-Kei region as the separate Crown Colony of British Kaffraria and announced plans to appoint magistrates with authority in place of the diplomatic agents, to reduce the chiefs to salaried officials, and to locate Mfengu settlers holding quitrent title, interspersed with white military villages, in the Ceded Territory, which was now named Victoria. This was to be done at a considerably lower cost than Pottinger had anticipated, even though Smith's appetite for expansion led him to advance British rule not merely eastwards into Kaffraria, but northwards, first to the Orange, and soon afterwards to the Vaal.

Smith's self-confidence knew almost no bounds, and the over-assertiveness of Maitland apparently taught him nothing. His magistrates might contain the situation for a while, and create the illusion of peace; but underneath there was smouldering resentment among the subjects of expropriated chiefs, and a good deal of inertia among those ordered to move out. Chiefs also grew to resent the attempts of Colonel Mackinnon, the Chief Commissioner of British Kaffraria, to short-circuit their authority, and when Smith arrived on the frontier in October 1850 to meet the Ngqika and Ndlambe chiefs and headmen, he realised that Mackinnon had gone too far. On the same occasion, however, he dismissed Sandile from the Ngqika paramountcy for refusing to meet him – from fear of being arrested, Sandile explained. Meanwhile Mlanjeni, a prophet, was beginning to unsettle the people and appeared to the Government as a mouthpiece of chiefly resentment; but it had become too dangerous to arrest him by the time the Government was convinced that he was guilty of incitement. On Christmas Day 1850, three of the military villages in Victoria were surprised and destroyed by the Ngqika. Maphasa's Thembu north of the Amatolas joined the Ngqika, as did Mhala, son of Ndlambe, and even the Kat river Khoi, driven to desperation by the drought and the growing insecurity of their settlement. Most of the Ndlambe, the Mfengu, and Phato's Gqunukwebe on the coast remained loyal to the Government; but the opposition was strong enough, and the terrain so difficult, that it was not until early 1852 that Smith began to get the measure of his opponents – by which time Earl Grey had decided to recall him.

Smith's policy of direct rule therefore went down in ruins. Sir George Cathcart, the appointee of the succeeding Tory régime in Britain, viewed the frontier initially as a logistic problem and reverted to the strategy of creating a defensible boundary as a first priority. Hence the settlement of the 'loyal Mfengu' in the Crown Reserve which he created at the foot of the Amatolas. He also buttressed the east bank of the Keiskamma with a string of trusted Gqunukwebe chiefs (Phato, Siwani and Khama), and placed whites on land confiscated from the Kat river rebels, and in the area north of the Amatolas from which Maphasa was evicted, and where Queenstown was laid out in 1853. He also created the Frontier Armed and Mounted Police. But Cathcart also came to appreciate the importance of establishing a viable relationship with the chiefs in general, especially after tasting defeat at the hands of the Sotho [see p. 135], and therefore learned to reject Smith's brand of paternalism. Chiefs had to be recognised as men of status, he considered; so Sandile was restored to his position, and not driven over the Kei. Care was also taken not to override customary law.

Sir George Grey and the cattle-killing of 1857

This last aspect of Cathcart's policy was followed by his successor, Sir George Grey (1854–61), who tried to bring about the maximum socio-economic integration of black and white on the frontier, hoping to make the Xhosa 'a part of ourselves, with a common faith and common interests, useful servants, consumers of our goods, contributors to our revenue'. He therefore proposed to fill British Kaffraria with 'a considerable number of Europeans' who would settle among the indigenous blacks, teach them the Christian religion and the arts of European farming, and give them an understanding of the white man's law, as well as a vested interest through the grant of individual title. In describing this policy as 'civilization by

2   **Rivals (1) Sarhili and Sir George Grey**

mingling', and linking it with the outstanding medical work of J. P. FitzGerald and the educational achievements of the Lovedale mission, Monica Wilson laid emphasis on a distinctive feature of Grey's policy which has led several historians, notably A. E. du Toit, to rate his humanity very highly indeed. This policy must be viewed, however, from several sides. Grey miscalculated in trying to apply the land policy he had developed in New Zealand, where land was relatively plentiful, to British Kaffraria, where it was not. His plan to penetrate tribal territory with white-owned farms and military roads was as widely resented as his plan to substitute European for traditional cultural values.

This resentment erupted in the cattle-killing tragedy of 1857, when, following the prophecy of a young girl, Nongqawuse, the Xhosa people slaughtered their stock and destroyed their crops in the expectation of the resurrection of ancestral spirits, accompanied by the provision of food from heaven. Although there was an evident correlation between the cattle-killing and a serious outbreak of lung sickness among the cattle which reached a peak late in 1855 (Peires), this was primarily a millenarian movement of genuine and passionate intensity; but it does seem probable that the Christian belief in the resurrection of the dead had a direct influence on events. A Xhosa tradition which ascribes the tragedy to the manipulations of Grey and the missionaries lacks weight because it has no basis in any known acts or statements of the people concerned. Nor has the allegation commonly made at the time, especially by Grey, that it was the result of a chief's plot, master-minded by Sarhili and Moshweshwe any substance, even though these two rulers were in communication with each other at the time. On the other hand, Rutherford and Peires have argued that the human mortality which resulted from the cattle-killing did remove a major obstacle to Grey's plans for the white settlement of the Ciskei. The population of the affected chiefdoms (excluding Sarhili's trans-Keian lands) fell from an estimated 105,000 to a mere 38,500, those who died of starvation approximating in number to those who poured into the Colony in desperate search of work and food (who increased from 31 in 1856 to 28,892 in 1857). The Government provided emergency relief, but also went ahead with the settlement of German immigrants – mainly Crimean veterans and peasants – on the East London–Stutterheim axis, grouping the Xhosa survivors into villages and setting aside some 317 farms for whites in British Kaffraria on simple military quitrent tenure. Furthermore, Grey's allegations of conspiracy, which led to the trial of fourteen chiefs and senior headmen (among them Mhala, the Ndlambe paramount, Maqoma and Phato, all of whom had promoted the slaughter) were used by him to justify the clearing of Xhosaland on both sides of the Kei for white settlement. But Grey's bid to expand the Colony was ultimately thwarted in the Wodehouse era by the decision of the British Government not only to rescind all annexations beyond the Kei, but even to coax the Cape Government into taking over responsibility for British Kaffraria (thereafter generally referred to as the Ciskei) in 1865.

The second of these decisions was determined mainly by British reluctance during the lean 1860s to spend money on the protection of an exposed Crown colony. The first resulted from the sheer difficulty of finding an easy solution to the problems raised by the resettlement of peoples beyond the Kei. These were: first, the colonial Thembu from the Glen Grey area (Matanzima and others) who were planted in Emigrant Thembuland east of the Indwe river; second, the Gcaleka, who were deprived of their lands around their great place at Butterworth though not those at the coast, and were allowed to expand across the Mbashe in Bomvanaland; third, a large number of Colonial Mfengu, who were moved from locations in the Victoria district into the lands previously held by the Gcaleka, partly to ease overcrowding, and partly to establish a community whom the Cape Government could trust beyond the Kei; and fourth, Mhala's Ndlambe, who were settled west of the Mbashe in a reserve at Idutywa [see Map 5].

The Thembu experience

Severe tensions ensued as a result of these arrangements, between the Thembu and Mfengu on the one hand who were both able to pose, to some extent, as friends of the Colony [see pp. 56–7] and the Gcaleka on the other.

The Thembu had never been directly at war with the Cape Government, though Maphasa, the chief of one of their clans, the Tshatshu, had received stolen cattle in the war of 1834–5, and rashly joined Ngqika in the wars of 1846 and 1851. Nonesi, the queen-regent after the death of Mtirara in 1848, had refrained from taking sides against the Colony, and although she and her people were expelled over the Mbashe for a while on account of a clash with white farmers which was not of her making, she was established in a new 'Tambookie Location' (later known as Glen Grey) by Sir George Cathcart in 1853, and was recognised as ruler over the whole chiefdom. The cattle-killing of 1857 split the Thembu, for although Joyi restrained the eastern Thembu, Nonesi could not keep all her western subjects in check. The Thembu were consequently divided when a move started in the 1860s for the settlement of the land east of the Indwe river, lying between the Location and the main Thembu settlement area on the Mbashe. It originated, on the one hand, with chiefs in the Location who had special reasons for acquiring land elsewhere – among them Matanzima, younger brother of Ngangelizwe, the emergent paramount (1863–84), who desired to become a chief in his own right; Gecelo, a regent about to lose authority when his son came of age; and Ndarala of the Ndungwana, who had an insecure title to that chiefdom (Wagenaar). On the other side, there was a growing demand among frontier whites to engross all land as far as the Kei, and this had the backing of the Cape Government and of J. C. Warner, the Colonial agent among the Thembu, who worked hard to clear Glen Grey of its Thembu settlement by encouraging the would-be trekkers, and threatening loss of land rights and the imposition of Colonial law on those who refused to go. The upshot was a partial eastward movement into what came to be known as Emigrant Thembuland, but there was also stubborn resistance from Gungubele, heir to Maphasa, and from the dowager Nonesi, so that although Emigrant Thembuland was occupied, the Location was by no means abandoned. The two Thembu territories on the Kei and the Mbashe were in fact now linked by a continuous belt of settlement. Warner's relationship with Ngangelizwe was crucial because he hoped to persuade Mtirara's successor, in return for official support for his paramountcy, to agree to the abandonment of Glen Grey. Ngangelizwe resisted. By early 1869 he was turning the tables on Warner, whose attempts to discredit the chief led to his own dismissal. Yet Ngangelizwe's difficulties were immense. His quick temper drew him perhaps wittingly, into a losing war with Sarhili in 1872 for the maltreatment of his great wife (Sarhili's sister), and to dismissal by the British authorities following the murder of a concubine (who happened to be Sarhili's niece). He had been unable to cope with the complexities of rival Gcaleka and Mfengu claims on territories the Thembu had traditionally regarded as their own, and on to which these participants on both sides in earlier frontier wars had been driven. But Ngangelizwe retained his headship of the royal Hala clan until his death, and the Thembu, though incorporated under British rule, kept as much land as they had had in the days of their independence.

The Gcaleka in exile: the war and rebellions of 1877–80

Sarhili's Gcaleka, by contrast, paid the penalty for defeat in the frontier wars of 1846 and 1851 by being exiled to Bomvanaland, and felt very insecure in occupation of territory over which the Thembu had historical claims. Sarhili also resented the loss of his hereditary lands to the Mfengu – that is, to Hintsa's refugees, back in Hintsa's country, but this time as rightful settlers backed by Colonial titles and Colonial power. To avenge a personal affront, as noted above, Sarhili marched right into Thembuland, and then pulled out again, in 1872, causing Ngangelizwe to throw himself on the protection of the colony. The two chiefdoms would have come to blows again in 1875, if the Cape had not managed to pacify them.

In 1877, a Gcaleka was killed in a brawl at the kraal of a Mfengu headman, who gave his name to the 'War of Ngcayecibi' which grew out of this incident – the ninth and last of the Cape–Xhosa wars (1877–8) in which the Colony became involved, first in defence of the Mfengu, and ultimately in war against the Colonial Ngqika under Sandile, who came to the aid of Sarhili's chiefdom in what developed into the bloodiest of all the frontier conflicts. (Over 3,500 blacks lost their lives, as against sixty whites and 137 of their black allies. Black losses exceeded those in the wars of 1835, 1846 and 1851 put together.) What gave this war a special significance was that it occurred at almost the same time as the Transvaal–Pedi war [see p. 141], the Anglo-Zulu war [see p. 151], the Sotho 'Gun war' [see p. 138], and the rebellion in Griqualand West [see p. 133], and led within two years to a further major rebellion among the trans-Kei Nguni. Taken together, these constituted by far the greatest trial of strength between the blacks and the whites to have happened in southern Africa.

Sprigg's Government, which had taken office on the dismissal of Molteno in 1878 [see p. 93] after prosecuting the war with vigour, determined to rule the trans-Kei, and pushed through a Peace Preservation Act in the same year to control all firearms. It confiscated the lands of the Ngqika and of the Gcaleka, and split the chiefdoms into smaller locations, with the clear intention of breaking chiefly power and releasing labourers to work in the Colony. But the extension of political control over the remainder of the trans-Kei proved to be a complex task.

Fingoland (including Idutywa) and Gcalekaland were first on the list. Retroceded in 1865, they were claimed by Molteno by right of conquest from Sarhili in 1875, and consolidated as the Chief Magistracy of the Transkei in 1878. The royal assent to their incorporation was given in that year, and annexation to the Cape took place in 1879.

'Nomansland' (subsequently named Griqualand East) was annexed at the same time, after earlier confusion which had resulted from competition for the territory between Nehemiah Moshweshwe, who had moved into the Matatiele district in 1859, and the Philippolis Griqua, who had moved into the Kokstad region with the permission of Sir George Grey soon afterwards [see p. 130]. The trial and conviction of Nehemiah for rebellion in 1877, and the subsequent suppression of the Griqua rebellion [see p. 131] ensured the passage of the territory under Cape control despite strong protest from Natal.

In the case of Thembuland, Ngangelizwe's request for British rule, out of fear of a Gcaleka attack in 1875, was supported by the Cape Parliament in 1876, but blocked by the British Government unless the annexation could be dovetailed into its developing federal schemes, which the Cape consistently opposed until they were abandoned in 1880 [see pp. 175–9]. A chief Magistracy of Thembuland (including Bomvanaland and Emigrant Thembuland) was nevertheless created by the Cape Government in 1878, at the same time as it set up the Transkeian magistracy, and placed under the High Commissioner.

But the trans-Keian rebellions of 1880 threw the whole annexation question back into the melting-pot. These rebellions were a delayed consequence of Sprigg's disarmament legislation and of the imposition of magisterial rule at the expense of chiefly power, and they were ignited from the Sotho rising of the same year [see p. 138]. Revolt first broke out in the Matatiele region, and spread to the Mpondomise of Qumbu (whose magistrate, Hamilton Hope, was murdered), and into large areas of Thembuland and Emigrant Thembuland. The Cape lost control over nearly all of the trans-Kei, and the whites of Umtata, Kokstad and other centres went into laager. With the assistance of Bhaca and Mfengu troops, however, the Cape forces were able to put the rebellions down, without having to call on British forces, early in 1881.

One obstacle to the transfer of the Territories to Cape rule was the insistence of the British humanitarian lobby that the incorporation of African territories in the Colony should only be done if Britain kept control over the character of the administrative system and the laws to be imposed – a precaution inspired by the record of south African frontiers in general and Sprigg's performance in particular. Scanlen's Government, however, showed some signs of measuring up to the required standards. It appointed the Cape Native Laws (Barry) Commission in 1881 – one of the strongest commissions ever to look at African affairs in the history of south Africa – to devise a pattern of law and administration for a politically tense and culturally discrepant post-conquest society. The Scanlen Government also had to handle the unauthorised settlement of white squatters, who had taken part in suppressing the Emigrant Thembu rebellion, in the Xalanga river district – a problem charged with difficulty on account of the support enjoyed by the squatters among members of the Afrikaner Bond, on whose votes Scanlen depended for survival. But Scanlen handled the squatters with tactful firmness, thus restoring some of the British confidence in the Cape's capacity to govern.

The war of 1877–8, followed by the rebellions of 1880–1 had, however, been extremely costly, and during the economic recession of 1882–3 a strong mood developed in the Cape, reminiscent of that which had prevailed in 1865 over the incorporation of the Ciskei, against the retention of responsibility in the trans-Keian territories. The retrocession of Basutoland in 1884 was a product of this mood [see pp. 138–9]. Had Scanlen formally asked for a British takeover of the trans-Kei, there was a reasonable chance that this might have been accepted (Saunders); but he refrained, he fell from office for other reasons in 1884, and the Upington Ministry which took over was able to carry the Cape Parliament behind its decision to retain the Territories, relying largely on the Bond's mistrust of British rule over blacks in the light of tensions between the Boer republics and the British on this score. Incorporation of Thembuland, Bomvanaland and Gcalekaland into the Cape was eventually completed by August 1885, and formal responsibility transferred from the High Commissioner (whose authority had been used to cover provisional annexations prior to that date) to the Governor of the Cape.

The incorporation of Pondoland

All that remained for incorporation after 1885 was Pondoland. The Mpondo chief, Faku, who had successfully weathered the Mfecane, was recognised by the British in 1844 as lord of the whole area contained by the Drakensberg and the Mzimkulu and Mtata rivers; but the chiefdom split before his death in 1868, when his military commander and right-hand son, Ndamase, was sent by Faku to rule west of the Mzimvubu, to avert a threatened conflict with Faku's heir, Mqikela. This resulted in a weakening of Mpondo assertiveness in relation to outlying areas such as Griqualand East and the lands of the Xesibe and Mpondomise, and – the real Achilles heel of Pondoland – Port St Johns, for which Wodehouse had made a bid in 1866, and which Frere eventually took over, without Mqikela's assent, by 'deposing' Mqikela and buying it from Nqwiliso (son of Ndamase) in 1878. The Mpondo reacted, under the inspiration of Mhlangaso, chief councillor for East Pondoland. With the support of powerful white trading interests in the territory they imposed levies on Cape wagons in transit, and created a new harbour, Port Grosvenor, to compete with Port St Johns. The challenge was accepted. With some slight reason for fearing German intrusion at the height of the Scramble, the British Government declared a protectorate over the whole Pondoland coast in January 1885. Mqikela would have none of this, but division had begun to appear in Mpondo ranks, and he found he had to allow the Cape to take over the Xesibe country the following year.

What eventually broke Mpondo resistance was the outbreak of civil war, after the death of Mqikela, in 1888, when his successor, Sigcawu, was challenged by Mhlangaso, and the Imperial Government let it be known that it would support Cape claims to Pondoland against those of Natal, and raise no objection whatever to a Cape takeover. Sigcawu, whose tactic was to conciliate the Cape authorities, won the civil war. Rhodes moved into Pondoland in 1894, without the maxim-gun demonstration usually attributed to him on this occasion. But no sooner had Sigcawu become a Cape subject, than he began to test the Cape Government by granting concessions of which they disapproved, and resisting the payment of hut tax until Mhlangaso had been punished to his satisfaction. For this he was arbitrarily detained on Rhodes's orders in 1895, only to be released on the orders of the Chief Justice, who delivered a sharp rebuke to Rhodes on hearing Sigcawu's appeal. In 1897 the Cape Parliament took its revenge by amending the Transkeian Territories Annexation Act to give the Governor the power to detain individuals for three months without bringing them to trial – a mere shadow of the powers enjoyed as Supreme Chief by the Governor of Natal, but a handy enough instrument of control. Thenceforth the powers of Sigcawu were contained (Welsh), and Pondoland had been fully incorporated in the Transkeian administrative system by 1902.

After incorporation, representation? The Ciskei in 1865 had been granted two parliamentary constituencies, and retained a non-racial franchise. Basutoland, during the period of Cape rule from 1871–84, had been ruled as a dependency without any political representation. The Transkei, like the Ciskei, was granted two constituencies, Thembuland and Griqualand East; but it became very clear from the parliamentary debates that the sudden addition of black territories to the Colony was not to be allowed to overturn the political dominance of the white electorate. Hence the franchise restrictions of 1887, 1892 and 1894 [see p. 97]. Yet the Transkei remained African territory, partly because settlement schemes offered to whites had not been taken up on a large scale; partly because it had been used as a dumping ground for blacks expelled from the Colony proper; partly because methods had been developed throughout the century, but especially during the war of 1877–8, and under Rhodes's Glen Grey Act of 1894 [see p. 164], of using the Territories as a labour pool for colonial needs; and partly because of the long-standing efforts of missionaries in the field and humanitarians in the Colony and overseas to protect the blacks in at least the residue of their rights.

From the black side, the Colonial advance presented insoluble problems. Militarily, they could not win, either by using surprise to make up for their defective weaponry, or by turning to war doctors to break white power. Despite the common European belief that the black chiefdoms were coordinating their strategy to drive them back, the evidence points rather to a lack of combined effort among the chiefdoms, which also accounts for the long duration of the Cape frontier conflict. Those who accepted conquest, and the mission education that went with it, included some remarkable people; but they were no more than a few thousand by the end of the century, and, as already noted [see pp. 97–8] the educated elite and a good many of the rank and file were already looking for a political solution to their problems.

7.4   THE CONFLICTS ON THE GRIQUA AND ORANGE FREE STATE FRONTIERS

The Cape–Kora Wars

In the region of the Orange River, where the hold of the Oorlam Afrikaners began to relax from about the 1850s [see above, p. 29], lordship among the Khoisan passed to the Kora and the Griqua. Kora dominance was restricted to the lower Orange from Kheis to the Aughrabies because, as Van Aswegen has shown, their earlier control over regions east of the Orange–Vaal confluence and the Vaal–Harts area had been destroyed by white acquisition of their lands. Several Kora leaders – Jan Bloem, Goliath Yzerbek and Kousop in the late 1850s – had lost their power in this way and then either trekked across the Vaal or entered the service of farmers. In the west, however, the Kora remained strong because, though lacking in political unity and organisation, they had firearms and excellent defensive positions on the thickly wooded islands of the Orange River.

Accounts of Kora history by Ross and Strauss have revealed intense conflict between rival groups for paramount control during the 1860s, when Cupido Pofadder and Klaas Lukas, aided by whites, were able to dominate their rivals. But there was a breakdown of order after the drought of 1868. The colony set up a border police force to check Kora raids up the Hartebeest river valley; but even with Pofadder's help they could not prevent the outbreak of war in 1869–70. The Kora raiders were with difficulty put down, and Lukas and Klaas Pofadder (Cupido's son) recognised as the rightful rulers of the north bank. But there were many Kora who resented their exclusion from the islands and the south bank, and therefore reoccupied them when the Government was attempting to locate whites in the area. In 1876 the Government began to evict them. Kora hostility, further sharpened by drought in 1877, resulted in many of them joining forces with the rebels of Griqualand West who took up arms in 1878 [see p. 133]. Between January 1878 and July 1879 all chiefdoms along the Orange River except the Bondelswarts were up in arms. The Kora fought hard, but they lost the war, and therefore the right to continue living as frontier bandits. They also lost Korannaland itself, which was opened to white settlement and renamed – after the eighteenth-century pioneer – as Gordonia.

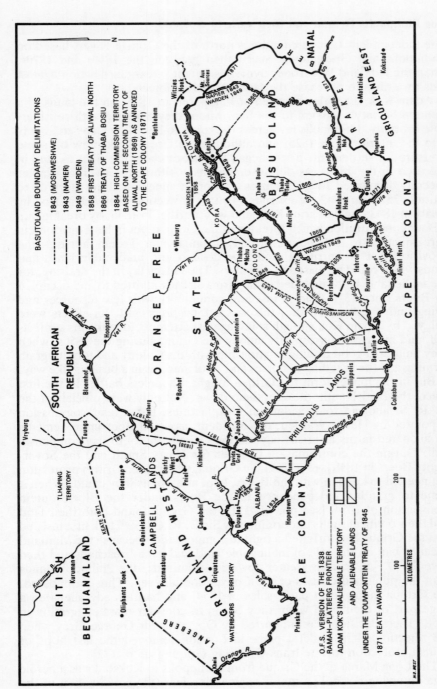

Map 6 Encounters of the Griqua, Sotho and Tlhaping with the Orange Free State in the mid-nineteenth century

BASUTOLAND BOUNDARY DELIMITATIONS

1843 (MOSHWESHWE)
1843 (NAPIER)
1849 (WARDEN)
1858 FIRST TREATY OF ALIWAL NORTH
1866 TREATY OF THABA BOSIU
1884 HIGH COMMISSION TERRITORY
BASED ON THE SECOND TREATY OF
ALIWAL NORTH (1869) AS ANNEXED
TO THE CAPE COLONY (1871)

O.F.S. VERSION OF THE 1838
RAMAH–PLATBERG FRONTIER
ADAM KOK'S INALIENABLE TERRITORY
AND ALIENABLE LANDS
UNDER THE TOUWFONTEIN TREATY OF 1845
1871 KEATE AWARD

0   100   200
KILOMETRES

N.G. WEST

The Philippolis Griqua and their exile to Kokstad

The independent Griqua chiefdoms north of the Orange River, based on Philippolis and Griquatown, succumbed between the 1840s and 1870s, when the Kok and Waterboer dynasties fought a rearguard action against bids by whites to purchase the farms of their subjects.

Adam Kok II's Griqua settled at Philippolis in 1826, on the lands of a London Society's mission to the San, whom they expelled with considerable brutality. Philippolis lay across the route followed by Cape trekboers into the interior from 1825, and although the Great Trek drew off some pressure for settlement, Boers began to seek or claim the right to land in the area in the 1830s, as 'fellow-emigrants'. Although Governor Napier speedily disavowed Judge Menzies's action in annexing all territory up to latitude 25° S. in 1842, he extended British protection over Adam Kok by treaty in 1843. Sir Peregrine Maitland went further in 1845, by breaking up a Boer concentration which threatened the Griqua; but in his Touwfontein agreement with Kok he unwittingly insinuated a Trojan horse – the provision that his territory should be divided into inalienable lands and lands which could be leased to outsiders. The fallacy lay in the drafting, for the *in*alienable lands included some farms already allotted to and occupied by Boers since 1840. For an insecure community with few resources and living under individual title, this was a fatal precedent. Its effects were delayed by Adam Kok's tough stand against attempts to make his subjects sell, and by growing prosperity among the Griqua during the 1850s, when they built up a good trading relationship with the Colony and took to grain farming and the breeding of horses and wool merinos in a businesslike way.

But in the longer term the Griqua fought a hopeless battle. In the first place, the British authorities let them down. Not only were officials of the O. R. S. allowed to speculate in Griqua titles, but a land commission appointed by Henry Warden, the Resident, assessed Boer improvements on alienated farms at prices beyond the Griqua ability to pay compensation. During the confrontation between Sir Harry Smith and the Sovereignty Boers in 1848 [see p. 169] the Griqua, who valued British protection but needed to keep in with the Boers, kept as aloof as they could. When it came to granting independence to the Boers under the Bloemfontein Convention of 1854, [see pp. 74, 171], the Griqua found both their land and their political rights undermined by Sir G. R. Clerk. Clerk first insisted that the Griqua had forfeited a right to compensation because the Maitland Treaty's ban on the sale of inalienable land had been breached, and then gave the O.F.S. officials greater powers to administer the Philippolis lands than the published clauses of the Convention allowed. Thus intimidated, the Griqua indulged in panic sales in 1854, and had already alienated a large part of their land when they began to consider mass emigration in 1858. Their decision was supported by Governor Sir George Grey when the rejection of his federal plans in London removed the last hope of British protection for the trans-Orangian Griqua [see p. 172].

The Long March of the Griqua from Philippolis to Kokstad was a heroic saga involving not only a major engineering feat (the construction of the pass over Ongeluks Nek) but also great hardship through stock losses during their wintering at Hangklip in the Drakensberg in 1861. But the migration succeeded in spite of heavy odds. Ross has shown how, before the founding of Kokstad in the early 1870s, Griqualand East became a magnet for other unsettled groups like Smith Pommer and his *banditti* (survivors of the Kat river rebellion). The Church followed the migration. Traders moved in and did business with the help of a paper currency. The people settled down to a life of farming and other supporting activities with the help of a far better land registry than they had in Philippolis days. Adam Kok III ruled with the aid of a written constitution which gave him executive and legislative councils. He ran an administrative system which maintained control over and empowered him to tax African communities within the territory. Public life was not without friction, though Kok himself was generally popular. Plans for the takeover of Griqualand East by the Cape were, however, already in hand, partly in order to pre-empt a similar move by Natal. In October 1874 Sir Henry Barkly visited Kokstad, announced that the government was to be placed under the supervision of J. M. Orpen, and Kok, who was unsure of himself in the situation, was persuaded to become a paid official. Then tragedy descended on 31 December 1875, when Kok himself was killed in a road accident. Matthew Blyth, who had long administrative experience in the trans-Kei, was sent as Resident, but he antagonised the Griqua. The new Government destroyed the two pillars of Adam Kok's land settlement – his ban on alienation and his ban on the sale of liquor in the territory – and with this the intrusion of whites began. In 1878 rebellion broke out, following the arrest of Lodewyk, a young member of the Kok family. His brother 'Muis' joined forces with Smith Pommer, while at a gathering outside Kokstad, Blyth confronted Adam Kok's widow, who refused to hand over the keys of the powder magazine. The rising was easily put down, and its suppression signalised the disintegration of the East Griqua community, for whom the growing pressures of white racialism and land hunger, accompanied by considerable African immigration from the trans-Kei (Beinart), had proved too strong.

Yet not all Griqua took landlessness lying down. It was a non-participant in the original trek who arrived only in the 1880s, Andries Stockenstrom le Fleur, who, after serving part of a fourteen-year sentence for sedition in 1898–1903, tried in 1917 to organise a trek of landless Griqua from Griqualand East to Touws river in the western Cape, where he hoped to establish a farming community which could prosper by sending its produce to Cape Town and Johannesburg by train. It failed, thanks to the hostility of the Karoo climate, financial mismanagement, and the Spanish flu. Undaunted, Le Fleur tried to organise another settlement on the Olifants River, this time of people from the Coloured mission reserves of Namaqualand, in 1922, and another near Victoria West in 1926. Both failed. Indeed, the only scheme of this kind which did prosper, a trek from the Cookhouse–Bedford district to Plettenberg Bay and Knysna, was at first repudiated by Le Fleur. This community subsequently moved a short distance inland to Krantzhoek, which became a symbolic focus for Griqua aspirations and, in 1941, Le Fleur's appropriate burial place (Edgar and Saunders).

The Griqua of Nicholas Waterboer, the land court, and the rebellion of 1878

Nicholas Waterboer of Griquatown, son of the Andries who had concluded a treaty of alliance with D'Urban in 1834, fell victim to the pressure of land-seekers from the Cape, and to diamond-hunters from many parts. The alluvial diggings at Pniel, on the right bank of the Vaal, first worked in 1869, were claimed not only by himself, but by the Tlhaping chief Mahura, by the South African Republic, by the Orange Free State, and by the diggers, who set up their own republic on territory belonging to the Berlin Missionary Society. When the Dry Diggings at Du Toit's Pan (the site of the later Kimberley) were opened in 1870, further dispute arose among the surveyors as to whether they were located east or west of the boundary dividing the lands of Kok from those of Waterboer; for if they were east of that line, they were unquestionably in the Free State [see Map 6]. David Arnot, a Colesberg law agent with an eye for the main chance, undertook in 1867 to defend Waterboer's territorial claims. His price included the right to survey and settle a tract named Albania, to the east of the Vaal–Orange confluence, with whites brought up from Albany who were prepared to recognise Waterboer's authority over them (Kurtz). Having thus strengthened Waterboer's sovereignty up to the Ramah-Platberg line agreed as a boundary with Adam Kok in 1838, Arnot then constructed a case for his northern border on a line agreed with the Tlhaping chief Mahura in 1842 and confirmed in 1864, and successfully defended his case to the satisfaction of Lieutenant-Governor Keate of Natal in October 1871. Having secured recognition as a territorial sovereign, Waterboer then offered his territory, referred to as Griqualand West, to the Crown for protection, and Sir Henry Barkly, the High Commissioner, accepted it. This new British colony came into being within a few months of the rush to the dry diamond diggings on the site of the present Kimberley. It soon became a white speculator's paradise.

After the discovery of the dry diggings, black and white prospectors moved to the Fields to stake their claims, though many of the blacks went there as servants of their white masters. Before the installation of Sir Richard Southey as Lieutenant-Governor of the new colony in January 1873, the diggers had set up their own committees as an informal government. In theory they had to comply with Cape law, which contained no barrier to the pegging of claims by blacks. But in practice the diggers' committees applied pressure to have the allocation of claims limited to whites, urging that to admit blacks as claimholders would be to destroy the possibility of controlling diamond smuggling. They never obtained a colour bar as such from the Colonial Government; but they achieved the same result by means of master–servant legislation administered by white officials sympathetic to their aspirations, under a proclamation dated 10 August 1872. Claimholders were made to acquire a certificate of good character from a magistrate; persons found loitering within range of a mining camp could be accosted by any registered claimholder and asked to produce a pass, which – if they were servants – they were obliged to carry. Kimberley was the first place in South Africa where the practice developed of trying pass offenders in a special Police Magistrates' Court, which was set up in 1876 to conduct mass summary trials (Worger).

When the diggers took their opposition to Southey's regime almost to the point of violence in 1875, this was not because Southey had encouraged claimholding by Coloured people, though he would have liked to be able to do so, but because under the constitution of 1873 the diggers had not been given as much power in the Legislative Council as they wanted, and because some of the diggers' leaders on the new Mining Board (constituted in July 1874) had developed a personal hostility to Southey and to J. B. Currey, his Colonial Secretary, and claimed – it seems, erroneously – that Southey had been involved in corrupt land deals. Southey and Currey were recalled by the Secretary of State, Lord Carnarvon, as scapegoats for a social policy whose failure they had not been given the resources to prevent. But the *de facto* colour bar in the matter of mining claims remained. Circumstances were less easy for the labourers when Sir Owen Lanyon was Administrator in 1876–80 than they had been in the Crown Colony period. They became harder still when the Cape took over the territory, for then the process of capitalist consolidation went ahead fast, labour controls were further tightened, and the closed compounds were introduced.

A Griqualand West Land Court was set up in 1875, under the presidency of Judge A. Stockenstrom, to resolve land questions and test the legal basis of the Keate Award. Although he accepted some of Waterboer's grants as valid, he rejected others and cast doubt on the legitimacy of the Griqua chief's role as a grantor of title. It was partly to meet Griqua protests arising out of Stockenstrom's awards that Colonel Charles Warren was appointed in October 1877 to reopen the land question. Warren was more sympathetic to the Griqua cause. If he recommended the placing of Waterboer's subjects in locations rather than on land of their own, he did this in the belief that 'a large number of natives will sell any property they possess [and] when this takes place the locations will be required'. He had made provision for a number of locations to be proclaimed, and for many more Griqua claims to be confirmed, before he was called away to serve on the Cape eastern frontier in January 1878. By the time he completed his report in August 1879, the Griqualand West rebellion had begun and ended. There can be no doubt that it was in part a protest against the alienation of land, for several leaders of the rebellion – notably Donker Malgas and Jan Pienaar (Gamga) had had their claims refused both by Stockenstrom and by Warren. But its causes were more complex, and because it was never officially investigated, they are not yet fully understood. It was a widespread rebellion which covered most parts of Griqualand West as well as territories to the north and west of it. It involved not only Griqua but also Kora [see p. 128], and Botlatsitse's Tlhaping who resented their inclusion in Griqualand West without consultation, as a result of Waterboer's submission to Barkly in 1871. There are some grounds for thinking that the rebels were encouraged by events on the Cape frontier, in Griqualand East, and in Sekhukhuneland [see pp. 125, 131, 144]. Their piecemeal suppression resulted in a weakening of the black chiefdoms, and of the position of blacks in the Crown Colony, in the years immediately before its incorporation in the Cape in 1880.

Moshweshwe's Sotho, the Free State, and the British, 1833–84

The Sotho under Moshweshwe had established their base in the Caledon river valley by the time the Paris Evangelical Missionary Society arrived in 1833 [see p. 54], and in association with the Paris missionaries they dominated the whole length of the river from the Phutiatsana confluence between Mekoatleng and Cana (the northernmost Paris Evangelical Missionary Society stations) to Bethulie, below the confluence with the Orange. In this area Moshweshwe was able, with Imperial backing at crucial moments in the struggle, to fight a relatively successful rearguard action, and ultimately preserve in reduced form the territory which would eventually become the independent state of Lesotho in 1966.

The immediate problem of trans-Orangia in the 1830s was the regulation of conflicting land claims and border banditry among the regrouped African and Kora chiefdoms of the immediate post-Difaqane era, and between them and the small number of trekboers who immigrated into the area as settlers during the 1830s. The first attempt to do this was that of Sir George Napier in 1843. Napier's settlement recognised Sotho rule to a limit of approximately thirty miles west of the Caledon river, either touching or marginally including lands occupied by Sekonyela's Tlokwa, Taaibosch's Kora, and Moroka's Rolong; but it left doubt as to Moshweshwe's dominion both over the lands which he had leased to the Rolong and over those abandoned to the Tlokwa and the Kora, peoples over whom he did not claim to exercise personal rule. He accepted the treaty without prejudice to his land claims, but these he attempted to enforce, and was ably supported by his Paris Evangelical Missionary Society allies against the efforts of the Wesleyans to claim them for the immigrant chiefs. Governor Sir Peregrine Maitland convened a meeting of all the chiefs concerned at Touwfontein in April 1845, because the situation had been rendered more complex by the movement into the area of trekboers from the Cape, who had begun to erect permanent structures on land to which Moshweshwe had granted them transitory rights. Maitland did not try to adjudicate between rival African claimants, but rather to find a basis for a peaceful settlement of the immigrant Boers, by proposing to the Sotho, as to the Griqua [see p. 130] that part of their lands be made alienable under safeguards. Moshweshwe accordingly released a wedge of land between the Caledon and Orange rivers for white settlement; but so far from reaching an agreement with the Tlokwa and the Rolong, he encouraged his subordinates Molapo, Moletsane and Posholi to hold on to their settlements in the territories claimed by these people.

When Sir Harry Smith became High Commissioner in December 1847, the Maitland formula was therefore in ruins. Smith's solution was characteristically simple: let the whites keep what they had, let the Africans continue to govern themselves, and let troubles cease. This did not help the Sotho. Moshweshwe supported Smith over his confrontation with the Boers at Boomplaats in 1848 [see p. 169], but without giving up his occupancy of the western lands. Smith's reply was to commission his secretary, Richard Southey, to investigate the dispute between the African chiefdoms and to impose a settlement. This involved Warden in a new demarcation – the celebrated 'Warden Line' of 1849, which detached from Basutoland in Thompson's calculation (supported in substance and in considerable detail by Sanders) over a hundred villages, with several thousand Sotho inhabitants, in the interest of a dozen or so white farmers. At the same time Warden deprived Moshweshwe of sovereignty over the territories of the immigrant chiefs beyond the Caledon. Relations between the Sotho and the British consequently came near to breaking point, and there was a widespread rejection of the missions by the Sotho leaders as a whole. Yet Moshweshwe accepted the Warden line, still calculating that Smith was behind Warden's policy, and that prudence still required that he keep in with the British. His subordinates thought otherwise. Posholi in the south, Moseme among the Rolong, and Moletsane among the Tlokwa refused to give up their lands. Warden tried to evict them, clumsily and without sufficient force, and he was humbled by the Sotho in 1851 at Viervoet. Moshweshwe's forces again stood their ground against an expedition under the new High Commissioner, Sir George Cathcart in 1852, in the battle of the Berea. But the Sotho king, as always, made a gesture of friendship to the British, this time from a position of strength. It was a crucial gesture for in the course of 1852–4 the British Government decided to withdraw from the territory north of the Orange and he needed to ensure their backing once the Free State whites were in control.

The first President of the Orange Free State, J. P. Hoffman, achieved a good personal relationship with Moshweshwe – too good for the likings of his people, who took the opportunity of his gift of a small keg of ceremonial gunpowder to the Sotho king to run him out of office. His successor, J. N. Boshoff, was altogether more formal in his approach, and reacted to Moshweshwe's penetration of disputed territory in 1858 by mobilising a commando, issuing an ultimatum, and – on receipt of no reply – declaring war. Having provoked the Boers into a conflict, however, the Sotho managed to hold their own, and when Sir George Grey responded to a Free State request for mediation, the Sotho received some territorial compensation between the Caledon and the Orange in return for loss of land on the west bank. This was the moment of Moshweshwe's greatest triumph, which was symbolised by Boshoff's resignation in 1859. There followed a few years' respite during which President M. W. Pretorius tried and failed to end Moshweshwe's occupation by a return to the personal diplomacy of the Hoffman era. The Free Staters, with understandable frustration at the manner in which the Sotho king manoeuvred to avoid the

3　Rivals (2) Moshweshwe and President J. H. Brand

implications of a diplomatic face-off, took their stand on the conventions of behaviour between high contracting parties. Moshweshwe took his stand on the fact of expropriation without his willing consent, in a nightmare world of unfamiliar conventions in which survival depended on the possession of powerful friends and an ability to outwit one's opponents.

Things changed in 1864 with the accession to the presidency of J. H. Brand. The new president, far superior to his predecessors in political acumen, was able to win the ear of the High Commissioner, Sir Philip Wodehouse, and to persuade him in 1864 to beacon off the northern end of the Free State–Sotho frontier, which had not been completed by Grey. Adhering correctly to the documentary evidence, Wodehouse in effect confirmed the Warden Line, and his award provoked intense anger among the Sotho. Brand mounted a new, tough diplomatic offensive, spelling out the treaty terms to Moshweshwe and giving him till 30 November 1864 to remove his people from Free State land, and backed this with a border force. The Sotho agonised, but agreed to move, even Molapo and Paulus Mopedi, who had much to lose. But it was beyond Moshweshwe's power to control the actions of all his subordinates, and when his nephew Lesaoana deliberately overstepped Wodehouse's beacons and raided both the Free State and Natal, Brand authorised a full-scale attack on the Sotho while Natal angrily demanded compensation. Although Commandant Fick failed to take Thaba Bosiu, this time the Free Staters got the better of the Sotho by means of attrition. Molapo, Moshweshwe's son, capitulated to the Boers and for a while became a Free State subject in terms of the Treaty of Mpharane (Imperani), and shortly afterwards in April 1866 Moshweshwe agreed to accept terms imposed by Brand in the Treaty of Thaba Bosiu (the 'Peace of the Millet') whereby the Sotho surrendered two-thirds of their arable land and paid over 3,000 cattle, but – as Sanders has observed – kept their horses, their sheep and their independence against the day when the crops would ripen and the war could be resumed.

Under the Occupation Law of 1866, Brand tried to establish a barrier of white-owned farms, three deep, along the border of the 'Conquered Territory'; but he could not obtain buyers for more than a fraction of them on account of the insecurity of the area. In their desperation, the Sotho were therefore tempted to move back again. Now the Free Staters resolved to punish their adversaries once and for all, to break their power, take over their territory and turn it into a labour reserve. Commandos moved through northern Basutoland in March 1867 and secured the submission of Mopedi in Witsie's Hoek. Early the next year the southern parts were overrun, and Posholi was among those killed. Refugees streamed into Natal and the trans-Kei, and Wodehouse even feared that the Free Staters might break through to the coast at Port St Johns.

At this stage Moshweshwe, despairing of effective aid from the High Commissioner, appealed for annexation by Natal, where the earlier anger against Lesaoana had begun to cool. The Natal government, urged on by Shepstone, was coming to see the acquisition of Basutoland as a means of reducing the congestion of its own blacks. Disraeli's Colonial Secretary, the Duke of Buckingham, actually assented to annexation by Natal. But Wodehouse sent in the Frontier Armed and Mounted Police under Sir Walter Currie to check the renewal of hostilities by the Free Staters (whose access to ammunition was cut off) and persuaded the ageing Moshweshwe to change his mind in a crucial encounter on 15 April before Keate and Shepstone could persuade him otherwise. By adroit manipulation he then prevailed on his masters in London to place Basutoland directly under the High Commission. In doing this, Wodehouse was reversing the policy of the Bloemfontein Convention by committing the High Commission to a protective function short of full annexation, through the agency of police and administrators of the Cape Colony, which had not yet been granted responsible government.

Free State anger at being thus deprived of the opportunity to crush the Sotho was considerable, but Brand was persuaded to tear up the peace treaties of 1866 in return for the cession of all territory lost by the first Aliwal North Convention in 1858, under the second convention of the same name in 1869. To the anger of the Sotho, he was able to keep all territory gained on the right bank of the Caledon, and agreed to an Imperial take-over of Basutoland itself.

In 1870 Moshweshwe died, to be succeeded by his son Letsie; but the substance of his paramount authority passed to Charles Griffith, who was appointed as the High Commissioner's Agent, or Governor's Agent from 1871, when the Cape Government agreed to take on the responsibility. Griffith, who relied on the advice of Emile Rolland, a French missionary who accepted a magisterial appointment, set about the reduction of chiefly power with determination, notably by the introduction of a hut tax (which the chiefs were required to collect in return for an honorarium) and the suppression of obligatory labour service (*letsema*) which, in Burman's estimate, had become burdensome in recent years. Magistrates in the four districts into which the territory was divided managed to attract increasing judicial business at the expense of the chiefs. Until 1879 it was arguable that Cape rule was not unpopular, because it provided the subjects with some protection against the excesses of their traditional rulers.

Of the leading sons of Moshweshwe, Letsie seems to have equivocated – understandably, in view of his difficult position – but he accepted the change. Molapo was bought over by the Government's strategy of involving him in the arrest and return of Langalibalele, the rebel Hlubi chief, to Natal [see p. 102]; but the tensions in the Leribe district lived on in a violent conflict between his own sons – Jonathan, who accepted Colonial rule, and Joel, who did not. The main opposition, however, came from Masopha, who inherited the lordship of Thaba Bosiu, and remained defiant of Cape, British, and even paramount Sotho authority until as late as 1898; yet it is arguable that Masopha did more than any Sotho chief to ensure the long-term achievement of independence. He worked in association with Letsie's son and successor, Lerothodi.

But it was the resistance of Moorosi, a Phuti (non-Sotho) chief from the Quthing district in the south, which set in motion the acts of physical defiance, even though, when he defended his mountain from Colonial forces from April to November 1879, he acted alone. Moorosi was not a rebel at heart, but he was badly served by two successive magistrates, and – like Masopha in his declining years – driven into rebellion rather than surrender a law-breaking son to justice. Moorosi's mountain was a kind of African Masada, for the chief and all his senior sons perished in its defence, and the survivors of the chiefdom were dispersed on defeat.

Moorosi's resistance might have been an isolated incident but for the crisis over disarmament which had started with the passage of Sprigg's Peace Preservation Act in 1878, and reached its first climax in Basutoland when its terms were extended there in July 1880. The so-called 'Gun War', in reality a rebellion, then broke out. The Sotho, who had learnt the value of firearms in their wars with the Free State, were simply not prepared to hand them over, though Letsie tried conciliation at first. Sprigg, the Cape premier, was insensitive to Sotho feelings, and received too much encouragement from the High Commissioner, Sir Bartle Frere. Disarmament proved to be the issue which showed that, in the final resort, the magistrates could not lay down the law for the Sotho. Chiefs who defied the proclamation gained in stature among their people, as one expedient after another was tried by the Government. Frere's successor, Sir Hercules Robinson, offered an amnesty to rebels who agreed to surrender their weapons, and pay a £1 registration fee and fine in cattle; but this produced little response. Scanlen, who succeeded Sprigg in 1881, sought to disengage Cape magisterial authority and entrusted the running of the Native Affairs Department to J. W. Sauer. Sauer employed two officers who mistrusted each other, J. M. Orpen and General 'Chinese' Gordon, on mutually exclusive strategies, the one for using force against Masopha and the other for talking him round. So disastrous did this prove that in 1883–4 the Cape

Government decided to ask the Imperial authorities to take over the burden. What they had at first looked upon as a political challenge with good economic prospects (the incorporation of the Sotho for trade and labour purposes in relation to the quickening pace of life at the diamond fields) looked far less attractive during the severe depression of the early 1880s. The British Government was willing to resume control, in return for a contribution from the Cape's customs revenue. Thus the first of the protectorates (later known as High Commission Territories) came into being.

The Rolong of Thaba'Nchu and the Orange Free State

Adjacent to Basutoland, but different from it in its background and associations, was Moroka II's chiefdom of Thaba'Nchu, peopled mainly by Seleka-Rolong but also by smaller groups of Tshidi- and Rapulana-Rolong, Kwena, and others. These had migrated in 1833 from the Platberg region south of the Vaal under Wesleyan guidance, to escape the Difaqane. Moshweshwe sold the land to the Wesleyans for a payment of cattle – or, as he saw it, granted them usufruct. When Napier's treaty of 1843 left Moroka's lands outside his own borders, Moshweshwe was angry. Moroka meanwhile, fearing Moshweshwe, supported the British in their confrontations with the Sotho in 1849–52. Not surprisingly, therefore, when the British withdrew from the Sovereignty in 1854, Moroka was driven into the arms of the O.F.S. President Brand eventually drew him into a defensive alliance in March 1865, with appropriate agreements covering ammunition supply, extradition, and the control of stock theft; but throughout the conflict between the Free State and the Sotho in 1865–7 the Rolong chief kept an extremely low profile for fear of attracting Sotho attacks on his territory. After winning the war of 1866, the Free State extended its borders towards the Caledon river, and Thaba'Nchu became an enclave. The Free Staters could not immediately occupy their new farms on the Sotho border on account of continuing Sotho resistance; but this changed with the British occupation of Basutoland in 1868, when the relative peace on that frontier brought problems in the relationship between Bloemfontein and Thaba'Nchu to the fore.

These were of several kinds. In 1874 there was a move initiated by Matlabe, a Rapulana chief, to draw the Thaba'Nchu Rolong back to the lands west of the Transvaal set aside for them under the Keate Award. Moroka blocked this with the help of President Brand, who denied Matlabe's followers transit rights through the Free State. More serious was the growing resentment among Free State Boers over stock thefts reported to have taken place from 'squatter farms' in Thaba'Nchu. This led, as Van Aswegen has shown, to a toughening of O.F.S. squatter and vagrancy legislation, and although Moroka tried to control abuse through ordinances of his own, the O.F.S. intensified its control over his state by insisting, for example (under an ordinance of 1865) that the O.F.S. courts had jurisdiction over any Free State subjects who committed crimes in adjacent territories other than the Cape and Natal.

Moroka died on 8 April 1880, and his death was followed by a succession dispute. Power passed *de facto* to Tsipinare, son of his second and favourite wife, Nkhabele, for he had been effective regent for five years; but Tsipinare did not test his legitimacy in the normal way, by convening a *pitso*. His claim was not accepted by Samuel Lepulere Moroka, the only surviving son of Moroka's great wife, a man who had been educated at Zonnebloem College, Cape Town, and at St Augustine's, Canterbury, and was an Anglican convert. It has been assumed by many that denominational rivalry lay behind the dynastic dispute, but the view that this was at most marginal has been expressed by Janet Wales, who notes that when the Anglican mission was set up near the Wesleyan in 1863, this was with the approval of Moroka himself. Neither the Anglicans nor the Wesleyans appear to have made much of the religious differences between Samuel and Tsipinare (a Methodist) in the early stages. The dispute, as Murray has stressed, developed after Brand, who offered to arbitrate and was eventually accepted by both parties, decided in favour of Tsipinare on 17 July 1880. For whatever reason, he ignored the Rolong custom which required ratification of the successor by the people, and he chose in Tsipinare a member of the minority Tshidi-Rolong, whereas Samuel looked to the Seleka- and the Rapulana-, as well as to the Sotho and Kwena elements for support. After some provocation, Tsipinare banished Samuel, who moved into the Free State in August 1880, where, with the help of land-hungry Free Staters, he began to prepare his counter-revolution. In 1884, by which time he had placed his case before the Volksraad and lost, he visited Basutoland, Cape Town and Britain, all to no avail. Brand, meanwhile, behaved with scrupulous correctness, recognising Tsipinare as legitimate ruler but also refusing to take seriously a continuous stream of warnings that Samuel was planning a coup. He also resisted a plea by a minority in the Volksraad to annex Thaba'Nchu. Eventually, on 10 July 1884, Samuel headed a force of at least 400 men, including eleven white O.F.S. farmers, who attacked Tsipinare's home in Thaba'Nchu and shot the chief. Brand's Executive Council immediately called out a large commando, which marched on Thaba'Nchu, where Brand raised the Free State flag, annexing the territory.

Whether the annexation was a precautionary measure taken to forestall the spread of lawlessness, or an opportunist bid engineered by frontiersmen in the hope of seizing land, may never be fully known. Samuel and the white participants were subsequently held by a Free State jury and discharged. The aftermath, as was common in like situations, was the sale of large numbers of farms which Tsipinare, the moderniser, had had surveyed, to white settlers, under land settlement schemes approved by the Volksraad in 1885–6. Nearly all the title deeds were destroyed in the attack on Tsipinare's home. Only 51 of the original 142 farms were still in Rolong hands by 1904, while only 6 per cent of the land in Thaba'Nchu was set aside for reserves. It is possible, as Murray suggests, that some of the farms had been sold to settle Tsipinare's debts. One of his creditors, a Kimberley magnate, obtained 56,000 morgen which were later resold to promote British settlement in the Orange River Colony [see p. 205]. There was a major exodus of Rolong either to the lands west of the Transvaal or to the Free State farms as labourers.

7.5   CONFLICT ON THE EASTERN AND NORTHERN FRONTIERS OF THE TRANSVAAL

The Pedi, the Boers and the British, 1845–83

The Pedi (Maroteng), or northern Sotho, were less successful in their conflicts with the white authorities in the trans-Vaal. They had endured tribulation at the hands of the Zulu, Swazi and above all the Ndwandwe during the time of the Difaqane and the Trek. Their able leader, Sekwati [see p. 53], made an agreement with Hendrik Potgieter in 1845, the details of which have been lost, under which he almost certainly granted the Boers a right of settlement without relinquishing lordship over their land. Meanwhile the Volksraad party in Ohrigstad, Potgieter's rivals, took the line that the Pedi were tributary to the Swazi, and won recognition of their title to the land west of the Steelpoort river from Mswati in 1846, though it was occupied by Pedi at the time [see p. 163]. The relationship between the Pedi and the Boers understandably went sour. The Soutpansberg and Lydenburg commandos attacked their *stad*, Phiring, in 1852; but, though they lost many stock, the Pedi withstood the siege and then withdrew to Thaba Mosega in the Leolu mountains. A treaty between the Boers and the Pedi followed in 1857, under which the Steelpoort was recognised as the boundary, and the parties reached an agreement for the restoration of stolen cattle.

When Sekwati was succeeded by Sekhukhune in 1862, after a civil conflict in which Sekhukhune's brother and challenger, Mampuru, was beaten, this short-lived harmony was shattered. Mampuru fled the chiefdom and began a parasitic existence at the courts of various chiefs hostile to Sekhukhune, notably among the Swazi, and remained a thorn in his paramount's side. Relations between Sekhukhune and the Lydenburg Boers, who had broken away from the other trans-Vaal Boer communities improved again, for each sensed the need for the other in a fluid military situation in which the maintenance of a power balance was the safest road to peace. But when, in 1869, the Pedi routed a major Swazi attack in a skilful defensive action fought with breech-loading rifles from good cover, they came to be seen as perhaps the most formidable power in the eastern trans-Vaal.

For several reasons this fact heralded trouble. In the first place, the Berlin Missionary Society, whom Sekwati had admitted to his territory in 1861, fell foul of Sekhukhune when he inherited the paramountcy in 1862. Sekhukhune resented the missionaries' criticism of traditional rituals and polygyny, and the fact that Alexander Merensky, the missionary at Khalatlolu, appeared to champion the interests of the Z.A.R. in a manner which would have been repugnant, for example, to the Paris Evangelicals in Basutoland. In 1864, Sekhukhune turned against the Christian converts

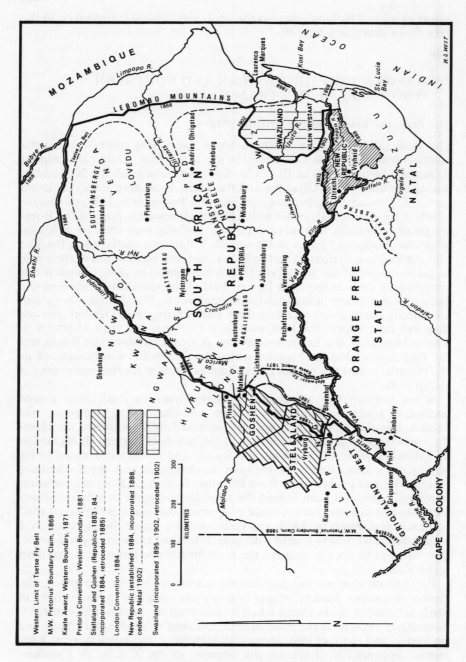

Map 7   The expansion of the South African Republic, 1858–98

Western Limit of Tsetse Fly Belt

M.W. Pretorius' Boundary Claim, 1868

Keate Award, Western Boundary, 1871

Pretoria Convention, Western Boundary, 1881

Stellaland and Goshen (Republics 1883 - 84, incorporated 1884, retroceded 1885)

London Convention, 1884

New Republic (established 1884, incorporated 1888, ceded to Natal 1902)

Swaziland (incorporated 1895 - 1902, retroceded 1902)

at a *pitso*, flogged their leaders, took their guns and their means of livelihood, and expelled them from the capital. Merensky discreetly departed with his converts beyond the boundary to Botsabelo. But these events had an unfortunate sequel for the Pedi, for they meant that they had lost the support of the B.M.S. in their dispute with the Z.A.R. The missionaries even fell out with Johannes Dinkwanyane, Sekhukhune's brother and a Christian convert, who walked out of Botsabelo in 1873, asserting that the missionaries had wrongfully refused to recognise his right, as chief, to tribute from his subordinates. He also found himself in competition with Nachtigal, another of the missionaries, over land to which both men claimed title.

Equally serious was the friction which developed with the Z.A.R. over the linked issues of land, labour and taxation. A confusion of titles had developed, especially in the northern part of the Lydenburg district, following the decision of the Republican Government to invite burghers to claim as many farms as they liked subject only to an annual quitrent of 30s per farm. Much of the land claimed was already occupied by blacks, and in some cases apparently selected for that reason, because their presence guaranteed water and a possible solution to labour difficulties. Delius quotes Merensky as having described 'the whole of the western portion of the Pedi heartland' as being in white hands. To make matters worse, unlike Sekwati's agreement of 1857, Sekhukhune's accession treaty with the Republic was silent as to boundaries.

As whites from the Transvaal, Cape and Natal took the land, the Republic claimed the Pedi as its subjects, and therefore held them liable for taxation and labour services – a point which Sekhukhune in no way conceded. These were crucial issues because the Z.A.R. had run into serious difficulties trying to raise money in taxation from its black 'subjects' generally. A common reaction of the Pedi, when accosted, was to affirm their allegiance to the Pedi paramount, and perhaps to take refuge in his territory. Their resistance to labour demands was similar. The Pedi did not supply the Boers with children captured from their neighbours, as did the Swazi. To an unusual degree, they preferred to seek their work far away – at Port Elizabeth, for example, where hundreds went annually from the 1850s, or at the Diamond Fields, where Pedi were more numerous than any other black work group from the early 1870s (Siebörger).

Thus, although Sekhukhune began to strengthen his resources by sending out migrants to get work and firearms, and welcomed refugees from the Zulu, Swazi and other chiefdoms to swell his numerical strength, and although he defied the Republic on the matter of his status, it should not be taken for granted (as is commonly done in the literature) that the outbreak of war with the Z.A.R. in 1876 was simply a result of Pedi aggression. The land in the Steelpoort valley was disputed territory in which the Z.A.R., the Pedi, and even some of the missionaries were claimants. It was also rich territory, and known to be, for the Lydenburg gold rush started in 1874. President Burgers, moreover, as heir to the government which had lost a territorial claim against the Tlhaping and Rolong in the west under the Keate Award, through supposedly failing to present its case with sufficient

4   Rivals (3) President T. F. Burgers and Sekhukhune

force and clarity [see p. 175], was not disposed to give way over the issue of sovereignty any more than Sekhukhune himself.

To Sekhukhune's apparent surprise, Burgers declared war on him on 16 May 1876, and in August sent in his commandos. But even with Swazi reinforcements they failed to take Sekhukhune's strong defensive positions. By switching to a war of attrition, however, they induced Sekhukhune to sue for peace in February 1877, to offer a fine of cattle, and to acknowledge Transvaal suzerainty. But mystery surrounds the terms of the surrender, for it emerged that Sekhukhune was not made fully aware of the meaning of the document placed before him by a group of over-hasty Boer commissioners. Meanwhile Sir Theophilus Shepstone entered the South African Republic to take over its government [see p. 177]. Sekhukhune accordingly approached Shepstone through Merensky, asking for protection from the Boers and denying that he was a subject of the Republic.

But the British annexation of the Transvaal in April did not end his troubles. Sekhukhune continued to object to incorporation. When Shepstone demanded the 2,000 cattle he had undertaken to make over to Burgers, Sekhukhune offered a tenth as a first instalment. Shepstone returned them and demanded the full consignment. Delius has argued that delivery was impossible for the Pedi ruler, for at that moment Pedi were bartering cattle for grain with the northern chiefdoms on account of a severe famine, while political tensions among the Pedi as a result of the current conflicts underscored the paramount's need to have loan cattle available with which to bind his subordinates to loyal service. For the British authorities, as for the Z.A.R., the effective government of blacks presented a challenge, especially in view of the emptiness of the Transvaal treasury and the recognised need to keep the supply of labour flowing.

There was also provocation from the Pedi side, notably with the burning of Fort Weeber. But, as had been the case in 1876, it cannot be taken for granted that the resumption of war in August 1878 was a simple British response to Pedi aggression. It is unlikely that Sekhukhune was in league with Cetshwayo, just at the moment when Cetshwayo was in open confrontation with Frere [see p. 150], though not hard to understand why Shepstone should have feared this to be the case. It is rather more likely that he was in contact with the Boer dissident, Abel Erasmus, field cornet of Lydenburg. In response to white fears of Pedi aggression, to which Nachtigal seems to have added his authority, a British force was sent against the Pedi great place in October 1878, and, like Burgers's commando two years earlier, it was repulsed. Thereafter the campaign against the Zulu monopolised British attention, and it was only after the capture of Cetshwayo that Sir Garnet Wolseley marched against Sekhukhune with a mixed force of over 14,000 men in September 1879. The Pedi, who had abandoned Thaba Mosega for a more defensible hill named Tsate, resisted until November, with a determination comparable to that of Moorosi at exactly the same time [see p. 138]. Three of Sekhukhune's brothers and nine of his sons were killed during the heavy slaughter.

Wolseley, who had taken over the administration as High Commissioner for South East Africa, then had the Pedi removed to two settlements, Mathebi's Kop and Maleo's Kop, fifty miles from their Leolu strongholds, and appointed Mampuru, Sekhukhune's old rival, over the chiefdom. Though Sekhukhune escaped, he was captured and detained in Pretoria. After the restoration of Republican independence in 1881, he was released to challenge Mampuru again for the supremacy. But in August 1882 he was murdered at Mampuru's instigation. Mampuru himself was pursued and finally tried and executed by the Republican authorities in November 1883, after a war of attrition conducted by General Piet Joubert.

A Pedi location of some 400 square miles was beaconed off by the Republican Government in 1885, as a home base for workers engaged to build the Delagoa Bay railway (which, as De Kiewiet noted, had never been planned to run through Pedi territory). By this time, the Pedi were deeply divided and broken. Kgolokoe, regent for the next chief, Sekhukhune II, accepted subordination to the white government. In 1896 his Geluks Location was split, and this led to a political division among the Pedi leaders on geographical lines, which erupted into warfare in 1900 between the younger Sekhukhune and Malekutu, son of Mampuru. A rhythm of internal conflict had been started which continued to trouble Pedi society well into the twentieth century, above all during the major land and political conflicts of the 1950s [see p. 347].

The Ndzundza, or Transvaal Ndebele

The consolidation of Afrikaner rule in the eastern Transvaal involved the overthrow, not only of the Pedi, but of their neighbours in the Middelburg district, the Sotho-speaking Kopa chiefdom of Maleo, and the Ndzundza chiefdom of Mabhogo (Mapoch), who were descended from the original

Ndebele inhabitants of the region [see pp. 53–4]. After the expulsion of the Khumalo Ndebele across the Limpopo in the 1830s, large chiefdoms like the Pedi had managed to preserve their autonomy *vis-à-vis* the Afrikaner successor state; but lesser chiefdoms had to enter into a client relationship with the Boers, make payment for the use of the land which they were assigned, and take orders from the commandant of the district. Maleo's lands were beaconed off in 1859, Mabhogo's in 1860; but the latter was accused of cattle-rustling and defied repeated summonses from the Republican authorities, who made threats but were in no position at the start of their civil war to launch an attack. At this point the highly volatile nature of political relationships in the eastern Transvaal became apparent. Maleo and Mabhogo chafed under Boer domination, and joined forces to win their freedom in 1860–5; but as a result of Ndzundza aggression they were also drawn into war with their old enemies, the Pedi, in 1863. Mabhogo survived the conflict but died in 1865, and his people were quietened for a decade (Van Jaarsveld). In 1876 the Ndzundza supported Burgers, and in 1879 Wolseley, against the Pedi. They stayed neutral in the Transvaal's war of independence in 1880–1, and their chief at that time, Nyabela, handed over Mampuru, the Pedi rebel, to Republican justice in 1883. But in the same year, as the price for attempting once more to assert his people's independence, he was attacked by a Boer commando, and his lands divided among the members of the attacking force.

The Lovedu and the Venda

The Boer Republic similarly assumed the right, as heir to Mzilikazi's power, to rule and tax the tribes of the northern Transvaal. The Schoemansdal settlement at the foot of the Soutpansberg, named after Potgieter's son-in-law and rival Stephanus Schoeman, was set up by Hendrik Potgieter as a centre for elephant hunting, after he had moved up from Ohrigstad, which lay on the Tsonga trade route between the Soutpansberg and the coast. These Schoemansdal settlers had as neighbours not only the Transvaal Ndebele in the Waterberg, but also the Venda in the Soutpansberg and the Lovedu to the east. In the early years the game was prolific, and there was enough to satisfy the ambitions of all four communities which were involved in the acquisition of ivory for the trade with Delagoa Bay and, to a lesser extent, Inhambane. One Portuguese entrepreneur, João Albasini, conducted an operation through Tsonga ('Knobnose') marksmen on a grand scale, while the Tsonga hunters enjoyed a special advantage in the eastern tsetse country where the Boers would not risk their horses. Albasini and his Tsonga vigilantes also had the role of taxgatherers for the Republican Government. When the Lovedu of Queen Modjadji defied his demands for a cattle payment in 1861, Albasini's commandos went against them and brought back a number of beasts together with 'about 400 little kaffir boys and girls' to train as labourers. Resistance proved beyond the power of the Lovedu, though they tried it again in 1894, the year of Modjadji's death.

The Venda were initially more successful. Republican authority was not strongly entrenched at Schoemansdal, and the commandos manifested considerable resistance to going so far north on campaign. After the death in 1864 of Ramabulana, the Venda paramount, the authorities in Schoemansdal backed as his successor his disinherited son Davhana, who received Albasini's protection. But the majority of his tribe suspected him of having poisoned his father, and rallied behind a rival Machado. So great was the pressure built up by Machado and his allies against Schoemansdal that, even though the Executive Council sent up a relief commando, it was decided in 1867 to evacuate the town, which the Venda then proceeded to sack. It was reoccupied by the Boers in 1868, and large farms again advertised for sale; but the episode highlighted the Republic's difficulty in maintaining control in these distant border areas in the face of black hostility and a lack of the sinews of war. The ease with which blacks could obtain firearms as their price for allowing whites to hunt in the area ensured that the political situation would remain unstable, especially when the game fell in numbers and the Boers began to hunt in the tsetse areas on foot. For some years, the mutual respect which prevailed between Machado and Kruger kept the peace; but after Machado's death in 1895, the Republican Government backed the claims of Sinthumule to the chieftainship against those of Machado's legitimate heir, Mphephu. With Boer support, Sinthumule drove Mphephu across the Limpopo in 1898.

7.6   THE SWAZI AND THEIR 'DOCUMENTS'

The Swazi (or Dlamini Ngwane), who had survived the Mfecane relatively unscathed [see p. 60], lived a troubled existence on the eastern highveld until the reign of Mswati, who succeeded Sobhuza I in 1838/9, and took over the reins of government from the Queen Mother Thandile in 1846. By checking a political split within the ruling family, and by incorporating some of the neighbouring chiefdoms within the Swazi age-regiment system, she had prepared the ground well for him; but Mswati would continue to be dogged by family opposition and by pressure from his Zulu adversaries for half his reign, and it was largely thanks to support from the Boers of Ohrigstad-Lydenburg that he was able to hold his state together. Bonner has demonstrated that the treaty of 1846 between the Swazi and the Boers, so far from being made on Boer initiative as has often been stated, was in origin a bid by the Swazi to counter a threat from the Zulu by seeking aid from the Ohrigstad Volksraad party, who were in conflict with Hendrik Potgieter. Potgieter had obtained a cession of land from the Pedi ruler, Sekwati, in 1845 [see p. 141]. The following year the Swazi offered the cession of a large area of their 'raiding grounds' (Bonner) between the Olifants and Crocodile rivers to the Volksraad party in return for cattle, and the offer was gladly accepted. But internal jealousies wracked the Swazi royal house just at this time, when Mswati was coming of age. Two of his brothers sought Zulu support against himself, and Mpande needed no urging. Meanwhile Potgieter made an alliance with Mswati's eldest rival brother, Somcube, who nearly staged a successful coup in 1847–8. Only in

1855 did Mswati emerge as a clear victor, by which time Potgieter was in self-imposed exile in the Zoutpansberg, the Zulu were in retreat thanks to Boer help for Mswati, and Somcube had been banished from the kingdom.

But in the next few decades the Swazi lost (or threw away) the advantages gained from a convenient association with the trans-Vaal whites.

Mswati followed up his offer of 1846 with a further concession in 1855, offering a buffer strip along the north bank of the Pongola for white settlement, thus cordoning off Zululand. At first this buffer was ineffective, for few whites settled there. But by 1866 the situation had significantly altered as a result of increased Boer settlement of the Wakkerstroom and lower Komati districts, with wool production as a leading incentive. Now it was the Boers who took the initiative and proposed a treaty, as President Pretorius began to pursue with some energy his desire to gain a corridor to the Indian Ocean. In taking over this strategy President Burgers in 1875 secured from the Swazi a treaty under which they accepted subject status, and agreed to keep trade routes open and allow a railway through their territory, and surrendered to the Transvaal the right to appoint a 'supervising official' to control their external relations but not (it was emphasised) to rule them. For all this the Swazi gained little beyond the expectation of Boer assistance in the event of attacks by Sekhukhune or Cetshwayo.

The Swazi played their cards tactfully during the confrontations of the late 1870s and early 1880s, at first declining to support either Boers against the Pedi or the British against the Zulu; but they came in convincingly to help the British defeat Sekhukhune and Cetshwayo in 1879. Such diplomacy and military helpfulness, however, profited them little. They failed in 1880, despite British support, to obtain from the Transvaal Boundary Commission the grazing lands on the lower Komati of which they were in actual occupation. Similarly, a Portuguese boundary commission of 1888 deprived them of all territory gained in Mswati's day to the east of the Lebombo mountains. And they allowed all this to happen without resistance.

There was a collapse of Swazi morale at the centre, without the fighting of a single campaign against a white government in defence of their rights. Mbandzeni was inadequate for the task, though it was not until the late 1880s, after he had been on the throne for over a decade, that the real collapse came. By the end of 1886 the Swazi had lost most of their winter pasturage to Transvaal trekboers, and most of their (imagined) mineral wealth by the end of 1887, largely to English-speaking prospectors, some of whom operated from the Transvaal, others from Natal. From 1888 onwards, a serious invasion of Swazi sovereignty began with the sale of monopoly concessions 'ranging from exclusive control over pawn-broking and patent medicines, to sole rights over the King's revenue' (Bonner). Individual members of a white Governing Committee which arranged the distribution of monopolies had business arrangements with individual Swazi councillors. General Piet Joubert, Vice-President of the South African Republic, and Landdrost Krogh of Wakkerstroom developed an efficient technique of threatening a political take-over in order to extract land concessions; while Offy, a younger member of the Shepstone family, obtained considerable personal benefits after accepting the position of government secretary. The final development, before the ultimate collapse of Swazi authority and the transfer of political control to the South African Republic after negotiations between President Kruger and the British Government, was a frantic spate of political killings, as Mbandzeni eliminated the councillors who opposed him, prior to his own death in October 1889. The Swazi, encircled as they were by potential predators, black and white, had survived remarkably well in the 1840s and 1850s against their black opponents. But where their relationship with the whites was concerned it was truly observed that 'the documents had killed them'.

Kruger's Government saw Swaziland as a strategic area blocking its access to the sea, and although the London Convention of 1884 set precise limits on the expansion of the Republic, it pressed hard for incorporation. To this end, Kruger signed the first Swaziland Convention with Britain in 1890, but failed to acquire the control of the territory because his Volksraad would not join the Cape customs union as part of the price. In 1893 the Imperial Government agreed that Kruger should negotiate with the Swazi for the right to control whites in the territory, while leaving the Swazi to govern themselves under their own paramount. But the Swazi refused to ratify this arrangement. At the end of 1894, therefore, the Republican and Imperial governments agreed to dispense with the need for Swazi consent, and the South African Republic established a protectorate over the territory. Three years later the king's chief minister, Mbhabha Sibandze, was killed at the royal residence, apparently on King Bhunu's orders. Bhunu was summoned to Bremersdorp for trial. He arrived in his own good time, accompanied by his warriors, but was advised by his indunas to seek refuge in Zululand rather than directly confront Transvaal authority.

The Anglo-Boer war brought the rule of the South African Republic to an end. The Imperial Government took over the territory in 1902, and placed Swaziland under the Transvaal Crown Colony government; but when self-government was restored to the Transvaal in 1907, Swaziland was placed directly under the High Commission, under whose authority it remained after the unification of South Africa in 1909. Lord Selborne, as High Commissioner, had the concessions reviewed by a commission in 1907, but his proclamation of the same year, laying down the lines of a new policy, left only one-third of the land in Swazi hands. The remaining two-thirds were to remain with the concessionaries, in freehold now, instead of on terms of long lease with reversionary rights to the Swazi.

7.7 THE SURVIVAL AND OVERTHROW OF THE ZULU MONARCHY, 1838–1906.

The Republic of Natalia had tried to establish a firm northern frontier along the Black Mfolosi river beyond the Tugela line recognised by Dingane as the limit of his cessions to white settlers in 1836 and 1838. To cope with a supposed influx of 100,000 Africans into Natal after the Mfecane, the British colonial authorities agreed in 1845 to a boundary along the Buffalo–Tugela line. They attempted to stabilise this frontier by setting up a series of African locations along much of its length. The success of this arrangement depended on three factors: its acceptability to the Zulu; the willingness of the Natal colonials to tolerate the continuance of an independent chiefdom whose power they feared; and the self-restraint of the Boers in the north, for whom expansion down the Mfolosi, Mkuze and Pongola river valleys provided a considerable temptation. Zulu aggression never became an issue for Natal during the long reign of Mpande (1840–72), owing to Mpande's non-provocative diplomacy and to the tactical skill of Sir Theophilus Shepstone who, as Secretary for Native Affairs, prided himself on the relationship which he had built up with the Zulu king. At first he achieved the same relationship with Cetshwayo, but this relationship was soured as a result of his own annexation of the Transvaal in 1877. The Zulu had protested frequently against the Boer infiltration of northern Zululand between 1861 and 1876, and Shepstone at first earned their support by warning the Transvalers that he could not hold Cetshwayo's anger in check indefinitely; but when he met a Zulu deputation near the Blood river in October 1877, six months after he had taken over the Transvaal, he spoke in favour of the Boer settlement and was told in no uncertain terms that he had forfeited Zulu confidence. Etherington's suggestion that his change of attitude reflected a realisation that the disputed territory lay across Natal's obvious route for expansion into the interior makes good sense. Natal at that time was generating the kind of visionary excitement that fired the imagination of many besides Cecil Rhodes, as they watched the early growth of Kimberley and of gold-prospecting in the eastern Transvaal, and of sugar-planting on the Natal coast, and sought to relate these developments to the largely untapped labour supplies of the eastern half of the sub-continent. The following year the Natal Government appointed a boundary commission to investigate the dispute; but when the High Commissioner, Sir Bartle Frere, found that its report vindicated the Zulu to a considerable extent, he delayed its publication until November, and in the meantime found other reasons for not implementing its proposals. Frere, with the backing of leading opinion in Natal, had reached the conclusion that Zulu power had to be broken. Advantage was therefore taken of the violation of the Natal border by a party of Zulu who kidnapped two fugitive wives of the Zulu chief Sihayo, and put them to death. Cetshwayo was willing to compensate Natal by a payment in cattle, but not to extradite the offenders. Frere served a very stiff ultimatum on Cetshwayo, requiring not only full compensation for the Sihayo affair and another border incident, but also the disbandment of the Zulu army and of the age-regiment system, and the acceptance of a British Resident in Zululand without whose assent the Zulu were not to be allowed to make war.

Cetshwayo rejected these unreasonable demands, and Frere sent in his troops in December 1878. A combination of poor generalship and unwise provocation by one of the three British invading columns resulted in the

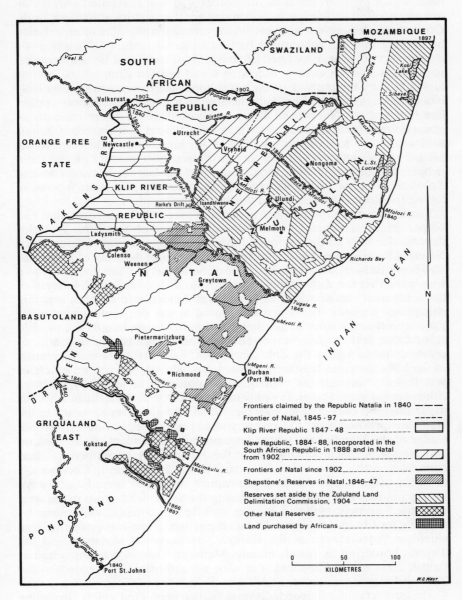

Map 8   Natal and Zululand

total annihilation of a British unit at Isandlwana in January, by a Zulu force which then advanced to the border and was prevented only by an extremely resolute defence from winning another victory at Rorke's Drift. Guy has assailed but not necessarily overturned the common interpretation by arguing that the subsequent battle of Ulundi in July 1879 was not a decisive act of revenge by Lord Chelmsford for the initial British reverses, so much as a token victory, following a half-hearted Zulu attack, merely highlighted by the burning of the royal homestead after a brief, relatively bloodless engagement. The Zulu armies, he argues, melted away (rather like those of the Ndebele in 1893) on account of the sheer difficulty of maintaining a force in the field for a sustained campaign, whereas Chelmsford was willing to settle for a victory of any kind for the sake of restoring his military reputation. Chelmsford professed no quarrel with the Zulu people, but only with their king, and when Sir Garnet Wolseley toured Zululand in preparation for the post-war settlement, he made a point of telling the Zulu that they would not be dispossessed.

Cetshwayo was captured in August, and taken to Cape Town, and had no part in the settlement which Wolseley imposed on the Zulu. Wolseley depended mainly on the advice of John Shepstone, Assistant Secretary for Native Affairs in Natal and a brother of Sir Theophilus, and of Governor Sir Henry Bulwer, whose earlier opposition to the war had given way to a conviction that the Zulu paramountcy had to be broken. Guy's analysis of the settlement, under which Zululand was divided into thirteen separate chiefdoms, suggests that it was not rooted in any deep understanding of Zulu society and tradition, but that it was nevertheless based on a twofold calculation: first, to restore pre-Shakan political units; and secondly to create divisions among the Zulu. Examples of the first were the recreation of the Mthethwa and Ndwandwe chiefdoms, whereas the second objective was realised through the promotion to positions of authority of three controversial men: Hamu, the only major defector to the British, who was made chief not only over his own Ngetsheni, but also over elements of the Buthelezi, whose loyalty to Cetshwayo had been close; second, Zibhebhu, leader of the Mandlakazi, whose lineage was independent of the Shakan, and who was given lordship over the homesteads of numerous clans connected with the royal house; and third, John Dunn, Cetshwayo's turncoat white counsellor and gun-runner, who had served Cetshwayo loyally but failed to keep his trust during the weeks leading up to the war, then tried unsuccessfully to remain outside the conflict, and ended by scouting for Chelmsford in the Ulundi campaign. Dunn was given the large chiefdom, later known as the Reserve, between the Mhlatuze and the Tugela, bordering on Natal. Finally, Melmoth Osborn was appointed as British Resident in Zululand, but with no authority to give orders, for Zululand was not annexed.

The predictable happened. Several of the appointed chiefs, including Zibhebhu, Hamu and Dunn, took advantage of their positions to victimise supporters of the exiled king. Cetshwayo, from the Cape, and his Usuthu supporters at home, put pressure on the British Government with the help of Bishop Colenso, to review the settlement. As a result, the king was

5   Rivals (4) Cetshwayo and Sir Theophilus Shepstone

eventually allowed to visit England; and Gladstone's Government, its confidence in the settlement eroded by events, allowed Cetshwayo to return to Zululand in January 1883, as ruler, not of his whole kingdom, but only of the central part of it, leaving Dunn's authority unimpaired in the Reserve, and Zibhebhu an independent ruler in the north. Cetshwayo was at first extremely reluctant to accept this limitation.

Zibhebhu's Mandlakazi did not take the king's restoration lying down, but opened hostilities against him. In two decisive actions, in the Msebe valley in April and in the second battle of Ulundi in July 1883, thanks to Zibhebhu's military skills and the arms provided by an unscrupulous white operator, Johan Colenbrander, they wiped out the Usuthu leadership. Cetshwayo fled into the arms of the British authorities, in whose care he died of causes unexplained on 8 February 1884, having named his youthful son Dinuzulu as his lawful heir.

Bulwer had reservations about the appointment of Dinuzulu, while Zibhebhu's victories commended him to the British authorities as the man to support. That was why some of the new generation of Usuthu leaders risked an approach to the Boers in May 1884 for help in breaking the Mandlakazi power. The Boers helped too well. They not only contributed to the defeat of Zibhebhu at Etshaneni in June, but for their efforts claimed five-sixths of Zululand outside the Reserve, including farms which gave them access to the sea at St Lucia Bay. This was too much for the British at a moment when Bismarck's colonial initiatives gave the whole coastline of Africa strategic significance, but they resolved the matter by negotiation with the Boers rather than by making a stand on behalf of Zulu rights. Under the leadership of Coenraad Meyer, the Boers in Zululand had constituted themselves as the New Republic, comprising the districts of Vryheid, Wakkerstroom and Utrecht. This had the effect of excluding from Zululand 'nearly all its highland grazing, and the mixed veld in the upper reaches of the major river systems' (Guy), as well as the sacred region of Emakhosini, where the pre-Shakan kings had been buried, and the main homesteads of many prominent chiefdoms. Accepting that their post-war settlement had collapsed, the British Government countered by annexing the remainder of Zululand in 1887, by agreement with the Boers. In return they recognised the incorporation of the New Republic in the Transvaal.

But this was far from the end of the Zulu tragedy, for Sir Arthur Havelock, the new Governor of Natal, who ruled British Zululand as Supreme Chief, allowed Zibhebhu and his Mandlakazi, who had lived in exile in the Reserve, to return to their own lands, at the cost of the displacement of some Usuthu settlers. Dinuzulu attacked and defeated them at Nongoma, only to be put to flight by British troops. He escaped to the Boers, but on Harriette Colenso's urging surrendered himself to the British authorities, who then tried him for high treason and sentenced him in 1889 to exile on St Helena.

The eventual return of Dinuzulu to Zululand in 1897 was part of a deal between the British Government and the Natal leaders which accompanied Natal's acquisition of Zululand itself. It was a step long urged in Natal, notably by Sir Theophilus Shepstone, but resisted by Britain for fear that the Zulu might lose yet more of their land. This was a very reasonable fear, but its realisation was stalled for five years, at the end of which time a land delimitation commission recommended the release of 2.6 of the remaining 6.5 million acres for purchase, which meant in practice – and also, it transpired, as a matter of policy – purchase by whites only. In 1905 Zululand was thus made available for the expansion of commercialised sugar farming; but the pressure on the remaining Reserve land which resulted had an important influence on the outbreak of the Zulu rebellion of 1906 [see p. 208].

7.8 THE FRONTIER CONFLICTS OF THE TSWANA ON THE 'ROAD TO THE NORTH'

The Tlhaping and Rolong

The Tlhaping of Mahura suffered for the benefit of Waterboer's Griqua when Lieutenant-Governor Keate made his Award [see p. 175] in October 1871. But they and their neighbours, the Rolong, who occupied the region between the Boer farms of the western Transvaal and the Kalahari desert, soon found themselves under growing pressure as the Republican Government and its subjects ignored the terms of the Keate Award. Conflict arose between the Kora of Mamusa under David Mossweu (Massouw), who lived on the frontier laid down by the Pretoria Convention, and Mankurwane's Tlhaping, based on Taungs. Further north, a similar conflict arose between Moswete, a Rolong chief based on Kunwana in the Transvaal, and Monthsiwa at Mafeking. Massouw and Moswete engaged white 'volunteers' from the Transvaal in return for promises of land. Mankurwane and Monthsiwa also engaged white supporters, some of whom came from the Cape. When the former pair, aided by covert supplies of arms from the Transvaal, were able to beat their rivals, their white allies set up two independent republics of Stellaland and Goshen, divided them into farms for themselves, and embarrassed British and Cape commercial and missionary interests by straddling the 'Road to the North', the only remaining access route from the Cape to central Africa outside the Boer republics [see pp. 180–3 for discussion of the Anglo-Boer conflict over territory].

The land problem arose out of the wholesale dispossession of Tlhaping and Rolong villagers as a result of the laying out of white farms in the area (Davenport and Hunt). To deal with it, a committee was first set up under the Rev. John Mackenzie. It found that Mankurwane's Tlhaping were in a state of 'extreme and increasing destitution', and recommended the setting aside of a well-watered block of land in the south of Stellaland for them. When Sir Sidney Shippard took over as Resident Commissioner, however, Mackenzie's proposal was rejected, and the Tlhaping were placed instead on a few scattered farms further north. Shippard was relatively more generous to blacks in Goshen, perhaps because it had been settled mainly by Transvalers, and set aside two reasonably large Reserves based on Kunwana and Mafeking, both considerably smaller than, and falling within, the region claimed by Monthsiwa as belonging to his tribe. The fate of the Kora of Mamusa, who were incorporated in the South African Republic under the London Convention, was less happy. In 1885 they attempted to take control of a white-owned farm by force. The Boers thereupon destroyed Mamusa, which was later rebuilt as the white town of Schweitzer-Reneke, and the Kora chiefdom was broken up.

The northern Tswana kingdoms

In the Bechuanaland Protectorate, as in Basutoland, the establishment of British paramountcy preserved most of the land for the inhabitants, though this was as much the result of accident as of design. Warren's protectorate of 1885 had not been in response to any Tswana invitation. He had proclaimed it as much to keep the Germans away from the South African Republic as to protect Tswana land rights from white encroachment (Agar-Hamilton), but the protection of these rights did enter into his calculations. Ever since Carl Mauch had found gold at Tati in 1867, the hope of an El Dorado had survived among white speculators, and every Tswana chief became involved, as Maylam has shown, with at least one concessionaire. By the end of the 1880s the control over the lands of the Tswana had become a bone of contention between the Protectorate Administration and Rhodes's British South Africa Company. In the early years the administration itself was weak. Shippard, as resident commissioner, was known for his lack of sympathy for the Tswana and his

6   Rivals (5) Kgama III of the Ngwato and Lobengula of the Ndebele

support for Rhodes; but the Protectorate Government at first refrained from direct administration, and when Shippard called a conference in January 1889 to discuss not only defence but hospitals, taxation, water-ways, railways and telegraphs, it failed because he did not have the means of persuading the assembled chiefs to accept such inroads into their sovereignty. Power to control these matters, however, was taken over by High Commissioner Sir Henry Loch in 1891, on the basis of orders-in-council of that and the previous year.

Of the Tswana chiefdoms which played key roles at this time, the most prominent were the Ngwato under Sekgoma and (from 1875) Kgama III, the Kwena under Setshele (to 1892) and Sebele (to 1911), the Ngwaketse under Gatseitswe (to 1889) and Bathoen (to 1910), the Lete under Ikaneng (1886–96), and the Kgatla under Lentswe (1875–1924). Kgama (Khama) stood out above them all. Shrewd as Moshweshwe, he had first applied for the Queen's protection against a threatened Boer encroachment in 1876. He resisted the importunities of white 'volunteers' who sought to interest him in a campaign against Lobengula in 1885, with the object of acquiring farms. In 1893, however, he did contribute a small force to aid in the British invasion of Matabeleland, but withdrew it before the campaign was over.

The real crisis for the Tswana came in 1895, when Rhodes's Chartered Company put in a strong bid to take over the administration of their territory from the Colonial Office. Kgama, Bathoen and Sebele went on a deputation to London. After being lionised by the London Missionary Society in the course of its centenary celebrations, they obtained an interview with Joseph Chamberlain, the new Colonial Secretary, and received from him the assurance of being allowed to remain masters in their own houses, free from Company control, in return for the loss to the Company of a hundred square miles of territory to the west of their now defined Reserves, and a border strip which the Company required for its railway into Matabeleland – and more covertly as a launching pad for the Jameson Raid. Maylam has shown that the Tswana chiefs who did not go on the deputation, notably Lentswe, Ikaneng and Monthsiwa, whose lands lay largely along the Transvaal border, lost both land and jurisdiction under Chamberlain's award, while the security won by Kgama and his companions was extremely precarious. What eventually saved their independence – and that of the three who had not gone – was the Colonial Office's refusal to allow the Company to administer the Protectorate after Jameson's invasion of the Transvaal.

From their first contact with white traders in the 1840s, the Tswana had dealt profitably in karosses, ivory, maize and cattle. But with political incorporation, accompanied by natural disasters like the rinderpest of 1896, they gradually lost their economic independence. Though some, like the Ngwato, might continue to thrive for a while – particularly Kgama himself – the Tswana were drawn increasingly to work in the mines of Kimberley and the Rand, for the loss of good lands in the east meant an unequal struggle for survival on the edge of the desert.

7.9   THE KHUMALO NDEBELE AND THE BRITISH SOUTH AFRICA COMPANY

Kgama made a deal with the Imperial authorities and saved his lands for his people. Lobengula likewise made a deal with the Imperial authorities, but in his case it was through their sub-contractors, the British South Africa Company. The difference was crucial, for whereas Kgama survived with his sovereignty largely intact, within four years Lobengula was to lose both his lands and his life. On assuming power in 1868, Lobengula had at first been generous in granting mining concessions, though these were normally small. After the Witwatersrand gold discoveries of 1886, the interest of speculators in Mashonaland increased, attracting men like Lord Gifford and E. R. Renny-Tailyour, and the Capetonians Frank Johnson and Maurice Heany. Piet Grobler arrived in Bulawayo on a mission from Kruger in July 1887, to ask for a treaty of mutual friendship and the appointment of a diplomatic representative at Lobengula's court. He was successful, but on his way home – under circumstances which are far from clear and were even thought by some to implicate Rhodes – he was killed in a skirmish with some of Kgama's Ngwato subjects.

Meanwhile John Moffat, acting on the instructions of the High Commissioner, Sir Hercules Robinson, who had in turn been prompted by Shippard and Rhodes, managed to obtain a treaty from Lobengula in February 1888, whereby the Ndebele ruler undertook to 'refrain from entering into any correspondence or treaty with any foreign state or power to sell, alienate or cede' any part of his territory without obtaining the High Commissioner's approval. The Moffat Treaty cleared the path both for

Rhodes and for the Exploration Company of Gifford and Cawston. But while Gifford's agent, E. A. Maund, took his time to reach Bulawayo, a team appointed by Rhodes comprising C. D. Rudd of Consolidated Goldfields, F. R. Thompson (an experienced African linguist) and Rochfort Maguire (a lawyer), reached Lobengula's court and with Shippard's help sought to persuade the Ndebele king to concede to their 'Matabele Syndicate' the 'complete and exclusive charge over all metals and minerals in his kingdom'. In return, Lobengula was to receive £100 monthly, together with 1,000 Martini-Henry breech-loading rifles, with ammunition, and a gunboat on the Zambesi with which supposedly to scatter the canoe flotillas of his rivals. As Cobbing has shown, he refused until 1893 to take delivery of the rifles, while no gunboat could ever in any case have got beyond the Kebora Bassa rapids to a river which Lobengula did not control. Nor was any copy of the concession apparently left in Lobengula's possession, though Rudd returned to Cape Town after a harrowing journey professing to carry a document bearing Lobengula's authenticated mark. The King subsequently claimed to have been tricked, and to have granted a mere right to 'dig a hole in the ground' in an area (near Tati) disputed between the Ngwato and the Ndebele. But what was more important, he listened to the advice of E. A. Maund, representing the Exploration Company, began to suspect Rudd's credibility, executed his *induna* Lotje (supposedly for having advised him to grant the concession), and appointed Maund to escort two of his *indunas* to London to protest against the arrangement. Maund, after taking a devious route to avoid being apprehended in the Protectorate, met Rhodes first in Kimberley, where he stood up to the latter's blandishments, and again at the end of January in Cape Town, where Rhodes entirely changed his tune – probably in response to a hint from the Colonial Office – and began to talk of a possible amalgamation of interests. The shepherd of Lobengula's *indunas* was therefore persuaded on his arrival in Britain in February 1889 (where Rhodes and Beit arrived soon afterwards) to work against the wishes of the king who had sent him. In May, the founding of a Central Search Association signalised the marriage of the Rhodes and Gifford groups. Two developments might still have thwarted their objective, which was the granting of a royal charter to exploit the Concession. One was the continuous propaganda of the Rev. John Mackenzie's missionary lobby, but its influence was blunted by the discordant views of the missionaries among the Ndebele. The other was Lobengula himself, who renounced the Rudd Concession in two letters despatched in April and June. But the second and more damaging of these, in answer to a direct word of caution from Queen Victoria herself, was held back in Cape Town by Shippard until after the royal charter had been granted to the British South Africa Company on 29 October 1889.

This charter gave the Company the authority to operate in the quadrant formed by the northern frontier of the Transvaal and the western frontier of Mozambique, to institute a government, issue shares, mine, and improve and distribute the land. The main limits on its power of action were the obligation to report annually to the Secretary of State, to maintain order, check slavery, and promote free trade. It could only assume such powers as were granted to it by indigenous rulers; its charter was subject to review after twenty-five years and every ten years thereafter, and all its directors had to be British subjects. But these were not onerous restrictions. Rhodes advertised farms as well as mining prospects on the strength of the Rudd Concession, thus exceeding his rights; but this was noticed by would-be investors, whose enthusiasm faltered to such an extent that the Company accepted the need to regularise its position. E. A. Lippert, the only concessionaire to have acquired land rights, indirectly, from two independent Shona chiefs, held out for a high price. It was Alfred Beit, according to Galbraith, who advised the Company Board against trying to call Lippert's bluff. Instead, they persuaded him in 1891 to seek a further concession, this time from Lobengula himself, posing as a rival to the Company. When Lippert achieved this the Company bought it from him in November for a large portfolio in B.S.A.C. and related United Concessions Company shares, £5,000 in cash, and the offer of 75 square miles of his own choosing in Matabeleland (where, until then, the Company had presumed to claim no rights at all).

The Company's Pioneer Column had left the Protectorate in July 1890, and reached its destination, which it named Fort Salisbury, in September, having skirted Lobengula's domain without his permission but also without incident. L. S. Jameson, appointed Administrator of Mashonaland by Rhodes, thought in terms of a fixed boundary between Lobengula's territory and the Company's along the line of the Umniati and Shashi rivers. He assumed authority over the Shona living to the east of this line. Lobengula, for his part, seems to have contended that Jameson's rule was limited to white settlers, and that his own right to collect tribute from his Shona 'Mahole' east of the line remained unimpaired. At first the Company made no difficulties over this, being aware of its precarious financial position which had necessitated the reduction of its police force to forty men at the end of 1892, and provided a powerful argument against the starting of hostilities. But Rhodes, Jameson and Loch, the High Commissioner, all seem to have reached the conclusion that it would be necessary to smash the Ndebele both for security reasons and to revive the dwindling fortunes of their enterprise by throwing Matabeleland open to mining and farming activities. To provoke a crisis before the acquisition of the Lippert Concession would have been unwise; but once that had been gained the legal need for restraint was less. Lobengula was aware of this and his *indunas* on tribute raids behaved with exemplary restraint where the white settlers were concerned. But in September 1893 the Company's forces marched into Matabeleland, supported by an Imperial contingent from the Protectorate. They had no difficulty in defeating the Ndebele with their superior weapons. The Company beat Loch in the race to Bulawayo. The invading armies suffered almost no casualties apart from the elimination of Alan Wilson's Shangani Patrol, which became the material for a settler legend. Lobengula took to flight and perished obscurely in the bush.

The Company, aided by the provocative tactics of Johan Colenbrander in Bulawayo, put it about that the Ndebele had been the aggressors. This is not an easy construction to place on the events around Fort Victoria in May 1893 and afterwards. An alternative theory has been advanced, on the basis of the Victoria Agreement in August, that it was the settlers of Mashonaland who initiated the war in order to obtain farms, digging rights and 'loot' in Matabeleland. But if this was the case, Stigger's observation that most of the grantees who obtained land in return for participation got rid of it to speculators soon afterwards, deserves notice. The argument advanced by Glass that the war was in essence the result of a conflict between the Company and the Imperial High Commissioner for control of the region north of the Limpopo seems exaggerated in view of the evident agreement between both parties that 'Lobengula must be destroyed'. It seems more reasonable, in short, to accept the dominant argument put forward by Galbraith, Samkange and others, that the war was started by the Company's leaders in order to check a 'slide into dissolution' and revive the Company's prospects.

The B.S.A.C. took over the control of Matabeleland, and authorised the volunteers to choose farms in the conquered territory. They reduced the African population to the status of squatters, save for those who lived in reserves set aside on the Shangani and Gwaai rivers by the Land Commission of 1894. But the Ndebele power had not been broken, and resentment grew among the blacks at their loss of land and at the large cattle fine imposed by the victors for distribution by the loot committee. The severe rinderpest epidemic of 1896–7 increased their sense of frustration, and perhaps supplied the occasion for the renewed outbreak of conflict in 1896. Not only did the Ndebele rise both north and south of Bulawayo, but there was even a rising among the western Shona as well, though some Shona had previously offered help against the Ndebele. Some encouragement undoubtedly came from the religious leaders of the Mware fertility cult recently taken over by the Rozvi from the Venda, and from the *mhondoro* spirit media among the Shona; but these cults did not play the dominant role assigned to them by Ranger. The rebellion was costly in lives, both black and white. The Ndebele leaders were able to buy good terms when they met Cecil Rhodes in the Matoppos in October 1896; but the Shona rebellion dragged on and was put down only in late 1897, at a far greater cost of human life, including the lives of a number of leaders who received the death penalty for participation.

7.10 THE ROLE OF THE MISSIONARIES

One thread in the incorporation of black chiefdoms within the matrix of a white-controlled state system was the extension of European values and cultural influences, especially as these were promoted by European missionary societies. Early missionary activity was exclusively Protestant. It began with the Moravians who encountered opposition from white colonials and the local church authorities, as a result of which Georg Schmidt's work, started in the Baviaans Kloof in 1737, had to close down in

1743. It reopened in 1792, and their station, now renamed Genadendal, flourished from the Batavian era onwards.

The first British occupation saw the arrival of the London Missionary Society (1799) which set up missions at Bethelsdorp under the Rev. J. van der Kemp, and at a number of other points in the eastern Cape, in the Orange river valley, in Namaqualand and among the Griqua. Their station at Kuruman, founded in 1829 by the Rev. Robert Moffat, provided a base for a forward move across the Limpopo in the 1880s, to take Christianity to the Ngwato and the Ndebele. The L.M.S. owed much of their success and many of the difficulties they encountered to the concerned but domineering character of Dr John Philip. The Glasgow and the Wesleyan Methodist Missionary Societies both arrived on the heels of the 1820 Settlement. The former concentrated in the Tyumie valley, where Lovedale was founded in 1824, and its school in 1841. The latter built a chain of stations through the territories of the coastal Nguni eastwards from Grahamstown in the direction of Natal, of which the furthest, Buntingville, had been founded by 1830, some 200 miles into African territory. The Methodists also penetrated Little Namaqualand and the region north of the upper Orange, where the station at Thaba'Nchu, among the Rolong, was of great strategic importance.

Other societies followed. The American Board Mission sent workers to Mzilikazi's Ndebele, which brought them into contact with the Voortrekkers. This led one of their number, Daniel Lindley, to remain among them while Adams and Grout moved to Natal, where they entered into an agreement with Dingane. This association was broken during the crisis of the king's demise, but the American influence survived in an important educational enterprise which grew into Adams College. The Paris Evangelical Missionary Society began work among the Sotho in 1833, when Arbousset and Casalis gave valuable political support to Moshweshwe, who also learned to lean on the French Catholics and derive what he could from each party. There were several German societies apart from the Moravians, notably the Rhenish, which was as old as the L.M.S. and operated mainly in the north-western Cape (Wupperthal) and among the coloured people of Namaqualand north and south of the Orange. The Berlin Missionary Society, arriving in 1834, set up a station at Pniel on the Vaal river, shortly before the diamond rush, for which it was embarrassingly well situated, and then extended its work – and its experience of the difficulties of African politics – by operating among the Pedi of the eastern Transvaal. If one adds to these the work of missionary societies from Norway, Sweden and Finland during the late nineteenth century, and the Roman Catholic return to Great Namaqualand, Basutoland and Natal, the impression is left of an enormous effort by the churches, after a slow start, to bring Christianity to the Africans. There was a time when their work tended to be viewed by historians (who, like J. du Plessis, also happened to be churchmen) simply as a story of success or failure in bringing souls to Christ. A later generation of Marxists, like Majeke, wrote rather of the 'role of the missionary in conquest'. Historians today, while accepting the importance of both these approaches, tend also to show greater interest in problems of culture contact more broadly conceived.

In the extension of conquest the missionary had a role as well as the trader, though its exact nature was less straightforward than has commonly been supposed. The two activities were not unrelated. The caricature, first fluently drawn by Majeke, of missionaries as promoters of a revolution in social taste for the benefit of the producers of Manchester cotton-piece goods, has a factual basis as any biography of Livingstone makes clear, but this kind of activity should not be seen as more than a by-product of missionary endeavour. Missionaries were sometimes embarrassed by the actions of unscrupulous traders, and driven to urge a policy of segregation on the frontier to clear the way for the gospel. For most missionaries the propagation of the Christian religion was an absolute priority – they were 'teachers of religion and that alone should be kept in view', as the Methodist instructions of 1821 expressed it (Cragg). But missionaries were not at one over the question of whether conversion required the adoption in full of the culture of the 'civilising' power. A minority, like Van der Kemp and the Reads, became totally absorbed in the way of life of the people they served. But the great majority, and above all those, like the Scots of Lovedale, who developed extensive educational activities, were convinced of the need to purvey the total package. There was a similar divergence over the issue of political control. Some, like the Wesleyans among the Mpondo and above all C. D. Helm at the court of Lobengula, promoted the extension of white political influence; but the Norwegians in Zululand worked hard to oppose it. Generalisations are therefore unwise.

The reception accorded to the missionary by the African ruler depended largely on the quality of the political relationship at the moment when the encounter took place. In the early days of the open frontier, chiefs commonly accepted missionaries, less perhaps for the content of their preaching than for their usefulness as advisers in negotiations with white governments. Moshweshwe, for example, responded to the Paris Evangelicals for their diplomatic *savoir faire*, while Dingane welcomed A. F. Gardiner as a musket instructor as well as preacher. But on the evidence supplied by Williams, Etherington and others, doubts generally arose in the minds of African rulers over the more subtle influence of missions on the political order. Chiefs resented the removal of converts from their jurisdiction, and the loss of their services in time of war, which was a matter of particular concern to Cetshwayo, king of the Zulu. Opposition to missionary requirements itself discouraged conversion, above all those which related to rites of passage. It was not easy for a chief, as the price of adopting Christianity, to have to dispense with circumcision rituals, because these were in turn connected with the organisation of labour and military age-sets. Nor could they easily accept the one-wife rule in a society traditionally polygynous, where judicious marriages – as, for example, among the northern and southern Sotho – often helped to confirm or extend political control.

It was no matter for surprise, therefore, that at first the Christian missions made few converts, and that they succeeded best in those communities, like the Mfengu of the eastern Cape, in which traditional disciplines had broken down. The missionary breakthrough among the Xhosa and the southern Nguni did not really happen until after the 1857 cattle-killing tragedy. In Sekhukhuneland it took root only after the conquest of the kingdom by white arms. Moshweshwe, who appreciated missionaries, was more cautious over baptism than Constantine the Great. Robert Moffat's writings suggest that the London missioners had little success at first among the Tswana; but in due course Setshele of the Kwena, Lentswe of the Kgatla, and Kgama of the Ngwato accepted conversion on behalf of their peoples in a manner which would have done Aethelbert of Kent credit, and then made courageous if only partly successful attempts to overhaul the customs of their people. All three abolished male and female initiation ceremonies. Kgama, whose laws were so prolific that, in popular minds, they constituted a distinct corpus apart from that of tradition, presumed to get rid of the *bogadi* (cattle bride-price) and imposed a ban on the brewing of strong drink throughout his chiefdom. Setshele, who had been baptised by Livingstone against Moshweshwe's advice, sent all but his great wife home on his conversion, but arranged things satisfactorily for all but one of the others. The Ngwaketse prohibited polygamy altogether.

There was a gulf between the traditional religious beliefs and experiences of the peoples of southern Africa and those of the churches whose representatives came to live among them; but from the work of Pauw, Setiloane, Wilson, Hodgson, Elphick, and others, it is clear that the concept of the Judaeo-Christian creator God had its equivalent in the remote figure of Modimo (or Qamata). Christian standards of behaviour were comparable for the most part with those accepted in African society. What was lacking, as Elphick has stressed, was any belief in a God who intervened decisively in history, though African minds may well have been more attuned than those of their Protestant teachers to the thought of arbitrary divine intervention in the affairs of men. The role of the ancestral shades, and of witchcraft, and the art of rain-making, were realities for the blacks to which the missionaries found adjustment far from easy. Similarly, for the African neophyte the Christian gospel presented problems of comprehension. In the Xhosa cattle-killing of 1857 it led to a tragic misunderstanding (Peires). Yet many Africans moved into the Christian churches during the post-conquest years, drawn as much by 'affective and emotional factors' (Elphick) as by any theoretical argument, though without necessarily abandoning belief in ancestral influences or the rituals which accompanied them. Therefore, the Christian religion had a deep influence on Africans during the century of conquest, and must have aided rather than delayed incorporation. The extent to which it fulfilled a role in latter-day resistance to or accommodation with colonial rule is discussed later [see pp. 209, 537].

7.11 THE CHANGING OWNERSHIP OF THE LAND

By the close of the nineteenth century the frontier wars were over, and nearly all the land that was to pass into white hands had done so; but the problems that were to arise from the transfer were only just beginning.

In traditional society the African chief normally held the land on behalf of his people. He had the power to allocate arable land for use but never outright ownership, though a son could normally expect to obtain the use of his father's holding. Grazing land was held in common, but the chief could control access to it by the villagers' livestock. White conquest greatly reduced the amount of land available for African use, and for farming communities used to shifting agriculture and regular transhumance, this was serious. It raised the question whether traditional rules of ownership and land use should continue, or be replaced by those which operated in the European community.

The answers given by the white colonial and republican governments were not uniform. The Cape Government expressed a preference for a uniform land system, but was reluctant to introduce individual tenure unless the Africans in the community concerned were in favour of it. Among the detribalised Mfengu of the eastern Cape, and among the Griqua, freehold and quitrent titles were made available. The Mfengu found security in them, the Griqua insecurity. Although the extension of such tenures throughout the Cape became lawful under the Native Locations Act of 1879, not much action followed.

The Glen Grey Act of 1894 had a special importance, for it was designed to set a pattern of African land-holding throughout the Cape African reserves. It was a multi-purpose law to whose making there were many contributors. Glen Grey was a problem area. It was overpopulated. Rhodes, though he purchased the nearby Indwe coal-mines for De Beers in 1894, seems to have been mainly concerned to draw out labour for the Colony. His method was to convert the form of tenure to perpetual quitrent, limit the size to four morgen (largely from Afrikaner Bond pressure), and impose a labour tax on non-title-holders to check squatting. Ally has stressed that this did not imply a calculated attempt to promote labour migrancy as such. The parallel reform of local government by the creation of district councils was largely contingent on the land reform (though it overtook it in importance) and further limited the powers of chiefs and headmen, who were – perhaps for that reason – generally well provided for under the new distribution.

Although Bundy's research has shown that a prosperous African peasant class had begun to appear in parts of southern Africa, notably in the Herschel district of the north-eastern Cape, before the end of the century, these were not, on the whole, tenants under the Glen Grey rules. Moreover, this class of producers was on the decline by 1900, partly because of the pressure of squatters on their land, partly on account of natural disasters such as the very serious rinderpest epidemic of 1896–7, and partly from the growing competition of white farmers who had larger farms, better access to markets, and better access to capital. Thus, although individualisation of African land tenure remained the theoretical aim of the Lagden Commission in 1905 [see pp. 207–8], it ceased to attract the support of politicians or the public service.

Outside the Cape, individual title remained for the most part the white man's privilege, communal tenure in Reserves or on Crown land being the normal form for blacks. Individual tenure was denied by law to blacks in the Orange Free State, save on the Wesleyan Thaba'Nchu mission lands among the southern Rolong, most of which passed out of African hands between 1884 and 1890. In Natal, where there was some black syndicate land purchase along the south-western border, the Governor and Executive Council were constituted as a Native Trust in 1864, and in that capacity held title to all communal land on which Africans resided. The same rule was adopted in Kruger's Republic, where it was assumed that blacks could not hold title to land, until the opposite was established by Tsewu's case in 1905 (Burton). On the strength of this case, several African syndicates in the Transvaal clubbed together to purchase surveyed farms from whites, paying up to £10,000 for a farm, sometimes to men impoverished by the war and obliged to sell. The prices were eloquent commentary on the scarcity of available land for black settlement, for if over fifty men clubbed together to buy a single farm, as happened on occasion, this could hardly have been with the expectation of a return on the investment. It meant a reversion to one-man-one-lot agriculture with communal grazing, and threatened to bring major problems of succession were subdivision of title to become the rule. Similar concern was shown over the subdivision of white-owned farms under the Roman-Dutch Law of succession, by the Transvaal Indigency Commission of 1908. Whether for black or white, there was a shortage of farming land from the 1870s onwards. Widespread squatting, share-cropping ('farming on the halves') and labour tenancy resulted. These practices were common enough in rural areas the world over, but they caused concern because they militated against efficient commercial farming by threatening to overburden the soil and block the supply of labour. With the growth of urban markets and the flow of money into the region, land values had begun to rise. A new generation of white entrepreneur landowners had come into being, who desired to exclude the competition of the smallholder, or considered that, if squatters there had to be, these should be white not black: the independent black peasantry should rather be drawn into the labour force. It was in this mood that the Parliament of South Africa tackled the land problem and carried the Natives Land Act of 1913, subordinating the interests of black farming to the demands of a new racial ideology called 'Segregation'. But this had at least as much to do with the preservation of cheap labour, and created far greater difficulties for later generations than were appreciated at the time [see pp. 486–8].

7.12   THE ROLE OF TRADE IN COLONIAL EXPANSION

The role of trade in the extension of the European frontier in south Africa was considerable, though it has not been widely explored in all its aspects. From the researches of Elphick, Peires and Harinck something has been recovered of the trade relationships between Xhosa and Khoi before the arrival of the white man, while Robertson, Neumark and others have stressed its importance to the East India Company during the Dutch period. With the coming of the 1820 Settlers there was a burgeoning of trading activity across the Cape eastern frontier, by which time the authorities at the Cape had realised that they could not prevent the activity and should therefore seek merely to regulate it. The sale of European trade goods in return for ivory and hides now began to escalate as the frontiers of settlement advanced. The European frontier advanced, by the same token, as game retreated from the hunter's rifle. The role of trade as a contributory explanation of the Mfecane, has been emphasised by Smith and by Monica Wilson, while the range of trade items imported by the Zulu is well represented by the inventory of goods found at Dingane's kraal after the battle of Blood River, and recorded in the *Voortrekker Argiefstukke*. The direction of white settlement was determined to a considerable extent by the trade routes used by African traders in pre-colonial times. A clear example of this was the ivory route from the Zoutpansberg down to Lourenço Marques, which seems to have determined the siting of the Voortrekker bases at Ohrigstad and Schoemansdal (Wagner). Of even greater consequence was the main axis of commercial advance, the 'road to the north', which ran from the Cape through the region of the Vaal–Orange and Vaal–Harts confluences and along the edge of the Kalahari to the interior. Trade not only determined the main routes of expansion, but also provided some of the means. With the incorporation of territory, and sometimes ahead of it, came the transport rider and the trading store, as European merchants moved into the African territories generally with sufficient capital to be able to extend credit and realise good profits from a sizeable sales turnover. It was common for such traders to promote the extension of white control, though there were some notable occasions when they could be seen to be promoting the independence of African rulers from shrewd calculations of self-interest. This was the case with the wholesale firms in Pondoland whose business prospered at a time when the capacity of the paramount ruler to control trading was on the decline (Beinart). Kgama III of the Ngwato, by contrast, drew much of the trading profit of his country, which was considerable, into his own coffers (Parsons).

8 Empire and Republics: the Breaking of Boer Independence, 1850–1902

8.1 FORMAL AND INFORMAL EMPIRE

Successive British cabinets through the nineteenth century debated the merits of formal and informal empire in southern Africa. After many changes of policy it was eventually decided in 1899 to make war against the Boer republics in order to establish a firm paramountcy over the whole region. The events leading up to this decision have provided much fodder for the twentieth-century debate over the meaning of imperialism, in which several strands of argument may be discerned. Thus the role of the humanitarian lobby, seldom if ever dominant, yet seldom so insignificant that politicians of either party could afford to ignore it, was deplored in the later writings of G. M. Theal, and commended in those of W. M. Macmillan, but neither doubted its importance. Others, notably J. S. Galbraith, have seen the hand of the British Treasury as the ruling influence in the formulation of British policy, 'reluctantly' extending the imperial frontiers, and economising in the use of governmental and military resources. Considerations of grand strategy dominated the thinking of leading imperialists, in the view of Robinson and Gallagher. Others have traced the key initiatives less to the Colonial Office than to the periphery. Benyon, for example, has displayed the innovatory role of a succession of Imperial high commissioners. 'Peripheral imperialism', as Kubicek and Schreuder have described it, was rather the work of 'subcontracting' merchants and land-seekers in the colonies themselves. This is to pick up the very important economic argument for empire, which must be seen as having special relevance for southern Africa, for it was a visit to Kruger's Transvaal that gave rise to J. A. Hobson's *Imperialism: A Study* (1902), the classic exposition of the original 'colonialist' thesis. This was to the effect that colonialism resulted primarily from a bid by financial pressure groups in the metropolis to find new fields of investment in order to combat under-consumption and circumvent the resultant over-saturated money market in the home country. Derivative theories, relating to the economic *rapport* between metropolis and colonial satellite first propounded by Hobson, enjoyed a heyday following the work of later Marxists and of dependency theorists like A. G. Frank from the 1960s, but it would be unhistorical to

167

attribute any significant 'development of underdevelopment' to southern African conditions much before the twentieth century. What does emerge from the literature is the clear need to integrate the more traditional approach to the partition of southern Africa on political lines with the more recent work, initiated by De Kiewiet and expanded by Marxist writers, which has sought to explain the political changes in terms of the new economic imperatives of an industrial age.

8.2   THE PURSUIT OF THE VOORTREKKERS

The Voortrekkers burst the banks of Colonial society in a surge of land hunger spiced by political protest, which had had no parallel in the *trekboerdery* of the Company era, and presented a difficult control problem for the authorities. Lord Melbourne's Government tried to assert control over regions beyond the frontiers with its Cape of Good Hope Punishment Act in 1836, proclaiming the extension of British jurisdiction (but not sovereignty) as far north as latitude 25° S. This law was of considerable value in buttressing magisterial authority beyond the borders. Even if it did not deter the Trekkers, it enabled Governor Sir George Napier (1838–44) to appoint a magistrate at Port Natal in January 1842, though Natal itself was not annexed as a colony until 15 July the following year.

It also became the precarious basis of Napier's settlement in trans-Orangia. There he tried to impose a settlement by treaty, hoping that the Sotho and Griqua, once fortified in their rights, would resist Voortrekker attempts to obtain their land. But Boers who had encroached on Sotho and Griqua territory had already called his bluff in 1842, when he had invoked the Punishment Act, while the excessive enthusiasm of a circuit judge in proclaiming British sovereignty up to the territorial limits of that Act had not helped. Napier's treaty system had further drawbacks. It placed within Moshweshwe's jurisdiction Rolong, Kora and Tlokwa chiefs who did not recognise his lordship, while Adam Kok was encouraged by it to assume British support for acts of state against whites in his territory, which was not Napier's intention. Friction between the Griqua and Boer communities resulting from Kok's enforcement of his sovereignty led to violence at Zwartkoppies in April 1845. A British force intervened on behalf of the Griqua. As a result, the Winburgers under Mocke were further alienated, while the Griqua received little comfort from Maitland's settlement the same year [see p. 130].

Lord John Russell's Whigs took office in July 1846, and the objections of their predecessors to annexation north of the Orange were no longer heeded. Earl Grey, the Secretary of State for the Colonies, shared his Prime Minister's enthusiasm for throwing British protection over any chief who needed it. With the appointment of Sir Henry Pottinger to succeed Maitland in 1847, a new post was developed for doing this: that of High Commissioner. This Imperial officer was given an extremely vague authority beyond the frontiers involving, in Benyon's words, 'an uncomplicated if sometimes arbitrary pattern of rule that the governed could readily understand' because appropriate tribal authorities and African customs were retained in a supportive role. By degrees, the high commissionership would grow into the chief bulwark of Imperial paramountcy in southern Africa.

An energetic wielder of the high commissionership was Sir Harry Smith (Governor, 1847–52), who, without waiting for orders, persuaded Kok to surrender all authority over the alienable lands in his territory, to give up their quitrents in return for £300 a year, and to agree not to evict any Boer on the inalienable lands without compensating him fully. He next persuaded Moshweshwe to place his chiefdom under the British Crown. Andries Pretorius and the Boers who were in the act of leaving Natal were then given to understand that he would not act without evidence of their support, as he declared the Queen's paramount authority on 3 February 1848 over 'the territories north of the Great Orange River, including the countries of Moshesh, Moroko, Molitsani, Sinkonyala, Adam Kok, Gert Taaybosch and other minor chiefs, so far north as to the Vaal River, and east to the Drakensberg or Quathlamba Mountains'. But this was 'something short of outright annexation' (Benyon).

Pretorius, who had travelled six hundred miles to plead the cause of the Natal Boers before Pottinger in October 1847, only to be refused an interview, now emerged as the leader of trans-Orangian resistance to British rule. He discussed the proclamation with the Boers of Winburg, Potchefstroom and Ohrigstad, and on 22 April demanded from Smith 'the same privilege which you are giving to the coloured population, namely self-government', for the white Afrikaner emigrants. Boer resistance, however, did not measure up to such boldness. Other leaders, among them Potgieter and Jacobsz, the landdrost of Winburg, preferred to avoid open confrontation; but Pretorius issued an ultimatum in the name of his *krygsraad* on 12 July 1848. He sent his commandos into the southern district of trans-Orangia, forcing Oberholzer's supporters into defensive laagers, and with his lines extended he seems to have been prepared to do a deal with Smith. But Smith, who had already outlawed Pretorius, brushed overtures aside, and with help from a force of Kok's Griqua beat Pretorius in a skirmish at Boomplaats, on 29 August, forcing the latter to retreat northwards. He then set up a provisional government for the new Orange River Sovereignty, with Major H. D. Warden as his deputy and Bloemfontein as its capital.

There was peace at first, but within four years the British retreat had begun. Smith ran into difficulties on the Cape eastern frontier in 1850–1, while on the Sotho frontier Moshweshwe was in conflict with his Tlokwa, Rolong and Kora opponents and with the white farmers of the Sovereignty over land. Moshweshwe defeated Warden at Viervoet and reached an understanding with Andries Pretorius. Prompted by news of the Cape frontier crisis, the British Government decided on caution. To work out a viable policy in the light of the military failures, Grey appointed two men with Cape experience, Major W. S. Hogge and C. M. Owen, to assist Smith in establishing a secure system of government in the adjacent territories, and report directly to himself. Before long, Hogge had so undermined Grey's confidence in Smith by demonstrating that his military appraisals had been consistently oversanguine, that by September 1851 Grey and Russell had begun to think seriously of abandoning the Orange River Sovereignty, whose annexation had in any case never been properly promulgated by letters patent.

8.3 REPUBLICAN INDEPENDENCE: THE SAND RIVER AND BLOEMFONTEIN CONVENTIONS, 1852–4

When Pretorius threatened to side with Moshweshwe against the Sovereignty unless Britain recognised the independence of the Boers north of the Vaal, the situation became very delicate. Smith agreed to revoke Pretorius's outlawry, which enabled him to enter the Sovereignty for negotiations with Hogge and Owen at the Sand river in January 1852. At this meeting the British representatives agreed to recognise 'the fullest right of the emigrant farmers beyond the Vaal River to manage their own affairs and govern themselves according to their own laws, without any interference on the part of the British Government'. They disclaimed on behalf of the Imperial Government 'all alliances whatever and with whomsoever of the coloured nations to the north of the Vaal River', while the Transvalers agreed to prohibit slavery. The balance of advantage clearly lay with the Boers, who were guaranteed access to supplies of ammunition (which were to be denied to the blacks), and granted the right to receive immigrants from British territory, as well as extradition agreements.

The success of the Sand River negotiations reduced the urgent need to ditch the Sovereignty, but the Sovereignty itself lasted only two more years. First, its author, Smith, was recalled and replaced by Sir George Cathcart (1852–4), who had been Wellington's aide at Waterloo. Cathcart was sent to devise a cheap and effective post-war settlement and, as already noted with regard to his policy for the eastern Cape [see pp. 120–1], he saw his task as a simple one of logistics without philanthropy. Where the Sovereignty was concerned, Cathcart's main contribution to peace was his willingness to suffer a military setback at Moshweshwe's hands in December 1852, and then to accept his overtures for peace without having another go at so astute an opponent.

Britain was not chased out of the Sovereignty either by Boer antagonism or by inability to cope with the frontier problems, over which she had not really been put to the test. By 1854, the Cape frontier had been pacified and Moshweshwe, who had finally beaten Sekonyela in October 1853, was unquestioned master of his black rivals yet on good terms with the Imperial authorities. There were interest groups in the Sovereignty which wished Britain to continue her rule – English-speaking landowners and merchants, and whites of both language groups who feared for the security of the Caledon frontier if British troops were withdrawn. Some Boer diehards had moved north across the Vaal after Sand River, and there was no deep rift over frontier policy between the Imperial authorities and those who remained. Philanthropic pressures were now recessive. Sir George Russell

Clerk, who had been sent as a Special Commissioner to work out the terms of Boer independence, was prepared to ditch the Griqua, and did so. Moreover, Hogge, Clerk and Cathcart, supported by Lord Aberdeen's Colonial Secretary (the Duke of Newcastle) and Chancellor of the Exchequer (W. E. Gladstone), and above all by Sir William Molesworth, all considered the maintenance of British rule north of the Orange a waste of resources. The decision to withdraw was taken, therefore, not as a result of any opinion poll in the Sovereignty, but primarily for economic reasons by the British Cabinet in March 1853, before Clerk had even set foot in the territory. Quite simply, informal empire had become a better proposition than formal.

A Royal Proclamation renouncing sovereignty over the territory, including by necessary implication the territories of the chiefs, preceded the Bloemfontein Convention, which in turn made the 'Orange River Territory' independent without qualification. The British Government undertook not to make any treaties 'prejudicial to the interests of the Orange River Government'. Maitland's treaty with Adam Kok, which had been ineffective, was to be revised by the removal of restrictions on Griqua land sales, in return for a guarantee that the Griqua themselves would not suffer 'vexatious proceedings' and would be 'guaranteed in the possession of their estates'. Extradition arrangements, an embargo on slavery, and a guarantee of access to ammunition supplies followed on the lines of Sand River, though no mention was made of the sale of arms to blacks. Finally, the British Government undertook to station an agent 'within the Colony near to the frontier' for liaison purposes. Less than two months later, the new Orange Free State had a constitution of its own [see p. 74], though the repeal of the Punishment Act, which was technically necessary to free British subjects north of the Orange from the jurisdiction of the Crown, did not take place until 1863.

8.4 THE HIGH COMMISSIONERSHIPS OF SIR GEORGE GREY (1854–61) AND SIR PHILIP WODEHOUSE (1862–70)

The appointment of Sir George Grey as high commissioner in 1854 was a strange decision at that moment in time, for Grey viewed the settlement of Cape Colonial and extra-colonial disputes as part of a common political problem and clearly intended to turn the high commissionership into a positive office. After first visiting the eastern Cape frontier, and receiving appeals from the Orange Free State to restrain the Sotho, he spoke in Parliament in 1855 about the need for a common southern African native policy, centrally controlled. Before the year was out, he had visited the Free State and held triangular talks with President Hoffman and Moshweshwe over unrest on the Caledon border. He had also been to Natal, drafted a constitution for that Colony, and taken its land policy in hand. But of all the problems which he had to handle, that of the eastern frontier, which he saw as a continuous line from the mouth of the Kei river to the upper Caledon valley, was the one which exercised him most. At the southern end, unrest among the dispossessed Ngqika and Gcaleka erupted in the cattle-killing in February 1857, and a rising among the Thembu followed in its wake. At the northern end of the frontier, meanwhile, Moshweshwe and President Hoffman had failed to bring under control the raids of Witsi in the neighbourhood of Harrismith, of Molapo in the Winburg area, and of Jan Letelle and Posholi around Smithfield. Grey believed the advisers who told him that Moshweshwe and Sarhili, the Gcaleka chief, were in league with each other against the whites. [For Grey's Cape Governorship, see pp. 91, 121–3].

Within his own area of control, Grey adopted tough measures against several chiefs for criminal and political offences, and commissioned Currie to drive both Sarhili and the Thembu rebels across the Kei. But across the Orange he could not act. As early as August 1856 he tried unsuccessfully to persuade the Colonial Office that the policy of the Conventions was outdated, and that the Orange Free State should be included in a federation with the Cape in the interest of trade and defence. This would prevent the merging of the Free State with the trans-Vaal Boers, which M. W. Pretorius was trying hard to bring about. An attempted coup by Pretorius in 1857 failed; but in March 1858 Boshoff declared war on the Sotho against Grey's advice, found he could not prevent their crippling sorties against his border farms, and appealed to both Pretorius and Grey for help [for details of the O.F.S.–Sotho wars see pp. 134–7]. The Transvaal Volksraad's price was political union, whereupon Pretorius and Boshoff met at Winburg, and arranged a truce with Moshweshwe. Grey prohibited Colonial volunteers from helping the Free State, and threatened to cancel the Conventions if the two republics amalgamated. This worked. The Free State Volksraad suspended closer union talks, while Grey went to much trouble to track down Moshweshwe and persuaded him, at Aliwal North in September 1858, to agree to peace on the basis of a new boundary giving him the Kora and Tlokwa lands, and substantial gains in the south.

While he was north of the Orange, Grey canvassed support for a federal South Africa, and on 6 December obtained a favourable vote of twelve to eleven from a Free State Volksraad anxious to escape its Sotho entanglement. He had already urged Lord Derby's new Secretary of State, Bulwer Lytton, to support a federation of the Cape, Natal and the Orange Free State, embracing Kaffraria and perhaps other territories, under a governor appointed by the Queen, and with a responsible federal legislature elected by the people of the various states in proportion to their financial contributions, on the lines of his New Zealand constitution of 1852. But by attacking past British policies he invited – and received – criticism of the cost of his own military establishment and his apparent lack of concern to cut expenditure. Grey, it was observed, had not shown how British forces could be reduced, or indicated how the Cape itself would react to being fragmented into 'two or three . . . states', as he had proposed. It was not politically easy to reverse the new orthodoxy of non-intervention north of the Orange, and Lytton did not propose to try, though he encouraged Grey to explore further the idea of federating the British coastal colonies, excluding the Free State. Grey then acted as if this was a sign that Lytton was open to persuasion on his own scheme, and recommended the Free State Volksraad resolution to the Cape Parliament in March. For this, and for what Rutherford sums up as 'a long series of past offences, great and small', Grey was recalled in June 1859, though a change of government in Britain gave him a short second term until 1861.

Though Grey failed to restore the Imperial presence north of the Orange, his successor, Sir Philip Wodehouse, succeeded. After showing an initial reluctance to intervene in the O.F.S.–Sotho conflict of 1865–7, he acted vigorously to curb Free State expansion, and blocked Natal's effort to acquire Basutoland as well, by persuading the Colonial Office to let him annex the latter territory directly to the High Commission [see p. 137]. He followed this up, after the renewal of hostilities in 1867, by cutting off Free State ammunition supplies and sending his frontier police into the territory in the Queen's name. When Wodehouse and Brand later confronted each other at Aliwal North in February 1869, he persuaded the Free State, which had no faith in the power of the Imperial Government to pacify the Caledon river frontier, to accept a major revision of the treaties imposed on the Sotho. Wodehouse was willing to restore some lands to the O.F.S., including the region lost to the Sotho in 1858 under the earlier Aliwal North Convention, and the Volksraad ratified the agreement. Republican resentment over Imperial intervention had been rekindled, but this was not a high price to pay for letting the Republics know that from the Imperial angle – despite the Bloemfontein Convention – South African frontier problems were seen to be indivisible.

During the late 1860s the clash of Boer republican and British imperial interests began to spread, following the discovery of diamonds near the Orange–Vaal confluence, and of gold north of the Limpopo. President M. W. Pretorius of the South African Republic, who had tried unsuccessfully to gain St Lucia Bay since 1861, proclaimed new frontiers for his state in April 1868, extending west and north as far as Lake Ngami, so as to incorporate the traders' route from the Cape to central Africa as well as the gold- and diamond-bearing regions, and east to include a stretch of coastline south of Delagoa Bay [see Map 7]. The Portuguese objected, and their possession of Delagoa Bay was recognised by the South African Republic in 1869. The British Government also objected in more general terms, while the Ngwato under Matsheng, the Tlhaping under Mahura, and the Rolong of Monthsiwa, voiced their opposition through the British High Commission. The Colonial Office, by an act described by De Kiewiet as bringing about the 'virtual end' of the Sand River Convention, decided to 'disallow' the proclamation.

Behind this decision lay economic and philanthropic pressures. Cape and Natal merchants had clamoured for reannexation north of the Orange, especially during the depression years before 1868, and Shillington has shown how active they became after the discovery of diamonds in the area. Meanwhile philanthropist agitation had grown from persistent reports – often based on hearsay – that the Transvalers were a slave-owning community, or at least guilty of black-birding on a considerable scale. Wodehouse, with the annexation of Basutoland behind him, argued that Britain had a duty to hold on to the sub-continent in the interest of order and justice, and began to revive the idea of federalism, pointing towards the reincorporation of the Boer Republics. C. B. Adderley, Under-Secretary in the Colonial Office, saw merit in the proposal, and talked his minister, the Duke of Buckingham, round. But the Tory Ministry took no positive steps. When Gladstone assumed office in December 1868, however, a new policy began to take shape, in which federalism came to be linked with the devolution of power to the Cape – which was anathema to Wodehouse – in a plan to promote economy and justice. Sir Henry Barkly arrived as High Commissioner in December 1870, to put this policy into effect. He persuaded the Cape to relieve the Imperial Government of Basutoland in 1871. He managed, on the second attempt, to persuade it to accept responsible government in 1872, with the increased defence and administrative commitments which that entailed. The only piece of the puzzle which conspicuously refused to fall into place was that territorial creation of the Colesberg lawyer David Arnot, soon to be known as Griqualand West.

8.5 SIR HENRY BARKLY AND THE DIAMOND FIELDS, 1870–7

It is not possible to reconstruct the problem of Griqualand West as it appeared to the Government in London without first realising that when the discovery of diamonds followed on the conflict over land rights which had already bedevilled the fortunes of the Griqua [see above p. 132], a major transformation of the South African society and economy had begun and was soon apparent to contemporary observers. 'The diamond fields', De Kiewiet wrote in an early, masterly attempt to place these events in perspective, 'were South Africa's first industrial community', the place where governments first had to face modern problems of industrial peace-keeping, complicated by the emergence of black–white confrontation in a new sphere. Of necessity, the mines had massive capitalisation thrust upon them, they provided the magnet for government-sponsored railway construction, and they were so situated geographically on the frontier between a British colony and the two Boer Republics, that their very location was an argument for closer political cooperation, not least because the Republics stood between the diamond fields and their main sources of black labour in Basutoland, the eastern Transvaal, and Mozambique.

The political problem presented itself to Barkly as one best resolved by arbitration, and in terms of the doctrine of British paramountcy that arbitration had to be British. But in an area which contained farms granted under Sovereignty, Free State, Transvaal, Tlhaping and Griqua title, and where evidence of effective political administration was almost non-existent, there were good arguments for granting the dry diggings at Du Toit's Pan to the Free State and the river diggings at Pniel to the South African Republic, and even better ones for ensuring that the wealth of the area, and perhaps the sovereignty as well, were preserved for the communities which lived there. The Free State Government, convinced that it had a strong case, insisted on foreign arbitration so as to demonstrate the reality of its independence, and when this was refused took no part in the arbitration court which sat at Bloemhof in October 1871. Pretorius and his attorney, Kleyn, appeared on behalf of the Transvaal, but failed to convince the court, either because their case was weak (as Agar-Hamilton argues) or because they put a good case badly (the view of Theal, supported by Van Jaarsveld). Lieutenant-Governor Keate of Natal, the chosen arbitrator, seemed to be disposed in advance to accept Arnot's arguments on behalf of Waterboer (Shillington). He recognised the latter as territorial sovereign of Griqualand West, and upheld the Tlhaping claim only by pushing the border of the South African Republic back to the Makwassie Spruit. The victorious Waterboer then asked Barkly to take over his territory, and Barkly accepted it on behalf of the Crown, expecting that the Cape would relieve it of the burden. But the Cape Parliament, despite having accepted Basutoland, was not prepared to help out. The value of the diamond mines to the Colonial economy did not depend on annexation; the administration of the area would not be easy; and acceptance could only damage the Cape's relationship with its Republican neighbours.

8.6   FEDERAL STRATEGIES, 1874–80: CARNARVON, FRERE, SHEPSTONE AND THE ANNEXATION OF THE TRANSVAAL

To incorporate Griqualand West within the formal Empire was to go back both on the strategy of, and on the undertakings entered into by, the Sand River and Bloemfontein Conventions of 1852 and 1854. The British action must therefore mean that new factors had entered into their policy calculations. Even in the years of informal paramountcy between 1854 and 1875, the federation of the South African states and colonies was never far from the minds of both the political parties in Britain. We have noted its attraction for Bulwer Lytton in Derby's second (Tory) Government of 1858–9, and for the Duke of Buckingham in his third (1866–8), while Goodfellow has noted its appeal to Lords Granville and Kimberley, successive Colonial Secretaries in Gladstone's Liberal Ministry of 1868–74; but in general, the reasons behind their support for federalism had been to bring about a limitation rather than the extension of the Imperial involvement, and it had been linked with plans to reduce military commitments by entrusting maximum responsibility to the Government of the Cape Colony. Lord Carnarvon, who followed in Disraeli's Tory Government of 1874, was the most positive federalist of them all, but his motivation has become a subject for debate. Goodfellow looked upon his plan to 'expand British control northwards from a confederate Southern Africa until eventually her paramountcy . . . should extend over the greater part' of the continent as little more than a personal quirk shared between the Secretary of State and his top permanent official, Sir Robert Herbert. Against this Atmore and Marks, and in more detail Etherington, have argued that Carnarvon was alive in 1874 to the mineral possibilities of south-central Africa, anxious to find a political solution for the growing harassment of migrant blacks who crossed the Republics on their way to and from the Diamond Fields, nervous of the possible intervention of other European powers in the early years of King Leopold's Congolese adventure, and above all attentive to the suggestions made to him by Shepstone on a visit to London in 1874.

Shepstone's involvement in the broader strategy of empire prior to 1876–7 has so far attracted little attention, but enough light has been shed by Etherington to make it clear that (at the time when indentured Indian recruitment to Natal was temporarily suspended in 1871) Shepstone and a small coterie of associates were actively concerned to promote the inflow of black labour into Natal from the east coast regions as far north as the Zambesi, and to check its outflow to the Diamond Fields at a time when the hazards of such a movement had been highlighted by the Langalibalele affair of 1873–4 [see p. 102]. Carnarvon's decision, after the trial of Langalibalele, to subject Natal to the discipline of the 'Jamaica' reform of 1875 [see p. 104] has usually been seen as punitive, which in part it was. But from the Imperial angle it can also be seen as a bid to consolidate the Natal base of operations, a stepping stone towards the expansion of Natal's influence northwards to link up (via the incorporation of northern Zulu territory) with the newly opened Lydenburg goldfields – or perhaps as a first step towards what Brookes, with considerable insight, later described as the annexation of the Transvaal, 'not to the British Empire but to Natal, by Natal's uncrowned king'.

Carnarvon took advice from his roving ambassador, the historian J. A. Froude, who visited South Africa twice between September 1874 and November 1875, and saw one thing clearly to the obfuscation of much else: that if Britain was to maintain her influence in southern Africa, this had to be in association with the Boer governments, not in opposition to them. This meant redressing the injury caused by the annexation of the Diamond Fields and the mismanagement of native policy (above all by allowing traffic in firearms) which had gone with it. Froude urged a reversal of the Keate Award, which the Transvaal Government explicitly rejected in September 1875, whereas Carnarvon upheld it. Froude was prepared to hold on to the 'Table Mountain peninsula' and allow friendly white governments to control the rest of southern Africa, whereas Carnarvon, for whom military and naval considerations were paramount, doubted whether the Cape could be held without firm control of the hinterland. Froude later professed not to have had any enthusiasm for federating southern Africa, and though he spoke in favour of it, he certainly hindered its cause by his inflammatory speeches. Carnarvon, on the other hand, warmed to federalism by rapid stages, and on 4 May 1875 authorised the calling of a conference of delegates in Cape Town to discuss it. Unfortunately for his own plans, he alienated Molteno's Cape Government, first by suggesting names of possible delegates and including among them Paterson, the leading advocate of Eastern Cape separatism, and second, by putting pressure on the Colony to take over the running of Griqualand West, under a loose federal arrangement, as a condition for the incorporation of Walvis Bay, which the Cape coveted. The Cape Town conference therefore never took place. Carnarvon toyed with the idea of snubbing the Cape by calling one in Pietermaritzburg instead, but eventually switched the venue to London for August 1876.

The London conference achieved little. Molteno, who refused to attend the proceedings, met Carnarvon beforehand. He was now more amenable to incorporating Griqualand West, but refused to consider federal proposals emanating from outside southern Africa. Brand, after accepting a monetary award for the loss of Griqualand West, agreed to attend the conference; but he insisted that no representative from Griqualand West should be there, and refused to discuss federation. President Burgers of the South African Republic was visiting Europe to raise a loan for a railway from Lourenço Marques to Pretoria, but was apparently not invited owing to an administrative error. Those who did attend came mainly from Natal, notably Sir Garnet Wolseley and Sir Theophilus Shepstone, while Froude stood in for Griqualand West. The conference spent much time discussing the defence of the white territories against the military threat of African chiefdoms armed with guns, and the desirability of achieving common native policies throughout the region.

Deadlock over federation, and reports of severe reverses to the Transvaal commandos in their war against the Pedi in August, lay behind Carnarvon's sudden decision in September to annex the Transvaal. Wolseley had suggested that Shepstone be sent to carry out the annexation. Intelligence reports by Colonel G. P. Colley from the Transvaal and Major W. F. Butler from the O.F.S. a year earlier seemed to indicate that English influence was 'likely before long to become dominant' in the former territory, but not in the latter. To annex the Transvaal, indeed, seemed to Carnarvon a good way to promote federation. So far was he from abandoning that aim, that in December 1876 his department drafted enabling legislation very similar to the British North America Act of 1867.

But the Transvaal annexation and the Permissive Federation Bill both backfired sensationally. Shepstone entered the Transvaal from Natal with a small force of police in January 1877, with secret instructions to annex the Republic with or without popular consent. He received plenty of encouragement from the English-speaking community to take the government over. He made much propaganda out of the Zulu threat to the Republic's south-eastern border, and may have believed much of what he said. He found the Executive Council sullen rather than hostile, and divided. He saw a Volksraad unwilling to carry out the reforms which President Burgers placed before it, and a people unwilling to submit to the emergency taxation imposed by the Volksraad. Burgers, aware of the challenge of Paul Kruger to his own presidency, merely offered token resistance when Shepstone proclaimed the Transvaal a British colony on 12 April. The deed was quietly and skilfully done, but that proved to be no index to its popularity.

Meanwhile Sir Bartle Frere, who had an impressive record as Governor of Bombay, which included a visit to Zanzibar in 1872–3 to negotiate the ending of the slave trade, was chosen by Carnarvon to succeed Barkly, in the hope that he would become the first Governor-General of a united South Africa. His main contact with southern African developments had been through Frederic Elton, an ex-member of Shepstone's staff who had served also as Protector of Indian Immigrants and, in April 1875, been made Britain's first consul at Mozambique.

Frere ran straight into difficulties on his arrival. He reached Cape Town in March 1877 to find that the Cape Parliament had rejected the Permissive Federation Bill while he was still on the high seas. The Transvaal Volksraad had likewise rejected it already, while the O.F.S. Volksraad followed suit in May. Despite these setbacks, the measure received the royal assent on 10 August, and it was left to Frere to call a conference to promote the measure when the right moment arrived. It did not, for by mid-year the war crisis on the eastern Cape frontier had arrived, and would not end until after the new High Commissioner's quarrel with the Ministry which resulted in the dismissal of Molteno from the premiership in February 1878 [see pp. 92–3]. Molteno's successor, J. G. Sprigg, was far more amenable to federation; but not even Frere and Sprigg, working together, could make such a policy acceptable in the Colony.

Within a few days of his arrival, Frere learned of the annexation of the Transvaal by Sir Theophilus Shepstone, as a Special Commissioner acting under orders from the Secretary of State. Frere was presumably privy to the decision to annex, but it was not until mid-1878 that he became 'Governor-in-Chief' over the northern possessions, in anticipation of the coming federation of South Africa. Meanwhile he had to witness the enormous 'let-down' of the first months of British rule: the paltry grant-in-aid of £100,000 made by the British Parliament, and the chaos of Shepstone's financial administration. When Kruger and E. J. P. Jorissen visited London in July 1877 to ask for a plebiscite to test the popularity of the Queen's sovereignty, it was Carnarvon who vetoed the request. A year later, however, it was Frere who parried a demand for self-government by insisting that this could only be granted in the context of a federation, linked with a single, coordinated system for administering African affairs in the whole sub-continent. He worked for the incorporation of the whole Transkei in the Cape, for the setting up of a British protectorate over the Tlhaping and Rolong north of Griqualand West, for the destruction of Zulu military power, even for the incorporation of South West Africa and the Ngwato and Ndebele peoples north of the Limpopo. But his designs were shaken by a crisis in the British Cabinet over the Balkans, which gave the 'little England' faction the ear of the Secretary of State. They were finally wrecked in January 1879 by the disaster of Isandhlwana, at the start of a war which Hicks Beach, Carnarvon's successor, had failed to stop Frere from provoking.

It was therefore at a moment when his 'grand design' was already in tatters that Frere met the Transvaal leaders at Hennopsrivier in April 1879. The Boers had already held protest rallies in January and March. Encouraged by the signs of British military weakness, Kruger now told Frere that he did not know how much longer he could restrain his people from active resistance. Frere failed to trade self-government for a Boer acceptance of federation, but he won Boer respect by offering to forward their demands to London. Soon afterwards, as part of its retreat from the Zulu débâcle, Disraeli's Government saved Frere from the need to resign by dividing the High Commissionership and giving Natal and the Transvaal, together with the supreme military command, to Sir Garnet Wolseley. But Wolseley, expert dispenser of patronage though he was, offended the Boers by bringing them an Assembly with no representative element, and by arresting M. W. Pretorius and Eduard Bok on a frivolous pretext. He also insulted them in dispatches subsequently published. Not surprisingly, therefore, at a gathering at Wonderfontein in December the Queen's sovereignty was publicly denounced, and talk of passive resistance began, with strong support from the Dutch press at the Cape. The Liberals' election victory in April checked talk of rebellion for a while, for Gladstone had criticised Disraeli's South African policy in his Midlothian speeches; but attacks were focused on the federation policy, which was the main excuse Gladstone gave Kruger on 15 June for not letting go of the Transvaal. In April Kruger and Joubert had already started a tour of the Cape to mobilise Afrikaner opinion there. As a result, the Cape Parliament rejected Sprigg's federal motion without a division in June. Gladstone, reading the signs, recalled Frere on 1 August.

Perhaps, at this point, a generous grant of self-government might have preserved British authority in the Transvaal; but Gladstone's Cabinet was too preoccupied with the Irish crisis to give the Transvaal proper attention, while Sir Owen Lanyon, the Administrator of the Transvaal, and Sir George Colley, who had succeeded Wolseley as High Commissioner for South East Africa, had been so reassuring about the mood of the Transvalers that the issue never reached the cabinet agenda between 24 July and 30 December (Schreuder). Furthermore, the Cabinet was divided over policy. Humanitarians like W. E. Forster urged the retention of British rule to protect the blacks; Whig peers like Kimberley urged a strong hand so as to preserve the Imperial image; while Bright, Dilke, Gladstone himself and, above all, Joseph Chamberlain sympathised with the local Boer demand for self-determination. In the end, events moved too fast. The seizure of a Boer wagon because its owner had refused to pay a tax led to violence at Potchefstroom on 19 December, and in the next two months, the leaders of the resistance broke the myth of British military supremacy in engagements at Laing's Nek, Ingogo and Majuba, none of which need have occurred if Colley, who had commanded the British troops and was killed in action, had been clearly informed of the start of negotiations and refrained from unnecessary bravado.

8.7   REPUBLICAN INDEPENDENCE AGAIN, 1881–4: THE
      PRETORIA AND LONDON CONVENTIONS; CONFLICT
      OVER BASUTOLAND AND THE ROAD TO
      THE NORTH, 1880–5

These engagements on the Drakensberg escarpment did not develop into a
full-scale war because the shock of Majuba enabled the moderates in
Gladstone's Cabinet to gain control, and because the leaders of the Boer
resistance proved amenable to the mediation of President Brand. By
remaining flexible in their demands, Gladstone and Kimberley persuaded
the Boer leaders to sign a Convention at Pretoria in August. This made the
'Transvaal state' independent, left its frontiers intact but prohibited Boer
settlement beyond them, defined the extent of the Transvaal's debt and the
size of a small Imperial grant-in-aid, and placed a British Resident in
Pretoria as local agent of the Queen's suzerainty. 'Suzerainty' was a
smokescreen term, adopted after considerable Cabinet discussion, which
reserved 'certain portions of sovereignty' to the Crown. Gladstone defined
these in the Commons as 'those which relate to the relations between the
Transvaal community and foreign countries', together with 'sufficient
power to make provision for the interests of the natives'. The Pretoria
Convention, though subsequently ratified by a reconstituted Volksraad,
was not a treaty between two high contracting parties, but a prerogative act
conferring rights on the Transvalers. These rights did not amount to a
simple return to the position of 1852, for the British presence north of the
Vaal remained. The Boer leaders were consequently unable to persuade
their countrymen at large that they had made the best possible bargain.

   They also discovered that when they or their subjects took liberties with
the terms of the Convention, the British Government showed reluctance to
risk a confrontation. Lord Kimberley and his successor, Lord Derby, were
very conscious of the difficulty of effectively confronting Afrikaner challenges on the frontiers of the Boer Republics, especially at a time when the
Cape Government was itself largely dependent on Afrikaner votes [see
p. 94]. But Sir Hercules Robinson, high commissioner in 1881–9, whose
experiences included the governorships of Hong Kong, Ceylon, New South
Wales and New Zealand, recognised that the Cape Government needed to
be involved in the making and implementing of Imperial policy if that
policy was to be effective. He was unable to avoid recommending the
restoration of Basutoland to Imperial control in 1884, on account of the
Cape's failure to deal with the problems arising from the 'Gun War' [see
p. 138], but he did put pressure on the Colony to take over large areas of
the trans-Kei in 1885 and 1886.

   In the problematic regions of the south-western and south-eastern
borders of the Transvaal, the situation was rather more complex. The
white frontiersmen who had flouted the provisions of the Pretoria Convention in 1882 by taking sides in the quarrels of rival Tswana chiefs as
mercenaries in return for the promise of land grants [see p. 155] had set up
the independent Republics of Stellaland and Goshen, based on Vryburg
and Mafeking respectively, but could not secure incorporation in the

Transvaal, because two pressure groups in Britain stiffened the Colonial Office's resistance. One was the missionary lobby, led by Rev. John Mackenzie of the London Missionary Society. The other was the traders' lobby, led by John X. Merriman and Cecil Rhodes in the Cape Cabinet, who insisted that the Road to the North along the eastern edge of the Kalahari be kept out of Republican hands.

By the end of 1883 Kruger, who had been elected President of the Transvaal Republic in April, was back in London with Rev. S. J. du Toit and General N. Smit, engaged in talks aimed at revising the Pretoria Convention. They demanded a return to the conditions of 1852, complained that the Pretoria Convention had been imposed on them against their will, and objected to its boundary provisions, the suzerainty reference, and the financial arrangements. With the Cabinet divided by the Egyptian and Reform Bill crises, Derby played defensively, directing discussion towards the contentious issue of the Road to the North, hoping thereby to enlist the support of the Cape as an interested party, and avoiding being drawn on the other points, on which concession would be easier to make. Scanlen's refusal to step out of line with the Transvaal made Derby's task difficult; but Sir Hercules Robinson, the High Commissioner, not only visited London in late 1883 to stiffen the Colonial Secretary's resolve, but on his return to the Cape early the next year he persuaded Scanlen to share in the cost of maintaining a British Protectorate over Bechuanaland. This offer, which amounted to very little in practice, gave Derby the chance he needed to tie Kruger down to a new definition of his western border 'which kept the Road to the North open'. In return, he agreed to reduce the Republic's debt, remove the British Resident in Pretoria, recognise the name 'South African Republic', and – all subsequent protestations by Derby, Chamberlain and others notwithstanding – abolish the Queen's suzerainty, save in so far as specific powers, not referred to by that name, were retained under the new Convention.

But unsettled conditions on the Republic's western border persisted into 1884. Robinson secured the appointment of the Rev. John Mackenzie as administrator of Stellaland; but with the small police force supplied by the British Government his task was beyond him. Cecil Rhodes, member for Barkly West (the river diggings) and a staunch advocate of annexation by the Cape, then persuaded Robinson to appoint him in Mackenzie's place. Rhodes tried to win over the Stellalanders by generous recognition of their land titles, in the hope that they would help oust the Goshenites. In this he signally failed. Anarchy in the area persisted, and eventually, in September 1884, Kruger forced the issue by 'provisionally' annexing the two Republics to his own, on the plea that this was necessary to restore order. But when the Rev. S. J. du Toit was sent to raise the Transvaal Vierkleur at Vryburg and Mafeking, the Imperial Government reacted strongly on the ground that this was a violation of the London Convention agreed only in the previous February. Kruger climbed down. The British Government sent a force to the area under General Sir Charles Warren in January 1885, ignoring signals from the Cape Government that it was now prepared to take the initiative. Warren, with an impressive military equipage behind him, met Kruger at Fourteen Streams on the Vaal and persuaded him to accept British responsibility for the area. He then established British jurisdiction over the area south of latitude 22° S. and between the Transvaal and 20° E. longitude, by an Order-in-Council of 27 January. Warren's aim was to have the whole area declared a Crown Colony, administered by British officials, and in part opened for white (but not Boer) settlement on portions of land offered by Kgama, chief of the Ngwato and two other Tswana chiefs. Robinson, however, strongly attacked these proposals, fearing above all that they might involve Britain in conflict between the Ngwato and their enemies in relation to land claims. He had them modified so that the Crown Colony was limited to the region south of the Molopo River, and a very loose Protectorate was established over whites to the north of it. Only in 1890–1 was an administrative Protectorate set up in Bechuanaland, giving authority to the High Commissioner, as Governor, to make laws, administer government, and impose taxes on the people as a whole. Prompted by Bismarck's surprise proclamation of a Protectorate over South West Africa in August 1884, the Imperial authorities had dug in their heels to prevent Transvaal expansionism on their western border, and in so doing – as Agar-Hamilton observed – they 'barred the land-shark' from the northern region and secured the black residents of the Crown Colony 'in at least the remnants of their land' [see p. 155]. Although the British South Africa Company obtained the right to develop large areas of western Bechuanaland in 1895, its right to this area lapsed through non-usage after the Jameson Raid, and it confined its activities to the promotion of white ranching along the whole length of the eastern border in what came to be known (from south to north) as the Lobatse, Gaberones and Tuli blocks.

It is not immediately obvious why the Imperial Government, which successfully blocked Transvaal closure of one 'road to the north' along the edge of the Kalahari should have so signally failed to block the other one – Shepstone's road which ran due north from Natal, through the disputed territories of northern Zululand and the eastern Transvaal gold fields to the Zambesi. The eastern region was also a region of unofficial Republican expansion through the movement of Boers into good winter grazing lands on the upper Pongola and Mfolosi rivers. In the east, too, a splinter Boer republic was formed to match Stellaland and Goshen in the west – Lukas Meyer's New Republic, proclaimed by Cetshwayo's moral heir, Dinuzulu, in 1884, with General P. J. Joubert in due course as its elected president. Here, too, there was a German presence – the coastal nibblings of A. F. Schiel and August Einwald – to create consternation in Britain and lead her in December 1884 to annex St Lucia Bay. But whereas the western 'road' could be kept open with the help of strong commercial pressure from the Cape, the leverage of Natal business was relatively less. Natal expansionism, too, had received a direct rebuff following the overthrow of Shepstone's annexation policy. Further, the Lydenburg district was unquestionably part of the Transvaal after the military defeat of the Pedi, and any bid to reopen an Imperial line of advance in that direction would have been strongly resisted by Kruger's Republic, for it would have cut off the Republic's access to the outside world to a much greater extent than the closure of its access to German South West Africa had done.

Therefore the Imperial Government, which had needed the energetic prodding of Mackenzie and Rhodes, and then of Warren and Robinson, before it agreed to act decisively over Bechuanaland, took the line of least resistance over Zululand. The mood of the Colonial Office, as Schreuder has emphasised, was to assume that any settlement in this area required Boer support if stability were to be achieved, especially after the morale of the Zulu had been broken and their resistance disorganised through the break-up of their state after Ulundi [see pp. 153–4]. The British Government, therefore, insisted on the independence of the Zulu Native Reserve (as the territories of John Dunn and Hlubi, two of the chiefdoms recognised in 1879, were named in 1882), for this lay along the Tugela river and protected Natal's flank. It was also prepared to recognise the New Republic which became incorporated in the Transvaal in 1888, in return for Transvaal acquiescence over St Lucia Bay, and over the annexation by Britain of the rest of Zululand in 1887. The only positive achievement of the Imperial Factor, for which the Zulu – and at a later stage the Swazi and the Tsonga – were to pay the price, was the denial to the South African Republic and to the Germans of access to any point on the coast where they could establish harbours of their own.

8.8   THE SCRAMBLE FOR SOUTHERN AFRICA: GOLD, RAILWAYS AND RIVAL IMPERIALISMS, 1880–95

The discovery of gold on the Witwatersrand [see p. 84] had a greater impact on the relationship between the Imperial Government and southern Africa than even the discovery of diamonds had had two decades earlier. It so transformed the economic balance of the subcontinent to the advantage of the South African Republic at the expense of the Cape, that in the first instance it caused a polarisation of interest on territorial rather than ethnic lines; but in the longer term it led to a resurgence of Anglo-Boer conflict. The Boer Republics, for all their anti-Imperial fervour in the early 1880s, desired closer economic liaison with the coastal Colonies, and, above all, a share in the customs duties collected at the ports, to help stimulate their struggling economies. Both Brand and Kruger tried in 1884–5 to interest the Cape in a customs union, but the Cape Government was not interested. Then the opening of the Rand goldfields radically altered the balance of advantage. There was a rush to the Rand from the coastal Colonies as well as from abroad, and the coastal states sought to attach themselves to the Rand commercially. The Cape provincial *bestuur* of the Afrikaner Bond became as interested in a customs union as the various chambers of commerce of the Cape and Natal. The Cape pursued this goal with the doggedness which eventually resulted in a free trade area comprising the Cape, the Orange Free State, Basutoland, Bechuanaland, Southern

Rhodesia and even Natal (which at first stood out) by 1899. But the South
African Republic held aloof, fearing that economic cooperation might lead
to loss of independence.

A parallel move to establish rail links between the coastal Colonies and
the Rand [see Map 12] had similar results. When E. McMurdo, an
American, obtained a concession from the Portuguese Government in
1882 to construct a railway from Lourenço Marques to the Transvaal with
the help of British money, the restored Republic seemed to be assured of
economic independence. But McMurdo's line, which was later taken
across the Transvaal by the Netherlands South Africa Railway Company
holding a concession from the Transvaal Government, only reached Pretoria in 1894, after many hazards. The Transvaal and the Free State
Governments discouraged the construction of lines from British colonies to
the Rand. The Cape and Natal Governments, however, built lines from
Cape Town, Port Elizabeth, East London and Durban to Fourteen
Streams, Colesberg, Aliwal North and Charlestown respectively, hoping to
wear the Republics' resistance down. Between 1888 and 1890 the Cape
broke through. Sprigg, prime minister in 1888, devised a plan to extend the
Colesberg line into the Free State under the threat of extending the line
from Fourteen Streams into the Transvaal if the Free State refused, thus
threatening to by-pass the southern Republic. If both Republics refused to
admit a line, he proposed to extend the Fourteen Streams line through
Bechuanaland, thus threatening to establish rail links with central Africa
which left both Boer Republics in the shallows. This persuaded Kruger to
put pressure on President Reitz of the Free State, who agreed to admit the
Colesberg line. The subsequent extension of this line into the Transvaal
resulted from the financial embarrassment of the Netherlands Company
during the gold crisis in 1890. Rhodes, by that time Premier of the Cape,
agreed to advance funds to the Company provided that the first call on
them should be a line from the Vaal river, connecting the Port Elizabeth
line to the Rand, in terms of the Sivewright Agreement, named after the
Cape's chief negotiator, in 1892. The Cape line reached the Rand the same
year. That from Delagoa Bay, with the help of Cape Government money
and a Rothschild loan which Rhodes also helped to arrange, reached
Pretoria in 1894. The Natal line via Charlestown, which encountered
continuing opposition from the Republican and Cape governments, was
only expected to be completed at the end of 1895.

In anticipation of a loss of revenue, the Cape Government Railways
asked the Netherlands Company to guarantee them half the traffic on a
continuing basis, when Rhodes's Commissioner Laing met G. A. Middel-
berg in August 1894. The latter would only offer the Cape one third of the
value of the receipts, and Laing's truculent tone helped to bring about an
early deadlock. There is some evidence, which Wilburn cites, that this may
have been deliberate, and that Rhodes was already using the transport
issue as a device to force a confrontation with Kruger in order to overthrow
him.

From about the beginning of 1895 goods had been banking up in the
Johannesburg railway yards owing to the inability of the authorities to cope

with their distribution. To alleviate the pressure, the Cape Railways had begun to offload goods at the Vaal river drifts and convey them to the Rand by ox-waggon. But on the collapse of the negotiations in August 1895, Kruger closed the drifts to imported goods, leaving access still free to Cape and O.F.S. produce. Rhodes, supported by the Colonial Office, which was now led by Joseph Chamberlain as Secretary of State, decided to confront Kruger with a demand to reopen the drifts on the ground that his action was in violation of the London Convention, and sent Kruger a threatening note on 3 November. Continental advisers told Kruger that he was within his rights, though it does seem that he had broken a 'solemn promise' made at the time of the Sivewright Agreement not to discriminate against the Cape. But the Republican Government was not seeking a confrontation if it could be avoided. They offered to reopen railway negotiations, and had already agreed to a temporary reopening of the drifts in a proclamation of 28 October. Even though the railway conference, which met between 4 and 9 November, failed to reach agreement, Kruger announced on 6 November that he intended to leave the drifts open to traffic.

The argument advanced by Wilburn that this action of Kruger's headed off a confrontation which Rhodes and Chamberlain intended to keep on the boil until their collaborators on the Rand were ready to start a rising, makes good sense in terms of chronology. On this interpretation, the Jameson Raid of December 1895 [see p. 188] would have to be seen as an abortive substitute for a plot which had already gone awry.

The years 1884–5 saw a marked increase in the tempo of the Scramble for southern Africa, following the decision by Bismarck, the German Chancellor, to challenge British imperial hegemony in these parts. There has been much debate as to why Bismarck, who had at first been indifferent to colonisation, began to throw his weight behind German colonial schemes from about August 1883. Views have ranged from those who saw Germany's first bid for colonies as little more than the working out of European conflicts in peripheral arenas, to those who take the lobbying of German colonising interests seriously, and interpret Bismarck's actions primarily as a response to economic and party political pressures at home. Whichever explanation is preferred, a conflict developed between Britain and Germany over South West Africa and the Zululand and Pondoland coasts, as well as over Germany's relationship with the South African Republic, which grew in intensity as a result of diplomatic misunderstandings on both sides, complicated by a lack of proper rapport between the British Government and those of Scanlen and Upington in Cape Town.

Angered by what looked like attempts on the British side to book parts of the African coastline for later colonisation, Bismarck became secretive over his colonial intentions. The British, who were still sensitive over the defeat of Majuba, were understandably suspicious over any approach made by Germany to the Transvaal, such as the fêting of Paul Kruger when he was over in Europe while the London Convention was being negotiated. Out of Bismarck's pro-colonial stand there gradually emerged a new strategy referred to as that of *Mittelafrika*, in terms of which Tanganyika and South West Africa were to be linked across the Zambesi. But in point of time, *Mittelafrika* came later than the *contra costa* aspirations of the Portuguese, which had grown out of the Macmahon Award of 1875 [see p. 82], received nourishment from Serpa Pinto's successful journey from Angola to Mozambique in 1879, and grew by the 1890s into an adamant refusal to consider the sale of Lourenço Marques to any bidder. Both these notions were incompatible, in turn, with the 'Cape to Cairo' dreams of Harry Johnston and Cecil Rhodes. The rhetoric of the Scramble thus became loaded with conflicting ambitions, until these were reconciled by the diplomatic arrangements of 1890 and 1891. Under the Anglo-German Treaty of the former year, spheres of influence were defined over the whole continent. In the southern part the Germans added the Caprivi Strip to South West Africa, and so gained access to the Zambesi; but they left the British in control of the region later known as Northern Rhodesia (Zambia), thus accepting defeat over their *Mittelafrika* dream. Similarly, the Anglo-Portuguese Treaty of 1891 allowed Portugal trans-continental telegraph rights from coast to coast, but no continuous land bridge.

The Anglo-German and Anglo-Portuguese treaties of 1890–1 kept open the southern extremity of the British Road to the North, consolidating the territorial gains made by Britain through the proclamation of the Bechuanaland Protectorate in 1885 and the granting of the B.S.A.C. charter in 1889. Although Rhodes had originally urged an advance into Bechuanaland in the early 1880s, and deplored the operation of the 'imperial factor' there, it was the British Colonial Office which took control in that region. Nevertheless, it was Rhodes who saw to the construction of the railway north from Vryburg, while the B.S.A.C. charter gave the Company the right to exploit the region north of latitude 22° S. (which would have given it access, other things being equal, to the greater part of Kgama's territory). In 1895 Joseph Chamberlain made a very substantial grant of land in Bechuanaland to the Company; but the Company had its wings severely clipped after the Jameson Raid, and was only able to keep control of the three white farming blocks along the Transvaal border. It was excluded from all other Tswana territory by the Southern Rhodesian Order-in-Council of 1898.

North of the Protectorate it was a different story. Here the Chartered Company was the government, and the Colonial Office operated by remote and not always very vigilant control. After allowing the Company to build its legal title on the distinctly doubtful Rudd Concession, it stood aside as whites from all parts of southern Africa, British and Boer, set off with the Pioneer Column in search of farms. A second wave of land purchase followed the defeat and death of Lobengula in 1893. Chartered shares, like farms, found their way into Boer as well as British hands, though the bulk of them were distributed in London, not South Africa. Rhodes's agents, Sharpe and Lochner, consolidated the Company's influence in North-Eastern Rhodesia and Barotseland, and were unfortunate not to acquire Katanga as well, while other Company servants moved east into Manicaland and tried unsuccessfully to establish control over the Pungwe River route to Beira. But the mineral wealth in Mashonaland on which much speculation was based was shown to be largely illusory by the Hays-Hammond Report of 1894. Most of the mineral wealth in the territories occupied by the Chartered Company lay to the north of the Zambesi, and remained largely unexploited until the opening of the Copper Belt in the 1920s. For immediate practical purposes, it had to be recognised in the 1890s that the key to the political control of southern Africa lay in the Transvaal.

8.9 CHAMBERLAIN, RHODES, MILNER AND THE CONFRONTATION WITH KRUGER, 1895–9

The encirclement of the Transvaal was one aim of British Imperial strategy in the 1890s. Political federation had ceased to be practical politics after the recall of Frere. Economic federation by means of a customs union and the integration of separate railway systems fell short of the target owing to Transvaal resistance in the 1890s. Kruger exposed his state to the danger of encirclement by revoking the provisional annexation of Bechuanaland in 1884 and by renouncing all interest north of the Limpopo in negotiations with High Commissioner Sir Henry Loch in March 1890. Having made engagements, however, he honoured them, and disowned the Bowler and Adendorff treks across the Zambesi in 1890 and 1891, staking all on the acquisition of a seaport, which he never obtained. But at least his Republic was never cut off, even though by 1895 the whole coastline from the Orange River mouth to Tongaland was in British hands. When Kruger agreed to abandon the north in 1890, it was in the hope of acquiring Kosi Bay in Tongaland, but this was made conditional on the Republic's joining the Customs Union, which the Volksraad refused to do. Thereafter the emphasis of Kruger's policy, like that of Rhodes, was on the acquisition of Lourenço Marques, which seemed to be within reach after the Imperial Government had agreed to the Republic's administering Swaziland in 1895. But the Portuguese, sheltering behind protracted litigation in Switzerland over McMurdo's complicated debts, adamantly refused to sell.

British Imperial strategists who recognised that Rhodesia could not become a second Rand came to realise that the Transvaal held the key to southern Africa as a whole. By the early 1890s, it was becoming clear that the Republic was already surpassing the Cape in the value of its exports, and that if it continued to remain outside the southern African common market, which it showed every sign of wanting to do, then Imperial paramountcy would soon become a meaningless phrase. On this line of thinking, the only hope of assured British political dominance was to transfer political control of the Rand to the Uitlander element. But this was not easy to achieve in Kruger's Republic, where the Afrikaner community, though divided, was firmly entrenched in power [see pp. 84–5]. When Kruger introduced constitutional reforms in 1890 to make sure that the Uitlanders were given representation, but at the same time effectively denied the hope of real power, the beginnings of a self-explanatory Uitlander agitation were set in motion. But although rooted in popular disabilities, it came to be used to further the cause of British paramountcy. No less a person than Sir Henry Loch turned his mind in 1894 to the idea of an Uitlander rising in Johannesburg to be followed by an invasion by a British force from the Protectorate, as a means of achieving a British takeover of power less subtle by far than Shepstone's takeover of 1877. Loch's idea provided a blueprint for the Jameson Raid of 1895, with the important difference that the intention behind the Jameson Raid was that the tracks of the Colonial Office should be properly covered by the use of the Company's private army rather than men in British military uniforms.

The plan promoted by Rhodes and the Reform Committee (Charles Leonard, Frank Rhodes, George Farrar, Lionel Phillips and John Hays-Hammond) – was that a rising should take place in Johannesburg, followed by an invasion from the Bechuanaland Protectorate, after which the High Commissioner was to proceed to the Rand from Cape Town and proclaim British sovereignty over the Transvaal. The plan ended in a fiasco because Jameson decided on 30 December 1895 to invade, even though he knew that the Reform Committee had postponed the rising, and because Rhodes, who could have called off the invasion, did not act (Rotberg). Jameson relied on his force of 500 men and the power of the maxim gun to reach Johannesburg. But the Raiders' cover was blown by poor security, and they were stopped at Doornkop and forced to surrender by Cronje's commando on 2 January 1896.

There is no longer any reason for supposing that Joseph Chamberlain was ignorant of Jameson's planned invasion of the Transvaal, or that he had made over to the Company a force of Bechuanaland Border Police and a strip of land along the Protectorate's border without knowing that these were to be used for the Raid. The best explanation of his position would seem to be that his knowledge was unofficial rather than official – a distinction explored by Butler – and that his awareness of Rhodes's planning did not in itself make him a party to Rhodes's schemes (Porter). But it is very difficult to accept Porter's claim that, because Rhodes was so hard to control there is 'no ground for assuming that Chamberlain could have acted otherwise', even if evidence for this is provided by Flint and Galbraith. At the very least, Chamberlain could have threatened to blow Rhodes's cover, and thus averted the irreparable damage done to the trust between the South African Republic and the Colonial Office by an unsuccessful *coup d'état*.

The involvement of Chamberlain, of Sir Hercules Robinson, now enjoying his second term as governor, and of other key figures, was suppressed by the Committee of Inquiry sitting in London in 1897, but this did not allay Transvaal suspicions. The Republic was given a genuine pretext for rearming in self-defence, which it now proceeded to do. But the act of rearming gave currency to the idea in British circles that Kruger aimed at the 'dominion of Afrikanerdom' (or Transvaal republican rule) from the Limpopo to Simonstown. That he had any such aim is improbable. The case against him depended largely on the revamping of Bond propaganda utterances dating from the early 1880s, when the mood of Afrikaner nationalists had been far more flamboyant. This could have deceived Chamberlain, for it was as a member of Gladstone's government during the trying negotiations over the Pretoria and London Conventions that he had first met Paul Kruger, then an angry, assertive political opportunist, keen to exploit the position of strength in which he found himself, equivocal in debate but expecting to win rather than lose. Kruger had better reason for anger in 1896–9 and the confidence his people reposed in him was now much stronger; but he was under much greater pressure than before, and if he equivocated now it was to avoid direct confrontation with skilled opponents on their ground rather than his own. They pulled him into the arena of Uitlander rights. His task was to keep the debate going on the issues related to British paramountcy, but that was not easy [see pp. 86–7].

The exact relationship between the strategy of the Imperial Government and the actions of the Uitlander leadership in the mounting crisis has been much debated. De Cecco and others have drawn attention to the development of South African gold-mining in the context of a fluctuating decline in the value of silver, until then the accepted monetary standard for many countries, from 1872, and its rapid replacement by gold between 1873 and 1896. This process was of particular advantage to the industrial states of Europe. The international gold standard was also of advantage to Great Britain, which had maintained gold parity since the end of the Napoleonic wars. The London money market had thus built up sufficient confidence among the world's investors to be able to supply nearly half the loan capital required for development by other countries in the late nineteenth century. The Rand gold discoveries gave the backing required for an increase in the volume of available currency at a time when the world was entering a period of major industrial and commercial expansion. Under such circumstances the continuing flow of 'Cape bars' to the Bank of England vaults helped to maintain investors' confidence in the London money market even if – as is now apparent – there is no documentary evidence of attempts by the Bank to engineer increased political pressures on the Kruger regime (Van Helten).

Whether the mining houses became either the manipulators of British policy or the tools of British imperial interests is therefore another question. Their orientation was not unambiguously British. The Corner House (Wernher–Beit) group, heirs to the French (Porges) Company which had first established itself in Kimberley, was by far the largest of the 'stables'. It was an international body with branches in Paris, in London (where it established Rand Mines in 1893), and a local south African office run by Hermann Eckstein and Co. Wernher seems to have been concerned to preserve the independence of the South African Republic in order to ensure that the Transvaal did not become a preserve for exclusive British investment, even if other members of his company, like FitzPatrick, made common cause with Milner. Wernher–Beit, who had acquired valuable long-term deep-level interests on the Rand, as well as extensive land-holdings in the Transvaal and a huge portfolio of investments around the world, stood to lose from the outbreak of war in 1899, as Kubicek makes very plain. Consolidated Goldfields of South Africa, as the Rhodes–Rudd venture had been renamed after its enlargement to include other interests, had also begun to invest in deep levels in the late 1890s. This development could only have been dislocated by war, even if the firm was much more 'solidly British' than Wernher–Beit. It could not therefore be assumed that the mining houses and the Imperial Government would act together in the crisis unless explicit steps were taken to ensure that they did. For this reason special significance may well attach to the relationship which developed between Milner and FitzPatrick.

The main thrust of the Imperial attack came not from Chamberlain but from Sir Alfred Milner, High Commissioner from May 1897. Milner had a very clear picture of the way events were shaping in South Africa, and of the probable changes in the balance of power, an equally pronounced confidence in the ability of a Balliol scholar to play and beat an unschooled Voortrekker at diplomatic chess, a very fluent pen full of adjectives, and a large share of the condescension too often found among *fin de siècle* imperialists who spoke of Britain's civilising mission within earshot of the Jameson Raid. But he had little apparent understanding of the points of view of the more or less Calvinist Afrikaners. Milner was interested in power. His decision that Kruger's power had to be broken probably dated from the latter's overwhelming victory in the presidential election of February 1898, for soon afterwards he confided to FitzPatrick in Cape Town that war 'has got to come' before a settlement could be achieved. But the mounting of his diplomatic offensive was delayed by the Bond's triumph over the Progressives in the Cape lower house election in July, and by the counter-influence of General Sir William Butler, who acted as High Commissioner while Milner was in Britain at the end of the year, and had the advantage of a longer, if broken, experience of South Africa. Butler could count on a body of opinion in Britain who, without being blind to Republican faults, did not think that these justified a war. They included Gladstonian Liberals and the main body of the Labour press. He was able to block an irregular Uitlander petition to the Queen arising out of the shooting of an Uitlander by a Republican policeman (the 'Edgar incident') in December 1898, though Andrew Porter has shown that the Colonial Office gave Butler little support, and rather treated the incident as a civil rights issue which extended beyond the narrow limits of the London Convention.

Milner returned in February 1899, and soon rebuilt the alliance between the Colonial Office and the anti-Government Randlords which had been shattered by the failure of the Jameson Raid. In the same month, with the help of Greene, the British Agent, and of W. F. Monypenny, a *Times* journalist who had recently arrived at Milner's behest to edit the *Star*, he brought the Uitlander petition movement alive again in response to a fresh succession of incidents which had inflamed relations between the Uitlanders and the authorities. On 26 February, in response to renewed pressures from the British side, J. C. Smuts, the State Attorney, made an offer to reopen negotiations with the Rand Capitalists over the dynamite monopoly and other contentious issues. FitzPatrick acted as intermediary between the organisers of the petition and the capitalist negotiators, between the negotiators and Smuts, and between both groups and Milner. Though the

Republican offer may have been genuine, FitzPatrick was not satisfied that the Government could carry sufficient reforms through the Volksraad. He and Milner agreed, therefore, that in the interest of rebuilding pressure against the Government it was necessary that the negotiations should fail. FitzPatrick told Julius Wernher, his London principal, on 6 April that he had acted discreetly as a negotiator; but he later claimed in his *South African Memories* that he had arranged for the details to be leaked before Kruger's Government had had a chance to make a definitive offer. At the same time, he began to organise a series of meetings along the Reef to agitate for franchise reform, and hoped that these might lead to the calling of an 'Uitlander Parliament' which would force Kruger's hand. Because of the efforts of the Republican Government to drive a wedge between the capitalist Uitlanders and the rank and file [see p. 86] this Uitlander agitation no longer seems as contrived as it was once thought to be; but from Milner's point of view it was closely tied to the paramountcy issue. Wilde's observation that the Colonial office only began to test the South African Government's franchise proposals in July 1899 has led Benyon to suggest that Milner 'had *all along* intended to exploit the Transvaal's tardy minor concessions in order to drive the political temperature high enough for him to move, imperceptibly, away from the franchise and forward to acceptance of imperial supremacy as the only alternative to war'.

At all events, Milner was ready, after the collapse of the negotiations, to forward the second Uitlander petition to London along with his so-called 'helot' dispatch of 4 May, in which he stated that 'the case for intervention is overwhelming'. But his triumph was not yet. The Cape Government and President Steyn undermined his strategy by carefully preparing the ground for a meeting between Milner and Kruger at Bloemfontein at the end of May, and obtaining Chamberlain's agreement in such a way that Milner could not refuse to take part. But, against Chamberlain's advice, he decided to exclude the moderating influence of the Cape premier, Schreiner, from the proceedings. At the Bloemfontein meeting Milner then worked for public confrontation rather than private negotiation, and got it. Thereafter events played into his hands. He secured the publication of the 'helot' dispatch, with its many gratuitous insults to Kruger's Government. In mid-June the Uitlander Council came out with a Declaration of Rights, which asked for considerably more than Milner had demanded at Bloemfontein, and made Milner's bid to force reform look insincere. The Transvaal Government made a succession of compromise offers over the controversial Uitlander franchise, realising that active support from Cape Afrikaners could not be taken for granted. Chamberlain was half persuaded by terms offered by Smuts on Kruger's behalf in August. But Milner professed to suspect a trap, the negotiations broke down and in October 1899 both sides resorted to the arbitrament of force.

8.10 THE ANGLO-BOER WAR OF 1899–1902

The Boers began the war on 11 October 1899 because, with an initial military advantage, they appreciated how important it was to seize the initiative. Smuts had calculated that they could bring about 40,000 men into the field – a slight over-estimate – against a British garrison which he slightly under-assessed at 15,000, at the outbreak of hostilities. A large British expeditionary force was expected, which began to arrive in November. Commandos from the Transvaal and Orange Free State moved into Natal, and after a few sharp early engagements invested Ladysmith and advanced to Estcourt and beyond. The Free Staters delayed their crossing of the Cape frontier on account of an earlier plea by Schreiner to help him maintain a non-combatant role. But faced with the prospect of attack by Cape-based Imperial troops, Steyn sent his commandos across the Orange on 1 November, and they soon brought a large number of Colonial Afrikaners out in rebellion. But there was no concentration on Boer forces for a drive into the Colony, and no determined attempt to take Mafeking, Kimberley or Ladysmith. In his discerning *Memoir* of the Anglo-Boer War, General Smuts strongly criticised this lack of offensive spirit among the Boer leadership during these early critical months, when Louis Botha and Koos de la Rey were refused permission to drive deep into Natal and the Cape respectively. The ability of the Boer forces to contain the initial British counter-offensive in tough operations on the Tugela, in the Stormberg and at Magersfontein in mid-December, perhaps lured them into a belief that defence was the best form of attack – unless, as Breytenbach has suggested, the Republican Governments were deliberately avoiding major confrontations so as to conserve manpower; but he agrees that at the start of the war they had enough numerical superiority to penetrate deep into the coastal colonies and thus increase their manpower strength to meet a British offensive.

Sir Redvers Buller, the first British Commander-in-chief, lacked the resourcefulness needed to take an army on to the attack, though he has been well portrayed by Pakenham as a humane general who deserved a greater measure of trust from the War Office than he received. His early failures, reaching a climax in the 'Black Week' in mid-December, led to his replacement by the legendary but semi-retired Lord Roberts, to whom history has, on the whole, been excessively kind. Roberts arrived from Britain in January, with Kitchener as his second-in-command, and brought a new plan of campaign: to advance up the line of rail from Cape Town to the Modder river, and then send his main force eastwards to cut the Free State line south of Bloemfontein, thus threatening to isolate the Boer forces in the south. Buller, who continued to serve under Roberts, and had meanwhile relieved Ladysmith with the help of troop reinforcements, completed the reconquest of Natal. Roberts's force advanced with relative ease into the Free State, taking Bloemfontein on 13 March after capturing Cronje's large commando at Paardeberg. They entered Johannesburg on 5 May and Pretoria on 6 June. Roberts proclaimed British sovereignty over the 'Orange River Colony' and the 'Transvaal Colony' on 24 May and 1 September respectively. Kruger left via Lourenço Marques for Europe in a vain bid to seek Continental aid, and Boer resistance dwindled as the commandos began to trickle home, leaving a mere 8,000 Free Staters and 7,000 Transvalers under arms (in the calculations of De Wet and Smuts).

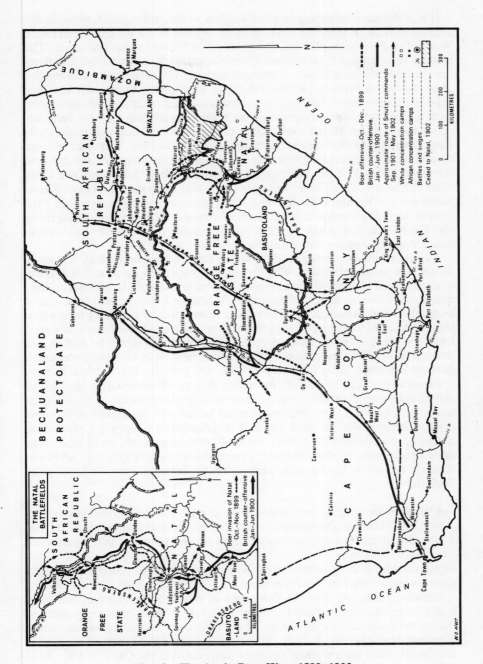

Map 9   The Anglo-Boer War, 1899–1902

It was the determination of a few leaders at this point which brought the commandos back into the field, notably President Steyn and General de Wet in the Free State, Botha, De la Rey and Smuts in the Transvaal. The leaders reappraised their tactics. Cronje's defeat had destroyed the glamour of the traditional laager. The experience of Diamond Hill, fought soon after the fall of Pretoria, showed the folly of allowing manpower losses in set-piece defensive actions. The accent now was on a war of movement with local commandants operating on their own initiative under centrally coordinated plans. Botha took charge of the eastern Transvaal, while De la Rey returned to the western. In the Free State, De Wet was elected Commandant-General in June. He organised the return of commandos to the Cape led by J. B. M. Hertzog, Kritzinger, Gideon Scheepers and (very briefly) himself. These invasions spread the war deep into the Cape. Smuts wrote on 3 February 1901 that 'the Afrikaners are rising everywhere', the Free State commandos having reached beyond Willowmore, Fraserburg and Carnarvon (all in the Karoo), with Colonial rebels active at Clanwilliam, Van Rhynsdorp and Tulbagh.

The Boer commandos proved a match for the British military machine, which was provided at first with far too few mounted men, and was quite unused to this kind of warfare. Under the inspiration of Danie Theron they quickly became masters of scouting, sabotaged the railway lines, and learned how to turn flight into an offensive weapon by suddenly turning on their exhausted pursuers. Smuts detected in the British field commanders a lack of confidence in themselves comparable with that which he had earlier noticed in the Boer veterans, Piet Joubert and P. A. Cronje – a weakness particularly discernible in Baden-Powell, the popular hero of Mafeking.

Faced with a type of warfare for which they were unprepared, the British commanders reacted with a good deal of unfeeling brutality. S. B. Spies has shown that the farm-burning started before the departure of Roberts in November 1900, so that the full responsibility cannot be placed on Kitchener. His calculation that about 30,000 farmsteads were destroyed during the course of the war, and approximately twenty villages, bears out Smuts's report to Botha from the northern Transvaal on 22 September 1900 that

> whenever the enemy now appears, he carries out indescribable destruction. All houses are burned down, all fields and gardens utterly destroyed, all cattle and foodstuffs carried off and all males taken prisoner!

Margaret Marquard's letters from Winburg tell a similar story with reference to one district in the Free State.

Because farms were in the front line in a war of movement, burnings could be militarily justified; but they led to the spread of atrocity stories, the truth of which is in the nature of the case very difficult to assess. Some involved high-ranking British officers, like General French. The stories became the fuel for a women's protest movement in the Cape, led by Olive Schreiner and Marie Koopmans de Wet. When the Opposition newspapers took up the stories, their editors were tried and convicted on charges of

7 **Commentators in continental Europe were often fervently pro-Boer in sympathy. A representation of a concentration camp in Jean Veber's *Das Blutbuch von Transvaal***

seditious libel, and the newspapers themselves were suppressed.

Train-wrecking became so frequent – Spies notes 135 incidents between December 1900 and September 1901 – that it was treated as a criminal offence, and in a vain attempt to stop it the military authorities made Boer hostages ride on the trains, or destroyed homesteads close to the places where sabotage had occurred. De Wet's accounts of successful attacks on trains passing through the Free State show how vulnerable the British supply lines had become.

Boers caught wearing British military uniforms were sometimes executed, the shooting of Jack Baxter of Klerksdorp being a case in point. Miscarriages of justice for which the military courts were held responsible formed the theme of G. Jordaan's later *Hoe Zij Stierven* (1915) and of Gustav Preller's edition of the diary of the colourful Boer martyr, Gideon Scheepers. The first work in Afrikaans to defend these military tribunals on the ground that they did what was expected of them under circumstances of martial law, appeared only in the very different climate of 1962. J. H. Snyman has demonstrated that if the military authorities were sometimes over-hasty in securing convictions, they were commonly lenient in the matter of sentence, for of over 360 death sentences passed in the Cape Colony only 35 were carried out.

To deal with the elusive Boers, the British authorities cordoned off enormous areas of South Africa with fences guarded by blockhouses, and then carried out organised sweeps. At first the commandos generally managed to cut their way through the obstacles, but by the end of the war

Kitchener's 'new model' sweeps were making evasion extremely difficult, and even De Wet was fully extended to break out of his cordon in February 1902.

The British also made use of surrendered Boers as peace propagandists. Burgher Peace Committees were promoted by brothers of De Wet and Cronje from December 1900. The same A. P. Cronje was the moving spirit behind the National Scouts, composed of Boers who had 'hands-upped' from conviction that their cause was hopeless and only surrender could bring relief. From the end of 1900 groups later known as the Volunteers in the O. R. C. and National Scouts in the Transvaal were established, placed under British military discipline, and attached to British units. There were 1,359 National Scouts and 448 Volunteers in the field at the end of the war. Their leaders were generally men like the diarist, P. J. du Toit, who saw no hope in further resistance and looked beyond surrender to recovery after the war. The rank and file were in many cases the rootless members of Afrikaner society, notably *bywoners* on the lands of the more prosperous (Grundlingh). The Boer leaders were very bitter about the 'joiners' and Scouts, some of whom were summarily executed when captured, and acknowledged that they substantially undermined Boer morale in addition to helping the British with their local knowledge.

National Scouts and their families were particularly vulnerable to Boer retribution, and it was in the first instance to protect them that the British military authorities decided in the second half of 1900 to set up concentration camps. But before the end of the year the concept was enlarged to include civilians cleared from their homes as a result of farm-burnings and military sweeps. Two categories of camp inmate were soon distinguished: those who were non-partisan or had taken oaths of allegiance to the Queen, and those whose husbands or sons were on commando and were regarded as hostile to the Imperial cause. The former received more considerate treatment. Some forty-four camps for whites were set up altogether, most of them in the Transvaal and the Orange River Colony. They were transferred to civilian control in November 1901, after Milner had protested to Kitchener about the harshness of the system and the high mortality rate, which had risen to 344 per thousand during October. The camps became a public scandal on account of the high incidence of disease in them (mainly measles and amoebic dysentery), and their administrative defects to which Emily Hobhouse and Joshua Rowntree drew attention during their visits in 1900–1. As the war drew to a close, conditions in the camps improved until the death rate was not abnormal, but by then 27,927 inmates had died, of whom about 22,000 were under the age of 16. Milner criticised the camps because of the adverse publicity which they gave to the British cause. The military authorities, however, would have had fewer problems if they had been allowed by their civilian counterparts to make peace with the Boers and leave them some measure of independence.

Demands for peace on such terms split and then destroyed the Schreiner Government. Merriman and Te Water, who had both been distressed by Schreiner's refusal to take a more public stand against hostilities before the outbreak of war, campaigned against martial law and against the disfranchisement of rank-and-file rebels. The best tribute to Merriman's 'stately' minute on amnesty (Lewsen), based on the analogy of the Canadian rebellion of 1837, was that even in April 1900 it won the support of the whole Cape Cabinet; but Chamberlain rejected it out of hand, managed to hold Schreiner to obedience, and in doing so created the split which forced the Cape Cabinet out of office in June.

Control of the campaign for civil rights and Republican independence now passed to the South African Conciliation Committee, which had been set up in January with branches in England and at the Cape. This body organised a massive public meeting at Worcester, Cape Colony, in December, as a result of which Merriman and Sauer tried unsuccessfully to deliver a 'grand remonstrance' to the House of Commons in March 1901. The Conciliation Committee deplored the inroads made by the war into the rights of the subject, denying – as Sir Edward Coke might equally have done – that reason of state justified any action done under martial law. In doing so, they struck a common chord with the British Liberal left, who deplored the Tory victory in the general election of October 1900, so often – but in the view of Davey and M. D. Blanch, erroneously – referred to as a 'khaki election'. They were shocked by Emily Hobhouse's revelations concerning the camps. At the end of Merriman's visit, and shortly after he had met Miss Hobhouse, Sir Henry Campbell-Bannerman spoke for many of them in his celebrated reply to A. J. Balfour's claim that British actions were justified on the ground that the war was already over: 'When is a war not a war? When it is carried on by methods of barbarism in South Africa'.

People throughout the land experienced real loss of liberty and material deprivation in 1901. Farmers in the Cape did not know whom to fear more, the Boers who moved in and commandeered their stock, or the military authorities who took their stock and destroyed their crops to prevent them from falling into Boer hands. Relations between Dutch- and English-speaking communities in the towns deteriorated. Boer supporters dressed provocatively in Republican colours. Supporters of the Empire joined Vigilance Associations or enlisted in the Natal-based South African Light Horse or in the (Cape) Colonial Volunteer Corps, whose members were freed for active service by the formation of town guard units from December 1899.

Militarily the year 1901 was indecisive. Invasions by Boer commandos at the beginning of the year had helped to bring about a second Cape rebellion, which resulted by mid-year in most of the north-west Cape falling into rebel hands. In February Kitchener offered to meet Botha at Middelburg, Transvaal, to discuss terms of peace. Botha accepted the invitation but negotiations broke down because Kitchener had refused to offer elective self-government, let alone independence, to the Boers. On 10 May, however, the Transvalers asked the Free Staters to agree to seek Kruger's advice on future policy. Though Steyn was strongly opposed, Smuts cabled Kruger after getting Kitchener's permission. He painted the situation of the Boers in gloomy colours. Kruger's reply indicated that foreign support could be discounted, but that so long as the Cape rebellion looked promising they should fight on. Eventually, on 20 June, the two governments managed to renew contact with each other and publicly renounced all thought of making peace unless their independence was assured.

The situation in the Cape remained fluid. The Boer Central Peace Committee had corresponded with T. P. Theron, then chairman of the Afrikaner Bond, in February, trying to get the 'Afrikaner Party' to support its peace efforts by publicly refusing to assist the commandos. Theron declined to negotiate with them, and would only work through the 'constituted authorities'. The times were out of joint, with the treason courts sitting in the north-east Cape, the editors of *Ons Land* and the *South African News* behind bars for publishing seditious libel, and the Progressive campaign for the suspension of the Cape constitution beginning to get under way. In August came Kitchener's 'paper bomb', requiring the commandos to surrender by 15 September on pain of life banishment. Three commando leaders, Lötter, Kritzinger and Scheepers were all caught by the British in the eastern Cape in September and October. But Smuts also arrived there in September, eluded capture and moved down into the western province, where he eventually linked up with Maritz's rebels in the north-west, who controlled the whole area except for Kenhardt and Upington. Yet Smuts's field report of 16 December, optimistic though it was as to the mood of Colonial Afrikaners, made it clear that the rebellion could not become mobile because of the scarcity of horses. Meanwhile Kitchener's drives in the northern Free State and eastern Transvaal were placing De Wet and Botha under severe strain, forcing De Wet to quit the eastern Free State and move westwards. De la Rey's capture of Lord Methuen in March was an insignificant if spectacular reversal of fortune.

Devastating attrition was the brute fact underlying the Boer situation. It was not so much the distress in the camps which weighed on the Boers, as that of the many families – 2,540 in the Transvaal alone, according to Louis Botha – who were struggling to survive on the bare veld outside the camps. Understandably, the numbers ready to make peace grew. On 4 March Kitchener was instructed to pass on to the Boer leaders a dispatch from Lord Lansdowne which, in rejecting a Dutch offer to mediate, made it clear that the Boer governments were once again recognised by the British as the spokesmen of their people. Schalk Burger, acting president of the Transvaal, asked for a safe conduct, and managed to persuade even Steyn to talk. The two Boer governments therefore met at Klerksdorp on 9 April, in tents supplied by the British. On 31 May they agreed to terms [see pp. 201–2] and the war ended.

The Anglo-Boer War was fought to determine which white authority held real power in South Africa. In scale and in temper, it was vastly different from all previous Anglo-Boer military encounters. The variety of moods – exalted and cynical, genuine and meretricious, perceptive and banal – which emanated from the white societies in South Africa and the western world, have been well captured in Malvern van Wyk Smith's *Drummer Hodge*, a study of the popular culture in poetry, and verse, of the Anglo-

Boer War. A British officer might publish his diary under the title *The Last of the Gentlemen's Wars*. De la Rey might give point to this by handing over the wounded Lord Methuen to the British and then sending a personal message of condolence to his Lady. But these were at best civilised moments in a war of considerable brutality. Kipling, lionising 'Piet' in his *Five Nations*, reflected this mood. But his vitriolic attack on the Cape partisans in his *Science of Rebellion* and Leipoldt's tragic *Oom Gert vertel* were more in keeping with the dominant mood of the war.

Because it was a war between whites, it was not allowed, save in a marginal sense, to become a black man's war. What was total war for a fifth of the population was therefore no war at all, in theory, for the other four fifths. This was symbolised by Sol Plaatje's description, in his Mafeking diary entry for 9 December 1899, of Rolong herdboys openly guarding their stock in the no-man's-land between the Boer and British lines, and casually picking up the fragments of shells which burst nearby. Yet the role of blacks was by no means as passive or as immune as this description suggests.

Republican laws forbade the carrying of arms by blacks, and Breytenbach affirms that the Boer authorities enforced this rule, limiting blacks who accompanied the commandos to the roles of wagon-drivers or servants. Warwick's observation that the Boers conscripted Africans and Coloured people 'to dig trenches, drive wagons, collect firewood, attend to horses and . . . perform other duties related to their campaign' carries the implication that the ten thousand or so *agterryers* who accompanied the commandos were of at least some military value. Blacks were also commonly required to stand in on the farms of commandeered burghers. On the British side, Roberts and Kitchener used blacks from the farms and the mines as labourers, drivers, convoy guards, dispatch riders, watchmen in blockhouses, and scouts. The black residents of the Mafeking *stadt*, who could move into and out of the town more easily than the whites, often carried messages and raided Boer farms for cattle, which they brought into the town, sometimes after armed clashes with groups of Boers. Further north, where Colonel Herbert Plumer fought a war of movement with the Boer commandos, in competition for the loyalty of the Tswana chiefdoms, mutual raiding occurred between the Boers and Lentswe's Kgatla, who at first planned to be neutral. Boer relations with black chiefdoms depended in large measure on the degree of their economic distress. At the beginning of the war, black levies stationed on the borders of the Transkei, with the support of Cape Mounted Rifle detachments, successfully deterred the commandos from moving into the area; whereas the arming of Zulu in the Nqutu district with 'sticks and assegais' was not sufficient to deter a big Boer cattle raid in September 1901. The Zulu revenge on the Vryheid commando in May 1902, when fifty-six men were speared to death at Holkrans, showed, however, that as a force they were not to be discounted. General Kemp, urging his compatriots to fight on at Vereeniging, claimed to have no problem where food supplies were concerned because he 'took what he wanted from the Kaffirs'. There were, on the other hand, many Boer complaints that the British armed the blacks in order to cause trouble for the Boers. Thus Smuts, in a propaganda letter to W. T. Stead on 4 January 1902 alleged that all the tribes in and around the South African Republic, had been armed by the British military authorities and had 'committed horrible atrocities on fugitive or peaceful women and children'. Ben Viljoen's *Reminiscences* likewise deal with black violence in the Lydenburg district, in association with a troop of white thugs known as Steinacker's Horse. The truth of such reports is hard to ascertain, but increasing deprivation was likely to make Boer–black relations more tense, and in proportion as Boer fortunes declined, so their fear of black molestation grew.

Blacks also found their way into concentration camps, without the same amount of publicity as the whites because neither Emily Hobhouse, who was aware of their situation, nor Dame Millicent Fawcett's Ladies' Committee had the time to pay much attention to them. The British created camps for blacks from the start. In general, African locations were not disturbed, but Africans living on Boer farms were removed, the women and children into camps, the men into labour service. A separate Native Refugee Department was set up in June 1901, and about 4,000 (largely ex-mine workers) drafted into the Army Labour Department for railway maintenance – of whom De Wet captured three hundred in June 1900. Maintenance in African camps was calculated at $4\frac{1}{2}d$ per day, as against $8\frac{1}{2}d$ for whites, partly because Africans were encouraged to grow their own food and build their own huts. There were twenty-nine African camps housing 107,344 by the end of the war. The death toll was not as high as in the white camps during the early months, but at the end of the war it was considerably higher, for the figures did not drop as quickly as they did in the white, and rose to the very high figure of 372 per thousand (as against the highest white figure of 344 in October 1901). The African camps remained under military control after the white had been transferred to civilian. The official figure for African camp deaths was 14,154.

9 The Shaping of a White Dominion

9.1 THE TREATY OF VEREENIGING, 31 MAY 1902

When the Boer leaders met at Klerksdorp in April 1902 to consider making peace, they rallied to the exhortations of the ailing Steyn and proudly approached Kitchener with a peace offer which took their continued independence for granted. They would demilitarise the republics but asked for a treaty of friendship which would settle future economic relationships and political rights, and provide for the arbitration of disputes, equal language rights, and a mutual amnesty. Kitchener agreed to relay their offer to London, knowing that the British Government would not contemplate such a basis for talks. He insisted that the annexation was a *fait accompli*. They retorted that they had no authority to sign away their independence. But Kitchener allowed them facilities for convening a representative assembly of the people with plenipotentiary powers. The two Boer governments accordingly met again on 15 May at Vereeniging, in company with thirty delegates representing the commandos of each republic. These reported on the situation in their districts, which in many cases was critical. Those who still had cattle, grain and horses were generally prepared to fight on, and De Wet in particular, keeping faith with his diehard president, brushed aside obstacles in a rousing speech. But it was Botha and De la Rey who best represented the majority view, as they weighed logistic possibilities, and concluded that to continue a hopeless fight might well weaken their bargaining position in the long run. On the 17th the delegates decided that they could accept a British protectorate, surrender control over foreign policy, and if necessary give up some territory – for example, the Rand and Swaziland.

For a second time Kitchener, who was now joined by Milner, rejected the basis of the Boer offer. This time they insisted that the Boers return to the Middelburg terms as a starting-point for talks. These had treated the annexation of the Republics as irreversible, but included the honouring of war debts incurred by the Republican governments among their own people, loans for the reconstruction of destroyed farms, and an undertaking by the British Government not to enfranchise 'kaffirs' before granting representative government to the Boers, and even then with securities for 'the just predominance of the white race'.

Conversion of the Middelburg terms into those eventually agreed to in

201

the Treaty of Vereeniging was assigned to a committee consisting of Smuts, Hertzog, Kitchener and Sir Richard Solomon, whose work was then reviewed by the British Government. The log-jam among the Boers was largely broken when Botha and De la Rey approached De Wet, to whom Steyn had handed over his authority, and persuaded him in private to agree to peace. The Boer leaders then agreed by 54 votes to 6 to surrender their independence in return for the repatriation and release of prisoners of war, the limited protection of their language in court and school, the expectation of ultimate political autonomy with no target date set, the right to keep firearms, and certain economic safeguards – the right to their property, protection against a land tax to pay war expenses, the honouring of republican war debts to a maximum of £3 million, and the provision of extensive relief for the victims of war. The British also promised not even to consider the enfranchisement of 'natives' until self-government had been introduced, thus giving the Boers a decisive say in the matter. It seems clear, from the explanations given by Worsfold and Marais, that the use of the term 'natives' (where the Middelburg terms had referred to 'Kafirs') left it open for the British to grant political rights to coloured people in any constitution restoring self-government to the new colonies; but when the time came they refrained from doing so. It is not fanciful to see in these terms the delayed influence of the pro-Boer agitation of the war years, which had so attuned British opinion to the wrongs done to the Afrikaners that it was thought necessary to compensate them at the expense of other groups.

9.2   THE CAPE AND NATAL IN THE POST-WAR ERA

South Africa was at last at Milner's feet. He had already moved with the high commissionership to Johannesburg in February 1901, and then received a peerage in England before returning in August to preside over the reconstruction of British South Africa.

Natal, under the governorship of Sir Henry McCallum, presented no problems where Milner's plans were concerned. With its northern boundaries extended by the inclusion of the Vryheid and Utrecht districts of the Transvaal, the Colony received its due reward for faithfulness to the Imperial cause even before the Vereeniging negotiations took place. But the period of peace and quiet which followed during the early years of Reconstruction belied the turbulence in some African locations and in Zululand which were to erupt in rebellion during the premiership of F. R. Moor in 1906. Natal was overtaken by considerable domestic turmoil which brought the Government into conflict with its own African and Indian communities, as well as with the Cape over railway tariffs. The Bambatha rebellion of 1906 [see p. 208] caught the Smythe Government utterly unprepared. Its exemplary execution of rebel leaders after a premature imposition of martial law, and in the face of a British attempt to intervene, together with Moor's unsuccessful attempt to pin responsibility for the events on Dinuzulu in a show trial, gave the Colony a great deal of adverse publicity. At the end of this unhappy period Natal sent a delegation to the National Convention which secured very little of what might have been termed Natal's special interests, until a referendum among the whites indicated that federal safeguards meant less to them than the fear of losing the more material benefits of incorporation in the Union.

In the Cape, the possibility of a Bond majority in the next election seemed to Milner to endanger the British character of South Africa as a whole. For this reason he had urged the suspension of the constitution since early in the war, with considerable support from the Progressives, whose campaign reached a climax with a well-signed petition on 10 May 1902. But the movement was killed by the resistance of a few Cape parliamentarians, led by Sir Gordon Sprigg, who made his second major defence of Cape parliamentary privilege at the Colonial Conference of 1902 in London (the first having been in 1869, his first year as a member of the old Cape House, when he had confronted and helped to defeat the suspensionist plans of Sir Philip Wodehouse). On this occasion he won the ear of Joseph Chamberlain and of the conference as a whole, despite the opposition of Natal's premier, Hime. So serious was the rift between Chamberlain and Milner on this issue, that it must be seen as one of the main reasons for Chamberlain's visit to South Africa in November 1902. But suspension ceased to matter in practice because the disfranchisement of Cape rebels by the military courts ensured a Progressive victory in the Cape elections of 1904, despite signs of an electoral swing in favour of the Bond. Sprigg undeservedly lost the East London seat which he had held for over forty years, and the Progressive leadership fell into Jameson's hands.

Jameson's victory postponed the political crisis; but ironically it did not preserve that sure base for British power which all parties had expected of such a premier. In a fairly successful bid to befriend Afrikanerdom, he carried out a redistribution of parliamentary seats with mathematical objectivity which only gave his party a very slight advantage, and then reduced the disfranchisement of rank-and-file rebels from a lifespan to five years, thus preparing the ground for his own defeat in 1908. For the rest, he tried to secure financial compensation for the victims of war damage (until this was killed by the financial crisis in 1907), worked hard to satisfy the farmers' interests by irrigation and agricultural credit legislation, coupled with protective tariffs, and sought popularity with the white electorate by measures to curb Chinese immigration and entrench white privilege in the government schools.

9.3 MILNER AND RECONSTRUCTION

As Governor of the Transvaal and the Orange River Colony, Milner had the help of Lieutenant-Governors Sir Arthur Lawley and Sir Hamilton Goold-Adams respectively, each with an executive council which took over from the military authorities in June 1902. Legislative councils consisting of officials and nominees were appointed soon afterwards, both holding their first sessions in 1903. In June that year an Inter-Colonial Council of four nominees (later raised to twelve) and fourteen officials came into being. This was Milner's brainchild, and it was given special responsibility for certain key agencies which straddled both the new colonies in a calculated bid to break down the provincial spirit – notably the Central South African Railways (an amalgamation of the Free State governmental and Transvaal private companies), Baden-Powell's South African Constabulary, repatriation, and schools. For administrative skill, Milner relied on the talented but controversial group of Oxford bachelors dubbed by Merriman his 'Kindergarten'.

To achieve the political conversion of the new colonies, Milner attached great importance to their economic recovery. Indeed, the significance of his efforts in this direction has been re-emphasised in recent years by a fresh look at his activities in the light of an assumed neo-mercantilist concern in the British banking world to maintain London's importance as a money market in an era of rapidly expanding international trade. The Bank of England was not vulnerable to foreign competition before 1914; but this need not detract from the suggestion of Marks and Trapido that Milner, profiting from financial experience gained in England and Egypt, strove to make southern Africa a place fit for finance capitalism to work in, and that he succeeded in this aim. He and the maverick FitzPatrick spoke with a common mind on many matters, while it is clear from accounts of Milner's approach to the labour problem by Denoon, Richardson and Levy that he was keen to promote the prosperity of the Chamber of Mines. He clearly saw that his urgent task was to bring the mines back into full production as quickly as possible, get the farmers back onto the land and their desolated farms re-stocked, build up railway communications for the proper flow of goods, and complete the drive towards a customs union which had stopped short before the war.

He received authority to raise a loan of £35 million under Imperial guarantee, and this, with an increase of the gold profits tax from 5 to 10 per cent to bring in an extra £500,000 a year, served to prime the pump, even though only £10 million were available for development as distinct from other commitments. Gold mining returned to its pre-war production level by 1904 and expanded steadily thereafter, the value of gold mined rising from fractionally over £1 million in 1901 to £20.9 million in 1905 and £32 million in 1910. This happened in spite of a serious labour crisis which Milner resolved, first, by a not very advantageous *modus vivendi* concluded with the Governor of Mozambique in December 1901 for the engagement of Shangaan workers, and second, by the introduction of indentured Chinese labourers from 1904.

The Chinese made it possible for expansion to take place while the machinery for the recruitment of African labour was getting into gear again, which it did from about 1907. This ensured the continuity of labour patterns on the mines which might otherwise have been subjected to severe pressure from the advocates of a 'white labour policy'; but the very fact that continuities were not broken at this stage helped to nurture tensions for a later age, as is argued elsewhere [see pp. 499–500]. Meanwhile the demand for labour remained greater than the supply, largely on account of the need for workers to man the railway construction projects and rebuild the farms, and a tendency for Africans to withhold their labour from the mines in response to substantial wage reductions.

The establishment of the Central South African Railways at the Bloemfontein railway conference in March 1903 resulted, during the next few years, in the completion of lines from Kimberley to the Rand, from the Rand to Zeerust, and of another joining the Natal and Orange River Colony systems between Ladysmith and Kroonstad, as well as the doubling of the line from Lourenco Marques to Witbank [see Map 12]. At the same time an experimental pan-South African Customs Union was set up in 1903, all internal customs dues were abolished, and a 10 per cent *ad valorem* duty imposed on imports from outside, with 25 per cent Imperial preference – all for a two-year trial period. Never had southern Africa had such a fluid circulatory system. It would not be long before the blockages reappeared; but when they did, the experience of internal free trade and open rail communications had created sufficient momentum to bring about political unification [see pp. 220–1].

Restoration of the farms and the repatriation of Boer prisoners was the task of a central committee operating through local commissions. The £3 million allotted under the terms of Vereeniging were to be divided among the ex-burghers of the Republics who could prove war losses, whichever side they had fought for. The actual sum spent on relief and repatriation amounted to over £16 million, in grants and loans administered by a Repatriation Department in the case of whites, and a much less well endowed Native Refugee Department in the case of blacks. Complaints among the Boers that those who had supported the British were favoured at the expense of those who had not were frequently made – without justification, it seems, for it was only after the Scouts had made special representations that they received repatriation benefits at all. Grundlingh comments that 'the great bulk of them . . . were landless men, and the bitterender landlords usually refused to take back *bywoners* who had fought on the British side'. But in practice the new administration worked hard to provide the Boers with ploughs, seed, and rations until they could feed themselves, and introduced veterinary services to deal with stock disease. By the end of 1902, most of the people were back on the land, and the problem of planting food for the following year more or less solved. What Milner could not have reckoned with, however, was the sustained drought conditions of 1903–8, which made rural recovery very difficult.

Milner hoped also to place English-speakers on the land so as to break down the sharp occupational division between rural Afrikaners and urban British. He wanted a massive infusion of English-speakers into the new colonies – 'a good class of settler – not "tommies" but men with farming experience and a little capital – Australians, Canadians, Scottish Lowland farmers, the best of the Yeomanry, and the best of the young British Colonists from the Cape and Natal'. He wanted to bring in 10,000 settlers 'within a twelvemonth'. Schemes for land settlement started by the Duke of Westminster, Lord Lovat and Sir Percy Fitzpatrick received his support.

But he complained to Chamberlain in January 1902 that the means at his disposal for acquiring land were 'quite inadequate' because it was difficult to allocate the money needed for land purchase from the funds available, and he lacked sufficient power of expropriation. All told, Milner's immigration policy settled only about 1,300 English-speaking heads of families on the land, and therefore failed in its political purpose.

Milner denied that his purpose was to plough the Afrikaner under: 'I no more want to exterminate the Dutch than I want to exterminate the British,' he wrote; but he wished to ensure the dominance of the British element, politically and culturally. Therefore instruction through the Dutch language was not to be allowed in the government schools: 'Dutch should only be used to teach English, and English to teach everything else.' He attached special importance to school textbooks, in particular, history books:

> A good world history would be worth anything. . . . Everything that makes South African children look outside South Africa and *realize the world* makes for peace. Everything that cramps and confines their views to South Africa only . . . makes for Afrikanerdom and further discord.

An Englishwoman, Bertha Synge, obliged with a *Story of the World* in five substantial volumes of equal length and difficulty, covering everything from the ancient world to the Victorian Empire (which formed the theme of the final volume). The tone was conciliatory towards the Boer, flattering his physique and his courage but not his culture, and setting out a new political orthodoxy: 'Today Boer and Briton stand shoulder to shoulder, "forged in strong fires, by equal war made one", both members of one great Empire, and as time rolls onward into space, they may feel

> The touch of human brotherhood, and act
> As one great nation, true and strong as steel.'

In the final resort, Milner intended to withhold political power from the whites of the new colonies until British ascendancy was assured, arguing that 'if, ten years hence, there are three men of British race to two of Dutch, the country will be safe and prosperous. If there are three of Dutch to two of British, we shall have perpetual difficulty.' But, rather like Lord Durham on French Canada, Milner miscalculated. Possessing in Stokes's words, 'faith in a planned society conceived and ordered by the scientific intelligence', he ran into serious opposition from those who lacked his kind of confidence, and from those who objected to their allotted place in his scheme of things. Afrikaners, in general, intensely resented his programme, but also discovered a way of defeating it. The English-speaking whites were divided over his aims, and ended by failing to give him the degree of support which he required if his policies were to succeed.

9.4 THE MILNER REGIME AND SOUTH AFRICAN BLACKS: THE LAGDEN COMMISSION, SEGREGATION AND THE ZULU REBELLION OF 1906

Meanwhile Africans, Asians and Coloured people experienced during the Milner era a series of attacks on their position in society which effectively cut them off from access to full citizenship. It is even arguable, as Odendaal has shown, that they were worse off in the new colonies after the war than they had been in the old republics, and now living under stricter laws more strictly enforced. African access to political power was blocked off by Article 8 of the Treaty of Vereeniging which made their enfranchisement dependent on the consent of the white majority. This was a victory for Milner, for Chamberlain had at first insisted on the enfranchisement of blacks as a condition for self-government. In December 1901 Milner had privately rejected the desirability of political equality for blacks, and recommended that they should be represented in the legislatures by whites nominated for the purpose. He told Chamberlain that the blacks should not be forced to change their ways or to work for whites, but that the whites should teach them 'habits of regular and skilled labour' and keep them severely away from strong drink. He placed blacks low on the Great Chain of Being, as people to be 'well-treated' and 'justly governed'.

To achieve uniformity in native policy, Milner appointed a South African Native Affairs Commission in 1903 to make recommendations to the various governments 'with the object of arriving at a common understanding' against the day when South African federation would be achieved. Sir Godfrey Lagden, his Commissioner for Native Affairs, presided over this almost exclusively English-speaking body. It produced a report in 1905 which reflected the High Commissioner's own concern for social planning, and introduced new rigidities into South African thinking about race relations which had an immense influence on later political debate. It formalised the idea of segregation in a new way. In the first place, it envisaged the territorial separation of black and white as a permanent, mandatory principle of land ownership. The background is important for an understanding of its proposals. In 1904 the redelimitation of Zululand had been completed, and a handy precedent created under which two-fifths of what was left of that territory was thrown open to competitive purchase by whites only. In 1905, by contrast, the Transvaal Supreme Court reversed, in *Tsewu's case*, a Republican rule of 1881 which had laid down that all black privately-owned land had to be held on their behalf by the Native Locations Commission in trust. The rule was now declared void because it rested on the authority of a mere resolution of the Volksraad. Its revocation accelerated a process which had already started, under which black syndicates raised substantial sums of money to buy white-owned farms, which often belonged to people who had been impoverished by the war and needed to sell. There was dismay in the white community at the reversion of land under quitrent title to a form of traditional tenure, and over the thought that land acquired by conquest should be lost through resale in this manner. The Lagden Commission therefore sought to put their minds at rest by urging that the separation of black and white areas should be brought about 'by legislative enactment . . . with a view to finality'. The Commission also gave approval to the systematic establishment of segregated locations for urban Africans, though – to its credit – it saw these less as dumping grounds for black labour, than as places where blacks could set up comfortable homes of their own. The Lagden Commission also urged the separation of blacks from whites in political life, with Africans in all the colonies represented by whites only in the federal legislature of the future. The Commission's territorial and urban proposals were implemented in 1913 and 1923 respectively [see pp. 234–6]. Its proposals for political segregation, after rejection by the National Convention in 1909, were later carried out in modified form under Hertzog's legislation of 1936 [see pp. 280–4].

There was a good deal of open violence between black and white during the first decade of the twentieth century, for which the Zulu rebellion of 1906 provides the chief focal point. The suppression of the Herero and the Maji-Maji rebellions by the Germans, and of the Zulu by the Natalians, involved the shedding of a lot of blood. Whether these risings were coordinated in Rand mine compounds seems at best speculation, but Denoon's suggestion that black worker consciousness was growing, is a point which needs to be stressed.

The Zulu rebellion took the authorities by surprise, but ought not to have done so. Shepstonian authoritarianism, streamlined and consolidated in the Natal Native Code of 1891, had given the Governor almost unlimited powers over blacks, which he used on the advice of the Executive Council rather than as a reserve power as was originally intended. This power had already been used to dismiss chiefs without trial, and to enforce the *isibalo* (labour tax), a *corvée* imposed arbitrarily on nearly a tenth of the male black population in return for rations and a small wage. Land shortage aggravated discontent, especially in Zululand, where the final report of the Delimitation Commission in 1905 had set aside 2.6 million acres for white settlement (mainly for the extension of sugar plantations), leaving only 3.9 million acres in tribal hands. Stock and crop diseases compounded the rural distress, while in 1906 the Government imposed a poll tax of £1 on every male not liable for the hut tax, hoping thus to catch the young (who were frequently the ones who raised the cash to pay the hut tax anyway).

Against a background of rumour, much of it relating to the supposed restlessness of the evergreen but not irresponsible Dinuzulu, the Zulu rebellion developed out of a series of small incidents initially connected with refusals to pay the poll tax. After the killing of two white Natal policemen at Byrnetown, the Government imposed martial law, and over a dozen men who had resisted were summarily executed, despite remonstrations by the British Government which caused the Natal ministers to resign in protest. When Bambatha, a petty chief in the Greytown area, rose in April and fled across the Tugela to Sigananda's kraal in the Nkandla Forest, the black resistance assumed more serious proportions. But Bambatha, the head of an impoverished tribe (the Zondi), had a long history of conflict with the authorities, and left no reason for going into rebellion, or even any indication of what he hoped to achieve, beyond what can be inferred from his actions: he had refused to pay the poll tax, failed to report that some of his men were armed, and then reacted to his own deposition by kidnapping his successor, before fleeing across the Tugela to avoid capture by Colonial forces. Sigananda, his Chube host, a man reputedly in his nineties, who had served Shaka, helped to increase the rebel force. But the rebels had no apparent plan of campaign. They were defeated with heavy losses in the Mome Gorge, near Cetshwayo's grave, by Col. D. Mackenzie, Bambatha himself being killed and Sigananda captured. Only after they had been defeated did rebellion flare up in Natal proper, in the Mapumulo district. There, too, the resistance was weak, the rebels' strategy directionless, and the slaughter massive in relation to the losses on the Colonial side. Altogether, only twenty-four white soldiers and about six white civilians were killed during the rising, as against over three thousand blacks (Marks).

9.5 INDEPENDENT CHURCHES AND THE GROWTH OF AFRICAN AND COLOURED POLITICAL MOVEMENTS

Black protest took other forms than that of uncoordinated civil disobedience. Independent churches had begun to spread as vehicles of religious enthusiasm and political protest, at least since Nehemiah Tile's Thembu Church had been set up in 1884. The founding of Mangena Mokone's Ethiopian Church in Pretoria in 1892, after Mokone and others had been excluded from a meeting of white Wesleyans in Pretoria, was an important occasion. He was joined four years later by James M. Dwane (like Tile and Mokone, and ex-Methodist minister) and they both affiliated to the African Methodist Episcopal Church, an American foundation, in 1896. Two years later, Bishop H. M. Turner of the A.M.E.C. visited South Africa, consecrated Dwane an assistant bishop, and ordained over sixty priests. So rapidly did the movement spread that it claimed 10,000 members distributed among 73 congregations by 1898. Dwane led his followers out of the A.M.E.C. as a result of a dispute with its American leaders, and after a decade of negotiations they entered into communion with the Anglicans as the Order of Ethiopia. Other groups split away from the A.M.E.C. in quest of black religious autonomy. In a similar manner, the Rev. Pambani Mzimba broke away from the Presbyterian Free Church of Scotland Mission in 1898 to set up a Bantu Presbyterian Church.

The extent to which the black separatist churches which broke away at this time were politicised is in dispute. Wallace G. Mills has argued for a 'pre-millenarian' revivalism in black Christianity which preceded political separatism, and the 'Taylor Movement' at Healdtown in 1866 gives a certain support to his theory. Sundkler has drawn a broad distinction between religious movements of 'Zionist' (revivalist) and 'Ethiopian' (political) characteristics. It is not always easy, as Saunders has suggested, in reply to Mills, to separate the two. Odendaal has pointed out that it was as important for the Ethiopians to have a political thrust as it was for them to conceal it. The very name suggested black nationalism in the decade of the Ethiopian victory over the Italians at Adowa, but the founding of the church had preceded that event. Mzimba may not have taken a political stance at first, but he did become involved in political activity after his secession. To some extent the separatist movements of the 1890s and after were drawn into a loose association across the sub-continent from the Cape to Nyasaland by the efforts of the radical British missionary, Joseph Booth, who visited the Cape and Natal in 1896–97, and published his pamphlet *Africa for the African* in the latter year. There was also some Ethiopian involvement in the Zulu rebellion of 1906, but as Marks has shown, the connection was not at all straightforward. The movement was accepted as legitimate in the Cape and the Transvaal, but denied legal status in Natal and the O.R.C., where it was officially linked with black nationalism by the authorities.

There was also a plethora of explicitly secular black political movements dating from the last century like the South African Native Congress founded in 1892 [see p. 98] and the Transkei Native Vigilance Association of Enoch Mamba of Idutywa. Martin Luthuli described a Natal Native Congress, of which he had been chairman, to the Lagden Commission in May 1904. It had close mission associations, a secretariat based on Verulam, a scattering of branches, and an ability to draw up to a hundred people to its meetings, which had tried to put pressure on the Natal Government over such issues as political representation, education and forced labour. The O.R.C.'s Native Vigilance Association of 1904 (sometimes known as the O.R.C. Native Congress), which had an executive composed of Africans from all four colonies and one Coloured man, was described by one of them as 'more or less governed' by the Church's laws, two of its members belonging to the A.M.E.C.. It campaigned to promote industrial education, location self-government and urban property rights. It stressed political rights and civil liberty in the urban areas, and denounced casual labour regulations about to be imposed, and the carrying of passes by African women. In 1907 it petitioned the King for the franchise. In the northern Colony there was a Transvaal Congress, a Bapedi Union and a Basuto Association, while a United Native Political Association of the Transvaal Colony made several appeals to the Imperial Government which were ignored, among them a petition for the franchise in April 1905.

The leading political organisation to emerge among the Coloured people, namely the African Political (later People's) Organisation, was established in 1902. The A.P.O. was divided over whether to support Jameson's Progressives or the Bond-dominated South African Party, its members falling in behind F.Z.S. Peregrino and John Tobin respectively; but in 1905 it elected Dr A. Abdurahman, a Cape Malay doctor as president, and tried to drive a hard bargain for Coloured rights without downplaying those of Africans. Under his leadership it fought against the Cape School Board Act of 1905, which made schooling compulsory for white but not for Coloured children. It also sent a deputation to London in 1907 to ask for political rights under the new Transvaal constitution though without success. The A.P.O. also sent delegates to the S.A. Native Congress gatherings from time to time.

9.6   GANDHI

The decade also witnessed further friction between the Indian community of the Transvaal and the Colonial Government, in which M. K. Gandhi again took up his compatriots' cause [see p. 106]. Gandhi had been in touch with Protestant Christian influences. His newspaper, *Indian Opinion*, attributed some of his inspiration to great figures such as Socrates, Ruskin and Thoreau. He named his Transvaal commune after Tolstoy, though his settlement at Phoenix in Natal seems also to have drawn on the planning of J. L. Dube (Swan). Before 1906 he had started to turn more deliberately to the teachings of the Jain sect of Hinduism, in which he had been brought up, linking their pacifism with an ascetic dedication to poverty and a renunciation of sexual activity in marriage, both forms of self-discipline which he found necessary for the kind of resistance to his people's oppression which he put into practice. This was the exercise of *satyagraha* ('soul force'), involving totally honest non-violent non-compliance with the offending law, the endurance of suffering or imprisonment if necessary, without ceasing to show respect to those who made the law or enforced it. The issue on which he first tested his method was the Transvaal Registration law of 1906, under which Indians were obliged to carry passes bearing their fingerprints. Prior to the grant of responsible government to the Transvaal, Gandhi was able to persuade the British Government to disallow this objectionable measure, and when it was brought back in 1908, after the grant of self-government, the Indian community organised a massive pass-burning demonstration, as a result of which Gandhi and many of his associates were arrested. While in prison, he worked out an acceptable formula with Smuts for the registration of Indians, only to fall out with Smuts afterwards, following a misunderstanding of the nature of their written agreement over which, as discerning commentators concur, there is room for more than one interpretation. Pillay and Swan have described the campaign of 1906–8 as a failure, and attributed this to Gandhi's excessive reliance on the older merchant elite as the basis of his support; but even if this was true, it served to establish Gandhi as a brilliant leader of protest and gave publicity to the methods of *satyagraha*, which would be used again.

9.7   THE REVIVAL OF AFRIKANERDOM

The Afrikaners took less time than might have been expected to organise their opposition to Milner's regime. Chamberlain's visit in November 1902 gave Botha, Smuts, Hertzog and others an opportunity, which they used, to cross swords with a long-standing adversary. On 2 July 1903, Botha and

Smuts, supported by Emily Hobhouse, addressed a protest meeting at Heidelberg, held with Milner's permission and in the presence of a good spread of ex-commando leaders as well as the South African Constabulary. Their mood was basically unconciliatory. On the argument that nothing short of self-government would satisfy them, they subsequently refused to serve on Milner's Legislative Council, a nominee body which included FitzPatrick and Farrar, a nucleus of English-speaking businessmen, a few *hensoppers*, and a small group of Afrikaner officials from republican days. In May 1904 several hundred Boer representatives met in Pretoria to establish their own political organisation, *Het Volk*, which was formally constituted on 28 January 1905. This movement, built up at first under cover of farmers' associations, spread through the activities of ex-Republican leaders who went through the districts in pairs, sometimes the same districts they had toured in 1900 to bring the commandos back into the field.

In the O.R.C. a congress met at Brandfort on 1 December 1904, to act as a sounding board for Boer grievances against the post-war settlement, and this led to the founding of *Orangia Unie* in July 1905.

These meetings represent the beginnings of a return by Afrikanerdom to a purposeful role in public affairs, and it is now possible, thanks largely to the analytical studies of Moodie and Hexham, to see these activities in overall perspective. The meetings displayed a good deal of pent-up anger, above all over the introduction of the Chinese [see p. 498], and the supposedly inequitable distribution of relief funds (though it was repatriated ex-commandos rather than *bywoner hensoppers* who did most of the complaining). But the meetings also signified a major reshaping of Afrikaner political attitudes in response to the experience of suffering and defeat. The Second Afrikaans Language Movement was born. It was a much more mature movement that its predecessor of the 1870s. Once again, the rival merits of simplified Dutch and Afrikaans were debated, with 'Onze Jan' Hofmeyr maintaining his earlier conservative line, while others like Gustav Preller and D. F. Malan argued in favour of Afrikaans. This time the supporters of Afrikaans, with the poetry of 'Totius' (Ds. J. D. du Toit, S. J.'s son), Jan F. E. Celliers, and Eugene Marais to back their cause, spoke with more confidence, so that the campaign which they started gained steadily until Afrikaans eventually became recognised as an official language of the Union in 1925. It was the experience of wartime suffering that produced poems of the quality of *Dis al, Winternag*, and *By die Monument*. But it was the rootlessness engendered by the drift of unemployed *bywoners* to town – the first major migration of Afrikaans-speaking poor whites – that caused real anxiety in the minds of the cultural leaders of Afrikanerdom. The Afrikaner people, saved from physical obliteration by Vereeniging, now needed to be saved from cultural obliteration at the hands of Milner's regiment of English-speaking teachers.

The battle for the minds of the Afrikaners centred largely on the classroom, and a new drive was started to establish Christian National schools in which the language of instruction could be Dutch, not English, and in which the educational rationale could be cooperation between

Church, school and family in the upbringing of the child. The Christian National Education (C.N.O.) movement succumbed, largely for financial reasons, within a year or two of its inception, and its failure to take root created a new ideological rift within Afrikanerdom. As Moodie has emphasised, the N. G. Kerk, claiming a membership of about four-fifths of Afrikanerdom, found a way to identify itself with the sufferings of the Afrikaner people without being untrue to its theology. It may have felt obliged to impose a ban on clerical participation in politics, but it took up the cause of the poor white in the name of social welfare, backed the C.N.O. movement, and in doing so became increasingly a *volkskerk*, directing its charity inwards, in the promotion of what Moodie has helpfully called a 'civil' religion. The Doppers, though only a small minority, went even further. Hexham has stressed the positive character of their early post-war gatherings, the firm reassertion of their expectation of divine favour after chastisement, their commitment to a policy of religious isolation as the way to rebuild their strength, and their anger at Botha and Smuts for abandoning the C.N.O. movement for fear of offending the British on the eve of self-government in 1907. The Doppers, with the help of the newspaper, *Het Westen*, started the political ferment which would eventually provide General Hertzog – though he was far from being a Dopper himself – with considerable supportive propaganda at the time of his breach with Botha in 1912. In their promotion of Dingaan's Day (later the 'Day of the Covenant') as a *volk* festival, and in their strong republican ideology at a time when republican thinking was discouraged, they suggest a continuity between the Calvinism of Kruger's Transvaal and the resurfacing of that ideology (if that is the appropriate term) in the Afrikaner Broederbond after 1918. Their principle of 'strength in isolation' would find a secular equivalent in Hertzog's doctrine of 'two streams', and there is ground for thinking, with Hexham, that it provided a philosophical basis for latter-day apartheid, so long as the point is not made more forcefully than that.

But if the mood of the Afrikaner revival had remained exclusively bitter, or exclusively preoccupied with questions which concerned the Afrikaner alone, it could have produced a series of barren confrontations, leading perhaps to another trial of strength with the British, and achieved nothing. It developed into a dynamic movement because its more sophisticated leaders realised the importance, in context, of conciliation. Conciliation was necessary to heal the rifts within Afrikanerdom between the *bittereinder* and the National Scout. It was necessary, further, to destroy the ill-feeling between Dutch- and English-speaker on South African soil, to say nothing of the gulf that had to be bridged between the Imperial Government and its new subjects north of the Orange. The Cape Bondsmen were the first to appreciate the value of a change in tactics, which they put into practice with great success during Chamberlain's tour in February 1903 (Davenport). At the emotional level they showed that concessions could follow from ostentatiously burying the hatchet. Before long, however, Afrikaner leaders began to realise that it was not merely possible to de-claw the lion by gentle words: one could actually divide the South

African British and derive political advantage from the exercise, by exploiting the growing opposition between capital and labour. Het Volk and the Orangia Unie began to open their doors to the English-speaking artisan, and the latter began to respond. The issue of Chinese labour was at first ideally suited to this purpose, for while the Afrikaner viewed the Chinese as an unnecessary complication of an already difficult racial problem, the English worker saw him as a potential rival.

Botha and Smuts developed the new tactics with finesse. While setting their sights firmly on responsible government, they cultivated an approach to the British authorities which became more accommodating with the passage time. The prospect of governing the Colony led them to suppress republican leanings and to cease to regard the sectional promotion of Afrikaner interests as a top priority. Whether they fully saw the political dangers of this may be doubted, and their reputations suffered enormously in Nationalist circles because of it. But in moving closer to the Rand capitalists they lost their contact with the English-speaking working man.

9.8   THE TRANSVAAL BRITISH

The political behaviour of the Transvaal British in the period after the Anglo-Boer war has been much debated in recent years. The debate has centred on the question whether the Uitlanders were a single, coherent political group; or whether they were fundamentally split on interest lines between capitalists and workers; or whether the capitalists were divided into two distinct groups – that is, long-term investors in deep level operations on the one hand, and quick-profit outcroppers linked with the Premier diamond interest on the other. One also needs to ask whether the workers, in turn, were a single group, or split between genuine socialists who desired no colour bar, and an 'aristocracy of labour' bent on maintaining white privilege.

The unity of the Uitlander community appeared to hold good at the end of the war, when Milner was careful to include workers' leaders in his nominee council for Johannesburg in 1901. But he soon ran into trouble. The British victory had raised Uitlander expectations, their leaders looked forward to political opportunities and to office, and when some (but by no means all) of the top political posts went to Milner's young men from Oxford, there was manifest resentment, which was not assuaged when Milner gave Johannesburg an elective council in 1903 because he also decided against making Johannesburg the capital.

Uitlander impatience for political change found expression in August 1902 with the founding of a Transvaal Political Association under the leadership of Dale Lace, a diamond magnate. This body, which arose out of a meeting called to oppose Chamberlain's proposed war levy on the Transvaal, and to demand political reform, at first enjoyed the support of 'virtually the whole English-speaking white community' (Denoon). But it was soon weakened by the withdrawal of several of its leaders – not so much gold magnates with deep level interests, as Denoon initially supposed, as 'the leading men of Johannesburg of all walks of life, mining, professional, commercial and other men', in Mawby's words. FitzPatrick, one of the prime objectors, wrote that they were 'not going to have any manufactured agitation of this sort to hamper Lord Milner', and set about the reduction of the war levy in more subtle ways.

On 22 November 1904, these dissidents formed a Transvaal Progressive Association under the chairmanship of Sir George Farrar, though the moving spirit was really FitzPatrick. The Progressives came into being with a six-point manifesto which included a demand for representative but not responsible government. They were not anxious for self-government until they could be sure that, as a community, the English-speakers could retain control of the Colony, and for that reason they would not be drawn into open confrontation with Milner. They quickly expanded into a large organization, claiming forty-three branches scattered through the Rand and Pretoria, and 32,000 members by February 1905. Their membership was too diverse to give them an obvious class character, though members of the Chamber of Mines were prominent in the organisation.

Meanwhile a Transvaal Responsible Government Association under the leadership of E. P. Solomon, brother of Sir Richard, Milner's Attorney-General, was formed in December 1904. These 'Responsibles', were almost entirely Johannesburg-based, and by May 1905 had a mere 5,000 members. Their distinguishing feature, as their name implied, was a common desire for immediate self-government, and this drew them into an agreement with Het Volk in March 1905, under which Het Volk undertook to refrain from criticising Chinese labour, to which the Responsibles were committed, while the Responsibles agreed to withdraw their support for Milner's policy of anglicising the educational system, and to accept the restriction of the franchise to whites. This association between Het Volk and the Responsibles was very influential in undermining Milner's strategy, especially after the return of the British Liberals to power in 1906.

Light has been thrown on the leading white workers' organisations in the political and industrial fields by the researches of Ticktin and Katz. The Transvaal Labour Party (founded in November 1904), the Political Labour League (September 1905) and the Labour Representation Committee (December 1906) were the most significant political groups. They were not in any significant way socialist. Their main preoccupation was the protection of white artisan interests, and subject to this qualification they were not unsympathetic to the Afrikaner who still stood on the edge of industry. Several craft unions – notably the Engine-drivers, the Engineers, the Tramway employees and the Typographers – together with the Witwatersrand Trades and Labour Council (formed in 1902), attended the opening meeting of the L.R.C. A notable absentee from this meeting was the Transvaal Miners' Association (formed in April 1902), which stayed out of labour politics until 1912, partly on account of its opposition to Creswell's white labour policy [see p. 498]. The miners, who were well organised, and launched strikes on Crown and Village Main Reefs in 1902, and at Knight's Deep in 1907, had a memory of unsuccessful industrial action in the years before the war, and were embittered by the high mortality rate from

GOING   COMING

8   The cartoonist D. C. Boonzaier gives a white workers' view on the importation of Chinese labour to the Transvaal, 1905

phthisis among underground workers. They were also apprehensive over the introduction of Chinese labour, which was at first widely held to be a threat to white employment on the mines, though in the longer term it was seen to have increased white opportunities and even to have saved white industrial privilege. The white miners and the labour groups in general had it in for the Rand capitalists, and to this end they made common cause with the Responsibles and Het Volk, with whom they made election pacts in respect of some Rand seats, but not all, in the 1907 general election.

9.9   THE MOVE TOWARDS RESPONSIBLE GOVERNMENT IN THE TRANSVAAL AND ORANGE RIVER COLONY

British policy after the Peace of Vereeniging was more responsive to trends in white politics than in black. Milner knew well before his recall in March 1905 that his bid to establish British dominance north of the Vaal had failed. On 2 May 1904 he suggested to Alfred Lyttelton, Chamberlain's successor, that electives might replace the nominees in the Transvaal Legislative Council. Lyttelton agreed in principle in July, so in December Milner outlined proposals for representative government, based on £100 property, £10 rent, or £100 income qualifications, which were low enough to admit most adult white townsmen, but too high for most white rural squatters. For the electoral divisions, Milner put forward two alternatives: either a system of equal constituencies, each returning three members (Scheme A), or a system of single-member constituencies corresponding approximately to existing magisterial districts (Scheme B). He envisaged a legislature of thirty under Scheme A, and thirty-five under Scheme B, plus six to nine officials. He evidently did not anticipate the reactions which greeted his plan. The Colonial Office, which already looked askance at his Inter-Colonial Council, felt that it would give the electorate enough power to make government impossible. Het Volk and the Responsibles protested that the scheme did not go far enoough, while the Progressives expressed fears of an Afrikaner takeover, and only gradually began to change their tune as the possibility of winning an election under Milner's rules occurred to them. Although Milner began to recoil from the idea of change, Lyttelton felt that the withdrawal of the offer was now unthinkable, and the British Government came out with a new constitution for the Transvaal to take effect on Milner's retirement. This, the Lyttelton Constitution, was based on Milner's Scheme B. It met the Progressives' wishes, which had been energetically canvassed by FitzPatrick, with a legislative assembly of up to thirty-five white members, elected by whites only, in single-member constituencies. These were to be delimited so as to contain an equal number of voters, with a maximum variation of 5 per cent from the average, and to be regularly revised. But before the new constitution could be implemented, it was necessary to draw up new voters' rolls.

In the meantime the Unionist Government in Britain fell from power in December 1905. The new Liberal Ministry under Sir Henry Campbell-Bannerman reconsidered Lyttelton's document, and on the recommendation of a cabinet committee under Lord Loreburn decided to offer the Transvaal full responsible government. Churchill, Under-Secretary of State for the Colonies, argued eloquently that nothing less would do for a 'war-torn country still red-hot from race hatred'. Several cabinet ministers saw responsible government as a means of facilitating the decision, already taken, to ban the further importation of Chinese labour (Bennett); but – as Hyam notes – the decision to grant greater political freedom was not seen by them as a concession made necessary by this economic clampdown. It was a calculated decision taken on its own merits.

Smuts visited London in January and February 1906, bearing a memorandum in support of responsible government which asked for a white 'population' rather than a white 'voters' basis in the new delimitation. He came away from the meeting with Campbell-Bannerman feeling that he had convinced the Liberal premier that this was the way to settle the future of South Africa. But Smuts's tactics aroused suspicion. Julius Wernher, whom Smuts also called on, found him 'intelligent and shrewd', and almost trusted him. The Cabinet had been put on its guard against Smuts by Selborne. As it had already decided to grant responsible government, the only doubts still to be cleared up were procedural and tactical: how to set about the dismantling of the Lyttelton constitution, which was technically in force, and whether to present the policy of the new Government as a stage in a continuously evolving bi-partisan colonial policy, or as a dramatic break with the past, intended to bring about a miracle of reconciliation. It does not seem necessary to belittle the personal impact of Smuts on Campbell-Bannerman, or – as Le May stresses – that of Campbell-Bannerman on Smuts. The rapport which clearly grew between them,

nurtured on Smuts's side by the memory of the 'methods of of barbarism'
speech, gave Campbell-Bannerman encouragement to present his government's policy in the shape of a dramatic new deal, a 'magnanimous gesture'
for the world (and above all the imperialists in his own party) to take note
of. There was a stormy cabinet meeting on 8 February, the day after the
interview, when Campbell-Bannerman argued in favour of sending a Royal
Commission to South Africa in face of Elgin's resistance. But it was Elgin
who told Selborne on 18 February that the Lyttelton Constitution had been
abandoned, and that the intention was to give the Transvaal full self-
government. The magnanimity of the offer received wide acclaim, even if
to Milner's supporters it was a 'great betrayal'. It was less widely realised
that the British Government was 'absolutely determined', in the words of a
secret memorandum by Churchill, 'to maintain . . . a numerical majority
of a loyal and English population', and that it had come to see the grant of
self-government on the basis of 'one vote, one value' as the only possible
way of retaining influence, short of the uneconomical use of force, in a part
of the world where Afrikaner power was bound one day to reassert itself.

The Committee of Inquiry which the British Government decided to
send to South Africa was led by Sir Joseph West Ridgeway, an ex-
Governor of Ceylon. They were to take soundings of opinion in the
Transvaal and supplement the not altogether welcome communications of
Lord Selborne, who was fighting a rearguard action on behalf of the
Transvaal British. The West Ridgeway Committee first interviewed Het
Volk's leaders in Pretoria, and was struck by their moderation, and their
preparedness to accept a constitution which did not give them an immediate majority in the legislature, if only control were not allowed to pass into
the hands of the Chamber of Mines. (Smuts had also taken this line in his
February memorandum.) The Progressives, by contrast, appeared dis-
united, and by stressing the danger of Boer dominance they failed to get
their objections across to the Committee when Het Volk's approach
appeared so sweetly reasonable. Farrar's men weakened their case by first
accepting a seat distribution for the Rand, Pretoria and the platteland of
29–5–29 respectively on 10 May, and then changing their minds in the light
of information (which West Ridgeway would not accept) that the 1904
census returns on which that calculation had been made were faulty. The
Committee seems rather to have warmed to the approach of the Responsibles and the labour representatives when they endorsed Het Volk's fear
of the power of the Chamber of Mines. It cast these smaller English-
speaking groups as mediators between the Progressives and Het Volk. It
therefore overruled Het Volk's objection to a voters' basis in constituency
delimitation (which FitzPatrick had pushed in Progressive circles), and
favoured the Progressive desire for single-member constituencies; but it
also backed Het Volk's request that the constituencies should comprise
existing magisterial districts, allowing for a fifteen per cent unload for rural
constituencies. After hearing evidence in secret from all parties, to the
consternation of the Progressives, the Committee settled for the 1904
census figures as their guide, rather than the voters' rolls drawn up under
the Lyttelton scheme. Finally, on 23 June, West Ridgeway proposed a new

distribution of 33–6–30, calculating that this would give 'a British majority, but not a mining majority' (Elgin) if they all pulled together – but on the almost unbelievable assumption that an undertaking once made by Het Volk not to contest any Rand seats would be honoured in practice (Bennett).

This new proposal – as Duminy has shown – was accepted by Farrar, and recommended for adoption by Selborne and even by Milner. FitzPatrick, by contrast, calculated that the Progressives could not win under such conditions, and set off for London with a demand for the Lyttelton voters' roll and a 37–7–27 share-out. He found the Liberal leaders reluctant to talk, and Elgin 'hostile throughout'. He was granted one extra seat for the Rand, and could derive some consolation from the fact that an initially nominated upper house gave the Transvaal British a safeguard for four years. But in his calculation that the West Ridgeway Committee had underrated the subtleties of Het Volk's approach, and overrated the capacity of British Transvalers to work together and clear nearly all the Rand and Pretoria seats, FitzPatrick was shown to be right. What he does not seem to have appreciated – as others like Farrar did – was that it might be more prudent to come to terms with Het Volk over the question of mine labour, so as to adjust to the contingency of a Het Volk victory, than to risk all in an attempt to outvote them.

When the first general election was held in 1907, Het Volk was returned with 37 seats against 21 for the Progressives, 6 for a new National Association (which included the Responsibles), 3 for Labour and 2 for Independents. The Committee had tried both to be fair and to ensure a British majority; but divided counsels and political calculation combined to bring about an opposite result.

The constitution framed for the Transvaal in the light of the West Ridgeway recommendations provided for an elective Legislative Assembly of 69 members and a Legislative Council of 15, nominated in the first instance. English and Dutch were both made official languages, English being the language of record. The electorate was limited to whites, the Liberals having decided that to attempt to impose conditions for the safeguarding of blacks was likely to alienate Transvaal white opinion to the ultimate disadvantage of the blacks. The Liberals were subsequently accused of having defaulted on undertakings made by the Unionists, in terms of Article 8 of the Treaty of Vereeniging, for the enfranchisement of blacks on the grant of self-government. In defence of their actions, however, Hyam has noted Elgin's concern to do justice by the 'natives' (a term now taken to include Coloured and Indians) in his minute of 5 April 1906, as well as Elgin's interviews with those who sought ways of entrenching black rights. All the Government eventually did was to confer formal powers as Supreme Chief on the Governor, to provide for the reservation of legislation affecting blacks, to provide for the convening of assemblies of chiefs if the Governor thought fit, and to place Swaziland directly under the High Commission instead of under the Governor of the Transvaal. The political climate which had developed in South Africa in the aftermath of the Zulu rebellion was not one in which rights could easily be extended to blacks. Nor, as Mansergh argued, could black rights be easily defended from London, once self-government had been granted to a South African colony, unless there was a substantial body of white opinion in the Colony determined to maintain those rights.

The Orange River Colony likewise received self-government, on the recommendation of the West Ridgeway Committee, on 5 June 1907. Selborne had ingeniously proposed a restoration of the old Republican constitution with a mere substitution of a nominated governor for the elected president, but this was strongly attacked by the Afrikaner leaders on account of the real powers previously enjoyed by the president, which would thus be placed outside political control. A constitution on the lines of that of the Transvaal was consequently introduced, with a nominee upper house of eleven, which would be subsequently elected, and a Legislative Assembly of 38. In the first elections, held in 1908, Orangia Unie won thirty lower house seats, to the eight won by Sir J. G. Fraser's Constitutionalists.

9.10　THE FORMATION OF THE UNION OF SOUTH AFRICA, 1908–10

When Milner created a South African Customs Union for an experimental period of two years, and amalgamated the Transvaal and O.R.C. railway systems into a single Central South African Railways, his hope was that these arrangements would justify themselves, and thereby further the federal cause. The Transvaal would be drawn into an already existing common market, while the possession of a considerable length of rail traversing the O.R.C. would incline the C.S.A.R. to do as much business as possible through the Cape ports. But two awkward facts stood in the way of Milner's plans. One was the growing economic dominance of the Transvaal, and the danger that, when it achieved self-government it would follow its own interests, if need be by cutting economic ties with the south. The other was the Portuguese stranglehold over the Rand's rail traffic, linked with Mozambique's power to give or withhold labourers for the gold mines.

On the customs front, the Transvaal needed to impose high duties for revenue purposes at the end of the Anglo-Boer War, and began in 1902 to tax Natal sugar and Cape wines. The Customs Convention of 1903 stopped this practice, and the Transvaal Government began to rely on an increased gold profits tax, which amounted to approximately three-quarters of the annual railway revenue from 1906 onwards. But on achieving responsible government Botha's ministry came under very heavy pressure to protect the Colony from Cape farm products and in June 1907 gave notice of its intention to withdraw from the Customs Union. The customs dispute suggested that the only way to eliminate harmful inter-colonial competition was to unite the colonies politically.

On the railway front the problems were more intricate. Milner had allocated money for railway expansion, and set in motion the construction of lines from Witbank to Springs, and from Ladysmith in Natal to Kroonstad in the O.R.C., as well as from Fourteen Streams in the Cape to the Rand. These works were completed by the middle of 1906 [see Map 12]. But the creation of new lines brought fresh friction. Thus the entry of goods into the O.R.C. from Natal led to so much bitter competition between the Cape and Natal systems that Selborne had to threaten to impose countervailing tariffs on the Free State Sections in order to offset attempts by either colony to undercut the other. A similar conflict developed between the Cape and the O.R.C. over the C.S.A.R.'s plan to build a line from Bloemfontein to Kimberley, which threatened to admit goods landed at Durban into the Kimberley market. Meanwhile deadlock developed between the High Commissioner and the Portuguese authorities when the former insisted that the privileges guaranteed to the Portuguese under the *modus vivendi* of 1901 did not apply with regard to the Springs–Witbank line, and the other routes to the Rand which had not existed at the time of that agreement. This became a cause of bitter dispute on account of the relative growth of rail traffic between Lourenço Marques and the Rand as a result of the *modus vivendi*: it had increased from 30.9 per cent of the total in 1903 to 51.5 per cent in 1905, during which time Durban's proportion had fallen from 44 per cent to 36.5 per cent and that of the Cape ports had fallen to a mere 12 per cent.

The bitterness behind these quarrels ran deep, and formed the subject matter of Lord Selborne's Memorandum of 1 January 1907, with its urgent plea for political federation as a means of staving off economic catastrophe. Conferences at Johannesburg (1905) and Pietermaritzburg (1906) merely bought time. It was therefore a matter of great significance that when the representatives of the Colonies met again at Pretoria in May 1908 they should have adopted Smuts's proposal to seek a political solution of their economic divisions, by calling for a National Convention. As this Pretoria conference failed like its predecessors to reach agreement on the economic issues, the adoption of Smuts's proposal was timely. As a by-product of Union, the National Convention managed to set up a central Railways and Harbours administration taking over all the railways systems and running them on a commercial basis under a separate budget. At the same time it accepted a new agreement concluded by the Transvaal with the Portuguese, which gave Lourenço Marques the lion's share of Rand traffic but guaranteed minimum percentages of the traffic for Durban (30 per cent) and the Cape (15 per cent).

It had always been unquestioningly assumed that if the political unification of southern Africa was to be brought about this would have to be done on federal rather than unitary lines, on account of the cultural differences and regional disparities, which seemed to require the maximum possible devolution of power. So Milner thought. So thought the Afrikaner Bond when it reviewed its political objectives in 1903. F. S. Malan and Jameson moved a joint motion to the same effect in the Cape Assembly in July 1907. Lionel Curtis, who master-minded Selborne's Memorandum of January 1907, the document through which, in Thompson's words, the Kindergarten took the initiative in the unification debate, was also a convinced federalist. But the Kindergarten was not allowed to retain the initiative, for the leaders of the Afrikaner movements began to suspect that their schemes would place power in unfriendly hands. Hence the decision, taken by Merriman, Steyn and Smuts in the course of 1906, to discourage any closer union movement until self-government had been restored to the new colonies, and until power had passed to Het Volk and the Orangia Unie, and returned to the South African Party in the Cape.

By February 1908, with the South African Party's victory in the Cape general election, these conditions had been realised. The leaders of the Afrikaner movements had also reached the conclusion that a unitary rather than a federal form of government would suit their interests best. Lionel Curtis and other members of the Kindergarten began to move in that direction too. Federalism still had its supporters; but its most convinced spokesmen, W. P. Schreiner, his sister Olive, and J. H. Hofmeyr, were not at the Convention, while the Natal delegates, who wanted as decentralised a constitution as they could get, and actually produced a draft federal scheme at the Convention, had neither the skill nor bargaining strength to force their views on to the other delegates. The triumph of unitary over federal thinking is to be explained primarily by the convictions of Smuts and Merriman, who led from the time of the Pretoria conference onwards. Both men were attracted by British constitutionalism, while Merriman was driven by a desire to reduce costs to favour a centralised system, and Smuts became convinced that it was necessary to concentrate power at the centre to prevent the structure from being shaken apart:

> What we want is a supreme national authority to give expression to the national will of South Africa, and the rest is really subordinate.

Together with Sir Henry de Villiers, Chief Justice of the Cape, who presided over the Convention, they examined and took what lessons they chose from the federal constitutions of the United States, Canada and Australia, looking to the American civil war and to Australian inter-state wrangles as powerful arguments against federalism, and ignoring the proffered advice of expert defenders of these constitutions.

The national Convention was primarily concerned with the distribution of power. In this sense, it must be seen against the background of confrontation between the racial and ethnic groups which had battled for possession throughout historic times in the sub-continent, but more especially during the preceding hundred years. The power situation was reflected in the actual distribution of delegates. There were no Africans, Coloured People or Asians present. The Government and Opposition white parties of the four Colonies were represented in almost equal proportions and in the numbers agreed at the Pretoria Conference, though there was rather greater cohesion among the Governmental representatives of the Cape, O.R.C. and Transvaal than among the groups of Opposition leaders. Southern Rhodesia, still a non-self-governing colony, was represented by observers with speaking but not voting rights, two appointed by the British South Africa Company and one by the Legislative Council; but Rhodesian settler interest in joining the Union was at best marginal.

After the completion of preliminaries, Merriman moved on 13 October in favour of a legislative Union of South Africa, of which the existing self-governing Colonies were to be constituted provinces, with provision for the incorporation of 'all such parts of South Africa as are not included from its establishment'. He and Smuts put their case for a unitary constitution, basing it on the correspondence which they had shared since August over a 'Suggested Scheme for South African Union' drafted by Smuts, on which Merriman, Sir Henry de Villiers and Steyn had passed comments. This scheme had been revised by Smuts and R. H. Brand, who became secretary of the Transvaal delegation. Having cleared up the constitutional flaws in his proposals, Smuts had then summarised them for the members of the Transvaal delegation, who had discussed them during the week before the Convention met and arrived with their differences ironed out. As the Transvaal and Cape Opposition parties arrived in Durban without alternative schemes of their own, and the Natal delegates were taken unawares by Merriman's opening motion and had not canvassed their federal alternative, the Merriman–Smuts proposal was carried without dissentient voice after a Natal amendment to place residual powers in the 'states' had been voted down. As a result, the Convention settled for a sovereign central Parliament with authority to amend the powers of provincial councils, or even remove them altogether, by ordinary simple majorities, and it made short work of attempts by Natal to increase the scope of provincial councils. Their authority was carefully circumscribed, while the provincial executive committees were placed under administrators appointed by the Governor-General, rather than under provincial premiers.

Thompson pertinently observes that the Natal delegates missed an opportunity, after losing the battle for federation, by not insisting on the entrenchment of provincial rights with special majorities for their removal. To obtain this alternative security, however, they would have had to vanquish the strong disposition to favour a flexible rather than a rigid constitution in South Africa at the time, rooted in the somewhat irrational notion that full autonomy required full flexibility. What emerged from the Convention was a flexible constitution like the British, albeit a written one, in which sovereignty (subject to the limitations of the Colonial Laws Validity Act of 1865 and the safeguards for the Royal prerogative) lay with the Union Parliament. Any part of the constitution could be amended by a simple majority of each House, but for the section protecting the voting rights of the non-white people of the Cape (Section 35), on which the Cape delegates dug in their heels, and the section defining the equal status of the English and Dutch languages (Section 137), over which the O.R.C. delegates were adamant. These could only be amended by a two-thirds majority at the third reading in a joint session of both Houses. Whether this involved granting a testing right to the courts, as had existed in the O.F.S. but not in the Transvaal, was not clearly stated in the Act, though by implication such a power had to exist.

The Convention agreed that the executive government should be headed by a Governor-General as the representative of the King, aided by an Executive Council composed in practice of the Ministry of the day. It settled for a two-chamber Parliament without great enthusiasm. This was to comprise, first, a Senate of forty members with a ten-year term (eight for each province, elected collegially by proportional representation, plus eight nominated by the Governor-General, of whom four were to be chosen for their 'thorough acquaintance . . . with the reasonable wants and wishes of the coloured races'). The House of Assembly was to have an initial membership of 121, rising to 150, as the size of the electorate increased. Each Province could acquire extra members as its total voters increased by multiples of the Union quota (obtained by dividing the total number of electors by the total number of seats).

The composition of the House of Assembly involved crucial decisions over the distribution of power. After sustained debates it became clear that on the question of black representation neither the northern Colonies nor the Cape was prepared to compromise. Walter Stanford of the Cape, supported by several of his colleagues, tried to have the political colour bar removed. De Villiers and Fitzpatrick proposed a civilisation test for blacks, while Botha and Moor adamantly refused to admit blacks to political rights in the Transvaal and Natal respectively. Rather than break up the Convention, the delegates therefore agreed that the franchise system in operation in each province should continue. The Convention refused to allow the election of non-white people to Parliament. On this point the Cape gave ground for it had never admitted them in the past, though at a late stage the Convention opened the door for black membership of the Cape Provincial Council.

In determining the allocation of seats between the provinces, several criteria were discussed. The basis of total population, which would have greatly favoured Natal with its large black population, was rejected. The Cape would have stood to gain from a distribution on a basis of total voters, on account of its relatively greater black electorate. But the basis eventually agreed on was that of the total white adult male population, which was a voters' basis in the northern colonies. The 1904 census returns were apparently taken as the basis for calculation, save that the delegates allowed the Transvaal an upward adjustment of its figures on account of the sizeable immigration to that colony since 1904, and allowed the Orange Free State (as the O.R.C. was renamed) and Natal an inflated number of 17 seats each for ten years, as against the Cape's 51, and the Transvaal's 36. The upshot was that the Cape had an initial average of 2,791 voters per constituency, the Transvaal 2,715, the O.F.S. 2,131 and Natal 1,647.

When it came to distributing the seats within the provinces, the main problem was to balance the interests of town and country, which largely corresponded with those of the English- and Dutch-speaking populations. The Afrikaner parties, on the whole, favoured unequal constituencies and the loading of the urban electorate, for which strong precedents already existed in all colonies, whereas the Progressives of the Transvaal, mindful of the Uitlander franchise wrangles and keenly led by Fitzpatrick, wanted 'one vote one value' and regular redistribution to ensure that constituencies remained equal. After one of its toughest debates, the Convention appointed a committee which recommended that delimitation commissions of three judges should be empowered to vary the size of constituencies up to 15 per cent either way from the provincial average (or quota), applying any of five criteria in the process: community or diversity of interests, communications, physical features, existing electoral boundaries, and sparsity or density of population. This allowed a measure of judicial discretion, and the guidelines were by no means precise, but at this stage in proceedings the delegates accepted Smuts's proposal for large multi-member constituencies linked with a system of proportional representation, as likely to protect minority interests. It was only at the final Bloemfontein session of the Convention in May 1909 that proportional representation was dropped in favour of single-member constituencies and simple cumulative voting procedures on account of the fear of Cape Bondsmen that Smuts's plan and the principle of equal constituencies might be to their disadvantage. At this late stage, too, came the Transvaal Progressives' first determined insistence on 'one vote one value', sparked off by the Cape resolutions. When the Convention was close to breaking up, De Villiers suggested the abandonment of proportional representation. The Progressives tried to insist on the entrenchment of 'one vote one value'. For several days the delegates deadlocked, before compromising on the acceptance of equal constituencies (subject always to the principle of loading), the abandonment of proportional representation, and the reservation for the royal pleasure of any bills to alter the sub-chapter dealing with the House of Assembly.

The federation of Australia had taken about ten years from the initial moves in 1890, and the federation of Canada three. With relatively much bigger differences to bridge, the South African National Convention completed its work in less than a year. After a brief Durban session, it had moved to Cape Town in November 1908, and deliberated there (with a Christmas recess) until February. The draft legislation was then submitted to the Colonial Parliaments in March, and the proposed amendments then debated at the Bloemfontein session between 3 and 11 May. The Colonial Parliaments approved the amended draft at the beginning of June, and it was approved in Natal by a referendum on the 10th. The draft South Africa Bill, having gone through all the formal procedures thought necessary, was then taken to London by a delegation from the Convention (in which Hofmeyr was also present) and went through all stages in the British Parliament between 22 July and 19 August, eventually receiving the royal assent on 20 September.

But although the South African Convention had bigger difficulties in its path, it overcame these as much by avoiding them as by facing up to them. The decision over the capital was a case in point. This, above all, was the issue on which local pride was most intimately touched. But a decision which made the Mother City the seat of Parliament, gave the most economically active Province the seat of administration, and placed the judicial capital in the centrally situated Bloemfontein did justice of a kind to all save Natal, at the cost of sending the civil servants on an expensive annual trek.

9.11   THE UNACKNOWLEDGED PROTEST OF THE BLACKS

Far more consequential was the agreement to differ over the treatment of blacks. The intense activity among African and Coloured leaders in face of the proposal to exclude them from an effective role was almost entirely ignored in earlier accounts of the Convention. It was, however, under-scored by Thompson and has now been described in some detail by Odendaal.

The Cape African newspapers *Imvo* and *Izwi* both criticised the draft South Africa Bill in strong terms, and welcomed a call from the O.R.C. Native Congress for a black Convention. The S.A. Native Congress, based on the Cape, and the leading political bodies in the Transvaal and Natal, all wanted a gathering of representatives to meet in Bloemfontein. Meetings were accordingly called in all the Colonies to elect delegates. At Emgwali, near Stutterheim, on 17 March 1909, Dr Rubusana, A. K. Soga, and T. Mqanda were chosen to represent the Cape; but Tengo Jabavu, the patriarch of Cape black politics, insisted on King William's Town as the venue for a Convention, and ignored the Emgwali meeting.

Thirty-eight delegates attended the Native Convention in the school-room of the Waaihoek Location, Bloemfontein, on 24 to 26 March. Despite the exhortation of a guest speaker, Dewdney Drew, to accept the draft constitution in the hope of improving it at a later stage, the Conven-tion reacted angrily to the exclusion of blacks under the draft Bill, and adopted resolutions criticising all the clauses which contained colour bars. Other resolutions urged tight safeguards for the incorporation of the Protectorates in the Union. The Convention decided, finally, to establish itself as a permanent body, and elected Rubusana as its president. It did in fact continue to meet, and its members later transformed the Native Convention by a deliberate act into the South African Native National Congress (the original form of the A.N.C.) in January 1912.

Jabavu's meeting in King William's Town on 7 and 8 April was attended by a rather larger number of delegates, but they came from a compact region of the eastern Cape only, and there were none present from any of the larger Cape towns. This was a meeting, not of men who had been denied a place under the new constitution, but of men who had been allowed to remain on the voters' roll and were anxious to safeguard the rights they still had. They therefore expressed approval of union in prin-ciple, but they found time to thank Hofmeyr and the Schreiners for their support, and they decided to send copies of their resolutions to the executive of the S.A. Native Convention 'for concerted action in the prosecution of the cause'. In other words, they were not promoting themselves simply as a rival show.

Meanwhile, despite the undermining of its efforts by the cautious Tobin and Peregrino Abdurahman's A.P.O. was politically very active, holding over sixty Coloured meetings before mid-April. Their objections to the draft Bill were as forthright as those of the two African conferences, and they agreed even before the final session of the National Convention to organise a deputation to London on the assumption that their protests would be ignored (Lewis).

They were in fact ignored, no amendments being called for by any of the white parliaments in the light of the objections raised, even in the Cape, where W. P. Schreiner had tried very hard to promote a series of amendments. Schreiner therefore led a deputation to London consisting of Abdurahman, Rubusana, Jabavu and several other black leaders, on the heels of the official 28-member delegation, to try to prevail on the British Parliament to reject a political colour bar. They made contact with Gandhi, who was in London for the same purpose. They won support from the Anti-Slavery and Aborigines Protection Societies, and from several other humanitarian bodies and radical M.P.s; but they found the press, with the exception of the *Manchester Guardian* and the *Review of Reviews*, generally unsympathetic. They found the contrary influence of Merriman and other 'friends of the natives' on the official delegation hard to combat. They were unable for technical reasons to obtain a hearing at the bar of the Commons; and, although they obtained an interview with Lord Crewe, the Secretary of State for the Colonies, this was not until after the Government had committed itself to an acceptance of the South Africa Bill without any substantial amendments. The Liberals in Britain were not in fact insensitive to the problem. Hyam has made it clear that the Protectorates were withheld, and barred from incorporation save under the stiff conditions laid down in Section 151 and the Schedule to the Act, to provide some kind of lever on white South African opinion. The South Africa Act had, however, created something rather different: it had given South Africa that 'supreme national authority to give expression to the national will' which Smuts originally desired, and provided a boxing ring in which the contenders for different principles could confront each other until the palm of victory went one day to the stronger.

The promulgation of a constitution for the Union of South Africa could have become the occasion for a fresh start in public life, and for this the orgy of 'convention spirit' which had accompanied the compromises of 1908–9 seemed to prepare the public. In the nature of the case, though, the earlier party lines re-emerged, and the notion of a 'government of all the talents', on which Jameson was encouraged to pin his hopes, was stillborn. Things could hardly have developed differently, with the limited spoils of office available after the merging of four administrative systems into one, and the need for whoever became prime minister to satisfy his own faithful followers.

Lord Gladstone, the first Governor-General, acting on both local and London advice, invited Louis Botha to form a government. Ex-President Steyn, an obvious alternative, was not available on account of ill-health. John X. Merriman, veteran prime minister of the Cape, who had shown by his heroic defence of the Boer cause in the war of 1899–1902, and by the toughness of his financial administration during the economic crisis of 1908–10 that he was a very strong candidate, did not enjoy the backing of

an Imperial Government anxious to demonstrate how well it could make
amends to the Afrikaner. There was even more to it than that. The
political leaders of the Transvaal, the richest of all the provinces, had
entered the compact of Union knowing that they could have afforded to
stay out, and were determined to secure the direction of affairs in their own
hands. They therefore worked hard to achieve this goal, in a manner with
which the more scrupulous Merriman would not compete, and they won.

Part Two
The Consolidation of a White State

Section I
The Road to Afrikaner Dominance

10 Union under Stress: Botha and Smuts, 1910–24

10.1 BOTHA'S ACCESSION TO POWER AND QUARREL WITH HERTZOG

General Louis Botha's Government took office on 31 May 1910 in the sunshine of Imperial approval, and dedicated to conciliation between Briton and Boer. The ministry contained almost as many British as Dutch names. In choosing it, Botha had drawn carefully from all provinces. Because of the manoeuvrings which had preceded his own appointment and the pressure inside his own party for the spoils of office, Botha could neither abandon party lines and choose a ministry of all the talents, nor divide the nation along lines which he would probably have preferred – with Jameson and the Unionists on the government benches, and Hertzog in opposition. This was ironic, for when the electorate went to the polls in September 1910 the policies of the South African and Unionist parties were difficult to distinguish. As Thompson has noted, both stressed the idea of a single South African nation (white by implication), both professed a non-doctrinaire native policy, both wanted white but not Asian immigration, material development, and Imperial preference, and neither sought special protection for the Afrikaner. Both hoped, in effect, that the spirit of tolerance would continue to grow in an atmosphere of ethnic peace. Problems arising from the relationship between blacks and whites did not appear to cloud the scene, for all save a few discerning thinkers like Abdullah Abdurahman, Olive Schreiner and M. K. Gandhi were inclined to leave these for the broader shoulders of the future. The bitter memories of the Anglo-Boer war, which was still less than a decade away, were probably much more present in their minds, as wounds to be healed by gentle medication and the passage of time.

But Botha, though he won the general election by a substantial majority, reckoned without Barry Hertzog, and the elements which he represented. Though Hertzog had won his campaign at the National Convention for the equal status of Dutch and English in public business, and for a bilingual public service, he was not convinced that equality would be achieved in practice unless both languages were used as media for the instruction of all white children. Two principles were at issue here: the right of parents to

231

choose the language medium of their children's education, and the right of society to expect pupils to have those linguistic skills which would make for proper social understanding, which was Hertzog's main argument, as it would be for the proponents of dual-medium education in later years. The atmosphere was poisoned by the recent controversies arising out of Smuts's Education Act of 1907 in the Transvaal (Hancock), Hertzog's of 1908 in the O.F.S. (Van den Heever), and by Botha's feeling that Hertzog's campaigning had caused his personal defeat by FitzPatrick in the Pretoria East constituency during the general election of September 1910.

Because of his performance in the election, Hertzog's cabinet colleagues regarded him as a cuckoo in the nest, but recognised his power as the leading representative of latent Afrikaner republican sentiments which, for reasons of expediency, had been suppressed since the end of the Anglo-Boer war. He was not consistently immoderate. The Fremantle Commission, which investigated the working of the provincial education laws in 1912, vindicated the O.F.S. system as the only one which did not discriminate against Dutch. The Commission recommended a margin of choice for parents over the language medium, but Hertzog signed the Report for the sake of cabinet unity, though he did not agree with this policy and he resented Botha's subsequent attempts to identify him with the majority view. His controversial public statements about the Imperial connection were of special importance, however, for acceptance of that connection had been a central feature of the conciliation policy since Vereeniging, though in places it was deeply resented.

The constitution of 1910 united South Africa under a single government but did not make her in all respects a sovereign independent state. Above all was this the case with reference to external affairs, for South Africa was bound by the decisions of the King, acting on the advice of his British ministers of state, on questions of war and peace. South Africa was represented by Botha at the Imperial Conference of 1911, at which Sir Joseph Ward, premier of New Zealand, moved for the setting up of an Imperial Council of Defence. Acting on the assumption that the United Kingdom could commit the Dominions to participation in war, he sought collective participation in the making of Imperial external policy. Botha led the attack on this plan, which was withdrawn in the face of general opposition. The Union's Defence Act of 1912 accordingly provided for a completely autonomous defence force, limited to military operations in any part of South Africa whether within or outside the Union. When Asquith, the Prime Minister, invited Dominion representatives to attend meetings of the Committee of Imperial Defence the same year, the principle of consultation over policy decisions was established. It was extended when Dominion governments were represented in the Imperial War Cabinet, but consultation had not made the King's declaration of war against Germany in August 1914 a collective Imperial decision.

Hertzog embarked on a campaign to assert South Africa's right to control her own international destiny in 1912. Speaking at Nylstroom, Smithfield and De Wildt at the end of the year, he insisted on the priority of South Africa's interests without insisting on a severance of the Imperial tie. This kind of utterance would hardly have caused a ripple if it had been uttered after 1931, but it provoked a strong reaction at the time, because he described Sir Thomas Smartt, ex-Afrikaner Bondsman and leader of the Unionists, who had recently been urging contributions to the British navy, as a 'foreign fortune-seeker', just when Botha was about to campaign among English-speakers, whose leaders controlled the mining, industrial and commercial assets of the country, and whom it was important for Botha's entire strategy not to antagonise.

There had already been a Cabinet crisis in May 1912, when the Treasurer, H. C. Hull, had crossed swords with J. W. Sauer, Minister of Railways and Harbours, for failing to coordinate the railway budget with the Treasury, and resigned. After Hertzog's De Wildt speech, Sir George Leuchars, the Minister of Public Works, asked Botha to accept his resignation. Botha tried to persuade Hertzog to resign as well, and when the latter refused he resigned himself. Asked to form another government, he then left both Hertzog and Leuchars out. But the dropping of Hertzog stirred up the feelings of fellow Free Staters. In November 1913, Hertzog and General C. R. de Wet walked out of the S.A.P. congress in Cape Town, taking a handful of the parliamentary caucus with them. In January, a congress of dissidents in Bloemfontein decided to form a new National Party, on a platform of South African self-sufficiency, dual-medium education, and compulsory bilingualism in the public service. At their first Transvaal congress in August 1914, they opposed South African participation in the Great War and any contemplated attack on South West Africa.

If the international crisis had not arisen, perhaps the Government might have come to terms with Hertzogism. But once the threat of war appeared, it was to the magnates' party, the Unionists, rather than the Nationalists that the Government had to look for support. This in turn helped to revive anti-capitalist sentiments among the Afrikaner rank and file. The Government experienced head-on collisions with the power of Afrikaner nationalists and white workers on two occasions, first in 1913–14, before and after the outbreak of the First World War, and again in 1920–4. These carried a serious challenge to the legitimacy of the new South African state, as Yudelman observes. But they are most conveniently handled in the light of attempts by the Government to consolidate the foundations of white power.

10.2 THE SEGREGATION STRATEGY OF THE BOTHA–SMUTS REGIME

The differences in outlook between the South African and Unionist parties, which dominated Parliament, were not marked where 'native policy' was concerned. Both disapproved of racial miscegenation; both regarded the idea of a black political majority as unthinkable, though the Unionists may have been less antagonistic to the retention of the Cape non-white franchise than the S.A.P.; both desired to see the restriction of African land ownership to the Reserves, and both wished to see African urban immigrants segregated in locations. In their various ways – some as farmers, others as mine-owners or industrialists – S.A.P. and Unionist politicians were anxious to safeguard their supplies of black labour. If this meant deliberately depressing wage rates, or preventing the growth of labour's bargaining power, or playing off white against black workers, or keeping land for Africans in short supply to force men on to the farms or down the mines, the power balance arrived at in the South Africa Act made it possible to do these things.

In its attitude towards the African people, the Government's thinking was characterised, as Kallaway has shown, by an inability to reconcile the northern and the Cape approaches, especially in the matter of political representation. But it was dominated by the segregationist arguments of the Lagden Commission. In most respects segregation enjoyed the support of the white electorate, and no violence is done to the evidence by the suggestion that, as a political ideology requiring the physical separation of people on racial grounds, it was more actively promoted in the period 1910–24 than it was in the period with which it is more commonly associated, namely the years of Hertzog's premiership (1924–39) [see p. 518].

The South African Party's programme extended segregation in areas where it already existed, and imposed it in others where it had never existed before. In the 1911 session it shackled African labour by prohibiting strikes by contract workers, and in regulations promulgated under the Mines and Works Act it reserved certain categories of work for white people, following a precedent in Transvaal law. Its Defence Act of 1912 provided for a white Active Citizen Force. Before it fell from power in 1924, it also made access to skilled trades safe for the white community by insisting on minimal age-linked educational qualifications for entry to apprenticeship, which youths of other race groups could not easily attain (1922). In its Industrial Conciliation Act of 1924, which represented a major intrusion by the Government into the field of labour regulation, the ruling party restricted the use of new collective bargaining machinery to unionised white and coloured people only [see pp. 507–8]. Other laws which left their mark on South Africa and stamped the Botha–Smuts period as the most formative until the era of Verwoerd, were the Natives Land Act of 1913, the Native Affairs Act of 1920, and the Natives (Urban Areas) Act of 1923.

The Land Act imposed a policy of territorial segregation with a very heavy hand. It aimed specifically to get rid of those features of African land ownership and share-cropping which white farmers found undesirable, and enlarge reserves to ease congestion and facilitate the recruiting of labour for the mines. The law dealt cautiously with Cape Africans because of the link between land-holding and franchise qualifications, though Bundy has also suggested that share-cropping presented less of a threat to white farmers in the Cape on account of the long succession of colonial anti-squatter laws between 1869 and 1909. African squatters living in Natal and the Transvaal were also spared from eviction 'until Parliament has made other provision' – that is, until a commission under the chairmanship of Sir William Beaumont, appointed under the Act to find more land to add to the Reserves, had completed its task. But Free State legislation which restricted squatting was confirmed, and the moratorium which applied to all other provinces, explicitly excluded that province. The influence of Hertzog seems to have dominated the thoughts of Sauer, as he introduced the bill (Grobler). Many farmers in the Free State proceeded to evict their squatters, rightly thinking that the law required them to do so. The sudden uprooting of large numbers of Africans from Free State farms, and the migration of many of them northwards across the Vaal, to the accompaniment of widespread forced stock sales at bargain prices, were movingly described by black witnesses before the Beaumont Commission, and in his memoirs by Sol Plaatje. The tough resistance to black squatting among Free State farmers seems to have arisen not only from a deep-rooted objection to black share-cropping, which undermined the master–servant relationship, but also from a growing desire to maximise favourable market opportunities [see pp. 485–8, 520–3].

Botha tried in 1917 to give effect to the segregationist provisions of the Land Act by introducing a Native Affairs Administration Bill which sought to impose a uniform system of control over all the Reserves scheduled under the 1913 Act. He was encouraged to do this by a Cape Supreme Court judgment in the case of *Thomson and Stilwell* v. *Kama* (1916) to the effect that Section 8(2) of the Land Act which protected Cape African voters from disfranchisement did not render the segregationist section 1(2) invalid in cases where black property owners who sold or were deprived of their land, like Kama, already had voting rights. The implication of this judgment was that, in principle, segregation could be applied in the Cape without infringing the constitution. But when Kama took his case on appeal, the Appellate Division ruled that because the effect of the segregationist section of the Act could be to deprive an African of the vote, the Act was *ultra vires* in the Cape after all. Botha therefore withdrew his Administration Bill, and it was left to Smuts to bring in a revised measure in 1920 (Lacey). Meanwhile five local committees were set up in 1918 to revise the Beaumont Commission's proposals in the light of objections raised.

Like its predecessor, Smuts's Act was segregationist in structure. It built on the Glen Grey system of district councils, which by then extended across the greater part of the Transkei (excluding Pondoland), by providing for their extension throughout the Union, and their grouping into general councils as at Umtata. The Act also set up a Native Conference of African leaders to be nominated by the Government and meet annually in Pretoria, together with an all-white Native Affairs Commission of experts, who were to maintain contact with the African population through its leaders, report annually to Parliament, and act as a liaison between the white legislators and African opinion.

Conceived within the framework of the Land Act, the Natives (Urban Areas) Act emerged from the matrix of the Milner regime, with its compulsion to achieve regularity and order. It was part of the legislators' intention to promote public health, under the inspiration of the commissions on Assaults on Women (1913) and Tuberculosis (1914), and the fear of epidemic disease such as the bubonic plague of 1900 and the Spanish 'flu of 1918. But alongside the clearance of slums, there developed a campaign to keep the urban areas in white hands, blacks being allowed there on sufferance and only for so long as they served the needs of the white man, as was stated in the report of the Transvaal Local Government Commission in 1922. Administratively, the aim of the Government was to separate the location from the town, through the establishment of a separate self-balancing native revenue account. Advisory boards were provided for, in an attempt to ensure some kind of local government by consent. Measures for the control of location trading, location brewing, and the pursuit of the idle, dissolute and disorderly, completed the range of this many-faceted law, but not until much later did it contain rules to control black influx into town [see pp. 524–30].

10.3 THE GROWTH OF AFRICAN POLITICAL OPPOSITION: THE S.A.N.N.C. AND THE I.C.U.

In face of their political exclusion and the tightening of controls over their daily lives, it would have been surprising if the African political organisations of the Union had not attempted to improve their capacity to resist. The founders of the South African Native Convention in 1909 had intended to set up a continuing organisation, and the Convention did continue to meet regularly, as Odendaal has shown.

During 1911 Pixley Ka I. Seme, a Zulu lawyer trained at Columbia, Oxford and the Middle Temple, who had met Schreiner's deputation in London in 1909, joined the Johannesburg branch of the Convention and appears to have put the idea to the other members including Sol Plaatje, to form a Native Congress – perhaps on the Indian analogy. There was strong support throughout the country, and a conference was called to take place in Bloemfontein from 8 to 12 January 1912. Only Jabavu presented a problem. He was in London towards the end of 1911, linking his own *Imbumba* movement to a Universal Races Congress which was in the course of formation. Seme tried to reassure him that his own Congress was not the Native Convention in sheep's clothing – 'an old idea, but as a society it is absolutely a new one' (cited by Reed). But it seems that Jabavu did not show willing. Dr J. L. Dube, an America-trained Zulu who had returned in 1904 to edit the new *Ilanga lase Natal* in Durban, and subsequently set up the Ohlange Institute at Inanda in 1909, was elected president *in absentia*. Rubusana was accorded an 'honorary' presidency, and vice-presidents were elected from Mafeking, Basutoland, Pretoria, Johannesburg, Natal, Bloemfontein and Cape Town. Seme was elected treasurer, assisted by Thomas Mapikela of Bloemfontein, and Plaatje given the role of corresponding secretary. Thus was born the organisation which would become the African National Congress before the decade was out.

Jabavu's South African Races Congress was formally constituted in April 1912, as the editor of *Imvo* continued on his independent line. His real test came over the issue of the 1913 Native Land Bill, which *Imvo* supported in its columns, on the assumption that the Government's intentions were above suspicion and that real advantage was to be gained from fair territorial segregation. Jabavu's reaction was understandable in the light of the widespread conviction among prominent liberal thinkers that segregationism should be given a chance to show that it could be fairly applied. Just at that time John Harris, Secretary of the amalgamated Anti-Slavery and Aborigines Protection Society was conducting a well orchestrated double campaign in Britain in defence of Botha and the Land Act, and in defence of a parallel bid to enlarge the reserves of Southern Rhodesia in order to restrict the power of the British South Africa Company (Willan, Whitehead). The flaw in Jabavu's approach came, as Willan has expressed it in the case of Harris, from a failure to distinguish 'the principle of separation from the question of its practical implementation'. The leadership of the S.A.N.N.C. was also divided over the merits of segregation, with both Dube and Selope Thema expressing some support for the principle; but Congress did send four deputations to remonstrate with Sauer, and tried to persuade the Governor-General to withhold his assent, and ended by sending Plaatje and Mapikela to London on a mission to the Imperial Parliament. Plaatje's campaign against the Land Act, with support within the A.P.S. committee coming from two formidable widows, Mrs Richard Cobden and Mrs Saul Solomon, resulted in the publication of his hard-hitting *Native Life in South Africa* with the help of a public subscription. This did much to counter the influence of Harris, but not enough to secure the repeal of the Act. When the land issue was raised again in Congress in 1917, after the publication of the Beaumont Commission's Report recommending a small extension of the reserves in each province, the majority came out strongly against the legislation, and Dube lost the presidency to S. Makgatho. By this time Jabavu was also disenchanted with the legislation.

During the world conflict of 1914–18, African political leaders generally held their followers in check, despite the distress which they experienced from a dramatic rise in living costs which was not balanced by any significant wage adjustments. Not unreasonably, therefore, some hope that the fruits of victory would fall into African mouths touched their feelings at the end of the war. Meshach Pelem's Bantu Union, which emerged in 1919 from a Native Convention held in the Transkei shortly before, was a naïve pressure group nurtured on this sentiment, and it never spread beyond the eastern Cape. The S.A.N.N.C., by contrast, took on a more aggressive air under the presidency of Makgatho between 1917 and 1924, sponsoring both a passive resistance campaign against the pass laws on the Rand and a spate of strikes.

Charlotte Maxeke, science graduate of an American college, wife of an A.M.E.C. missionary and founder of the women's section of the S.A.N.N.C., had conducted a moderately successful campaign against the carrying of passes by African women in the Orange Free State in 1913. After the war, Witwatersrand branches of the Congress, taking a leaf out of Gandhi's book, organised the collection of passes in sacks and persuaded thousands, without the use of picketing or physical force, to hand themselves over to the police for disobeying the law. These demonstrations were broken up by the authorities, however, amid considerable violence, which Makgatho angrily denounced in his presidential address in May 1919. The Government's subsequent appointment of the Godley Committee to review the pass laws seemed at first to vindicate the organisers of the campaign; but that committee's recommendations in favour of simplification of the system were not implemented, and failure cost the S.A.N.N.C. some support.

More serious for its image, however, was the overall failure of African strike activity. The consolidation of an industrial colour bar by the legislation of 1911 did not ban but did inhibit African strike action. African gold miners came out in support of the Kleinfontein whites in July 1913, but arrests and an official inquiry followed. African diamond miners came out at Jagersfontein in the Orange Free State, following the killing of one of their number by a white man in 1914; but this resulted in the shooting of several more black miners. In 1918, the S.A.N.N.C. took a lead in organising a strike of the poorly paid Johannesburg sanitary workers, but the strike leaders were arrested. The following year Selby Msimang, a lawyer and Congress member, engineered another wage strike in Bloemfontein which for a change was partly successful, but Msimang was arrested though not convicted. In 1920, a strike of the Port Elizabeth municipal workers organised by Samuel Masabalala of the Cape Provincial Native Congress resulted, after a riot in which the police failed to control *vigilante* strike-breakers, in nineteen deaths (Baines). When a major black mine strike broke out in the same year [see p. 253] the police were soon able to suppress it.

The failure of this industrial action caused new divisions in the African political movements. Clements Kadalie, an expatriate Nyasalander who had taught and held clerical posts in Southern Rhodesia and Mozambique before going to Cape Town, organised a moderately successful strike of African and Coloured dock workers, members of an Industrial and Commercial Union of which he was honorary secretary, in 1919. They refused to load maize for export at a time when it was in short supply, and received some backing from the white Railways and Harbours Servants. They also won higher wages, but not as a direct result of the strike. Following this limited success, wage demands among unskilled workers there and elsewhere began to proliferate. Kadalie in Cape Town and Msimang in Bloemfontein accordingly discussed the establishment of a general workers' union for skilled and unskilled, industrial, domestic and rural workers, which could organise industrial action and provide a wide range of benefits. At a conference in Bloemfontein in May 1920, they established a new Industrial and Commercial Workers' Union (I.C.W.U.) which, if more widely supported, might have formed the nucleus of a formidable labour movement. But there was no representation from Natal, where African labour was still very poorly organised, or from the Transvaal where workers on the Rand were still licking their wounds after the 'bucket' and mine-workers' strikes and the pass-law demonstration. To make matters worse, the I.C.W.U. suffered loss of face from the Port Elizabeth riot in October, for Masabalala's workers had joined the new labour organisation. Partly for personal reasons, the alliance between Msimang and Kadalie became strained. The I.C.W.U. disintegrated, Msimang withdrawing from trade union politics, while Kadalie reconstituted his earlier I.C.U. which became essentially a Cape-based organisation, and began to take on the character of a political movement rather than an industrial pressure group. According to Wickins, the I.C.U. lacked the three essential qualities for success: a firm base in large-scale industry, recognition by employers, and a record of successful strikes. These deficiencies were plain to see during 1920–4; but the I.C.U. nevertheless survived as a dynamic movement in the countryside [see pp. 270–3].

10.4 INDIAN AFFAIRS: THE CLIMAX OF THE GANDHI–SMUTS ENCOUNTER AND THE DEFIANCE OF SAPRU

Smuts and Gandhi had reached an uneasy truce when the separate existence of the Transvaal Colony came to an end. Gandhi, like the Coloured and African leaders, went to London to object to the draft South Africa Bill, which gave no political rights to Indians at all. He returned at the end of the year to Tolstoy Farm, but also kept in touch with Indian leaders, notably G. K. Gokhale, a prominent member of the Viceroy's Council, about the disabilities which continued to plague his fellow-countrymen. One of these was the £3 tax in Natal, which applied only to Indian contract labourers and their families, for whom it was ruinous, and which had failed both as a means of raising revenue and as a means of encouraging Indians to return home. Another was the restrictions on the immigration of Indians and on their freedom of movement between provinces. A third was the restrictions on their property and trading rights.

The immigration problem was the first to raise its head after Union. The Government of India placed a ban on further emigration to South Africa in 1911, at Lord Crewe's behest, partly to save Botha embarrassment. Botha's Government, thus given a breathing space in which to devise its own rules, tried three times to bring in a satisfactory immigration law between 1911 and 1913, and although Parliament carried a Bill in the latter year, no formula was found which satisfied white South African fears of swamping on the one hand, and Indian dignity on the other.

Gokhale visited the Union in October 1912, and returned to India under the impression that the Government had agreed to abolish the Natal tax in return for his acceptance of Union legislation which informally restricted Indian settlement. But he was not to know that a concession which allowed the immigrant to choose the European language in which he would have to take a dictation, rather than have it chosen for him, would be rendered ineffective by an announcement by the chairman of the Durban Appeal Board (endorsed subsequently by Botha) that all Asians by definition would be declared undesirable immigrants on economic or cultural grounds.

9   Rivals (6) Gandhi and J. C. Smuts

This offensive pronouncement provided the catalyst for Gandhi's last and most effective South African *satyagraha*. Its success has been attributed by recent scholars to a conscious decision by Gandhi to pick an issue which brought an important new element into the resistance movement, identified by Ginwala as the 'petty bourgeoisie', and by Swan as the 'new elite' (descendants of the first indentured labourers who had risen to become lawyers, civil servants, teachers, small businessmen and farmers). Gandhi made a point, however, of keeping other controversies on the boil, and by 1913 he was laying stress on four major issues apart from the head tax: property rights, Indian entry into the Cape under the restrictive Immigration Act of 1906, restrictions on Indians in the Orange Free State dating from the 1880s, and the legality of Indian marriages (arising out of recent judgments in the Transvaal and Cape Supreme Courts, in which the courts had made it progressively harder for Indians to bring into South Africa, first more than one wife of a polygamous marriage, then any such wives, and finally – by Judge Searle in Cape Town on 14 March 1913 – any wives who were not Christians). But as Gandhi later recorded, 'The undertaking given to Gokhale cleared the way for the satyagrahis.' Some moved out of Natal across the Transvaal border and were arrested under the Transvaal Immigration Regulation Act of 1908. Others moved from the Transvaal and went to the Natal collieries, where they organised the non-payment of the £3 tax by those liable to it, and a strike by those who were not liable, until the tax should be withdrawn. Strike action spread to the coastal sugar estates. Gandhi was arrested and released on bail several times before being sent off to prison in Bloemfontein. But the demonstration was publicised across the world. The Government of India and the

Viceroy, Lord Hardinge, were outspoken in their criticism. After Lord Crewe had proposed an informal inquiry into the South African Indian problem, Botha appointed a commission chaired by the South African judge, Sir William Solomon, to which Sir Benjamin Robertson gave evidence on behalf of the Government of India, after inclusion of an Indian had been refused by Botha. The Indian community boycotted the Solomon Commission on account of its membership; but Smuts and Gandhi met on 16 January 1914 and with the help of Robertson and Gandhi's missionary friend, the Rev. C. F. Andrews, the terms of a compromise were hammered out which came to be embodied in the Indian Relief Act of the same year. This Act abolished the £3 tax entirely, recognised marriages performed by accredited marriage officers of any Indian religion, and made it possible for children of Indians domiciled in South Africa to join their families; but it did not remove restrictions on Indian residence, land ownership and trading where these existed.

When Gandhi finally left South Africa in July 1914, to the great relief of Smuts, he had made a few explicit gains, but knew that the legislation of that year could not be the end of the story. Very soon renewed friction developed under the existing restrictive laws. Thus, in the Transvaal, Indians discovered that it was possible to evade the Gold Law and Townships Act of 1908 by establishing businesses under the Transvaal Companies Act of 1909, and to evade Law 3 of 1885, respecting the ownership of property, by registering it in the names of companies, which was declared lawful by the courts in 1916 and confirmed on appeal in 1920. The number of Indian private companies in the Transvaal grew from three in 1913 to 103 in 1916. Whites of Krugersdorp initiated a South Africans' League in 1919, under the chairmanship of Sir Abe Bailey, the local M.P., to work for the expropriation of Indians who had acquired property in defiance of the Gold Law. An Anti-Asiatic League congress met in Pretoria in September that year, attended by twenty-six local authorities, thirty chambers of commerce, nine agricultural societies, twelve religious congregations and forty trade unions. The parliamentary select committee under E. Rooth, which was appointed to look into the problem, came up with milder recommendations than might have been the case, given the state of white public feeling. From its report emerged a Transvaal Asiatic Land and Trading Amendment Act in 1919 which exempted Indians with businesses in mining areas if they still occupied the sites, but prohibited the ownership of fixed property by companies in which one or more Asians had a controlling interest. On acceding to the premiership, Smuts appointed another commission under Judge J. H. Lange, to which Sir Benjamin Robertson was again attached. In 1921 this body rejected suggestions that Indian traders be required to live 'at some distance outside the town proper', considering it 'unjust and unreasonable to force men who had been trading in the centre of the town for many years, and established businesses there, to remove to an outside location'. It recommended voluntary segregation, and voluntary repatriation to India. It thought that the Transvaal Land and Trading Act of 1919 should be retained, and that Indian land purchases in Natal should be restricted to the coastal belt. But white public opinion was beginning to demand radical solutions, and the extent of their pressure can be gauged from Smuts's willingness, even after a serious clash with Dr Sastri at the 1921 Imperial Conference, and with Sir Tej Bahadur Sapru at the conference of 1923, to allow Patrick Duncan to introduce the segregationist Class Areas Bill in 1924.

It was at the 1917 conference that the Government of India had first given clear warning that it intended to press for fair treatment for Indians in Commonwealth countries. Smuts played for time. In 1921 and 1923 his encounters with Sastri and Sapru carried the controversy deeper. Most Dominion prime ministers accepted that their policies towards Asians were capable of improvement. Smuts alone took the line that, because of the peculiar racial balance of his country, and the difficulty of granting rights to Asians without extending them also to the African majority, his Government was not in a position to make concessions. For Sapru, it was a matter of *izzat* (honour); for Smuts, a question of the white man's position in society, and in the last resort of his continuing presence in southern Africa. But it was Sapru who won the battle of words, and he made one remark which threw a long shadow:

> I tell him frankly that if the Indian problem in South Africa is allowed to fester much longer it will pass . . . beyond the bounds of a domestic issue and will become a question of foreign policy of such gravity that upon it the unity of the Empire may founder irretrievably.

For a start, the political organisations which had been set up to represent Indian interests in Natal, the Cape and the Transvaal amalgamated to form the South African Indian Congress in May 1923. But like the African people, the Indians found no effective way of asserting their power. It had been established by 1924, therefore, that the direction of South African public life was assuredly in the white man's hands. But over the question of which whites were to do the controlling, there was still room for doubt.

10.5 WHITE WORKER RESISTANCE, 1913–14

In May 1913 a dispute took place at the New Kleinfontein mine over the relatively minor issue of Saturday afternoon work. Mishandling by the management resulted in a walk-out, which was used by the strike committee as a lever to force the recognition of the Transvaal Federation of Trades (which had come into being in 1911) as a legitimate negotiating body for the labour movement. This was a much more important issue of principle, especially in the light of Yudelman's well-grounded observation that a close understanding had developed in mining and government circles from the time of the 1907 strike that it would be necessary to subjugate white workers in the interest of both political and economic stability. The potential gravity of the crisis was underestimated by the Minister of Mines, F. S. Malan, while the Chamber seems to have overestimated the ability of the state to deal with a major worker confrontation, once a white work force of 19,000 men from all the mines had come out on strike by 5 July. Smuts, as Minister of Defence, was aware of the unpreparedness of the new Active Citizen Force to cope with such a crisis, especially when Imperial troops released for action by the Governor-General proved unable to maintain order and prevent the burning of Park Station and the offices of the *Star* in Johannesburg. He and Botha, at some personal risk, braved the anger of the strikers and made terms with their leaders at a meeting in the Carlton Hotel, agreeing on behalf of the management to reinstate the workers if they ended their resistance.

It was fortunate both for the Government and the Chamber that the strike leaders proved so accommodating. Katz has emphasised the moderation of the Federation of Trades and rejected the suggestion that they were involved in any syndicalist conspiracy to overthrow the state. Yudelman goes further, and argues that the strikers 'missed a clear opportunity to seize control of the state, by wavering between purely industrial demands and radical political goals'. Never again would they be in so strong a position to do so, especially if – as seemed possible at that stage – they could make common cause with Afrikaner opponents of the Government in the rural areas. Afrikaners, after all, were beginning to join the trade unions despite some discouragement from Dutch Reformed clergy, while Afrikaner-dominated branches of the Labour Party were coming into being on the Transvaal *platteland*.

But the opportunity passed by. The general strike of 1914 showed that real bonds of unity between the mineworkers and the Nationalists did not exist.

This strike, which broke out in an atmosphere of continuing tension after the tame resolution of the 1913 crisis, began on 8 January, on the heels of a government threat to lay off Railway and Harbour employees. The Federation of the Trades backed the railwaymen with a call for a general strike on the 13th. As the Railways were an essential service, precluded from strike activity by special legislation, their confrontation was a special challenge to the Government, especially when workers from some fifty-three mines came out in their support. But by now Smuts's Active Citizen Force was in a position to act. He brought 10,000 troops to the Rand and had martial law proclaimed on the 14th. Nowhere was the division between the English-speaking workers and potential Afrikaner opponents of the regime more clearly demonstrated than in the arrival on the Rand of A.C.F. commandos under Generals Beyers and De la Rey, with supporting artillery. Both men would lose their lives, as promoters of the Afrikaner rebellion against the Government, before the year was out. But now their forces surrounded the Johannesburg Trades Hall and secured the arrest of the executive of the Federation of Trades, along with many other strikers. These included Creswell and Boydell of the Labour Party (both cabinet ministers under Hertzog from 1924) and W. H. Andrews (then Labour Party chairman and later leader of the Communist Party). In a demonstration of *kragdadigheid* (power play) which deeply offended many believers in the rule of law, notably Hertzog and Merriman, Smuts deported the nine strike leaders on 30 January, and then covered his actions by an Indemnity

(a) F. Holland of the *Star* balances phthisis deaths and profits (1913)

(b) Boonzaier of the *Burger* links the Botha Government with capitalism, martial law and repression (1914)

10   Hostile views of Hoggenheimer in relation to the 191 strike and the 1914 Afrikaner rebellion

and Undesirables Special Deportation Bill. To ensure public order, he then introduced a Riotous Assemblies Bill in the Assembly, which prohibited recruitment to unions by force, banned violent picketing and any strikes in the public utility services, permitted magistrates to prohibit meetings thought likely to endanger public peace, and greatly increased police powers of law enforcement.

When the Labour Party won a majority of seats in the Transvaal Provincial Council in the elections of March 1914, even constituencies like Krugersdorp and Pretoria West returning English-speaking Labour candidates, it looked as if the suppression of the strike had merely tensed the spring of worker opposition. But the realities of the situation were different. The state was now armed to deal with unrest. The steps it had taken to secure the recognition of the right of white unions to take part in collective bargaining, with the agreement of the Government and the Chamber, should be seen rather as part of a strategy of cooptation than as a concession to union strength (Yudelman). Furthermore, both the Labour and the Afrikaner opposition movements soon lost their capacity to resist as a consequence of their own actions after the outbreak of the First World War.

The Labour Party split on the issue of participation in the war. A minority of convinced socialists, led by D. Ivon Jones, S. P. Bunting and Colin Wade, set up a War on War League in September 1914 and carried an anti-war resolution at the Party conference at East London in January 1915. But the majority under Colonel Creswell, who favoured participation in the war, soon regained control over the Party, and in doing so lost the contact with the rural Afrikaner which their Rural Propaganda Committee had cultivated assiduously.

10.6   THE INVASION OF GERMAN SOUTH WEST AFRICA AND THE AFRIKANER REBELLION OF 1914

There was real opposition in the Afrikaner camp in August 1914, when the Imperial Government asked the South African Government to invade German South West Africa, the colonial territory of a friendly power, to immobilise radio stations and capture Swakopmund, Luderitzbucht and Windhuk. Botha was told that, if South Africa did not act, other Imperial forces would be sent. The Government therefore had to view the matter in the light, not only of immediate military necessity, but also of longer term national interest, with incorporation of the territory in the Union as a possibility. The opponents of invasion took various stances and, as Spies has shown, were by no means confined at first to the Opposition ranks, since four members of the Cabinet, including F. S. Malan, were among them. Hertzog was not prepared to admit that South Africa was legally involved in Britain's war. General C. F. Beyers, who was commander of the Active Citizen Force, J. H. de la Rey, who was now a Union senator and still a close friend of Botha, and General de Wet, who was now a Nationalist, were all opposed to the invasion of German territory, and all may have thought that the time was ripe for a restoration of republican independence. Others, of whom General S. G. ('Manie') Maritz was the most prominent, quite clearly desired a republican restoration, if necessary with German support. Maritz, whose commandos had ranged over the north-western Cape with those of Smuts at the end of the Anglo-Boer war, was in command of the military district which covered the South West African frontier, and had been appointed, like Beyers, by Smuts.

Botha and Smuts underrated the opposition to the proposed campaign, which a special session of Parliament had agreed to by 12 September with big majorities in the Assembly and in the Senate. The Nationalists opposed invasion at their August congress. The Transvaal and Free State commandants dissented at a special briefing, and there was an excited republican demonstration at Lichtenburg in the western Transvaal on 15 August, apparently inspired by the dreams of a local 'prophet', Van Rensburg. The Government therefore stated that only volunteers would be asked to cross into German territory, but this assurance was not punctiliously carried out. On 15 September, Beyers resigned his commission. That night, after failing to stop at a road block in Langlaagte while he and Beyers were on their way to Potchefstroom, De la Rey was shot and killed (accidentally, according to Judge Gregorowski, who made the official investigation) by troops who were under orders to intercept the criminal Foster gang. The shooting of De la Rey may have delayed the outbreak of a planned rebellion. But on 9 October, cornered by Smuts into admitting treasonable intentions, Maritz went over to the Germans, who were embarrassed by his action because they were not anxious to provoke hostilities on their poorly defended frontiers. Beyers and De Wet then faced a hard choice. Beyers rebelled after being physically assaulted while addressing a meeting in Pretoria. De Wet also went into open rebellion. Soon afterwards his son was killed by Government forces while he himself was on his way to seek ex-president Steyn's mediation.

The rebels were put down in a few weeks, and Botha, who waited for over two weeks before declining a secret British offer of Australian and New Zealand troops, decided in the end to use only Afrikaners against them. De Wet's defeat at Mushroom Valley demonstrated that evasive commando action was less easy to contrive in the age of the motor car. Beyers perished while in retreat across the Vaal river. General J. C. G. Kemp, who crossed the Kalahari in a vain attempt to join Maritz, surrendered in January 1915. Maritz himself escaped to Angola. The sentences imposed on the rebels were generally lenient – seven years for the ringleaders, but none served more than two. Yet the rebellion added to the Afrikaner hall of fame, producing more legends and martyrs to inspire a new nationalist movement in the 1930s. De la Rey was held to be a murder victim; Beyers came to be seen as a martyr to his conscience who had died without having fired a shot in anger, symbolically uniting Transvalers and Free Staters by his death in the river which divided them; while Jopie Fourie, who had not resigned his commission before rebelling, and had been executed for shooting at Government forces under a flag of truce, excited feelings rather by the manner of his death – facing his executioners without a blindfold, on a Sunday, singing a psalm, after Dr D. F. Malan had tried unsuccessfully to find Smuts to intercede on his behalf. Not surprisingly, the rebellion consolidated Nationalist forces behind Hertzog, who himself stood up to a severe grilling by a parliamentary select committee under Patrick Duncan, and cleared his party of the allegation of collective treason. To help pay the fines of the rebel leaders, the *Helpmekaar* society was born. Competitive giving to a popular cause, which had created *Helpmekaar*, was extended in 1916 to the subscription lists of the first Nationalist newspaper, *De Burger*. The Nationalists made impressive gains in the 1915 general election, taking 16 out of the 17 Free State seats, as well as 7 in the Cape and 4 in the Transvaal, and netted 77,000 votes to the S.A.P.'s 95,000. Despite the victory of Union arms in South West Africa, the S.A.P. lost eight seats and the Unionists (if one includes the Natal Independents of 1910) a further ten.

10.7 SOUTH AFRICA IN THE GREAT WAR

The war brought and held the S.A.P. and the Unionists together in competitive enthusiasm for the Allied cause. The organisation of the South West African campaign, which was over by 15 July 1915, was essentially the work of the Government. Botha himself overran the north. Smuts, taking over from Van Deventer, completed the conquest of the south, and then – after some initial reluctance to assume command – began the conquest of German East Africa in February 1916. He was denied the fruits of victory, however, by the brilliant rearguard defence of the German commander, Von Lettow-Vorbeck. Botha had meanwhile responded to pressure from his Unionist allies and offered to send a South African contingent to Europe. A brigade of 6,000 men was accordingly sent to Britain in December 1915. It was almost immediately switched to Egypt to help defend the Suez Canal against Turkish attacks, but after successfully concluding the Egyptian campaign it was sent to France in April 1916, where it took part in the battle of the Somme in July, and won great military distinction by taking and then holding Delville Wood on an exposed salient of the British line, losing over two-thirds of its strength in the process. After playing a prominent part in the advance into Belgium in 1917, the South African brigade was almost exterminated before it surrendered during the German offensive of March 1918.

Apart from their continuing opposition to the Land Act and to the segregationist features of the Native Administration Bill of 1917, African politicians restrained their utterances during the war years. They generally gave support to the Allied cause, even though the Defence Act made no provision for the arming of non-whites, and offers to recruit Coloured and African troops for the armed forces were initially rejected. Considerable numbers served in the South West African, East African and Western Front campaigns in non-combatant roles, and when the troopship *Mendi* sank on the way to Europe in 1917, some 615 Africans lost their lives. Total South African fatalities on all fronts amounted to 7,304.

10.8   PARTY REALIGNMENTS, 1915–21

The loss of electoral support which the Unionists suffered, accompanied by resignations of their leaders (Farrar, Jameson, Chaplin, Phillips, Abe Bailey, and ultimately FitzPatrick) in the period 1911 to 1920, induced a mood of frustration among them. The few who hung on, like Smartt, Duncan and Jagger, began to talk of coalition, which Merriman had resisted so firmly and Botha so deviously, on the eve of Union. But the South African Party did not reciprocate since their support against the Nationalists was assured, the desire to bring the Hertzogites back into their fold was always present, and the fear that Afrikaner working men might move across to Labour was always real.

At the end of 1919 the Unionists and the S.A.P. merely flirted discreetly with each other. Smartt reverted to the 'best man' theme at his party congress in October, and spoke favourably of 'fair amalgamation' without surrender of identity by his own party. Smuts replied at the S.A.P. congress the same month with a carefully limited request for their 'hearty co-operation'. The general election of March 1920 made the Nationalists, with 44 seats, the largest party in the Assembly. The S.A.P. dropped back to 41 seats, the Unionists to 25, while the Labour Party, profiting from triangular contests and from popular discontent during the post-war depression, won 21 seats as against the four previously held. Smuts, after failing to persuade the other parties to form a non-party government, decided to woo the Nationalists again. A private congress at Robertson, however, followed by a public one at Bloemfontein in September 1920, broke down over the definition of South Africa's relationship to the Empire, chiefly because the Nationalists had decided in 1919 to make republicanism a permissible article of faith, and sent a deputation to Versailles in a futile bid to ask for a restoration of freedom. Smuts therefore circularised all S.A.P. branches with a call for the establishment of a new centre party dedicated to support of the British Commonwealth. A special S.A.P. congress at the end of October accepted a resolution standing in Smuts's name, which discreetly discouraged aspirant republicans, recognised the priority of South African interests as a condition for the maintenance of the Imperial bond, and asserted the equality of the two white language groups and the need for them to work together. The Unionists accepted this overture, and, at a special congress in Bloemfontein at the beginning of November, gave their executive discretion to act. Most delegates were willing to join the S.A.P. on the latter's terms, after Smuts had appealed through Smartt for an understanding of his special difficulties. Although Sir Edgar Walton wanted fusion on equal terms, Smartt thought that the strengthening of the S.A.P. was necessary to keep the Nationalists out of power. The Unionist Party was accordingly dissolved, and its members encouraged to join the S.A.P. as individuals. Smuts announced publicly that there had been no amalgamation of parties, but that the Unionists had joined the S.A.P. 'unconditionally and without bargaining'. He told Hofmeyr privately that 'the dissolution of the party of Rhodes and Jameson is one of the greatest victories ever obtained on the road to "het Zuid Afrikaanderisme"'. He then had Parliament dissolved, and in the 1921 election the enlarged S.A.P. was returned to power with 79 seats, won mainly at the expense of Labour, who were cut back to 9, while the Nationalists increased their holding to 45. Smartt, Jagger and Duncan received posts in the new Cabinet.

10.9   SMUTS AT VERSAILLES, THE SOUTH WEST AFRICAN MANDATE AND THE BID TO INCORPORATE SOUTHERN RHODESIA AND THE PROTECTORATES

Among the factors which aided the rapprochement of the S.A.P. and the Unionists must be included the contributions made by Botha and Smuts at the Paris peace conference, and to the debate on the nature of the emerging Commonwealth, and their attempts to secure an extension of South African influence on the African continent.

Lloyd George had appointed Smuts to the British War Cabinet in January 1917 in the hope that he might be able to deal with pressures on the Government by the General Staff. Smuts's military advice proved to be of little consequence; but the ideas expressed in his pamphlet of 1917, *The League of Nations: A Practical Suggestion*, had a direct influence on the formulation of President Wilson's plans for a post-war settlement. Wilson took from Smuts several key features of his League proposals, among them the idea of a strong League Council composed of the Great Powers, joined by representatives of smaller states in rotation, and the device of a veto to restrain the League from acting if three council members exercised it.

Smuts's influence at the peace conference, as a member of the British delegation, had one serious result not intended by himself. He gave an opinion that war widows' pensions could legitimately be charged against the German reparations account. The effect of this was to escalate the Allied demands for compensation to the massive sum of £6,000 m. Smuts then signed the peace treaty only with great reluctance, for, with the memory of Vereeniging still green, he saw no virtue in a peace which fostered resentment.

Smuts gave Wilson the idea of the League Mandate system, but intended that it should be applied to the satellite provinces of the broken Central Powers. Wilson adopted the idea, but insisted that it be applied to all conquered colonial territories such as German South West Africa, which Smuts intended to annex. Smuts countered with a proposal for three categories of mandate, and was able to arrange that the 'C' class, in which South West Africa fell, allowed for the government of the territory under the laws of the mandatory power, an arrangement stopping just short of annexation.

The extent to which Smuts and Botha had taken part in the war in Africa in order to be able to extend South Africa's influence on the Continent, and that with Colonial Office approval, was not clearly revealed until the 1970s. Apart from the incorporation of South West Africa, Smuts had hoped in 1915 that the conquest of German East Africa would lead to its being exchanged with the Portuguese for the whole of Mozambique south of the Zambesi (including Lourenço Marques and Beira), which could then be incorporated in the Union. Difficulties with the Portuguese over the 1909 tariff agreement, and problems associated with the negotiation of a new one, were seen as strong arguments for this alternative approach. If the Protectorates were then to fall into the Union's lap, and if Southern Rhodesia were to vote itself into the Union, as Smuts hoped it would, then territory more than three times the size of the Union would fall under the control of Pretoria. Nor was revisionist cartography (see Chanock) confined to Smuts, for in 1916 Lord Buxton, the High Commissioner, submitted a memorandum to the Colonial Office proposing the partitioning of southern Mozambique and Bechuanaland between the Union and Southern Rhodesia, the incorporation of Barotseland in Southern Rhodesia, and the amalgamation of North-Eastern Rhodesia with Nyasaland in a new Central African Protectorate – the creation, that is, of two British territories to the north of the Limpopo as a counterweight to the enlarged Union to the south of it. But without Portuguese cooperation, these remained merely interesting dreams.

Smuts tried but failed to incorporate Southern Rhodesia. Successive amendments to the original Order-in-Council had resulted in an elective majority in the Southern Rhodesian Legislative Council, and Settler support for Chartered Company rule had diminished on account of the Company's assumption of vested rights in unappropriated land, which a Privy Council judgment in 1918 allocated to the Crown. Meanwhile Charles Coghlan, who had originally favoured incorporation in South Africa, joined the newly-formed Responsible Government Association to press for political autonomy for Southern Rhodesia. By 1923 the two main alternatives offered to the electorate in a referendum were self-government and incorporation in the Union. Strong pressures were applied in favour of incorporation. Milner, now Colonial secretary, threw his weight behind it, as did the *Argus* press, though Winston Churchill, Milner's successor, was less inclined to force the issue. From the South African side, Smuts desired it for reasons of political strategy – the extension of Union influence northwards, and the incorporation of a territory likely to support the S.A.P.–Unionist fusion against Hertzog's Nationalists. The incorporationists found a Rhodesian leader in Drummond Chaplin. Smuts offered attractive terms: incorporation as a fifth province with ten members in the Assembly, the promise of railway and harbour development, the establishment of a land settlement board to bring in a large white settler population, and respect for the borders of existing native reserves. By a fairly narrow majority of 8,774 votes to 5,989 in an 80 per cent poll, the Southern Rhodesian electorate voted in favour of independent self-government. Apart from those English-speaking voters who were frightened by Hertzog's success in the South African election of 1920, the majority seems to have consisted largely of farmers who depended on world rather than South African markets, employers of black labour anxious to inhibit its southward flow, white workers angered by the Union's suppression of the

1922 rebellion, and white women who enjoyed the franchise (whereas their South African counterparts did not).

The High Commission Territories, excluded from the Union under the National Convention on account of the British Government's reservations over white South African ideas on native policy, continued to attract the interest of Botha and Smuts in spite of this initial rebuff. Botha had begun to urge their incorporation even before the outbreak of the First World War. He first made a special plea for Swaziland on the ground that it was already extensively occupied by white people, in face of a warning by the Secretary of State, Lewis Harcourt, not to alienate African feelings by trying to force the pace. Botha also put in a bid for Bechuanaland, acting on information (which proved unreliable) that the B.S.A. Company might be about to extract land rights there from the British Government under the terms of its charter. The Colonial Office steadily refused to part with any of the Territories, on the ground that African opinion was strongly opposed to transfer. After the First World War, Botha raised the question of Swaziland's transfer again, claiming that this territory was the best suited of the three for an experimental takeover, and urging that this would make it possible to give whites in Swaziland political representation, and at the same time enable the Union Government to extend rail communications from the Transvaal through the mining districts of Swaziland to the coast. Smuts kept up the pressure after Botha's death. Lord Buxton, the Imperial High Commissioner, was more sensitive to African desires than his predecessor, Lord Gladstone, had been, and it was partly to meet his objections to transfer that Smuts introduced his Native Affairs Bill of 1920, which provided for a statutory Native Affairs Commission of the kind defined in the Schedule to the South Africa Act. Once the Bill had become law, Smuts asked for the transfer of Swaziland, offering immediate railway development and representation for whites. But the newly installed Paramount Chief, Sobhuza II, led a deputation to London at the end of 1922 to protest against transfer and fight the British Government's land apportionment of 1907 before the Privy Council.

By the time of its fall from power in 1924, therefore, the South African Party Government had achieved most of what it wanted in relation to South West Africa, but failed to obtain either Southern Rhodesia, or the Territories, or any portion of Mozambique. In the last resort, these bids for territorial expansion had failed because Imperial support had been withdrawn. The new doctrine of the paramountcy of African interests, which had been clearly expressed by the Duke of Devonshire in relation to Kenya in 1923, lay behind the British attitude. It formed no part of Smuts's vision, for Smuts had come to look upon the extension of 'a great White Africa along the Eastern backbone, with railway and road communications connecting north and south', as a necessary guarantee for the long-term security of the white south. His correspondence with Lord Delamere during the 1920s, and his Rhodes Lectures at Oxford in 1929, amply demonstrate this point.

It is now recognised that, by his performance at the Imperial War Conference of 1917 and at the subsequent Imperial Conference of 1921,

Smuts went a long way towards bringing about the definition of dominion status for which General Hertzog received most of the credit in 1926. There had been a tendency for Commonwealth solidarity to grow during the war years. Smuts himself strongly supported the idea of the Commonwealth, as a comity of nations held together by consent, in stark contrast to the Hohenzollern, Habsburg, Romanov and Turkish Empires, which had not been based on government by consent, and had also failed to survive the war. But, with the lesson of Ireland much in mind, he warned against over-centralisation, and spoke in support of Sir Robert Borden's Resolution Nine at the 1917 conference. This Canadian proposal called for a special conference after the war to readjust the constitutional relationships of the component parts of the Empire, stressing Dominion self-government, and proper participation by the Dominions, as autonomous states, in the framing of a common foreign policy by means of continuous consultation. At the Prime Ministers' Conference in 1921 Smuts put in a plea for 'the practical recognition of the equality of statehood of the Dominions with the United Kingdom', and for legislation by the British Parliament to remove both the restrictions of the Colonial Laws Validity Act of 1865 on dominion law-making powers, and also the right of the British Parliament to legislate in respect of the Dominions, as well as to limit the Governor-General's powers to those of a viceroy. The Prime Ministers, however, swayed by the rhetoric of W. M. Hughes, who spoke for Australia, rejected Smuts's proposals, which covered in their main features the subsequent provisions of the 1931 Statute of Westminster.

10.10   SHADOWS OVER THE SMUTS REGIME, 1921–2: BONDELSWARTS, BULHOEK AND THE RAND REBELLION

But if Smuts's imagination grasped the concept of dominion autonomy without managing to steer the British Commonwealth in that direction, his government also had the short-sightedness to steer South Africa into the minefield of international disapproval over racial policy. In 1921 it crushed the Bondelswarts, a Khoi chiefdom in southern South West Africa, whose hopes for redress of grievances when the Union Government took over the territory were soon disappointed. They complained about the non-restoration of their captain, Jacobus Christian, about continuing white penetration of their land, and the new Government's imposition of a graded dog tax which severely limited their ability to keep packs of dogs for purposes of hunting game. Christian was arrested without proper cause, while he was on his way to the police station to report his return from exile. Abraham Morris, who had led the Bondelswart resistance to the Germans and had fled to the Union for sanctuary, had returned in May 1922, still a popular hero, with a group of armed companions. Violence broke out between the Government and the Bondelswarts because Morris's followers would not allow him to surrender their guns, and because Christian and the new Administrator of South West Africa, G. R. Hofmeyr, failed to reach a proper understanding about their surrender a fortnight later. Hofmeyr resolved on a punitive expedition, but aircraft used to bomb the Bondel-swart flocks killed some women and children, and drove the menfolk into rebellion in the mountains. They were soon suppressed by Union troops and aircraft; but the affair was given widespread international publicity and was debated over a full year in the Permanent Mandates Commission of the League of Nations. Smuts attempted in private to restrain Hofmeyr, but defended him in public at the cost of his own reputation.

In the following year there was violence at Bulhoek, when Enoch Mgijima, leader of the Israelite sect, squatted with his followers on the commonage at Ntabelanga, near Queenstown, and defied all government attempts to persuade them to depart. In the end they suffered grievous loss of life when blind faith in their leader's words drove them to attack the police. This seems to have been a tragic example of group resentment among landless blacks, seeking an outlet in the millenarian teachings of a leader whose message drew on Jewish and Christian symbolism, having been initially inspired by the passage of Halley's Comet.

Bondelswarts and Bulhoek, coming after the suppression of the Afri-kaner rebellion of 1914, made inroads into the popularity of the S.A. Party which the absorption of the Unionists in 1920 barely counteracted. But the event which really destroyed the image of the Government in the public mind was its handling of the Rand crisis of 1920–2.

At the end of the First World War the sterling value of gold was allowed to float, and reached an average price level of about 26 per cent above the figure of 85s an ounce which had prevailed during the War. But between the beginning of 1920 and the end of 1921 deflationary policies in Britain and South Africa restored the relative value of their currencies at the expense of gold. The South African mines found it difficult to face the fall in the gold price because of a marked increase in costs since 1914, and when the Low Grade Mines Commission reported in May 1920 it warned that with the decline in prosperity which was expected to continue, some twenty-one mines, constituting about half the Rand gold industry, and employing over ten thousand whites and over eighty thousand Africans, were in danger of becoming unprofitable. These facts need to be set against the tendency during the war years for white miners' wages to rise in step with the cost of living, at a faster rate than those of blacks (Davies), whose resentment was reflected in a series of strikes, culminating in a major one in February 1920 (Bonner). This strike, which broke out after the arrest of two miners who had campaigned for a pay increase, was impressive for its range, in that twenty-one of thirty-five mines, and altogether 71,000 Africans were involved. It was led mainly by Shangaan and Pedi elements, a number of whom lived outside the compounds and thus had political contact with wider African opinion. But despite its widespread nature, and the fact that it was the climax of several years' unrest, the strike was quickly put down. The police, profiting from the recommendations of

Commissioner Buckle's report on African grievances after the 1913 strike, dealt with the mine compounds piecemeal, and broke resistance by destroying communications between them. There was some loss of life at the Village Deep compound.

In 1920, according to Hancock, 21,455 whites employed on the mines earned a total of £10.64 million, whereas 179,000 blacks earned £5.96 million. The wage bill was the one area in which costs could be cut to meet rising expenditure, and this made the 'grey area' of semi-skilled employment, that is jobs related to 'drill-sharpening, waste packing, pipe and track laying, rough timbering, whitewashing' and similar types of work (Johnstone), the most sensitive area, for blacks and whites were commonly employed in these tasks. To maintain an equilibrium and keep the peace among both black and white miners, the Chamber had persuaded them to accept a *status quo* agreement in September 1918, under which the existing allocation of work to the different race groups had been frozen. This was, in Johnstone's words, 'a strategy of extreme accommodation, designed to minimise class conflict and to stem a rising tide of workers' militancy'. It was accompanied, writes Davies, by 'the greatest proliferation of negotiating machinery in the industry's history, before or since'.

But in November 1921, in face of the growing economic crisis, the Chamber gave notice of its intention to abandon the *status quo* agreement by eliminating a colour bar in any semi-skilled work. Though over 15,000 white workers might ultimately lose their jobs, the Chamber intimated that it did not expect more than 2,000 to be retrenched, and replaced immediately, on the implementation of its policy on 1 February 1922.

The South African Industrial Federation, to which the trade unions related to mining were affiliated, could have asked for a board of conciliation under the Transvaal Industrial Disputes Prevention Act of 1909; but the legislation was unpopular, according to Davies, because awards under its rules were mandatory, and it was largely discredited in the workers' view because the owners had tried to circumvent its procedures in 1913 (Katz). Nor could the Federation handle developments on the gold mines in isolation, because the Chamber's abandonment of the *status quo* agreement coincided with a new bid by the coal-owners to depress wages, and a refusal by the Victoria Falls Power Company to agree to higher wage demands. Meanwhile Percy Fisher, the irregularly elected and subsequently deposed secretary of the S.A.M.W.U. announced the formation of a new and militant Miners' Council of Action, which had managed by January 1922 to infiltrate many of the unions and set up a Red International of Labour Unions with revolutionary intent.

Thus pressurised on two sides, the S.A.I.F. balloted its members and brought the coalminers out on 2 January and the goldminers, engineers and power-workers out on the 10th. It put the direction of the strike in the hands of an augmented executive, and organised the strikers into unofficial commandos across the Rand and in the country districts to meet force with force – an indication of the growing Afrikaner presence in the Mineworkers' Union, many of whom were political supporters of Hertzog.

The Labour and Nationalist Parties were quick to identify themselves with the cause of the strikers. On 14 January the former publicly backed the S.A.I.F.'s action, while the *Vaderland* carried a letter by Tielman Roos, the Transvaal Nationalist leader, urging Active Citizen Force members to disobey the call-up, if it were made.

Immediately after the start of the goldminers' strike, Smuts arranged for direct negotiations between the Chamber and the S.A.I.F., under the chairmanship of Judge Curlewis; but after two weeks of bargaining, these meetings broke up in failure on the 27th. The Chamber now insisted, instead of abrogating the *status quo* agreement, on an employment ratio of two whites to twenty-one blacks for a two-year period, which implied more white dismissals than would have been the case under their earlier offer. The Federation demanded nothing less than two whites to seven blacks, which was an abnormally high ratio of whites, and followed the breakdown of the negotiations with a public attack on the Government on the 29th, alleging that it was in collusion with the owners. This was to turn an industrial struggle into a political conflict. An unofficial 'Parliament' convened by Nationalists and Labour members in Pretoria on 30 January heard an appeal by R. B. Waterston on 5 February to proclaim an independent republic.

These developments cut across a new round of negotiations between Smuts and the moderate members of the S.A.I.F., which made some progress. On 5 February Smuts accordingly persuaded the Chamber to modify its earlier terms by agreeing that the *status quo* arrangements could continue on all save the low-grade mines until an impartial report had been considered by the Government. The S.A.I.F. tried on the 6th to have these terms further modified, but to this the Chamber would not agree. Next day Crawford, the moderate Mineworkers' leader, backed the strike committee's approval of the use of commandos against scabbing. But the workers' feelings now appeared to be wavering, and the augmented executive of the S.A.I.F. rejected a call for a general strike on 8 February, even after the arrest of Percy Fisher and Ernie Shaw of S.A.M.W.U. for incitement.

On 11 February Smuts came down clearly on the side of the owners (Simons) with an 'abrupt change of front' (Hancock). He called on the owners to restart the mines, and on the workers to go back on the owners' terms, with an assurance that the Government would protect those who did and that Parliament would see that right was done. He then returned to Cape Town to attend Parliament, whose opening had been deferred until 17 February to enable him to take charge of the Rand crisis on the spot. He justified his actions to Parliament during a debate on a confused motion by Hertzog; but the tough line he took against the commandos by declaring them to be unlawful assemblies on the 22nd and authorising police action against them on the 27th, led to the death of three men at Boksburg. The Nationalists demanded an official inquiry. From that moment the crisis escalated fast, yet probably need not have done so. On 2 March, in view of the general move by the miners back to their jobs, the augmented executive of the S.A.I.F. asked the Chamber for a conference without conditions in order to try to end the strike. The Chamber returned an unqualified refusal on the 4th, and in doing so created the conditions under which the revolutionary Miners' Council of Action could seize the initiative and force the S.A.I.F. to proclaim a general strike on the 7th. Smuts mobilised the A.C.F. on the 9th, after violence had already broken out on the Rand, and proclaimed martial law on the 10th. It took several days of bitter fighting between the A.C.F. and the commandos before the insurrection was put down on the 16th. Smuts then followed this at the end of the month with an Indemnity and Trial of Offenders Bill, which set up a special court to try those accused of murder. All other accused were given jury trials. In retrospect, Smuts rejected the Opposition charge that the Government had sat idly by while the rising got out of hand, contending that before declaring martial law the Government was 'bound in the interest of the country to let the situation develop, . . because it was possible that the situation might develop peacefully'. Hertzog misrepresented Smuts's claim to have 'wanted the situation to develop', by deliberately portraying him in a miscast Krugerian role of 'sitting behind the tortoise to stick his fork into its head when it should put its head out', which was proper treatment only for the likes of Jameson. The trouble, from Smuts's point of view, was that Hertzog's mud stuck, because his handling of the strikes of 1913 and 1914, and of the Afrikaner rebellion, and of the shooting of Africans at Port Elizabeth in 1920 and Queenstown in 1921 made it easy to caricature him as one whose footsteps 'dripped with blood'.

African mineworkers had more to gain from supporting the mine-owners in 1922 than from supporting the white mineworkers, for abandonment of the 1918 *status quo* agreement which the owners desired would have made twenty-five extra categories of semi-skilled work available for black and Coloured workers. African coalminers in fact continued to work, and with the help of a few officials brought up the coal while the white miners were on strike. But the Chamber sent large numbers of black goldminers back to the Reserves when the strike started, in a necessary move to reduce working costs. The white Mineworkers' Union, consisting largely of men whose past relations with African workers, as Simons has shown, gave them little enough reason to feel a sense of class solidarity with them, had struck with the primary purpose of maintaining the colour bar, and the communist leaders of the strike justified the slogan carried by the Fordsburg commando – 'Workers of the World Unite, and Fight for a White South Africa' – with the suspect plea that the struggle would build up class-consciousness among the white workers, opening the way for the disappearance of the colour bar at a later date. Meanwhile it was necessary to build up an alliance between white townsmen and countrymen to break the Rand tycoons, on whatever terms this could be arranged. Even S. P. Bunting, who later became a dedicated supporter of black emancipation, thought like this. Not surprisingly, the A.P.O. and the I.C.U. both condemned the actions of the white workers in strong terms. There was a good deal of violence between white strikers and Africans, and perhaps thirty Africans lost their lives from the actions of white strikers' commandos. Even so, one should note the argument fully elaborated by Johnstone that much of the opposition of black miners in the years down to and including 1922 was directed against low wages and economic exploitation of blacks under the system, rather than against the job colour bar as such [see pp. 503–12].

10.11 THE NATIONALIST–LABOUR PACT AND THE 1924 GENERAL ELECTION

The growing unpopularity of the South African Party, which was reflected in several by-election defeats, encouraged Hertzog and Creswell to conclude an electoral pact in April 1923. The two leaders condemned the Smuts regime as a tool of 'big finance' and harmful to the country, and stressed that they wanted to save South Africa from a minority government after the next election. They admitted that Nationalist secessionism and Labour's 'bolshevism' were mutual stumbling blocks, but Hertzog assured Creswell that his party would not change existing constitutional relationships with the British Crown if it were returned to power at the next election. The two leaders rejected party fusion, and limited their agreement to an electoral pact under which they shared out controversial seats to avoid mutual contests, and undertook to support each other's candidates. By killing secession as an immediate prospect, Hancock writes, Creswell and Hertzog 'sank the ship which had brought Smuts triumphantly to port in the elections of 1921'. Their alliance also profited from the hard times of 1923, when the mine-owners were trying to turn their victory after the strike of the previous year to good account, and white workers in both language groups looked to government to secure them in their jobs at rates of pay which would enable them to keep up their 'white' standards.

Meanwhile in 1919 Hertzog had started to make a strong bid for Coloured support, and helped to found a United Afrikaner League to build on the cultural links between Coloured and Afrikaner and to weaken the links between Coloured and African (Lewis). In preparation for the election, the Nationalists now proposed to release the Coloured people from the economic colour bar, even to extend the vote to Coloured people in the northern provinces. At a time when the A.P.O normally supported the South African Party, Hertzog's overtures also brought into being an Afrikaner Nasionale Bond in 1925 – a Coloured political movement led by W. H. le Grange, which offered him electoral support. He also won support from M. A. Gamiet's Cape Malay Association, which also took shape after the 1924 election. The Nationalists benefited from Coloured support in every election between 1920 and 1929, notably in 1924, when Dr W. B. de Villiers captured the Stellenbosch seat.

Hertzog also won Kadalie's ear. At its 1923 and 1924 conferences, the I.C.U. decided not to align itself with either white party, and when it convened a 'united Non-European congress' in Cape Town after the dissolution of Parliament in April 1924, its neutral stand alienated both the A.P.O. and the Cape Native Voters' Association, both of which inclined to the S.A.P. The African National Congress (as the S.A.N.N.C. had renamed itself in 1923) went further in its May conference, by urging the black electorate 'to vote solidly' for a change of government. A mixed deputation of I.C.U. and A.N.C. leaders (Kadalie, Thaele, Masabalala and Dlwati) then called on Hertzog in Bloemfontein. Apart from Hertzog's contribution to I.C.U. funds in 1921 and his offer to cover the costs of an election edition of their *Workers' Herald*, there is no evidence that the Nationalists made any specific undertaking to Kadalie in return for the support he then offered.

Smuts, sensing the swing of opinion against the S.A.P., resigned after the loss of a by-election at Wakkerstroom on 5 April 1924. In the ensuing general election, victory went to the Hertzog–Creswell Pact. The Nationalists won 63 seats and Labour 18, giving a total of 81, against the 53 won by the S.A.P., and one by an Independent. This represented a gain for the Nationalists of 16 seats, mainly in the Transvaal and Cape rural areas, a gain of 5 by Labour on the Rand, and a loss of 19 by the S.A.P.; but in terms of votes cast, the S.A.P. polled 47.39 per cent of the total (over 150,000) whereas the Nationalists polled only 36.34 per cent (under 120,000). This was because the Cape, where the S.A.P. won most of its seats, had numerically inflated constituencies, and because the S.A.P. was most successful in the urban constituencies, some of which had been loaded in the 1923 delimitation by as much as 10 per cent. On top of this, the Pact won the propaganda battle. Its call for more segregation, its playing down of the secession issue, its defence of white workers against black competitors and the capitalists, its overtures to Coloured voters and its charges of bloodthirstiness, or lassitude, or economic stringency, levelled against the S.A.P. cumulatively produced the swing which carried Hertzog to power.

The fall of Smuts left big questions about the direction of South African history, perhaps even the viability of Union under the terms of 1910, still largely undecided. On the inter-white front, the coalition rejected by Botha in 1910 had been accepted by Smuts in 1920, but no longer satisfied the electorate on account of the revival of discontent among Afrikaners, which the fathers of Union had tried very hard to avert. From this angle, the Great War could not have come at a worse time, for it had widened the alienation of capital from labour as well as of Nationalist Afrikaner from Briton. On the front of black–white relations, the Botha–Smuts ministries had insisted on white political and economic hegemony, and placed segregationist legislation on the statute book without being entirely convinced of its desirability, which had led them to suppress black discontent rather than seriously try to satisfy it. The resultant growth of inter-racial tension, as reflected in the violence of 1919–22, made the removal of inhumanity in the law harder to contrive, and this fact played into the hands of the more ideological politicians who took over the reins in 1924. At the international level, the first clouds of isolation began to gather, but the weather prophets were not yet insistent with their warnings.

11 The Afrikaner's Road to Parity: Hertzog, 1924–33

11.1 1924 – A TURNING-POINT?

1924, a turning-point in South African history in the popular imagination, is now seen not to have been so to anything like the extent previously envisaged. This is because an earlier view that the Hertzog government was a white workers' government antagonistic to the interests of mining capital, has been substantially dented [see pp. 508–9]. As a 'South Africa First' government it did not generate the kind of campaign which friends of the Empire feared, on account of Hertzog's restraint on Imperial issues. As an Afrikaner nationalist government it was a pale reflection of what was to come later. As a government committed to segregation, it attempted considerably less in that direction than its predecessor. Yet it was a government elected at a moment of public anger, a coalition consisting of elements dissatisfied in various ways, and it is not difficult to pick up changes of emphasis in its public stance – always subject to the limitations of practical politics.

The government which took office on 30 June 1924 was almost devoid of men with cabinet experience, but several of them had won reputations as public figures. Hertzog himself, the stormy petrel of South African politics for over a decade, had sat on the Free State bench with distinction, and led a commando during the war of 1899–1902, before becoming Minister of Education in the O.R.C. Piet Grobler, J.C.G. Kemp and N. C. Havenga were also Anglo-Boer War veterans, while Dr D. F. Malan, who had an important assignment as Minister of the Interior, Education and Public Health, had already displayed a variety of skills as philosopher, cleric and editor of the *Burger*. Tielman Roos, leader of the Party in the Transvaal, was a personable but volatile lawyer. The two Labour men in the coalition cabinet, Colonel Creswell and Thomas Boydell, had both been imprisoned for leading the 1914 strike.

These ministers set about a busy legislative programme. Havenga, as Minister of Finance, made the South African economy fully protectionist in a succession of budgets and tariff bills, each geared to the market needs of the moment, but all designed to pull South African industry on to its feet. Creswell brought the Iron and Steel Corporation (I.S.C.O.R.) into being in 1927 as a public utility, in face of Opposition criticism that this profit-making enterprise should have been entrusted to a syndicate of steel

producers. Kemp (Agriculture) and Grobler (Lands) took steps to promote the external marketing of fruit, dairy and other produce by means of
land and sea transport subsidies. They also offered fiscal relief on imported
fertilisers and farm implements. But it does not seem that the progressive
farmers were their main concern. Their main efforts were directed 'less at
nurturing capitalists than at saving stragglers' (Bradford). Agricultural
credit associations were set up under Land Bank auspices, available even
for farmers who lacked the security for raising loans, as well as work
colonies for those in need of social salvage. The white working class,
brought under the ministerial heads of a new Department of Labour
(Creswell, until his transfer to Posts to appease the Chamber of Mines, and
his successor Boydell), experienced industrial peace and limited material
advance. The Government increased the protection of white urban tenants
against eviction at a time when houses were short, overhauled the law on
miners' phthisis, and brought the Factories Act into line with current
international standards with regard to the length of the working week and
the employment of child labour. More controversial were the Wage Act of
1925 and the 'Colour Bar' Act of 1926. After being rejected in the Senate
in 1925, the latter measure was opposed at every reading when it was
reintroduced in the Assembly in 1926, but the Government forced it
through by 83 to 67 votes in a joint sitting. The former law was designed to
help unskilled white workers, in particular poor whites, whereas the
Colour Bar Act was meant to protect the skilled and semi-skilled [see
pp. 508–10].

The Afrikaner, whose cultural needs Botha and Smuts had played down,
was also made to feel that he mattered to the new regime. Malan began a
campaign for bilingualism in the civil sevice, and in so doing opened job
opportunities for his people in a new and important field. In 1925, the
meaning of 'Dutch' in the constitution was extended to include Afrikaans,
which thus became an official language for the first time. It had already
been adopted in the schools and by the Dutch Reformed Churches, whose
Afrikaans Bible was completed in 1933.

11.2 DOMINION STATUS, THE FLAG CRISIS AND THE
PROTECTORATES

Hertzog followed up the work of Smuts between 1917 and 1923 by tackling
the question of dominion status with great singleness of aim, asserting
South Africa's right to full international sovereignty, and within three
years of taking office he had contributed substantially to the formula
agreed at the 1926 Imperial Conference.

'South Africa first' was a satisfactory election slogan for Hertzog's
Nationalists in 1915 or 1920. Under the Pact with Creswell he was obliged
to treat the Imperial relationship with circumspection during the election
campaign of 1924; but, in his own view at least, he held to a consistent
policy from the De Wildt speech of December 1912 until his participation
in the 1919 deputation to Versailles, and beyond. Much of what Hertzog

said was by implication secessionist, though whether he would at that time have seceded from the Empire had he been in a position of power could be debated. During the 1925 budget debate, he described secession as a right, but went on to say that for South Africa to secede from the British Commonwealth could be 'a flagrant mistake and a national disaster'. He made two key speeches in April and May 1926, the first in the Assembly, the second at Stellenbosch, before going to the Imperial Conference in London in November. These indicated that he regarded South Africa as already in practice 'completely independent . . . just as free as England itself', but he rounded on Smuts in Parliament for having questioned South Africa's right of secession from the Commonwealth, saying that this committed Smuts to a view of the Commonwealth as 'a kind of super-authority . . . a super-State'. For Hertzog, the only legal tie was the 'personal bond of a common king', as distinct from the formal bond of King-in-Parliament. He contended that the Dominion Prime Ministers should have recognised this in 1921; but instead they stuck to 'the idea of the unity of the Empire group', envisaging 'nothing less than a quasifederal Empire, with the highest authority vested in the Imperial Conference', and with Great Britain enjoying the decisive voice as the only member with accepted international standing. But, Hertzog continued, events since the peace conference had shown that the international standing of the Dominions remained ambiguous, while the non-participation of the Dominions in the Locarno treaties had shown that the idea of a common foreign policy was a myth.

Smuts referred to the Stellenbosch speech as one of 'first-class importance', but in certain respects 'contentious'. He asked Hertzog for an assurance that if the forthcoming Imperial Conference did not reach agreement on the status of the Dominions, he would not publish a declaration of South Africa's external sovereignty without reference to Parliament. Hertzog reassured him, replying that international recognition of South Africa's independence was an important consideration, and that if the Imperial Conference did not reach agreement 'then we shall have to wait and see whether it cannot be got later'.

An important feature of the prepared speech which Hertzog gave to the secret session of the Committee of Prime Ministers at the Imperial Conference in London in November 1926 was the central position which he gave to Smuts's memorandum of June 1921. Picking up the sense of urgency in Smuts's memorandum, he stressed the need both to clarify and to publicise the equal status of the Dominions, while insisting that it would be 'monstrous, and certainly disastrous, if the freedom of one dominion, or its exercise of the rights pertaining to that freedom, were made dependent upon the will of, or upon the exercise of similar rights by, the other[s]'. His warning of the dangers of separatist movements if a clear definition of equal status were not achieved and made public, and his references to the confusion of foreign governments over the Dominions' legal position, had an important influence on the deliberations. They were of major importance in the drafting of the Balfour Declaration which stated that Great Britain and the Dominions were 'autonomous communities within the

British Empire, equal in status, in no way subordinate one to another in any aspect of their domestic or external affairs, though united by a common allegiance to the Crown and freely associated as members of the British Commonwealth of Nations'.

Intelligent discussion in Parliament of the report of the Imperial Conference was delayed until March 1928, chiefly on account of the extremely acrimonious reaction of members to Dr Malan's Nationality and Flag Bill, first introduced on 25 May 1926, shortly after Hertzog's Stellenbosch speech. The definition of South African nationality and the achievement of a distinctive national flag could not be separated from the issue of Dominion autonomy, from which in the view of Hertzog's Government they flowed naturally. Contention arose, however, because the Government's proposal to adopt a flag which contained neither the old republican colours nor the Union Jack seemed to the Opposition to have secessionist implications, even though Dr Malan, when introducing the second reading, referred to the Union Jack as the 'flag of the Empire', to be displayed 'officially on all occasions which are intended specifically to represent or indicate our relationship to the British community of nations'. The Government decided not to proceed with the measure in 1926, and deferred it. But when the measure was reintroduced in May 1927, fur flew once more. It was only in October, after Hertzog and Smuts had held private talks, that the Prime Minister climbed down. He now offered to incorporate both the Union Jack and the Republican flags in a new Union Flag, and to accept the Union Jack as a flag to be flown alongside the new Union flag as a symbol 'giving expression to our relationship with the other members of the commonwealth of nations'. Smuts congratulated Hertzog on 'the most important, statesmanlike and wise speech he has just made to the House'.

When Hertzog introduced the debate on the Report of the 1926 Imperial Conference on 8 March 1928, he laid stress on the attention paid by the Conference to the practical aspects of Dominion participation in international affairs – procedure to be adopted over international treaties, their representation at international conferences, the practical conduct of foreign policy, the granting of authority to foreign consuls, and means of communication between Dominion and foreign governments. He then switched to the question of Dominion neutrality in the event of British involvement in war, arguing eloquently (as Botha and Smuts had done with Lloyd George in 1919) that if the right to neutrality did not exist, then equality of status meant nothing. These remarks were controversial, because the question of Dominion neutrality had been deliberately avoided at the Imperial conference on account of its potentially disruptive side-effects. Smuts warned of these in his reply to Hertzog, referring to the unresolved legal problem of the divisibility of the Crown which had not yet been fully faced, but which was implicit in Hertzog's stance, and, above all, the danger to Commonwealth solidarity if hypothetical discussion of neutrality were to get out of hand. 'So long as our cause is just and good', Smuts said, 'and the danger is really one of first-class character, it will be practically impossible for any dominion to declare its neutrality in a great war in which Britain is involved.' Smuts also picked on Hertzog for his emphasis on Dominion independence, on the ground that the Conference had not discussed this either, but dwelt rather on the need to ensure the voluntary cooperation of the Dominions as equal members of the Commonwealth.

The Balfour Declaration of 1926 gave the green light for the creation of a South African Department of External Affairs, of which Hertzog assumed the portfolio on 1 June 1927. This was followed by the appointment of ministers plenipotentiary at the Hague, Washington and Rome, together with the raising of the London High Commissionership to diplomatic rank, and the establishment of a network of trade commissioners in Europe and North America. The Union was also represented at the League of Nations Headquarters in Geneva, notably by Charles te Water and E. H. Louw.

Separation of the offices of Governor-General and Imperial High Commissioner followed logically if the King's deputy as head of state were not also to hold a British ambassadorial role. Smuts warned against such a separation in May 1927, on the ground that a combination of these offices made it easier for the Union Government to deal with Britain on matters affecting the High Commission Territories. But the change was effected in December 1930, at the end of the Earl of Athlone's term of office, when the Earl of Clarendon was appointed Governor-General, and Sir Herbert Stanley High Commissioner. Once this step had been taken, it became more appropriate to select a local person as head of state. Hence Hertzog's choice of a resident South African, Patrick Duncan, as Governor-General at the end of the Clarendon's term. Smuts later trumped this move, on Duncan's death in 1942, by securing the appointment of Gideon Brand van Zyl, a Governor-General who was an Afrikaans-speaking South African by birth.

Botha and Smuts had shown considerable enthusiasm for territorial expansion in Africa. Hertzog's designs were less wide-ranging, but at least he desired to consolidate the Union's control over the southern end of the continent by obtaining the High Commission Territories, while he accepted as a *fait accompli* the mandate over South West Africa. Hertzog wasted no time in asking for the transfer of Swaziland and Bechuanaland to the Union in 1924, but his lack of finesse made it relatively easy for the High Commissioner, Athlone, to turn his demand down. From 1926, when the Territories were placed under the Dominions Office in London, Hertzog's case for incorporation became harder to defend on account of the unpopularity of his colour bar legislation both among the residents of the Territories and in London. L. S. Amery, as Secretary of State for the Dominions, toured South Africa in late 1927, and began to urge the development of the Territories, to preserve them as bases of continuing British influence in an Afrikaner-dominated region, and because he realised that the Territories were in urgent need of development as Sir Alan Pim's reports of 1932–5 were later to make clear. His visit stiffened the British Government against early transfer, and no more was heard from the South African Government until 1932.

Hertzog did not help his cause in that year by demanding the incorporation of the Territories on the argument that, if this were denied, the Union might have to withdraw economic favours to protect herself from competition. This threat of economic pressure, to which Smuts gave some support after joining Hertzog's Government in 1933, was turned by the British Government into an argument for promoting economic cooperation, and London's refusal to talk of transfer remained obdurate. It remained a live issue, however, enlivened further by a debate in *The Times* between Margery Perham of Oxford, who opposed incorporation, and Lionel Curtis, who supported it. An *aide mémoire* presented to Hertzog by the Dominions Secretary, J. H. Thomas, in May 1935, seemed to break the deadlock by offering the Union Government an opportunity to cooperate with the territorial administrations economically, so that an appetite for incorporation in the Union could be whetted among the African populations. Hertzog made an offer of £35,000 for aid to the Territories, but spoiled the effect of this by asserting on at best dubious grounds that Thomas had agreed to a definite transfer in 1937. He was persuaded to withdraw this assertion, but not before it had done its damage by implying that the South African offer of money was a Trojan horse. Malcolm Macdonald, who succeeded Thomas in 1937, was keen to effect transfer if at all possible. Hertzog met him in June, while in London for the Imperial Conference; but he again spoiled a promising atmosphere, this time by an untimely press interview. Macdonald gave him an opportunity to recover by suggesting that the Union prepare a policy statement indicating what it would do in the Territories after transfer had taken place. Hertzog's Government accordingly did so, in a memorandum completed in August 1939; but by offering to maintain rather than to extend the services started by Britain, and by failing to over-trump the British record of expenditure under the Colonial Development Act of 1929, it did nothing to counter black fears generated afresh by its own restrictive legislation for Union Africans of 1936–7. African opposition was in fact becoming more and more public, even if King Sobhuza of the Swazi seemed to flirt with incorporation from time to time. Against such a background. Smuts's bravado in attempting to wrest the Territories from British control, by an appeal to the Dominions Office to relinquish them in October 1939 (Hyam), could hardly have been expected to succeed.

11.3 HERTZOG'S POLICIES FOR ASIANS AND AFRICANS

Compromise, which unlocked the tensions over the Flag Bill, also provided an 'Open Sesame' for Hertzog's Indian policy during his early years of office. When Dr Malan introduced his Areas Reservation Bill in 1925, to stiffen the Class Area proposals of the Smuts Government and make the repatriation of Indians easier to effect, this threatened to ruin the atmosphere for round-table discussions which had been proposed both by the Indian Government and by J. H. Thomas in the Colonial Office. But the South African Government agreed in 1925 to receive a fact-finding commission from India, led by G. F. Paddison, Commissioner of Labour in

Madras, and containing two Indian members of the Council of State. At the same time the S.A.I.C. sent a deputation to India led by Dr A. Abdurahman, to interview the Viceroy and put its case to the Indian National Congress, over which Mrs Sarojini Naidu, who had recently visited South Africa, presided. The two missions crossed each other at sea. Abdurahman's won world-wide publicity for the South African Indians' cause, while Paddison's negotiated patiently for the holding of a round-table conference, which eventually took place between the South African and Indian governments over four weeks from 17 December 1926. The subsequent Cape Town Agreement was the product of an exceptionally harmonious encounter. It contained provisions for the assisted emigration of South African Indians, for the entry into South Africa of the wives and minor children of Indians with domiciliary rights, and included an under-taking by the South African Government to withdraw the Areas Reserva-tion Bill. What was more, the policies of Hertzog's Government continued to reflect the afterglow of this encounter for several years, as it agreed to condone illegal entries of the past and to radically overhaul the Indian educational system. But this mood disappeared in the early 1930s, when the repatriation provisions of the Agreement proved unworkable, the attitude of white Natal and Transvaal townsmen gradually turned sour, and backbenchers renewed the onslaught on Indian trading and property purchases in those two provinces, and tried to make the marriage of Indians with whites illegal.

Hertzog had taken the portfolio of Native Affairs, which he had previously held until Botha dropped him from the Cabinet in 1912. Though commit-ted in general terms to a policy of segregation, he marked time for over a year before giving any details. 'This Government has no native policy at this moment,' he asserted defensively in Parliament in 1924. In March 1925 he criticised the Smuts Government for not purchasing land released on the recommendation of the local committees of 1918 [see p. 522] and affirmed that 'territorial segregation of the natives is the only sound policy that can be followed both for the natives and the Europeans in South Africa'. It depended, he said, on the Africans' learning how to develop the Reserves both agriculturally and industrially; but he linked this with the notion that in the towns, on the railways, in existing industrial undertak-ings, the white man was entitled to first consideration: 'the native cannot blame us if in the first place we try to find work for our own class.' Thus the reverse side of segregation (which was conceived as a favour conferred on the black man) was the industrial colour bar, which Hertzog saw in 1925 as a means of redressing wrongs done to the white worker in 1922, even if – as he disingenuously admitted in the second reading debate on the 1925 Mines and Works Bill – such a policy was morally below par.

Hertzog spoke at Smithfield on 13 November 1925 of the need to provide the extra land promised for Africans under the 1913 Land Act, as if they would find this, together with a form of communal representation, a completely adequate substitute for the common roll franchise. On 23 July 1926, therefore, he tabled three bills on native affairs as well as a Coloured

Persons Rights Bill to secure their representation (but not that of Asians) in Parliament by whites. The Native Land Act Amendment Bill was presented as an attempt to fulfil the Union Government's obligations under the Land Act. It has sometimes been treated in the literature as a prototype for Hertzog's better known Native Trust and Land Act of 1936 [see p. 522], but the emphasis of the 1926 Bill differed from that of both the 1913 and the 1936 Acts. It scaled down the scheduled reserves of the 1913 Act from 11.2 to 10 million morgen, and decreased the areas to be made available for release to black buyers outside the reserves to 7 million morgen, which was rather less than the area proposed by the local committees of 1918 which had already revised the Beaumont recommendations downwards. It seems clear that the Bill, read in conjunction with Hertzog's public statements, was designed to encourage African acquisition by purchase rather than by parliamentary grant, and it sought to restrict African purchases mainly to land adjacent to districts already in African hands. This bid to consolidate areas of black and white settlement fits in with the notion that Hertzog's thinking was segregationist; but the reduction in the overall size of the scheduled reserves seems to have been more in keeping with farming than with mining interests, above all with regard to the needs of labour recruitment. Lacey has suggested, with good insight, that 'the main aim of [Hertzog's] farm labour policy was to immobilise labour in the white rural sector, not in the African reserves'.

The second measure introduced by Hertzog, a Union Native Council Bill, aimed to establish a Council of fifty Africans, of whom thirty-five were to be elective, as a substitute for the nominated Native Conference set up under Smuts's Native Affairs Act of 1920. The purpose of the third measure, the Representation of Natives in Parliament Bill was to remove the African voters from the common roll in the Cape, and as an alternative to give seven white representatives in the House of Assembly to Africans from all provinces, with the power to vote on measures affecting Africans only. Hertzog hoped to make this legislation bipartisan, and approached Smuts on 23 January 1926; but when the latter asked to see the draft legislation before committing himself Hertzog alleged that Smuts was dragging his heels and closed the correspondence. In August, Smuts criticised the Bills severely in a memorandum which found the land proposals far less generous to Africans than his own Government had been in practice, but then – with the electorate perhaps in mind – went on to criticise the proposal to give Africans separate representation in Parliament as an attempt to weaken the political influence of the white man (Van der Poel).

On 28 March 1927 the House agreed to send the Bills to a select committee, which reported on 17 June, too late for them to be handled that session. Meanwhile Parliament took through all its stages a Native Administration Bill, which extended over Africans in every province except the Cape the authoritarian powers enjoyed by the Governor-General in Natal under the Natal Native Code of 1891. He was made Supreme Chief over all Africans, with authority to appoint native commissioners, chiefs and headmen, define boundaries of chiefdoms, alter their composition, and move chiefdoms or individuals at will 'from any place to any other place within the Union upon such conditions as he may determine' (provided Parliamentary approval was obtained if a chiefdom – as opposed to an individual – objected). His powers were also made to cover the registration and ultimate control of African-owned land, and all judicial procedure affecting Africans, both civil and criminal, through a separate system of courts surmounted by a Native Appeal Court, which was given the right to refuse appeals from its own judgements to the Appellate Division in Bloemfontein. The Governor-General was also empowered, subject to Parliamentary veto, to legislate by proclamation for the scheduled Native Areas, such legislation to have effect unless and until abrogated at the request of Parliament. He was also given authority, in this portmanteau law, to impose rules on Africans governing censorship, control of weapons, wearing of clothes, carrying of passes – and, in a controversial Section 29, he could punish 'any person who utters any words or does any other act or thing whatever with intent to promote any feeling of hostility between Natives and Europeans'.

This law, together with a stiff amendment to the Riotous Assemblies Act in 1930, provided a strong rampart behind which the Hertzog Government could build up a system of controls which were designed primarily to provide effective machinery for the direction of labour. These included the Wage Act of 1925 and the Mines and Works Amendment Act of 1926, dealing with conditions of industrial employment [see pp. 509–10]. An amendment to the Native Administration Act in 1929 extended the network of labour districts across the entire country, thus bringing all potential black workers anywhere in South Africa under the discipline of pass laws and movement control (Lacey). The Natives (Urban Areas) Act was amended in 1930 to introduce tighter controls over the recruitment of farm workers by urban employers, and this was followed in 1932 by the Native Service Contract Act, which enabled farmers to call on the labour of their workers' families as well as the workers themselves, to evict them summarily for non-performance of labour obligations even if there were no written contract of service, and if need be to have their workers magisterially whipped. This was to consolidate in spirit a system of arbitrary labour controls which had existed at the Cape before the administrative and legal clean-up of 1809–28 [see pp. 42–4], which also reflected some current practice (Bradford).

Meanwhile pressure from his own supporters caused Hertzog to modify the Parliamentary Representation Bill by offering Africans from the northern provinces a mere two senators in place of five members of the Assembly. In a series of private conversations in February 1928, Smuts pushed him the other way, urging him to consider 'a common franchise all over South Africa, based on occupation and income or salary which was to apply to all, black and white alike', but be high enough to exclude the bulk of the African population, together with a civilisation test from which white people would be exempt. If he could not accept that, then Smuts suggested that 'the least he could do would be to offer the Cape natives representation according to their present voting strength' – perhaps five or six seats in the Assembly, and five in the Senate for the northern provinces, the Cape seats to increase as the number of qualified voters increased, until a permitted maximum was reached. Hertzog professed to be attracted by Smuts's idea of a high uniform non-racial franchise, backed by a civilisation test, but he did not follow it up, on the ground that the time was not yet ripe. Smuts also criticised the proposed Native Council by expressing the fear that it would 'collect all the Kadalies and Communist agitators in South Africa into a body which might have a very unsettling effect on the native mind'. He urged Hertzog 'to let the General Council stand over, to establish councils under the Act of 1920 in the various territories, and when these were in full and efficient working order, then to consider the question of a General Council based on them as a superstructure' (Van der Poel). Hertzog took this advice, and dropped the Native Council Bill during a joint sitting called before the 1929 election.

The South African Party decided to oppose the Natives' Parliamentary Representation Bill and the Coloured Persons' Rights Bill at the joint sitting, in the knowledge that Hertzog had timed the sitting with an eye on the forthcoming election, and that they could prevent him from getting a two-thirds majority. For Hertzog it was an unhappy moment. He was obliged to recognise, and did, that his attempts to consult African opinion had brought an adverse response. In 1926 the Transkeian Bunga had given signs of equivocation. But the Native Conference was outspoken. Selope Thema said that under the Representation Bill 'all hope of getting full citizenship rights was closed', and carried a motion for its rejection by a big majority. He carried another for the extensive modification of the Land Bill, in a debate in which one speaker said it reminded him of 'lysol', and another called it a 'jackal trap'. The Union Native Council Bill, the only one to fall by the wayside was, ironically, found to be acceptable. Now, in 1929, Hertzog contended that the Africans had been more than adequately consulted by the Native Affairs Commission and by himself, but because they had refused to accept any alteration of the Cape system only Parliament could resolve the difference.

The Coloured Rights Bill now came under Smuts's attack as 'a raw uncouth immature scheme' which threatened surreptitiously to undermine the security of Cape voters by placing their registration under the scrutiny of magistrate and Minister for the first time. He repeated a proposal first made in 1925, for an inquiry into the economic and other relations of the European, Coloured and African population of the Union by 'a national commission or convention' on which the views of all sections of the people should be represented. Although the Nationalists held together in the divisions (Roos being absent), only one backbencher from a northern constituency, who was provoked, actually spoke in favour of enfranchising Coloured people in the northern provinces. When the third reading division on the Native Representation Bill failed to produce a two-thirds majority, Hertzog announced the withdrawal of the Coloured Bill as well, since the measures had been made interdependent.

11.4 THE GENERAL ELECTION OF 1929

The Government's failure to carry the Native Representation Bill set the stage for the 1929 general election, when questions of native policy were placed before the voters as never before. In fact, the election battle had begun before the joint sitting, sparked off by two speeches at Ermelo, Transvaal, the first by Roos in September 1928, the second by Smuts in January 1929. Roos selected native policy, and in particular the restriction of the Cape African franchise, as the issue on which he hoped the election would be fought. Smuts, who was particularly disturbed by the paramountcy accorded to black interests in Kenya by the Colonial Office, spoke of a 'great African Dominion stretching unbroken throughout Africa' as 'the cardinal point in my policy'. His opponents reacted, in the words of a manifesto put out by Hertzog, Roos and Malan, by pouring scorn on 'the apostle of a black Kaffir state'. It was a bitter election, in which the Nationalists and the S.A.P. fought each other almost to the exclusion of Labour. Nationalist slogans notwithstanding, the S.A.P. stood for the policies implicit in the Land Act, the Native Affairs Act and the Natives (Urban Areas) Act, involving a substantial measure of segregation on the land, in politics and in the towns. Segregation was not in fact the issue which divided the major parties, and when Smuts delivered his Rhodes memorial lectures at Oxford in November, he laid special emphasis on the

11 **Crisis in the Pact Government during the 1929 general election, as portrayed by E. A. Packer of the *Star***

need to prevent the excessive integration of the black man in white society. The aims of the National Party were hardly different from this, but as they relied almost entirely on white votes they could pose as the more robust defenders of white security. Emphasis on justice for the black man was therefore played right down.

On polling day the Nationalists picked up fifteen seats to give them 78, the S.A.P. eight to given them 61. Labour fared disastrously. The Party had begun to fall apart through internal dissension over the government's illiberal labour legislation as early as February 1928, even before Hertzog had a major confrontation with Madeley, who defied his instruction later in the year not to handle an indirect approach from Kadalie over a wage dispute involving the I.C.U. When Hertzog reformed his Government with H. W. Sampson taking Madeley's place, Creswell remained at the head of a section which still professed loyalty to the Pact, and that section won five seats in the general election. Madeley's rival National Council group retained a mere three. Altogether, the Labour representation declined by ten seats, and the Government no longer needed Labour support in the House. In the Depression years which followed, the Pact itself collapsed (September 1931), after which some National Council Labourites like Morris Kentridge joined the S.A.P. while some ex-Pact supporters found a home with the Malanite element of the N.P.

11.5   THE I.C.U. AND THE A.N.C. IN THE 1920s

The cordiality which had prevailed between the Nationalists and selected Coloured and African organisations had already worn thin. Coloured people, even if pleased at being distinguished from Africans in the Coloured Persons Rights Bill, tended to resent being equally clearly distinguished from Europeans. Their leaders had begun to draw away from Hertzog when the Transvaal Nationalists resisted the meagre extension of their political rights (one white representative in Parliament for all three northern provinces) which Hertzog proposed to allow (Lewis). Despite the Colour Bar Act, Coloured people also began to find that, like other non-white groups, they were being eased out of jobs on the railways and in other public and private concerns, as a result of governmental pressure, to make way for unemployed whites. After the 1929 election this became pronounced, as it had been for Africans (but not Coloured people) between 1924 and 1927.

The A.N.C. and the I.C.U., which had made gestures to Hertzog in 1924, had even less reason for supporting him. Those who accepted territorial segregation doubted whether the proposed land distribution was fair. Very few thought that the loss of parliamentary representation in the lower House was a fair price for communal representation in the upper. And the Native Administration Act of 1927 called forth angry denunciation, both for the extension of arbitrary powers which the Governor-General could exercise over Africans, and for the 'race hostility' clause which gave the Government power to act against people or organisations deemed (without judicial testing) to have acted in an inflammatory manner.

Strong government initiatives in racial policy during the early Hertzog era were countered by a mood of euphoric Garveyism which spread through the A.N.C. and the I.C.U. during the period 1920–40, linking with the independent churches and leading to demonstrations of extravagant optimism, as in Wellington Buthelezi's movement in the Transkei (Hill and Pirio). But although the African movements adopted a variety of defensive tactics, they failed to act together. The I.C.U. and the Communists fell out, while the A.N.C. was torn asunder through marginal involvement in the conflicts of the other two.

The I.C.U. grew into a mass movement. It enlarged its organisation by adopting a new constitution in 1925. In the same year it scored minor strike successes in East London and Johannesburg, and in 1926, after strongly opposing the Colour Bar Bill, Kadalie made an approach to the British trade union movement. Working through Mabel Palmer, Ethelreda Lewis and Winifred Holtby, he made contact with the Fabian movement, and applied for I.C.U. membership of the International Federation of Trade Unions. I.C.U. branches increased in 1927 and 1928, those in the Transvaal and Natal growing fast under the respective influences of Thomas Mbeki and A. W. G. Champion. A membership of over 50,000 was claimed – not unreasonably – in January 1927, rising to about 86,000 (Wickins), or perhaps 250,000 (Bradford).

By exploring the rapid expansion of I.C.U. branches in the rural areas of the eastern half of South Africa after 1926, in the face of measures to deprive blacks of access to land, and to double the obligations of labour tenants to 180 days in the year, Bradford has redressed an imbalance in the historiography of the movement and provided an important link in the continuing history of peasant protest since the 1890s [see pp. 208–9, 252–3, 346–9], but without suggesting that the movement gave its adherents more than a transitory taste of freedom. Kadalie's bid to secure international recognition of his union was defeated by the South African Department of Labour. There were more failures at home – to launch successful strikes among the Durban dockers, Natal coalminers and Johannesburg railway workers in 1927; to protect I.C.U. farm workers from eviction by their landlords, and to launch a land-buying scheme for the homeless; or even to reach agreement at a special conference called in Kimberley in December 1927 over the I.C.U.'s relationship with white unions and the Communists. Soon afterwards a personal feud developed between Kadalie and Champion, which focused on Kadalie's refusal to charge the I.C.U. with the costs of Champion's semi-private litigation, and on Champion's counter-allegation that the head office had regularly failed to present proper financial statements. Kadalie's attempt to humiliate the Natal leader resulted in the latter's decision to break away and establish a rival *I.C.U. yase Natal*, in May 1928. Meanwhile the national council of the I.C.U. sought the help of a financial organiser from Britain; but William Ballinger, the Scottish trade unionist selected, found the affairs of the Union in chaos, and in the course of trying to impose discipline on its operations he antagonised Kadalie, who broke away to form an Independent I.C.U. in

March 1929. The I.C.U. proper held its last congress at Kroonstad in June 1929, and thereafter led no more than a twilight existence until its final disappearance in 1933. The first mass movement in the history of black South Africa, it died essentially of its own weakness in the face of steady but not overbearing pressure from outside.

There had been very little effective liaison between the African political leaders and left-wing political thinking before the general strike of 1922. The Labour Party had given only grudging admission to non-white people in 1913, while the International Socialist League (established in South Africa in 1915) had failed to build up meaningful contact with the black masses. During the 1922 strike the Communists had obviously put skin colour before class. After 1922, however, they began to pay more attention to the Africans, without at first abandoning the hope of influencing white labour. They tried to affiliate with the Labour Party in 1923, in accordance with instructions from the Comintern and in defiance of the facts of the South African scene, even at a time when the passions generated during the Rand rebellion had given rise to a good deal of superficial left-wing propaganda on the platteland. The Communists failed to make headway with white labour, and in 1926 began to cross swords with the I.C.U. as well. In the Communist view, Kadalie had become a 'respectable trade union bureaucrat', who was financially corrupt and had refused to launch a proper mass movement. From the angle of the I.C.U., the Communists' profession to give priority to black interests was suspect. It was Champion rather than Kadalie who took the initiative against Communist influence in the movement, though personal animosity between Kadalie and Bunting played its part. When James la Guma, general secretary of the I.C.U., accepted the Communist Party's nomination to attend a Congress of Oppressed Nationalities in Brussels in 1927, without consulting his executive, the National Council of the I.C.U. decided to make its officers relinquish C.P. membership.

The Communists set up their own trade union movement in opposition to those affiliated to the I.C.U. In the Federation of Non-European Trade Unions, established in 1928, they fathered an organisation which committed itself to the separation of black from white workers, which succumbed during the Depression. But Communist influence endured in some of the stronger unions which flourished during the 1930s, notably the Garment Workers' Union, which had a non-racial membership and seasoned leaders like Solly Sachs and Leo Weinbren among the whites, and Alex La Guma, Moses Kotane and Gana Makabeni among the blacks. Makabeni and Max Gordon, a Trotskyite, successfully amalgamated several of the leading African unions during the late 1930s. Gordon's internment in 1940 was a setback to left-wing influence, but it was still dominant in the spate of strike activity which characterised the early war years.

Following the Comintern line, the Communists also began in 1928 to work for a black Republic in South Africa, dissociated from the British or any other Empire. The classless society, as La Guma saw it, was to be introduced via a period of African rule, and African nationalism encouraged as the first stage of a social revolution. Bunting resisted the implications of such a strategy, which he feared would result in race conflict and the elimination of the whites, but subsequently accepted Comintern discipline and preached black republicanism when he contested the Tembuland seat in the 1929 election – unsuccessfully, it was alleged, owing to police interference with his campaign.

The professedly political African movements reacted cautiously to Hertzog's policies at first. Davidson Jabavu, who took over his father's mantle as leader of a Cape Native Voters' Convention, tried hard to keep lines of communication with the Government open, and petitioned Hertzog to withdraw his bills in 1928. The A.N.C., under the presidency of the Rev. Z. R. Mahabane from 1924, strongly attacked the bills in 1927, but otherwise refrained from protest activities save among western Cape farm workers, where the A.N.C. took on a role similar to that of the I.C.U. elseshere. It also sought links with the Coloured and Indian movements, and participated in the conciliatory work of the Joint Councils of Europeans and Natives which had been established since 1921.

Black republicanism of a Leninist kind appealed to Gumede, the next A.N.C. President, as a result of his trip to Europe (which included Moscow) in 1927–8. In 1928–9, the Communist Party attracted several capable leaders of the A.N.C., like J. B. Marks and Moses Kotane, into its ranks. But liaison between the Communists and the A.N.C. barely survived the 'white terror' of Pirow's campaign against left-wing political activity during the 1929 election and afterwards, particularly when he armed himself with new powers under an amended Riotous Assemblies Act in 1930. Pressure to dissociate from the Communists now built up within the A.N.C. Mahabane, John Dube and Thomas Mapikela managed to remove Gumede from the presidency in April 1930, though Gumede could call on the personal support of Champion and several other prominent leaders. Pixley Seme's election in Gumede's place heralded a return to caution in the African Congress.

11.6 THE GREAT DEPRESSION AND THE POLITICS OF COALITION AND FUSION

Hertzog made few cabinet changes after the 1929 election. Oswald Pirow took over the Department of Justice, because Roos was ill and critical of Hertzog's agreement with Labour. Roos argued that Madeley's office should have gone to a Nationalist, not to H. W. Sampson, and defied Hertzog almost to the brink over the allocation of the Brakpan and Germiston seats to Labour in the election. He soon found a release from politics on the Appeal Court Bench. Hertzog made another significant cabinet change by relinquishing Native Affairs to E. G. Jansen of Natal, whose task it became to shepherd the 'Native bills' through another unsuccessful joint sitting, and then through the Joint Select Committee which presented its report in 1935.

The Government now had to face the Great Depression of 1931–2. After the Wall Street collapse of 1929, the outside world found it increasingly hard to pay adequate prices for South Africa's main export products. Consequently South African diamond exports fell in value from £16.5 million in 1928 to £1.4 million in 1934, and although South African wool exports did not vary much in quantity during the period 1926 to 1934 – never less than 235 million pounds weight, never more than 336 million – the world price of wool fell from 16.6 pence in 1927–8 to 4.4 pence in 1931–2. At 1932 prices, therefore, it would have been necessary to export four times as much wool as in 1927 to earn the same amount of foreign exchange. World wool prices had started to fall in August 1929. Australia, whose product amounted to about three times that of the Union, devalued her currency in February 1931, and Great Britain followed suit in September. At the end of the year and in early 1932, £100 sterling bought £125 Australian but only between £70 and £75 South African. With the South African pound valued at nearly double the Australian, competition on the world wool markets became almost impossible for South African growers. Havenga announced on 20 November 1931 that 'South Africa is on the gold basis and will remain on the gold basis'. He and his young Opposition counterpart, J. H. Hofmeyr, were both orthodox financiers who rejected devaluation. Gold-producers feared that higher import prices would force wages up, and perhaps cause marginal mines to close down. So instead of devaluing, as the Opposition urged during the Finance Emergency Regulations Bill debate, and as Smuts strongly urged while overseas, Havenga clapped duties of up to 12.5 per cent on nearly all imports and offered a bounty of 10 per cent rising to 20 per cent on nearly all exports, hoping to achieve a balance of payments by fiscal measures. Prompted by Hertzog and Havenga, a select committee appointed in January 1932 recommended that South Africa stay on the gold standard. But fiscal measures could not stop a flight from the South African pound if this looked like a promising speculative risk. People began to gamble on the possibility of the South African pound following sterling, and bought extensively on the London stock exchange, thus creating a currency famine in South Africa itself. It was a situation in which, as Schumann observed, 'political and psychological issues may emphatically not be neglected by the economist'.

At this point, after a young S.A.P. politican, and protégé of Smuts, J. G. N. Strauss, surprisingly beat the Nationalist and Labour candidates in a triangular by-election at Germinston, Tielman Roos suddenly embarked on a flamboyant personal crusade for devaluation on 16 December 1932. On the 22nd he resigned from the Bench, and people supposed that he was making a bid for the premiership. Whatever truth lay in that supposition, it is clear that he had been approached by Ewald Esselen of the S.A.P. and by Oswald Pirow of the N.P. in 1931 to try to bring Hertzog and Smuts closer together, and that after he had returned from a visit to Europe in February 1932 he, Arthur Barlow and Colin Steyn had begun to work together to urge Hertzog to abandon the gold standard. Roos is unlikely to have wanted to weaken the N.P. to the advantage of the S.A.P., and Turrell's suggestion that he promoted devaluation in order to deprive

Smuts's party of kudos for recommending the same line of action has some merit. His actions at any rate brought the desired results, for they increased speculation to such an extent that on 28 December Havenga was forced to announce the abandonment of the gold standard. Within a month, emancipated from the control of the Reserve Bank, the South African pound had fallen to parity with sterling, and many fortunes had been made.

Roos's return to politics came as no surprise to Hertzog, who had expected it. Early in 1933 Smuts, who depended on Hofmeyr for information about Roos's intentions, was persuaded by him, and against Duncan's advice, to offer Roos the deputy premiership under himself, together with three extra cabinet seats. Roos replied with an offer of equal representation in a cabinet of ten, under himself as premier. Smuts learned from his parliamentary colleagues in Cape Town in mid-January that party feelings in favour of coalition were strong, but that the idea of serving under Roos was not popular. F. S. Malan, Heaton Nicholls and Stuttaford backed an agreement with Roos, as did the leading representatives of the mining interest in the party caucus, who seemed ready to ditch Smuts (O'Meara); but Duncan, Reiz. Hofmeyr and Van der Byl were against. Roos improved his offer to a ratio of seven to four in favour of the S.A.P., with himself still as premier, shortly afterwards; but when the party caucus debated the question between 25 and 31 January, Smuts resolved the dilemma in which it found itself by personally deciding to reject Roos's offer. He had by this time received information that Hertzog was prepared to talk terms.

On 24 January, Smuts had moved in the Assembly for a new start in politics, calling on Hertzog, in a gesture of conciliation, to resign in the expectation of being asked to form a national government. Hertzog had to rebut this initiative in public. But things were moving behind the scenes. Hofmeyr seems to have told 'Pen' Wessels, the Nationalist member for Frankfort, that Smuts was willing to cooperate, and to have reported Wessels's favourable response to Smuts (Paton). Pirow claimed to have received a conciliatory message from Hertzog for Smuts, and to have passed it on through Duncan, on 25 January , – that is at the time that Smuts was turning his back on Roos. When the Cabinet met on 28 January to discuss an approach to the S.A.P., Havenga, Grobler, Kemp and Pirow were in favour of Hertzog's proposal but Malan, Jansen and Fourie were opposed. Hertzog, who clearly lacked confidence at that moment in the ability of his party to win a general election, its rural base largely destroyed by the gold standard crisis, authorised a firm approach to Smuts to be made. Smuts did not find it easy to agree to serve under Hertzog; but Hofmeyr persuaded him to meet the premier on 17 February. Havenga and Duncan were brought into the discussions.

The advantages of coalition were clear to both parties. The Roosites would in any case be the losers, their market value having slumped once devaluation had been authorised. An election was due at the latest in 1934. Hertzog might count on his followers to close their ranks to some extent; but on the evidence of the parliamentary by-election at Germiston and a provincial one at Roodepoort, both of which the Nationalists had lost, and a narrow victory in the normally safe Colesberg parliamentary seat, he could not be sure of victory. Disenchantment over the Government's handling of the economic crisis was real, though this did not mean that the Nationalist caucus found it easy to swallow coalition, especially as Hertzog made no attempt to take the caucus into his confidence while he was negotiating with Smuts. Hertzog also knew he had lost the support of the I.C.U. and of his erstwhile Coloured allies, though the enfranchisement of white women in 1930 had halved the efficacy of the non-white vote. Meanwhile the passage of the Statute of Westminster through the British Parliament seemed to give South Africa in general, and the Afrikaner people in particular, real security – greater by far than Kruger had received under the London Convention – thus enabling Nationalist Afrikaners to risk lowering their defences. Equally important, a coalition with the S.A.P. could result in an agreed measure to limit African representation in Parliament, however unhappy some S.A.P. members might be over this, and thus obviate the hurdle of the two-thirds majority.

The S.A.P., for its part, may or may not have smelt electoral victory. It is by no means certain that Smuts really wanted it, but as O'Meara has noted, he had to listen to representations by the Chamber of Mines that coalition might be a way to avoid a heavy tax on the gold premium then being mooted in government circles. In a speech at De Kroon in August 1932, Smuts had soft-pedalled the party line and advocated 'a new philosophy of non-racial, inclusive South African nationalism' (which almost certainly was not meant to include blacks). He told Gilbert Murray on 20 April 1933 that he wanted 'a cessation of the orgy of racial politics which has been the stock-in-trade of our public life' – possibly, as Turrell has proposed, in the hope that the S.A.P. might 'secure a party advantage through the appearance of abandoning purely party objectives'. He was currently troubled, too, by a schismatic movement in Natal, represented by Stuart Helps's Devolution League, which had been formed in 1931 to give expression to Natal fears for the future of the provincial system. This mood was only contained by the Natal Congress's acceptance in 1933 of a memorandum by F. C. Hollander, proposing the extension of provincial control over such areas as immigration, higher education, native affairs and the police. Furthermore, Smuts had accepted the machinery of a Select Committee, on which his own party was well represented, for ironing out the 'native bills', and they were not yet free to walk out of its deliberations.

The S.A.P. caucus adopted the coalition proposal unanimously, the N.P. only by a majority of forty-two to twenty-eight votes.

In March 1933, therefore, Hertzog and Smuts formed a Coalition Ministry, on a basis of seven agreed points, some clear, some opaque: the maintenance of South African autonomy as defined in the Statute of Westminster; acceptance of the national flag; equal language rights for Afrikaans- and English-speakers; the safeguarding of a 'sound rural population'; acceptance of a 'white labour' policy; the solution of the 'native question, through the maintenance of 'white civilisation' and political separation; and the protection of South Africa's currency and economic assets. In the distribution of Cabinet offices, which were shared equally between the parties, Hertzog kept External Affairs, while Smuts received the deputy premiership and the portfolio of Justice, which he had first held as a young man in Kruger's Republic. His protégé Jan Hofmeyr took over the Interior, Education and Public Health, and Duncan was given Mines and Industries. On the Nationalist side Pirow, a white supremacist and versatile outdoor man with something of Roos's opportunism, moved from Justice to take Defence and the Railways from Creswell, who, despite Hertzog's desire to find him a post, went out of office with his defeated Labour colleague, Sampson. Jansen, the recently appointed Minister of Native Affairs, gave up that portfolio and was in due course elected Speaker, so that Grobler (Nationalist) could have Native Affairs and give Lands to Deneys Reitz (S.A.P.). It was not a coalition which satisfied all, and Esselen gave Smuts a full catalogue of Cape S.A.P. frustrations, centring on the disappointment of F. S. Malan, for whom nothing had been found. His namesake, Dr D. F. Malan, refused a post. He and his followers met in special congress on 15 March and decided to accept coalition, however, for this would enable them to take part as coalition candidates in the general election which Hertzog called in May, thus avoiding likely defeat, for Hertzog and Smuts had agreed that sitting members had first option on the seats they currently held.

The coalition parties were returned with a massive majority of 144 (75 Nationalists and 61 S.A.P. candidates) to 14. Only two of the latter were Roosites, though 21 had contested seats. The fact that there had been no significant swing in the electorate apart from the threatened division in the Nationalist camp showed that the S.A.P. had been wise to accept coalition. Some thirty Malanites were among the Nationalists returned, and they soon chafed at having to work with Smuts. Hertzog did his best to reassure them, through meetings with W. Visser, M.P. for Senekal, in August, and Dr N. J. van der Merwe, a prominent Free State Malanite, in September, telling the latter that he would not agree to fusion with the S.A.P. as it was then constituted 'without differentiation', nor accept a ban on the making of republican propaganda which Smuts appeared to be demanding as his price for closer association with the Nationalists.

The implication of his remarks was that fusion would be acceptable on his own terms; and in the apparent belief that he had reassured Malan on this point, Hertzog spoke out in favour of fusion with the S.A.P. at the Transvaal congress of the National Party on 8 and 9 August, where a motion in its favour was carried by 281 votes to 38. Later the same month the Natal congress voted for fusion with only two contrary votes. When the Cape Congress at Port Elizabeth rejected fusion by 142 votes to 30 on 5 October, therefore, Hertzog was taken aback – still more so when Malan turned up at the Federale Raad of the party later in the month to say that negotiations with Smuts could not be entertained by his section of the party. A major reaffirmation of fusion by the Free State congress immediately afterwards gave the prime minister some reasurance, but in Basson's view this is to be explained by an estrangement between N. J. van der Merwe and Malan which was only made up in January 1934.

With the coming of the new year the situation remained fluid. On 30

January the Roosites stopped preaching party amalgamation and decided to form a new Centre Party; but both Malan and Smuts kept their lines to Hertzog open. Malan, despite the disapproval of hardliners like Strijdom and Swart, approached Hertzog on 4 February, and received his assurance that the amalgamated party would permit the making of republican propaganda, work for the abolition of appeals to the Privy Council, and seek the appointment of an Afrikaner as Governor-General. Malan's colleague, F. C. Erasmus, then wrote to Hertzog to ask for further assurances that he would work for the sovereign independence of South Africa, for the divisibility of the Crown, for the right of South Africa to opt for neutrality in a British war, and for secession from the Commonwealth. The publication of this correspondence on 16 February brought a letter from Smuts to Hertzog on the 18th in a bid to firm up the premier's adherence to his earlier commitments. Smuts insisted that in any party fusion there would have to be room for differences of opinion on three issues on which Malan demanded a firm stance: first, the definition of South Africa's sovereign status, but so as to avoid explicit standpoints on the divisibility of the Crown, the right of neutrality, and secession; second, the formulation of a doctrine of nationality which recognised 'our common status within the British Commonwealth'; and third, safeguards against the under-mining of South Africa's status in the Commonwealth by excessive propagation of republican doctrines. Hertzog met all Smuts's points the same day, and in the course of the next few weeks the leaders of the Nationalist and S.A. Parties together nursed the Status of the Union and the Royal Executive Functions and Seals Bills through Parliament. These measures, by which the South African legislature helped itself to the legal freedoms offered by the Statute of Westminster, put the reality of South African autonomy beyond reasonable doubt, and for the time being closed the debate between Smuts and Hertzog on the relationship between South Africa and the Empire. Not only had the South African Parliament become a completely sovereign legislature, but the placing of a Great Seal for the Union in the custody of the Prime Minister, for use by the Governor-General, who was now to be regarded as the King's complete *alter ego*, ensured that all acts of state, even the making of war and peace, even secession from the Commonwealth, could now be performed legally on local authority alone.

The Programme of Principles of the combined party was published in the press on 5 June 1934. Fusion was accepted by the Nationalist Federale Raad later in the month, and by the S.A.P. congress in August by a massive vote of 453 to 8. In December the United South African Nationalist Party (more familiarly, the United Party) was brought into being. The seven points of the agreement of March 1933 formed the basis of the amalgamation, with slightly greater emphasis given to dominion status within the Commonwealth, the autonomy of the provinces (out of consideration for Natal), and the removal of native policy from the party political arena. Turrell's analysis of Fusion as a tactical victory for Smuts, even though it involved serving under Hertzog, seems to be borne out by what happened. The S.A.P. had been placed at a disadvantage through coalition without fusion, as the 1933 election agreement had shown; but

Smuts had regained ground by forcing Hertzog to choose between himself and Malan, without giving significant ground to Hertzog in the matter of the Commonwealth relationship or losing too many of his English-speaking followers. Smuts's gamble was later vindicated in the general election of 1938, after which the S.A.P. element came to constitute the majority within the U.P. parliamentary caucus.

It would have been beyond the powers of Hertzog to hold the followers of Smuts and Malan together by some clever semantic formula. They had been pulling in opposite directions. In the course of July and August 1934, therefore, the opponents of Fusion in the four Nationalist provincial congresses broke away to form the *Gesuiwerde* (Purified) *Nasionale* Party, whose Federale Raad met in Bloemfontein on 5 July 1935 to work out its own republican political programme.

The published principles of the United Party, and in particular their flexibility on the topic of constitutional change, drove out Colonel Stallard and a handful of supporters for reasons diametrically opposed to those which had driven out Malan. They formed a Dominion Party at a meeting in Bloemfontein on 23 August, with a concern to preserve the Union's ties with Britain, rather than the issues of provincial autonomy or native policy, as the nexus which held them together.

12 White Unity, Black Division, 1933–9

12.1 THE FUSION GOVERNMENT AND THE 'NATIVE BILLS'

The Fusion Government was born of a common desire to settle the constitutional relationship within the Empire and to pull South Africa out of economic crisis. The Status and Seals Acts, carried without any recrudescence of party hostility within its ranks, had taken care of the first issue by the middle of 1934. The economy had taken a remarkable upswing after devaluation, with gold shares well over twice their January 1931 listed prices by May 1934, and manufacturing industry booming in a variety of fields – food and drink, metals and engineering, clothing and textiles in particular, both on the Rand and in the main coastal cities. If the English-speaking community was growing rich on the proceeds, Afrikaners and Africans were moving to town in large numbers, and the former were building up their influence through the trade unions.

There remained one task of special difficulty, which could have broken the coalition, but which the amalgamation of the parties was able to bring to a conclusion – whether that conclusion was a settlement, as Hertzog saw it, or the 'new unsettlement' of which Smuts complained. This was to complete the work of the Joint Select Committee of 1930 on the Native Bills. Any interpretation of the strategy of Hertzog's Government and of its S.A.P. rivals or associates in the Joint Select Committee before and after Fusion must take into account both the traditional explanations, which are best represented in the work of C. M. Tatz, and the more recent revision by Marian Lacey. Tatz understood Hertzog's policy, in the latter's own terms, as a bid to give Africans the 'substance' of more land in return for the loss of a 'shadowy' common-roll franchise, and presented the events as involving a conflict of ideas leading to a compromise between the parties over the franchise question in 1936. Lacey, by contrast, has argued that the parties reached substantial agreement over the franchise issue as early as 1932, even before the formation of a coalition government, and that a compromise was reached rather on the questions of land and labour, with the Native Trust and Land Act of 1936 as the more contentious issue. The interpretation offered here follows Lacey's analysis in some of its socio-economic aspects, but adheres to Tatz and Turrell in its handling of the relationship between the parliamentary parties.

Of the twenty-seven members of the Joint Select Committee, twelve belonged to the S.A.P., but by agreement between the parties there was to be a free vote on all issues. In practice, when the Committee divided, most of the S.A.P. representatives commonly voted in the minority, though Heaton Nicholls and Colonel Stallard generally sided with the Government on the more controversial questions. The key amendments proposed to the Natives Parliamentary Representation Bill which were laid before the Committee in 1930, came from the Opposition side. They may be sorted into three categories. First, F. S. Malan proposed the enfranchisement on the common voters' roll in all provinces of all Africans who passed a high qualification test, and his proposal was modified by J. H. Hofmeyr, who urged, rather incongruously in the light of his later attitude, that the level of the qualifications should be altered periodically to ensure that the African electorate did not exceed 10 per cent of the total. Second, there were proposals by G. B. van Zyl and by Smuts that the representation of Africans should be developed through the establishment of further General Councils in the Reserves, which should be politically correlated, and the parliamentary vote restricted to Africans who passed a test of civilisation. Third, there were proposals related to Hertzog's of which those put forward by Heaton Nicholls on 2 May 1930 were accepted by the Committee for discussion.

Nicholls moved that, apart from the Governor-General's nominees, Africans should elect four representatives to the Senate, namely one each for Natal, for the Transvaal and Orange Free State, for the Transkei, and for the rest of the Cape. These were to take the place of elected African representatives in the lower ('democratic') house, for Nicholls asserted that democracy was alien to the African outlook, and that their representation in the Assembly, if conceded in principle, would undermine his objective of preserving white supremacy 'for all time'. He suggested that Africans might elect black senators in the Cape, and in other provinces too if, after ten years, both houses of Parliament were agreeable; but he later withdrew this proposal.

To these proposals, Stallard added the idea of a Senate Grand Committee on Native Affairs, consisting of 'all native representatives and at least an equal number of Europeans with a chairman', to consider and, if it desired, also initiate legislation and tax proposals affecting Africans, together with matters referred to it by the Minister of Native Affairs or by any General Council under the Act of 1920.

By 25 February 1931 the Committee had accepted the revised Nicholls–Stallard electoral proposals by 17 votes to 9 (with eight S.A.P. members in the minority), and the fact that no Opposition member used his right to reopen the debate has enabled Lacey to argue that the S.A.P. had accepted the Government's franchise proposals at an early date. Whether this indicated an agreement by the S.A.P. to accept the Hertzog proposals, as Lacey implies, may be doubted. From very different perspectives, Nicholls and Smuts noted a growing lack of enthusiasm for the proposals among the S.A.P. members of the Committee in 1932. Nicholls resented what he diagnosed as an attempt to encourage the S.A.P. members to undermine the proceedings. Smuts told his English Quaker friends that 'the Native Bills Committee is getting worse and worse. We shall not arrive at an agreement and the Natives will be deprived of such scanty rights as they still possess'. This last remark may well refer to the systematic efforts of Hertzog's Government to destroy the effectiveness of the African vote in the years 1929 to 1933. It enfranchised white women in 1930, thus reducing the African electorate from 3.1 per cent to 1.4 per cent of the total. It liberated white male adults in the Cape and Natal from the property and income test in 1931, thereby adding another 10,000 to the roll. And it managed to remove some 5,000 Africans from the roll over the same five years by a new and perhaps irregular requirement that those claiming income qualifications had to prove employment for eleven of the preceding twelve months, and by amending the electoral law in 1931 so as to make objections to names on the voters' roll easier to lodge and more costly and inconvenient to contest (Lacey).

There was no progress in 1933, the year of election and political crisis. In 1934, the achievement of fusion may have robbed the Committee of its freedom, but it gave additional weight to the views of the majority, despite a brave attempt by the drafters of the United Party's programme of principles to leave the door open as wide as possible, by laying down that the 'solution of the political aspect of [the Native] question might be on the basis of separate representation of Europeans and Natives "or otherwise"', and that consensus was to be sought through 'the free exercise of the discretion of individual members representing the party in Parliament'. Therefore the Nicholls–Stallard formulation remained in tentative possession of the field; but there was room for change, and the Cabinet's new initiative brought some fresh surprises.

The first of these came in 1935, when Hertzog moved the rejection of Stallard's Grand Committee, and proposed instead the establishment of a Natives Representative Council of twenty-two, presided over by the Secretary for Native Affairs. It was to be attended by the five Chief Native Commissioners (non-voting), and include four nominated Africans and twelve Africans elected by colleges in the Transkei, in the rest of the Cape, in Natal, and in the Transvaal and Orange Free State together, some of the representatives being chosen by the urban Advisory Boards. This was a much smaller body than that originally proposed by Hertzog in 1926 [see p. 266], and because the Natives' Representatives could attend, it has been described by Tatz as a 'compound' between Stallard's Grand Committee and the original council of 1926. The influence of Smuts may be discernible here; but if so, he and the minority continued to oppose the Natives Representation Bill in which it was incorporated, for it still embodied Nicholls's rejection of African representation in the lower house.

The Nicholls Bill, then, as amended by the inclusion of Hertzog's plan for a Natives Representative Council, was the measure published on 31 December 1935 for debate in the Joint Sitting of February 1936. There was doubt, however, as to whether it could gain sufficient support. The efforts of men such as Sir James Rose Innes (ex-Chief Justice of the Union) and Eric Walker (Professor of History at the University of Cape Town) had helped to build up a hostile climate of opinion in urban Opposition circles, and Hertzog had reason to fear for his two-thirds majority if Smuts's followers withheld support. Smuts himself had constantly voted with the minority in the Joint Select Committee.

Despite the apparent disarray of the African political organisations in the early 1930s, the African reaction was, in the words of Karis and Carter, 'unequivocal in its opposition and Unionwide in its expression'. On the one hand the A.N.C., the Cape Native Voters' Convention, I.C.U. remnants, advisory boards and vigilance committees uniformly damned the proposed land legislation which was intended to compensate Africans for loss of common-roll voters' rights. Their opposition to the proposed abolition of Cape African representation in the lower house was equally widespread. Even conferences of black leaders which had been arranged by Hertzog at best tried to buy time. The decision to set up an All African Convention in December 1935, so as to co-ordinate resistance to the legislation, stemmed from consultation between D. D. T. Jabavu, leader of the Cape Native Voters' Convention, and Seme, president-general of the A.N.C.; but they were able to attract to their conference in Bloemfontein some four-hundred-odd representatives of many different kinds of organisation who reached a high degree of unanimity, and ended by sending a deputation to Cape Town led by Jabavu, with a petition of protest and an instruction to seek an interview with the Prime Minister.

Before meeting Hertzog on 7 February, members of Jabavu's deputation met a number of Eastern Province and Border M.P.s and discussed the idea of a compromise measure, on the lines of the 1929 Bill, which adhered to the principle of a separate voters' roll but allowed for some black representation in the lower house. They wired Jabavu, after he had returned to Alice, to convene the A.A.C. executive in Cape Town, so as to obtain a mandate for negotiating with Hertzog on these terms. But the arguments of Mofutsanyana, Xuma and Moroka, all members of the A.A.C. executive, as well as the concern of white liberals associated with the Institute of Race Relations, seem to have convinced Jabavu that compromise would be a mistake. Consequently, when the deputation met Hertzog on 13 February it knew it had no mandate, though Hertzog insisted that it was they who had brought up the idea of discussing the 1929 proposals, not himself. A memorandum by D. L. Smit, Secretary for Native Affairs, drawn up on the 14th, makes it clear that this was the basis of their negotiations. Hertzog gave the African leaders until the following Wednesday (the 19th) to come up with positive proposals, which he agreed to submit to his colleagues. On the day after the interview, however, he went ahead with his December Bill, which made no provision for black representation in the lower house, while Jabavu and his associates tried to have their case presented at the bar of the Assembly through the good offices of F. S. Malan and Sir James Rose Innes.

Hertzog surprised the House on the 17th by withdrawing the controversial Bill and replacing it by a second, which would give the Africans three white representatives in the Assembly. This drew the fire of D. F. Malan and the Purified Nationalists, who now moved an amendment to place Coloured as well as African voters on a separate roll, while Colonel

Stallard tried in vain to disinter his Senate Grand Committee proposal from the archives of the Joint Select Committee. But neither of these extreme groups had much influence on the debate. What Hertzog apparently did was to accept overtures from the group of eastern Cape members who had negotiated with Jabavu on the 7th and were prepared to do a deal with the Prime Minister even without African support, perhaps not realising that Jabavu had failed to get the mandate from his executive which such a deal clearly required. L. D. Gilson justified the support of this group for Bill Number Two on the ground that the decision of the Purified Nationalists to support Hertzog meant that they had no prospect of voting Bill Number One down if Hertzog decided to revert to it. Bill Number Two, he argued, at least provided for the 'retention of the individual vote', and still made it possible for black men's advocates to sit and debate in the Assembly. For Smuts and his S.A.P. followers who had consistently voted against the Nicholls proposals in the Joint Select Committee, retreat still had merit. Smuts saw himself as a 'Fabian' seeking to delay the complete exclusion of African representation from the lower house.

Only eleven members voted against the third reading, which received 169 supporting votes – a result greeted by spontaneous cheering, in defiance of convention, as members recognised the triumphal ending of Hertzog's ten-year campaign. The eleven opponents consisted, in about equal numbers, of S.A.P. liberals like F. S. Malan, Morris Alexander, and, above all, J. H. Hofmeyr, and Dominion Party representatives – liberals like C. W. A. Coulter on the one hand, and the segregationist Stallard on the other. Unlike Malan's Nationalists, Stallard preferred to throw the whole matter back into the melting pot rather than abandon Bill Number One. Hofmeyr's third reading speech made an impact because he was a cabinet minister, though he had arranged with Hertzog beforehand that his action would not be construed as involving an issue of confidence. He tore into the principle of communal representation on the ground that it involved inferior citizenship, and objected to the destruction of the 'vested right' of Africans in the existing political system because it involved a breach of faith by the white man which was likely to destroy the trust of the black. He accused Hertzog of lack of courage, as he retreated by stages from the relatively generous Bill of 1926, and prophesied that there would be no end to the retreat.

12.2   THE BLACK REACTION TO HERTZOG'S 1936 LEGISLATION

Despite the sweeping majority for Bill Number Two, Hertzog had not had things all his own way over the African franchise. Yet Lacey has correctly observed that he had no real need to tie his land offer to a deal over the franchise, because the black vote was neither a danger to the white man's political domination, nor really seen to be such. He feared the black vote only in the sense that it could determine electoral results in marginal constituencies, and might perhaps enable his white opponents to beat him

12 An African view of imperialism from Umvikeli-Thebe: The African Defender,
January 1936. The caption, 'Tata amakatango ako. Angiwafuni' means 'Take
away your chains. I do not want them!' Mussolini's invasion of Ethiopia and
Hertzog's 1936 'native bills' are equated

in a general election. If he was to free himself from this threat by placing
black voters on a separate roll, he needed to offer his parliamentary
opponents, who included leading representatives of the mining houses,
some kind of equivalent security, such as a guarantee of their labour
supply, without at the same time depriving his farmer supporters of their
land or their access to labour.

Hertzog did reassure the mining houses, in two main ways. First, he
reopened the doors to labour recruitment north of the Limpopo, which had
been closed since 1928 [see p. 499], as a special concession to the mines. In
the second place, he adopted a new-style Native Trust and Land Bill
introduced by Heaton Nicholls, which not only incorporated the Natal
principle of a native trust to control new lands acquired on behalf of
Africans, but reverted to the principles of the 1913 Land Act in its planned
extension of the reserves to the amount of 7.25 million morgen over a
period of years, with a fixed quota set for each province. This, Lacey urges,
was the main compromise of 1936 [see pp. 522–3].

At the same time, he looked after the farmers. The controls over black
labour introduced between 1927 and 1932 [see p. 511] had already given
them enormous powers. To these he now added a major attempt to keep
farm labourers on the land by means of a curb on the urban inflow of blacks
through the Native Laws Amendment Act of 1937. Influx control, a notion
closely associated with the thinking of Colonel Stallard, who had advocated

it as chairman of the Transvaal Local Government Commission in 1922 [see pp. 266, 526–7] had not at first commended itself to Hertzog. But Stallard promoted the idea in the Joint Select Committee, and although it was rejected with vigour by a departmental committee under J. M. Young and A. L. Barrett in 1935, it was accepted by Parliament as a third leg to the land and franchise policy of the Government (Davenport). The 1937 law sought to control black influx by a most elaborate provision for biennial industrial censuses in each municipality, as a basis for the removal of 'surplus' blacks from the towns by ministerial decree.

Whether to reject the new institutions imposed on the African people, or to make use of what was offered in the hope that it could be turned to some good purpose, greatly troubled the A.A.C. The moderates prevailed, and Jabavu, with understandable inconsistency, was among them. In December 1936, the Convention damned the Government's policy but authorised its executive to investigate how common citizenship could be restored and extended. A disenfranchised African, Ndlwana, took his case through to the Appeal Court in 1937, in an unsuccessful bid to have the Representation Act invalidated. Counsel argued on his behalf that he had been wrongfully removed from the common roll on the ground that Parliament had been incorrect to follow the unicameral procedure after the Union's adoption of the Statute of Westminster; but the Court ruled that the Union Parliament, being fully sovereign, could adopt any legislative procedure which it thought fit. Recourse to the law having thus proved fruitless, some leaders of the A.A.C. decided to recognise the new Native Representative Council, and some (though not Jabavu himself) fought for and obtained seats. They also swallowed their pride and backed white candidates for the Natives' Representatives' seats in Parliament and the Cape Provincial Council. Finally, in December 1937, despite opposition from Seme and others, the A.A.C. adopted a constitution which turned it into an umbrella for any African organisations, political or other, which wished to affiliate. This action made it a potential rival to the A.N.C., which had clearly lost the initiative to it. But the A.N.C.'s longer history and the wide range of its African membership, together with some measure of built-in sensitivity to a Jabavu challenge, led men with as differing views as James Calata (Anglican priest and Cape president), Selope Thema (Representative Councilor and editor of the *Bantu World*), on the one hand, and the communists J. B. Marks and Moses Kotane on the other, to propose a silver jubilee revival conference in 1937. This took place. The re-election of Mahabane as president-general did not rebuild the organisation's fighting efficiency, but at least it filled it with a bit more potential fire and helped prepare the movement for a new lease of life during the Second World War.

In the Cape Coloured world, where pressure for greater segregation from the Malan Nationalists and lack of real concern for Coloured interests in the U.P. presented a challenge to which the A.P.O. could give no answer, important new developments took place on the left. The Communist Party, which moved its headquarters from Johannesburg to Cape Town in the late 1930s, linked up with Abdurahman's daughter, Zainunissa ('Cissie') Gool in an attempt to create a united black–white workers' front. Her brother-in-law, Dr Goolam Gool, and I. B. Tabata (who was also related by marriage) meanwhile worked through the A.A.C. leadership to set intellectual ferment going through the New Era Fellowship, a Trotskyite discussion group. Both movements combined to form a National Liberation League (N.L.L.) in December 1935, Cissie Gool being chosen as its first president, though she was briefly replaced by Goolman Gool in 1937. Mrs Gool's return to power in 1938 marked a desire among most non-white groups, in associaton with the Communist Party and the Trades and Labour Council, to set up a Non-European United Front to contest the parliamentary election. But although its candidates obtained reasonably good support in three peninsular seats, none were returned to Parliament. What brought the new Front alive in 1938–9 was a move among the Nationalists, backed by a section of the ruling U.P., to promote the segregation of the Coloured people from the whites in public places, on public transport and in residential areas. A fiery demonstration occurred in Cape Town on 27 March 1939, when Mrs Gool attacked a draft Cape ordinance on these lines. A riot ensued, the police intervened; but the Administrator withdrew the ordinance.

Mrs Gool toured Natal and the Transvaal in June and July 1939, encouraging the Indians of Johannesburg to begin a passive disobedience campaign in August, in opposition to the Transvaal Asiatics (Land and Trading) Bill, which gave two years' grace only to Indians living in areas exempted from the provisions of the Gold Law, empowered the Minister of the Interior to refuse trading licences, and pegged the Indian occupation of the land to existing bazaars, save with ministerial consent. The Indians themselves were divided. Conservatives hoped that the Government would accept the findings of the Feetham Commission of 1934–5, which recommended a slight extension of Indian land rights; but the militants led by Dr Y. M. Dadoo favoured a passive resistance campaign, and – despite Gandhi's discouragement on account of the international situation – won the general support of Indian opinion when friction between the two sides erupted in violence.

While backing the United Front, the Communists also approached the A.A.C., urging it to fight the Hertzog bills by refusing to pay taxes. They hoped to transform it from within and persuade the A.A.C. and the A.N.C. to affiliate. This involved a return to their earlier tactic of joining hands with African nationalism, but even though men like E. Mofutsanyana sat on the executives of both bodies, they failed.

12.3 THE PARTY SPLIT OF 1934 AND THE RISE OF 'PURIFIED' AFRIKANER NATIONALISM

Unlike the African organisations, which discovered between 1935 and 1937 that they could not hold up the will of a determined white parliament either by political demonstration, or by appeal to the Government, or by action through the courts, the Purified Nationalists could at least make a noise in

Parliament. Yet Malan could not count on more than twenty votes in the Assembly, and the prospect for his *Gesuiwerde* followers looked bleak, even if they did manage to win over some Afrikaner members of the Creswellite Labour rump, who were encouraged by an economic programme published by Malan in January 1934.

Nevertheless, within fifteen years the Malanite Nationalists were to become the government of South Africa, so their success needs to be explained. For the sake of presenting the rise of Malan's Nationalists in perspective, it will be helpful to focus attention on the current debate between those, like Moodie, who have concerned themselves with the ideological aspects of the movement, and those, like O'Meara, who have seen it primarily as the outcome of a change in the balance of class forces.

Afrikaner nationalist thinking has often been described as Calvinist. But this means little, as writers like Hanekom, Oberholster and Moodie have shown, unless one distinguishes between two major streams of local Calvinist thinking – the dominant *Volkskerk* (People's Church) Calvinism of the N. G. Kerk, with its view of the Church as an institution separate from the state yet at the same time supportive of the nation, and the dogmatic neo-Calvinism associated originally with Dr Abraham Kuyper of the Netherlands, with its view of human society as a complex of overlapping theocracies ranging from the family to the state, each sovereign in its own sphere under God. Malan and the Cape Church in general held a *Volkskerk* position, whereas neo-Calvinism had a strong following in Potchefstroom in the 1930s, where it was well represented among lay writers by the political philosopher, H. G. Stoker. But there was, in addition, a distinctly secular nationalist tradition, which Moodie has helpfully labelled 'neo-Fichtean' for its preoccupation with the idea of the *Volk* as an organic body held together by a common historic culture. This was brought back to South Africa by a group of scholars who had studied in Germany in the 1920s, some of whom later became well known in public life – Nico Diederichs, P. J. Meyer, H. F. Verwoerd, Gert Cronje, and others. Diederichs's *Nasionalisme as Lewensbeskouing* (Nationalism as an Outlook on Life) exemplified their kind of writing. What happened in practice, as might have been expected, was that the neo-Calvinist and the neo-Fichtean influences played upon each other to produce an array of political doctrines, some totalitarian like those of Hans van Rensburg and Oswald Pirow, some democratic like the parliamentary credo of D. F. Malan, some with theological and others with secular rationales, whose variety in itself helps to explain the political turbulence which characterised the politics of opposition between 1933 and 1948.

O'Meara, however, arguing that one cannot judge a political movement 'by its own consciousness', finds an explanation of the Afrikaner nationalism of the period 1934–48 in 'an organised attempt by specific class forces to secure a base for capital accumulation in the industrial and commercial sectors of the economy'. Most accounts of Malan nationalism give prominence to the economic movement, the fullest being that of E. P. du Plessis. O'Meara's differs from the others in the questionable priority which he assigns to these class forces against an ideological explanation. Like

Moodie, he attaches importance to the Afrikaner 'civil religion', but essentially as a device for the concentration of diverse interests on a common materialist purpose: the rescue of all Afrikanerdom through the promotion of a shared *volkskapitalisme*.

Rescue was certainly necessary, and that on a big scale. About a fifth of the Afrikaner population could be loosely classified as 'poor whites' in 1930, in the sense in which J. F. W. Grosskopf of the Carnegie Commission used the term. He defined a poor white as 'a person who has become dependent to such an extent, whether from mental, moral, economic or physical causes, that he is unfit, without help from others, to find proper means of livelihood for himself or to procure it directly or indirectly for his children'. The incidence of poor whiteism, which was regularly discussed at Afrikaner Bond congresses in 1890s, increased markedly as a result of the rinderpest epidemic of 1896–7, the burning of farms by the British army during the Anglo-Boer war, and the sustained drought of the years 1903–8. These catastrophes led to the eviction of white *bywoners* in considerable numbers, many of whom migrated to the towns in search of livelihood, but without qualifications for jobs. At first the authorities hoped to rehabilitate such people by enticing them back to the land; but land was short, and too many poor whites lacked sufficient initiative, as the Transvaal Indigency Commission stressed in 1908. Van Onselen has pointed to a further category of urban whites who had been thrown out of trades such as brick-making and cab-driving by the expansion of capital enterprise on the Rand. In 1916 the N. G. Kerk convened a conference at Cradock, which concerned itself with a variety of remedial measures, including the provision of sheltered employment combined with suitable training, where possible, in the towns, on the railways, and in organisations where the discipline was strict (as in the police force). Eventually the Carnegie Commission of 1929–32 carried out a Union-wide investigation, again on the initiative of the churches, and its report in five volumes, dealing with rural impoverishment, the psychology of the poor white, and with educational, health and social aspects of the problem, suggested leads which the Hertzog Government began to follow up, offering privileged employment for white workers, setting up a Department of Social Welfare in 1937, and in other ways.

The Afrikaner was helped by the expansion of opportunities in the towns. Some had moved into the mines after the strike of (mainly British) workers in 1907, and by 1922 three-quarters of the white miners on the Rand were Afrikaners. As already noted, this brought the Afrikaner workers into close association with English-speaking workers, from whom they were able to pick up the techniques of industrial organisation which would enable them at a later stage to take control of the industrial unions and turn them to their own purposes. One immediate result of this contact was the establishment of close links between urban and rural Afrikaners and the Labour Party, which had notable results in the capture of the Transvaal Provincial Council by Labour in 1914, and in the electoral victory of the Pact in 1924. But a fully bilingual labour party, capable of drawing on the support of large numbers of Afrikaans- and English-speaking workers, never emerged. 'Aristocrats of labour' even if they were a 'bounded working class' [see p. 506] could not combine under the banner of socialism, while common cultural ties between Afrikaans- and English-speaking workers could hardly grow in the face of determined efforts by politicians to divide them over issues such as republicanism or the flag.

The Botha–Hertzog split, the neo-republicanism of the Nationalists after their breakaway in 1913, the Afrikaner rebellion of 1914 with its new list of folk heroes, and the deeds of community self-help which saw the establishment of the *Helpmekaar* (mutual aid) movement in 1915, the launching of *De Burger* in 1916, the creation of the *Arme Blanke Verbond* (poor white alliance) in 1917 to facilitate job-seeking by poor whites, and in 1918 of *Ons Eerste Volksbank* (our first people's bank) for savings, S.A.N.T.A.M. (for insurance) and S.A.N.L.A.M. (for investment and endowment), were key developments in a popular *risorgimento*. 'Jong Suid-Afrika', which came into being in May 1918 and soon changed its name to the *Afrikaner Broederbond*, began as a modest attempt to 'propagate the Afrikaans language and bring together serious-minded young Afrikaners in Johannesburg and along the Reef' and was at first 'nothing more than a semi-religious organisation', according to L. J. du Plessis, who later became its chairman. It was however, a growing force in public life, whose activities – secret since 1921 – have been opened up not only by enterprising news-papermen, and by E. G. Malherbe (who studied them from the perspective of military intelligence during the Second World War), but also by their official historian, whose reticent narrative adds confirmatory detail in the safer areas. As had been the case with its prototype, the *Genootskap van Regte Afrikaners*, the Broederbond saw the need to branch out into the cultural and economic fields, and this made the launching of the *Federasie van Afrikaanse Kultuurverenigings* (F.A.K.) in 1929, as a public front organisation for the Bond, an important landmark. This body, whose leaders were prominent Broeders, saw to the cultural isolation of Afrikaner youth by setting up the *Voortrekker* movement as an alternative to the Boy Scouts, and by promoting the Day of the Covenant festival so far as possible as a private Afrikaner occasion. It also looked after the economic needs of Afrikaners during the Depression years in a variety of ways: by promoting the launching of *Volkskas* as a cooperative (later a commercial) bank in 1934; by the promotion of chains like *Uniewinkels* in the context of a 'Buy Afrikaans' campaign; and by the organising of conferences to deal with poor whiteism and other issues. The climax to its activities on this front was the *Ekonomiese Volkskongres* in Bloemfontein in October 1939 [see p. 292].

How early the Bond began to engage directly in politics was never disclosed by its members, nor the manner in which this was done. But it followed from its first premises that it should seek to dominate the public life of South Africa, since only in that way could it ensure the restoration of authentic Afrikaner republican and Calvinist institutions to a position of ascendancy. People who thought in this way deplored the pact with Labour in 1922, alleging that it involved 'the continuous trafficking in principles, . . . the violation of consciences, . . . doubleheartedness', and other undesirable things. Under coalition, Malan said, problems could not be tackled or solved 'in a manly way'. Strong, purposeful action, *kragdadigheid*, came to mean a great deal to the neo-Nationalists. Hertzog's fault, whether his compromise was with English-speaking labour or English-speaking capital, was that he had diluted the Afrikaner cause. His gesture of bilingualism in education was looked upon as a risk not worth taking because the English-speaker did not want to learn Afrikaans or identify himself with South Africa, and would continue to try to preserve the towns as bastions of his culture, and keep alive and spread among Afrikaners the humanitarian (but, as they would urge, unpractical) notions regarding colour policy which had marked official British attitudes from the start. Hertzog's faith in the Statute of Westminster was subject to the same criticism: it was satisfactory as far as it went, but until the right to contract out of the Empire, and the right to stay out of Britain's wars, and the right to have a South African head of state, and to dispense with judicial appeals to the Privy Council were all clearly asserted, the Afrikaner cause was not secure. Coalition with Smuts's half-English S.A.P., or worse still fusion, therefore put much at risk.

The Broederbond had become involved in a campaign to break Hertzog's leadership of the National Party soon after his return from London with the Balfour Declaration in 1926 [see p. 261]. It also promoted a Republican Union started by N. J. van der Merwe within the Nationalist caucus in 1930 with the same object, and took active steps to stimulate the growth of a rival leadership in 1933–4 by drawing in men such as D. F. Malan, J. G. Strijdom and C. R. Swart as members (Serfontein). How far the Bond intended to dominate party politics has been disputed. The conspiracy theory advanced by Serfontein and by Wilkins and Strydom rests largely on documents like the circular distributed to members by J. C. van Rooy and I. M. Lombard, chairman and secretary respectively, on 16 January 1934. This referred to the proposed 'Afrikanerisation of South Africa in all its spheres', and ended with the slogan that 'our solution for South Africa's troubles is not that this or that party shall gain the upper hand, but that the Afrikaner Broederbond shall rule South Africa'. Though these words seem plain enough, some modern historians with good insight prefer to regard the Bond as primarily exercising a watchdog role over political standards according to their own criteria (Moodie), and as building up the complex organisational structure which was necessary to make the economic movement effective (O'Meara). Above all, it seems to have devoted its energies to holding the *volk* organisations together in the face of increasingly powerful centrifugal forces.

The governmental regrouping of 1933–4 gave it a political role in the north which it had not had before, because although Malan managed to take most of the Cape Nationalists with him in his 1934 breakaway, nearly all the parliamentarians in the northern provinces, who included the parliamentary representatives of the wealthy maize-producing districts of the south-western Transvaal and northern Free State, followed Hertzog into the United Party. It was therefore the Broederbond, O'Meara argues, which held together the politically weak *Gesuiwerdes* in the Transvaal during the 1930s, eclipsing the Party in importance. The fusion crisis also helped to shape the organisation itself, by turning it into an alliance between the Purifieds of the Transvaal (mainly small stock farmers, teachers and civil servants, together with the intellectuals of Potchefstroom) and the influential Malanites of the western Cape, in association with S.A.N.L.A.M. and the press leaders of Keerom Street.

With the support of the Broederbond to make up for their parliamentary weakness in the north, the Purified Nationalists attacked boldly, but at first made a poor showing as the official Opposition in Parliament. Malan's 'no confidence' speech on 15 January 1935 was long-winded, vague and trivial. He did not repeat the tactics in the years immediately following. But there were moments during the sessions of 1934–7 when his party took a distinctive stand. Thus they rejected Hertzog's demand for sanctions against Italy during the Abyssinian war [see p. 295]. They drew Hertzog's fire by demanding a bilingual chairman for the select committee on public accounts in 1936, and they explicitly demanded an amendment to the Aliens Bill in 1937, asking for a ban on the immigration of 'persons or classes of persons or races, who, such as among others the Jewish, cannot be readily assimilated', together with the abolition of Yiddish as a specially recognised European language. But on the whole they were unable to make the Government take them seriously.

Change came, though, in 1938. This was the year of a general election which boosted their strength in the Assembly to twenty-seven, though only one of these, J. G. Strijdom, was elected in the Transvaal. It was also the year of Malan's celebrated Day of the Covenant address at Blood River, when he exhorted the Afrikaner people to fresh efforts in their new and 'greater' trek, not away from the centres of civilisation and into the wilderness as in 1838, but back from the platteland to the town where their new Blood River, the new locus of conflict with black power, now lay.

The Nationalists had managed to win the initiative in the stage-management of these centenary Voortrekker celebrations, which were sponsored by the F.A.K. and placed under the chairmanship of Henning Klopper, one of the original founders of the Broederbond, in whose imagination the ritual reenactment of the Great Trek had been born. They were able to exclude Hertzog from a prominent role in the celebrations, remembering his blistering attack on the Broederbond at Smithfield on 7 November 1935 (Wilkins and Strydom), and in Parliament in 1936, when he had accused the Bond of being a self-elected élite in unholy alliance with the *Gesuiwerdes*, playing politics in the guise of a cultural organisation, and arrogating to themselves a monopoly of patriotism. During the organisation of the Voortrekker centenary celebrations J. D. Kestell, the much-respected commando chaplain of Anglo-Boer war days, appealed to save the living descendants of the Voortrekkers, and this led, under the auspices of the F.A.K., to the calling of an *Ekonomiese Volkskongres* in Bloemfontein in October 1939 to discuss the future of the Afrikaner. New ground was broken here, and the speakers who broke it were in a number of cases men who later played a prominent role in public life: among them Dr C. G. W. Schumann, the Stellenbosch economist, who spoke on the economic position of the Afrikaner; Dr T. E. Dönges, later cabinet minister and State-President elect, and M. S. Louw, later chairman of the *Ekonomiese Instituut*, who both spoke on the mobilisation of capital; Dr H. F. Verwoerd, who spoke on consumer cooperatives; Dr Albert Hertzog, son and rival of the Prime Minister who spoke on the organisation of labour and made a strong attack on communism in the trade unions; and others who dealt with peoples' banks, the Afrikaner's role in manufacturing, and other topics. The most significant result of the congress was the promotion of Afrikaner businesses, great and small, and the concentration of Afrikaner economic power in large investment corporations. Of these, *Federale Volksbeleggings* (Federal People's Investments) was the most impressive creation. This was a Transvaal-based financial house at first under the control of SANLAM. But it grew into the pioneer Afrikaner business concerned with mining finance, in this respect matching the achievement of Willem Boshoff, whose gold-mining empire had already begun to take shape in the early 1930s (Du Plessis). Out of the conference also grew an *Ekonomiese Instituut*, which undertook a variety of functions among them the setting up of a *Reddingsdaadbond* (Rescue League) devoted not so much to saving poor whites as to making Afrikaners economically conscious and saving them from 'the un-national power of the trade unions' (O'Meara). Trade schools, labour bureaux, insurance schemes and worker entertainment emanated from this active body. So did the *Afrikaanse Handelsinstituut* (Afrikaans Business Institute), formed in 1942, to promote large- and small-scale manufacturing and commercial businesses, and guard against excessive company taxation, foreign investment damaging to local production, and the too rapid growth of black wages and unemployment insurance [see p. 489].

The Broederbond also kept a careful watch over developments within trade unionism. It recognised the growth of class divisions within Afrikanerdom as lethal to the collective interests of the *volk*, and thus saw the Labour Party and the South African Trades and Labour Council as *volksvreemde* (hostile) bodies whose power needed to be broken. Hence the forming of a *Nasionale Raad van Trustees* (N.R.T.), under Albert Hertzog, P. J. Meyer and others, in 1936, to promote a new Afrikaner unionism imbued with Christian National principles, prepared to negotiate rather than strike, to give value for wages, to resist the moral undermining of socialist doctrine, and to keep blacks out of 'white' jobs. The N.R.T. had limited success, but the *Arbeidsfront* (Labour Front) of the Ossewa Brandwag which appeared in 1943 as a rival, together with the Nationalist Party's *Blanke Werkers Beskermingsbond* (White Workers' Protection League) of 1944, left little room for doubt as to how important it was to the Nationalist leadership to keep the Afrikaner worker within the movement. Apart from the *Spoorbond*, however, which successfully drove the National Union of Railway and Harbour Servants out of business in 1937, Afrikaner industrial unions had little success before 1948, and did not manage to destroy the older craft unions.

The *Ossewa Brandwag* (Oxwaggon Sentinels) was another movement to grow out of the Voortrekker celebrations. Rather like the Broederbond itself, it started as a cultural organisation officially founded under the leadership of Colonel J. C. C. Laas in Bloemfontein on 4 February 1939. But in the context of a tense international situation, marked by the rise of Nazi Germany, it underwent a fundamental change, becoming a paramilitary body with its own storm troopers under a new commandant-general selected in December 1940, the ex-Administrator of the Orange Free State, J. F. J. Van Rensburg, who would soon be fighting Malan for control of the nationalist movement.

The *Nasionale Instituut vir Christelike Onderwys en Opvoeding* (National Institute for Christian Education and Instruction) was established under the F.A.K. in July 1939, under the chairmanship of Professor J. C. van Rooy of Potchefstroom, who was also chairman of the F.A.K. and a leading Bond member. Its aim was to apply in the schools the culturally separatist doctrines which had been developed in Purified Nationalist circles, involving a revival of the defensive educational strategy which had been developed in the Transvaal and Orange River Colony in opposition to Milner's anglicisation policy after 1902. A third of the Broederbond's members were teachers, wrote I. M. Lombard in the *Transvaler* in December 1944.

Teaching, broadly conceived, involved also the means of propaganda. By the outbreak of the war in 1939, the Nationalists could rely on a spread of newspapers in the main centres. The *Burger*, founded by *Nasionale Pers* in Cape Town in 1915, remained faithful to Malan after 1934, while the same company's *Volksblad* took the Purified line in the Free State. To counter the influence of the Hertzogite *Vaderland* in the Transvaal, the *Nasionale Pers* decided in 1936 to set up a new company, *Voortrekkerpers*, in the hope that they could keep control over its new paper, the *Transvaler*. In this, however, they miscalculated, for its editor, Dr H. F. Verwoerd, though he came from the Cape, decided from his appointment in 1937 to pursue an independent line, strongly republican, strongly racist, and in some degree anti-semitic. A measure of north–south friction resulted from these developments, but in general the Nationalist press companies played a major supportive role behind the political movement. They put out a series of volumes, some commemorating the Afrikaner's historical past, like Gustav Preller's *Voortrekkermense* series, some to boost the Afrikaans language and literature; while the political tracts of the *Tweede Trek* series put across the programme of the Afrikaner revival in handy pocket editions.

As the Malan Nationalists grew in confidence from 1938 onwards, the United Party found it increasingly difficult to hold together in face of their attacks. At first, the issues which divided it were domestic, but it was the decision to enter the war against Nazi Germany which eventually drove Hertzog and Smuts apart. Tea-cup storms over the national anthem plagued 1938 – when *Die Stem van Suid-Afrika* was played together with *God Save the King* at the opening of Parliament, when *Die Stem* was played at military parades on Union Day and *The King* was not, and when, because the organisers of the Voortrekker Centenary would not allow the playing of *The King* at their celebrations, the Governor-General (and therefore the Prime Minister) felt unable to take part. But these storms were damaging to government morale, for on the second occasion Richard Stuttaford temporarily resigned from the Cabinet, while Leslie Blackwell, a leading back-bencher, openly dissented from his leader's policy. A ministerial decision, taken without Hertzog's knowledge, to give Roberts Heights, the military base south of Pretoria, the new name of Voortrekker-hoogte in December 1938 had similar repercussions, appropriate though the gesture may have been to the occasion. Rather more serious were the effects of Hertzog's decision in 1938 to appoint A. P. J. Fourie, the ex-Minister of Labour, who had been defeated in the general election, as a senator selected for his knowledge of native affairs. Hofmeyr resigned from the Cabinet in protest, feeling that Fourie was not properly qualified, and Sturrock followed, believing Hertzog had forced Hofmeyr out. Smuts, who felt strongly about Hertzog's choice of Fourie, lost face in some quarters for not resigning, but made it clear that he was still more concerned over the implications of the current crisis in Czechoslovakia, and saw this as a compelling reason for staying in office.

12.4   THE FOREIGN POLICY OF THE FUSION ERA

Rising international tension during the 1930s gave point to the growing desire in governmental and private circles for an independent foreign policy released from the constraints of decisions taken in London, and in the spirit of the new freedom attained under the Statute of Westminster. The Union Government began to assert its point of view, often hesitantly, but with occasional bursts of surprising conviction, between 1931 and 1939. Both Hertzog and Smuts were 'League of Nations men', for both Fusion partners found it politically less controversial to talk of support for the League than of identification with the Commonwealth, for so long as the League seemed to have a chance of success. Yet it was hardly an intimate partnership, in that Hertzog kept foreign policy largely to himself, and seldom brought the issues before the Cabinet. Smuts, though a father of the League, never went to Geneva to attend its sessions, but maintained contact with world political leaders like L. S. Amery, Gilbert Murray, Tom Lamont of New York and Chaim Weizmann through regular correspondence.

The main burden of expressing South Africa's official viewpoint overseas fell upon two men in particular, Eric Louw, who represented the Union Government successively in London, Washington, Rome and Paris in 1929–37, and Charles te Water, who held the London High Commissioner-ship from 1929 to 1939, and spent much time in the General Assembly of the League of Nations, of which he was elected president in 1933 (Pie-naar). Te Water denounced the Japanese invasion of Manchuria on behalf of his government, though no follow-up action resulted. In the case of Ethiopia, the Union Government adopted a markedly inconsistent policy, some of its members (notably Hertzog and Smuts) lending energetic support to a policy of economic sanctions against the aggressor, Italy, while others backed the commercial and farming interests which continued to win subsidies for Italian shipping lines which frequented the Cape route, and to export large quantities of farm produce to the Italian forces in East Africa. In Geneva, Te Water shocked the British authorities by his outspoken opposition to the Hoare–Laval Pact of December 1935, and by his strong advocacy of an oil embargo against Italy the following month. Supporters of sanctions were, for the most part, men who saw them as necessary if the authority of the League were to be maintained. But with Italy's victory in 1936, soon followed by the Spanish civil and Sino-Japanese wars, faith in the efficacy of the League diminished among South African politicians, and this opened the door for negative criticism of its role from members of the Purified opposition, whose support had been at best equivocal.

The League of Nations never subjected the South African Government to the intensity of moral pressure which bore down on it after 1946, largely – it seems – because the political values of the League, and of the members of its Permanent Mandates Commission, were intrinsically European, and harboured certain colonialist assumptions. Even so, Pienaar writes that 'the virtually unanimous judgment of those who have examined South Africa's record' is that she failed to fulfil the trust placed in her under the South West African mandate. Criticism stemmed from the degree to which governmental policy favoured the growing number of white settlers (who were at the same time the leading tax-payers), giving them generous treatment in the matter of schooling facilities while black education was left entirely to the missionary societies until 1935, and the segregated black reserves were largely starved of public funds. Throughout the period of the mandate the Union Government was involved in a verbal fencing match with the League over the issue of sovereignty, after the Appellate Division had laid down, in the aftermath of the Bondelswarts rising, that 'the Government of the Union of South Africa, as mandatory of South West Africa under the Treaty of Versailles, possesses sufficient internal sovereignty to warrant a charge of high treason against an inhabitant who takes up arms . . . against the Government of that territory'. The sovereignty issue was sensitive because of the ease with which it could be linked with possible incorporation of the territory, especially after the beginning of the 'Fifth Province' agitation started by the dominant white political movement, after the upsurge of German irredentist feelings at the start of the Nazi era. A constitutional commission under Judge van Zyl in 1935 observed that there was 'no legal obstacle to the government of the mandated Territory as a province of the Union subject to the Mandate'; but the Union Government refrained from following the logic of this statement through, and at the same time stood firm against Hitler's bid to regain the territory after 1936, dealing with manifestations of Nazism with considerable vigour.

Hertzog and Smuts reacted in rather different ways to the growth of German assertiveness, and this mattered for local reasons because of the pull exerted on Hertzog by his ex-colleagues, the Malan Nationalists, some of whom saw in Hitler's racism a credo which could be adapted to South

African needs. Both Hertzog and Smuts had reacted against the severity of Versailles, Smuts as a participant who had had to shoulder more of the blame for the harshness of the treaty than his role at the peace conference warranted, Hertzog with the uninhibited judgment of one who had not been involved in the settlement. Smuts tended to see the rise of Hitlerism as a monstrous consequence of an unjust peace, Hertzog as the legitimate reaction of a downtrodden nation. Hertzog was prepared to trust Hitler's undertakings right down to the outbreak of the Second World War, whereas Smuts, who shared Hertzog's feeling that the posture of neutrality in a European conflict was desirable, felt unable to recommend neutrality after the rape of Czechoslovakia. Their differing assessments of the international danger became tied up, in the course of time, with their differing attitudes to the role of South Africa in the British Commonwealth, above all the right of South Africa to participate or not, at will, in any war in which Britain became involved. For Hertzog, even after the Sudeten crisis of September 1938, neutrality was a right which it was still prudent to exercise. For Smuts, too, it was a legal right; but he denied that South Africa had the political right to use it in the international crisis of 1939. Both men probably realised the dangers to white South African unity involved in making war against Germany for the second time in less than twenty-five years, when the unpleasant memories of the first occasion were still green; but for Smuts the international dangers outweighed the domestic, whereas for Hertzog it was the other way round.

Hertzog considered that a statement which he had placed before the Cabinet in September 1938, setting out a firm neutralist line in the event of Britain becoming involved in war against a European power, was still binding on Smuts, who had originally approved it, a year later. Smuts, whose public utterances reflected a growing anxiety for the preservation of civilised values, rejected this argument. A special session of Parliament was called for 2 September 1939, primarily to prolong the life of the Senate, which was due to expire on the 5th. If, at this point, Hertzog had asked for a dissolution of Parliament in order to seek support for his policy of neutrality in the war which had just broken out between Britain and Germany, the Governor-General, Sir Patrick Duncan, might have found it difficult to avoid his request, especially as the issue of foreign policy had not been tested in the general election of 1938. But Hertzog, apparently acting on mistaken advice that he could command a majority in the Assembly, moved a motion in the Assembly on the 4th to reaffirm his policy of neutrality in a European war. Smuts carried an amendment in favour of breaking off relations with Germany by 80 votes to 67. The Cabinet was split down the middle, and when Hertzog asked Duncan for a dissolution the latter refused, on the ground that a viable alternative government could be formed. If he had dissolved Parliament and an election had been called on the war issue, a great deal of public violence might well have broken out. As it was, there was a new and threatening polarisation of political forces, as the Labour and Dominion parties fell in behind Smuts, and the Malanite Nationalists backed Hertzog. The experiment which was Fusion thus came to a dramatic and fateful end.

13 Smuts and the Liberal–Nationalist Confrontation, 1939–48

13.1 SOUTH AFRICA ENTERS THE SECOND WORLD WAR

Smuts took South Africa into the Second World War out of concern for the future of the human race, and in particular for that of Europe, 'this glorious mother continent of Western civilization – the proudest achievement of the human spirit up to date', which seemed to be in danger of destruction in the short term by Hitler, or in the longer term by Stalin. It was a choice, as he put it, 'between the Devil and Beelzebub', since Hitler was 'another Attila', whereas Stalin and the communists, the 'looters' who grabbed half of Poland, had taken the wrong turning, 'for man is primary, not society'.

The team which he selected to take South Africa into the war consisted largely of survivors of the Fusion Government who had remained with him in the September division – notably Harry Lawrence (Interior), Claude Sturrock (Railways), Deneys Reitz (Native Affairs), Stuttaford and Clarkson. He brought Hofmeyr back (Finance and Education), put Collins and Conroy, ex-Hertzogite colleagues from the Anglo-Boer War, into Agriculture and Lands respectively, gave Justice to Colin Steyn, son of the last O.F.S. president, and found places in his coalition for the Dominion Party leader, Stallard, and the Labour leader, Madeley. They were men of uneven competence, though some – notably Hofmeyr and Sturrock – achieved much during their period of office. What mattered most to Smuts was that he should be able to devote his energies to the winning of the war. The management of parliamentary business was therefore left mainly to Hofmeyr, while Louis Esselen took charge of party affairs. Smuts himself concentrated on external affairs and defence, the military aspects of which were handled through the Chief of General Staff, Sir Pierre van Ryneveld, and the economic through Dr H. J. van der Byl, the first chairman of I.S.C.O.R., who was made Director-General of War Supplies.

The needs of war required changes in the methods of administration, though parliamentary government, including the contesting of elections, was kept going and served as a lightning conductor for the release of public emotions, which – as will be shown later – were extremely volatile. Indeed, one of the outstanding characteristics of the Smuts wartime government was the coolness with which it handled threats to the security of the State. Like all belligerents, it armed itself under a War Measures Act of 1940, with the power to intern suspects and enemy aliens, and used them; it called in all firearms; and it helped itself to a range of arbitrary powers, including powers to control supplies and curb industrial unrest. But, profiting from the lessons of the First World War, Smuts pulled his punches in handling the most provocative opposition to his war policy, and refrained from the use of the death penalty even for blatant acts of treason.

The Treasury was required to relax its controls over defence expenditure by acceding as a matter of routine to all requests made by a new combined Defence Authorities Committee. Thus released from the economics of peacetime, the Department of Defence spent close on £650 million between 1939 and 1945 on the war against the Axis. The demands of war, in consequence, resulted in considerable industrial expansion, above all in mining, steel and textiles, as factories turned to the manufacture of armoured cars, artillery pieces, ammunition, boots and uniforms, using a good deal of unskilled black labour, diluted with that of white artisans, in order to meet production targets.

Defence of the Cape sea route was South Africa's first duty to her allies, and Smuts cast South Africa, in the first instance, for an otherwise passive military role, while raising sizeable forces against contingencies elsewhere. But once France and French seapower had been lost to the Allies, and Italy had entered on the German side, the continent of Africa became directly involved. The Defence Act limited the operational area of South African forces to 'any part of South Africa whether within or outside the Union'; but in 1940 the Smuts Government made it possible for volunteers to offer their services anywhere in Africa. Only white troops, however, were permitted to join combat units, the Coloured and African soldiers being confined to auxiliary services. Union forces took part in the reconquest of Ethiopia from the Italians in 1940–1. They seized Madagascar, which had thrown in its lot with Vichy France, in 1942, in order to forestall any possible landing by the Japanese. Two South African divisions took part in the north African campaigns against German and Italian forces in Egypt and Libya, the second being captured by Rommel's Afrika Korps in Tobruk. After taking part in the battle of El Alamein in September 1942, and the final expulsion of the Axis forces from Africa, the 6th South African Armoured Division was sent to Italy as part of the American Fifth Army, its members having volunteered to serve anywhere in the world, and fought its way up the peninsula from Salerno to the Po valley. Altogether some 200,000 uniformed South Africans took part in the war, of whom close on 9,000 were killed.

13.2   THE AFRIKANER OPPOSITION, 1939–43

Although the Government relied on volunteers for all operations outside the Union as a way to avoid provoking its opponents, the world-wide ideological conflict cut deep into South African public opinion. Those who were attached emotionally to Britain, and those who deplored racial fanaticism, were concerned to ensure the victory of the western Allies. But whites who felt that the preservation of the existing South African race – class structure was necessary for European survival in the sub-continent, or who were emotionally drawn to the Germans as to near-kinsmen, or who were excited by the vigour or the doctrines of Nazism, backed the Axis; while those who merely wanted to implement South Africa's constitutional right to control her own destiny, and saw this as of greater importance than the issues at stake in the war, opted for neutrality. Others, like the Communists, who saw the war as a civil conflict between rival capitalist factions, tended at first to be neutral by conviction, but partisan from the moment of Russia's entry in 1941.

The Broederbond, working through the F.A.K., had advertised a republican demonstration on Monumentkoppie, outside Pretoria, for 9 September 1939. The occasion was used to celebrate reunion (*hereniging*) of the Nationalists under Malan and Hertzog, thirty-seven Hertzogites having crossed the floor of the Assembly to vote against the decision to enter the war. *Hereniging* was a difficult assignment, however, for in five years the U.P. and the G.N.P. had drifted apart in sentiment and objectives. Basson has noted the latter's fear that Hertzog might become the focus of a revived personality cult, and the fear of some northern Nationalists that Malan's resistance to him might be too soft. But *hereniging* was achieved in December 1939, so far as a form of words could do this, on the basis of making South Africa a white man's country, with a republican constitution based on the 'broad foundation of the people's will' as expressed in a referendum, and on the equal language and cultural rights of the two sections of the white population. This, however, was an awkward formula, for the more rigorous Nationalists like J. G. Strijdom and H. F. Verwoerd of the Transvaal, and N. J. van der Merwe and C. R. Swart of the O.F.S., firmly believed that an Afrikaner Republic had to be created as a precondition for the build-up of a right relationship between the two white groups, and that remained anathema to Hertzog. Malan and Hertzog, working together, put pressure on the Government to leave the war; but they could not stop the Free State Nationalists, in the heady atmosphere engendered by Hitler's campaigns of May and June 1940, from calling a republican rally in Bloemfontein on 20 July against Hertzog's express instructions. They used the occasion to propagate not only republicanism but also Christian National (single-medium) education, of which Hertzog strongly disapproved, and to attack the party fusion of 1934 as a product of 'British–Jewish capitalist' influence. An anonymous attempt was made at about this time to smear Hertzog and Havenga by 'discovering' evidence in a freemason's private suitcase which suggested that they had connived with Smuts to make South Africa (including English-speaking Rhodesia) a Republic within the British Empire. This rumour helped to erode Free State Nationalist confidence in Hertzog, and confirmed Hertzog in the belief that he was being extruded from a position of leadership.

The issue on which the attempt at *hereniging* finally broke down was the adoption of a programme of principles for the new party. This happened in November 1940, but the rumblings had started as early as March, when the *Volksparty* (as Hertzog's followers were now called), unlike their colleagues in the other provinces, had decided to defer party fusion until October, and in the meantime to draw up their own programme of principles. The document which Hertzog then drafted, for which he obtained press publicity in October, made explicit reference to the equal rights of English- and Afrikaans-speakers, and it was lukewarm towards republicanism. At the O.F.S. provincial congress on 5 and 6 November, where a clash between the two sides seemed inevitable, the Nationalists used their majority to reject a Hertzogite as chairman, and then went on to turn down Hertzog's draft programme as a basis for discussion. They decided instead, on a motion by C. R. Swart, to debate the draft of the Federal Council of the H.N.P., which that body had prepared, in the self-chosen absence of the Hertzogites, in October. Hertzog ducked a fight on the procedural point, but challenged Swart to explain the omission from the Federal draft of any reference to equal political rights for English-speakers. Swart's reply, which referred to linguistic and cultural equality in the federal draft, did not satisfy him, so for the second time in his career, Hertzog stormed out of the party congress with a small group of followers (among them Havenga), this time not to found a nationalist party but to dissociate himself from the Free State section of a party of which he intended to remain a member. But he could not remain a member, for shortly afterwards the Transvaal congress, on Strijdom's initiative, quietly withdrew its support. Malan did not defend him. His contribution at this stage, by drawing a smokescreen in public over what had happend at the conference in Bloemfontein, was to ensure that when the Hertzogites rallied at the end of the year and went on to form their breakaway Afrikaner Party in January 1941, only a small number of the H.N.P. supporters went with them.

In the distractions of the *hereniging* crisis which lasted through 1940, the H.N.P. may have missed an opportunity to strengthen its own hand by turning its back on a new and popular movement, Gert Yssel's *Handhawersbond* (League of Defenders). Like another body of the same name which had enjoyed a brief existence in 1930 (Moodie), Yssel's movement had a paramilitary structure, based on a network of local commando units. It aimed to protect persecuted Afrikaners, teach desecrators of monuments a lesson, and work for a republic. It undertook, if necessary, to use 'abnormal methods' to achieve its ends. But the *Handhawersbond* failed to win the confidence of either the H.N.P. or the Broederbond leadership. Verwoerd thought the movement had Nazi tendencies – a suggestion to which Pirow's hovering in the wings gave some colour – while Strijdom (whom Roberts and Trollip criticise for rejecting what might have become a private *Ossewa Brandwag* within the ranks of the H.N.P.) saw the Handhawers as potential troublemakers whose keenness to restore the Hertzog connection presaged only difficulties (Basson). The movement dissolved itself in February 1941, Yssel joining up with Pirow's New Order Group, while the bulk of its members went over to the O.B. As a result,

Malan's party was faced, right through to the general election of 7 July 1943, with the problem of coordinating rival groups which doggedly retained their own identities rather than combine, some committed to peaceful change, but others appearing to welcome violence.

Despite the precedent of Hertzog's deposition, personalities remained important, among them Malan's chief rival, J. F. J. van Rensburg, ex-Administrator of the O.F.S., who succeeded a discredited Colonel Laas as Commandant-General of the O.B. in January 1941. The O.B. was committed broadly to the maintenance of the Afrikaner values, the nurturing of patriotism and group pride, and the vigorous defence of their way of life, through participation in festivals, heroes' days, wreath-layings, target-shoots, *jukskei* matches, public lectures on folk history and folk literature, camps, and in other ways. Its leaders were doubtful whether the Afrikaner cause could be adequately served by orthodox political action alone, and some of them, like Van Rensburg himself, were sufficiently influenced by developments in Europe to doubt the value of the parliamentary system at all. In this they differed fundamentally from Malan. They gambled on a victory for the Axis, encouraged from 1942 by Zeesen radio's support for Van Rensburg against Malan. Malan, however, insisted on constitutional procedures, arguing that they alone were capable of producing the right results, whichever side eventually won the war. On 29 October 1940 he obtained from Dr C. R. Kotze, chairman of the O.B. Groot Raad, a document subsequently known as the Cradock Agreement whereby the H.N.P. was to operate on the party political level and the O.B. on the non-political, the latter to refrain from subversive activities or force directed against friendly political movements. But the militant Van Rensburg had not yet been elected Commandant-General when this agreement was drawn up; and the O.B. was already linked under a common command to a para-military movement, the *Stormjaers*, whose potential danger to public security – not to mention that from various other Nazi-type movements like L. T. Weichardt's anti-Semitic Greyshirts – had already led Smuts to order a general surrender of rifles to the authorities. Members of the O.B. tended not to commit acts of sabotage and public violence until 1942, and then they were denounced by the H.N.P. for so doing, but their attraction to Nazism and what they termed 'the revolution of the twentieth century' and their liking for the Nationalist virtue of *kragdadigheid* made the restraints of the Cradock Agreement wise policy from the H.N.P.'s point of view – if they could be enforced.

Of the H.N.P.'s other rivals, the least significant was the Afrikaner Party of E. A. Conroy and N. C. Havenga, which was formed in December 1940 as a political home for Hertzog's Free State faithful, on the basis of their retired leader's now apparently outdated policy of promoting Anglo-Afrikaner political cooperation. The seats vacated by Hertzog and Havenga were easily captured by H.N.P. rivals, and the Afrikaner Party was reduced to ten members in the lower house, plus a handful of senators. Weakened by desertions to either the government benches or the Nationalists, they cast around for political allies, sometimes in unlikely places, such as the O.B., which at least shared a common dislike of the

13 **Afrikaner nationalist views of Smuts as a tool of British imperialism, 1943 (top) and 1948 (bottom), both by T. O. Honiball of the *Burger*. In the lower cartoon, which represents Hofmeyr, Smuts and Colin Steyn astride the South African Party nag, Smuts's *A Century of Wrong* having fallen to the ground, Steyn asks his leader: 'Daddy, is the snake really dead, or is he just lying and digesting his prey?' Smuts replies 'No, my child, I'd say he's been dead for years.'**

H.N.P., but Havenga failed to reach an agreement with Malan before the 1943 election, and the Party failed to win more than a handful of votes.

The most original member of the Hertzogite diaspora was Oswald Pirow, ex-Minister of Defence, who had travelled in Nazi Germany on government business and expressed in his *Nuwe Orde vir Suid Afrika*, which was frequently reprinted between December 1940 and May 1941, what he later described as an attraction for the national socialism of Salazar. Pirow remained in the Nationalist Party, but set up a separate New Order Group within it on 29 September 1940, that is before *hereniging* had collapsed. Its posture was anti-capitalist and 'Christian-republican', but – in the Hertzog tradition – not exclusively Afrikaner-oriented. Most of its members were Transvalers. Its political objective after the split was to keep a Hertzogite circle alive within the Party, and for this reason it came under heavy fire from Strijdom, who seems to have feared Pirow as a potential rival for the party leadership, and from Verwoerd's *Transvaler*, which objected to his attacks on parliamentary government in defiance of the Party's policy (Basson). Malan began to move against him in August 1941, the month in which the Transvaal caucus decided to ban the formation of groups within its own ranks. The next January Pirow and his parliamentary followers left the Nationalist caucus without formally seceding from the Party. But they walked out into the wilderness, refusing on the one hand to attach themselves to the O.B. despite their common contempt for the parliamentary system, and on the other to contest seats in the 1943 general election.

Malan's offensive against the New Order turned out to be the catalyst for a period of open conflict between the H.N.P. and the O.B.. Van Rensburg reacted to the attack on Pirow by throwing down the gauntlet to Malan. On 3 July 1941, supposedly believing that Malan approved of the decision, the O.B. distributed throughout the land 100,000 copies of a draft republican constitution which had been drawn up by a committee of the Broederbond. It was very much less national socialist in tone than an earlier one published in O.B. circles in April 1940, which had featured a dictatorial president and carried heavy racist overtones (Moodie). Like it, however, it laid emphasis on Afrikaans as 'the only official language', with English relegated to a secondary role. Malan was angry. He had not given his assent to publication, and regarded Van Rensburg's action as a violation of the Cradock Agreement. At first, the leaders acted with restraint, and Malan accepted Van Rensburg's apology. But Malan's attack on Pirow was the signal for Van Rensburg to assume responsibility on behalf of the O.B., not only for the publication of the constitution, but for its contents as well, in a speech at Elsburg on 9 August. In what looked very much like a bid for Nationalist leadership, he presented the O.B. to his audience as a movement above party which all could join, and which would not take sides in the dispute between Pirow and Malan. On 4 September the O.B. decided to withdraw its controversial constitutional circular of 3 July, but replaced it with another which, while repudiating any desire to undermine the Party, nevertheless criticised Malan for not referring his complaint to the *Afrikaner Eenheidskomitee* (Afrikaner Unity Committee) before making a public protest (Basson).

This *Eenheidskomitee* had come into being in June, chiefly on the inspiration of Professor L. J. du Plessis of Potchefstroom, to coordinate the activities of the various Afrikaner groups. Du Plessis was a neo-Calvinist political philosopher and chairman of the Broederbond committee which had drafted the controversial constitution (O'Meara). He had come to believe that Calvinist theology, linked to cultural nationalism and held together in a totalitarian frame, would provide a better political system than liberal democracy, which, like Hertzog, Pirow, Van Rensburg and others, he had come to regard as decadent. The aim of the *Eenheidskomitee*, as he saw it, should be to end the divisions within the Afrikaner opposition, and harmonise the activities not only of the H.N.P. and the O.B., but of the F.A.K., the R.D.B., and the Afrikaans churches as well. At the H.N.P. congress in the same month, Malan was elected *Volksleier* (Leader), but the chairmanship of the *Eenheidskomitee* was left in the hands of Du Plessis.

The *Eenheidskomitee* tried in September to patch up the dispute between Malan and Van Rensburg, using ingenious formulae which granted the essence of Malan's case but enabled Van Rensburg to cover up for the O.B., in the matter of the embarrassing publication. But the O.B. had not eaten its pie with sufficient humility for Malan's liking, and he resolved to break Van Rensburg as he had broken Pirow. Zeesen's support for Van Rensburg stimulated Malan's determination. The *Eenheidskomitee* soon found it could no longer hold the ring. In September 1941 Malan sought to increase his control still further by instituting a shadow cabinet of his own choosing, to be called the *Nasionale Komitee*. Later, in January 1942, after further abortive attempts to close the breach, he purged the O.B. members from the Cape H.N.P. ranks, and publicly declared war on the movement for carrying out acts of sabotage.

By the time of the general election of 1943 the H.N.P. had clearly emerged as the dominant political mouthpiece of Afrikanerdom. Malan's ruthlessness and his rejection of para-military activity were much resented. There was even a possibility during 1942 of an alliance against the H.N.P. by the combined forces of the O.B., New Order and the Afrikaner Party, with perhaps even support from the Greyshirts, held together either by an attraction for national socialism or by a penchant for direct action in politics. But when election time came the Greyshirts adopted a neutral stance. New Order put forward, but later withdrew, a plan to allow its members to stand as independents. The O.B., for its part, decided it could neither participate as an organisation in the election, nor refuse to support candidates put forward by the H.N.P., especially after that party had shown in a series of by-elections in 1942 that it was making ground against the ruling United Party.

This trend continued in the 1943 general election. The United Party retained a massive majority, as was to be expected, and was returned to power with 110 seats. Malan's party had a mere 43, which meant that 23 opponents of the war policy had now disappeared from the Opposition benches; but all those defeated were Afrikaner Party supporters or members of Pirow's New Order, which had been swept from the board. The H.N.P., as the only Opposition party facing the Government coalition, had won two extra seats and polled 343,000 votes against the 619,000 polled by the government parties, and cut the U.P.'s share of the Afrikaner vote from 40 to 32 per cent (Heard).

One reason for the electoral success of the H.N.P. had been the manner in which it shifted its attack away from the war policies of the Government, on which it began to realise that it had been wasting its breath, to domestic issues, especially those touching on race relations, which could not fail to increase in importance and urgency.

13.3 LIBERAL REFORM INITIATIVES AND A POLARISED RESPONSE, 1942–3

On assuming power, the Smuts Government had inherited the Hertzogian racial policy, with its five defensive bastions against African pressure: communal representation under the 1936 Representation Act, territorial segregation under the 1936 Native Trust and Land Act, urban segregation with influx control under the 1937 Native Laws Amendment Act, authoritarian rule under the Native Administration Act of 1927, and the Riotous Assemblies Act of 1930 as a security back-stop. In the case of the Indian population of the Transvaal and Natal, the restriction of land and trading rights remained the dominant features of government policy, and there was no thought of extending political liberties to Indians anywhere. Hertzog's economic and political 'new deal' for the Coloured people was a thing of the past, his Coloured allies in disarray and his intentions exposed by the A.P.O.'s refusal to buy Coloured rights at the expense of Africans (Lewis). The Willcocks Commission, appointed by the United Party in 1934 to assess and if possible put right the damage done by Hertzog's policy had reported in 1937. Comprising both segregationists and anti-segregationists in equal numbers, it had no clear prescription for the future of the Coloured community.

When the Smuts Government took office in 1939, instead of promoting segregation it preferred to allow that policy to run down, and perhaps even contemplated its reversal. Labour shortage was the likely reason for this. Industrial growth, which had already been remarkable during the 1930s, proceeded even faster during the war years, as South Africa began to manufacture munitions and military equipment. The systematic enforcement of influx control had begun only in 1938, and even then the municipal labour censuses carried out under the Native Laws Amendment Act of 1937 showed that there were relatively few able-bodied African workers in the towns who could reasonably be driven out to work on the white-owned farms, because of growing industrial labour demands. The labour shortage became still more noticeable during the war years when, to keep the war industries going, the dilution of skilled with unskilled labour was increasingly practised in government factories.

Another reason for the slowing down of segregation was the appearance in Parliament in 1938 of a well-coordinated group of white Native's Representatives, whose influence was strong enough to transform the debate over native policy from a discussion of control techniques into a discussion of immediate and long-term welfare. Margaret Ballinger and Senator Edgar Brookes led this team, the former spearheading their attack in the Assembly, while Brookes concentrated his efforts mainly in the Native Affairs Commission, and put his constituents' case in the Senate with consummate tact. Together they saw to it (in a way which Hertzog had perhaps never calculated) that African demands were continuously and accurately put. In 1941 Senator J. D. Rheinallt Jones set a precedent with a motion commending the resolutions of the Natives' Representative Council to 'the careful consideration of the Government'. It produced a hostile reaction in some quarters, but ensured that the statutory tabling of the resolutions on this occasion was more than a formality. A corresponding change of outlook began to appear in the Department of Native Affairs, through the initiative of its Secretary, Douglas Smit.

The Government's appointment of a Social and Economic Planning Council to devise blueprints for post-war reform, and of an Inter-Departmental Committee under Smit's chairmanship to investigate the social, educational and health conditions of urban Africans in 1942, gave promise of important reforms. The Government introduced improvements in the fields of workmen's compensation, pensions, unemployment insurance, public health and secondary education in particular. While none involved the spending of large sums of money, they established areas of public responsibility where this had not been acknowledged before, extending to other races benefits which the Hertzog Government had introduced for white (and sometimes Coloured) people. In May 1942, following ministerial consternation at the increase in the number of Africans arrested for technically infringing the pass laws, the abolition of which was in any case recommended by the Smit Committee, the Departments of Justice and Native Affairs agreed to restrain the police from demanding the production of passes save by individuals who seemed to be breaking the law. There was a dramatic reduction in the number of pass arrests in the second half of 1942. At about the same time Madeley, the Minister of Labour, let it be known that he was considering the inclusion of African workers in the collective bargaining procedures of the Industrial Conciliation Act, and he personally opened the inaugural conference of the Congress of Non-European Trade Unions.

The liberal reforms adumbrated in 1942, however, unleashed a predictable reaction, and the Nationalist counterattack started in Parliament as the two sides squared up for the general election. In the Assembly, Malan moved a highly eclectic social security motion on 19 January 1943. He dissociated himself from both Nazism and Communism, attacked the Social and Economic Planning Council as 'neither representative nor competent' and professed a faith in segregation while at the same time identifying himself with the current interest in general social welfare. A week later, Eric Louw asked the House to deplore the spread of communism (Soviet Russia being by this time an ally of the West and under strong German attack), and this produced heated exchanges which had obvious electioneering value. Mrs Ballinger counterattacked with a motion urging a new beginning in native policy, through the adoption of the Smit Report; but the new Minister of Native Affairs, Major Piet van der Byl, countered with a defensive amendment asking the House to endorse 'the Native Policy envisaged in the 1936–'37 legislation' as well as the policy of providing 'improved health, housing, education and other social services for the Non-European population'. Brookes, whose approach was more conciliatory, had a similar experience in the Senate. The task of the Natives' Representatives in this changed atmosphere was beginning to require the avoidance of collision with the United Party, for fear of losing the chance of influencing its majority.

Between 1943 and 1946 the African population suffered many new hardships. On the Witwatersrand a committee under S. H. Elliott, Chief Magistrate of Johannesburg, recommended a return to pass law enforcement in 1943, not because it could demonstrate a causal connection between policy relaxation and the increase in crime (which was the field of its inquiry) but because it was able to show that the relaxation of the policy had led to fewer Africans registering for work on arrival in the municipalities, and therefore threatened to undermine the policy of influx control itself. The measure of African disappointment at this reversal of their hopes can best be seen in the determination with which an Anti-Pass Campaign was set in motion in Johannesburg in May 1944. The organisers made repeated approaches to the Government and obtained no concessions, save that the pass laws were eventually placed on the agenda of the 1946 Fagan Commission.

Rising transport costs for Johannesburg Africans led to a series of bus boycotts between 1940 and 1945, which helped to politicise African opinion on bread-and-butter issues, and to promote confrontation with the authorities, which had at first not been unhelpful. The same effect resulted from an acute housing shortage which reached crisis point in 1944 when the first of seven substantial squatter movements was launched. The problem could not be resolved with any speed owing to the shortage of building materials and the continuing ban on the training of blacks as builders. The squatter movements did not derive much support from the Communists, and even less from the A.N.C., though its Youth League [see p. 347] realised that they were rooted in the kind of mass grievance that could be used to inflame opinion. They were led by a handful of individuals, of whom James Sofasonke Mpanza was the most noteworthy (Stadler). They defied the law and moved their followers on to the Orlando commonage, provided hessian for shanties, employed camp guards to prevent looting, sold trading rights and levied an *ad hoc* rate from the squatters. They eventually forced the central Government and the Johannesburg City council to set up emergency camps. But the episode left a bitter legacy, above all in the relationship between urban Africans and the police, which eventually led to riots in August 1947, the climax of a series of confrontations which had in recent years alone produced violence at Vereeniging in September 1937, at Marabastad in December 1942, in Sophiatown in October 1944, and at Springs in July 1945.

13.4   THE MINEWORKERS' STRIKE OF 1946 AND THE FAGAN REPORT

A rapid spread of African trade unionism characterised the middle war years. This owed a good deal to Communist Party influence [see p. 272]. By the 1930s African workers, realising they could expect little support from white artisans, had formed their own African Federation of Trade Unions, which had been incorporated in a Council of Non-European Trade Unions by November 1941. There were frequent African strikes during the second half of 1942, and a good many resulted in redress of grievances, especially where it could be shown that employers had been paying low wages; but, so far from Madeley's hint of collective bargaining rights being extended, successive war measures tightened the controls over black workers. Of these, War Measure 145 of January 1942, which outlawed strikes by Africans under threat of heavy penalties, and required them to accept arbitration of disputes at ministerial discretion, was regularly re-newed until permanently embodied in a statute (the Native Labour Settle-ment of Disputes Act of 1953). Both the parliamentary Labour Party and the Trades and Labour Council opposed the extension of bargaining rights to Africans, and when the Council of Non-European Trade Unions se-cured an interview with Madeley in October 1943, it came away empty-handed. Black workers in more menial positions had little chance of exploiting their scarcity value. Hemson's account of the epic struggle of the Durban dockworkers between 1940 and 1959 has shown how the Govern-ment and the stevedoring companies, by using extra-economic controls and building up a reserve army of labour, could keep wages down and outblud-geon and outwit even a tough and subtle labour leader like Zulu Phungula. The African mineworkers learned an even sharper lesson in 1946.

The mineworkers' basic wage of two shillings a shift was low because families had to be maintained in the Reserves under the mines' scheme of deferred pay, and because the miners had to buy their boots, blankets and any supplementary food at normal prices. They had tried as early as 1943 to obtain four shillings a day, plus better food and free equipment, but failed to persuade the owners. In August 1941 the African Mineworkers' Union was formally constituted under the energetic leadership of S. P. Matseke (chairman of the Transvaal A.N.C.), Gaur Radebe and J. B. Marks (communist members of the A.N.C. executive). The energy they put into their recruiting campaign enabled them to claim over 25,000 members in 1944. In that year the Lansdown Commission recommended that African miners should receive an extra fivepence per shift plus threepence cost-of-living allowance, together with a boot allowance, overtime pay, and, in the case of permanent workers, increased cost-of-living and two weeks' paid leave. The Government and the Chamber accepted the overtime proposal, and rejected cost-of-living and boot allowances, but agreed to a wage increase of fourpence and fivepence for surface and underground workers respectively. This cut the extra expenditure recommended by Lansdown from £2,642,000 to £1,850,000. The Lansdown Commission also advised against the recognition of the African Mineworkers' Union, though it recommended the recognition of African trade unions in principle. Its case was based on the arguments that 'no movement . . . has emanated from the mine native labourers themselves', and that the communists had manipulated the workers. The Commission therefore looked rather to the appointment of suitable welfare officers under the control of the Department of Native Affairs, who should keep close contact with the workers and report their needs to the Department and to the mine managements.

The miners were dissatisfied on both counts, and soon had other grievances. By War Measure 1425 of 1945 the Government then sought to contain union resistance by prohibiting gatherings of more than twenty people on mine property. The Union-wide famine in that year necessitated a cut in mine rations, and violence resulted at the Modderfontein East compound. In April 1946 the Mineworkers' Union put in a claim for a basic wage of ten shillings a day and demanded the repeal of War Measure 1425. The Chamber repeatedly ignored the wage demand on the ground that the union had no *locus standi*. Eventually, on 4 August, over 70,000 African miners went out on strike. The strike was put down by the police, as that of 1920 had been, at the cost of several lives lost and many injured. It was soon followed by the arrest and trial of leading communists, notably W. H. Andrews (the national president), Moses Kotane (the general secretary), and Betty Radford, editor of the *Guardian*, which had supported the strikers and incurred a libel action for publishing extracts from the African Mineworkers' Union's evidence before the Lansdown Commission.

Two days after the start of the miners' strike, the Natives' Representative Council reassembled in Pretoria, each of its members having been asked on 26 July by Xuma, as president-general of the A.N.C. and chairman of the Anti-Pass Committee, to adjourn their session unless the Government agreed to abolish the pass laws, recognise African trade unions under the Industrial Conciliation Act, and repeal the oppressive sections of the Native Administration Act of 1927 which permitted banishment without trial. The action next taken by the Natives' Representative Council, therefore, seems to have been deliberate rather than spontaneous. The Under-Secretary for Native Affairs opened the Council because the Secretary, Dr G. Mears, was absent on account of the miners' strike. He made no reference to the strike in his opening address, and had no information for members when he was pressed by them. The Council reacted angrily. Dr Moroka, who in any case thought there was no substitute for direct representation in Parliament and had no love for the Council as an institution, moved the adjournment of the session with a motion that was antagonistic in tone and obviously intended to be so.

Significantly, his motion was supported unanimously by radicals, moderate intellectuals, and even chiefs.

The Natives' Representatives tried to bring the parties together, without avail. Brookes approached the Native Affairs Commission and Hofmeyr (the acting Prime Minister), urging them to consider a meaningful programme of reform, and not take umbrage as Hofmeyr was inclined to do. The pass laws, the educational system, the status of the N.R.C., the recognition of African unions and the miners' strike, Brookes urged, were all nettles that needed to be grasped in a new initiative. Hofmeyr discounted this advice, telling Smuts, who was at the United Nations Conference in Paris, that he thought the whites would look on such proposals as surrender. He preferred 'a friendly and conciliatory but firm statement of government policy as at present followed', with an offer that went no further than Lansdown on the subject of trade unions. Smuts, however, saw something in Brookes's proposal, and asked for a draft on those lines to be approved by the Cabinet and sent to him, remarking that 'our native policy would have to be liberalized at modest pace but public opinion has to be carried with us . . . Practical social policy away from politics as stated by me still holds, is being carried out, and will be so more and more as finance permits.'

The Native Affairs Commission agreed that Hofmeyr, rather than the less popular Van der Byl, should address the N.R.C. on 20 November to give the Government's reply; but the reply given dwelt more on the Government's past record than its future plans, and above all offered no collective bargaining concessions to the African miners. The N.R.C. accordingly replied on the 26th, repudiating Hofmeyr's censure on its earlier action, indicting the Government with responsibility for lives lost during the miners' strike, and rejecting Hofmeyr's defence of government action because it 'made no attempt to deal with . . . the Pass Laws, the colour bar in industry, the political rights of Non-Europeans' and did not recognise the miners' union. It ended by demanding direct African representation at all levels from the municipal councils to Parliament.

Smuts said on his return to South Africa that he understood that the N.R.C. would be satisfied with nothing less than effective political power, which to him was an unthinkable concession; but he did listen to Mrs Ballinger's suggestion in February 1947 that if he were to recognise the existence of permanent African communities in the towns, make some plan for the better training of increasingly scarce African farm workers, set about the establishment of efficient labour exchanges so that the pass laws could be dispensed with, give the N.R.C. a promise of proper consultation in the future, and extend African representation in some form to the municipal and provincial councils, he might buy ten years in which to persuade the white electorate to adjust to a sharing of power. Much of this was already being considered by the Fagan Commission, appointed before the strike. The Native Affairs Commission was now asked to prepare proposals for constitutional reform; but when Smuts met a group of members of the N.R.C. on 8 May, he was not yet in a position to make them a meaningful offer.

The constitutional plan proposed by the Native Affairs Commission, which resembled Smuts's advice to Hertzog in 1928, was for the democratisation of African government downwards rather than for an extension of African influence upwards. It suggested a council of fifty (as Hertzog had proposed in 1926, only this time all members were to be elective) which was to be the apex of a country-wide representative system, based on General Councils in the Reserves (as established under the Native Affairs Act of 1920), and on an official Location Advisory Boards Congress for the representation of African interests in the urban areas (as distinct from the unofficial congress which had met annually since 1929). But without the Fagan proposals, which were not available until February 1948, the constitutional offer looked singularly meagre, while on the trade union front the Departments of Labour and Native Affairs were still unable to improve on Lansdown. Consequently Smuts's overtures proved unacceptable, and although Smuts urged Parliament in January 1948 not to break off relations with the N.R.C. he gave the Council no real reason for expecting better things at the political level.

The Fagan Report, which was eventually published in February 1948, contained much that was acceptable to moderate black opinion. Its proposals for a Union-wide system of labour bureaux, which might eventually provide a substitute for influx control, can be traced back to the Smit Report. Its proposals for the stabilisation of African labour in the towns, which meant encouraging workers to bring their families with them, was an idea which the N.R.C. had been pressing very hard. Fagan did not think that the system of migrant labour could be legislated out of existence, or stopped by administrative decree, any more than he thought stabilisation of labour could be forced on employers. But he urged that they be encouraged to experiment, for example on the new O.F.S. goldfields. He also recommended that villages should be built in the Reserves for the concentrated settlement of the landless; but this aroused apprehensions on account of the overcrowding of the Reserves and the constant demand of the white farmers to be relieved of their black squatters. On the pass laws, the Fagan Report was strangely equivocal, for it recommended the retention of passes as a control device, but also proposed that, under the new name of identity cards, they could be voluntarily applied for if they were also linked to the provision of secure employment. The Report exhibited positive qualities. It recommended a change of direction, as Smit had done in 1942, and represented the most considered view of which the combined thinking of the Smuts ministry, prodded by the Native's Representatives, were capable under conditions of extreme political stress. Published two years earlier, in time to enable the Government to put some of its ideas into practice, there was an outside chance that it might have changed the direction of South African policy; but appearing so near the end of the Government's term, with none of its recommendations yet tested in practice or in public debate, it offered the electorate a liberal aspiration rather than a policy, and if the choice for voters was between aspirations, the Sauer Report of the Nationalists, with its early spelling out of the gospel of apartheid, seemed to offer more security on more familiar lines [see p. 323].

13.5   XUMA'S A.N.C. AND THE RISE OF THE YOUTH LEAGUE

The N.R.C. was demanding 'a policy which recognises that Africans are citizens of this country and not things apart'. How to give content to such an aspiration was the difficulty which the Smuts Government could not surmount. It required that they should take a chance on the good faith of the black man, and assume that the moderate leadership of black political opinion both meant what it said and was able to hold in check such radical elements as there were in their rank and file. They saw this as at best an open question, for the mood of the black political organisations was far more purposeful after 1945 than it had been before 1940.

When Dr A. B. Xuma became president-general of the A.N.C. in December 1940, he worked hard to transform it into an efficient, central-ised national body. He refused to allow provincial branches to step out of line in the formulation of electoral policy, as the Cape Congress discovered in 1942, and stepped in to take over the running of the Transvaal Congress when rifts developed among its members on ideological grounds. Under his supervision, Congress adopted a new constitution in December 1943, which allowed it to include people of other races, eliminated the House of Chiefs (which had proved largely ineffective, especially since the Native Affairs Department had discouraged chiefs from participation in Congress activities), provided for the election of the secretary and treasurer by a free vote at the annual conference, instead of from a list submitted by the provincial presidents, and set up a working committee consisting of mem-bers living within fifty miles of the national headquarters, with power to take day-to-day decisions. The 1942 conference initiated a million-member campaign. This failed to achieve its object because the A.N.C. could not sustain its drive,owing to the fickle and uneven enthusiasms of its local organisers; but it was good for Congress morale. Another of Xuma's contributions was to introduce regularity into Congress's accounting pro-cedures. It never became a wealthy organisation, and the balance of £800 which it achieved on one occasion was hardly enough to sustain any kind of political campaign; but the fact that it could collect subscriptions and have them transferred to the centre made it potentially a force to be reckoned with.

On the propaganda front, Xuma's A.N.C. encouraged the hope of better times in the post-war years. The 1942 conference empowered Xuma to set up a committee to study the Atlantic Charter and draft a Bill of Rights to present to the peace conference at the end of the war. Xuma interested some thirty leading African intellectuals in the task, and aroused public interest by inviting individuals to submit essays for the committee to consider. Professor Z. K. Matthews of Fort Hare was chairman of the committee, which included conservatives like Selope Thema and Richard

Godlo, and left-wingers like Kotane, Marks and Mofutsanyana. The Bill of
Rights which they eventually issued demanded the 'freedom of the African
people from all discriminatory laws whatsoever', as well as something very
like adult suffrage – a more ambitious claim than the 'equitable' representation asked for in 1919, or the 'equal rights for all civilized men' asked for
in an earlier bill of rights in 1923. The pamphlet *African Claims*, which
embodied this Bill of Rights, was adopted by conference in December
1943, but turned down by the Government as unrealistic. It was, however,
a demand couched in the moderate language of western liberal thinking.

As was the case with the Afrikaner Nationalists, who divided over the
rival merits of parliamentary methods and direct action, so the African
Nationalists, for whom the option of parliamentary methods was scarcely
available, tended to divide into those who relied on the Natives' Representatives and the N.R.C., supported by well-signed petitions and deputations, and those who wanted to force the hand of the Government by
strikes, boycotts and passive resistance. In the first group fell nearly every
member of the N.R.C., with a few possible exceptions like Dr J. S.
Moroka, together with the 'old guard' of the A.N.C., Xuma himself
included. Not too far removed ideologically from this group was a new
African Democratic Party founded by Paul Mosaka and Self Mampuru in
1943, with the encouragement of Senator H. M. Basner, a provocative
ex-Communist Natives' Representative for the Transvaal and Orange Free
State. It developed loose Trotskyite leanings, largely as a result of a brush
with the Communists, but never developed a policy of boycott, never
pressed for Non-European unity, and maintained a friendly contact with
whites through liberal bodies like the Institute of Race Relations and the
Friends of Africa. But it soon wilted before the attacks of Xuma, who, with
the instincts of a Malan, berated it for trying to divide African loyalties and
took care that the Transvaal A.N.C. did not fall into its hands.

In the second, more radical group were the Communists, who had
opposed South Africa's entry into the war in 1939, while taking care to
remain aloof from the Nationalists, but changed their tune when Soviet
Russia, 'the motherland of socialism', was attacked by the Germans in
June 1941. At first they failed to make much headway with the A.N.C.,
who rejected their anti-war stand just as the Communists rejected the
exclusive Africanism of some A.N.C. elements. By degrees, however, they
were drawn closer to the A.N.C. Three leading communists, Moses
Kotane, J. B. Marks and Dan Tloome, were members of the A.N.C.
national executive in 1945. The Communists gradually came to accept that
the way to a socialist revolution lay through the promotion of African
nationalism, and in this they were influenced by the thinking and the
dynamics of the A.N.C's new Youth League. They encouraged participation in Advisory Board elections, which some elements preferred to
boycott, while on the white political front they achieved minor successes
when Sam Kahn and Betty Radford were elected to the Cape Town city
council in 1943.

The A.N.C. Youth League was founded in 1943–4. Its founders were for the most part talented professional men in their early manhood, many of them teachers, with a high proportion of mission school graduates, though they included no clergy. The group was first led by the intellectually sensitive Anton Lembede, a graduate in philosophy and law who was to die at 33 in 1947. Other leaders who won celebrity in later years were Jordan Ngubane (who was to join the Liberal Party), W. F. Nkomo (a medical doctor attracted to Moral Rearmament, whose long career ended when he died in office as president of the S.A. Institute of Race Relations in 1972), Walter Sisulu and Nelson Mandela (who were sentenced to life imprisonment in 1963 for their part in the 'Rivonia' conspiracy), A. P. Mda and Robert Sobukwe (men of strong Africanist inclinations, one the brains of the movement on Lembede's death, the other the founder of the Pan-Africanist Congress in 1959), the lawyers Duma Nokwe and Joseph Matthews (son of Z. K. Matthews), and J. C. M. Mbata, a teacher. Their posture was originally anti-communist, the committee which drafted their manifesto recording 'the need for vigilance against Communists and other groups which foster non-African interests'. The group originally came together to lobby for Self Mampuru as Transvaal A.N.C. presidential candidate in 1943, before Mampuru joined the A.D.P. It owed something, too, to Xuma's encouragement in December 1943, though Champion's warning that a youth league would destroy Xuma's presidency seemed prophetic when the group attacked Xuma's new constitution at the 1943 conference as 'collaborationist', on the ground that it did not encourage the adoption of an exclusivist posture by Africans at that stage in their struggle (Karis and Carter). Lodge finds evidence that Xuma's reservations about the Youth League stemmed from a sense that their skilful exploitation of African gut reactions for nationalist ends was insufficient unless backed by greater organisational forethought than they seemed capable of. In March 1944 the Youth League published its Manifesto, a document designed to promote African unity and high standards of moral conduct, Christian by implication. They saw themselves very much as an elitist pressure group within the A.N.C., analogous to the Afrikaner Broederbond. They were strongly influenced by the boycott tactics adopted by the Non-European Unity Movement, though they stayed outside it, and above all by the passive resistance campaign launched by the Indians in 1946, which especially impressed Mandela. The hardest decision for the Leaguers to make related to the degree of cooperation they should offer to other movements which shared some of their objectives. Garveyite exclusivism had its attractions, and several of the basic documents of the Youth League focused on African nationalism to the exclusion of the wider community. But a document on 'Basic Policy' put out by the League's national executive in 1948 stressed the importance of collaboration with the 'national organisations' of the Indians and Coloured people, as oppressed communities, on issues of common concern. The idea of driving the whites into the sea was explicitly disavowed, though the League expected whites to accept majority rule. But the document most frequently quoted as evidence of the League's political stance was the 'Programme of

Action' adopted by the A.N.C's annual conference in December 1949, after the rise to power of Dr Malan's Nationalist Government [see below, p. 332].

13.6 'C.A.D.', 'ANTI-C.A.D.' AND THE NON-EUROPEAN UNITY MOVEMENT

The Cape Coloured people, deeply injured by Hertzog's legislative record, and stirred up by the segregationist outburst of 1939 [see pp. 256–8, 306], were further shocked in January 1943 when H. G. Lawrence, the Minister of the Interior, announced his intention to create a separate section within his department to deal exclusively with Coloured affairs. This proposal, for which some support had been given in the Cape Coloured Commission report of 1937, aroused popular fears that the end result would be a Coloured Affairs Department analogous to the Department of Native Affairs. The Government affirmed that it did not intend to set up a separate department, or to attack Coloured political rights, or to press ahead with compulsory residential segregation; but the community's suspicions were aroused after the appointment of a Coloured Advisory Council in March under the leadership of S. Dollie, G. Golding, and other prominent community leaders, several of whom were office-bearers in the Teachers' League of South Africa. The event brought Coloured teachers into the forefront of the political battle, though they were not sufficiently united as a profession to make much impact on the 1943 elections. A movement known as the Anti-C.A.D. came into being in May, its most dynamic leader being B. M. Kies of the T.L.S.A.. At the T.L.S.A. conference at Kimberley in June, those present denounced the C.A.C. in robust terms; but supporters of the C.A.C. captured the executive on the strength of previously garnered proxy votes. The T.L.S.A. split, the bulk of its urban membership supporting the Anti-C.A.D. Another body, the Teachers' Educational and Professional Association, was set up to cater for the wishes of the more cautious, because the radicals had politicised the T.L.S.A. (Lewis).

Support for the C.A.C. also proved fatal to the A.P.O., now led by Dr F. H. Gow after the deaths of Abdurahman in 1940 and of his successor S. Reagon in 1942. Gow tried unsuccessfully to keep the C.A.C. issue under wraps, for the Anti-C.A.D. element captured the A.P.O.'s executive in April 1944. But they then turned to the All-African Convention, in which Goolam Gool and Tabata had influence, as a vehicle for promoting unity among non-Europeans.

To this end the A.A.C.'s triennial conference in December 1940 had tried to set up a committee to coordinate its activities with those of the A.N.C., but a year later its leaders objected to a scheme to make the A.A.C. a mere coordinating body for all manner of African organisations, while the A.N.C. concentrated on politics. Consequently the A.N.C. and the A.A.C. stayed apart even though men like Z. R. Mahabane were office-bearers in both.

The A.A.C. and the Anti-C.A.D. delegates, however, held a 'unity conference' in Bloemfontein in December 1943, to which Coloured and Indian organisations had been invited. They drew up a Ten-Point Programme for the Non-European Unity Movement which they launched. This was not so much a programme of action as a list of demands, including demands for political rights and a fairer division of the land. They took into account the broad interests of all black communities. But the conservative section of the Coloured community, for the most part those who had supported the C.A.C., rejected the new Movement and, under the leadership of George Golding, formed a Coloured People's National Union of which Golding was leader until his death in 1967. The C.P.N.U. eschewed ideological issues in favour of bread-and-butter politics, and in its support for the United Party it largely filled the vacuum left by the dying A.P.O. Indian support for the N.E.U.M. was equally hesitant. The Natal Indian leaders were currently engaged in their own battle with the Union Government over the Pegging Act of 1943, [see p. 318] and still attempting under A. I. Kajee's leadership to win concessions by a policy of non-provocation. The Indians therefore agreed to cooperate on specific issues such as the pass laws, the Pegging Act or the C.A.C., but rejected a formal alliance based on the Ten-Point Programme. They stayed away from the second unity conference in July 1944, though they attended the third in January 1945. By this time they were beginning to find that their closest ties were with the A.N.C.. This was partly because the N.E.U.M., consisting largely of Coloured intellectuals who wanted to direct and broaden the ambitions of the potentially much more powerful African nationalists, preferred to take part in peaceful protests well within the law, rather than to defy the law by means of organised passive resistance. It was primarily in their mutual preparedness to defy the law that the Indian congresses and the A.N.C. found that they could make common cause; but this became true only after the radicals under Y. Dadoo and G. M. Naicker had captured the Indian congress in late 1945, and set in motion the Indians' passive resistance campaign.

13.7   DURBAN'S INDIANS AND THE 'PEGGING' AND 'GHETTO' ACTS

At the beginning of the war, when it was rumoured that the Transvaal land and trading legislation affecting Indians was to be extended to Natal, the Natal Indian leaders put pressure on the Government to settle questions of property transfer informally, and to this end a Committee under H. G. Lawrence was appointed in March 1940. But pressure from Durban whites induced the Government to appoint an Indian Penetration Commission under Judge Broome in May. In his first report, Broome found no significant penetrations by Indians in any area of Natal or the Transvaal which could be said to have precipitated a white exodus. His second report, published in 1943, demonstrated that there had been a significant Indian takeover of a smalll section of the Durban Berea, though for investment rather than residential purposes. What it did not make clear was that this was an area of 'white' Durban which the building societies had decided to regard as suitable for Indian settlement, and where they were therefore prepared to advance loans, and that the Indian population of Durban, which was not far short of the white in total numbers, owned a mere 4 per cent of the land in the Old Borough.

Against this background, the Government's decision to introduce 'pegging' legislation in April 1943 (shortly before the general election) caused a sharp reaction. All white–Indian property transactions in Durban were to be frozen for three years, and the Transvaal land legislation extended for a similar period. Objections were widespread, and Hofmeyr, the Deputy Prime Minister, contemplated resignation. The Natal Indian Congress protested vigorously. The Government of India protested, got nowhere, and began to consider economic sanctions against the Union. The South African Government immediately tried to damp down the crisis by putting Judge Broome at the head of another commission to investigate the 'uplift' provisions of the Cape Town Agreement, and as a result of a compromise gesture by the N.I.C., sponsored by A. I. Kajee and P. R. Pather, the Pegging Act was suspended in terms of the Pretoria Agreement of 18 April 1944, whereby a board consisting of two whites, two Indians and a lawyer as chairman was to control inter-racial property transactions. This, however, proved no more than a brief respite. The Natal Provincial Council was allowed under the agreement to legislate to prohibit whites and Indians living next to each other. It accordingly drafted an ordinance, which was withdrawn after N.I.C. objections. It drew up a second, to which whites took exception. Its third attempt, a Residential Property Regulation Draft Ordinance, was regarded by the N.I.C. as a violation of the Pretoria Agreement in that it provided for the control of purchase by Indians, whereas the Pretoria Agreement was concerned only with occupation, and because it extended beyond Durban. The Natal Provincial Council was also seeking to restrict Indians in other ways, by means of Housing Board and Expropriation ordinances which were enacted with the Residential Property Ordinance in November 1944. So sharp was the public outcry that the Broome Commission found it could no longer hold public hearings. The Indian Government immediately began to apply retaliatory legislation against white South Africans. A deputation of the N.I.C. saw Smuts at the end of the month, drawing from him the comment that the Pretoria Agreement was now 'stone dead'. Shortly afterwards the N.I.C. split into a militant section under Dr G. M. Naicker and a moderate under Kajee and Pather, who later broke away to form the Natal Indian Organisation. Smuts's response to the collapse of the Pretoria Agreement was to introduce new legislation in March 1946, the Asiatic Land Tenure and Indian Representation Bill, which would restrict Indian ownership and occupation to particular 'uncontrolled' areas of Natal, but attempt to buy their support back by an ironic reversal of Hertzog's tactic with the Africans – the offer of token political representation in place of land rights: three white representatives in the Assembly and two in the Senate, plus two provincial councillors who could be Indians.

14 **Afrikaner nationalist propaganda in the 1948 general election. In the upper cartoon, Honiball of the *Burger* has Smuts, 'who once blessed Russian weapons and doffed his hat to Stalin', now making an urgent appeal for the stopping of Communist imperialism'. (Contrast the representation of Smuts as a tool of the capitalists in the lower cartoon in Plate 10.) In the lower picture the same artist portrays Smuts reminding readers that they need have no fear of Hofmeyr's liberalism**

The N.I.C. scorned the offer and went for world-wide publicity for its cause, through the Government of India and the United Nations. When the Union Government refused to alter its course and allowed this 'Ghetto Act' to become law, the N.I.C. began a passive resistance campaign. Some two thousand went to prison for squatting in batches on a vacant 'controlled' site in Durban. It was during this passive resistance campaign that the N.I.C. leaders began to make common cause with African and Coloured movements. In March 1947 a 'Joint Declaration of Co-operation' was drawn up by Naicker of the N.I.C., Dadoo of the T.I.C., and Xuma of the A.N.C., to work together for full franchise rights, equal industrial rights, the removal of land restrictions, the extension of free compulsory education to all non-Europeans, freedom of movement (involving the abolition of passes for Africans and of restrictions on inter-provincial travel for Indians), and the removal of all-discriminatory legislation.

13.8   THE NATIONALIST VICTORY IN 1948

It was unfortunate for the United Party, but fortunate for the Nationalists, that the development of robust opposition by African, Coloured and Indian elements should have occurred at the same time as the beginning of the Government's serious difficulties on the international front. It was perhaps not surprising, under these circumstances, that the H.N.P. and their allies won the general election of 26 May 1948 by 79 seats to the 71 gained by the U.P. and its associates. It was an important event in the history of South Africa, the consequences of which it is still too early to assess in full. The Smuts Government appeared to be in an unassailable position, even though it had been losing ground in recent by-elections. It entered into an electoral agreement with the Labour Party, thus protecting marginal urban seats. It could draw immense credit from having successfully brought South Africa out of the war on the winning side. But it seems to have overrated this achievement as a vote-catching factor, and to have over-capitalised on its successes, above all in two ways. One was by using a royal visit to project the image of South Africa as a leading Commonwealth country, in order to douse the republican propaganda of the Opposition. When King George VI and Queen Elizabeth toured the Union with their two daughters in early 1947, they endeared themselves to the South African public without apparently making many political converts among the Nationalists. The other counter-productive strategy was Smuts's postwar immigration scheme, announced in 1946 as an attempt to recruit European skills to beat the manpower shortage. Some 60,000 immigrants entered under the scheme in 1947–8, the largest number ever to enter South Africa under an organised scheme before the 1960s (Bradlow). It came under strong attack from various quarters, but especially in Afrikaner opposition circles on the ground that it was an attempt to 'plough the Afrikaner under', which is unlikely to have been the main objective of the Government.

Some allowance must be made for political pin-pricks in any explanation of the Government's fall, such as the restlessness of ex-soldiers who did not adjust easily to civilian occupations in spite of the overall efficiency of the Government's demobilisation scheme. On the domestic front, some resented the slow progress of the Government's housing programme, others the lack of tax relief for wage-earners in Hofmeyr's budgets, others the irritations of wartime controls over food distribution. More seriously the Government's major policy decisions aroused opposition. Where these were illiberal, as was the case with its Indian policy, they came under pressure at the United Nations. In so far as they were either liberal or unsuccessful, the Nationalists knew how to capitalise on this, and set out to convince the electorate that the U.P. either consorted with or was not tough enough with the Communists, and the Communists were a danger to South Africa. They fastened their attention on the Springbok Legion (the more socialist-inclined of the two main ex-servicemen's organisations), and on Jan Hofmeyr, the Deputy Prime Minister and Smuts's heir apparent, as a man of dangerous liberal tendencies.

The Nationalists had in fact prepared the ground far better than their opponents. In place of the U.P.'s cumbersome campaign organisation of provincial head committees and regional councils, they had a small steering committee consisting of the provincial party leaders only; they had professional organisers in place of the U.P.'s reliance on voluntary help; and they had an active cell system, copied from the O.B. in 1941, as against the relatively inactive branch system of the U.P.. The lethargy of the U.P. organisers was noted by its candid friends before the election, but the lesson was not sufficiently appreciated. With the help of a dedicated press and some brilliant cartoonists, the Nationalists also won the propaganda battle even though their opponents had a call on the loyalties of newpapers with far greater circulations. They won it too, because they stripped their policy of its prickly attributes, explicitly refrained from asking for a mandate for a Republic, stressed their change of front in the matter of rights of English-speakers, and undertook to honour all obligations entered into by the Smuts regime towards ex-servicemen.

The Nationalists had also worked hard to build up their position within Afrikanerdom, notably by reversing their stand of 1943 and entering into an electoral pact with Havenga, despite indignant remonstrances by Strijdom and Verwoerd over the prospect of an arrangement with the Afrikaner Party and the hitherto critical *Vaderland*. Havenga had unsuccessfully tried to do a deal with Smuts by offering support in return for the succession to the premiership and eight Assembly seats, but despite E. G. Malherbe's exhortation to clinch a deal, Smuts evidently doubted Havenga's ability to win marginal seats against H.N.P. opposition. Havenga's other tactic was to negotiate with the O.B. and try to piece together a united front composed of Hertzogite elements in all parties. The upshot of this was an agreement by the A.P. and the O.B. to work together in the election. He even allowed an O.B. general, B. J. Vorster, to stand as an A.P. candidate for Brakpan; but this violated an understanding he had made to the H.N.P. not to put prominent O.B. candidates in the field, in return for the right to contest eleven seats without H.N.P. competition.

Vorster therefore stood as an independent, to the embarrassment of the
H.N.P., which hesitated but connived, according to his own account, and
was narrowly defeated (D'Oliviera).

Relations between the H.N.P. and the O.B. had not materially improved since their confrontation prior to 1943. The Transvaal congress of
the H.N.P. in September 1947 rejected by an enormous majority a proposal that O.B. members should be readmitted to party membership, while
the Cape congress made it clear that no O.B. member could be readmitted
without first resigning from the O.B. (Basson). But as Moodie has explained, what counted in 1948 was not the failure of the Party and the O.B.
to reach an agreement at the leadership level, but the success of individual
H.N.P. candidates in wooing the support of O.B. voters at the constituency level. In this the association of Havenga with the O.B. was undoubtedly an important consideration.

Questions of electoral arithmetic raised by political scientists also have a
bearing on the results of 1948. It was well known that the birthrate among
English-speakers was appreciably lower than among Afrikaans-speakers,
so that the successes which the Nationalists had come to expect as a result
of several by-election victories could be put down to demographic as well
as political factors. But the Nationalists actually did far better than their
popular support warranted, for they won a majority of the seats after
polling 39.4 per cent of the votes (including an estimate for uncontested
seats), against the 53.3 per cent picked up by their unsuccessful opponents
(Heard). Their success therefore derived largely from the work of the
delimitation commission, which had produced this result partly by the
loading and unloading of constituencies, but more especially by the drawing of constituency boundaries in such a way that the Nationalists were able
to waste fewer votes than their opponents. (Stultz, Heard).

Prior to the researches of Legassick and O'Meara, little work had been
done to interpret the general election of 1948 in terms of the changing
political economy of the Union. Heard's figures show that the main
electoral swing in 1948 involved a twofold movement towards the H.N.P.,
first by Transvaal farmers who deserted the U.P., which gave the H.N.P.
fifteen extra seats, and second, by white working-class voters in the
Witwatersrand constituencies, which gave the H.N.P. six extra seats.
O'Meara explains the former trend as a protest among the farmers generally at the failure of the Smuts Government to look after their black labour
supply, through relaxing the controls on black urbanisation during the war
years. He also argues that the Smuts Government had begun to undermine
the financial interests of the farmers by interfering with producer control
over prices through the boards set up under the Marketing Act of 1937.
The drift of white workers towards the H.N.P. occurred at a time of
considerable industrial unrest among both white and black workers, when
there was a large-scale movement of Africans into jobs in industry at
semi-skilled rates of pay, to the point at which white workers had begun to
feel threatened in their jobs. They turned to the Nationalists because the
influence of the Labour Party and of their traditional unions had begun to
come under heavy attack from the Christian National agencies of the

Afrikaner revival. When Legassick described apartheid as a cheap forced labour system extended beyond the mines and farms to black workers in industry, he was really articulating the policy of job reservation which white workers were coming to regard as a solution to their problems.

Apartheid became the central slogan of the Nationalist propaganda. It was really an elaboration of earlier segregationist traditions derived partly from Stallardism, partly from the thinking of the Broederbond in the 1930s (Serfontein). According to M. D. C. de Wet Nel, who later became a leading exponent of the doctrine as Minister of Bantu Administration under Dr Verwoerd, the apartheid concept originated in the mid-1930s, among Afrikaner intellectuals who wanted some 'vertical' separation of the races. To that end they founded a *Suid-Afrikaanse Bond vir Rassestudie* (South African League for Racial Studies) in 1935, with Mrs E. G. Jansen in the chair and De Wet Nel himself as secretary. The Malanites had not agreed with several aspects of Hertzog's policy in 1936–7, standing out in particular against the continued presence of Coloured people on the Cape electoral roll, and resisting the purchase of more land for Africans by the State (as distinct from purchase by blacks themselves). They had also objected to the watering down of the clause in the Native Laws Amendment Bill of 1937 which aimed to prohibit the establishment of churches and schools for Africans in white urban areas. During the war years, as racial integration speeded up, the Nationalist intellectuals worked hard on the problem. Thom notes the appointment of a commission by the H.N.P. in 1943 to work out the main lines of party policy. This commission reported in 1946. P. O. Sauer was the chairman, and P. W. Botha its very active secretary. In the same year the *Burger* became in N. J. Rhoodie's words, 'the mass-ventilator of apartheid theory'. Meanwhile active thinkers like Professor Gert Cronje of the University of Pretoria, who had published *'n Tuiste vir die Nageslag* ('A Home for Posterity') in 1945 and *Regverdige Rasse-apartheid* ('Justifiable Racial Separation') in 1947, helped to create the intellectual climate for the founding of a Nationalist-orientated research body, the *S.A. Buro vir Rasse Aangeleenthede* ('S.A. Bureau for Racial Affairs', or SABRA) in 1948.

Further, with a view to the general election, the Nationalist Party appointed a second committee, also under P. O. Sauer, and of which De Wet Nel was a key member, to draft an apartheid policy with an electoral appeal. The Sauer Report gave the word apartheid full prominence, contrasting it with the rival notions of integration and domination. It was forthright in its rejection of South African Indians as an *uitheemse* (alien) element who were unassimilable, and in its proposal to separate the Coloured people from the whites with regard to transport, education, amenities, residence, and politics, perhaps even through the provision of a separate territory for them. For Africans, it reaffirmed the earlier intention to consolidate the reserves, and urged that these should be taken in hand by a Native Industrial Development Corporation. It also endorsed the Broederbond's notion of a separate political system for the reserves, based on traditional forms of government, together with the abolition of such 'un-African' devices as the Native Representative Council and the representation of Cape Africans in the House of Assembly and the Provincial Council even by whites. The report also recommended the removal of control by anti-Government missionary bodies over black education, and an embargo on the movement of blacks into the urban areas save as contract labourers. This last point, as O'Meara notes, reflected the material interests of white farmers and urban workers. The strength of the Nationalist manifesto thus lay in its simplicity, and in its appeal to the voters' desire for security in a world which seemed to be moving too fast in a liberal direction and turning its wrath against South Africa as it did so. The weakness of that manifesto, considered as a contribution to South African development, lay in the way in which it made the country's problems seem easier to resolve than they really were, and in the way it rode roughshod over the dignity and ultimately the physical welfare of those who were at the receiving end of the policy.

Section II
The Designing of a 'New Model' State

14 The Age of the Social Engineers, 1948–60

14.1 THE FIRST PURELY AFRIKANER GOVERNMENT

Dr Malan's coalition Government was the first fully bilingual government in the history of the Union, and the first to consist of Afrikaners only. Its members had resolutely opposed taking part in the war against Nazi Germany. It was not easy under these circumstances for ex-soldiers and English-speakers to see that some members of the ruling party had been less attracted to Nazism than others; nor was it easy for the Nationalists, who had been bred on resentment at the treatment of their own people by Imperial Britain, to understand the revulsion with which their wartime attitude was regarded by Europeans (Continental as well as British) who had suffered as a result of the war.

From the start, parliamentary relations between the Government and the Opposition got off on the wrong foot. The Government broke with tradition by failing to consult with the Opposition over the choice of a Speaker. In the first two sessions of the new Parliament, despite the care taken by Malan to reassure English-speakers that they were not destined to second-class citizenship, the Government took steps to weaken their dependence on the Commonwealth association. The United Party's plan to recruit British and Continental immigrants was immediately suspended, and although the Government sponsored white immigration again after a short interval, it tried to give Continentals, including German children displaced by the tragedy of war, relatively greater encouragement (Bradlow). The South African Citizenship Bill of 1949 resulted in an acrimonious series of debates because, though Canada and Great Britain had both revised their own citizenship legislation, the South African measure made it considerably harder for immigrants to acquire citizenship, and as expensive for them to do so as it had been in Kruger's Republic between 1890 and 1899. It also narrowed almost to vanishing point the advantage previously enjoyed by British subjects (including all white citizens of the Commonwealth) over aliens. This seemed ominous to English-speakers, in view of the development of separatist republicanism in J. G. Strijdom's wing of the National Party. The Strijdom challenge was in fact a serious matter. He rejected the stand taken by Malan, made possible by a decision taken at the Prime Ministers' Conference of 1949, that South Africa should become a Republic and stay within the Commonwealth. Their disagreement lasted until the middle of 1951, when Malan and Strijdom were persuaded to agree that the issues of Republican status and Commonwealth membership were separable, and that the latter should be considered in the light of circumstances when the Republic was introduced.

The new Government also showed from the start that it intended to check and eliminate the trends towards inter-racial integration. One can distinguish here between legislation to establish distinct biological categories among the population groups, and legislation to prevent their residential mixing when the biological sorting had been done. The Prohibition of Mixed Marriages Act of 1949, which made all future marriages between whites and members of other groups illegal, rested on a Hertzogian precedent banning marriages between whites and Africans. It was followed by a Population Registration Act in 1950, designed to allocate everybody to a racial group, and by a stiffening of the Immorality Act to make extramarital intercourse a more serious offence if indulged in across racial frontiers. Later on, when members of all races were required to carry identification documents which clearly stated the race they belonged to, the sorting procedures became more foolproof than they were at first, when they often depended on the impressionistic decisions of officials. But 'trying for white', and the harrowing social consequences which it entailed for the Coloured community through the severing of contact between close kinsfolk, was not eliminated by these new rules (Watson).

The Group Areas Bill, introduced by Dr Dönges in 1950, to empower the Government to proclaim residential and business areas for particular race groups, incorporated much of the machinery devised for the restriction of Asians under the Smuts Government's Asiatic Land Tenure Act of 1946. A Land Tenure Advisory Board was created (later renamed the Group Areas Board, and later still the Community Development Board), consisting of white officials responsible to the Minister of the Interior, who could recommend the setting aside of particular areas for the sole ownership or occupation (or both) of particular race groups. Provision was made for representations to be made by local authorities and other interested parties; but the object of the legislation was nothing less than a complete unscrambling of the residential patterns in South African towns. Africans were barely affected, for they were already controlled under the Urban Areas Act. But the Indian and Coloured communities were brought under strong pressure in ways which quickly became apparent. Dönges asserted that he had received many petitions from whites objecting to penetration by Indian and Coloured people into white residential areas, resulting in the depreciation of property values, though he was not prepared to divulge confidential details. In view of the class of Indian who normally sought to purchase in white residential areas, and the great difficulty prosperous Indians had in finding houses, such an assertion needs to be treated with some scepticism. When committees of the Land Tenure Advisory Board later visited towns in the Transvaal and Natal, they were generally presented with proposals by the local authorities for the removal of Indian homes and businesses a mile or more out of town, and occasionally for the elimination of Indian homes and shops altogether. Indian and Coloured opposition to the measure, at both the local and national levels, was intense. The United Party, which opposed the Mixed Marriages Bill at all stages, attacked the Group Areas Bill as well, for its members viewed it either as unnecessary, or as improper, or as likely to lead to unfair speculation in real estate on a grand scale [see pp. 538–41].

14.2   THE COLOURED VOTE ISSUE AND THE TORCH COMMANDO

The new Government also began to dismantle the political structures set up by the United Party regime to cater for the African, Asian and Coloured peoples. The token enfranchisement of Indians allowed for in Smuts's unpopular package deal of 1946 was reversed with no waste of time in 1948, after Indians had themselves rejected it as inadequate. In 1951, the Government abolished the Native Representative Council, which had persisted in its refusal to do business with the Nationalists, as it had previously with the United Party.

The Government wanted to remove the Coloured voters in the Cape from the common roll, but they met resistance from Havenga, who, out of loyalty to Hertzog, did not favour such action save on the basis of a statutory two-thirds majority in a joint sitting of Parliament. He apparently felt that if the constitutional objections to the creation of a separate roll for Coloured people were met, the question of a breach of trust did not arise. The constitutional point did not in itself trouble Malan. He accepted the view of the Government's law advisers that the decision of the Appeal Court in *Ndlwana's Case* (1937) [see p. 286] was definitive, and that after the passage of the Statute of Westminster the Union Parliament was sovereign over its own affairs, and therefore able to ignore the special procedures laid down for the amendment of the entrenched voting rights of the Coloured people. But rather than override Havenga, on whose party's votes the Nationalists were still dependent for survival, Malan let the Coloured vote issue lie dormant in 1949 (Schoeman). On 14 October 1950 he and Havenga agreed to go ahead with legislation the following year, to place the Coloured voters on a separate roll with power to elect four members to the Assembly, one to the Senate, and two to the Cape Provincial Council – whites only in the first two categories, but not explicitly so in the last, for on Malan's insistence it was decided in caucus to leave this detail unresolved. A Separate Representation of Voters Bill was duly published and introduced by Dönges in the Assembly on 8 March 1951. On 10 April the Speaker rejected the Opposition's submission that a joint sitting was necessary under the constitution, and the Bill went through all stages as a bicameral measure, to receive the Governor-General's assent on 15 June. A group of Coloured voters, however, contested the legislation. They lost their case before the Cape Provincial Division, but were vindicated by the unanimous decision of the Appellate Division in *Harris* v. *Dönges* on 20 March 1952. The court fully accepted the validity of Stratford's earlier judgment in Ndlwana's case where the sovereignty of Parliament was concerned, confirming that as a sovereign body Parliament could legislate in any manner it chose; but it also insisted that, in terms of the constitution, Parliament, for purposes of amending the entrenched clauses, could only be defined as a legislative body which functioned unicamerally: if it functioned in any other way, it could not be regarded as Parliament. Strauss moved in the Assembly on 16 April that the judgment of the Appellate Division be accepted; but the Government was unable to accept such a rebuff, and on the 22nd Dönges moved a Bill for the reconstitution of Parliament itself as a High Court with power to review all cases in which the Appellate Division declared legislation invalid. Despite Opposition protests, this legislation was then taken through all stages; but the same four Coloured voters appealed against this law too. The 'High Court of Parliament' duly sat in Pretoria and solemnly set aside the Appeal Court's judgment on 25 August, but the High Court itself was declared invalid by the Cape Provincial Division on the 29th, and subsequently by the Appellate Division on 13 November. The judges had no hesitation in rejecting such a court, as badly conceived in history as it was in law, and the Government discreetly dropped this constitutional fantasy.

Malan could then have forced the issue by interfering with the judges or by packing Parliament, or he could have worked to obtain a two-thirds majority and thus lift the vote legislation above legal controversy. What he could not do, having once accepted the jurisdiction of the courts, was to ignore that jurisdiction and proceed with the disfranchisement of the Coloured voters. He decided to use the Coloured vote as a platform for the 1953 general election. He did not get his two-thirds majority that way, but his government survived a tough confrontation.

The Nationalists had already increased their bare majority in Parliament by creating six new seats for South West Africa in the lower House and four in the Senate – ingeniously, without incorporating the territory in defiance of the Mandate – and then winning them. But they were now confronted by the War Veterans' Torch Commando, an ex-servicemen's extra-parliamentary movement which was established in April 1951 by Louis Kane-Berman, 'Sailor' Malan (an ex-Battle of Britain ace pilot) and others, explicitly to oppose the Government's Coloured vote policy. It achieved a paid-up membership which ran into six figures, and showed that it could bring very large crowds together to protest against the Government's policy. By joining a Democratic Front with the United and Labour Parties in April 1952, it was within reach of being able to endow the political Opposition with a winning combination of organising skill, political dedication, and an incisive political programme which catered for the main traditional fears of the white electorate without shedding the idealist mood of the post-war world or losing sight of the demand that in a politico-moral crisis right had to be done. But its political campaign became blunted. Rioting, followed by injury to well over a hundred people, occurred in the wake of a procession to Parliament to deliver a protest petition to Dr Malan on 28 May 1951. The angry exchanges between the Government and the Opposition which followed failed to establish how far this was the work of the Torch's supporters, and how far the work of provocateurs, but the unrest enabled the Government to brand it as a force for anarchy.

The Coloured community set up its own franchise action committee, but its links with the Torch were not close. The Torch, having taken up the cause, failed to agree over the admission of Coloured people as members, with the result that in November 1951 the Coloured ex-servicemen withdrew. It also allowed itself to be drawn into a new wave of Natal separatism, which weakened its links with the United Party. It also made the mistake of trying to split the Nationalists by attributing their racism to Nazi influences, which was an ineffective tactic because so much of it was traditional white South African practice. Moving on to the scene in force to help the U.P. in a by-election at Wakkerstroom in June 1952, the Torch failed to prevent the Nationalists from increasing their majority. The same year it failed to win U.P. support for its determined lobbying of the Tenth Delimitation Commission in favour of equal constituencies. The U.P. preferred, as Smuts himself had done in 1947, to propose a slight loading of the urban seats in the vain hope that the more radical loading proposed by the Nationalists would be rejected by the three judges of the Commission. When, after all this, the Nationalists won the general election in April 1953 with an increased majority, taking 94 seats to the U.P.'s 58 and Labour's 4, the Torch Commando faded out. Its divided spirit lived on in the U.P. and in the emergence of two new political parties, both formed in May 1953: the Union Federal Party, with its main base in Natal and the devolution of political power as its main platform; and the Liberal Party, which aimed to establish a common South African citizenship irrespective of race.

Malan's Nationalists monopolised the government benches after the 1953 election, for after the Nationalist and Afrikaner Parties had formally merged in October 1951, all the former A.P. members save Havenga were eliminated at the nomination meetings. The Government claimed that the increase in their following gave them a mandate to go ahead with their Coloured vote legislation, even though they still did not have a two-thirds majority. Undaunted, Malan announced a joint sitting for 14 July. He let it be known that if the requisite majority were not forthcoming, the Government would legislate to amend the constitution of the Appeal Court. Despite this threat, he was still sixteen votes short at the third reading on 16 September. An Appellate Division Quorum Bill was therefore introduced on the 18th by Swart, its purpose being to expand the court and divide it into three separate panels for constitutional, civil and criminal appeals. But rather than proceed with the second reading as planned on 28 September, Malan unexpectedly postponed the debate, reconvened a joint sitting on the Coloured Vote Bill on 1 October, and immediately had that legislation referred to a Joint Select Committee. His tactic now was to try to persuade dissidents in the U.P. to vote with the Government on an agreed measure, and thus defuse the constitutional crisis. A small group of U.P. members led by Bailey Bekker and Arthur Barlow showed signs of willingness to compromise with the Government, provided Coloured voters then on the common roll were left on it. Despite a great deal of opposition in the Nationalist caucus, which they handled firmly, Malan and Dönges, who were confident of a majority in the Cabinet, decided to make a deal with the U.P. rebels. But this gamble did not pay. Malan had reckoned without Strauss, who saw his own leadership of the U.P. threatened, and reacted by urging his party to rethink the fundamentals of its race policy, and in doing so to take a stand on the moral as well as the constitutional issues at stake. The United Party stood almost solid and the Joint Select Committee therefore reached deadlock when it began its work in February 1954. Even though the Bill which it produced for the consideration of yet another joint sitting in May was tailored to meet the susceptibilities of the Bekker group, half of whom supported it, it failed by nine votes to obtain a two-thirds majority on 14 June. Malan apparently began to consider the enlargement of the Senate as a way out of the deadlock at this stage, but his own resignation from office on 30 November left the next step in the hands of his successor [see pp. 342–3].

14.3   THE POLITICS OF THE DEFIANCE CAMPAIGN

All the main non-white groups – Coloured, African, Indian – had grounds for feeling that their interests were under attack under Nationalist rule, to an even greater extent than they had been under previous regimes. In face of this pressure, twelve African leaders, of whom half belonged to the Representative Council, met at Bloemfontein on 3 October 1948, and issued a 'Call for African Unity' under a new umbrella body to be called the 'All African National Congress' – an obvious olive branch to the A.A.C., whose leaders met with the A.N.C. leadership on 16 December. But the A.A.C. delegation under its new president W. M. Tsotsi considered the differences between the bodies were 'basic and fundamental', and although they agreed in principle to unity the A.A.C. leaders rejected the statement of 3 October as its basis chiefly because it said nothing about non-collaboration, on which the A.A.C. was taking its stand. Non-collaboration, however, later defined by I. B. Tabata for the A.A.C. as the rejection of the N.R.C., Bunga, advisory boards and parliamentary representation by whites, could too easily become a cover for simple inactivity, so the feelers came to nothing.

Meanwhile the A.N.C. did provide some leverage for a new stage in the development of black resistance through a Programme of Action which was presented for discussion at its annual conference in December 1949, in response to a growing feeling among Youth Leaguers in particular that something more than petitions and deputations to the Government was now imperative. The Programme demanded 'freedom from White domination' and the right of Africans to self-determination. It urged the use of boycotts, strikes, civil disobedience and non-cooperation as the weapons of the future. Despite reservations on the part of elder statesmen, the Programme was endorsed by the conference, and the change of policy further underlined by the election of Dr J. S. Moroka, the Youth League's candidate, in place of Dr A. B. Xuma as president-general. Lodge has convincingly suggested that the Programme derived its goal of political independence from Africanist sources, its non-collaborationist strategy from Indian and Communist roots, and its self-help enthusiasm from the economic nationalism of the A.N.C. of the 1930s – which would account for the readiness with which rival groups in later years could claim the document as their own. Its immediate value, though, was that it offered a formula which satisfied Africanists, yet offered a course of action to other groups which differed from them.

How deep those differences could be was shown by the Durban riots of January 1949, when 142 people were killed and over a thousand injured, after an African youth had struck an Indian shop assistant, whose employer in turn beat and inflicted accidental injury on the youth near a crowded bus terminus at the end of the working day. The riots exposed serious tension, which escalated into loosely organised attacks on Indian residential property over a wide area on the following day. Commercial exploitation by Indian businessmen, themselves disadvantaged *vis-à-vis* whites, had provoked African migrants with even less access to property, market opportunities and jobs. But if the riot was a tragic episode, the black leaders – Champion and Xuma in particular on the African side, and Naicker and Dadoo on the Indian – were able to end the conflict between their respective communities, and in the new atmosphere the African and Indian congresses began to work cautiously together on a basis of non-violent non-cooperation with the authorities, towards the partnership which led in 1952 to the launching of a joint Defiance Campaign.

Having by its policies precipitated an association between the black nationalists and the Communists, the Government then attempted to eliminate the latter. This task was allocated to C. R. Swart. On becoming Minister of Justice in 1948, he appointed a departmental Committee to investigate the influence of communism in South Africa, and told the Assembly in February 1949 that it had indeed found communism to be a 'national danger'. In May 1950, he brought in an Unlawful Organisations Bill, at first not explicitly directed against Communists; but it was soon withdrawn and replaced by a Suppression of Communism Bill designed to grant the minister very wide powers to deal with communism and a good deal else besides. This was one of a series of measures over the next few years which, on the plea of national security, ignored the principles of civil liberty on which the public law of South Africa was theoretically grounded. It made the Communist Party unlawful. It empowered the Minister of Justice to declare any kindred organisations unlawful too, and to 'name' the office-bearers and active supporters of such bodies (subject to their right to make contrary representations), and to prohibit named persons from taking part in their activities. He could also restrict the movements of named persons and prohibit any gatherings likely in his view to further the ends of communism. The Bill defined communism to mean not only Marxist-Leninism, but also 'any related form of that doctrine' which sought to establish the dictatorship of the proletariat, or to bring about 'any political, industrial, social or economic change within the Union by the promotion of disturbances or disorder', whether in association with a 'foreign government' or not, or by encouraging hostility between Europeans and non-Europeans. Both sides of the House, with the exception of one Communist member, Kahn, and at best a small handful of others, were antagonistic towards communism. This was not surprising in a society where wealth was so unevenly divided and at a time when the intensification of the cold war made Stalinist activity appear particularly subversive. The Opposition based its resistance, not on any defence of communism itself, but on the implied violation of civil rights which the Bill contained, in particular the recourse to arbitrary action in place of the usual reliance on the courts. J. G. N. Strauss, who succeeded to the leadership of the Opposition shortly before Smuts's death, confused the issues by introducing a personal amendment which aimed to preserve the role of the courts, yet placed the onus on the accused to show that he was not a Communist, and urged that Communist activities be declared treasonable and liable to the death penalty. The Government, which enjoyed the backing of the Afrikaner Party, stood up to the vigorous opposition of bar councils, English-language newspapers and the S.A.T.L.C.. The Communist Party dissolved itself on 20 June 1950, shortly before the Bill was due to become law. It seemed likely that this action would keep its property out of the hands of the liquidator provided for in Swart's Bills, and also make it possible for Kahn and Carneson to keep their seats in the Assembly and the Cape Provincial Council. But in the following year the Government amended the Act to extend the definition of 'communist' to include any who had ever professed communism, and to make its operation retroactive. Kahn and Carneson defended themselves before a select committee on which the United Party had agreed to serve, but were turned out by the House in a straight party vote on 26 May 1952, the United Party opposing such action. Two other Communists, Brian Bunting and Ray Alexander, who were successively elected to follow Kahn in Parliament in 1953, were both prevented from doing so. Meanwhile the Communist *Guardian* was suppressed, to reappear successively as the *Clarion*, the *People's World*, *Advance* and *New Age* until, as the *Spark*, it was extinguished in 1962.

Aided by the Suppression of Communism Act, the Government also began to move againt multi-racial trade unions, and more particularly against Communists in their ranks. The establishment of a number of breakaway Afrikaner unions under the auspices of the *Blankewerkersbeskermingsbond* had prepared the way for this, and the S.A.T.L.C. was further weakened in 1949–51 by the secession of several English-speaking craft and other unions, some of them as a result of the passage of the Act. Although some sixteen mixed-racial unions then formed a South African Federation of Trade Unions in a bid to continue their struggle, they could not resist the new ministerial powers effectively, though Solly Sachs, General Secretary of the Garment Workers' Union, immediately defied the ban imposed on him in May 1952 by addressing a public meeting outside the Johannesburg city hall. Over fifty union officials, several of them office-bearers of the S.A.T.L.C., were banned before the end of 1955, and all unions were compelled to segregate their membership in 1957.

It was the Communist Party which initiated the May Day strike of 1950, as a protest against the Unlawful Organisations Bill, and it resulted in the deaths of eighteen Africans following tough counter-measures by the police. It was the kind of incident needed to dispel the mutual suspicion between African nationalists and Communists, the former inclined to believe that the Communists were trying to manipulate the forces of African nationalism in the interests of ideological class warfare from which the Africans might not benefit, the latter tending to regard the Programme of Action as a blueprint for wealthy Africans to squeeze their own people under a free enterprise economy. After the dissolution of the Communist Party on 20 June, however, the organisation of the Day of Mourning called to honour the May dead on 26 June was taken over by the A.N.C. The two sides were beginning to discover that the achievement of their immediate objective, the destruction of unbending white supremacy, did not require complete identification of their ultimate aims.

A successful strike by Coloured and African workers on 7 May 1951, called in protest against the disfranchisement of Coloured voters, kept the mood of opposition alive within the non-white community as its leaders began to prepare for another confrontation with the Government, timed to coincide with the tercentenary of Jan van Riebeeck's arrival at the Cape, on 6 April 1952. Mass protest meetings were held in many parts of South Africa on that day, and the A.N.C. and S.A.I.C. capitalised on the enthusiasm aroused by them to set up a Joint Planning Council to organise a more ambitious demonstration on the next 26 June – not a general strike, for which they calculated the African workers to be unprepared, but a civil disobedience campaign designed to throw the administration of the law into confusion by Gandhian methods. They sought to remove six blemishes on the statute book which affected one or more of the black peoples adversely: laws relating to passes, livestock limitation, Bantu Authorities, Group Areas, the separate representation of voters, and the suppression of communism. At a number of centres in the Transvaal (notably Boksburg, Johannesburg, Vereeniging, Pretoria and Germiston) and in the Cape (notably Port Elizabeth, East London, Peddie, Uitenhage and Cape Town), though to a lesser extent in the other provinces until the campaign reached its climax in September, groups of protesters entered black locations without permits, broke curfew laws, and defied 'Europeans only' notices at railway stations and in post offices ostentatiously, so as to invite arrest. The campaign petered out before the end of the year, but not before some 8,326 people had been arrested, and in nearly all cases convicted of an offence (Lodge). A noteworthy feature of the campaign was the leading role played by protesters in the eastern Cape, where over 70 per cent of all the arrests took place. In Port Elizabeth a strongly politicised black trade union leadership took effective control of a poor and rapidly growing work force. In East London a determined Youth League elite group had built up a good rapport with migrant worker peasants. Despite the leaders' intention to keep the demonstrations non-violent, some twenty-six Africans and six Europeans lost their lives, including a nun in East London, Sister Aidan, who was brutally killed by demonstrators as they were being driven back into the location by the police.

Some demonstrators who were arrested for occupying premises reserved for whites won their cases in the Supreme Court by arguing that separate facilities should be equal. After losing the case of *Rex* v. *Lusu*, however the Government came back with a Reservation of Separate Amenities Act in 1953, which invalidated this construction. It also carried further draconian legislation – a Public Safety Bill which empowered it to declare a state of emergency over all or parts of South Africa and then to bring in emergency regulations to deal with any contingencies that might arise, and a Criminal Law Amendment Bill which imposed heavy sentences of fines, imprisonment and corporal punishment for breaches of the peace or incitement. Because of the imminence of a general election on 15 April, the United Party did not oppose these bills, though urged to do so by the leaders of the Torch Commando.

14.4   TOMLINSON, VERWOERD, AND THE IDEOLOGY OF APARTHEID

The early years of the Malan Ministry were thus marked by bitter conflict, giving an aspect of unrelenting toughness to the face of apartheid which hardly tallied with the idealistic image which its devotees wished to foster. Thom has corrected a view that Malan had little interest in 'native policy' – a subject significantly neglected in his memoirs – by showing that he paid a great deal of attention in his public speeches at this time to the promotion of apartheid. But he interpreted that word as not much more than a reaffirmation of traditional segregationism, with the emphasis to be placed on 'differentiation' rather than 'discrimination'. The Department of Native Affairs was at first in no hurry to give the word a new meaning. It was still controlled by officials appointed by the Smuts Government, notably the Secretary, Dr Gordon Mears, who, with Dr Edgar Brookes on the Native Affairs Commission, continued to maintain the liberal approach they had followed during the previous administration. The Minister himself, Dr E. G. Jansen, who had previously held this portfolio under Hertzog between 1929 and 1933, was not an ideologue. His policy statements in the Senate in 1949 and 1950 were almost empty of the jargon of apartheid; his approach was flexible, and he seemed mainly concerned with practical administrative problems, notably the rehabilitation of the Reserves and the shortage of housing in the townships. To this end he appointed a commission under F. R. Tomlinson to look into the socio-economic problems of the reserves with a view to increasing their human carrying capacity. The native affairs groups in the Nationalist caucus, however, consisting of men such as M. D. C. de Wet Nel, P. W. Botha, W. A. Maree, and Albert Hertzog, began to agitate for Jansen's removal, and his replacement by the dedicated Dr H. F. Verwoerd, whose omission from the Cabinet had angered some Transvalers. In self-defence, Jansen did get rid of Mears and Brookes; but the crusaders of apartheid won their way, and Malan, after appointing another apartheid enthusiast, W. W. M. Eiselen, to succeed

Mears, brought Verwoerd into the Cabinet as Minister of Native Affairs on 18 October 1950. The atmosphere and the pace of the Native Affairs Department now began to change.

As chairman of the Bantu Education Commission appointed in 1949, Eiselen moved against the control over African schooling achieved by the Christian missions, Catholic and Protestant, after over a century of work in the field. In its Report, tabled in 1951, the Commission argued the case for a separate educational system for the Bantu-speaking people, controlled by the central government rather than the provinces, and – in contra-distinction to Hofmeyr's reform of 1945 – by the Department of Native Affairs rather than by the Union Department of Education. It also argued for a differential syllabus for Africans, designed to prepare them for their special place in society, rather than give them what Heaton Nicholls had described in 1937 as 'a little clerkly instruction in individualism'. This meant, as Eiselen saw it, a greater emphasis on the use of the vernacular medium than was practised in any colonial territory in Africa, so as to anchor the African child in his own culture, combined with basic instruc-tion in both the official languages and special emphasis on manual training, to provide an avenue to employment in the white-controlled economy.

Verwoerd did not lag behind Jansen in noting the measure of distress in the Reserves and the urban locations. By 1952 he was beginning to expound a coordinated long-term policy to deal with it, undertaking to show the Senate 'how the various Acts, Bills and also public statements which I have made all fit into a pattern, and together form a single constructive plan'. He wanted to establish economic farming units in the Reserves, cultivated by 'full-time stock-farmers or agriculturists' producing for the market and resale to 'large non-farming native communities in the native areas' engaged in 'the rural type of urban development'. Although he disapproved in private of Jansen's appointment of the Tomlinson Committee, whose findings he would later reject on important matters of principle, he set up an inter-departmental committee to investigate the location of industry near the Reserves so as to cut down the black invasion of white urban areas. Two other departmental committees were investi-gating ways of reducing livestock and exploiting mineral deposits in native areas. Verwoerd also said he was 'training the Bantu for possible forms of self-government, based on their own traditions', and on the principle that 'sound evolution depends on starting with small responsibilities within a limited sphere'. In place of the Smuts system of 1920 [see p. 235] which was in conflict with Hertzog's system of 1927 [see pp. 265–8] and in place of Hertzog's N.R.C. which was 'an umbrella authority without proper props to keep it up', he planned a pyramid of Bantu Authorities in town and country, rooted in tribal custom. Starting from the Stallardian position that blacks in white towns could not have political rights, he argued that they could not complain if they were given adequate residential areas, adequate housing, and conditions for an orderly social life. It was therefore necess-ary to provide 'in every town, and particularly in every industrial area, a potentially comprehensive location site, virtually a native group area', large enough to house all Africans in the area, so that peri-urban and backyard squatting could be eliminated. He elaborated on general conditions to be observed in the siting of locations – above all their separation by a *cordon sanitaire* from the white urban area, and provision of easy rail transport to industrial sites, all of which required planning at the regional as well as municipal levels. He now saw the site-and-service scheme, as a complete answer to housing problems. Africans were allowed to build their own homes on surveyed plots, under the supervision of the local authority, which provided water and sanitary removals. With home-ownership (but never site-ownership) by Africans as an incentive, there was also a prospect of such housing schemes becoming economic, so that transfers from general municipal revenue to urban location revenue accounts (which in 1950 had amounted altogether to £358,774) could be reduced. Finally, Verwoerd announced a campaign to eliminate black land ownership in white farming areas, and to get rid of African squatting and labour tenancy on white farms through the conversion of all farm workers to wage labourers, and the revision of the 1936 Land Act to make its anti-squatting provisions enforceable.

Verwoerd's policy resulted in a crop of legislation. His Bantu Authorities Act went through Parliament in 1951, though the Urban Bantu Authorities Bill was a casualty of the debates, and became law in a revised form only in 1961. A Prevention of Illegal Squatting Act in 1951 empowered the Minister of Native Affairs to compel Africans to move off public or privately owned land, at the same time authorising local authorities to establish resettlement camps where squatters could be concentrated. The Native Building Workers' Act of 1951 and the Native Services Levy Act of 1952 took care of location housing policy, creating jobs for blacks, thus cutting costs, and ensuring that employers could be made to pay their share in the construction of location housing and amenities. The notorious Section 10 of the Native Laws Amendment Act of 1952 limited Africans with a right to live permanently in the urban areas to those who were born there, those who had lived there continuously for fifteen years, and those who had worked continuously for the same employer for ten. In the same year a Natives (Abolition of Passes and Coordination of Documents) Act required all Africans (including those exempted under the pass laws, and women for the first time, as well as men) to carry 'reference books' containing their photographs, and information about their places of origin, their employment records, their tax payments and their encounters with the police. This created the means of ensuring that control over African influx into the towns could be exercised. In the Bantu Education Act of 1953, which resulted from the work of the Eiselen Commission two years earlier, the Department of Native Affairs obtained control over all African schools. This involved financial pressure on the missions to hand their schools over to the Government. It also placed the immediate management of African schools in the hands of Bantu school boards, enforced vernacular instruction in the junior schools, made both English and Afrikaans compulsory subjects in the higher primary, and laid down a differential syllabus for Bantu schools, geared to what the Government considered African educational needs to be.

15 'Who cares whether it works? It's got apartheid, and, like Verwoerd says, it's better to travel hopefully than to arrive'. David Marais of the *Cape Times* frequently caught the absurdities of Dr Verwoed's doctrinaire apartheid

With a capacity for imagining social change greater even than that of Milner, and with more self-confidence than ever Milner possessed, Verwoerd imparted a crusading zeal to his fellow devotees of *apartheid*. That static term soon gave place to *aparte ontwikkeling* (separate development) in Government parlance. By May 1956, so systematic had been the development of his policy across a broad front that he felt able to set out his achievements against the declared goals of 1952, as evidence that 'the solid and sound foundation of a great reformation' had already been laid. It took him two hours to say what had been achieved. As for the future, Verwoerd saw the total separation of white and black as 'an ideal to aim at', but estimated in 1956 that it would take twenty years before the integrationist tide could be seen to have turned. There was more to apartheid, though, than the territorial separation of the races, for as he said in 1954,

Apartheid comprises a whole multiplicity of phenomena. It comprises the political sphere; it is necessary in the social sphere; it is aimed at in Church matters; it is relevant to every sphere of life. Even within the economic sphere it is not just a question of numbers. What is of more importance there is whether one maintains the colour bar or not.

As the ideology took hold, Verwoerd himself became its leading glossator.

It became possible to take stock of the Verwoerdian claims for the first time in 1956, after the publication of the massive report of the Tomlinson Commission. This commission was required 'to conduct an exhaustive inquiry into and to report on a comprehensive scheme for the rehabilitation of the Native Areas with a view to developing within them a social structure in keeping with the culture of the Native and based on effective socio-economic planning'. These terms appeared to be open-ended, but they precluded proper correlation in the Commission's Report of policy proposals for African life in both the white areas and the Reserves. The Commissioners pointed this out, but only one of them felt free to suggest that the policy of separate development should itself be looked into, and abandoned if found to be impracticable. The Commission as a whole took as its starting point the view 'that there is little hope of evolutionary development' towards a common society, and 'not the slightest ground for believing that the European population, either now or in the future, would be willing to sacrifice its character as a national entity and as a European racial group'. It considered that this should be accepted as 'the dominant fact in the South African situation'.

It accordingly tried to discover how far the Bantu Areas were capable of carrying the African population, and reached the conclusion that, if a gross income of £120 per annum per farming family were taken as a guide (being, on average, the figure preferred by witnesses), only 20 per cent of the families living in the Reserves could be adequately provided for on the land. That was too few. It therefore took as its standard an annual gross income of £60 for mixed and pastoral farming, and £110 for irrigation and cane farming, as being in practice 'large enough to attract a Bantu to full-time farming', but urged that with improved methods the land could be made to yield substantially better profits. As pastoral economic units required 275 morgen and agricultural units 52.5 morgen to yield the requisite income, this meant that there was enough land in the Reserves to support 51 per cent of the Bantu Reserve population as it stood at the time of the 1951 census. With a further three million morgen still to be bought under the 1936 Act, the Commission calculated that the Bantu Areas would ultimately be able to house 2,142,000 people in households engaged in commercial agriculture. This left some 16,300 pastoral farmers and some 282,000 mixed farmers in the Reserves for whom alternative means of livelihood had to be provided.

The Commission put in a plea for improved marketing methods for farmers, better credit facilities, better farm-planning and stabilisation of tenure, with limited encouragement for successful farmers to buy a second lot if they had paid for their first, and the canalisation of funds through a development corporation for the introduction of valuable plantation crops – sugar, fibres and timber in particular. They saw good prospects of mining development in the northern Transvaal and, to a lesser extent, in Natal. They also underlined the need for industrial development both in the Bantu Areas and on their borders. In the Bantu Areas, they wanted to encourage African entrepreneurs, who could receive assistance from the same development corporation, which might itself initiate its own enterprises. A majority argued that white-sponsored industries should be allowed in the Reserves, in order to increase the carrying capacity of the Bantu Areas sufficiently, create a better balance between urban and rural employment, and encourage Africans to acquire skills. As part of the process of establishing industry, the Commission had its eye on the twenty-six towns and villages of the Transkei, on thirty-four centres in Natal and Zululand, on the various *statte* of the Tswana in the western Transvaal, and other well-spread centres, as likely nuclei for town-building. Only in the Vaal triangle, the industrial heartland of South Africa, was it unable to find a satisfactory Bantu homeland, and concluded that 'the Bantu population of this largest development complex will, therefore, have to be concentrated chiefly in urban residential areas for Bantu . . . on a regional basis'. The Commission hoped, however, to draw African workers away from the existing industrial centres by encouraging industrial firms to decentralise their activities and set up factories on the borders of the Reserves, where labour was cheaper and basic resources (above all, water) presented fewer problems.

The Tomlinson Commission took the widest view it was allowed to take of its task, and included the provision of health, welfare and educational services in its recommendations. The churches were encouraged to do missionary work, even if they could no longer teach. The Commission calculated that £104,486,000 should be spent on development of the Bantu Areas in the first ten years, of which £55 millions would be recoverable in due course. The largest single item of proposed expenditure was £27.4 millions for soil reclamation. The budget of the Department of Native Affairs, which the Commission desired to see highly centralised, and as much revenue as possible derived from African sources, would have to rise from about £9 million in the next financial year to about £20 million at the end of the decade. Then, if the right tempo were kept up, the population of the Bantu areas could be expected to reach ten million by the end of the century (including dependants of migrant workers in the white areas), through the provision of 50,000 new jobs per annum, of which 20,000 were to be in secondary industry and most of the remainder in commercial and professional employment. In the Bantu areas there would also be local self-government under the Bantu Authorities Act. In the white areas, political power would remain in the hands of the whites; and there the African population, with no political rights, would not be larger than the white. It was all very cleverly worked out, but it hung on a faulty major premise [see pp. 368–71].

14.5 THE STRIJDOM INTERLUDE

When Dr Malan resigned on 30 November 1954, he was 80 years old; but the need to replace him by a younger man was not the only consideration for the National Party. Malan's Government, as first appointed, had contained seven Cape men to two Free Staters and three Transvalers, and there were strong feelings in the northern provinces both over this imbalance and over the apparent intention of Malan to determine his own succession. It was common knowledge that he favoured Dr Dönges; but Dönges's reputation had suffered from his introduction of the unfortunate High Court of Parliament Bill, while for Group Areas and the population register he was better liked in his own party than outside it. Malan therefore worked for the election of Havenga as a night watchman, hoping that he could keep the succession warm for Dönges and keep out Strijdom, whose health was not robust, and who was distrusted by Malan for his direct but unsubtle approach to public issues. Strijdom's supporters, mainly Transvalers such as Albert Hertzog and Verwoerd, felt that Havenga, who was not a dyed-in-the-wool Nationalist, was mainly responsible for the Government's failure over the Coloured vote issue. Malan resigned the Cape leadership in November 1953, so as to give Dönges, who became his successor, greater stature in the Party. He timed the announcement of his resignation from the premiership to coincide with the eve of Strijdom's visit to Europe a year later, hoping thereby to discourage his candidature; but Strijdom's allies in the caucus saw to it that his name was canvassed among the members, and eventually secured his election.

The choice of Strijdom as Prime Minister meant that Havenga followed Malan into retirement, and Parliament lost two devotees of constitutional restraint. Strijdom saw political problems in much simpler terms, as a succession of Gordian knots to be cleanly severed. Examples of this approach were his bland announcement in 1957 that *Die Stem van Suid Afrika* would henceforth be the only national anthem and his unopposed legislation of the same year that the Union Jack ceased to have any standing as an official flag of the Union. Issues which had led to displays of great political emotion in 1927 and 1938 were now settled arbitrarily and without a major outcry because there were more important matters to think about. Perhaps surprisingly, these issues did not include the introduction of a Republican constitution, to which Strijdom was dedicated. But a steamrollered Republic could have removed all chance of incorporating the High Commission Territories, on which he had also set his heart. Nor could he assume, even in 1958 after he had enfranchised eighteen-year-old whites, that the Nationalists were in a position to win a referendum on the republican issue.

14.6   THE DEFEAT OF THE COLOURED PARLIAMENTARY STRUGGLE

The Coloured vote issue remained unresolved on Strijdom's accession to power, in the face of growing opposition in the community, whose original Franchise Action Committee had been replaced by the South African Coloured People's Organisation (S.A.C.P.O.) after the calling of a People's Convention in August 1953. S.A.C.P.O. had run its own campaign against the vote legislation, and also participated in the running of the Defiance Campaign [see pp. 332–6].

Undeterred, and lacking Malan's concern for constitutional propriety, which seemed to him much less important than the vindication of the sovereignty of Parliament, Strijdom acted quickly to end the vote crisis. Without taking the caucus into its confidence, the Cabinet worked out a new strategy. The first step was to reform the constitution of the Appeal Court, not on the lines of the earlier bill moved by Swart, but by increasing its membership to eleven judges and requiring a full quorum of eleven for constitutional appeals. The second was to enlarge the Senate so as to ensure that the Government would get a two-thirds majority in a joint session of Parliament, and then to bring the Coloured vote Bill to a joint sitting of the enlarged Parliament. The Government made sure of appointing a majority of judges who favoured its case, even if all members of the existing Appellate Division handed down hostile judgments. Its second aim was achieved by increasing the membership of the Senate to 89, by giving the larger provinces proportionately more members than the smaller (in defiance of the federal principle of equal representation), and ordaining that the party which could muster the majority of votes in the electoral college in each Province (that is, the majority of Assembly plus Provincial Council members) could elect all the senators for that province. This involved a rejection of the other federal principle of proportional representation, and was to the advantage of the Nationalists, who commanded a majority in all provinces save Natal. There followed a rush for the plums of office. The constitution thus altered to suit its purposes without actual breach of the law, the Government validated the Coloured vote legislation with a manufactured two-thirds majority during the session of 1956. In Collins's case, heard before the eleven judges of the new Appeal Court in November, the Government won its fight, the only dissenting judgment being that of Judge O. D. Schreiner, who considered the legislation invalid because the intention behind it had been to circumvent the rules of the constitution. The Government did not deny this, but claimed to have acted on the higher morality of a popular mandate. It was not deterred even by the efforts of the Women's Defence of the Constitution League (more familiarly known as the Black Sash), which was established in May 1955 to propagate respect for the constitution, and sought to do this by doggedly 'haunting' cabinet ministers through the holding of silent stands on public occasions. The legislation, and the court judgment, have remained matters of controversy (Wiechers, Dlamini).

A Coloured Affairs Department was established in 1959, and a Union Council on Coloured Affairs, comprising fifteen government nominees and twelve elective members, was set up to advise the Government; but so hostile was the community to the Council that no Coloured opposition candidates stood for election.

14.7 RESIDENTIAL AND CULTURAL APARTHEID

During Strijdom's Ministry residential apartheid began to affect all dark race groups, even urban Africans living in those few suburbs like Lady

Selborne, Pretoria, where they could still own property in spite of the
Urban Areas Act. Under a Native Resettlement Act of 1954 the Government moved the African residents of the western suburbs of Johannesburg
to a new area called Meadowlands twelve miles from the city. Sophiatown
was re-zoned for whites and renamed Triomf in 1956, and the southern
part of the district was set aside for Coloured ownership and occupation in
1957. The removals were carried out with the precision of a military
operation, and left over a thousand 'unlawful' residents of Johannesburg
homeless. In Cape Town the City Council boycotted a public hearing of the
Group Areas Committee in August 1956, because of the many Coloured
homes and institutions affected, when it was proposed to zone the whole of
the Table Mountain area to the west of the suburban railway line from
Cape Town to Muizenberg for white people; but the main features of this
proposal were put into effect during the next few years, the loss to the
Coloured people of District Six and the Kalk Bay harbour settlements
being particularly resented. Many Group Area determinations had the
support of, or had been initiated by, white local authorities or pressure
groups. Thus the removal of Coloured people from the centre of Paarl to
the area of the Berg River, was endorsed by the white Ratepayers'
Association. Proposals for the removal of Indian shops and residencies
from the central business areas of many Transvaal towns were made to the
Group Areas Board by local authorities, and adopted, notably in Lydenburg (1952), Balfour and Carolina (1953), Nelspruit and White River
(1954), Ermelo, Wolmaransstad and Klerksdorp (1955), and Pretoria,
involving the removal of the wealthy Asiatic Bazaar area (1956). Meanwhile experience led the Government to increase its powers under the Act
in a series of amendments between 1952 and 1957. It set up a Group Areas
Development Board in 1955 to control the disposal of affected properties,
and overcame numerous legal snags with regard to the racial classification
of individuals and the meanings of 'occupation' of property which had
arisen in the administration of the Act [see pp. 562–3].

Cultural apartheid was also extended during the Strijdom era. A State-
Aided Institutions Act of 1957 empowered the Government to enforce
segregation in libraries and places of entertainment if they were controlled
by public authorities, whether the people gathered to read, to watch
boxing or to listen to Brahms. The Native Laws Amendment Bill of the
same year contained a clause to empower the Government to prohibit the
holding of classes, entertainments and even church services if they were
attended by Africans in white Group Areas. The public protest was sharp –
a good deal sharper, in fact, than had been the case in 1937 when the
Hertzog Government had introduced a not dissimilar proposal. Even in the
Nationalist caucus it was argued by a minority that the Bill violated the
Reformed principle of the sovereignty of the Church within its own sphere,
while the Anglican episcopal synod informed the Prime Minister that its
members would not be able to advise their clergy to obey a law which
excluded people from a church on racial grounds. The terms of the Bill
were modified but only so as to leave the initiative with local authorities

and to expose the offending African rather than the Church concerned to the risk of prosecution. It became increasingly difficult for whites to hold night schools for urban Africans, which were also brought under the Bantu Education Act and had to be held in African locations, and less easy than before for domestic servants to hold religious services in private suburban garages on Sunday afternoons [see pp. 537–8].

It was also in 1957 that the Government went ahead with its plans to attack integrated higher education, in the face of strong opposition from those universities (all of them English-medium) which were not already uniracial. Acting on the Report of the Holloway Commission, which had investigated the administrative aspects but not the principle of university apartheid, the Government made alternative provision under an Extension of University Education Act for four ethnic university colleges, in addition to Fort Hare, at Bellville, Ngoye, Durban and Turfloop, for Coloured, Zulu, Indian and Sotho-Tswana students respectively. Objections to its policy were overridden, whether these were based on the argument that segregated education was wrong if publicly endowed, or on the much more widely supported view – at least among whites – that the Government's proposals were an invasion of university autonomy. The measure was eventually carried only after widespread demonstrations and an all-night sitting on 11 June 1959.

By the end of the 1950s the work of the designers was substantially complete. Extraordinarily detailed rules had been made for the control of groups of people. But the laws, to be effective, needed to be enforced, and before the 1950s were out a great deal of resistance to living under them was beginning to break surface. The larger features of the Afrikaner Nationalist dream state – an independent white-dominated republic, surrounded by a cluster of economically dependent and therefore politically impotent black client states – also needed to be defined. These two themes are taken up in the following chapter.

15 Internal Combustion, 1956–64

15.1 RURAL RESISTANCE TO THE APARTHEID REGIME

South Africa is a country of many baffling contrasts. There have been few societies in history in which so much dedicated enthusiasm for the promotion of a cause had been manifested by one section of society, while another section complained so persistently to be suffering from a sense of indignity and pain as a result of policies ostensibly designed for their long-term benefit. Between the euphoric vision of Dr Verwoerd and the resigned apathy of a pass-law offender on his rapid progress through the magistrate's court stood a vast gulf of apparent incomprehension.

Police counter-measures, aided by the sanctions of the Public Safety and Criminal Law Amendment Acts, had brought an end to the Defiance Campaign of 1952, which was essentially an urban movement.

Peasant resistance to government policies was very common during the history of the Union, but it passed unnoticed for years because such resistance was normally localised, obtained relatively little press publicity, and was generally put down by the police after a fairly short confrontation at the cost of relatively few lives lost. But the growth of world-wide interest in peasant history, reflected in the writings of Beinart, Bradford, Bundy, Hirson, Keegan, Lodge and others in South Africa, has brought much new information to light on peasant conditions and modes of resistance since the end of the nineteenth century. After the initial stage of dispossession, which reached a climax with the Natives Land Act of 1913 [see Chapter 7 and pp. 520–3], the loss of land remained an underlying cause of resentment, and the ultimate explanation of why other remedies failed. But by the 1940s, after the blunting of the I.C.U's rural resistance campaign [see p. 271] African peasants were more likely to rebel against controls over their use of the land, such as the culling of cattle and the introduction of fencing in the name of a policy of 'betterment'. Resentment against such controls continued during the second half of the century, as was clearly shown in 1950 by disturbances at Witzieshoek, where the local community cut loose after a third attempt by the authorities to reduce their cattle, in an area where relations between the authorities and the local chiefs had been poor (Lodge).

The resistance of the Mamathola tribe to removal from their farm in the Wolkeberg mountains of the north-eastern Transvaal affords another kind of example. They had had title to their land on this watershed since 1907, and claimed a much longer occupation; but the beginning of soil erosion on their watersponge made remedial action urgent. In September 1956 they were given two weeks to move to another farm, but they objected and were then given until the end of June 1957 to move to the farm Metz, thirty miles away on the lowveld, so that their original Reserve could be planted with trees. Metz was well provided with amenities to receive them; but there was outspoken opposition to the removal, which grew when Chief Mamathola was himself deposed for non-cooperation. The tribe was eventually obliged to settle at Metz, but a third of them went off elsewhere. A migration which was probably necessary for ecological reasons had proved a disaster for good public relations on account of deep-seated opposition to the 1927 Native Administration Act, in terms of which they were moved, and on account of suspicion of the new Bantu Authorities system. It was only later, during the 1970s and 1980s, when many more groups of people with long occupational rights were required to move, not so much for ecological as for ideological reasons – the tidying up of the racial map – that real, large-scale bitterness over forced removals was widely experienced [see pp. 403–7].

After the accession of the National Party to power, a great deal of the peasant resistance which followed, and which increased in intensity between 1957 and 1964, resulted from opposition to unpopular legislation introduced after 1948. At the centre of the picture was the Bantu Authorities Act of 1951, which was an attempt to restructure the government of the reserves on more traditional lines, but in practice came to mean the establishment of a system of indirect rule through the medium of subservient and sometimes well-rewarded chiefs, chosen for their preparedness to enforce government policy at the expense of their own popularity. Under this new machinery, taxes were harder to evade and consensus between chief and people in matters of local decision-making less likely to happen.

Several major outbreaks of resistance occurred during these years. One was in Sekhukhuneland, where, in April 1957, the Government deported to Natal two Pedi councillors, Arthur Phetedi Thulare and Godfrey Sekhukhune, after they had begun to agitate against the rumoured deposition of their chief, Moroamoche Sekhukhune. The Government subsequently set up a Tribal Authority under Moroamoche in July, but dissensions persisted in the tribe, and were attributed by the authorities to the A.N.C.. Moroamoche was suspended in November. He successfully appealed against suspension in the following March, whereupon he was deported to Cala in the Transkei in terms of the Native Administration Act, and superseded by Kgobalela Sekhukhune, a retired policeman with whom the Pedi refused to cooperate. Riots broke out in May 1958 in this region with a long history of antagonism to white intrusion [see pp. 141–5], and to ease the tension the Government suspended the Tribal Authority. Over three hundred arrests followed the rioting, and twenty-one people were convicted of murder; but all sixteen of the death sentences imposed were commuted on appeal.

Further dissension arose all over South Africa when the Government began to compel African women to carry reference books (as the consolidated passes were now known) in 1956. Twenty thousand black, white, Indian and Coloured women from many parts of South Africa went on a peaceful march to the Union Buildings on 9 August to protest against the decision, but their leaders failed to obtain an interview with the Prime Minister, Strijdom. As might have been expected from the Orange Free State experience of 1913 [see p. 237], there were widespread acts of protest, accompanied by the burning of reference books by the women, often with the encouragement of their menfolk when they returned from working in Johannesburg at the weekends. Sometimes they stoned the officials who were sent to distribute the books. There were many arrests between November 1956 and February 1959. The violence was particularly severe in the Hurutshe reserve in the western Transvaal, particularly in the location of Chief Moiloa, whose deposition in April 1957 for refusing to cooperate over Bantu Authorities, the removal of residential 'black spots', and passes for women aroused much anger. A determined campaign of pass-burning took place in 1957–8, ending with the sealing-off of the location and a tough campaign of intimidation by the police, as a result of which many local residents fled into Bechuanaland. Charles Hooper, the Anglican priest at Zeerust, captured the pathos of the events in his *Brief Authority*. But by the middle of 1959 the unrest was over, and the reserve placed under Chief Lucas Mangope, head of a new Bantu Authority, for whom order, albeit on the Government's terms, became the rule of conduct.

The climax of rural violence was reached in Pondoland between 1957 and 1960. It began, as in Sekhukhuneland, with opposition to the introduction of Bantu Authorities. The chosen agent of the new system, Chief Botha Sigcawu, had been controversially appointed in 1939 under the old political order. Rioting broke out in the Bizana district in 1958, and the rebels formed an 'Intaba' (Mountain) Committee and took to the hills, where they set up a rival administration and sought to enlist popular support by burning the huts of government informers, and intimidating the waverers in unofficial courts. People serving on school committees under the Bantu Education Act were required to resign, and the 'selfish' were fined to provide defence funds for those charged with public violence by the police. The Government brought in mobile armoured units and aircraft, and beat down the resistance in a series of clashes culminating in a police onslaught on the rebel headquarters at Ngquza Hill on 6 June 1960, when between eleven and thirty Africans were killed. Inquiries conducted by the Government and by Mary Draper of the Institute of Race Relations revealed that much of the opposition could be ascribed to peasant conservatism in face of official attempts to introduce not merely Bantu Authorities but agricultural betterment schemes; but as in Sekhukhuneland and the western Transvaal, the atmosphere was vitiated by fundamental suspicion over Government intentions. In Pondoland, especially the eastern parts, the traditional leadership of the people had been almost completely incorporated into the Bantu Authorities system, argues Lodge. This meant that the resistance leadership arose among a different group, who had contact with the main political organisations in the urban areas, notably the Congress of Democrats, and they probably found that a slump in the Natal sugar industry at that time had released for service a number of potential followers.

Thembuland was the scene of unrest in 1962–3. Here the opposition to Bantu Authorities was led by the Paramount, Chief Sabata Dalindyebo, but in Chief Kaiser Matanzima of the Emigrant Thembu, a man who was prepared to conform with Government policy, he faced a tough rival. Matanzima tried to put in practice the land consolidation envisaged in the Tomlinson Report, but he did so at a time when the Government was applying pressure on Africans in the western Cape to return to their homelands. The conjunction of circumstances proved explosive. Many of the men affected came from Thembuland and there was a widespread fear that their land was being taken over in their absence. In 1962 a number of activists, who had come under the influence of Poqo, a black nationalist movement which had arisen after the Sharpeville crisis [see p. 395], were intercepted by the police as they were attempting to converge on Matanzima's great place with the object of murdering him. The following year, when the Transkei received self-government, Matanzima was chosen above Sabata as the head of the new state.

15.2 THE CONGRESS OF THE PEOPLE AND THE FREEDOM CHARTER, 1955

Meanwhile the urban African leaders had been forced by the defeat of the Defiance Campaign and by the Nationalists' victory in the 1953 general election to rethink their strategy. Here they received some encouragement from the support of Liberals, for one consequence of the Campaign had been to bring some whites out in support of the African resistance. A very few, like Patrick Duncan, son of the former Governor-General, had taken part fully and been arrested. The Liberal Party was committed to the support of a qualified non-racial franchise. At its congress in July 1954, it adopted the principle of adult suffrage, subject to suitable transitional safeguards, and was thus able to hold the support of a small section of moderate black opinion, of elder statesmen like Selby Msimang, and younger men like the Natal journalist, Jordan Ngubane; but in the western Cape it could not compete for African loyalties against candidates put up by the Congress of Democrats, who inherited the mantle of Kahn and Bunting.

Cooperation between the African and Indian congresses grew after the end of the Defiance Campaign. The N.I.C. invited Albert Luthuli, President-General of the A.N.C. (a man later to be awarded the Nobel Peace Prize, though a banned person, for his dedication to political reform by persuasion rather than by violence), to open their conference in Durban in July 1954. There had been a huge escalation in A.N.C. membership during the Defiance Campaign, rising it was said to 100,000. Defiance Campaign cadres later provided volunteers for the Congress campaign of 1955 (Suttner and Cronin), thus offsetting the effects of attrition caused by the banning of several of its leaders, and the inefficiency of its branch offices which Xuma had tried and failed to overcome (Feit). But it proved difficult to concentrate on humdrum organisational fund-raising activities when dramatic public issues like the Natives Resettlement Act and the Bantu Education Act invited political action; and it was bad for the morale of Congress when large numbers of Africans put security before principle by settling for homes in Meadowlands rather than find themselves in the streets, or chose Bantu education rather than no education at all. The numbers of Congress stopped growing. A mass national conference to adopt a charter was thus an imaginative antidote to frustration.

The idea of an Assembly of the People, for which a precedent had been set by the Communist Party in 1944–5, was proposed at the A.N.C. Cape conference in Cradock on 15 August 1953, not inappropriately by Professor Z. K. Matthews, who had been largely responsible for the drawing up of the pamphlet *African Claims*, [see p. 314]. In the following March, executive members of the A.N.C., S.A.I.C., S.A.C.P.O. and C.O.D. met at Frasers on the lower Tugela in Natal, so that Luthuli, who was under a restriction order, could take the chair. Further meetings were held in Johannesburg, Durban and elsewhere, and a National Action Council composed of eight representatives of each participating body was appointed to issue a 'Call to a Congress of the People' on 26 and 27 June 1955, at Kliptown, south of Johannesburg.

The meeting at Kliptown was attended by some 3,000 people of all races, representing a large spread of organisations and districts, which sent delegates in response to the Call. Individual sections of the Charter, which had in the meantime been collated by a small drafting committee from a large number of contributions imaginatively solicited by well-briefed volunteers, sometimes presented verbally, sometimes 'on brown paper', were read out to the accompaniment of speeches, and voted on by show of hands. The authorities merely watched on the first day, but on the afternoon of the second detectives, supported by police armed with Sten-guns, surrounded the concourse, took control of the platform, searched all those present, and confiscated many documents, anticipating that they had obtained evidence of an intention to commit high treason.

The Charter itself, which had not been distributed in advance to the branches of the participating bodies, had been checked by most members of the A.N.C. executive, though not by either Matthews or Luthuli. It affirmed that South Africa belonged to all its inhabitants, black and white. It demanded a non-racial, democratic system of government, and equal protection for all people before the law. It also urged the nationalisation of the banks, mines and heavy industry, as well as land redistribution. Finally, it sought equal work and educational opportunities, and the removal of restrictions on domestic and family life. It was avowedly non-racial. It contained no class war phraseology even if C.O.D. propagandists preached Marxism while distributing the Call. Its references to nationalisation were well within the limits of social democratic thought, though in so far as it advocated socialist redistribution, it went beyond the A.N.C.'s earlier Programme of Action. In his initial advocacy of a congress, Professor Matthews had used the term 'national convention' as an objective, and great efforts had been made to make the Congress as representative as possible of people of all races; but it was not so much an attempt to usurp the authority of the State, which may at first have been contemplated, as a bid to raise the awareness of the people as a whole. For this purpose, the wording of the Charter struck quite a good balance, with its omission of any reference to individual ethnic groups, and the stand which it took on behalf of all South Africans.

Not surprisingly, though, acceptance was difficult for some. The national executive of the Liberal Party was sufficiently wary of sharing a platform with the C.O.D. (its chief opponent in parliamentary elections for the return of Natives' Representatives) to decline to take part officially, though individual Liberals did. The Africanist element in the A.N.C. was extremely unhappy at what it feared was a Communist take-over bid. Potlako Leballo, one of its leaders, was at the Congress but not of it, selling copies of their paper, *The Africanist*. He was later to denounce the movement at the Transvaal conference of the A.N.C. in October. A month after Kliptown, the Africanists staged a memorial service to Anton Lembede, and used it as an occasion to honour the heroes of the African past. The real objection of the Africanists seem to have been to participate on an equal basis with the other organisations, in a Congress Alliance in which they saw themselves as the rightful core organisation in virtue both of their stand on behalf of the indigenous dispossessed, and of their enormous numerical ascendancy. Africa was 'for the Africans', and until they had learnt to participate as equals, not as overlords, the alien element was to be required to take a back seat. Their opposition caused turmoil in the A.N.C. which declined to endorse the Charter at its national conference in December. It did so at a special conference in April the following year, under circumstances which called forth further Africanist recriminations. But the A.N.C. leadership, Luthuli and Matthews in particular, though they had their reservations about the Charter, saw the Congress of the People for what it now clearly had been – an imaginative, skilfully orchestrated attempt to promote the unity of the politically deprived, the influence of which could only be countered by a conspicuous and morally damaging assertion of the authority of the State.

15.3 THE FIRST OF THE TREASON TRIALS

The Congress of the People showed the police how successfully the C.O.D., which provided a home both for ex-members of the Communist Party and for non-Communists of the stamp of Trevor Huddleston and Helen Joseph had moved into an alliance with the black organisations. Police raids on the homes and offices of those who had participated therefore followed in September, and at dawn on 5 December 1956 the police arrested 156 people from all races and all walks of life all over South

Africa and held them in the Johannesburg Fort pending an arraignment for high treason. Then began one of the longest and largest trials in the history of mankind. By August 1958 the Government had reduced the number of the accused to 91, and these were committed for trial in the Johannesburg Drill Hall, which was specially prepared for the purpose. Bail had meanwhile been allowed despite the nature of the charge. By November 1960 the number of the accused had been further whittled down to 30, and all without exception were eventually acquitted of the charge of treason by three judges of the Supreme Court on 29 March 1961. Some interpreters of the trial thought that – even without convictions – it demonstrated that there were many operating close to the edge of treason. Others considered that the Government had abused its own authority, and prematurely cried 'Wolf'. This is perhaps what it was really doing, if, as Karis suggests, the chief prosecutor, Oswald Pirow, considered the trial to be less a witch hunt than a bid to check agitation and give the police more time to acquire fresh skills.

15.4 VERWOERD'S 'NEW VISION' AND MACMILLAN'S 'WINDS OF CHANGE', 1959–60

Strijdom died in office on 24 August 1958, a man respected by his followers for the long and initially lonely stand he had taken on behalf of his party in the Transvaal. Though he had opponents in the party, above all in the Cape, he had controlled his Cabinet, stood up to the Broederbond in a way Malan had not, and left his mark on the policy of the country through his capacity for taking resolute decisions.

Dr H. F. Verwoerd emerged the victor over Dönges and Swart in the subsequent lobbying for the premiership, but although his victory in the caucus was fairly decisive, he had the greatest difficulty in winning the personal loyalty of Strijdom's cabinet and in rearranging the portfolios so as to placate disappointed supporters. But by giving Dr N. Diederichs Economic Affairs, releasing Dönges from the Interior and giving him Finance, and persuading Dr Albert Hertzog to take Health and Posts and Telegraphs, rather than Mines, he was able to minimise the tensions in a difficult team. A Hollander by birth, though he had lived in South Africa, and briefly in Southern Rhodesia, since early childhood, Verwoerd had received university training at Stellenbosch, and then in pre-Hitlerian Germany, before returning to Stellenbosch as professor of social psychology. He edited the *Transvaler* during the war years, provocatively enough to sting the *Star* into alleging that his editorials had supported the enemies of South Africa. Whether he ought to have lost the libel action which he brought against that newspaper seems at best doubtful, however, in view of the generally accepted hostility of the *Transvaler* towards the promotion of Nazism as a philosophy appropriate to South Africa. Verwoerd had certainly supported Malan during the same years, in his confrontation with Pirow and the New Order Group. A man of benign appearance, he both mesmerised and dominated his political followers to an extent not achieved by any of his Nationalist predecessors. Intellectually, he stood head and shoulders above most of his contemporaries in Parliament, while his self-assurance and his didactic manner led many to believe that he really could conjure into being the political objectives of his fertile imagination. Few parliamentarians, among them Margaret Ballinger, queried his genius.

The Verwoerd era began with two major changes in the political orientation of South Africa. One was the firm commitment of the Government to a policy of some kind of independence for the Bantu areas, which brought in its train a realignment of the forces of parliamentary opposition. The other was the decision of the Government to go for a Republic, which led to South Africa's departure from the Commonwealth. Both these developments occurred against a background of increasing tension which reached a climax at Sharpeville in March 1960.

As Minister of Native Affairs, Verwoerd had never committed himself to independence for the Reserves, always limiting his promises to self-government under Pretoria at the level of the Territorial Authority. Dr Eiselen, the Secretary for Native Affairs, stated very explicitly in *Optima* as late as March 1959 that the grant of independence was never intended, and confirmed that this had been the case in a press interview in October 1972, urging that he had always attached more importance to the economic development of the Bantu areas than to their political autonomy. As late as January 1959, Verwoerd hedged over the political future of these areas, referring to their ultimate independence only as a remote, unforeseeable possibility. When asked on 5 September 1958 about a related topic, the abolition of African representation in the House of Assembly, Verwoerd replied that the matter had not yet been considered. But during the 1959 session the Government introduced a Promotion of Bantu Self-Government Bill, the negative feature of which was the termination of African elected representation in Parliament, rounding off the policy for the elimination of African political influence in the white areas which had led to the abolition of the N.R.C. in 1951 [see p. 329] and of the Advisory Boards Congress in 1956–7. There was opposition in Nationalist circles, however, chiefly from Japie Basson, the member for Namib, who had crossed over from the United Party in 1948. Basson argued that only the grant of genuine political independence to the Bantu areas would justify such disenfranchisement. He was expelled from the party caucus in May. Meanwhile the new Bill made provision for the restructuring of the Bantu Authorities system on a framework of eight Territorial Authorities, and Verwoerd allowed the suggestion of eventual independence for these Territorial Authorities to creep into his introductory and second reading speeches. He repudiated Eiselen's *Optima* article, saying it had been written 'long before the latest official Government statement was made'. In reply to a question by the Leader of the Opposition, Sir de Villiers Graaff, whether the Union Government would retain control over the foreign affairs of the Bantu areas 'forever or merely temporarily', Verwoerd explicitly referred to the possible development of these areas to full independence. He saw analogies between the direction South Africa could

take and that being taken by Europe – a combination of national sover-
eignties with economic interdependence. He also repudiated the fear
expressed by Graaff that independent Bantustans might provide footholds
for Communist powers and hostile armed forces by saying:

> My belief is that the development of South Africa on the basis of this
> Bill will create so much friendship, so much gratitude, so many mutual
> interests in the propulsive development that there will be no danger of
> hostile Bantu states, but that there will arise what I call a common-
> wealth, founded on common interests and linked together by common
> interests in this southern part of Africa. In other words, I believe that
> these dangers of foreign ideologies, of foreign navies and so on, will not
> materialize.

There are good grounds for supposing that Verwoerd's 'new vision' of
1959, the authenticity of which has general acceptance among his biographers, was in part a tactical reaction to the decolonisation of Africa, which
was just beginning. His vision of a South African Commonwealth, in the
framework of which the independence of the Bantustans was to be considered, had the merit of being a mould into which a new policy for the
High Commission Territories could be made to fit in the event of their
becoming independent. They too might become Bantustans, perhaps even
with boundaries adjusted to mesh with South African reserves on their
borders, and the whole unhappy question of transfer be allowed to fall into
abeyance. This possibility was certainly noticed by Verwoerd, De Wet Nel
and Eiselen at the beginning of 1959. When Harold Macmillan, the British
Prime Minister, visited Cape Town in February 1960, Verwoerd held talks
with him over the future of the High Commission Territories, and on this
occasion he explicitly asked Macmillan's permission to present to their
governments his own ideas for the development of the projected South
African 'Homelands'. Thus the legislation of 1959, while it finally demolished the Hertzogian new deal of 1936 for Africans by silencing their voice
in the South African Parliament, also opened up an alternative route which
might help to inaugurate a new system of international relations in
southern Africa linked, as now suddenly became clear, with the introduction of a republican form of government.

The decision to go for a republic, which had not featured in the
Governor-General's speech at the beginning of the 1960 session, was taken
in cabinet on 18 January, adopted by the National Party caucus on the
morning of the 19th, and released by Verwoerd during the 'no confidence'
debate the same afternoon. The effect of surprise was complete, and the
Opposition was thrown into some disarray. But the drama of the 'no
confidence' debate was soon eclipsed by more sensational events.

Two weeks later the British Prime Minister, Harold Macmillan, visited
South Africa at the end of a tour through the African continent, during
which he had been impressed by the strength of African nationalism, and
convinced that these 'winds of change' blowing through the continent were
irresistible. Macmillan was invited to address both houses of Parliament on

3 February. He broke the normal rules of etiquette, clearly wanting to gain maximum advantage from surprise (as Verwoerd had done a few days earlier over the Republican issue), by not providing the South African Prime Minister with a text of his speech in advance. He made it clear that the South African Government's apartheid policy could enjoy no support from his Government, and that he thought access to political power should be extended in South Africa on the basis of individual merit, irrespective of race. Verwoerd's impromptu reply was a dignified restatement of his Government's position, a defence of the white man's rights as a European in the minority on a black continent, and a presentation of his own policy as something 'not at variance with a new direction in Africa, but . . . in the fullest accord with it'.

He spoke on behalf of a majority, but not of all parties in the South African Parliament, though his new Homeland policy had already divided the official Opposition. While the thinking of the Nationalists moved in the direction of a multinational South African commonwealth based on the conversion of the African Reserves to eight 'independent' units to be consolidated so far as possible into territorial states, the United Party retorted that the partition of South Africa was unthinkable. After emancipating itself in 1948 from the toils of Hertzog's policy of 1936–7, and adopting the Fagan proposals as its guidelines, the U.P. had discovered by 1954 that its lack of positive objectives placed it at a disadvantage in face of Nationalist propaganda. On Strauss's initiative, therefore, the party adopted a new statement of policy at its Union congress in November 1954. This accepted the African as part of a single South African political community, and justified white leadership only if the white man was prepared to share his civilisation with the African. It affirmed, as in 1948, the fact of economic integration, but now described political rights for the black man as 'an inevitable historical corollary to an increase in economic power', once he had undergone a 'long period of training in the ways of democracy' and after 'a decisive majority of the European electorate' had agreed that such rights should be conferred. This was a cautious, empirical approach with almost no electoral appeal at all, though it indicated a direction opposed to the Nationalist line of advance, and admitted the principle of greater African participation in parliamentary politics one day, which might be difficult to shrug off. The U.P. rejected the non-racial democratic ideas of the Liberals as electorally non-viable, which they were, and it rejected federalism as a device for the protection of minorities, no doubt because all the federal thunder had been stolen by the Union Federal Party, whose posture was closely linked with the historic 'Natal stand' of the early 1930s, and had more to do in their hands with provincial rights than with the solution of racial problems. After the 1958 election, when the Federal Party collapsed after winning a third of the Natal votes but failing to take a single seat, the federal option became more available, to be exploited in very different ways by the U.P. and the new Progressive Party.

Overtaken by Verwoerd's partition proposals, the U.P. reacted by asserting that it would oppose the transfer of any further land to the African Reserves if the destiny of such land was to be lopped off the

Union. But the liberal wing dissented, and the issue split the Party, eleven of its fifty-three M.P.s seceding in 1959 to form the Progressive Party. They contended that the obligation to find more land for the Africans was unaffected by Verwoerd's change of policy, and, once freed from the constraints of the U.P. caucus, they subjected their own standpoints to fundamental review. A new constitutional policy was adopted, known as the Molteno plan, for the protection of minority interests through a two-tier multi-racial common-roll franchise for the lower house, giving nine-tenths of the seats to people possessing fairly high educational and wealth qualifications. It also recommended the direct representation of all races in the upper house, through special voting procedures to ensure that no candidate could win a seat without receiving support from voters of all race groups. This was intended to ensure that the Senate would be disposed to veto racially discriminatory legislation. The Progressives also proposed to entrench a Bill of Rights, and to bring about a considerable devolution of power to bicameral provincial legislatures, each one a replica of the federal Parliament and possessing wider powers than the existing Provincial Councils. Despite the originality of these proposals, however, the urban voters rejected Progressive candidates in the general election of 1961, enabling the U.P. to recapture all their seats save that of Mrs Helen Suzman in Houghton, Johannesburg.

Having survived the Progressive challenge, but failed to prevent the Nationalists from increasing their seats by three, the U.P. came out with a new policy, described as 'Race Federation', in 1963. This envisaged a three-stage plan after the party's return to power. In the first stage, it would study and then dismantle what it could of the controversial apartheid laws. It then planned to restore the Coloured voters to the common roll in the Cape and Natal, and give those in the Transvaal and Orange Free State some representation in the Senate, to restore and enlarge African representation on a separate roll in both houses (up to eight seats in the Assembly, and up to six in the Senate), and to seek some formula for the representation of the Indians after consultation with them. In the third phase, it would set up a number of communal councils for each race, building on the structure outlined by Smuts in 1947 for the Africans, and allowing for the representation of each group, indirectly through these councils, in a central Parliament. As later elaborated in 1972, the U.P. policy allowed for the adaptation of the existing Provincial Councils and of the Territorial Authorities in the Bantu Homelands (assuming that the latter could be persuaded to reject independence) to become communal councils under this race federation plan; and the Party insisted that the white electorate, which was in possession of the field, should be able to control the evolution of the policy, and if need be stop it, at every stage.

15.5   THE A.N.C., THE P.A.C. AND SHARPEVILLE, 1960

Thus the whites debated about the future of the blacks. But it was a debate conducted in a political whirlpool, and had almost no relationship to the thinking of the black leadership, save in so far as a few thinkers like Ngubane were toying with a new kind of federal map. The unrest in Sekhukhuneland and the western Transvaal was still simmering, while the situation in Pondoland was highly volatile. Active opposition to reference books for African women, to Bantu education (especially, now, to its higher manifestations in the 'tribal colleges'), and to the new Bantu Authorities was still widespread. The A.N.C. was beginning to send emissaries into the rural areas to coordinate opposition, though it did not at this stage encourage violence. There were ugly scenes at Lady Selborne, Pretoria, in February 1959, when police broke up a protest meeting of African women. In June there was serious rioting in Durban's African townships sparked off by three rather more traditional irritants – low wages, shack removals, and liquor raids – during an epidemic of typhoid. Feelings there exploded again in the following January, when nine police-men were murdered in a riot after a liquor raid in Cato Manor. Meanwhile, on the night of 10 December, some eleven Africans had been killed and forty-four injured by police fire in the Windhoek location, after the residents had stoned them in a bid to resist removal to another township.

In this situation of unremitting tension, rifts which had already begun to appear in the A.N.C. now started to open wider. These had been evident in the Congress Youth League as early as 1952–3, when the new leadership elected that year began to take an interest in the Marxist apologetic now that the Congress of Democrats had emerged to take the public place once occupied by the banned Communist Party. But this caused an upsurge of Africanism on the rebound. Meanwhile the studied moderation of Luthu-li's leadership itself stimulated a new activism, especially after State harassment in 1955–6 had begun to expose some of the A.N.C.'s organis-ational weaknesses. The new 'Tambo constitution' of 1957, with its grant-ing of increased financial and disciplinary powers to the National Executive addressed these. But there were strong leaders among the malcontents, who still smarted under their defeat over what they contemptuously referred to as the 'Kliptown Charter' – men like Potlako Leballo, a talented public orator, Peter Raboroko, who had dreams of an African cultural renaissance, and the scholarly yet retiring Robert Sobukwe, who insisted that Africa was for the Africans, but added – like 'Onze Jan' Hofmeyr – that 'everybody who owes his loyalty to Africa' should be regarded as such. The break between the two sides came at the Transvaal provincial congress in November 1958, when the Africanists were physi-cally excluded from the hall, but avoided what might have been a very violent confrontation by deciding forthwith to withdraw and form their own organisation. In March 1959 the Pan-Africanist Congress was formed, with Sobukwe as its chairman, Potlako Leballo as its secretary, and the Youth League's Programme of Action and the Defiance Campaign as their main points of reference for the struggle they planned to continue.

Sensing competition from this breakaway activist movement, the A.N.C. conference at Durban in December 1959 decided to hold massive demonstrations on 31 March 1960 against the pass laws, linked with a national campaign for a minimum wage of £1 a day. But on 18 March, the

P.A.C. pre-empted this plan by announcing a campaign to defy the pass laws on the 21st, linked with a demand for a slightly higher minimum wage. Sobukwe and his followers, true to their word, defied the pass laws on the 21st and were arrested, as were many of their followers all over the country. Though the Government used aircraft in one place to scatter the crowds, the police reaction to a non-violent demonstration was itself in most places non-violent. At Sharpeville in the Transvaal, however (a so-called 'model location' unremarkable for its record of political violence, but situated in the Vereeniging area where large scale rustication to the homelands and sharply increased rentals had recently accompanied a local resettlement programme), sixty-nine Africans were killed and 180 injured when the police opened fire on a crowd of demonstrators. Some of these, according to a statement by Nyakane Tsolo, their spokesman, had arrived without reference books and merely wanted to be arrested. Some witnesses at the subsequent judicial inquiry regarded the crowd as noisy but not hostile, and composed largely of people who had gone to the police station expecting to hear an important announcement about the pass laws. The police, on the other hand, thought that the crowd was getting out of hand, and that the fence round the police station was in danger of collapsing under their pressure. What followed was not a calculated massacre like the slaughter of Indians at Amritsar in 1919, but a panic reaction, barely two months after the Cato Manor murders, by undisciplined police, who were probably not told to open fire before the first shot went off, and then went on firing after the crowd had been put to flight. The shooting was immediately condemned throughout the world, primarily because it exposed the harshness of a system of controls which the rest of the world condemned as inhumane, just the kind of bloody confrontation which could have been expected during what was, after all, not the first major protest movement against the pass system since Union, but the seventh. A similar tragedy, on a much smaller scale, occurred at Langa, near Cape Town, later the same day. There a crowd of 6,000 had gathered to await 'word from the national office', after an attempt to march on the police station in the early morning to surrender passes had been called off by their young student leader, Philip Kgosana, in response to a police threat to disperse the marchers by force. But news of the Sharpeville shootings was out by midday, the evening crowd was angered rather than intimidated by a police baton charge which followed an inaudible command to disperse, and when the police subsequently opened fire two people were killed. During the night the crowd rioted, burned the municipal offices, and went for the police reinforcements which had been brought in.

Cape Town Africans now began to stay away from work in growing numbers, though elsewhere it began to look as if the protest strike was over. On the 24th, a crowd of P.A.C. members led by Kgosana and others went to the Caledon Square police station, and there, through the mediation of Patrick Duncan of the Liberal Party, whose association with this anti-communist section of the African political movement was becoming closer, they managed to gain from the police officer in charge an undertaking not to carry out pass arrests for a month if they would return home, which they did. Pass arrests were suspended throughout the country later in the day, on the instruction of the Minister of Justice.

But this represented the illusion of victory for the P.A.C., not the real thing. As the ripples of shock at the Sharpeville killings spread across the country, the Government banned public meetings in all the disturbed centres. Luthuli identified himself with the P.A.C. protest even though he had not been involved in its planning, and on the 27th, after the Commissioner of Police had announced that Africans were not to be arrested simply for not carrying reference books, Luthuli publicly burned his own. He also declared the 28th a day of mourning for the victims of the 21st, asking people to stay at home, which many of all races did. On the 28th, the Government introduced legislation to declare the A.N.C. and the P.A.C. illegal organisations, and acted to control the situation in other ways before this ban became operative on 8 April. Thus at dawn on 30 March and on subsequent days, a total of over 18,000 people were detained under new emergency regulations. Many of these were released after screening, but over five thousand were convicted and sentenced for various offences, and others held for several months in custody. Sobukwe was subsequently given a three-year jail sentence but was actually detained for a further six years on the annual decision of Parliament. Over a hundred P.A.C. leaders were given the alternative of three years' jail or a £300 fine, but the sentence was subsequently halved. Luthuli and the A.N.C. leaders who had destroyed their reference books were sentenced to one year's imprisonment or a £100 fine.

The atmosphere of crisis was heightened on 30 March because the Government had decided to break what was already becoming a successful stay-at-home movement by the workers. But the violence of the police angered the residents of the townships and drove them to stage protest marches in Durban, where white vigilantes fired on crowds marching to the city centre, and in Cape Town, where about 30,000 Africans tried to march to Parliament (which was in session) to demand the release of their leaders. The Cape Town marchers seem to have set out without the foreknowledge of Kgosana, who joined them and stepped once more into the leadership. They were encouraged to go to Caledon Square by the persuasiveness of a police detective, rather than threaten the legislature. There, for the second time, Kgosana confronted the police commandant, and was persuaded once again to turn his men back in return for a police promise to try to arrange an interview with the Minister of Justice later in the day. When Kgosana returned to keep the appointment, he was arrested. (He later levelled the scores by estreating bail and leaving the country.) The same afternoon a state of emergency was proclaimed in altogether 122 of the Union's 265 magisterial districts. This empowered the authorities to prohibit gatherings, impose curfews, detain suspects, impound publications, search premises and do whatever was necessary to maintain public order. The Active Citizen Force was mobilised in strength, and used to cordon off the African townships of Langa and Nyanga in the Cape.

On 9 April there was an attempt to assassinate the Prime Minister, Dr Verwoerd, while he was opening the Rand Easter Show. He was shot in the head and badly injured by a white man who was subsequently declared to be mentally disturbed.

The South African state was shaken by these events, not least because the economy itself came under heavy pressure. Because of the danger that a mass stay-at-home by African workers might paralyse the industrial system, one of the tasks allotted to the police and to the troops during the crisis was to propel African workers out of the townships and back to their jobs, not to besiege them in their homes. Since 1957 there had been a net outflow of capital from the Union of over R20 million; but in the eighteen months to June 1961 a total R248 million left South Africa, while the gold and foreign exchange reserves fell from R315 million in January 1960 to R142 million in June 1961. A major loss of confidence by investors in the South African economy had been inspired by the disturbances and by the chain of events, during the same period, which led to South Africa's withdrawal from the Commonwealth.

But the Government managed within a few years to nurse the economy back to a level of unprecedented growth and prosperity. It imposed new controls on imports to take care of the balance of payments deficit; it blocked the repatriation of distributed profits earned by foreign investors, and imposed tight controls on the export of capital in general. This in turn built up reserves of private capital inside the country, and led to an expansion of economic activity and rising share prices as more and more public and private investors were attracted to the stock market. The upswing was discernible before the end of 1962, and by 1966 the prosperity was so marked that increased imports were already beginning to create inflationary conditions. There was a net capital inflow of R235 million in 1965 [see p. 514].

15.6   THE FIRST REPUBLICAN REFERENDUM, OCTOBER 1960

The full significance of the final stages of the Republican movement can be appreciated only if they are seen in the context of the political and economic crisis. Verwoerd had indicated that he intended to submit the republican issue to a referendum of white voters (excluding, he said, those of South West Africa), and to accept the decision of a bare majority if necessary, either way. This was a departure from the emphasis of Strijdom, who had generally insisted that a republic had to be based on the 'broad basis of the people's will'. The Commonwealth Prime Ministers' Conference in May 1960, which Eric Louw, the Minister of External Affairs, attended on Verwoerd's behalf, would not take a decision in advance on whether a Republic of South Africa would be allowed to remain within the Commonwealth, on the ground that this would constitute interference in the domestic affairs of the Union. Verwoerd therefore indicated before the referendum, which was scheduled for 6 October, that the constitutional changes would be formal only; that he intended to apply for continued membership of the Commonwealth should be voters choose a republic; but that he would proceed to the constitution of a republic even if this meant exclusion from the Commonwealth if the electorate voted accordingly. The Government had meanwhile decided in March to extend the poll to the whites of South West Africa, but to exclude Coloured voters everywhere. At no point did the inclusion of African or Indian voters arise.

The United Party told its supporters to oppose a republic in the referendum, while the Progressive Party urged theirs to 'reject *this* republic' on the argument that a weighted electorate could not provide a valid test of opinion.

The outcome of the referendum was a majority in favour of a republic of nearly 75,000 in a total poll of 1,632,583 votes cast. 52.14 per cent of the votes cast were favourable, and 47.42 per cent against. Majorities voted in favour of a republic in the Orange Free State (76,733), Transvaal (81,091), Cape (3,771) and South West Africa (7,921), and in Natal a majority of 93,399 voted against, the results in individual constituencies corresponding closely to those which might have been predicted in a general election.

Verwoerd accordingly took South Africa's application to remain in the Commonwealth as a Republic to the Prime Ministers' conference in March 1961. He worked hard for a final communiqué which South Africa could accept, without the inclusion of a partisan statement critical of apartheid and therefore repugnant to South African public policy. For the sake of obtaining such a formula, and because he did not want to throttle debate, Verwoerd did not insist on the exclusion of domestic political issues from the discussion. Once it became clear, however, that South Africa's remaining in the Commonwealth would probably lead other members to leave it, he formally withdrew South Africa's application. When the Union became the Republic of South Africa on 31 May, its membership of the Commonwealth therefore ceased forthwith.

A draft Republican constitution had meanwhile been debated in Parliament and received the Governor-General's assent on 24 April. It bore little resemblance to a traditional Boer Republican constitution or to the draft of 1941, either as to the form of government proposed, or as to its provisions for the relationships between the white communities. Its form was essentially that of the South Africa Act, with the new office of State President combining those of the Queen and the Governor-General: a head of state without a political role, elected by the legislature, not by popular vote, though like Paul Kruger he would wear a top hat and presidential sash on state occasions. The equality of the white language groups, and the English and Afrikaans languages, remained. Political power remained as before almost exclusively in the hands of the whites, who retained their monopoly of the seats in the two-chamber Parliament.

Verwoerd had achieved a masterstroke of moderation. He had stressed the need to conciliate the English-speaker in speech after speech. Whether, as one of the drafters of the more controversial republican constitution of 1941, he meant to stop at this point is less certain, though it is likely that he would have tried to carry English-speakers with him in any proposed change. As Scholtz noted, he reminded Parliament in January 1961 that the new constitution should be seen not as the end of a process, but as the 'start of an evolution towards a future'. Scholtz's later claim, made over the radio a long time after Verwoerd's death, that the master had told him verbally of a plan to move towards an executive presidency at the appropriate time, accorded with nearly everything that Verwoerd had said about a republic in the course of his political career.

15.7   POST-SHARPEVILLE RESISTANCE: B. J. VORSTER AND THE POLITICAL UNDERGROUND

The Republic invited a new start, and this meant different things to different groups. For the Nationalist Afrikaners it was, perhaps only in passing, the annulment of the defeat of Vereeniging; but it was also a step towards the creation of white unity, which meant that offence should not be given to the white English-speaker by introducing too radical a change in the form of the constitution. Politically conscious English-speakers, for their part, were divided. Some resented the severing of the umbilical cord which tied them to Britain – that, rather than the institution of a Republic, for it meant that they had to decide whether to remain British or become South African citizens. Others were driven into the arms of the National- ists by Britain's decolonisation movement in Africa and Macmillan's famous speech. Verwoerd was soon able to exploit this sentiment by persuading two English-speakers, Frank Waring and A. E. Trollip, to join the National Party and the Cabinet.

The Government had excluded all non-white people from any share in the making of the Republic. Although it took steps after 1960 to promote the economic and educational development of Coloured people, and gave recognition to Indian South Africans as citizens of the Republic for the first time in 1963, it did not give either of these communities a defined terri- torial base for even local self-government. Its apologists considered, how- ever, that by setting up the Bantu Authorities system, and above all by giving a form of self-government to the Transkei in 1963, it was restoring to the Africans a governmental system as rooted in their own soil as a republicanism was in that of the Afrikaner. But the Transkeian constitu- tion was drawn up in Pretoria, not in Umtata, at the request of a recess committee of the Territorial Authority, and Verwoerd himself had a great deal to do with it. It provided for a dyarchical system of government under which this 'self-governing territory within the Republic of South Africa' was to have a cabinet elected by a ballot in the Legislative Assembly, with initial control over the portfolios of Finance, Justice, Education, the Interior, Agriculture and Forestry, and Roads and Works. The Assembly in turn was to consist of the four paramount chiefs of the Transkei, together with the sixty chiefs of the Transkeian regional authorities and forty-five elected members chosen by adult suffrage, giving a clear majority of chiefs over commoners. This enabled the Government of the Republic to ensure that its own favourite for the premiership, Chief Kaiser Matan- zima, who had come out in support of the Government's Bantu Authorities and land consolidation proposals, was provided with a safe majority, though nearly all the elective seats in the first general election in 1963 went

16 'It works!' David Marais of the *Cape Times* marks the grant of self-government to the Transkei in 1963 – the first step in the development of the National Party's Bantu Homeland strategy

to supporters of Matanzima's opponents, the Paramount Chiefs Victor Poto and Sabata Dalindyebo. Something of the atmosphere of a democratic election was achieved, though it was contested in the shadow of emergency regulations proclaimed in November 1960 to deal with the Pondoland rising. Matanzima was appointed Chief Minister of the Transkei. He later founded his Transkeian National Independence Party, (T.N.I.P.) which professed allegiance to separate development, while the opposition Democratic Progressive Party cpposed the fragmentation of South Africa and favoured full African representation in the Republic's Parliament. The T.N.I.P. gave the Republican Government something that it had failed to get under the 1936 system of representation – a black political ally committed to its own policies. To grasp and sustain the initiative which the Republican Government handed to them by promising them 'independence' presented a challenge to the Transkeian Government, and Matanzima's team were able to show from time to time that they could stand up to Pretoria, even without the power to make their territory economically independent or militarily strong.

For the leaders of the black organisations outlawed after Sharpeville, the birth of the Republic became the occasion not for rejoicing but for going underground. Towards the end of 1960, when the Union-wide state of emergency had ended except in the Transkei, a group of African Liberals

and ex-members of the A.N.C. and P.A.C. called a consultative conference at Orlando, to work for a non-racial democracy and the continuance
of non-violent pressures against apartheid. This in turn sponsored an
African leaders' conference in Pietermaritzburg the following March, at
which plans were developed for the calling of a new national convention – a
different kind of fresh start altogether and involving all races. Several of
the organisers of this conference were arrested on charges of promoting the
aims of the A.N.C. but were cleared of guilt on appeal. Under the pressure
of events, however, the rifts in the African leadership were not healed.
Ngubane, one of the leading promoters of the conference (and, incidentally, one of those arrested) deplored the ease with which other elements
could take over the running after Luthuli had been restricted to Groutville
in Zululand by a government banning order. The conference chose Nelson
Mandela, a Witwatersrand University law finalist and ex-Youth Leaguer,
who had been born in the Transkei, as leader of a new National Action
Council. This council put out a demand for a convention of all races, but
coupled it with a threat that if the Government did not respond favourably
it would call a general strike between 29 and 31 May, during the inaugura-
tion of the Republic. The Government spurned the challenge and the
strike took place, with uneven effect because the strikers failed to gain the
support of the Opposition press. Mandela himself went underground and
began actively to establish a new militant wing of the A.N.C., *Umkonto we
Sizwe* (Spear of the Nation), with a plan to sabotage installations without
taking human lives. Their first acts of sabotage took place on the Day of
the Covenant, 16 December 1961.

Umkonto's sabotage activities were directed against such targets as
electric pylons, post offices, Bantu Administration premises, jails, and
railway installations, and some twenty separate acts were eventually admitted by its leaders. Lodge, following Feit, refers to over 200, not all of which
conformed to the leaders' injunction to avoid taking human life. Their
activities were supplemented by those of a white student group, the
African Resistance Movement. Cumulatively these were at least as widespread, and at least as destructive, as the sabotage acts performed by the
militants in the Ossewa Brandwag during 1942.

The P.A.C. also sponsored, and can in general be identified with, an
underground movement, *Poqo* ('We go it alone'), an organisation with
cells in urban compounds and on farms, as well as in the Reserves, light in
revolutionary theory but bent on insurrection, which turned to tactics of
intimidation and did not shrink from taking lives. Judge J. H. Snyman, in
his report on the Paarl riots of 20–22 November 1962, attributed eleven
murders of constables and suspected informers in the western Cape in
1962–3, to Poqo adherents, as well as the attempts referred to earlier [see
p. 349] on the life of Chief Matanzima. Poqo, as Lodge affirms, contained
many members who were hostile to Matanzima's land consolidation proposals, which seemed likely to throw more and more people on to the
labour market of the western Cape just at a time when the Government
was trying to turn it into a Coloured preference area. But the immediate
cause of the riots in Paarl, where black migrant workers and their families

had suffered a good deal from the effects of harsh residential laws corruptly administered, was the tough, provocative treatment of Poqo members by a black headman. This developed into a march on the police station and the jail which was repulsed, and ended with a rampage through one of the town's main streets.

While the Umkonto and Poqo campaigns developed in the townships, both the A.N.C. and the P.A.C. set up headquarters outside South Africa. Both established missions in Dar-es-Salaam and London, and offices in Cairo, Algiers, and elsewhere. For a short while they were able to hold a United Front together (1960–2), but the tensions born in South Africa soon drove them apart again. Together with African émigré political groups from South West Africa and Southern Rhodesia, these bodies became involved in the African summit conference at Addis Ababa in May 1963, which set up the Organization of African Unity, and under it an African Liberation Committee whose patronage they both came to enjoy. Through it they began to exert pressure on the United Nations and on the World Council of Churches, aiming at the moral isolation of South Africa as a prelude to the political, economic or military overthrow of white rule. They could count on the support of refugees and political exiles calculated variously at between one and five thousand by 1964. As will be shown later, the fortunes of the A.N.C. and the P.A.C. in exile were to vary considerably [see p. 388]; but neither would be able to muster the organisational and military strength to enable it to take immediate advantage of the next great South-African crisis – the Soweto unrest of 1976 [see p. 389].

The embattled South African Government had both a new kind of internal security problem and an external logistic problem of unpredictable long-term proportions. It tackled the former with a wider range of security laws touching many aspects of life. Wide discretionary powers were given to a new Publications Control Board in 1963 to prohibit the importation of works and films considered offensive, harmful to public morals, blasphemous, or prejudicial to state security or good order. The press escaped direct governmental control by drawing up its own code of conduct and establishing its own Press Board of Reference in 1962, to deal with complaints of misreporting. After Sharpeville the South African Broadcasting Corporation, a public utility, changed its neutral political stance for an 'editorial' policy more openly favourable to the policies of the Government. The Defence Act was amended in 1961 to enable the Government to handle the threat of internal disorder more effectively. The period of military training was extended, and provision made for the creation of a police reserve, in the same year. When B. J. Vorster took over the Department of Justice in 1962, the power of the police in the interrogation and control of suspected persons, and even over potential state witnesses, were greatly widened to help them uncover plots and obtain convictions. By successive stages, authority was granted to the police to detain suspects without putting them on a charge, and under conditions of solitary confinement, for single or successive periods of twelve days (1962), ninety days (1963), one hundred and eighty days (1965), and later for an unlimited period if authorised by a judge (1966), and even without such authorisation (1976). Sabotage and terrorism were defined as statutory offences. In 1962 the former was made to cover tampering with property, the illegal possessions of offensive weapons, and unlawful entry, as well as acts of wilful destruction; while terrorism was defined in 1966 to include training for terrorist activity, furthering the objects of communism, and committing acts of sabotage. The Government took power in 1962 to place individuals under partial or total house arrest, and this, when added to its existing powers of banning, banishing and listing individuals or organisations, gave it an overwhelming advantage in its conflict with active opposition movements within the frontiers. Restrictions imposed under the Prisons Act of 1959, which made the unauthorised reporting of conditions in prisons illegal, together with the power of the State to hold suspects incommunicado, made it impossible to corroborate or refute allegations of third-degree treatment of prisoners, except in a very few cases, though such allegations were commonly made and as commonly denied by the authorities. Some detainees committed suicide. The situation would soon arise, as the deaths in detention continued to mount, where suicide ceased to be a convincing explanation of why some deaths occurred, but where the conditions under which the detainees were held made any other explanation impossible to demonstrate [see p. 545]. The story of Adam Tas no longer made sensational reading.

Before long, the new draconian legal system achieved the results intended. Umkonto we Sizwe was broken after the capture of Mandela in August 1962, followed by the seizure the following July of its other leaders at Rivonia, near Johannesburg. They were tried in 1964, and sentenced to life imprisonment on conviction for sabotage, the State having withdrawn the charge of treason. Those members of the African Resistance Movement who had failed to flee the country were sentenced shortly afterwards to jail terms of up to fifteen years. In 1964 the security police also managed to infiltrate the underground Communist Party, and secured the conviction of its leaders for belonging to an unlawful organisation. One of them was Bram Fischer, a member of a prominent O.F.S. Afrikaner family, who had himself defended the Rivonia trialists. Fischer, after being allowed out of South Africa on bail to fight an important case for his country before the Privy Council, returned honourably to stand trial. When it became clear that police infiltration of the movement had established the State's case, he estreated bail and went into hiding to continue his fight, a Marxist for whom treason, patriotism and humanity were synonymous terms in the South African context. He was recaptured in November 1965 and sentenced to life imprisonment, to be released on compassionate grounds only shortly before his death from cancer in 1975.

After the retrial in 1966 of a number of Africans previously convicted and imprisoned for A.N.C. activities in 1963–4, the political trial became endemic to South African public life, despite the growing efficiency of the police in bringing activists to book, and the phenomenally long sentences imposed on those found guilty of political crimes [see p. 545]. From that date until 1985, without exception, every year was scarred by at least one major political trial.

15.8   THE MURDER OF DR VERWOERD

In the general election of 1966, the National Party increased its majority to 86, winning 126 seats to 39 won by the U.P. and one by the Progressives. The fifth anniversary of the Republic occurred two months later. The country was experiencing unprecedented economic growth, and to some extent overseas confidence in South Africa as a stable society seemed to have returned. But on 6 September, just before he was due to make a major policy speech, Dr Verwoerd was stabbed to death by a white parliamentary messenger as he sat at his desk in the House of Assembly. As with the earlier attempted assassination, the man was declared insane. To the nation at large, it seemed as if the architect of public policy had been suddenly removed, for although Verwoerd's critics within the National Party had become more outspoken of late, both on the right and on the left, there was a disposition on both sides of the House to view the recovery since Sharpeville as in a real sense his personal achievement.

His sudden removal, however, left no apparent political vacuum and hardly caused a hiatus in the continuity of government policy. The succession passed, by unanimous vote of the caucus after B. J. Schoeman, the Party's elder statesman, had withdrawn, to the Minister of Justice, B. J. Vorster. And the new Government would soon show clearly that Nationalist policies did not depend, in essence, on the brainwaves or idiosyncrasies of individuals, but on the collective determination of Party leaders and of top civil servants who had themselves advanced to positions of authority only after careful ideological screening.

16 Modification and Backfire, 1964–78

16.1 LIVING WITH THE TOMLINSON REPORT: INDUSTRIAL LICENSING AND RURAL RESETTLEMENT

The credibility of the Nationalist Government among its supporters depended at all times on its ability to find a workable solution to its population problems which would enable the white people to survive as a distinct community and at the same time permit other communities to share the decencies of life. The publication of Tomlinson's long-term plan was a source of confidence to it, though Verwoerd was not enthusiastic about the Tomlinson Commission, which had been appointed by his predecessor, Jansen. The Commission's chairman knew this well; but by the time the Commission had completed its work in 1955, it was able to make recommendations confirming the broad direction of government policy, while dissenting from it in key details. The main objections of the Government to the Report were set out in a White Paper in 1956. With regard to land policy, it rejected Tomlinson's proposal to allow individual tenure in tribal areas, or give preference to it in the released areas, or to allow the purchase of more than one lot by an individual, because it was not anxious to encourage commercial farming by individual Africans at the cost of 'the proper settlement of many'. It also held its hand over the immediate development of mining enterprise, and over the immediate setting up of a development corporation for the Reserves, but saw these as long-term projects. It strongly supported the principle of labour-intensive industries on the European side of the borders, but rejected absolutely the idea of allowing white-owned capital into the Bantu areas, thus siding with Young and Prinsloo, two of the commissioners, against the majority. But what was accepted by Strijdom's Government and by Verwoerd's was the recommendation to diversify the economy so as to enable the Reserves to house the 'surplus' black population of the white urban areas and the white farms. Verwoerd accordingly took the first hesitant steps towards the implementation of the Tomlinson Report.

The Tomlinson Commission thought that industrialists could be attracted to the neighbourhood of the Reserves to provide work for Africans taken off the land, by the lure of cheaper transport, power, water and African housing. It took the Verwoerd Government until 1964 to realise that Tomlinson had underrated the difficulty. The Government therefore tried to speed up industrial decentralisation by offering significant tax concessions, help over the erection of factories, and exemptions from minimum wage determinations and the statutory protection of public against private transport, to those industrialists who were willing to move to the border areas. But by the end of 1966, rather less than 45,000 new jobs for Africans had been created in the border areas and the Reserves, a slower rate of progress in ten years than the Tomlinson Commission required in one. This was in spite of the passage of a Bantu Investment Corporation Act in 1959 and a Bantu Homelands Development Corporations Act in 1965, enabling the Government to set up and capitalise individual entrepreneurs and a Development Corporation in each of the Bantu homelands. By prohibiting white-owned risk capital, in opposition to the recommendations of the Tomlinson Commission, the Government prevented the rapid diversification of the economy within the Reserves, and therefore their capacity to absorb more people.

To win the propaganda battle, Verwoerd had needed to be able to demonstrate that his policies could be effective in turning the flow of African migration back from the urban areas; but on his own statements it was too early for this to have happened. On the eve of his assumption of the premiership, he said in Parliament that it would take twenty years before the urban African population started to decrease. He did little before 1966 to help bring about that result, though an attempt was made in the Bantu Laws Amendment Act of 1964 to extend influx control beyond the urban areas to include peri-urban districts, (now known collectively as 'prescribed areas'), in order to plug gaps in the system of controls. His Urban Bantu Councils Act of 1961, by allowing for the democratic election of new bodies, with African chairmen and some administrative duties, to replace the Advisory Boards, was a measure curiously at variance with the terms of his Promotion of Bantu Self-Government Act of 1959, which aimed to give authority in urban locations to representatives of Homeland chiefs so as to promote awareness among residents of their identity with homeland areas in the Reserves and to play down electoral aspects. Because the Urban Bantu Councils Act seemed likely to promote rather than undermine the Africans' sense of belonging to the urban area, it tended to lose favour with the white and essentially conformist Institute of Administrators of Non-European Affairs, which had a growing voice in the detailed formulation of policy.

The Vorster Ministry was the first government which had to live with the implications of the Tomlinson Report, whose predictions of black population growth were shown to be extremely inaccurate by the evidence of the 1970 census. Projections made in 1972 on the basis of that census report gave a total African population of 36 million at the very least by the year 2000, as against the outside figure of 21.36 million calculated by the Tomlinson Commission. Subsequent estimates for the year 2000, by the Department of Statistics in 1976 and by Van Tonder and Mostert in 1980, gave figures of 34.7 million and 30.4 million respectively (Lötter).

Aware of the previous government's failure to achieve rapid industrial decentralisation, Vorster's Cabinet turned to the device of industrial

Table 1   Population growth in relation to the predictions of the Tomlinson Report

A. *Total Population by Registration Groups, 1911–80*

	1911	1951	1970	1980
African	4,019,006	8,560,083	15,057,952	18,965,327
White	1,276,242	2,641,689	3,752,528	4,453,273
Coloured	525,943	1,103,016	2,018,453	2,554,039
Asian	152,203	366,664	620,436	794,639
Total	5,973,394	12,671,452	21,448,169	23,771,970

B. *Recent Population Estimates for 1980 and 2000*

	African	White	Coloured	Asian	Total
1980 Census	18,965,327	4,453,273	2,554,039	794,639	23,771,970
1980 D of S	20,365,000	4,703,000	2,721,000	829,000	28,312,000
1980 L & M	19,643,000	9,705,000	2,539,000	813,000	27,494,000
2000 D of S	34,748,000	5,631,000	4,699,000	1,270,000	46,348,000
2000 L & M	30,441,000	5,209,000	3,572,000	1,128,000	40,550,000

Sources   H. Sonnabend, in E. Hellmann (ed.), *Handbook on Race Relations* (1949) p. 13; *Report of the Tomlinson Commission* (Summary) p. 29; M. Horrell *et al.* (eds.) *Survey of Race Relations* (1973, 1981); *Monthly Bulletins of Statistics*; J. M. Lötter, 'The South African Population, its growth and expected trends', *RSA 2000* 3, 2 (1981) 1–19.

D of S = Department of Statistics Projection, 1976.
L & M = Lötter and Mostert's Projection, 1980.

licensing and carried a Physical Planning and Utilization of Resources Act in 1967, under which they could hold up any new industrial development in what were termed 'controlled areas', or impose conditions regarding the employment of labour, the building of houses, and the utilisation of water or other resources in them. The southern Transvaal and the Port Elizabeth–Uitenhage regions were soon proclaimed as controlled, and applications for the employment of Africans in new enterprises in these areas were turned down or reduced in scale, employment for 61,908 extra individuals being refused to the end of March 1973. Meanwhile decentralisation was further encouraged by the positive offer, to industrialists who set up in the border areas, of up to five year's income tax exemption, together with specially favourable loan rates, road and rail tariff rebates, and other concessions. The Government, abandoning the policy of the 1956 White Paper on the Tomlinson Report, also offered to consider requests to develop industries inside the Homelands by white entrepreneurs who were prepared to operate on an agency basis, without acquiring ownership of

Table 1 cont.   C. *A Graph to illustrate A and B*

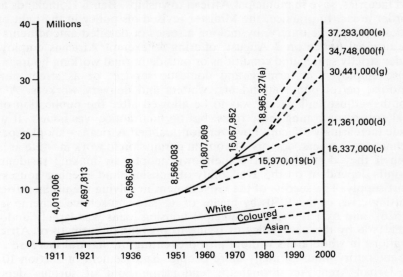

(a) = total African population, 1980 census
(b) = African population less Transkei and Bophutatswana, 1980 census
(c) = Tomlinson Commission's Projection A, 1955
(d) = Tomlinson Commission's Projection B, 1955
(e) = J. L. Sadie's Projection, 1972
(f) = Department of Statistics Projection, 1976 (D. of S.)
(g) = Lötter and Mostert's Projection, 1980 (L & M)

land or establishing links with foreign interests, and who would accept fixed-period agreements only, and give preference to the employment of Africans over whites. In consequence of these and earlier concessions, new jobs for 85,554 Africans were found in the border areas and the Homelands in the years 1960–72. But this figure of under 8,000 jobs a year was well short of the 50,000 jobs a year deemed necessary by Tomlinson, and it caused the Government concern because there was no evidence of acceleration in the latter years in the rate of employment, nor even as rapid a growth rate in these areas as in the country as a whole (Bell).

The Government tried at the same time to restrict the African presence in the white areas by whittling down residential rights and encouraging labour migrancy. An Act of 1970 empowered the Minister of Bantu Administration to prohibit the employment of an African in any specified area, or in any specified class of employment or trade, or in the service of any specified employer or class of employer. In terms of these powers, the Minister gave a month's notice on 3 April 1970 of his intention to ban the employment of Africans as counter assistants in shops and cafés; as professional or commercial receptionists; as telephone operators in shops, offices, factories and hotels; or as clerks, cashiers or typists in shops, offices and factories, save in municipal African townships, Bantu Homelands and Border areas. In practice, the Minister revised his policy in the light of a widespread public outcry, by making a series of detailed amendments to the original notice on 7 August, offering to exempt Africans employed under strictly segregated conditions or outside normal working hours, and those employed in farming and domestic service, or as street news-vendors, petrol pump attendants, waiters and delivery workers. A six months' adjustment period was to be allowed after the publication of a final notice confirming these rules; but no final notice was issued. It was made increasingly difficult, however, for qualified Africans – shopkeepers, technicians, lawyers, doctors – to obtain permission to work in white areas, even if they desired to serve their own people, by making residential permits dependent on the availability of housing, and keeping houses in short supply. The success of the Government in solving the urban African housing crisis in the 1950s by means of its 'site-and-service' scheme [see p. 526], and by authorising municipal housing loans was largely undone after 1966 by the new policy of trying to prevent the growth of African locations in white areas without also preventing the natural increase and the migratory influx of many more people. Enforcement of Section 10 of the Urban Areas Act through the 'endorsement out' of 'surplus' depen-dents of working people did result in a slight reduction of the total African population of the Cape Peninsula in 1967–8, and may well have helped to peg the growth of the urban African population in the Republic as a whole, for over 450,000 Africans from the white areas were resettled in the Homelands down to the end of 1968 (Baldwin), and any Section 10 rights they may have had were thus forfeited. But the Government dropped the plan, put forward in a Bill of 1969, to prohibit the further acquisition of Section 10 rights by anybody, on account of strong opposition from municipalities. Though the number of Africans increased in the white areas, however, they came to consist more and more of contract workers without residential rights, living in hostels or 'bachelor' quarters rather than private homes, or – on account of the growing housing shortage – as lodgers in the homes of others.

To accommodate Africans endorsed out of the white areas, whether from the towns or from the farms, where the squatter population was steadily increasing, the Government accelerated the development of Bantu towns and resettlement villages in the Homelands, laying down the main lines of this policy in instructions to magistrates issued in December 1967. R44.5 million were set aside for the development of rural townships in the Bantu Administration budget of 1966, representing just over half the total Department budget. Municipalities were given authority to make contri-butions from local revenue to Bantu Homeland development, and 80 per cent of the profits of municipal liquor sales to Africans was earmarked for this purpose. In 1968 it was officially stated that plans for 105 such villages had been approved, and that 54 were under construction, 55,000 houses having been built so far at a cost of R31 million.

Though seen by the Government as necessary to the implementation of

17   Don Kenyon of the East London *Daily Dispatch* catches the spirit of the liberal critique of apartheid policy in the Vorster era

its policy, the resettlement villages received a great deal of adverse publicity, above all as a result of the publication of Cosmas Desmond's *The Discarded People* in 1970; but the banning of Desmond in 1971 helped to scotch public debate by rendering his book unquotable. Critics of the policy focused attention on the manner of the removals (above all at Limehill, Natal, in 1968), and on the lack of amenities in the villages, especially in the early stages of settlement, on the general lack of jobs other than low-paid unskilled work, on the inadequacy of the statutory old-age pensions for Africans, which then amounted on average to R5 a month, and on the insufficiency of the rations supplied to non-pensioners for sustaining health. There was evidence by 1973 that in some of the villages, notably Sada, Ilinge and Dimbaza in the Ciskei, amenities and job opportunities were beginning to improve; but in the case of the great majority of settlements little information had been published. In its public utterances, however, the Government began to profess the intention of providing proper amenities in the future before it started to move people. Verwoerd's dictum that the care of the black aged was the responsibility of the extended family was quietly abandoned, but the scale of relief remained very low in relation to the rapidly increasing cost of living. The rate of removals was to increase enormously during the next decade [see pp. 403–7].

The Vorster Ministry made two important changes in the government of urban blacks. The first was an Act of 1971, which vested all urban Bantu administration in sixteen Administration Boards (later reduced to twelve) spread throughout the Republic, all reporting directly to Pretoria. This Act entirely removed responsibility from the town councils over their own African locations, but required them to contribute the income from their Bantu Revenue Accounts in the normal way, and to make the services of their officials available to the Boards on a *pro rata* payment basis. This law would generate further problems [see p. 529], but when it came into force in July 1973, the duality of control which had characterised urban African administration since 1910 was removed at a stroke, and the Government had an instrument in its hands for controlling the growth of urban African townships, directing the flow of contract workers (which was simplified by the Act), and overcoming either opposition or inertia in the local authorities. The second development, occurring after the Soweto riots of 1976–7 was the replacement of Urban Bantu Councils by new Community Councils, in an attempt to give urban blacks more local power (for example, control over their troublesome schools) as a pretext for excluding them from a new political deal to be worked out for the Coloured and Indian peoples.

16.2   THE EXTENSION OF HOMELAND SELF-GOVERNMENT: THE FIRST REACTIONS OF HOMELAND LEADERS AND LIBERAL WHITES

By way of compensation, the African control over the government of the Homelands was increased, as attempts were made through the Bantu Homelands Citizenship Act of 1970 to attach the citizenship of one or other of the Homelands to all Africans in the Republic (for domestic as distinct from international purposes), even if they had never lived outside the 'white' area. The Bantu Homelands Constitution Act of 1971 was enabling legislation, to empower the State President to confer self-government on any of the eight Territorial Authorities by proclamation, as had happened in the Transkei. In terms of this law, the Ciskei became a self-governing territory on 28 July 1972, with a Legislative Assembly of fifty and an elected Cabinet under the leading Mfengu chief, Justice Mabandla. Zululand became the self-governing though fragmented territory of Kwazulu on 30 March 1972, under its own King, Chief Zwelithini Goodwill Bhekuzulu. The sprawling territory of Bophutatswana, stretching in eight main territorial enclaves from north-east of Pretoria across to the borderlands east and south of Botswana, and taking in the Thaba 'Nchu enclave in the eastern Orange Free State, became self-governing in May 1972, with Chief Lucas Mangope's Bophutatswana National Party clear victors in the first election. Lebowa, Homeland of the northern (Transvaal) Sotho, followed in September. The policy of Homeland self-government had to be seen to be on the move, under the dedicated direction of M. C. Botha, Vorster's Minister of Bantu Affairs.

In granting self-government to the Territorial Authorities, the Government of the Republic had no intention of sowing dragons' teeth, and there was no real indication by the eleventh year of the Vorster Ministry that

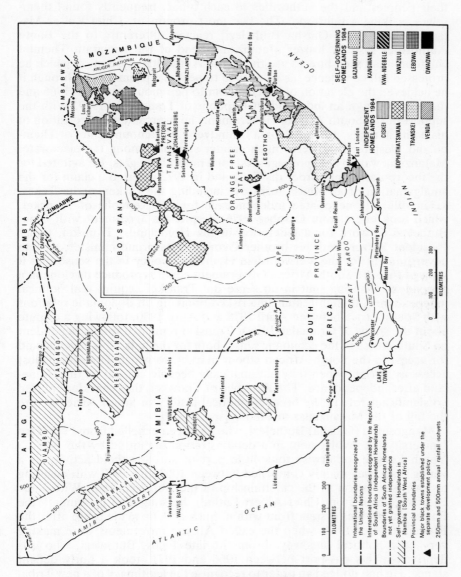

Map 10   African homelands in 1984

they had done so. But the black leaders of the new Homeland Governments, like chiefs in the past who had had the difficult task of interpreting their peoples and the authorities to each other, frequently found themselves walking a tightrope. The two most prominent, Chief Kaiser Matanzima and Chief Gatsha Buthelezi, reacted differently to the Bantu Authorities system. Kaizer Matanzima, head of the Emigrant Thembu chiefdom, had seen how to use the Bantu Authorities system, in which he professed full confidence, as an avenue to personal promotion. Through it he achieved the elevation of his chiefdom to paramount status in 1966 and the presidency of an independent Republic of Transkei in 1979. With the support of the South African Government, he overcame the opposition of his political rivals, notably Sabata Dalindyebo, Paramount Chief of Thembuland, despite the latter's much greater support among the electorate. Matanzima was an able propagandist for Transkeian rights. He agitated for the incorporation of border districts, and in 1972 asserted a claim for the amalgamation of all Xhosa territory, including the Ciskei, under Transkeian rule. He negotiated independence for the Republic of Transkei, which took effect from October 1976, despite his agreement with Chief Buthelezi to work for a federation of the Homelands. Transkei, under President Kaizer, with his brother George as its prime minister, was an advertisement for the Verwoerdian Homeland policy in the sense that it showed that the South African Government could reproduce its clone in a dependent offspring; but in no sense did Transkei acquire real political independence, though Matanzima risked breaking off diplomatic relations with South Africa between April 1978 and April 1980, following a dispute about the status of Griqualand East. Transkei remained totally dependent on South Africa in the economic sense, both for the bulk of its revenue and for access to the South African labour market, to which Transkeians lost access as of right when they automatically became citizens of the Homeland after independence. The Republic of Transkei, thus shackled, played no significant role in the broader political history of South Africa before the fall of the Matanzimas in 1986–7 [see p. 417].

Mangosuthu (Gatsha) Buthelezi, who had been expelled from Fort Hare University for involvement in a demonstration organised by the A.N.C. Youth League, otherwise took little part in anti-apartheid activity as a young man, was mainly concerned between 1953 and 1960 with ensuring his own succession to the chieftainship of the Buthelezi clan. With some encouragement from Chief Albert Luthuli, he sought to manipulate the Bantu Authorities system from within. Such a tactic made sense after the Rivonia trial of 1964, when the exiled African movements were making very little political headway. From the late 1960s, Buthelezi, who was deprived of his passport between 1966 and 1971, took a fairly defiant stance. He first dodged an order to recognise the legitimacy of a new Tribal Authority in his own Mahlabatini district (Mzala). Then, with brilliant sleight of hand, he ensured that, when a Territorial Authority was created for Zululand in 1972, it was based not on the supposedly traditional autocratic chiefdom in Zululand, but on the historical fiction that decision-making should rest on the head of the Buthelezi clan who had traditionally been the chief minister. Once in power, he repeatedly worked through the KwaZulu Legislative Assembly, which he dominated, to block the State's attempts to use King Goodwill as a puppet (in contrast to the situation in the Transkei, where Matanzima, who supported the Bantustan system, was used by the South African state to break the power of his paramount ruler, Sabata Dalidyebo, who tried to defy it).

Buthelezi pulled off this coup during the years when the Black Consciousness movement was beginning to emerge under the leadership of Steve Biko [see p. 378], and for a short while it seemed as if these two leaders would work together, that the Zulu cultural movement which Buthelezi restored to life in 1975, *Inkatha YaKwaZulu*, could develop into a broad black nationalist movement rather than an exclusively Zulu organisation (Mare). This was because, by 1976, Buthelezi had managed to draw together nearly all the Homeland leaders, as well as the (Coloured) Labour Party under the Rev. Allan Hendrickse, and the Indian Council under A. M. Rajab, behind the idea of a national convention to forestall the territorial disintegration of South Africa as envisaged in Verwoerd's Homeland policy, to give the Bantustans consolidated territories through the incorporation of key regions, and to ensure their effective participation in the government of South Africa under a federal system. Buthelezi was himself demanding the incorporation into KwaZulu of the new port of Richards Bay, as well as Empangeni and other white towns, and using the expulsion of Zulu labour tenants from northern Natal to resettlement villages in Nqutu and elsewhere as his justification for demanding more territory. His idea of a federation of the Homelands met initial resistance from the leadership of Ciskei and Bophutatswana; but all the Homelands except QwaQwa and Venda were represented at a meeting in Umtata in November 1973 to discuss a future federation of the Homelands. Almost immediately afterwards a further meeting at Bulugha, near East London, attended also by Coloured and Indian leaders and by the Progressive Party, heard Buthelezi propose the formation of a 'Federal Union of Autonomous States of Southern Africa'.

Behind the Bulugha conference was a decision by two bodies strongly critical of government policy, the South African Council of Churches and the Christian Institute, to set in motion a Study Project on Christianity in Apartheid Society (S.P.R.O.C.A.S.) in 1969. This body appointed a commission to discuss South Africa's political alternatives, whose report, published in 1972, was of interest mainly for its critique of Westminster-style confrontational politics, as these had been taken for granted, for example, by the Progressive Party's Molteno Report [see p. 356], urging that it had avoided facing the real causes of political instability in plural societies. At the Bulugha conference most speakers made a point of stressing federalism as the best approach to South Africa's constitutional problems, and Chief Buthelezi's proposal envisaged a society in the government of which all elements could participate. It was significant that, as a result of continuing discussions with the Progressive leadership over the next few years, Chief Buthelezi should have managed to win over Inkatha, to the support of a constitutional system based on the control of power, through procedures designed to promote consensus, rather than the exercise of simple majoritarian rule. This would constitute his chief claim to be taken seriously during the period of flux in South African constitutional thinking between 1973 and 1983.

But Buthelezi's challenge to the Bantustan concept induced Vorster to convene three meetings with the Bantustan leaders between March 1974 and October 1976, at the last of which he roundly rejected the suggestion of a new national convention, and in doing so forced the black leadership into a posture of confrontation with his Government. Immediately afterwards Buthelezi, in company with the heads of Lebowa and Gazankulu, and various Black Consciousness and trade union leaders, met to plan a Black Unity Front which would eventually grow by January 1978 into the South African Black Alliance. But by that time the initiative for which Buthelezi had been largely responsible had been overtaken by two key events: the first was the Transkei's decision to opt for independence, the second the outbreak of the Soweto disturbances in June 1976.

16.3   BLACK CONSCIOUSNESS

Within the Republic proper, as distinct from the Homelands, the banning of the A.N.C. and the P.A.C. in 1960 had left Africans relatively voiceless, and utterly vulnerable to the new, large-scale social engineering which the Homeland policy implied. But there were signs during the early 1970s of a new approach to politics less optimistically liberal than Luthuli's A.N.C. had been before Sharpeville, more realistic in its appraisal of political forces than Sobukwe's rival movement, and less vulnerable to the charge of collaborationism than the Homeland leaders in general. This was the approach through the philosophy of Black Consciousness, which may have taken inspiration from notions of Black Theology and Black Power, which had their origin in the United States, or from the challenging writings of Frantz Fanon in Algeria, though its aim, as Gerhart has well expressed it, was 'not to trigger a spontaneous Fanonesque eruption of the masses into violent action, but rather to rebuild and recondition the mind of the oppressed in such a way that they would be ready forcefully to demand what was rightfully theirs'.

The key figure in this movement was Steve Biko, who had been born in King William's Town in 1946 and attended the Catholic mission school at Mariannhill, near Durban, and then studied medicine at Natal University before devoting himself fully to politics. A man of refreshing candour and real leadership qualities, Biko saw a need for the black man to win psychological emancipation after generations of conditioning to see himself as the underdog. This meant freeing himself from the tutelage of white liberals, who assumed too easily that blacks wanted merely to become incorporated in a social system dominated by white cultural values. Biko looked beyond his own fellow Africans to include in his Black spectrum all the oppressed race groups of South Africa. He was scornful of the Bantustan policy as the policy of the oppressor, and ruled out the possibility of

even a Buthelezi being able to operate effectively from such a platform –
perhaps overrating the extent to which Buthelezi was in fact collaborating
with the system, and misrepresenting his position as narrowly Zulu in
focus. From about 1972, Inkatha and Black Consciousness as expressions
of African political strategy tended to go different ways; yet both, in
contradistinction to the A.N.C., were at least operating on South African
soil.

A host of new organisations sprang into life as a result of the spread of
Black Consciousness. The South African Students Organisation (S.A.S.O.)
broke away from N.U.S.A.S. in 1968, to provide black students with a
vehicle entirely their own. The Black People's Convention was formed in
1972 to operate on the political front, while Black Community Programmes were set up to promote black initiatives in the provision of health
and welfare services. A lot seemed to be going for Black Consciousness
when it first emerged. For a brief spell it even enjoyed some support in
government circles, at least so far as its withdrawal from N.U.S.A.S. was
concerned. But it ran into troubled waters when several of its leaders,
including Biko himself, were banned in March 1973 at the time of the
Durban strikes [see p. 515], while both S.A.S.O. and the B.P.C. attracted
the wrath of the Government for their indecent haste in welcoming the
installation of a Frelimo Government in Mozambique in September 1974.
Nine of their leaders were put on trial under the Terrorism Act for
fomenting student disorders on black campuses. They were convicted and
sent to Robben Island; but there can be little doubt that their boisterous
conduct in the dock did much to stimulate the mood of defiance which
would dominate the resistance movement which erupted in Soweto two
years later.

16.4 THE END OF INDIRECT REPRESENTATION FOR COLOURED PEOPLE AND THE FAILURE OF THE COLOURED REPRESENTATIVE COUNCIL

Vorster's Government wound up the defective Union Council for Coloured
Affairs and tried to set up a completely segregated political system for the
Coloured people, centred on a Coloured Persons' Representative Council,
in 1968. Unlike the Transkeian legislature, the C.P.R.C. had a majority of
elective members (40) over government nominees (20). In the first general
election held on 24 September 1969, 26 of the elective seats in a 48.7 per
cent poll went to the opposition Labour Party of M. D. Arendse, which
rejected the notion of a separate 'Coloured' identity and participated in
order to break the system. The Federal Coloured People's Party led by
Tom Swartz, which hoped, by accepting the Government's ethnic premises, to win improvements for the Coloured people, obtained only 8 seats;
but this was just sufficient for it to take power with the support of the 20
nominees, 13 of whom had been defeated in the election.

In August 1974, Sonny Leon, Arendse's successor, carried a motion
demanding representation in the Assembly and the abolition of the

C.P.R.C., which the chairman declined to accept as a motion of confidence. Leon initially turned down Vorster's challenge to take over the chairmanship of the Council. But in the 1975 election the Labour Party won an outright majority with 31 of the 40 seats in a 37.5 per cent poll. Leon then accepted office, again refused to 'compromise for anything less than full citizenship and direct representation', and his party threw out the Coloured Affairs budget. The drafters of the Council's constitution had anticipated such an emergency by enabling the Government to dismiss the chairman and appoint another, whom it was beyond the competence of the Council to remove. Mrs Alathea Jansen, an independent nominee, was appointed in Leon's place in November 1975. She proved more amenable to the Government, and the budget was forced through. But the image of the C.P.R.C. had been predictably destroyed. The F.C.P.P. lost confidence in its image under Swartz's successor, W. J. Bergins, and renamed itself the Freedom Party. Even Labour began to sense that the real political movement in the Coloured world was now happening outside the formal structures.

The feelings of Coloured people were further strained by developments on the Group Areas front. The Minister of Community Development revealed in the Assembly on 21 February 1973 that, whereas only 1,513 white families had had to move because they lived in the wrong group area, 44,885 Coloured and 27,694 Indian families had been moved by the end of 1972: 135 white families, 27,448 Coloured and 10,641 Indian still had to move, as well as 1,162 Chinese. In terms of geographical realities, the Coloured people of the western Cape had seen the central city area of Cape Town proclaimed for the white group in 1965, which meant that permits had to be obtained by Coloured people to attend the traditionally multi-racial occasions – concerts, receptions, public meetings, and so on – in the Cape Town city hall or on the Grand Parade. District Six, Kalk Bay and Simonstown were all proclaimed white Group Areas in 1966–7, which involved the displacement of families whose ancestors had lived there since the days of the Dutch East India Company, and the removal of fisherfolk from their homes near the sea to new homes on the Cape Flats. The construction of substitute Coloured townships went ahead at Factreton, Kensington, Bonteheuwel and Bishop Lavis on the Flats, and longer-term plans were laid for large Coloured settlements at Mitchell's Plain behind Strandfontein on False Bay, and at a new site called Atlantis, near Mamre, to the north of greater Cape Town; but the new settlements developed many of the problems of displaced communities, and a massive housing shortage (authoritatively calculated at over 43,000 houses in 1971) was in part the result of the enforced sale of Coloured homes in proclaimed white Group Areas. District Six, in Cape Town, and South End, in Port Elizabeth, were condemned for demolition – a testimony in uncertain proportions to the hard-heartedness of white political ideology, and the hard-headedness of white entrepreneurial ambition. Several large shanty towns developed on the Cape Flats.

The Coloured people were given generous opportunities for finding wage-earning employment in the western Cape through the proclamation in January 1957 of the area west of Aliwal North and the line of the Fish and Kat rivers as a Coloured labour preference area. This meant that Coloured employees were theoretically to be appointed in preference to African wherever possible, even in Port Elizabeth, where the Coloured population was a small fraction of the African, and the latter was growing fast.

In 1972, the Government abolished Coloured representation on Cape municipal councils by means of a provincial ordinance, and substituted nominated consultative committees, provided for under a Cape ordinance of 1963. Some of these were replaced by elective management committees, with a view to the eventual separation of Coloured and white municipalities in each urban area. This was a step which made limited geographical sense in larger urban settlements but none whatever in smaller, where the task of finding and paying people qualified to perform the work of senior municipal officials proved difficult. These bodies provided a sub-structure of a kind for the Representative Council; but the Representative Council remained a body in a vacuum, predictably unattached to any defined territory which it might one day be allowed to call its own.

16.5   THE ERIKA THERON REPORT AND VORSTER'S CONSTITUTIONAL REFORM PROPOSALS, 1976–7

The Government's policy towards the Coloured people had thus led to a considerable estrangement between the two sides. Like Hertzog in the 1930s, therefore, and for very similar reasons, Vorster appointed a commission, this time under Professor Erika Theron of Stellenbosch, to look at the problems again.

The Theron Commission began its work in March 1973, and reported in June 1976. A minority of its members were Coloured. Its recommendations are noteworthy for their departure from the hard segregationist line which had been typical of governmental attitudes to Coloured affairs since 1948, even if – as was hardly surprising – a reaffirmation of certain assumptions, such as the acceptance of segregation under the Group Areas Act, and of separate school educational systems, was largely taken for granted. The Commission was not happy about the inadequate availability of land for Coloured people, and about the poor provision for health, housing and welfare facilities. It proposed the abandonment of rigid apartheid through, for example, the admission of Coloured farmers to agricultural cooperatives with full rights, the admission of Coloured pupils to white private schools and universities if the institutions so desired, and the appointment of Coloured people to regional welfare boards and to the performing arts councils of the provinces. It also urged the total removal of government control over mixed white and Coloured access to theatres as performers or members of the audience, and the selection of sporting teams on merit save at the club level, where local options should apply. This was itself a striking departure from the decision taken by Vorster in 1968 to ban the visit of an English cricket team because a Cape Coloured cricketer, Basil d'Oliviera, had been selected to play in it, even though Vorster himself had already begun to move away from a rigid racist attitude to sport by that time.

At the level of constitutional change, the Theron Commission also broke some new ground. It attacked the Coloured Representative Council as an utterly inadequate legislative organ, lacking a basis of legitimacy in the community, lacking even a defined area of legislative competence from which other government law-making bodies could be excluded; a body whose petitions, like those of the Natives Representative Council in earlier years, tended to be acted upon only if they were inconsequential, and watered down or ignored if they touched upon real grievances. The Prime Minister had himself met the Federal Party leadership in January 1975 and offered to give the C.R.C. executive committee cabinet status and to experiment with a consultative Cabinet Council in which his own ministers and members of the executive of the South African Indian Council would also sit. He was also prepared to include Coloured people on statutory bodies such as the Group Areas Board, whose decisions affected their community. But the Prime Minister's Cabinet Council failed to take root, because the Labour Party had decided rather to make common cause with the Black Alliance brought together by Chief Buthelezi [see p. 378]. The Theron Commission therefore urged the appointment of a committee of experts to give the Coloured people a direct say, through their representatives, in matters concerning their own community, on the assumption that they would not be given their own territory and that 'the existing Westminster-based system of government will have to be changed to adapt it to the peculiar requirements of the South African plural population structure'. It did not amplify this statement with an analysis of the defects of the Westminster system, but the mere mention of it was taken in government circles, as well as those of the Opposition, as an invitation to devise another constitutional dispensation *de novo*.

Vorster initiated this process of constitutional change in 1977 by appointing a committee consisting of the four National Party provincial chairmen and the ministers of Bantu, Coloured and Indian Affairs, under the leadership of P. W. Botha, chairman of the Party in the Cape. This committee's proposals were included in the Party's election programme in November. Their plan made provision for three separate parliaments, one for whites, one for Coloured people, and one for Indians, each with its own prime minister and cabinet, and with authority to legislate for its own people alone. There was no provision for a parliament for Africans, who were to be catered for on the basis of Homeland independence. Common interest legislation would be referred upwards to a Council of Cabinets (modelled, presumably, on the Joint Cabinet Council of 1975), which would be presided over by the State President, who would thus have executive powers. The State President was to be elected by a college consisting of representatives from each of the three parliaments in proportion to their numerical ratio (50 whites, 25 Coloured and 13 Indians). The State President was also to be assisted by an advisory President's Council, consisting of white, Coloured and Indian experts. There were also to be white, Coloured and Indian local authorities, and regional administrations of some kind at the intermediate level. In so far as they brought Coloured people and Indians directly into the central legislative process, the proposals were innovatory; but when viewed in the light of the actual distribution of power, which in the last resort was left firmly in white hands, and in the light of the blanket powers which were to be conferred on the State President (who would almost certainly be the choice of the ruling white National Party), it was a very cautious document indeed. This was reflected in a statement to the press on 5 November by Dr Connie Mulder, Transvaal leader of the Party and a member of the committee, that

South Africa has found a magic formula for making cooperation with the Coloureds and Indians possible. The new Constitutional plan is an honest attempt at being fair towards everybody who will be in South Africa after the Homelands have obtained their independence . . . [yet] the policy is not a policy of abdication for whites and will not lead to it.

Mulder would later change his mind, and oppose the new constitutional dispensation after its amendment in subtle though minor ways after a political scandal in which he was directly involved provided extraneous reasons for doing so [see pp. 394–6, 428–34].

16.6 VORSTER AND THE OPPOSITION: THE EXTRUSION OF THE HERTZOGITES AND THE HARRYING OF THE LIBERALS

In so far as Nationalist governments toyed with changes of a relatively liberal kind, they were likely to arouse the concern of right-wing elements inside and outside their own ranks, who were quick to respond not so much to the immediate threats to white dominance, which in the case of Vorster's proposals were minimal, as to the indirect dangers which might ensue from such policy changes in the long term. This would be the chief tactical problem for Vorster's successor. Vorster himself had a simpler kind of problem to face: that of party members who were so caught up in the Verwoerdian slipstream that they felt any modification of his policy to be a downright betrayal. Vorster had acceded to the premiership as a junior in the Party hierarchy, apparently conscious of the void left by the charismatic Verwoerd, but determined – if the Party wanted him as leader – to assert his authority. By doing so, he provoked the first major split in the Nationalist ranks since 1948.

In the squabbles which eventually led to the dismissal of three Cabinet ministers – Dr Albert Hertzog (Health), A. E. G. Trollip (Indian Affairs) and P. M. K. le Roux (Interior) – in August 1968, it is not easy to distinguish between personality discords and issues of principle. It was accompanied by contested elections for party office. Beaumont Schoeman, himself a participant in the events as a member of the editorial staff of *Hoofstad*, a new right-wing newspaper under the editorship of Vorster's colleague Dr Andries Treurnicht, traces the conflict in the first instance to a dispute within the *Akademie vir Wetenskap en Kuns* (Academy for Science and Art), as early as 1966. In that year the Hertzog Prize for literature went to Etienne le Roux for his *Sewe Dae by die Silbersteins*, a highly symbolic novel which reflected the emancipated thinking of the liberal Afrikaner *Sestiger* School. The critics of the award were also concerned about the possible cultural undermining of the Afrikaner through American Field Service scholarships and Leader Exchange programmes. They viewed with mistrust Vorster's decision to admit black ambassadors from foreign states, and his guarantees to English-speakers not to let them down if they joined the National Party, and the element of equivocation which crept into his references to possible visits by Maori rugby players. Vorster, for his part, resented attacks from the right which focused on these relatively adventurous features of his policy. It was not good for the images of a prime minister who was in the habit of telling non-Afrikaner opponents to 'put their house in order' to be told by fellow-Afrikaners that there was something wrong with his own. He referred to them in public as 'Super-Afrikaners', or as 'Watchers on the walls of Zion', and was so infuriated by their evasiveness that he even turned the Security Police on to tracing the source of anonymous press correspondence addressed to the Cabinet. The dissident *verkramptes* (narrow ones, in Wimpie de Klerk's parlance) pulled out of the Party in September 1969, and reconstituted themselves the *Herstigte* (Restored) *Nasionale Party*. Their opponents, dubbed *verligtes* (enlightened ones), remained solid behind Vorster, and enabled him to contain their challenge. He advanced the general election a year, and eliminated their influence in Parliament before they had time to organise. The Broederbond came out for the National Party, though it ought probably to have stayed out of the ring. At bottom, the issue was between ideologues who saw apartheid as a self-contained system to be defended in its totality, as Verwoerd had envisaged it, and the politicians in power who, faced with mounting pressures in the outside world, required room to manoeuvre on such issues as mixed sport, the admission of black diplomats, and the defence of South Africa's position at the U.N.. Election contests between the Nationalists and the Herstigtes in 1970 and 1974 were very bitter, and to beat his opponents Vorster had to assert himself against the liberals and the blacks on the other flank, for he could not be seen to lack the courage of his convictions and still hope to stay in power.

Criticism of the Government by Bantustan leaders and by dissident Nationalists embarrassed the Vorster Government, but did not assail it at a strategic point. But criticism by groups ideologically at variance with it, emanating from the English-language churches, press, student organisations (black as well as white), and the Liberal and Progressive Parties were harder to suffer because they questioned the moral *bona fides* of the regime. Immediately after taking power, therefore, Vorster attempted to break the inter-racial contact fostered by organisations hostile to his own policies. His Prohibition of Improper Interference Bill of 1966 was a measure to block probable Progressive victories in the forthcoming elections for Coloured seats in the Cape Provincial Council and in Parliament. The Government tried to take more power than it needed for the purpose, and phrased the Bill so as to make it illegal for a person to belong, not merely to a mixed political party, but to any kind of mixed racial organisation, the objects of which were to propagate, discuss, study or encourage political views. There was a public outcry, in which the *Burger* shared. The Government covered its tracks by appointing a select committee, and the Bill, as revised, was enacted as a Prohibition of Political Interference Act in 1968, its terms now limited to membership of political parties and attendance at political meetings, which in either case had to be uniracial. Rather than continue under conditions which made nonsense of its basic values, the Liberal Party, several of whose leaders had been served with banning orders, decided to dissolve. Though deprived of the prospect of winning Coloured seats, the Progressives had retained a toehold in the white constituencies and felt justified in continuing as a white party, but it was not until the general election of 1974 that they were able to extend their representation. On that occasion they gained seven urban seats as a result of dissension in the United Party, but could not prevent the National Party from making up some of the ground lost in 1970 as a result of Afrikaner divisions.

The English language press, described by Elaine Potter as the real Opposition in the South African political system, had long been under attack in the National Party. The leading monument to this was the twelve-volume Press Commission Report of 1964, which had taken fourteen years to produce. By accepting the establishment of the Press Board of Reference in 1962, newspapers published by members of the Newspaper Press Union had avoided the threat of censorship. In 1967, however, the State placed the editor of the *Rand Daily Mail*, Laurence Gandar, and a senior reporter, Benjamin Pogrund, on trial for publishing statements about conditions in the Republic's prisons which, though attested on oath before publication, were held to be false. The sentences on conviction were nominal, but the legal fees incurred by the newspaper in what had become a show trial amounted to about R250,000, and Gandar subsequently retired from his post under strain. On occasion, decisions of the Publications Control Board to ban books and periodicals were successfully contested in the courts, one magazine winning its eighth appeal against a decision of the Board in 1973. The Government then appointed a Commission of Inquiry, and followed this with legislation to remove the decisions of the Board from judicial review. In 1974 a new chapter opened with the first banning of a literary work in Afrikaans – André Brink's *Kennis van die Aand*.

The censorship of literary works could be counted on to arouse very strong criticism in South African writers' circles. This was hardly surprising, in view of the quality of the best South African writing to emerge from the tensions and the tragedies wrought in so many lives by the toughness of the legal system – works of which Alan Paton's *Cry, the Beloved Country* was the pioneer. To it were soon added the graphic descriptive novels of

Peter Abrahams and Ezekiel Mphahlele, the sensitive writing of Nadine Gordimer, the calculated defiance of convention by the Afrikaans-speaking *Sestigers* (School of the Sixties), of whom André Brink was one, the stage plays of Athol Fugard, and – in more recent years – the highly evocative novels of John Coetzee and Etienne van Heerden, to mention only a few. They revealed a society in which the leaders of opinion were not only wrestling publicly with the moral issues presented by their situation, but were also free to do so to an extent which would not have been possible in Nazi Germany, and could only be done at considerable risk in Soviet Russia.

The English-language universities had fallen foul of the Government over the admission of non-white people as students in the 1950s, and lost this fight without abandoning their objection to this kind of interference by the State in their affairs. Student opposition to government policy, both in relation to the universities and to public affairs in general, remained vocal, above all in the ranks of the National Union of South African Students (N.U.S.A.S.), though hardly at all in the Afrikaans universities, whose Afrikaanse Studentebond (A.S.B.) was then committed to the support of government policy. Some ex-N.U.S.A.S. leaders became involved in the African Resistance Movement before 1964, though N.U.S.A.S. itself explicitly condemned acts of sabotage. N.U.S.A.S. successfully invited Senator Robert Kennedy of the United States to South Africa in 1966, but its president, Ian Robertson, was served with a banning order on the eve of his visit. Thereafter, Government attacks on N.U.S.A.S., combined with pressure on the English-language universities, began to intensify. There was a worldwide upsurge of student radicalism at the time, by which the relatively conservative English-medium universities in South Africa were marginally affected. They proved vulnerable to Government attacks because their criticism of the country's racial policies, combined with their rejection of some aspects of conventional morality, made it possible for the Government to draw a response from the much more conservative Anglo-Afrikaner electorate to its cry of 'the nation in danger'.

In February 1972, the Prime Minister appointed a Select Committee under the chairmanship of A. L. Schlebusch, on which both the National and the United parties agreed to serve, to investigate N.U.S.A.S. along with the University Christian Movement, the Christian Institute and the South African Institute of Race Relations. It started by investigating N.U.S.A.S. and held its hearings in camera. On the black campuses 1972 was a year of unrest. There the South African Student Organization (S.A.S.O.) had recently been formed to give expression to the principle of 'black power' rather than that of non-racialism in its public policy. When O. R. Tiro, a black student at the University of the North, was expelled for a public attack on the white control of black universities, a wave of support for him developed in the other English-language universities, black and white. N.U.S.A.S. identified itself with the black demands and held protest stands in June. Those in Cape Town and Johannesburg were broken up by the police, using batons and tear gas. Some students subsequently paid fines for unlawful marching or unlawful assembly, but all charges under the Riotous Assemblies Act, under which 118 persons were arraigned, either failed or were withdrawn. Early in 1973 the Schlebusch Commission issued an interim report on N.U.S.A.S., in which it recommended no action against the union as a body, but named eight leaders whom it regarded as dangerous to internal security. These, including the N.U.S.A.S. president, Paul Pretorius, were very soon served with banning orders, as were eight leaders of S.A.S.O., including their president, Jerome Modisane. The student demonstrations prompted a series of intimidatory attacks on the homes of some of their leaders, which resulted in the prosecution of one man. Tiro was subsequently murdered by a car bomb in Botswana, but his assassin was not identified.

The English-speaking churches were not easy to assail on account of the adverse effects of international propaganda likely to follow acts of persecution, and they had remained largely immune from attacks by the State since their defiance of the 'church clause' in 1957. But a full-scale judicial onslaught on the Anglican Dean of Johannesburg, G. A. ffrench-Beytagh, in 1971, on a charge of possessing subversive propaganda material and of having attempted to incite audiences to violence, got as far as the Appeal Court before the evidence of state witnesses was rejected and the Dean found not guilty. But this trial, helped by a decision of the World Council of Churches to make contributions for non-military purposes to guerrilla organisations operating in southern Africa, built up the atmosphere for a more direct confrontation. The withdrawal of passports from, or refusal of visas to, clergy (many of whom were not South African citizens) became more frequent. In 1972 the Schlebusch–Le Grange Commission investigated the inter-denominational Christian Institute, a body best known for its sponsoring of the S.P.R.O.C.A.S. [see p. 377]. The Institute, some of whose members were prepared to commit contempt of Parliament rather than appear before a secret quasi-judicial inquiry, was heavily censured in the final report of the Commission in 1975. The University Christian Movement had actually dissolved itself before the Schlebusch Commission sat, after black students had decided to pull out of this multi-racial body.

Before waiting for the result of the Schlebusch–Le Grange inquiry, the Government introduced an Affected Organizations Bill during the early part of the 1974 session. This measure empowered the State President to declare any organisation 'affected' if he considered it was dangerous to the security of the State, and it prohibited affected organisations from receiving foreign funds. N.U.S.A.S. and the Christian Institute were declared 'affected'. Organisations thought by those in authority to be subversive had thus been subjected to a non-judicial form of inquiry from which penalties could ensue.

The Government had outmanoeuvred the official Opposition, by inducing it out of concern for public security to participate in the Schlebusch Commission and endorse procedures which ignored normal judicial safeguards. At first the United Party was able to conceal its divisions, and it went into the general election of 1974 with its front unbroken, though it lost some ground. During 1975–7, however, the Party split twice and disintegrated. First, Harry Schwartz and his splinter Reform Party joined the Progressives in 1975. Then in 1977 Sir de Villiers Graaff tried and failed to reunite the Opposition. But so divided were his followers that his right wing broke away to form a new South African Party, the centre group renamed itself the New Republic Party in June 1977, while Japie Basson's more liberal element joined the Progressives under Colin Eglin, to form the Progressive Federal Party.

16.7   BLACK MOVEMENTS IN EXILE AND THE START OF THE TERRORIST CAMPAIGN

While the Opposition was thus fragmenting, the external and the internal situations became less stable. During the Vorster era the A.N.C. and the P.A.C., whose leaders had gone into exile, first infiltrated back into South Africa in an attempt to disrupt and if possible overthrow the regime. At first they acted together, but the United Front of 1960–2 collapsed in the face of leadership disputes (Lodge). Each group went its own way. The A.N.C. built up contacts with the Soviet Union, with the winning Portuguese colonial resistance movements, and with the Organisation of African Unity which had been set up at Addis Ababa in 1963. It made common cause with the Zimbabwe African People's Union, and took part in its attacks in Matabeleland in 1968, where it was confronted by South African police as well as Rhodesian forces. But although it sent a few infiltrators into the Republic, and exploded pamphlet bombs in the large centres in 1971, it was not able to cause any real disturbances or build any local base of operations. During the late 1970s there were signs of escalation in guerilla activity, especially after the political movements in exile had received an influx of recruits following the Soweto riots of 1976. Several acts of sabotage were carried out during 1977, and on 12 May 1978 the Minister of Justice, J. T. Kruger, reported thirty-one incidents to date, as a result of which 91 trained guerillas had been arrested and 594 suspects taken (Kane-Berman). They belonged either to the A.N.C. or the P.A.C.

The P.A.C. was, on the whole, much less successful than the A.N.C. Its link with the F.N.L.A. in Angola availed little in view of that body's defeat at the hands of the rival M.P.L.A.. Its courting of China was far less useful militarily than the A.N.C.'s approach to Russia. Although the P.A.C. established a base at Maseru in 1962, the senseless bombast of its leader, Potlako Leballo, led to the arrest and extradition to South Africa of many of its members. In the next few years (1964–8) the P.A.C. was expelled first from Maseru, then from Lusaka, and its attempt to send a few saboteurs into the Republic via Mozambique, in June 1968, met with failure.

In 1966–7 a few guerillas belonging to the South West African People's Organisation (S.W.A.P.O.) had entered South West Africa from Tanzania via Zambia and Angola, and it was known that perhaps 2,000 had left South Africa for training in various countries, mainly in the Communist bloc. In 1969 to 1972 there were several clashes between police and guerrillas in the Caprivi Strip.

To counter new threats beyond the frontiers [see p. 365], Vorster removed all judicial restraints from the 1967 Terrorism Act, allowing commissioned officers to detain suspects in solitary confinement, at will, for as long as they deemed it necessary. It took steps to tighten border control and extended compulsory military service to all young whites, making provision in 1967 for the training of Coloured cadets as well, and sending African as well as white police to patrol the borders. The military budget was greatly increased, and a factory set up for the production of jet aircraft. Legislation was passed to enable the Government to procure and conserve essential military supplies. The search for oil, started in the Verwoerd era, was continued, with special attention to off-shore exploration. Between 1969 and 1972 the Government brought into being a Bureau of State Security (B.O.S.S.) attached to the Prime Minister's office, and its members were accorded an unusual measure of protection from public discussion. A Security Services Special Account was set up, to enable the Government to invest funds secretly for the defence of the Republic.

16.8   THE SOWETO DISTURBANCES OF 1976–7

It was a boast of white South Africans in the post-Sharpeville era that, however much might be thought to be wrong with South African society, it was at least a country in which law and order prevailed, and in which investors could therefore safely invest. But unrest which developed during the middle months of 1976 disturbed this complacent assumption. On 16 June an illegal student march in Soweto, near Johannesburg, was stopped by police bullets, with some loss of life, after the firing of two warning shots and the use of tear gas had been met by stone-throwing. This incident was to set in motion a chain of disturbances throughout the country which continued spasmodically until 1980, and then returned in a different form in 1984–5.

The occasion for the march was a demand by pupils for the abrogation of the compulsory use of Afrikaans as a medium of instruction in black Transvaal schools, in the handling of which – on the evidence both of the Cillié Commission and Kane-Berman's analysis – the authorities from the Minister of Bantu Affairs downwards had been quite remarkably obtuse over a long period. Ideological issues apart, there clearly did not exist in Soweto a sufficient number of qualified teachers in the secondary schools who were capable of teaching their subjects in Afrikaans. But the Soweto troubles need to be viewed against a wider background of frustrations, of which the language issue was merely a part. They were 'riots looking for a place to happen', in the words of a *Sunday Times* editorial, and stemmed from a spirit of revolt among the youth which was partly rooted in their dislike of the Bantu Education system, to which Dr Verwoerd had publicly and very explicitly referred in earlier years as education for a menial place in society. At a time of rising unemployment, an 'inferior' education system could be expected to produce resentment, even if it had not been made to diverge from 'white' education to the extent that the original policy required. The looming independence of the Transkei was another cause for unsettlement, not so much in itself, as from a new and sudden realisation that the citizens of 'independent' states would lose their South African citizenship rights even if they had never lived in a Homeland, and with them the freedom of access to the job market in the Republic which they had enjoyed to that point. Then there was the severe, and largely contrived, housing shortage which reached a peak at the same time, as a consequence of the Vorster Government's decision to slow down the building of black houses in the 'white' area and rather to build them in the Homelands in order to encourage the growth of commuter-migrancy. Nor was this all. In his report on the riots, Judge Cillié concluded that there was 'so much dissatisfaction with administration boards', which had replaced the urban local authorites in 1972–3, 'that many Black residents were worked up to the point where they could easily resort to rioting'. The boards had led to a new and heavy financial burden on the black townships for two main reasons. One was the Government's embargo on the 'subsidisation' of township revenues from either its own sources or those of the white local authority, which in the case of Soweto meant the loss of a contribution from Johannesburg of over R1,000,000 a year. The other arose from an increase of salaried officials (many of whom were whites) whose cost, amounting to nearly half of Soweto's R58,000,000 budget for 1976–7, had to be met entirely from township contributions (Kane-Berman).

The student campaign was well orchestrated. On 13 June they had elected a Soweto Students' Representative Council under Tebello Motopayane, and thereafter led successively by Tsietsi Mashinini, Khotso Seathlolo and D. S. Montsitsi, until each found it necessary to flee abroad. Police arrests eventually drove the S.R.C. to vest leadership in a committee of nameless persons. The S.R.C. had planned the march on 16 June (Lodge). They organised work stoppages – two in August, one in September, and one in November, which were initially successful, thus demonstrating an awareness of the need to draw in the working man. But migrant workers, who risked deportation if they lost their jobs, were extremely vulnerable. On 24 August, after the hostel at Mzimhlophe station had been set on fire by over-enthusiastic students, residents who had not been drawn into the student protest, and who may have been egged on by individual policemen (Brookes and Brickhill), reacted and ran amok through the homes of residents. Chief Buthelezi arrived on the scene when the disturbances were past their peak to caution the Zulu element and denounce the police.

Neither the student leaders, nor their student followers, and least of all the 'tsotsi' element which took advantage of the unrest, went out of their way to avoid violence, as the Commission report makes plain; but Kane-Berman has made it clear that in so far as the S.R.C. was able to control events – and it succeeded to a remarkable degree – it kept its rank and file in check. The students attacked bottle stores and shebeens, in a bid to curb the excessive drinking of their elders they claimed – not irrationally, if they aspired to legitimacy as a leadership cadre, though the investigating judge favoured a less subtle explanation. Whatever the answer, the S.R.C. acted with considerable maturity in its handling of the Soweto workers (who, in the view of Brooks and of Hirson, took a more positive part than Kane-Berman allows), in its handling of sportsmen whose fixtures they wanted to have cancelled, and in its organisation of a Christmas shopping boycott. S.R.C. leadership emerged clearly in April 1977, when they appealed to their parents' generation through a campaign to stop pending rent increases, in the course of which they so discredited the Soweto Urban Bantu Council, that they compelled its members to resign, and won their battle over the rents. Out of the confusion, and with full student support, arose a Committee of Ten, led by Dr Nthatho Motlana, in June 1977. It claimed to be representative of Soweto opinion, and there can be little doubt that, if free elections had been held, its members would have been able to demonstrate their popularity, and provide a representative body with whom officialdom could negotiate.

The authorities, however, thought otherwise. Though the police seem to have learnt something from their early mistakes in the handling of crowds, it was no part of the Vorster Government's strategic outlook to handle opponents from a position other than one of strength. The police were therefore required to make their presence felt. Kane-Berman mentions incidents of what looked like calculated intimidation to a number of press reporters, when white men in camouflage drove around in Valiant cars (a model commonly issued to the Security Police) firing indiscriminately at bystanders; but no charges were laid as a result of this alleged conduct, and the episodes in question do not seem to have featured in the judicial report. The worst outbreaks of violence occurred at funerals, particularly that of Jacob Mashabane, who had died while in police custody, and was buried on 17 October. Police opened fire at a crowd estimated at 16,000, many of whom were students who used the occasion to distribute strike leaflets. Seven people died and fifty-one were injured. A rhythm of shootings at funerals, followed by further funerals and further shootings, occurred all too often during the next few years.

Since the unrest was led by youths, inevitably large numbers of those apprehended by the police were children. These were held at John Vorster Square in Johannesburg, either under preventive detention or to await trial. A second student march, this time to John Vorster Square, took place on 4 August. It failed to get through, three of its members falling to police bullets, and therefore failed to secure the release on bail of prisoners under age, though some of these were returned to the custody of their parents from time to time. But a demand for the release of their colleagues would feature from then on as a condition whose fulfilment would have to precede an instruction by the S.R.C. to its followers to return to school, especially after the beginning of November, by which time the police had conducted a number of raids on private homes in an attempt to winkle out the student leadership.

The troubles would have been difficult enough to handle if they had been confined to Soweto. But there were signs from very early on of keen student support for the Sowetans in other centres. The administration block and library at the University of Zululand were burnt down on 18 June, only two days after the initial outburst in June 1976. Attempts at arson led to the closure of the University of Fort Hare on 18 July. The Legislative Assembly building in Bophutatswana was burned down on 9 August. There was fierce rioting and real turbulence in the heart of Cape Town, as Coloured students came out in support of African grievances, in August and early September. This rose to a peak in November and December. The Cillié Commission report covers the violence of June 1976 to February 1977 in thirty-one chapters devoted to Soweto, the West and East Rand, the Vaal Triangle, the Central Transvaal, the Highveld and Southern Transvaal, the Eastern Transvaal and KaNgwane, Lebowa, (Kwa)Ndebele and Northern Transvaal, Venda, Gazankulu, Bophutatswana, the Western Transvaal, the University of Zululand, Durban and environs, the University of Durban-Westville, the rest of KwaZulu, the rest of Natal, the Northern Orange Free State, the Central and Southern Orange Free state and Thaba'Nchu, Qwaqwa, the Eastern Cape and East London, the Ciskei, Port Elizabeth, and the Cape Midlands, the Karoo and the Diamond Fields, the Northern Cape, the South-Western Cape, the Cape Peninsula, and Nyanga.

The start of 1977 brought little relief, for although the public examinations which had been postponed from November 1976 until the following March were held in spite of attempts to disrupt them, there was a further heavy police clamp-down, accompanied by over 2,000 arrests, in anticipation of renewed trouble in June 1977. A further spate of school-burnings followed, and by November the spread of the school boycott had led to the resignation of some 500 secondary teachers from schools in Soweto alone.

On 19 October the Minister of Justice, J. T. Kruger, banned all movements associated with Black Consciousness, to whom blame for the events was ascribed. S.A.S.O. came under the axe, as did the Black People's Convention, the South African Student Movement, the Soweto S.R.C., Black Community Programmes Ltd (an association which promoted health and welfare work in black communities), the Black Parents' Association (which had stood behind the S.R.C. and the parents of detainees in a supportive role), the Union of Black Journalists, and many other bodies. The *World*, the leading African newspaper on the Rand, was also banned, along with the Christian Institute, which had earlier come under fire from the Schlebusch Commission. The range of bannings was itself an indication of the extent to which black self-awareness had proliferated since the banning of the A.N.C. and the P.A.C. in 1960.

The extent of physical damage to property had been vast: it included over 100 buildings belonging to the Administration Boards, as well as '250 bottle stores and beerhalls, 170 shops, 25 clinics, eight banks, about a dozen libraries, and a score of post offices, as well as smaller numbers of hotels, cinemas, clinics, churches, community halls, magistrates' courts, and petrol filling stations' (Kane-Berman). Over 300 buses belonging to the Public Utility Transport Corporation (P.U.T.C.O.) were attacked. Over 200 private homes belonging to Africans, and at least 350 schools were destroyed or damaged.

The official figure for lives lost was 176, but this only covered events down to 25 June 1976. The Cillié Commission calculated that 575 persons had died in the riots by 28 February 1977, while Kane-Berman, who took the Cillié calculations into account, reached the conclusion that 'the total number of publicly recorded deaths arising from the disturbances between June 1976 and October 1977 is 700'. As had been the case during the Defiance Campaign of 1952, some of the victims were people who had given their lives to African welfare. Dr Melville Edelstein, the West Rand Administration Board's chief welfare officer, was a tragic example, for he had warned against the possibility of just such violence in a book entitled *What do young Africans think?* as early as 1972. Other common victims were blacks thought to be police informers – a reminder of how easily life under a suffocating political system can tear the moral fabric of a community apart. The casualty details given by Judge Cillié contain 104 names of children under the age of 17, not all of whom were killed by the police, but the great majority of those who lost their lives were under 25.

Many more were arrested or detained. The Cillié Commission, received information from the police that 5,980 people were arrested between 16 June 1976 and 28 February the following year. It made no mention at all of the numbers detained, for under the Terrorism Act there was no obligation on senior police officers to release any kind of information about detainees, and no restriction as to the place or duration of such detention. But the list of 360 names compiled by the *World* on 8 October corresponded more or less with the figure of 374 released by the Minister of Justice ten days later. Detentions apparently doubled in the next few months, and then fell away as detainees were either held, released, or appeared in court in one of over a hundred trials which were held throughout the country.

Some were less fortunate. Among those detained was Steve Biko, leader of the Black Consciousness movement, who was taken into custody in the Eastern Cape on 18 August 1977. He was interrogated and subjected to severe physical violence in the Security Police cells in Port Elizabeth, and then, critically ill, he was taken by road unclothed to Pretoria, where he died of his injuries on 12 September, as tragic a martyr to the cause of his people's emancipation as any person in the history of South Africa, black or white.

Two months after Biko's death, and one month after J. T. Kruger's clamp-down on the Black Consciousness organisations, white South Africa went to the polls for the 1977 general election. The Government played its cards well. Profiting from the break-up of the United Party, and making a special feature of their constitutional proposals, the Nationalists were returned with a record tally of 134 seats. Their tough handling of events in Soweto had won them more, not less support, however much they may have been to blame for the outbreak in the first place.

The following September Vorster resigned from the premiership, and was elevated to the office of State President left vacant by the death of Nico Diederichs in August. This was an honour for a leader who had acted so demonstrably in the tradition of Paul Kruger, yet his elevation was ringed around with disappointments and was to end, a mere eight months later, in public disgrace. The tragic events which scarred South Africa in 1976–7 drew a good deal of attention away from the successes of his 'outward policy' towards the less hostile black states of southern Africa [see p. 460]. There then occurred a scandal affecting his own Cabinet which a younger, fitter, more vigilant Vorster might have headed off, given a sense of political correctness sufficient to restrain the temptations of exaggerated party loyalty; but Vorster in 1977 was a sick man, as several of his colleagues testified, and he was not equal to the demands made upon him.

16.9   THE INFORMATION SCANDAL AND THE FALL OF VORSTER

To cope with the perceived needs of external security, the Prime Minister had obtained authority from Parliament to establish a Security Services Special Account in 1969, which was to be subject to official audit only to the extent that the Minister of Finance determined, in consultation with the Prime Minister. But the practice gradually developed under which such funds, though properly falling under the control of the Prime Minister, could be channelled through individual government departments after consultation with the Prime Minister's office.

In November 1976 the Auditor-General first became uneasy about the manner in which the Department of Information's secret funds were being invested, and he drew Vorster's attention to the matter in June 1977. Gradually rumours of irregular practices began to spread, and they clearly affected the succession to the premiership, for the minister in charge of the Information Department, Dr C. P. Mulder, was the main contender for the post in his capacity as leader of the Party in the Transvaal. When the National Party caucus met on 27 September, he was challenged by the Cape leader, P. W. Botha, while R. F. ('Pik') Botha, the Minister of Foreign Affairs, another Transvaler, stood as the third candidate. Mulder won on the first ballot, but failed to gain an overall majority. At the second ballot, from which 'Pik' Botha's candidature was withdrawn, his supporters gave sufficient votes to P. W. Botha to enable him to overtake Mulder and win the position.

The public had no hard information on which to base an opinion on the financial rumours until November 1978, when Judge A. Mostert of Natal, who had been appointed as a one-man commission to look into irregularities in exchange control practices, came across details about the activities of the Information Department which seemed to him so startling that, in possible defiance of the rules governing commissions, he made the evidence available to the press. It concerned, in particular, the use of large secret government funds to buy control of a part of the English-language press for the National Party and, in particular, to set up and pay for a new national daily paper, the *Citizen*. The Secretary of the Department, Dr Eschel Rhoodie, was named in association with the transaction.

Faced with a major crisis affecting a Cabinet of which he had been a member, the new Prime Minister P. W. Botha pitched into the matter as if pugnacity was the best means of defence. He wound up the Mostert Commission, of whose action he disapproved, and appointed a Free State judge, R. P. B. Erasmus, to investigate the Department of Information, which had in the meantime been closed down. Erasmus delivered his first report in time for a special session of Parliament on 7 and 8 December. It was nothing if not emphatic in its conclusions, separating the sheep from the goats with a little more haste than was wise, as later events were to show. Thus it cleared Vorster, in his capacity as prime minister, of conscious connivance in the Department of Information's irregular practices, and pronounced that the true facts about its activities had been concealed from him by Mulder and by General H. J. van den Bergh, the head of the Bureau of State Security and a close personal friend of Vorster's since the Second World War. It also cleared the new prime minister, P. W. Botha, then Minister of Defence, who needed clearance because some secret funds appeared to have been laundered through that department in his day in a manner which had drawn the disapproval of the Chief of the Army, General Magnus Malan. It also cleared the Minister of Finance, Senator O. P. F. Horwood, though Mulder had once persuaded him, on the ground of extreme urgency, to authorise the payment of a very large sum from the secret fund without making a careful check on the purpose of the expenditure. The charges against Rhoodie, on the other hand – that he had used nearly R32 million of state money to buy the *Citizen* and keep it on the road, that he had destroyed public documents to conceal irregularities in violation of the Archives Act, and that he had misled the Department of Defence over the use of secret funds – were sustained. Various transactions involving the purchase of properties on behalf of the State, some of them very select, in various parts of the world, were not investigated in the first Erasmus Report; but Rhoodie was later put on trial for these in October 1979, and sentenced to twelve years' imprisonment, only to win a reprieve on all counts a year later, in an Appeal Court judgement which gave him the benefit of the doubt. Van den Bergh was indicted for misleading both Mulder and Vorster over the *Citizen* deal, and – along with Mulder – for intimidating a subordinate official in the Bureau of State Security to produce a false report which cleared the Information Department to Mulder's political advantage (though not sufficiently so, as has been noted, to gain him the premiership). Mulder, for his part, was declared to have floated loans abroad without keeping the Treasury informed, and to have lent large sums of public money to a Nationalist supporter to buy control of Opposition English-language newspaper interests, without checking how that money was spent, and to have led the Minister of Finance into error by deceptive and urgent demands to have unlawful expenditure cleared. Mulder was later to hit back through *Rapport* in March and April 1979, by alleging that Vorster and Horwood had lied in claiming that they had not known in advance of the plan to set up the *Citizen*. He also stated that he, Vorster and Diederichs had met regularly to discuss the secret projects, including the establishment of pro-Government newspapers with state funds, and that they constituted the 'committee of three' about which Opposition spokesmen had asked questions in vain during the debate on the Report. So effective, it seems, was Mulder's counter-attack that Judge Erasmus changed his mind about Vorster's complicity, and declared in a final report on 4 June 1979 that Vorster had had foreknowledge of the Department of Information's financial operations. The State President had one course open to him to avoid possible impeachment: he resigned. In November 1980 further allegations were made by the *Rand Daily Mail*, but never tested in court, concerning improper handling of the Erasmus Commission's first and final Reports before they were presented to the State President; but by then the momentum had gone out of the public agitations. The Botha Government was firmly in the saddle. Mulder and his associates, who had formed a new National Conservative Party, were still in the political wilderness, though Rhoodie had no cause to feel dissatisfied. And the *Citizen* still existed as a pro-Government English-language newspaper. 'May one be pardoned', Claudius asked, 'and retain the offence?'

17 At the Crossroads, 1978–90

17.1 P. W. BOTHA'S POLITICAL STYLE AND AIMS

When P. W. Botha took power in 1978, he acquired the image of a reformer in a hurry. He told a conference of businessmen at the Carlton Hotel, Johannesburg, in November that apartheid was 'a recipe for permanent conflict', and when he opened the Transvaal National Party congress in September 1980 he treated it to a speech about economic realities rather than the usual exhortation to party loyalty. Unlike Vorster, who had allowed his ministers too much latitude and done little to control them, Botha employed tighter curbs, moving his own men into key positions in the top echelons of the civil service and so organising government business that a large part of it passed through the office of the Prime Minister, not least the control of the civil service itself, by means of a network of cabinet committees and advisory councils. This meant that even a maverick Nationalist like Dr A. P. Treurnicht, who was brought into the Cabinet in September 1980, could be kept under control.

The transfer of General Magnus Malan from his military post as Chief of the Army to the civilian position of Minister of Defence, which he took over from Botha himself, emphasised this trend towards centralisation still further. Malan was a key figure in the Afrikaner establishment, son of a speaker of the House of Assembly, brother of a Springbok rugby captain, a member of the Broederbond, and a soldier who not only had direct observer experience of the Algerian civil war but was a graduate of an American military academy and a close student of French, Israeli and Taiwanese military methods. He did much, in his capacity as commander of the South African armed forces, to coordinate the three services with each other and with the growing armaments industry. Under Malan as Minister of Defence, the notion of 'total strategy' to cope with what the Government presented as 'total onslaught' by Marxist enemies against the Republic became the mainspring of policy – perhaps even, 'in the absence of any alternative critique by more sceptical defence and civilian intellectuals, creating in a new generation of colonels and majors', as Spence suggests, 'a cadre of true believers'.

The exaggeration in such an appeal led commentators to consider seriously the possibility of a military take-over of government, a 'De Gaulle option', and to see in the State Security Council (S.S.C.), first

397

formed in 1972, some kind of rival to the Cabinet itself. B.O.S.S., renamed the Department of National Security and later the National Intelligence Service, had been discredited during the Information Scandal and the Seychelles coup [see p. 467], and lost its superiority to the S.S.C., which was remodelled by P. W. Botha as one of five cabinet committees in September 1979. This body acquired the informal status of an 'inner cabinet' to which the Ministers of Foreign Affairs, Defence, Police (Law and Order) and Justice had regular access, as did the chairmen of cabinet committees on Finance, Education, Development Aid, and Constitutional Development and Planning, as well as some senior civil servants; but other ministers attended only by invitation. The S.S.C. acquired a large secretariat under the control of a general of the S.A.D.F., who could report directly to the Prime Minister without going through the Cabinet. The S.S.C. sometimes exercised discretionary executive powers, especially when Parliament and the Cabinet were not sitting, even to the extent of ordering cross-border offensives (Jaster). Its contacts and its authority radiated downwards through eleven regional, sixty sub-regional and 448 local Joint Management Centres (J.M.C.s) operating outside the range of electoral politics and in close association with the S.A.D.F. (Grundy). By means such as these the State President, whose personality endeared him to his Party as 'Piet Wapen' or the 'Great Crocodile', achieved a dominance over the Cabinet at least comparable with that of Smuts and Verwoerd.

The South Africa which P. W. Botha took over in October 1978 was a politically chastened land. It was nevertheless enjoying a return to prosperity as a result of a massive upswing of the gold price. This had been pegged at $35 a fine ounce from 1933 to 1970. It had then been freed from the dollar, and rose to close on $400 at the end of 1979. At the beginning of 1980 it topped the $850 mark, and in the course of that year gave the Treasury a record revenue yield of R3,633 million from the gold mines alone, as against R446 million in the year of Botha's accession to power. Yet the sheer difficulty of predicting the performance of gold forced the Treasury to adopt a cautious monetary policy, and actually to reduce government spending during 1980 to under 19 per cent of the gross domestic product.

There were, nevertheless, real problems for public policy to overcome. These stemmed from a population increase which was seen by 1981 to be well above the Tomlinson predictions [see table on p. 371] thus largely negating the advantages of the gold price windfall. Dr S. du Toit Viljoen, Chairman of the Bantu Investment Corporation, had estimated in 1975 that South Africa needed an annual economic growth rate of 5½ per cent till the end of the century to absorb the increased numbers in her workforce. This would involve finding skilled work for at least three-and-a-half million blacks, the products of an educational system which had paid much more attention to primary than to secondary schools since the introduction of Bantu Education in 1953. It would also involve overcoming the other major economic obstacles to expansion, above all the scarcity of reliable water, the seriousness of which would be underscored by the mammoth drought of 1982–4.

There were several reasons, both political and economic – the shortage of water among them – for advocating the decentralisation of industry. But the failure of decentralisation during the premierships of Verwoerd and Vorster had made such a strategy unpopular among industrialists. P. W. Botha's Government set out to gain the same objective with a great deal more determination and self-assurance. The reports of two commissions, the one chaired by Dr P. J. Riekert of the Prime Minister's Economic Advisory Council, the other by N. E. Wiehahn, Professor of Industrial Relations at the University of South Africa, helped to set the scene at the urban industrial end in 1979.

The Riekert Report set down new conditions for the training, employment, housing and government of black workers in industry. It sought to marry the Tomlinson commission's support for influx control with recommendations akin to those of the Holloway Commission (1932) of drawing a clear distinction between those blacks who were already urbanised, and those who were not. The former, said Riekert, should be encouraged to work and live in town with their families (even if their wives did not possess Section 10 rights) and become full, though still residentially segregated, participants in the urban industrial culture. They should have first access among blacks to urban employment anywhere in the Republic. Those without legal rights in town, on the other hand, should be required to base themselves in the Homelands as before, and visit the urban areas of the Republic only as migrant labourers, after being screened at 'assembly centres' outside the borders of the Homelands for admission purposes. The report recommended maximum flexibility for work-seekers through abolition of the 72-hour period within which a job had to be found, and the abandonment in individual cases of the rule limiting contracts to one year. To ease the movement of black workers who possessed Section 10 rights, the labour districts had already been enlarged to coincide with the increased areas of jurisdiction of the Administration Boards, which were reduced in number from twenty-two to fourteen in April 1979. So long as housing was available, African work-seekers were to be free to move within the region without having to seek permission to move from town to town.

These were much more limiting provisos than at first appeared, however, as was shown by the Government's reaction to two court rulings in favour of black townsfolk. One was the case of Mrs Nonceba Komani, who in August 1980 won the right to live with her husband in an urban area even though she had not been entered by officials on her husband's lodger's permit. Administration Boards were commonly reluctant to apply this judgement in other similar cases but threats to take the Boards to court were sometimes effective. The other case was the successful application of M. T. Rikhoto to the Rand Supreme Court in September 1981 for permanent resident rights in an urban area, after he had worked continuously for ten years for one employer as Section 10 of the Urban Areas Act required. The judgement established that although he was a contract worker, and therefore required to return to his Homeland annually to break the continuity of his residence in town, these annual holidays did not destroy his Section 10 rights. Many thousands like him thus came within range of securing the right to live permanently in town. The Government took nearly three years to devise blocking legislation, but by August 1983 new laws were in force to undermine the effects of both the Komani and Rikhoto judgements. Thus, to prevent what might have become a large-scale reuniting of wives to husbands in the urban areas, the wives and children of urban Africans with rights were now required to prove that they had already been living with the qualified men of their choice before 26 August 1983, which meant that all who sought to qualify on the basis of residence taken up after that date would be excluded. Similarly, to contain the effects of the Rikhoto judgement, black contract workers seeking Section 10 rights were now required to show that they either owned, rented or occupied houses in their own names, the occupation of a room in another's house not being regarded as adequate. Thus rights became dependent on the availability of accommodation. The rearguard drag of influx control was to be made effective against Riekert's attempt to foster industrial streamlining and black urban renewal – but also, it should be stressed, in line with the less adventurous features of the Riekert Report itself.

The Riekert Report formed the basis for draft legislation released by Dr Koornhof in October 1980 and immediately referred to a committee under Judge E. M. Grosskopf for scrutiny. The history of this draft legislation reflects the tension in government circles generated by the Riekert Report in the light of the Komani and Rikhoto judgements. The Department of Cooperation and Development (as 'Bantu Affairs' was now called, after a brief spell as 'Plural Relations' when Dr C. P. Mulder had been minister) took a tough line on influx control. Its Orderly Movement and Settlement of Black Persons Bill, as revised in 1982, threatened to become, in the words of Sheena Duncan, National President of the Black Sash, 'the most effective form of influx control this country has ever experienced'. The intention was to remove Section 10 rights from all Africans who might subsequently qualify and all town-born black children who could not prove that both their parents possessed such rights. Draconian penalties of up to R5,000 were to have been imposed on those who employed, housed or admitted unqualified persons. But the Grosskopf Committee, rather like the Young – Barrett Committee of 1935 [see p. 286] took a very different line, gave the Government credit for intending to move away from hurtful discrimination, and proposed that existing Section 10 rights should be replaced by a permanent right of urban residence for Africans who had lived in town for a continuous period of five years, along with their children, with retroactive effect. The Department did not like the Report, and buried it, perhaps from a fear that it might increase the danger of urban terrorism (Savage). But the Select Committee on the new constitution under C. Heunis, Minister of Constitutional Development, seems to have had doubts about the stance of the Department, for in September 1982 it decided to postpone discussion till new black local authorities had been set up under another of the Koornhof bills, so that these bodies could be given a chance to advise. This meant no legislation until 1984. When Dr

Koornhof's departmental vote came up for debate in May 1984, the Minister announced that the Orderly Movement Bill had been scrapped. Instead, a new measure would be introduced after the implementation of the new constitution [see pp. 433–4], and after consultation with urban and Homeland leaders.

But on the positive side, the Government's concern for urban renewal should not be overlooked. Hence the Black Community Development Bill which Parliament carried in 1984. Likewise stemming from the Riekert recommendations, it made provision for the Administration Boards to be converted into Development Boards, the purpose of which would be to support the new black municipalities to be established under the third Koornhof measure, the Black Local Government Act of 1983. Urban renewal had been very much in the air as a result of the manner in which black townships had been allowed to run down during the Vorster era, with the object of encouraging urban growth in the Homelands alone. A conference of businessmen in November 1976, had set up an Urban Foundation to raise funds and stimulate urban development so far as this was allowed by the Government. Louis Rive, who had had a distinguished career as Postmaster General, was commissioned by the Government in 1980 to draw up a plan for the upgrading of greater Soweto, through the introduction of 99-year leasehold ownership and a massive electrification project, which was bound to have an important spin-off both for black domestic comfort and for industry.

The biggest problem for black township development was financial. It stemmed from the existence – for political reasons – of separate revenue accounts for white residential areas, to which the central business districts were attached in nearly every town in the Republic, and for black locations which could call on almost no wealth-creating enterprises at all. The growth of black business during the late 1970s [see p. 492] had begun to change this condition marginally; but the ruling party could not bring itself to consider the most straightforward way of solving the problem in economic terms – the amalgamation of black and white local authorities in a joint political system – because its electorate found such a solution politically unacceptable. Instead, the Croeser Committee was appointed to devise ways of financing black local government without diverting the revenue which existing local authorities would continue to need for their own purposes. The serious inroads which such a policy could have on the traditions of local government were not hard to see; but it was clear that a system under which a group of townships like Soweto, which provided at least half the revenue of central Johannesburg but could divert none of it to their own development, was in urgent need of overhaul. This was done in 1985, but the Regional Services Councils Act of that year proved to be so controversial that it was only implemented in 1987 [see p. 530].

The Wiehahn Commission, also appointed in 1979, concerned itself with the question of labour and industrial relations. Its influence led to the setting up in the same year of a National Manpower Commission to look into the rationalisation of labour usage in industrial production, and of an Industrial Court which was to busy itself with the interpretation of labour

laws, and to hear cases of irregular employment practices such as contentious dismissals, wage disputes, and the legality of strikes. Appeals from its
judgements lay to the Supreme Court. Wiehahn recommended further that
segregation, which was obligatory under existing factory legislation,
whether in regard to amenities or access to employment, should be made
discretionary within individual firms. He also recommended that the
mining industry, which had strongly resisted outside interference and
worker unionisation in the past, should be 'encouraged to conform' with
the new dispensation. That the Government was keen to follow Wiehahn's
advice was clear, not only from the provisions of the Industrial Conciliation
Amendment Act of 1979 under which the reforms listed above were
introduced, but also from its decision to allow Africans other than contract
workers to form their own trade unions. A Labour Relations Amendment
Act of 1981 abolished all racial distinctions with regard to union membership, and permitted the formation of mixed trade unions, but obliged even
unregistered unions to open their premises, their accounts and their
membership lists to the Registrar for inspection. Strict rules were also laid
down to prevent any direct association or financial links between political
parties and trade unions, whether registered or not, and to ban financial
assistance to members of unregistered unions if they went out on strike.
How far this was, however, from drawing the teeth of the trade union
movement can be seen in the 1987 amendment to the Labour Relations
Act, promulgated in September 1988. This threw down a new challenge to
the workers by barring unions from supporting community boycotts, or
indulging in sympathetic strikes, or encroaching on the bargaining rights of
non-members. It also laid down rules for dismissals and retrenchments
which took good care of employers' interests, as did the clause which made
unions liable for damage to property resulting from strike action.

Rationalisation of policies with regard to industry and the urban areas
needs to be placed in the context of the Botha Government's broader
economic policies for the Republic, the Homelands, and southern Africa
as a whole. He first elaborated his idea of a 'constellation' of southern
African states [see pp. 473–4] at a conference of businessmen at the
Carlton Hotel, Johannesburg, in November 1979. In May 1980 the Prime
Minister's office put out a more detailed statement of policy for the
economic development of the Republic, including the independent Homelands. Its assumption was that the Republic and its satellites had to be seen
as sharing a single economy in need of even development. There had to be
a new approach to economic decentralisation, and a unified financial
strategy through the setting up of a Development Bank, and the planning
of axes of development based on centres with already existing infrastructures, so that the Homelands could themselves contribute to and participate in the profits of economic growth. The axes identified were mainly in
the north, radiating from Pretoria northwards to Messina on the Limpopo,
eastwards to Nelspruit, and westwards via Zeerust, to the new mining
areas in the northern Cape, taking in as many of the African Homelands as
possible, and starting with the east–west axis between Bronkhorstspruit
and Rustenburg. The creation of eight development regions was linked

with this strategy, which was to be made as attractive as possible to investors through the removal of government restrictions on manpower.

It seemed good on paper, but when the Prime Minister reported back to the businessmen in Cape Town in November 1981 – the so-called 'Good Hope Conference' – there was some support but a good deal of scepticism about government intentions because so little progress appeared to have been made in two years. On 9 April 1982, however, the *Financial Mail* reacted very positively to a new government White Paper on regional development which recognised that the earlier schemes under the Physical Planning Act had not created sufficiently good opportunities for the border areas, and that the costs of financing new plant, transporting produce and training new workers outweighed the incentives offered in the form of tax holidays, cheaper labour and other 'border area' concessions. There was now to be a new Decentralisation Board with power to put pressure on the developed industrial areas by means of employer levies and a lowering of tariff subsidies on the one hand, and on the other to create more attractive opportunities in the Homelands with the resources of the Development Bank, which eventually became active towards the end of 1983. Whereas the initial development focus had been in the Transvaal, the 1981–2 policy now gave top priority to the eastern Cape, the most depressed region outside the Homelands in relation to population density. Next in order of priority came Natal and the northern Transvaal, then the western Cape, eastern and western Transvaal and the O.F.S.; and finally the Pretoria–Witwatersrand–Vereeniging area. It also looked as if the Government, by concentrating largely on the Homelands which had accepted independence, was trying to use economic carrots to promote its political ideals.

17.2 THE CLIMAX OF POPULATION RESETTLEMENT

The Homelands were to be key participants in the proposed socio-economic revival, and this gave P. W. Botha's Government a strong incentive for pressing on with the consolidation of these territories – a task which was assigned to the Van der Walt Commission. The continuity of the resettlement policy needs to be stressed, as does the fact that over the years there was a steady increase in the real *per capita* expenditure from government sources on Homeland development, despite the enormous growth of the Homeland populations as resettlement moved into top gear. Thus, according to C. Simkins in a paper on the economic implications of resettlement given in 1981, in 1960–1 the state contributed an average of R18.38 per head at 1978 prices on a population of 4,739,855, whereas in 1978–9 it paid R89.64 per head on a population of 11,338,308. But there was a strong tendency to sink much of the money into costly governmental buildings, rather than in the development of infrastructures for peasant subsistence. The sums spent on the relief of resettled people who had lost their means of livelihood were also considerable.

An unofficial five-volume report by a group of researchers calling themselves the Surplus People Project, published thirteen years after Cosmas

Desmond's *Discarded People*, came out in 1983 under the title *Forced Removals in South Africa*, and was later summarised by Platsky and Walker. It quoted official figures to show that in the interest of Homeland consolidation and for other reasons approximately 3,500,000 people had been moved, many of them under some measure of duress, between 1960 and 1982. Although accurate statistics are hard to come by, Platsky and Walker also calculated that a further two million people were 'threatened with removal in the near future'. In May 1984 the Department of Cooperation and Development, making use of a different set of figures, rebutted these allegations in Parliament with a statement that only 1,971,908 people had been removed, and that it was not possible to state how many were still under threat of removal. By common consent, however, the figures were massive.

The western Cape removals have to be related to the policy under which Coloured people were as a general rule to be granted employment in preference to Africans west of a line from the Fish and Kat rivers to Aliwal North, from which Port Elizabeth and Uitenhage were exempted only in 1978. Having established large settlements for Coloured people at Atlantis and Mitchell's Plain [see p. 380], the Government announced its intention in 1984 to allow their eventual expansion into the African settlements of Langa, Nyanga and Guguletu on the Cape Flats. But this was small compensation for the loss of the historic, predominantly Coloured suburb of District Six, which was flattened under powers acquired by Community Development in terms of the Group Areas Act, leaving a great scar on the slopes of Devil's Peak where a vibrant, poor, colourful, gang-ridden community had lived since about the time of slave emancipation in 1838.

Behind the western Cape removals lay the Government's desire to reduce the number of Africans with residential rights and replace them with contract workers. Hence the destruction of three squatter settlements on the Cape Flats in 1977–8, and above all the much publicised saga of Crossroads, a squatter settlement which had grown up close to the southern end of Cape Town's main airport. At the last of these, an energetic women's committee, with some backing from sympathetic whites and considerable international press publicity, encouraged the people to stand their ground despite forceful attempts by the authorities to disperse the settlement. Eventually in 1981 Dr Koornhof agreed to settle those with residential rights permanently at 'New Crossroads', between Guguletu and Nyanga. This partial concession, however, encouraged new would-be squatters on such a scale that the Government had come to realise by 1983 that no piecemeal settlement of the squatter problem could be achieved within the principles of influx control (as revised by Riekert) and the Coloured labour preference policy. So he tried first to deport Transkeian squatters, as illegal immigrants from a 'foreign' state; but with Matanzima's encouragement these deportees went straight back to the Cape. Meanwhile the population of Crossroads, calculated at about 10,000 in 1976, escalated to about 80,000 in a decade. The Government therefore decided, as an alternative, to set aside a large area on the False Bay coast for a permanent African residential township of Khayelitsha, and this change of policy was endorsed by the Party's congress in September 1984. But the Crossroads problem did not stand still. More immigrants arrived in the area and settled in the surrounding bush, fired with a determination to stay, notably a group which squatted without permission in the K.T.C. Bazaar area adjacent to New Crossroads. But residents of Crossroads proper, led by Johnson Ngxobongwana, resented an intrusion which appeared to cut across government plans for their own community development, and Ngxobongwana was able to enlist the support of the nationwide United Democratic Front, established in August 1983 [see p. 428], which made much political capital out of widespread opposition to the proposed concentration of African settlement at Khayelitsha. The state meanwhile resolved its dilemma by enlisting the support of Ngxobongwana, whose dictatorial landlordism played into their hands, by encouraging his private army of Crossroads followers, known as *witdoeke* from their white headbands, to attack and destroy the K.T.C. settlement, in the expectation of remaining at Crossroads themselves. This was achieved, with brutal violence and police support, during the troubles of May and June 1986 [see p. 439]. Broken and demoralised by this inexcusable misuse of state power, many of the K.T.C. refugees went of necessity to Khayelitsha, where they came under the comparable landlordism of one of their erstwhile squatter leaders.

In the eastern Cape, where a good deal of publicity had already attended the establishment of Dimbaza, near King William's Town [see p. 373], removals escalated with the migration of about 56,000 people from Herschel and Glen Grey into the Hewu district of the Ciskei to escape Transkeian rule, after the Transkei had taken transfer of the former districts on becoming independent in 1976. The settlers were moved on to very well-developed agricultural land in such large numbers that within a year or two the land had been reduced to near desert conditions, and the people became dependent on rations. The Government also began to clear politically inconvenient black settlements like that of the Mfengu community who had lived and farmed near Humansdorp, west of Port Elizabeth, since the 1830s. Their appeals to be allowed to remain rather than move to the Keiskamma valley in the Ciskei were rejected by Parliament. They went. The Coloured farmers of Stockenstrom district, descendants of the Kat River settlers of 1829, were expelled in 1988 from an area which had been included in Ciskei, no provision having been made for them by the State beforehand. Resistance to removals was also particularly strong at Mgwali, a Presbyterian settlement in the 'white corridor' between East London and Queenstown, which occupied land originally given to the Xhosa hymnologist Tiyo Soga by Sandile, the Xhosa paramount, and kept by the residents as a reward for their loyalty during the cattle-killing of 1857. Elsewhere, as at Cathcart, Potsdam and Thornhill, resettlement continued throughout Botha's period of rule. Incorporation of black communities in Homelands by means of frontier adjustments without physical resettlement, as occurred at Peelton, became common in the late 1980s. The African population of Ciskei grew from 357,801 to 630,353 in 1970–80, net immigration as a result of removals amounting to 142,350.

The drought of 1982–4, and the very undeveloped infrastructure of Ciskei added to the problems of resettlement there, despite efforts of the Ciskeian authorities to create more employment opportunities.

In the Orange Free State, the policy led to the building of an enormous location at Onverwacht, south of Bloemfontein, and to the packing of large numbers of people into the Rolong and Sotho Homelands of Thaba'Nchu and Qwaqwa. Onverwacht became, in the words of the Surplus People Project, a 'sprawling slum' of something between 100,000 and 200,000 people, a disease trap lacking most basic amenities and with very little grazing land on which the residents, most of whom had been brought from farms in the Free State, could run their few remaining stock. In 1988, known by then as Botshabelo, it successfully contested a proclamation by the State President incorporating it (without community consultation) in Qwaqwa, 270 kilometres away. Thaba'Nchu was equally crowded. Qwaqwa, the official name for the Mopedi location at Witzieshoek, was considerably worse, with a population which had risen very fast from 24,000 in 1970 to something between 200,000 and 300,000 in 1980, its density increasing over the same period from 54 to 622 per square kilo-metre – a settlement described by Benbo, a government agency, as 'overpopulated in relation to available employment opportunities . . . poorly situated with regard to industrial areas and markets . . . [possessing] no notable mineral or agricultural riches', yet with 'a limited tourism potential' close to the beautiful Golden Gate nature reserve.

In the Transvaal, where the largest amount of land for black settlement had to be found in terms of the Beaumont Report (1916) and the 1936 Land Act, most moves resulted from the policy of relocating Africans into territorial Bantustans. 1,153,000 had been moved by 1982, and another 585,000 were under threat of relocation. Of those removed, 400,000 had been taken from farms, 350,000 as a result of urban relocation, 280,000 in terms of 'black spot' removal, and 120,000 in the name of territorial consolidation. The Surplus People Project listed 58 black spots, and 29 towns whose black residential areas had been moved. Evidence of resistance to removal has emerged from some Transvaal localities such as Rooigrond, near Mafeking, whose turbulent history goes back to the days of the Republic of Goshen. The people of Mogopa, near Ventersdorp, who were moved with a considerable show of force to Pachsdraai at the end of 1983 resented actions by the Government in circumventing first an Appeal Court decision in their favour, and later a joint reprimand by three European governments to the Government of South Africa in May 1989 for blocking a further attempt by this community to buy their original land back. Parts of the farms Driefontein, Daggaskraal and KwaNgema in the Wakkerstroom district of the South-eastern Transvaal (a community comprising some 5,000 Swazi-, Zulu- and Sotho-speaking adults, 1,500 of whom were landowners in 1982) had been bought by P. ka I. Seme on behalf of the Native Farmers' Association of Africa in 1912, shortly before the Land Act made black purchases in this area unlawful. According to the Surplus People Project, the total population grew to between 30,000 and 50,000. The Government decided to remove this black spot, and to relocate the people to their respective Homelands according to their home languages, and also to build a dam covering part of their land. The first indications that removal was intended were given in 1965, but pressure was only brought to bear in 1981. At this point the residents elected a board of directors, with Saul Mkhize, a well-respected community leader, as its chairman. The authorities chose not to recognise the board. Relations between the community and the authorities deteriorated during 1982 and 1983, as a series of petty incidents showed. Eventually, on 2 April 1983 Mkhize called a meeting at the Cabanangi school, supposedly to discuss the move. Two policemen arrived beforehand to ban the meeting. There were altercations and the judge who later heard the case, accepted police evidence that stones had been thrown. Mkhize was shot and killed by a policeman, who was subsequently charged with murder and acquitted. The residents were eventually granted permission to remain on their land in 1985.

The number of people relocated in Natal between 1948 and 1982 was calculated by the Surplus People Project at 745,000, nearly half of whom were farm residents, 105,000 lived in 'black spots', and 295,000 had been moved under the Group Areas Act. A further 606,000 were said to be under threat of removal, mainly from black spots and urban areas.

Reports by the Association for Rural Advancement in Natal during the early 1980s reveal a gradual switch of emphasis from the removal of labour tenants on white farms to the clearing of black spots, especially in Northern Natal, where the squatters on white-owned land had attracted the attention of the Du Toit Commission in 1959–60 (Davenport and Hunt). By 1983 black freehold in northern Natal had largely been cleared, and the authorities were beginning to turn their attention to Ladysmith and the Natal Midlands. The Limehill example (Desmond) had alerted the authorities to the need for more careful preparation in the provision of infrastructures before relocating people, but the scale of operations made this extremely difficult to implement, as was the case in the eastern Cape, where the early publicity given to Dimbaza had been comparable. Consequently Natal removals were far from lacking in distress stories, as is shown by the detailed research which lies behind the Natal volume of *Forced Removals*, with references to places like Mzimhlophe, where no water supply had been laid on during the eight years since the removal in 1975, where unemployment was high, diet insufficient, and the provision of schools, clinics and shops generally inadequate.

17.3   THE CONSPIRACY OF GOLD AND MAIZE

The Resettlement policy, with its massive movement of people from places where they were trying to solve their own survival problems to places where survival was commonly very difficult indeed, presupposed the availability of emergency rations on an enormous scale. In a number of areas rations were indeed made available at state expense, though sometimes only for a brief initial period. But their availability needs to be seen against the background of food production in South Africa as a whole, and its cost, and this for most practical purposes meant one commodity above others: maize.

The published figures for maize production show a healthy excess of production over consumption for all years from 1968 to 1983, with the exception of 1973 and 1982–3, accompanied by enormous fluctuations in the size of the crop, largely owing to weather hazards. Exceptionally good harvests in 1981–2 were followed by the severest drought in living memory in 1982–4. In April 1981 the crop was estimated at 13.5 million tons – 25 per cent up on that for 1980, and more than double the local demand at the price at which it was offered. The maize Board, however, was obliged by agreement to buy 95 per cent of the crop, at a price fixed by the Minister of Agriculture at R146 per ton, even though it was unlikely to be able to sell a substantial proportion of it, and would have to make up any loss on stocks sold outside South Africa, where the ruling price was considerably below the South African. Although the subsidy amounted to several hundred million rands, the farmers for their part complained of a 25 per cent increase in production costs in 1980–1, as a result of increased prices for fuel and the protection of local industries engaged in the building of tractors and the manufacture of fertiliser and bags. This occurred in the aftermath of an overall doubling of costs, not matched by an equivalent rise in produce prices throughout the 1970s (Hugo). Cattle-ranchers were heavily hit by the rising cost of stock feed, especially those in the northern Transvaal, where their difficulties were compounded by the growing insecurity of the border region, which was reflected in a significant decline in the white occupancy of frontier farms. The National Maize Producers' Association also demanded the removal of protection so that it could produce more economically in a free market; but industry and commerce were less hopeful than farmers of being able to produce under open competition, and feared the influence of the maize lobby on Government policy.

In 1982–4 the drought obliged the Government to import maize and also compounded the farmers' debt. By June 1982 the Land Bank, which lent money via the cooperatives to farmers at well below the prime interest rate, was in debt to the commercial banks to the tune of R2,000 million and needed to raise further sums to fund the farmers for the next planting season. A table published in the *Financial Mail*'s agricultural survey in September 1982 showed that the farmers' burden of debt had risen from R1,384.2 million in 1970 to R4,883.3 million in 1981. Early in 1983 the Government took the pressure off the banks by converting the farmers' debt into mortgage bonds repayable over a long term, and based on a deliberately low valuation of agricultural land. By mid-1983, owing to the recent poor harvests, the maize farmers claimed a loss of R834 million. The Government, which had already allowed maize price increases of 35 per cent between 1981 and 1983, allowed two further increases of 10 and 18.5 per cent in January and April 1984 respectively, with the support of the official Opposition, on the ground that the number of insolvencies which would otherwise have occurred would have been unacceptably high. Understandably, when the maize farmers put in for a further governmental subsidy in 1985, the Government felt compelled to refuse the request.

Most of the Republic's maize production occurred in the white-owned farming areas; but the Homelands were also cereal producers, and food in these regions was so short in 1982 that nineteen districts were declared disaster areas, the whole region from Ciskei through to KwaZulu and the northern Transvaal being seriously affected. Voluntary drought relief organisations, of which the South African Institute of Race Relations project, Operation Hunger, and the American Christian relief organisation, World Vision, were among the more prominent, issued public appeals to which there was a good response from some business organisations and foreign embassies; but a larger part of the relief work was necessarily devoted to emergency feeding rather than to the promotion of agricultural self-help.

By early 1984 the possibility of agricultural disaster, unless the growth of population could be curbed and the misuse of land by incorrect farming methods halted, was causing much concern. On 17 March the Minister of Health announced a propaganda campaign to try to curb population growth. In April, the second Carnegie Inquiry, focusing mainly on black poverty, held a major conference in Cape Town in an attempt to promote a campaign as effective as that launched under the same auspices against white poverty fifty years earlier. One estimate made at the conference was that there were 1,400,000 destitute people in the Homelands, earning no income, and living on land whose populations had doubled in twenty years, causing a collapse of traditional subsistence agriculture. Nor was the disaster confined to South Africa and her satellite states. The civil war in Mozambique, linked with the lack of rains in early spring, resulted in such large numbers of people being taken into emergency camps that on 18 December the *Observer* referred to a crisis of Biafran proportions. The link between this fact and the Nkomati Accord of May 1984 [see p. 476] needs little stressing.

If the drought and the maize crisis had occurred on their own, they would have constituted very serious problems in their own right. The fact that they happened against the background of steadily rising defence costs [see pp. 499, 471] and massive public expenditure on population resettlement made them part of a much larger crisis. But on top of this, the Government found itself facing the most serious monetary crisis in the country's history. Gold did not maintain its high 1980 price of $850 but fell, unevenly, to below $300 by the beginning of 1985, owing to the surge of the dollar itself in the light of President Reagan's cut-back on possible spending. Unlike the years 1929–32, when the value of South African currency had been protected by the international demand for gold, this time the value of the rand was allowed to fall together with gold, in competition with the dollar.

An unexpected conjunction of circumstances had conspired to bring together all the weaknesses in an economic system which had to that point appeared to be proof against all kinds of onslaught: the country's over-dependence on gold, a wasting asset; its inability to sell sufficient goods either to the Western world or to Africa as a substitute for gold exports [see p. 466]; its failure to train and engage the whole population in productive activity and pay it an adequate wage, so as to build up industrial profits and head off the alienation of the black worker by opening up the domestic market. Meanwhile the Treasury and the Reserve Bank attempted to impose financial discipline, but the heavy commitments of the State prohibited proper recourse to this formula for success. The Government failed to hold back large increases in public service salaries, so that its rate of expenditure rose to 28 per cent of the gross domestic product in 1984 (against 19 per cent in 1980, when the gold price was right up). By September 1985 the value of the rand had fallen so low in relation to all major currencies that the Reserve Bank was forced to intervene both to block its further decline and to freeze foreign loan repayments without renouncing obligations.

17.4   SIGNS OF A WHITE BACKLASH

But in 1982, the full extent of South Africa's economic crisis lay in the future. A dominant feature on the political scene was the emergence of right-wing pressure groups, consisting largely of white workers who were beginning to feel the draught of unemployment, and farmers fighting the problem of rising costs. Not surprisingly, they found political homes in two right-wing movements which broke away from the National Party, as well as in various extra-parliamentary groupings which collectively signalled a return in Afrikaner politics something like the turbulence of the 1930s. There were some who had been excluded from power and the Party as a result of the Information Scandal. Others, led by Dr Andries Treurnicht from within the Party, were making it plain that they thought that P. W. Botha's liberalisation policies threatened to go too far.

Early in 1982 the pot began to boil. In February the Party leadership decided to force a showdown with the Treurnicht group, as Vorster had done with Albert Hertzog in 1969; but in the case of Treurnicht and his followers, it was likely to be far bigger affair. There was at least the possibility, as Ivor Wilkins suggested in the *Sunday Times*, that the rebel group had themselves planned a showdown at the same time. On 24 February, Treurnicht and twenty-one other members of the caucus refused to support a cleverly-worded motion, proposed by the Leader of the House of Assembly, S. P. ('Fanie') Botha, of 'full confidence and unqualified support for the Prime Minister, his leadership and his interpretation of National Party policy'. They objected to the Prime Minister's reference earlier in the week to 'healthy power-sharing' as being utterly foreign to Nationalist philosophy, even though Botha had then picked his words carefully and drawn a distinction between his own understanding of the term and that of the Progressives, stating that, 'For us the concept of consultation and co-responsibility is a healthy form of power-sharing, without undermining the principle of self-determination. Therefore we prefer the term co-responsibility.' The logic of Botha's argument, which had specific reference to the Coloured people, was that if there was to be no separate Homeland for them, then they would have to participate in some way in a common political system if they were to be given any power at all.

Treurnicht correctly analysed the constitutional proposals of 1977 [see p. 382] as stopping short of substantial power-sharing, because in their original form, and in the form in which they were gazetted on 3 April 1979 they left ultimate control, in the event of deadlock, in a Council of Cabinets dominated by the white Parliament. But he and his followers refused to resign from the Party, which they evidently intended to try to take over. Ex-President Vorster, acting with rather more conviction than discretion, came out publicly in support of them. The real showdown came at the Transvaal Head Committee's meeting on 27 February, when members had to brave a gauntlet of Treurnicht supporters holding large anti-Botha posters on their way into the hall. Circumstances seemed to favour Treurnicht, especially as an engagement in Namibia was expected to prevent P. W. Botha from attending. But Botha staged a surprise appearance at the meeting in person, replied at length to Treurnicht, and received a confidence vote of 172 to 36.

There still remained the Waterberg constituency, represented in Parliament by Treurnicht himself. But again the Party leadership used surprise tactics. F. W. de Klerk, the Minister of Mineral and Energy Affairs, called an urgent meeting of the Transvaal executive on 8 March, and this body expelled Dr Treurnicht from the Party, thus depriving him of the right of admission to the Waterberg meeting due to take place at Thabazimbi on 11 March, though in practice he was admitted to the meeting and allowed to speak. The Waterberg constituency remained loyal to its member, and gave him a strong vote of confidence after a tough verbal battle between De Klerk and himself. But De Klerk was able to commandeer the committee's books. Treurnicht was obliged to fight back from outside the Party. This he did at a mass meeting in the Skilpadsaal, Pretoria, on 20 March, when a crowd estimated at 7,000 gave him a rousing welcome. Thus the *Konserwatiewe* Party (K.P.) was born. It drew in the New Conservative Party which Dr Connie Mulder had formed after his own eviction, but not the H.N.P. of Dr Jaap Marais, who was still wedded to the Verwoerdian doctrine of total apartheid.

Botha needed to consolidate. He took the unusual step of calling a federal congress of the National Party to Bloemfontein on 30 July, in an attempt to set the tone for the Party as a whole and guide the individual provinces on the issue of 'healthy power-sharing' as laid down in the President's Council's draft constitutional proposals which had in the meantime been made public [see p. 434]. A federal congress could not lay down party policy, but no provincial congresses had ever in practice contradicted a federal decision.

In preparation for these developments, the Cabinet was reformed with a new portfolio of Constitutional Development instituted for Heunis, while De Klerk took over Heunis's Ministry of the Interior. It was necessary to give Heunis this additional authority in matters constitutional, to eliminate the influence of Dr Dennis Worrall, whose indiscretion in suggesting a possible future role for Africans in the proposed new constitution [see p. 431] had come at an awkward moment, for with the K.P. about to hold their first congress at the same time as the Nationalists, there was no point in offering hostages to fortune.

The danger of division within the Party thus removed, Botha enjoyed yet another triumph at Bloemfontein. The Federal Congress of the National Party gave its blessing to the President's Council's constitutional plan as interpreted for it by the Prime Minister. Meanwhile the K.P. were putting their own act together in Pretoria, and laying down the need for a separate Coloured Homeland.

Between August 1982 and May 1983 a hardening of the lines between the Nationalists and the K.P. took place in a series of by-elections, with the H.N.P. failing to make much of an impact. For the Germiston provincial seat in August, the K.P. ran in ahead of the Nationalists in a very low poll, but the Nationalists recovered at the expense of both the Progressives and the right wing in Stellenbosch in November, after launching a very determined election campaign. They also took the new seat of Walvis Bay. But at Parys and Bothaville, though the Nationalists retained both seats, the rival right-wing parties matched them in the number of votes cast. In an extraordinary challenge thrown down by Fanie Botha, the Minister of Planning, three northern Transvaal constituencies were thrown into by-elections; but although the Nationalist and K.P. faces were saved in this 'battle of the Berge', the Soutpansberg seat went to the K.P. in 1984 when the same minister resigned from Parliament. This gave the K.P. control of the rural northern Transvaal. It was a situation in which the Government might, in certain circumstances, have looked for support to English-speakers. Vause Raw's New Republic Party had little difficulty in offering it, but its weight was slight save in Natal, and several of its leaders went over to the Nationalists in 1984. The Progressives were alienated by the Government's constitutional proposals, and received no encouragement from the Government to draw closer. The middle ground, as one commentator noted, had come to be seen as a 'disaster area', and rational consensus between the thinking parties a forlorn hope.

Outside the formal right-wing Afrikaner party structures, the 1980s witnessed the growth of new movements, and new directions in old movements, in reaction to the reformist challenge presented by P. W. Botha's policies. An *Afrikaner Weerstandsbeweging* (A.W.B.) announced itself in history in 1978–9 by tarring and feathering a Pretoria professor, F. A. van Jaarsveld, for daring to discuss in a public lecture the historiography of divine intervention in the battle of Blood River. Some months after their conviction for assault, its leaders also received suspended sentences for possessing a cache of undeclared weapons and explosives. Soon afterwards a *Vereniging van Oranjewerkers*, whose secretary was Hendrik Verwoerd (Jr), grew out of a S.A.B.R.A. research project to locate a territory which Afrikaners could call their own, shortly before S.A.B.R.A. itself disowned the National Party's tricameralism (Zille). Two organisations emerged from the Broederbond in the early 1980s to provide a rallying point for people with Verwoerdian loyalties who were appalled at P. W. Botha's reforms. One was *Aksie Eie Toekoms*, which sought to provide a home for H.N.P. members who had been driven from the Bond in 1972. The other was an *Afrikaner Volkswag*, chaired by Dr Carel Boshoff (Dr Verwoerd's son-in-law), which aimed to infiltrate policy-making committees in order to preserve apartheid. The most radical of the new movements to emerge was a *Blanke Bevrydigings Beweging* (White Liberation Movement), led by an ex-professor of biochemistry, which stood on an explicitly racist platform, determined to defend whites against the 'mud races' and the Jews.

The A.W.B. maintained the highest profile of all, under the leadership of Eugene Terreblanche, an ex-policeman. Projecting a neo-Nazi image, it also registered itself as a *Boerestaat Party*, but preferred to regard the Conservative Party as its parliamentary front, though the latter was often loath to fraternise with it. It set up a hierarchy of councils at local and regional levels, under a central *hoofraad*, and encouraged members of its paramilitary *brandwagte*, which were set up in most northern towns, to carry their firearms in public. It developed its own youth movement (*stormvalke*), surrounded its leader with a bodyguard (*Aquila*), and announced as its goal the formation of an independent Afrikaner *volksstaat* when the moment was politically opportune.

Much of the ideological furniture of the Afrikaner nationalism of the 1930s reappeared in the thinking and the propaganda of these new movements. They proclaimed an ethnic nationalism rooted in language and cultural values, though with seemingly less dedication to orthodox Christianity, and a manifestly dangerous fascination for theological fantasies which on one occasion excited a vulnerable youth to go on a cold-blooded shooting spree as a deliberate act of racist brutality. This contrasts with the improved concern for the welfare of black labour noted by Hugo in their rural recruiting grounds, despite a shared feeling in all the movements that black-supportive reforms were dangerous, that township unrest should be more systematically suppressed and cross-border military retaliatory raids stepped up – all vote-catching ideas emanating from people whose expectation of success at the polls grew rather than diminished as a result of the elections of 1987–9.

17.5 REACTIONS TO DENATIONALISATION IN THE HOMELANDS

Whatever else 'healthy power sharing' might have meant in the Government's mind, it had no obvious reference to blacks as South Africans. The independent Homeland policy went ahead under Botha, as under Vorster. Transkei and Bophutatswana had obtained their independence in 1976 and 1977. Venda was to acquire it in 1979, and Ciskei in 1981. The Government intended that, as each Homeland acquired full sovereign status, so its citizens should lose their South African citizenship and retain that of the

Homeland alone, even if they continued to live and work in the Republic proper, as many thousands of them did. In such a way, South Africa could acquire an actual white majority to correspond with its political system.

There could have been few better catalysts than this for a black political revival, despite the suppression of the Black Consciousness organisations in October 1977, given a sufficient measure of unity among blacks. But the early years of the Botha Ministry were to be more marked for the varieties of black political activity than for its inner coherence.

The Homelands were slow to move away from a posture of subservience to the Republic of South Africa, chiefly on account of monetary transfers for which they were dependent on Pretoria, which in 1988–9 totalled R5,667,817,000, of which two-fifths went to the four which had chosen independence – Transkei, Bophutatswana, Venda and Ciskei (*Race Relations Survey, 1988–9*, pp. 62–4). These four had accepted independence on South Africa's terms without either preserving South African citizenship for their subjects, or gaining international recognition as sovereign states, or achieving territorial frontiers which satisfied them. All were to find the task of political management, particularly the control of graft in high places, beyond them. There were signs by early 1990, however, in all the states which had all accepted independence, as well as in Kwa Zulu, which had rejected it, of a renewed desire to end the apartheid system which had brought them into being.

The unhappy story of Venda, under its leader Patrick Mphephu, who had acquired a non-traditional paramountcy and the headship of a one-party state several years before his death in April 1988, was punctuated by a particularly unsavoury spate of ritual murders, some of which were hard to separate from the political tensions within the state, especially as cabinet ministers were thought to have been involved. Add to these events a sustained attack by the Government on leaders of the Lutheran Evangelical Church, who refused to be politically conformist or politically silent, in a country whose borders ran close to the 'frontline states' of Zimbabwe and Mozambique, and the sensitivity of the Government is not difficult to understand, however little there is to be said for the brutality of its police methods and its over-zealous efforts to serve the interests of Pretoria.

When the Government of the Ciskei accepted independence in 1981, it did so against the unanimous advice of the Quail Commission, a body of international experts who concluded that independence would be unpopular among Ciskeians, and recommended that the people would be better served by a 'condominium' under joint black and white rule over both the Ciskei and the corridor between East London and Queenstown, whose inclusion would provide a potential industrial nucleus around which economic prosperity could be built. Nevertheless, the referendum conducted by Chief Lennox Sebe in December 1980 gave him a Napoleonic majority of 295,891 votes against 1,642 on a 59.5 per cent poll. At the time it was generally assumed that King William's Town would be included in Ciskei, as recommended by the Van der Walt Commission; but in April 1981, shortly before the white general election, the exclusion of King William's Town was announced. The Status of Ciskei Bill was carried through the

South African Parliament on 9 October. Court applications subsequently brought to restrain the Ciskeian Government from taking independence were rejected on the ground that in strict law the conferring of independence was a unilateral action by the South African Parliament, 'whether the Ciskeians wished to accept it or not'.

Independence brought to Ciskei a considerable inflow of wealth through the establishment of industries which took advantage of the favourable short-term tax and labour concessions offered by the Government. Dimbaza, notorious for its squalor when attention was first drawn to this resettlement camp, acquired an industrial area of some size. Lennox Sebe, who, like Patrick Mphephu of Venda, was granted the office of president for life in 1983, travelled extensively to Europe and Israel to attract business ventures. Yet the resettlement of over 300,000 people in the territory during the 1960s and 1970s, some from the Transkei, some from other parts of South Africa, were an enormous incubus with which Ciskei did not have the resources to cope. Despite the prosperity of its new capital at Bisho, on which Sebe spent huge sums, Ciskei remained a poor country, and the distress of its peasantry was not alleviated by a land policy, similar to that of Venda, which gave the state wide powers to expropriate peasant holdings in the interest of development. Ciskei was held together by one of the toughest police forces in the whole southern African complex, and dominated by Sebe's Ciskei National Independence Party, whose powers of patronage effectively undermined formal opposition and made resistance to incorporation by alienated communities at Mgwali, Potsdam, Peelton, Thornhill and in the sprawling dormitory town of Mdantsane, on the fringe of East London, extremely hazardous. On top of all this, domestic political crises, notably a split in the presidential family which led to the detention of Sebe's brothers Charles (his Chief of Security) and Namba (his Minister of Transport) and other members of the family, helped to heighten public tension. So did a simmering conflict with the Government of Transkei arising out of the latter's attempts to promote Xhosa political unification, which reached crisis point when Charles Sebe was 'sprung' from the Bisho jail and escaped to Umtata, it was thought with Transkeian connivance. The deposition of Lennox Sebe by a military coup in March 1990 was cause for little surprise.

Bophutatswana had started on its course as an independent state in 1977 with confidence unshaken by the destruction through arson of its legislative building the previous year, because it had an economic growth potential higher than that of any other black South African territory. Its rigid constitution also represented a notable advance on those of other Homelands, for it contained an explicit Declaration of Rights enforceable by the courts on common law grounds. The constitution also allowed for a multi-party system, even if little was done to encourage it, and from 1984 it provided for the election of the president by direct popular vote rather than by an electoral college – itself a potential check on the ruling party.

But mere good fortune was not enough. Two-thirds of President Lukas Mangope's subjects were Tswana-speaking, the remainder either northern Sotho or Ndebele; and Bophutatswana faced major problems with the incorporation of minorities: both resistance to transfer from the Republic of South Africa, which was common to all Homelands on account of the concomitant loss of South African citizen rights, and resistance to the imposition of the Tswana language on non-Tswana-speakers. Whereas other Homelands were prepared to consider dual citizenship, Mangope insisted that Bophutatswana's citizens had to renounce South African allegiance, in the hope that this would conserve the territory's resources for its own residents, and perhaps also lead to amalgamation with Botswana (whence he received little encouragement). Political difficulties among the Rolong of Thaba'Nchu, who feared incorporation in QwaQwa, and above all in the Winterveld–Mabopane–Hammanskraal area north of Pretoria after the incorporation of new territory in 1983, shattered the harmony of the state. Repeated amendments to the Internal Security Act were introduced to tighten controls, especially when the university and the schools became centres of opposition. The safeguards of the Declaration of Rights proved ineffective in court cases brought after 1984. Police violence in the areas of turbulence was bad and well-authenticated, though – like South Africa's official report on Sharpeville – the report of a judicial inquiry into the violence was withheld from the public. Worse still, the Seoposengwe Party, which was opposed to the principle of separate Homelands, was intimidated into ineffectiveness, while a new People's Progressive Party led by Peter Malibane-Metsing, was kept waiting for three years for registration before fighting 54 and winning 6 seats (against the 66 gained by Mangope's Bophutatswana Democratic Party) in the general election of 1987. Leaders of the P.P.P. were involved in an army coup in February 1988, which briefly toppled Mangope's regime. The President, his minister of defence, his commissioner of police, his army chief and several seconded South African officials, were briefly held in the Independence Stadium and the army base at Mmabatho, until they were rescued by South African troops in response to a plea smuggled out by Mangope, and the rebellion suppressed. Though Mangope was restored to power, his stature as a political leader was greatly diminished by this last undignified failure and the publicity of the treason court which inflicted long prison sentences on the convicted rebels.

Transkei was able, on accepting independence, to persuade a number of foreign firms to establish industrial plant on its territory (Southall), but in several instances this resulted in the blatant exploitation of the fledgling state (Streek and Wicksteed). Kaiser Matanzima was kept in power by Pretoria with the help of tough legislation conceived on the South African pattern minus some of its racist attributes. In Transkei South Africa managed, as Southall has shown, to co-opt a small chiefly nucleus, which had been given an initial position of dominance in the legislature until it was possible, with the grant of independence, to give elected members numerical parity with chiefs in the sure knowledge that Matanzima's Transkeian National Independence Party (T.N.I.P.) would be able to fill the great majority of those seats either with other amenable chiefs or with members of the new entrepreneurial class which had been nurtured under the system. A cabinet crisis, following the dismissal of Stella Sigcawu, the

Minister of Education, brought an opposition Democratic Progressive Party (D.P.P.) into being in 1979, under the Matanzimas' longstanding rival, Paramount Chief Sabata Dalindyebo of the Thembu. Though shaken, the regime secured the conviction of Sabata on a minor charge, but his acquittal on all the serious charges brought against him, and the large amount of public support for him which emerged, were a propaganda disaster for the Government. Most members of the D.P.P. executive were arrested in 1980, and many others detained or banned (Streek and Wicksteed). Sabata fled to Zambia, where he made contact with the A.N.C., from which significant results would flow after his death in 1986.

Before long the Matanzima power base began to crack. Kaiser resigned the presidency in 1986, but retained his seat in the legislature as paramount chief of Western Thembuland, being succeeded as president by Paramount Chief Tutor Ngangelizwe Ndamase, son of Chief Victor Poto of Western Pondoland. Chief George Matanzima, the prime minister, whose animosity towards his brother was reflected in various attempts to exclude him from power, so weakened his own position by these efforts that the rising turbulence of Transkeian politics in 1986–9 resulted in the overthrow of both men. Charges of corruption in various government departments provided the necessary catalyst. One victim of the ensuing in-fighting was General Ron Reid-Daly, the ex-Rhodesian Selous Scout commander of the Transkeian Defence Force, who was replaced by General Zondwa Mtirara in April 1987. As a result of George Matanzima's influence, Mtirara was almost immediately superseded by General Bantu Holomisa (who had previously been detained by Reid-Daly). The crisis in the army high command, which reflected a much wider malaise, led in October 1987 to the flight of George Matanzima, who was later imprisoned on conviction for serious misappropriation of public funds. The T.N.I.P.'s first choice as his successor was Stella Sigcawu. But in January 1988 she was herself ousted in a military coup led by General Holomisa – it was thought at the time with South African connivance which, if true, is not likely to have been the whole truth.

It was at this point that the Dalindyebo succession acquired crucial importance. The burial of the traditional ruler of all the Thembu had become a matter of protocol. When Sabata's son Buyelekhaya brought his body back to the Great Place for public burial in April 1986, it was seized on the orders of Kaiser Matanzima, whose authority in western Pondoland still held, and given a covert pauper's burial despite the protection Buyelekhaya had received from the courts for his action. But Holomisa, himself a Thembu though he discounted this as the reason for his actions, supported Buyelekhaya's claim to succeed to the paramountcy and encouraged him to return. With the further support of a new Congress of Traditional Leaders of South Africa (Contralesa), which had first arisen among chiefs in KwaNdebele but spread to KwaZulu (in defiance of Buthelezi) and into Transkei, Buyelekhaya returned in October 1989 to participate in the public reburial of his father, in the presence both of prominent traditional rulers like King Mswati II of Swaziland, but also of leading political opponents of the South African Government, some of whom, like

Buyelekhaya himself, had close association with the A.N.C. These developments, occurring shortly after F. W. de Klerk had succeeded P. W. Botha as South Africa's state president, were followed by Holomisa's unbanning of the U.D.F. and other related organisations in November, and by his announcement that he intended to conduct a plebiscite to test Transkeian wishes for reincorporation in South Africa. The first Bantu Homeland to opt for independence appeared to be about to retrace its steps.

The success which Mangosuthu Buthelezi had enjoyed in building up his political programme before 1976 did not continue after that year, and the pointers to his change of fortune are clear. Transkei's acceptance of independence broke the solid front of resistance to the Verwoerdian programme which he had built up. His intervention in the Mzimhlophe hostel encounter during the Soweto disturbances [see p. 390] cast doubt on the extent of his support for the liberation movement, especially when the banning of the Black Consciousness organisations and the murder of Steve Biko carried black anger beyond the point at which clever strategies were sufficient to attract supporters. To maintain his position as a contender for black political loyalties he found it necessary to indulge in tactics which themselves proved counter-productive. The increasing militarisation of Inkatha illustrates the point: the setting up of its Youth Brigade (1976) and of its Women's Brigade (1977), its invasion of the teaching profession and the school syllabus (1979), its forceful suppression of school boycotts and university campus unrest (1980, 1983) and its promotion of paramilitary camps (from 1981) provoked a growing measure of mistrust from the radical movements, which Inkatha's periodical *Clarion Call* attacked relentlessly for their refusal to accept a 'multi-strategy' approach to liberation. When Buthelezi flatly rejected the requirement of the Minister of Justice, Jimmy Kruger, that Inkatha should limit its membership to Zulus, even this did not convince them that it had a place for outsiders. Suspicion of his intentions broke surface with the violent expulsion of Buthelezi and several white 'collaborators' and journalists, though they were guests of the family, from Robert Sobukwe's funeral at Graaff-Reinet in 1978. Nor was he able to achieve an understanding with other leaders of the black extra-parliamentary opposition – with Archie Gumede of the U.D.F., Nthatho Motlana of the Soweto Committee of Ten, Oliver Tambo, and other leaders of what he came increasingly to refer to with calculated provocation as the 'A.N.C. mission in exile'. In 1989 he crossed swords with General Bantu Holomisa of Transkei and with the leaders of the Contralesa movement which, perhaps more than any other, undermined his claim to represent the traditional in black politics.

But Buthelezi was nothing if not resourceful, and behind that resourcefulness it is possible to see a passionate longing to resolve the conflicts of South Africa by paying less attention to their ideological components (always with the exception of his irrepressible Zulu patriotism) and considerably more to the dynamics of the conflict, in which he saw himself as a gladiator in the middle, facing up to the harsh realities of a power struggle in which other participants had simply miscalculated the logistics of opposition to the South African Government.

In March 1980 the Inkatha Central Committee launched the Buthelezi Commission, consisting of 46 scholars, politicians, lawyers, educationalists, religious leaders and businessmen, to look into the possibility of reconstituting KwaZulu and Natal as a single self-governing unit, in the hope that it could provide a viable way of breaking out of the apartheid structures. A similar idea had already been scouted by a committee under Professor J. A. Lombard, who had been invited by the Sugar Association to look into the implications of a proposed consolidation of KwaZulu for the sugar industry. But the Buthelezi Commission took the idea further, and reported in 1982 in favour of the political unification of KwaZulu and Natal under a form of consociational democracy, claiming that this was 'acceptable to clear majorities', and that there was 'strong and consistent support' for 'the market economy system as opposed to socialist or communal alternatives'. The Government would not accept that a KwaZulu-appointed commission had the competence to probe the future of Natal, and declined an invitation to serve. Its disposition towards KwaZulu can hardly have been sweetened at the time by the loss of face which it suffered when Buthelezi successfully took his case to the appeal court against a government decision to make over the Ingwavuma district of KwaZulu to Swaziland, and won. Whether this defeat had any influence on the Government's decision not to allow African representation in the tricameral parliamentary system which it referred to a plebiscite in 1983 may be doubted; but the rejection of Buthelezi's constitutional initiatives, which had attracted considerable support from liberal thinkers in opposition circles (though some, like Southall, were very critical) deserves notice. The insult to Africans everywhere contained in their exclusion from power in the 1983 constitution, especially after four Homelands had rejected his advice and accepted independence, understandably soured the Zulu leader, especially since it is quite clear from the KwaZulu Legislative Assembly debates of 1980 that Buthelezi was able and willing to deliver the support of that body to a national convention to debate the sharing of power.

Even after the rebuff of 1983, the Buthelezi Report was not a dead letter, for the KwaZulu cabinet and a group of Natal politicians reached an agreement in 1984 to cooperate on common problems, and they hoped that this would lead to the setting up of a joint executive authority, and ultimately to a joint legislature. They submitted draft legislation to the Government in March 1986, and this time the National Party accepted observer status at an Indaba which met in Durban in April, though the Conservative Party and the U.D.F. refused to participate. The Indaba settled for a two-chamber legislature, one elected by proportional representation, the other based on ethnic groupings, each with a veto on any proposed legislation; but the Government, which now accepted the principle of a joint executive authority to the extent of actually introducing one in 1986, turned down the proposal for a joint Natal–KwaZulu legislature out of hand.

The resistance of the U.D.F. to the Indaba was an important pointer to the rifts within the extra-parliamentary Opposition. 'Mzala's' critique of the Indaba reflects a strongly-held belief in A.N.C. circles that no constitutional changes were acceptable unless they emanated from an expression of the dominant will of the people, and the Indaba was rejected because it had not arisen out of a decision of direct democracy, just as its federal ideas seemed inappropriate to the correction of a political system rooted in racial inequality and the unequal distribution of wealth. The Indaba also seems to have enjoyed less white support than its initiators imagined, in view of the National Party's success in winning most white seats in Natal in the general election of 1987, despite the support for it shown by the P.F.P.

Even worse for the Buthelezi option, and for the immediate peace of South Africa, was the growing confrontation between Buthelezi's followers and the U.D.F.- and C.O.S.A.T.U.-supported townships around Pietermaritzburg and Durban, where a slowly excalating civil war developed during the Emergency of 1985–90. In their total context these developments are not hard to understand, though the suppression of detailed information during the State of Emergency makes the precise attribution of responsibility difficult. At bottom, the growing polarisation between Inkatha and the Mass Democratic Movement (to use nomenclature which became formalised in 1989) can be seen in the differing attitudes of the mass democrats and the A.N.C., on the one hand, and Inkatha on the other, to the use of violence. The former regarded it as a legitimate option, and an important bargaining counter, in view of the banning of the A.N.C. and the use of force by the state, whereas Inkatha renounced violence as a method of engaging the South African state, but found little incentive to avoid using it against black political opponents who in theory had no such inhibition. A further point of disagreement was the identification of the mass democrats with militant trade union activity, which became important after the launching of C.O.S.A.T.U. in December 1985, especially in the light of the democrats' anti-capitalist stance and their approval of international sanctions and foreign disinvestment from South Africa. Inkatha, by contrast, set up its own rival trade union, U.W.U.S.A., in 1986, consistently opposed sanctions and disinvestment, and sought the support of business interests. These were points of political principle which went to the heart of the anti-apartheid debate.

It was in Natal, above all, that conflict between Inkatha and its opponents broke surface. Here Inkatha, whose opponents persisted in describing it as a Zulu nationalist movement, and the Mass Democratic Movement, which Inkatha derided with rather less justice as a Xhosa infiltration into Zulu territory, met head-on. The M.D.M. feared an Inkatha take-over of the Natal townships outside KwaZulu which it did not control, especially when KwaZulu asked for and received the right to place its own police force in those townships. On the other hand, KwaZulu feared that C.O.S.A.T.U. would expand its membership into Inkatha-controlled areas. There seems initially to have been considerably more provocation from the Inkatha side than from that of the U.D.F., especially since a group of ruthless warlords emerged from Inkatha's ranks, whom the movement could not or would not contain, some of whom were occasionally brought to justice. Inkatha also provoked violence by bussing armed bands of its supporters into U.D.F.–controlled townships and encouraging them to attack Inkatha's opponents, sometimes in the expectation of acquiring the homes of the refugees as a reward. This was the case in Inanda, a seething over-populated trouble spot north of Durban, and in places surrounding Edendale, outside Pietermaritzburg, where one particularly graphic account describes a group of youths who set up their own paramilitary organisation under a leader named 'Colonel Gaddafi', to defend the homes from which their families had fled from the threat of occupation by rural immigrants under Inkatha protection. 'Gaddafi's' boys outgunned their opponents with the help of home-made firearms acquired at R120 each from home industries in 'Moscow' and paid for with R20 weekly contributions made on pay-day by members of the community diaspora. Gangsterism, attributed to 'com-tsotsis' (thugs who had once supported the U.D.F. but now lived simply by brigandage) grew easily in the townships around Pietermaritzburg and Durban, in opposition to the warlords. Rival factions, formal and informal, adopted their own liveries, danced their own *toyi-toyi* dances and sang their own songs of war, especially at the peace rallies which each side convened from time to time, as the rival leaderships sought relief from the violence and a chance to outmanoeuvre their opponents in repeated public demonstrations. But peace moves had little chance of success when the state, for all its earlier antagonism to the Buthelezi approach, persisted in banning or detaining the U.D.F. leadership at critical moments in their discussions – all against a background of massive overcrowding in the fastest human growth point in South Africa which still carried signs of the disastrous flood havoc of October 1987. Behind the Natal violence, and a major contributory cause of it, was a large amount of sheer social distress.

To say that the Homeland policy was collapsing in disarray by the mid-1980s would be an understatement. Any advantage which it may have had as a means of buying time for white South Africa needs to be set against the deep and bitter divisions which it created within and between black communities. It was certainly not a way of saving public money, or even of spending it wisely, in view of the emphasis so often placed on prestige investments rather than social welfare. Even as a device for cauterising black political growth in the common area, the South African Government was beginning to see its limitations by the late 1980s, by adopting a much more flexible approach to the issue of citizenship, and by bending before the growing force of objections to political independence; for in Bophutatswana, in KwaNdebele, in Ciskei, in Venda, in Transkei, and above all perhaps in KaNgwane, where the Chief Minister, Enos Mabuza, was walking a moderate political tightrope with consummate skill, moves for the political reunification of South Africa under an entirely new dispensation were gaining ground (to the credit of Buthelezi, who had never abandoned this route since the early 1970s). A 1987 amendment to the South African National States Constitution Act of 1971 recognised this by giving non-independent Homeland governments access to a long list of new powers which they could have without sacrificing their South African ties, thus devaluing independence itself as a desirable goal.

17.6   RESISTANCE TO DENATIONALISATION IN THE COMMON AREA: SCHOOL BOYCOTTS, RESURGENT TRADE UNIONISM, AND THE REVIVAL OF BLACK CONSCIOUSNESS AND A.N.C.–RELATED ACTIVITIES

The shattering experience of the Soweto disturbances had induced in the Department of Bantu Education a mood of determined but extremely cautious reform. The word 'Bantu' was speedily removed from the Education Act. The Act itself was repealed in 1979, and replaced by an Education and Training Act, which relieved pressures in various ways: by lowering the level of instruction through an official language to Standard 2, and not insisting on both official languages; by making school education largely free; by enabling white private schools to admit blacks after special registration. Teachers were given freedom to establish their own associations, which could criticise the system without risk of being arraigned for misconduct. A new wave of troubles nevertheless broke out in 1980.

It started in Soweto on 2 February, with a boycott in protest over the employment of white national servicemen as teachers in black schools. Between then and early June it spread to Cape Town, Uitenhage, Port Elizabeth, Grahamstown, Durban, the Universities of the North and Fort Hare, Pietermaritzburg and the University of Transkei, involving African, Coloured and Indian centres of learning. In most of the places listed above the demonstrations were continuous, and marked by widespread stop-outs and the burning of classrooms. The grievances expressed varied from place to place: that teachers were unqualified, or poorly paid, or immoral; that Bantu Education (which had technically been abolished in 1979) was unacceptable because it was 'tribal', or because it was education for menial work; that buildings were inferior by comparison with those provided by the white and even the Coloured and Indian education departments, textbooks in short supply, and school uniforms costly and unnecessary. Above all, there were demands for the integration of the education departments into a single system, so that equality could be seen to be there, and for the right to elect student representative councils (with memories of Soweto) for the expression of student grievances. There was little demand for the racial integration of schools, because Black Consciousness did not want that.

1980 was a year in which almost no black education happened at all, for the boycott lasted well into September. In June the Government asked for a report on the educational system by the Human Sciences Research Council, which appointed the Rector of the Rand Afrikaans University, Professor J. P. de Lange, as chairman of its Commission. The De Lange Report, which was released in October 1981, gave the educational system very broad coverage from the pre-school to the tertiary levels, and laid special emphasis on technical education in view of the growing skilled manpower shortage in the country as a whole. Its most noteworthy political recommendations were for the establishment of a single ministry of education for purposes of determining national policy and the channelling of funds, and against 'differentiation based purely on differences of race or colour', which it saw as 'contrary to the social and ethical demands for justice'. These were carefully chosen words, but if they were meant to imply the integration of the races in one educational system, which might have been the best way to handle the insularity of Black Consciousness, the Government made it clear in an accompanying interim memorandum that this was unacceptable. Dr Viljoen, the Minister of Education, came out very clearly against racial integration in government schools on a number of subsequent occasions: he would go no further than allow private schools to admit pupils of other colours if they wished to do so – a practice which would not have been allowed in the Verwoerdian era. The stand taken by the Government was massively endorsed by an Afrikaner conference in Bloemfontein, well attended by thinkers of a conservative persuasion, who were told by their chairman that 'we will steer the congress on a middle path between the policies of Mr P. W. Botha and the H.N.P.'. That left little room for shared learning experiences, healthy or otherwise. A White Paper on Education was released by the Government on 23 November 1983, endorsing the existing structures, to the chagrin of eight of the commissioners, who were moved to dissent in public.

In the meantime the new Department of Education and Training (previously 'Bantu Education') had embarked on a massive schoolbuilding programme in the hope of killing discontent by the provision of amenities. It also started to implement a policy of compulsory education for blacks to bring them into line with other race groups. Channels of communication between the Department and the school communities still remained poor, chiefly on account of the Government's reluctance to allow the pupils to elect their own representative councils, in view of the influence exerted by the Soweto S.R.C. in 1976. Further class boycotts occurred in 1984, notably at Cradock, following the dismissal of a local teacher and community leader, Matthew Goniwe, who had refused transfer and was later to lose his life at the hands of unknown assassins in July 1985, after the local African community had come out strongly in his support. The school boycott movement also became linked with demonstrations against the new constitution in August and September 1984, and these became particularly active, provoking police counter-violence in the Vaal triangle at Sebokeng and Sharpeville, and in the eastern Cape. The use of troops acting in a police role showed how serious the situation had become.

There was also a good deal of movement on the workers' front, but black trade unionism had had a late start even if it had shown its potential strength during the early 1970s. The Report of the National Manpower Commission in 1982 disclosed a sharp increase in the African membership of registered trade unions from 56,700 in 1980 to 260,000 in 1981 – almost a quarter of the total membership, though under 20 per cent of African workers belonged to any union at all in 1983. Registered unions were looked upon increasingly, by politicised workers, as 'part of the system' and for that reason to be avoided, so that an organisation like T.U.C.S.A., which had made a strong stand for the recognition of mixed unions in the 1950s in order to preserve black access to bargaining power, now found itself threatened by the rise of new black unregistered unions, which did not feel so obliged to observe the conciliation procedures laid down by law, and preferred to press their claims by means of short unofficial stoppages rather than formalised collective bargaining. T.U.C.S.A., the largest of the workers' federations, found itself in crisis in 1983, with its black membership growing far too slowly, and that mainly through the enforcement of closed shop union rules by its own affiliates, rather than by voluntary association. Its conference called for a ban on unregistered unions and turned down a proposal that workers should be allowed to join the union of their choice.

Other labour federations were gaining ground at T.U.C.S.A.'s expense. One such was the Council of Unions of South Africa (C.U.S.A.), founded in September 1980, a generally moderate group of black unions which registered themselves properly, sought to maintain good relations with management, but on the whole had a rather light record of effective industrial action. More effective, in terms of their industrial but not their political militancy (Van Niekerk), were the unions linked to the Federation of South African Trade Unions (F.O.S.A.T.U.) formed in April 1979, a group of unions whose membership was multi-racial, which based themselves, like C.U.S.A., on individual factories, sent their officials to the training project instituted by the University of the Witwatersrand and concentrated on the employment of good shop stewards to fight for their member's interests in the workplace. There were other unions, like the African Food and Canning Workers' Union and the Western Cape General Workers' Union, which were characterised by a predominantly African migrant membership and covered a range of trades. They managed to organise very effective strikes in 1979–80, notably over dismissals by a food processing and a cold storage firm in the western Cape, and succeeded in each case by means of an effective consumer boycott. The influence of these community-based demonstrations spread to the Eastern Cape, where the South African Allied Workers' Union organised a protest around the boycott of a sweet factory in East London in 1980–1.

In Port Elizabeth and Uitenhage, disputes in the motor industry in 1980–2 highlighted several of the dominant issues in the changing pattern of industrial relations. One was the difficulty of determining when a trade union should take up or refuse to have anything to do with community as distinct from strictly industrial issues, especially at a time and in a place where continuous troubles in the schools were making people politically conscious. The leaders of a F.O.S.A.T.U.-affiliated African union at Ford Motors lost the support of the main body of their own workers through refusing to act over the dismissal of an employee, Thozamile Botha, who had been elected president of the Port Elizabeth Black Civic Organisation (P.E.B.C.O.) and then been told by the firm that the two positions were incompatible. The issue was complicated by friction between Coloured and African workers, who had separate unions, one registered, the other not, and worked at different plants. At Uitenhage, by contrast, where Coloured and Africans worked on the same assembly lines at Volkswagen, there was little friction, and the African union which had lost its following at Ford to a new Motor Assembly Component Workers' Union (M.A.C.W.U.S.A.) not only retained good worker support, but had a good working relationship with U.B.C.O., the equivalent local civic association, as well. The Port Elizabeth–Uitenhage experience showed how premature police intervention in a dispute could disrupt rhythms of collective bargaining. It also highlighted the difficulty experienced by the emergent, unregistered unions in assessing the limits of their bargaining power during a period of recession, when there was a danger of losing shop floor support if wage demands were set too high and maintained too rigidly, at a time when it was still against the law to provide financial help to members of unregistered unions on strike.

Strike activity in industry generally increased greatly during the period 1980–2, when the number of working days lost overtook the figures for 1973–4 [see p. 516]. At the same time, there were signs that industry was learning to ride the storm despite the fact that many of the strikes were illegal. But even the state was showing increasing reluctance to prosecute strikers who broke the law, since the number of arrests it might have had to make could have been unacceptably large. Early in 1984 the ground appeared to have been prepared for the amalgamation of F.O.S.A.T.U., C.U.S.A. and several Western Cape groups of unions into a single federation embracing nearly 300,000 black workers, but still without the inclusion of several leading community-based unions. Another important development, envisaged by Wiehahn, was the beginning of real movement among black mineworkers. Despite a slight backlash within the white Mineworkers' Union led by Arrie Paulus, the resistance of white mining unions had significantly diminished by September 1983, even to the point of their agreeing to major innovations like the training of black apprentices. Meanwhile a black National Union of Mineworkers, initially set up by C.U.S.A. and led by Cyril Ramaphosa, had achieved recognition by the Chamber and effectively challenged this tough but not fundamentally hostile employers' organisation, between 1982 and 1987, on issues relating chiefly to mine safety, wages, and labour migrancy, with tactical manoeuvres of growing sophistication (Van Niekerk).

Rougher by far were the encounters between trade unionists and the State. The South African Transport Services (S.A.T.S.) were accustomed to dealing only with their own staff associations until the new unionism confronted them in the 1980s. They employed nearly 100,000 black workers, as casuals liable to dismissal on twenty-four hours' notice however long their service, and in January 1982 they dismissed the chairman of their black dock workers' committee in this way. His case was taken up by the General Workers Union (G.W.U.), to which the stevedores belonged, with the support of the Midland Chamber of Industries and the stevedores themselves. But S.A.T.S. refused to recognise the union's standing, and in

September dismissed a further 900 dockers for taking part in a go-slow demonstration, because as state employees they were not entitled to strike, in an action which had major international repercussions. In April 1987 a further dispute developed between S.A.T.S. and 18,000 railway employees over the recognition of the S.A. Railways and Harbours Workers' Union (S.A.R.H.W.U.), for the Minister refused to deal with any body but the Black Trade Union (B.L.A.T.U.). Workers in 80 depots came out on strike (*Race Relations Survey, 1987–8*, pp. 670–5), and when the authorities persisted in rebutting S.A.R.H.W.U. they turned to violence, setting fire to railway rolling stock worth over R7 million. The dispute escalated to the point at which several lives were lost through police shootings and 'necklacings' by strikers, before a settlement on 6 June led to the re-engagement of all dismissed workers save those found guilty of intimidation, with permanent employment rights after two years' service but no claim to R40 million in forfeited wages. In December 1989 S.A.T.S. workers came out again, and this time 22,407 workers were fired in the course of a dispute which again saw widespread destruction of railway property, considerable intimidation among strikers and by the police, and 27 deaths. The S.A.T.S. confrontations were bitter because they brought workers and the State into collision course and neither side felt it could afford to back down. What gave them political significance was the linkage between S.A.R.H.W.U. and the most heavily politicised industrial federation of all, the Congress of South African Trade Unions (C.O.S.A.T.U.), which had been formed in November 1985 with an initial membership of 450,000 workers, combining the F.O.S.A.T.U. and U.D.F. unions and others, including the G.W.U. and the N.U.M. (which had left C.U.S.A.) in a common syndicalist strategy to fight apartheid and capitalism. C.O.S.A.T.U's president, Elijah Barayi, and general secretary, Jay Naidoo, had established careers as political activists. Soon after its establishment, C.O.S.A.T.U. was confronted in Natal by a new United Workers' Union of South Africa (U.W.U.S.A.), set up by Chief Buthelezi as a 'workerist' rather than a political organisation, and their mutual antagonism did much to inflame the situation in Natal, tempting the State to assume a partisan role. C.O.S.A.T.U. in fact had numerous confrontations with the police, in the course of which its headquarters in Johannesburg were mysteriously destroyed in May 1987, in what was recognised to be a very professional demolition job.

It can hardly be doubted that such linkage as did develop between black trade union and community-based political activities owed a good deal to the spirit of Black Consciousness which had grown up as a result of careful cultivation prior to October 1977. Black Consciousness survived even without institutionalised forms, in the enthusiasm which underlay the school boycotts and the strike action of emergent black trade unions. The Azanian People's Organisation, however was an institutional exception. A.Z.A.P.O. was founded in April 1978, in the view of its creators, to 'take black consciousness to the broad masses' and work towards 'a society where there would be a common educational system for all people and one parliament for a unitary state'. Despite the brief detention of its first executive, A.Z.A.P.O. held a congress in September 1979, and laid down a rigidly Africanist line, rejecting dependence on whites and dismissing one high office bearer who defaulted on this point of principle. It insisted on the fulfilment of very stringent conditions before it would consider attending any national convention: for a start, it wanted power transferred to 'the indigenous owners of the country', participation by the A.N.C., P.A.C. and B.P.C. in any such convention, the freeing of all political prisoners and banned persons, and a total restoration of civil liberties.

A.Z.A.P.O. sought to build a bridge with the trade union movement, and with the founding of C.U.S.A. in September 1980 it made some initial headway. Lodge has argued that A.Z.A.P.O.'s attitude to trade unionism was over-theoretical, and that its involvement in strike action was too limited to be effective. But the publication of the Koornhof Bills [see p. 400] and the new constitutional proposals of the Government gave A.Z.A.P.O. a new lease of life after its National Forum Committee had convened a massive conference at Hammanskraal, north of Pretoria, in June 1983. The conference looked to a black working class 'inspired by revolutionary consciousness' to set up 'a democratic anti-racist workers' republic in Azania, where the interests of the workers shall be paramount through worker control of the means of production, distribution and exchange'. The meeting displayed a widely held assumption that business interests and the National Party worked hand-in-hand, to which some credibility had to be given in the light of the Carlton Hotel and Good Hope conferences, though the Hammanskraal findings drew a stinging rebuke from the *Financial Mail* on 24 June.

A.Z.A.P.O. maintained its trade union links. Cyril Ramaphosa, the Mine Workers' leader, regaled its congress in January 1984 with a plan for the build-up of black workers' unions into a 'union of all the oppressed'. It also projected the image of a purified, hard-line body through its opposition to Senator Edward Kennedy's visit to South Africa in January 1985. Yet it was not A.Z.A.P.O., but an ideologically moderate movement which took centre stage when the Botha Government came out in 1983 with its proposals for constitutional reform.

The A.N.C., although it ran its operations from headquarters in exile, falls most appropriately into a discussion of domestic politics on account of its record as the longest-standing South African political party and its continuing if obscure participation in South African public affairs after its banning in 1960. Despite its ineffectiveness as a movement in exile during the years 1960–75 [see pp. 388–9], and its at best marginal role in the Soweto disturbances of 1976–7, it was able with the help of numerous recruits who then joined it from the Republic to step up its activities even though many were intercepted by the security forces on their return.

Lodge has outlined three stages in their guerrilla campaign, starting with the establishment of lines of communication, the development of a cell structure, and the setting up of arms caches (often discovered by the police) in 1977–9; then the start of attacks on strategic targets such as the

Sasolburg oil refinery and various power stations in 1980–1, leading in August 1981 to a declaration by Tambo that 'officials of apartheid' (many of whom, like the occupants of police stations, had already been hit) would now come under attack. In 1983 the A.N.C. went over with rather less restraint to the infliction of civilian casualties, as was shown by the explosion of a car bomb outside the Air Force headquarters in Pretoria on a Friday afternoon in May, when 19 people were killed and 200 injured, and by another bomb planted at the entrance to the Durban docks during the morning rush hour in March 1984. After April 1984, by which time the Nkomati Accords had been signed [see p. 476], and especially from 1989, when the settlement of the Namibian conflict deprived the A.N.C. of bases in Angola, its ability to cause disruption came to depend less on acts of terror and increasingly on the promotion of mass action within the Republic by new movements like the U.D.F. and C.O.S.A.T.U., and this needed time to organise.

The United Democratic Front (U.D.F.), whose existence and activities received the unstinting support of the A.N.C., announced its birth at a mass rally in Cape Town in August 1983. The idea of this movement came originally from the World Alliance of Reformed Churches. It acquired a figurehead in Dr Allan Boesak, the recently elected president of that alliance, who had been mainly responsible for persuading it to declare apartheid a heresy at its conference in Ottawa in August 1982. The U.D.F., like the All African Convention of 1935, arose out of the emotional distaste of millions of people at constitutional proposals which were intended permanently to exclude the entire African population of South Africa and the Homelands from the central parliamentary structures of the state. The movement came to boast an affiliated membership of over two million people, spanning all races and classes, and distributed through trade unions, local educational, religious and social groups, and sports clubs, which were said to have totalled over 600 by March 1984. It declined to form itself into a political party, perhaps out of reluctance to appear to compete with the A.N.C. (with which many but certainly not all of its members clearly sympathised). It accepted the Freedom Charter of 1955 [see p. 350] as its formula for a 'unitary socialist state'. It rejected out of hand the structures of the apartheid state, and therefore declined to participate in the politics of the white referendum in November 1983 or the Coloured and Indian elections of 1984 [see pp. 433–5].

17.7 CONFRONTATION ABOUT CONSENSUS: THE CONSTITUTIONAL DEBATE, 1978–90

The promotion of a new system of government received much attention from P. W. Botha and his colleagues during 1979–83, but the constitutional ideas put forward by the Government turned out to be so controversial that they led to a further breakdown of public order, followed by the reimposition of a state of emergency, between 1985 and 1990. This led eventually to the fall of P. W. Botha, as will be described in the final section of this chapter, and – perhaps consequentially – to the first substantial loosening of apartheid's grip with the accession to power of F. W. de Klerk.

That the constitution of 1961 was never intended to be a final resting place has already been suggested [see p. 361], as has the proposition that John Vorster was driven towards constitutional reform primarily by the fact of deadlock in the relationship between his Government and the Coloured people [see pp. 381–3]. The upshot had been a set of proposals designed to coopt the Coloured and Indian communities into the white political system, through the device of three separate parliaments under a single executive presidency, in such a way that effective power would remain in the hands of the whites.

The key to advance, somewhat simplistically placed in the door by the Theron Commission, was a suggestion that the 'Westminster system' was an obstacle to good government in a multi-cultural society, and therefore needed to be abandoned. The worst that could be said against Westminster – and it was hardly an objection that could have been anticipated from National Party circles – was that it encouraged confrontational politics, and in a plural society tended to lead to the permanent dominance of a single cultural group.

The task of devising a satisfactory form of government for plural societies had already begun to exercise the minds of prominent political scientists outside South Africa, like Arend Lijphart in California, and Robert Dahl of Yale, to name only two of a wide fraternity who had given a good deal of thought to ways of promoting consensus rather than confrontation under the democratic order. The essence of Lijphart's conclusions was that where identifiable communities need to be kept apart for political purposes in a single state, they should be separately represented in a 'grand coalition government' in which there can be discussion among community leaders before policies are put to their followers; that each element should be represented in the legislature according to its numerical strength, so that even minorities can be sure of representation, and given a blocking veto to prevent the enactment of thoroughly uncongenial legislation; and that each should possess 'segmental autonomy', that is the right to control those affairs which really are its own concern, above all in cultural matters.

This notion of 'consociational democracy' was a far cry from the existing South African constitutional system, though it had found its way into public debate through the work of S.P.R.O.C.A.S. [see p. 377] in the early 1970s. Liberal intellectual opponents of the Government had grasped the importance of the concept and paid considerable attention to its implications at two conferences in 1978, the first in Pietermaritzburg in February, the second in Grahamstown in August. On each occasion, conference reports of considerable substance were published, and these helped towards the formulation of new constitutional ideas by the leaders of the Progressive Federal party in particular. It became clear at these conferences that consociationalism provided no panacea for South African conditions, because of the deep cleavages in a society where differences of race were reinforced rather than obliterated by differences of class, and because there would be little chance of achieving consensus government unless steps were first taken to remove from the statute book those laws which offended the dignity and undermined the opportunities of particular sections – the Mixed Marriages and Group Areas Acts and influx control, to name but three examples. Contributors came out very strongly in favour of the introduction of a Bill of Rights, safeguarded by means of access to the courts. Participants questioned the logic of going for the protection of group rights against oppression by other groups, without at the same time protecting the rights of individuals against oppression by the state. The conferences also accepted that the only satisfactory basis of consociational government was consensus freely reached, not domination, and that if any new constitutional system introduced were characterised by the dominance of one group over others, the nest would be fouled in advance.

In so far as government thinking was informed by consociational principles, this was largely through the ideas of Dr Dennis Worrall, who was a National Party senator in 1975–7 until he won the Gardens seat in the House of Assembly, and was generally thought to have lent his authority as a political scientist to the 1977 proposals of the Vorster Government. He had been a member of the S.P.R.O.C.A.S. commission, and had emphasised its importance even though he dissented from some of its conclusions, and it was he who presented the Government's proposals to the Pietermaritzburg conference in 1978.

On accession to power, P. W. Botha appointed a parliamentary select committee to look into the 1977 constitutional proposals, which had been published as a bill in April 1979 and contained some important amendments, notably the renaming of the three parliaments as chambers of a single parliament. Converted into a commission under the chairmanship of Alwyn Schlebusch in July 1979, this body reported on 8 May 1980 and proposed a series of major changes in the constitution which were implemented during the 1980 session of Parliament. Thus the Senate was abolished with the minimum of fuss, with no opposition from the P.F.P., in a joint sitting on 21–2 May, and the entrenched clauses amended accordingly. More controversial was the proposal that the State President should be empowered to nominate twenty people, on the recommendation of party leaders and in proportion to party strength, as members of the House of Assembly. Both the P.F.P. and the N.R.P. opposed this, without success. Still more controversial was the proposal to set up a new body, to be called the President's Council, consisting of sixty members appointed by the State President for a five-year period, whose duties would consist in advising the State President on matters of public interest, including draft legislation. Its members could be white, Coloured, Indian or Chinese, but not African. The New Republic Party decided to participate in the President's Council, but added a proviso that there should be a 'single consultative council embodying elements of all groups'. The Progressive Federal Party representatives appended a minority report which asserted that the exclusion of blacks would not promote peaceful constitutional development in South Africa, and it therefore declined at first to serve on the

Council. The Government's response was that it had not yet worked out a scheme for the consultation of black communities.

When the President's Council took office in October 1980, its members were divided into a series of committees, one of which took over the work of the Schlebusch Commission and was placed under the chairmanship of Dr. Worrall. The Worrall Report (the First Report of the Constitutional Committee) was a well researched, well written document notable for the familiarity of its authors with up-to-date constitutional theory. It opted for limited segmental autonomy for white, Coloured and Indian groups, and argued for a confederal relationship of some kind with the black states, but with the accompanying assertion that 'a single political system in South Africa which includes Blacks on an unqualified majoritarian *or* consociational basis could not function as a successful democracy in current and foreseeable circumstances'. In taking this stand, it seems likely that the Committee was influenced by a paper given by Professor S. P. Huntington of Harvard at the conference of the Political Science Association at the Rand Afrikaans University in September 1981, above all his conclusion that on the issue of 'whether South Africa is a society of individuals or a society of racial communities', the record would suggest 'that it is far more the latter than the former'. In arguing that the numerical imbalance in South Africa was too great to allow black participation, especially since there was opposition among blacks to the protection of minority rights, and that cultural and class cleavages were too deep to make inter-group accommodation at all easy, the Committee of the President's Council was making valid points with which the official Opposition agreed, save in so far as the Buthelezi Commission had given grounds for thinking otherwise [see p. 419]. Because it thought this way, the Committee was not prepared to recommend a national convention. It hoped rather to find a basis for consensus in an indirectly elected president of the kind proposed in the 1977 plan, on the argument that if he were chosen by a multi-ethnic constituency (a college composed of members of the three ethnic parliamentary chambers) he stood a better chance of being 'supra-ethnic' than if he were elected by popular vote, even though the membership of the college was so defined as to leave the effective choice in the hands of the majority in the white chamber. If he presided over a multi-ethnic cabinet, whose members were to be drawn from the three ethnic chambers in a ratio to be determined by himself, the Committee thought that this would promote consensus politics, to which it felt committed. It paid respect to the theories of Arend Lijphart. It also wrote of 'considerable support' in written representations it had received for a Bill of Rights which could cater for groups as well as for individuals.

But at a Johannesburg business dinner on 24 May, Worrall had let slip a private suggestion that the proposals left room for the inclusion of blacks at a later stage, just at the time when the Government was in spasm over the Treurnicht challenge. He was accordingly sent to be ambassador in Australia, and his role as constitutional mentor taken over by Chris Heunis, though the chairmanship of the Committee of the President's Council was given to Dr S. W. van der Merwe. The tone of the Committee changed. With two of its three professional political scientists absent (for Professor A. de Crespigny had also left South Africa, somewhat unexpectedly), its Second Report, presented on 22 November, lacked the sophistication of the first, above all in its crude rejection of a Bill of Rights, and in the manner in which political considerations were allowed to override theoretical. This was noticeable in the Report's extraordinary preoccupation with the problem of deadlock and the need to give the Government authority to overcome it – a clear indication of the way in which its thinking was affected by its difficulties with the Coloured Representative Council. The Report paid extremely close attention to the Prime Minister's recommendations at the federal congress of the National party on 30 July. It was clearly a matter, now, of taking congress decisions to the electorate at large, and persuading that electorate, by whatever means necessary, to give support to the Government's proposals, even if this meant the expenditure of a large sum of money to ensure a propaganda triumph through the media, rather than through the encouragement of public debate between the contending parties on the actual merits of the policies advanced.

A referendum, rather than a national convention, was the Government's chosen path, and at the end of March 1983 the Prime Minister announced this for 2 November, with the promise of tests of Coloured and Indian opinion to follow. By this time the Constitution Bill had been drafted, and, though subjected to a massive kangaroo closure in the committee stage, it was debated in Parliament and passed.

Voters were asked to accept or reject the Constitution Act 'as passed by Parliament'. The question gave no opportunity for those like the K.P. and the H.N.P., who thought it too liberal, or the P.F.P., who felt it did not go far enough, to distinguish themselves from each other, and enabled the Government, to project it as a document of moderate reform acceptable to all but 'extremists'.

The Government was also greatly helped by the decision of the Labour Party, the leading Coloured political organisation, to support the measure. That party's calculation was foreshadowed by David Curry at the Congress of the Cape Association of Management Committees in September 1982. As the Coloured people did not have the 'political punch at this stage to force the Government to give us what we want', he argued, it was better to become actively involved in the negotiating process than be to left outside it. When the Party decided to accept the Government's offer at its annual congress in January 1983, this occasioned much surprise, though its leader, the Rev. Allan Hendrickse, stuck to this line, stressing that the proposals were 'a point of departure, not a point of arrival'.

To talk like this, however, was to breach the unity of the Black Alliance which Chief Buthelezi had been nurturing since the mid-1970s. Buthelezi had also managed by this time to bring to completion the commission report which carried his name for the political liaison of KwaZulu and Natal [see p. 419] and therefore had some reason for claiming to be able to deliver the support of the largest political organisation in South Africa –

18   Dave Gaskill of the Johannesburg *Sunday Times* captures the tension of the 1982 constitutional conflict. He shows F. van Zyl Slabbert (PFP) and Gatsha Buthelezi (Chief Minister of KwaZulu) attempting to promote change, while Jaap Marais (HNP) and Andries Treurnicht (CP) attempt to retard it, while a pensive P. W. Botha looks on – from a conservative position.

Inkatha – for the calling of a national convention to discuss real consociational planning on the basis of a sharing of power. He was understandably angered. The Progressive party had based its own constitutional planning on the assumption that Buthelezi's initiative at the very least needed to be tested, and Buthelezi himself conducted an active campaign before the white referendum, urging the voters to reject the constitution if they wanted to avoid an upsurge of black wrath, for it was clear that if the new constitution were adopted there could be no place for Africans within the new framework. As the Leader of the Opposition, Dr Slabbert, said, the Government had no 'hidden agenda'. The policy of turning the Homelands into independent black states, the inhabitants of which were to be deprived of South African citizenship, had at no point been arrested or denied. Yet the Buthelezi Report may well have been a two-edged instrument, for it seems to have alienated the New Republic Party, which dominated the Natal Provincial Council, and probably encouraged the N.R.P. to throw in its lot with the Nationalists.

The result of the referendum among whites was a two-thirds majority in favour of the new constitution, after an unprecedented propaganda onslaught on the electorate by the Government, through full-page advertisements in all the country's national and local newspapers, and full use of S.A.B.C. television. Like the K.P., the P.F.P. was handicapped by the refusal of the Afrikaans-language press to accept advertisements advocating a 'no' vote, and by its inability to persuade the S.A.B.C. to allow its leaders to take part in a live debate with the Government over the air. It was not altogether surprising that, in the face of such handicaps, the effectiveness of its propaganda fell far short of the quality of its arguments.

On 2 November the white voters endorsed a constitution which differed only in minor respects from the scheme first introduced by the Vorster

Government in 1977, which had then had the backing of those who later opposed it as members of the K.P. Common to both schemes were, first, an executive president, elected indirectly by a college of parliamentarians in which the majority white party would have control, and dismissable only if majorities in all three legislative chambers agreed, his term of office to be normally coterminous with that of the legislative bodies. Second, there were to be three legislative chambers ('parliaments' in the original plan to give a cosmetic impression that power was not being shared): a House of Assembly for Whites, a House of Representatives for Coloured people, and a House of Delegates for Indians, whose members were to be elected by voters on separate ethnic rolls. Black affairs were vested solely in the State President (a plan to create a Council for Blacks parallel to the President's Council having been rejected by African leaders themselves). Each House was to be responsible for legislation dealing with the 'own affairs' [sic] of its community, and each House was given the power, by simple majority vote, to block changes to the constitution in most areas relating to its basic structures, including the presidency, the three houses, the President's council, and the testing right of the courts (which was fairly circumscribed – Van der Vyver). Third, there was to be a presidential cabinet system (three separate cabinets in the 1977 plan, each under a prime minister, straddled by a council of cabinets under direct control of the President; three ministerial councils under the 1983 revision, straddled by a single cabinet under the direct control of the President). In either case, the body controlled by the President would be responsible for initiating legislation spanning all ethnic groups. Fourth, a President's Council with advisory, not legislative functions, was to come in as a substitute for the Senate. Most of its members were to be elected by the three chambers on a proportionate basis, though a minority were to be chosen by the State President, while there was provision in the 1983 Act for ten members (one sixth of the Council) to be chosen on a proportionate basis by Opposition parties in the three chambers. Fifth, deadlock between the chambers was to be handled by a joint (or standing) committee, supplemented in 1983 by further joint committees, in which most of the work in reconciling the views of the different houses and rival parties was intended to take place. Sixth, the judicial structure was unchanged. And seventh, tentative proposals were made for the overhaul of the provincial and local government systems. The primary motivation here was to arrive at a financially viable system of local government under which communities which had been largely excluded from the sources of local wealth under the Group Areas and Natives (Urban Areas) Acts could be given access to resources capable of matching their basic needs.

The Government subsequently announced that Coloured and Indian opinions would be tested, not by referenda, for which there was considerable demand, but by two separate general elections. The advantage of such an arrangement, from the Government's angle, was that these communities would not be able to vote on the question of accepting or rejecting the new dispensation. The denial of such an opportunity introduced an element of bitterness within the two communities, and this had much to do with the unrest which broke out at a number of polling booths when the elections were held for the (Coloured) House of Representatives on 22 August 1984, and for the (Indian) House of Delegates on 2 September. The United Democratic Front, which obtained wide support among South Africans of all ethnic categories, joined forces with the Transvaal and Natal Indian Congresses to persuade voters to abstain, and its supporters used much intimidation. The police tried to thwart their efforts, sometimes in over-robust fashion, and on the eve of the poll the Government detained a number of U.D.F. and Indian Congress leaders under the clause of the Internal Security Act (Section 29), which also prohibited the publication of any statement by persons so detained. By registering very low polls (little over 30 per cent in the Coloured election – very much lower in the Cape Peninsula, where the U.D.F. was strong – and 24 per cent in the Indian), these organisations were convincingly credited with having shown that the people rejected the new dispensation. The Labour Party of the Rev. Allan Hendrickse won nearly all the Coloured seats, and then caused consternation by appearing to stage a party split so as to give ('ex-') Party members access to the Opposition seats in the President's Council as well, but this ploy was not allowed. Amichand Rajbansi's National People's Party had a neck-and-neck race with Dr J. N. Reddy's Solidarity Party for control of the House of Delegates, each winning between 7 and 8 per cent support from the registered voters. Rajbansi was able to consolidate his position and win control of the House of Delegates in a deal which gave him the support of a Labour-backed independent, the Prohibition of Political Interference Act notwithstanding (Lemon).

Predictably, P. W. Botha was elected South Africa's first executive state president by the electoral college on 5 September. He announced his new ministerial team on 15 September. For the most part, he retained existing portfolios and their incumbents in the central Cabinet for general affairs, but reallocated certain functions, assuming a personal supervisory role, for example, over the Department of Cooperation and Development, of which Dr Gerrit Viljoen was made the minister in succession to Dr P. Koornhof; but the Deparment was relieved of the obligation to handle questions of influx control, which went to the Department of Internal Affairs, in whose hands already lay the issuing of passports. Similarly, the administration of the Group Areas Act was removed from the Department of Community Development and placed in the hands of the Minister of Constitutional Development, who would thus be in a good position to ensure that those who voted separately would continue to live separately. The chairmanship of the Coloured Ministerial Council was given to Hendrickse, and that of the Indian to Rajbansi, both of whom were admitted, as ministers without portfolios, to membership of the central Cabinet – the first people ever to attain such a position without being white.

In 1985 the new Parliament met. In spite of the complexities of the new constitution, the Government carried over a hundred bills in its first session, with the backing of the majority parties in the three houses and almost no opposition save in the white Assembly. Where necessary, bills were eased through the system by standing-committee discussions, though the repeal of the Mixed Marriages and Prohibition of Political Interference Acts were victories for the two smaller chambers.

Constitutional reforms in subsequent years included the abolition of white-controlled provincial councils and the establishment, in their place, of multi-racial provincial executives appointed by and taking orders from the State President. This centralisation of second-tier government was the price paid for a token extension of non-white involvement (including Africans) in administrative decision-making. More controversial was the gradual introduction from 1987 of Regional Services Councils set up under an Act of 1985. These bodies comprised indirectly elected representatives of black, Coloured and white local authorities, whose voting strength reflected the financial input of each local authority, when they met to allocate funds for capital development within the area of their jurisdiction.

As had been anticipated, the new constitutional dispensation gave rise to much debate precisely because of its incorporation of basic apartheid principles which were supposedly on the way out. Constitutional debate intensified in circles as far apart as the Government and the A.N.C., which were not yet talking to each other.

Both talked, separately, about human rights. In January 1986 the A.N.C. set up its own constitutional committee to look into the Freedom Charter as a basis for a fundamental law, and in October 1987 it published a 'Statement on Negotiations' outlining procedural strategy on the assumption that Pretoria was not in earnest about abolishing apartheid, and with the intention of entering into negotiations for a united democratic South Africa once the A.N.C. and other banned organisations and persons were set free to work in South Africa, and once violence by the State and its opponents had ceased.

In April 1986 the Government asked the South African Law Commission to make recommendations as to how group rights could be defined and protected, and individual rights extended, under the South African constitution. The Commission's report in 1989 urged the adoption of a Bill of Rights which would protect minority groups (as distinct from particular cultural, religious and linguistic interests, which could not be categorised as 'persons' in the legal sense). It admitted the need for affirmative action to grant temporary, non-mandatory privileges to disadvantaged groups as well. It insisted that discriminatory laws should be purged from the statute book before such a bill were introduced, and that the bill should be justiciable in the Supreme Court and entrenched by a three-quarters majority of those entitled to vote in each House. It thought that the process should be initiated in the existing Parliament, followed by a public education programme, and that it should then be refined by a council provided for in the Promotion of Constitutional Development Act of 1988 before being finally legitimised by means of a referendum. Opposition to the idea of a Bill of Rights was at first strong in A.N.C. circles, because the protection of group interests was seen as a bid by the white minority to consolidate its own position. But by the time of its conference in Harare in February 1989, the A.N.C. had moved towards the view that a Bill of Rights constructed like the Freedom Charter out of the generally-felt needs of the whole community (as distinct from those of groups) could well underpin a new South African constitution once victory in the forthcoming power struggle was assured. Their leading spokesman, Albie Sachs, saw such a bill as necessarily the creation of a new political order, which needed to be 'structured around a programme of affirmative action' and extended to 'every aspect of South African society' – health, education, work, leisure, housing and other areas. Their emphases were thus rather different from those of the South African Government in 1986, especially on the matter of group rights and affirmative action; but the Law Commission had moved much closer to their substantive arguments. When the Harare conference put out further guidelines in 1989, still taking the Freedom Charter as the basis for a form of majoritarian social democracy, these were criticised on various grounds – for their apparent faith in uncontrolled majoritarian rule despite the lessons of the South Africa Act of 1909 [see pp. 220–7], for their dismissal of federalism (apparently from an assumption that it had to be racially based or that it was somehow related to the retention of independent Homelands), for insufficient concern to ensure that the courts should be professional as well as elective, and for what looked like a doctrinaire determination to promote public ownership in certain spheres. But the demonstrated mental flexibility of the A.N.C. leadership, even in association with their S.A.C.P. allies, made it reasonable to assume that these were presented as talking points rather than as fixed principles.

17.8 THE EMERGENCY OF 1985–90, THE RISE OF F. W. DE KLERK AND THE RELEASE OF NELSON MANDELA

From the relative impotence of exile, the A.N.C.–S.A.C.P. alliance nevertheless maintained its stance of militant antagonism to the South African Government, while professing a willingness to negotiate a new dispensation provided that apartheid were removed, and banned organisations and political prisoners set free. Its chief assets were its growing success in persuading the outside world of the justice of its cause, as reflected in the growth of its semi-formal diplomatic network, and the steady increase of economic pressure on the Republic, especially in the United States, in most Commonwealth countries, and among member states of the European Economic Community.

In a pamphlet published in June 1986, the Government sought to portray the A.N.C.'s national executive committee as heavily dominated by communists. This assertion has been questioned (Karis, Phillips), primarily because it misrepresented political realities by underplaying the necessary dependence of the alliance on Eastern bloc sources for its weaponry (which the West would not provide), and encouraged the misleading assumption that its antagonism to the South African Government required the existence of an external threat. The Government found communist infiltration a handy cover for its 'total onslaught' propaganda, and tried to discourage but did not necessarily prevent contact between South African residents and these 'enemies'. It did not stop successive groups of prominent businessmen, Opposition politicians, community leaders and leading academics from visiting the A.N.C. in Lusaka (September 1985), Dakar (July 1987), Munich (October 1988), Paris (June 1989) and at other times. So long as the Government felt compelled to insist on a total renunciation of violence by the A.N.C. as a condition for negotiations, it could not itself initiate open discussions, though P. W. Botha broke the ice on 6 July 1989 by holding secret talks with Nelson Mandela. Nor, for its part, could the A.N.C. afford to renounce its option to use violence so long as the framework of apartheid remained on the statute book, for were it to do so it ran the risk of gaining neither a redress of grievances nor the constitutional means of redressing them itself. The confrontation between the South African Government and the A.N.C. thus resolved itself into a contest for the gaining or retention of the initiative, in which the A.N.C., largely deprived of the ability to infiltrate its own cadres into South Africa, was necessarily drawn into closer association with allied movements which were permitted to operate within the Republic, notably the U.D.F. and C.O.S.A.T.U. [see pp. 426–8], which it could not expect to control, though these movements, for their part, valued the A.N.C. link in their own struggle with Inkatha and other anti-socialist resistance movements for the loyalties of black South Africans.

It was the rejection of the 1983 constitution which provided the chief momentum for the next chapter in the resistance. The P.F.P., having fought and lost the referendum, decided that its role as an Opposition political party required it to remain in Parliament and oppose, though in the course of agonising over its future role it lost several of its caucus members, including its leader, Dr F. van Zyl Slabbert, who chose to leave Parliament and launch an Institute for a Democratic Alternative in South Africa (I.D.A.S.A.) and seek to sway opinion on the extra-parliamentary front. But the anger of excluded blacks was picked up in the posture of the U.D.F., which remained committed to a political boycott, and although the effective suppression of U.D.F. activism during the Emergency of 1985–7 showed up the movement's weakness [see p. 441], the Government did not repress the mass democratic movement which emerged informally out of its ashes.

The Vaal Triangle disturbances of September 1984, beginning on the day set aside for the swearing-in of the new Coloured and Indian parliamentarians, took the form of a mass protest against high rent and electricity charges imposed by the Lekoa and Evaton town councils, which controlled Sharpeville, Evaton, Sebokeng and Boibatong. The troubles spread to other centres in the Transvaal, and communicated a clear political message through the brutal murder of the Lekoa council chairman, Esau Mahlatsi, and the deputy mayor, Sam Dlamini, accompanied by attacks on the homes of councillors and policemen, government buildings, shops and liquor outlets, churches, vehicles, a service station and a beer hall: the new system of black local government, as a substitute for power at the centre, had been rejected. A widespread stay-away from work followed, among black residents of the Vaal Triangle and Pretoria, leading on to a school boycott the following year. Violence spread early in 1985 to the northern Free State and the Port Elizabeth–Uitenhage area, before extending to Natal and the western Cape.

The Uitenhage confrontation of 21 March, when 20 lives were lost during a funeral procession arranged (without subversive intent) on the anniversary of the 1960 Sharpeville shootings) was not, it seems, an incident planned by either the marchers or the police, and it had no trade union backing (Van Niekerk). The subsequent inquiry showed that policemen who had been provided with lethal rather than proper crowd-control equipment, and were neither properly trained nor competently led by officers who subsequently lied to the judicial commission, opened fire without good reason on a crowd which had used very little, if any, violence.

Uitenhage provided a flash-point. Demonstrations elsewhere led to the arrest of protest marchers in Cape Town and in other places, to class boycotts in schools all over the country, and to fighting between the police and the people, with further loss of life, and in due course to bomb explosions in Durban and Port Elizabeth on the anniversary of the Soweto risings on 16 June.

The Government declared a state of emergency on 20 July, and – apart from a short break between 7 March and 12 June 1986 – emergency regulations were reintroduced annually across all or most of the country for the remainder of the five years under discussion. These empowered police commissioners (subsequently widened to include non-commissioned officers in all branches of the police and prisons services in the Republic and the non-independent Homelands) to restrict the movements and access of people, or confine or remove them, and to control services, protect installations, distribute or withhold information, under the threat of penalties on conviction rising to a R20,000 fine or ten years' imprisonment, and without any public right to seek court interdicts, all with the protection of a blanket indemnity.

The Government used its emergency powers, as it had used its statutory powers after the Soweto disturbances of 1976–7, to impose severe restrictions on extra-parliamentary activities. The eighteen high-profile organisations so incapacitated in February 1988 and February 1989 included A.Z.A.P.O., the U.D.F., several black civic associations and youth congresses, the Release Mandela and End Conscription Campaigns, and – for sake of variety – the *Boere Bevredigings Beweging*. Bans were also imposed on individuals, and the Government took advantage of its new control over access to information to withhold the names of large numbers of detained people whenever Parliament, to which it was obliged to report, was not in session, and to exclude press and television reporters from the vicinity of violent confrontations on the ground that their presence could itself escalate conflict. The censorship of news, which became really effective for the first time, caused national newspapers to carry cautionary notices as a regular feature on their front pages, and drew much adverse comment overseas.

The resources of the state were more severely extended during the crisis of 1985–7 than they had been in 1976–7, for the township defiance was as widespread, and the Government found it necessary to deploy troops in the townships for the first time. The glare of international publicity was also greater, as became apparent in July 1985, when the funeral of a popular Cradock teacher, Matthew Goniwe, who had been waylaid and murdered, along with three colleagues, outside Port Elizabeth, after months of conflict with his government department, was attended by diplomatic representatives from France, Norway, Denmark, Canada, Australia and Sweden. A march to Pollsmoor prison to protest the continued incarceration of Nelson Mandela, scheduled for 27 August, was intercepted by the police; but the detention of the man chosen to lead it, Dr Alan Boesak, attracted international attention in virtue of his position as president of the World Alliance of Reformed Churches. During October the public was treated to a spectacular police demonstration, involving the use of a purple spray to facilitate the identification of crowd participants, in the heart of the Cape Town central shopping district – a technique which would be used again, four years later, to disperse protesters against the general election of August 1989.

The 1985–7 emergency revealed an organising capacity in the black townships which had not been evident a decade earlier. Protests against the Black Local Government Act, not in itself, but because it had been offered as a sop in place of parliamentary representation, led in one township after another to the resignation of councillors (who had invariably been elected on very low polls), and to the *de facto* but not *de jure* collapse of the system. Rent boycotts occurred in Soweto and many other townships, and were so successful that by the end of 1987 the total arrears owed to African local authorities amounted to R387 million (*Race Relations Survey, 1988–9*, p. 208). Township government in many places passed by default into the hands of paid officials, often supported by troops, whose presence provoked widespread protest both in black and in Progressive Party circles. In many instances informal street committees emerged to take the place of the formal structures. Clearly these were to some extent improvisations; but it is also certain that they were held in being by a centralised command structure, perhaps originating with the U.D.F. or the A.N.C., capable of coordinating activities to an unprecedented degree. These bodies proved their administrative competence in a number of ways, though they do not appear to have attempted to institute alternative fiscal procedures. Most criticised – and with very good reason – was the sheer brutality of the informal courts presided over by youthful 'comrades' (as distinct from the traditional but irregular 'people's courts described by J. G. van Niekerk), which carried out summary death sentences by 'necklacing' their victims with petrol-soaked motor-tyres, sometimes after mutilation, as a way of combatting the activities of informers with a brand of terrorism calculated to outweigh the severity of police inquisitorial methods [see pp. 547–8]. Not surprisingly, the State set a high priority on the smashing of these alternative structures, and with a heavy hand it succeeded. The appearance of vigilantes to help in the suppression of the comrades – the *witdoeke* of Crossroads and KwaNobuhle (Uitenhage), the warlords of Natal, and other such groups, can hardly be placed in any other context in the light of cumulative evidence of their association with local police units.

As a device for restoring order, if not respect for law, the emergency regulations worked. This can be seen, for example, in the admission of Murphy Morobe of the U.D.F., in an interview with an *E.P. Herald* reporter (13 November 1985) that in that year 8,000 U.D.F. leaders had been detained and most of their national and regional executives had either disappeared, or been killed, or emigrated. The State had devised its Joint Management Centres, linking the military with local government structures under a thick blanket of secrecy, in order to ensure its retention of control [see p. 398].

This was the context in which the Government, after extending its constitutional power of delay to the limit, announced a white general election in May 1987. For the first time, the Government faced well-organised opposition from right-wing Afrikanerdom, with Treurnicht's *Konserwatiewe* Party offering a much greater threat than Jaap Marais's *Herstigtes*, whose single seat (won in a recent by-election) was lost. Botha sought to fight them off by mounting his main attack on the P.F.P., which lost seven seats to the Government, which in turn lost eight to the K.P. The K.P., profiting from the rightward swing promoted by the Government, won enough to become the official Opposition with 22, thus significantly altering the balance of subsequent parliamentary debate and throwing the Progressives into crisis.

It would not have been easy, given the distractions from left and right, for P. W. Botha to maintain a constant reform initiative, especially after the reversal of 1987. But in its faltering, that initiative gave rise to criticisms that it had never been robust enough to succeed in the first place. Without discounting the imaginative steps taken in the aftermath of the Riekert and Wiehahn Reports of 1979 [see pp. 399–403], and the firm commitment to a very cautious form of power-sharing, which had led him to oust Treurnicht and his followers from the Party in 1982 [see pp. 410–11] and still keep 66 per cent of the electorate behind him in the referendum, his performance after 1983 lacked lustre. He never responded to the challenge of Buthelezi and Slabbert to make a clear declaration of intent as to his political goals, despite the world-wide disillusionment over the lack of content in his 'Rubicon' speech to the Natal party congress in Durban on 15 August 1985 when major policy changes expected by the American State Department were not announced, the Chase Manhattan Bank called in its maturing loans, and the market value of the rand fell sharply. Press commentators from the time of the Treurnicht split frequently drew attention to a lack of conviction in government circles, as if there was no clear objective in their minds, which seemed to focus rather on the 'totality' of the frontier onslaught. With his party split, Botha's dictatorial manner was a handicap in any attempt to maintain a loyal following within the Nationalist rump, for he lacked 'that endless patience to plough slowly towards consensus' which the *Financial Mail* ought perhaps to have attributed not to Botha's predecessor, Vorster, but to his successor, De Klerk.

This is not to say that Botha's later years saw no progress in the direction of fundamental reform. The repeal of the Urban Areas Act in 1986 (involving the removal of the pass laws under which over seventeen million blacks had been imprisoned since 1916), the introduction of uniform identity documents (even if the number codes yielded racial information), and the abolition of formal influx control (even if this could still be regulated in terms of the availability of housing) were not insignificant changes. Other laws to go were the Black (previously Bantu) Labour Act of 1964, the Black (originally Native) Affairs Administration Act of 1920, and the Black (originally Native) Prohibition of Interdicts Act of 1956, though interdicts were rigorously prohibited under the emergency regulations still in force.

But in spite of these more than cosmetic changes, there was no clear direction in the policy of the Botha Government over the central issue of power distribution. This could be seen in the lack of clarity over the Homeland policy. While insisting that, where independence had been granted and accepted, it could not be returned, the Government showed increasing preparedness to allow other Homelands which did not want independence to acquire all its trappings 'by stealth' (as one P.F.P. member expressed it) without accepting the status on paper. It was also willing to countenance dual citizenship, which all Homelands except Bophutatswana were beginning to demand, without making it clear what dual citizenship in the South African context would necessarily involve. Further, the establishment of a 'Secretariat for Multilateral Cooperation in Southern Africa' in 1986, with headquarters adjacent to those of the Development Bank, might lead to improved facilities and improved relations between the Republic and its satellites, but had no power implications.

Where blacks in the common area were concerned, the Government thought its way ponderously through a National Council Bill (first published in May 1986), which sought to provide a forum in which a small number of representatives of all races could meet together to discuss the outlines of a new constitution, to a Promotion of Constitutional Development Bill which was carried with separate voting at a joint session in June 1988. During the latter session the Government also tabled for comment an Extension of Political Participation Bill to provide for nine or more elective regional councils with limited legislative and executive functions for Africans living in the common area. But it failed to carry another Constitution Amendment Bill designed to empower the State President to appoint Africans to the Cabinet, because such a measure required the approval of each House individually, and the Labour Party majority in the House of Representatives turned it down. Certainly there was no lack of constitutional ingenuity in the mind of Minister Heunis, but the almost total lack of support for any of the proposals pur forward by the Government in 1986–9 must be seen as reflecting a hardening conviction among the disfranchised that South Africa's crisis could only be resolved by the involvement of communities in the drawing up of the broad outlines of a new political system. The sudden resignation of Heunis from the Cabinet in May 1989, whatever his personal reasons, reflected the weaknesses of an approach based on gimmickry without sufficient allowance for the political ground swell.

P. W. Botha resigned his presidential office, with reluctance, on 14 August 1989, seven months after a minor stroke had led to his hospitalisation, Heunis being sworn in as Acting State President. On 2 February, Botha had stepped down as leader of the National Party, following the advice of Heunis and 'Pik' Botha, clearly in the hope that one of these two would succeed him. But in the event both were heavily defeated in caucus, and Barend du Plessis, another close supporter, was beaten by the Transvaal leader, F. W. de Klerk, by 69 to 61 votes. A cautious group-minded Transvaler was not Botha's choice for a successor. He therefore stood his ground on 9 March, when his four provincial leaders met him at the Tuynhuys (his official Cape Town residence) and endorsed a caucus decision taken earlier in the day that he should be asked to resign. On 6 April he announced his intention to resign only after the forthcoming general election, the date of which he had not yet announced, and to continue to run the government until then. The showdown with his party leader was delayed until 12 August, less than a month before the election which had meanwhile been set for 6 September. The President, when advised by 'Pik' Botha that Dr de Klerk had accepted an invitation to visit President Kaunda on the 28th, claimed that the visit had not been cleared in the proper manner, and summoned the Cabinet to Cape Town on the 14th. This time De Klerk and his colleagues stood firm, and although there was some doubt, at a time when Parliament stood dissolved, whether any procedures existed for compelling the State President to stand down (other than a decision by the Cabinet that he was mentally incapable of holding office), Botha decided after a heated encounter to resign formally rather than accept 'Pik' Botha's suggestion that he was resigning for health reasons, which would mean leaving 'on a lie'.

Such a public display of cabinet disunity on the eve of a general election was bad for F. W. de Klerk's party, though it was better for him to lead the party as Acting State President than to have to defend his unsafe Vereeniging seat against a threatening *Konserwatiewe* challenge. All the same, the Nationalists made heavy weather of a contest forced upon them by the Labour Party's refusal to agree to a later election date, for in terms of Section 39(2) of the constitution, each House had the right to insist on a dissolution of Parliament after completion of its five-year term, and Labour had decided to force the Government's hand when its demand for the repeal of the Group Areas Act was turned down. National Party election propaganda lacked the sting and the confidence which it had displayed in the 1983 referendum and in 1987. The *Konserwatiewe Party*, by contrast, was in rampant mood, appealing to ethnic and racial emotions, and won 39 seats, mainly in the Transvaal and Orange Free State, with a few urban blue-collar footholds as well. A new Democratic Party had meanwhile come into being as an alliance between the P.F.P. under its new leader, Dr Zach de Beer, a small group of dissident Nationalists under Wynand Malan, and an Independent Party which had formed around Dr Dennis Worrall, when he had resigned his ambassadorial post in London in 1987 to fight the Somerset West seat, which he had nearly taken from Chris Heunis in that year. The D.P. was unable to prevent the K.P. from holding on to its position as the official Opposition; but its success in winning 33 seats showed that it had overcome the stigma of being 'weak on security issues' which government propaganda had previously fastened on to the P.F.P., by bringing in several leading military figures as candidates without having to make any meaningful policy shifts, by highlighting the economic crisis at a time when sanctions were beginning to bite, and by down-playing without underrating issues of racial policy.

De Klerk's Nationalists lost 27 seats, 16 to the K.P. and 11 to the D.P., and were thus narrowly able to avoid the embarrassment of a hung parliament for which the Opposition parties hoped. De Klerk's own performances in public and on television were remarkable for their bland-ness as well as their humanity, while the Party's propaganda gave few guidelines to the electorate. It announced 'an action plan which . . . deals with the full South African reality' to be 'implemented with great enthusi-asm' after 6 September; 'an honourable road back to South Africa's rightful place in the international community', which had been put success-fully at 'positive meetings' with German, British, Portuguese, Italian, Mozambican and other African leaders, but without any prior disclosure of its details to the South African public. A party which had so conspicuously failed to deliver its promises in Botha's later years was fortunate to retain as many seats as it did. Yet a Rooseveltian fireside approach was perhaps De Klerk's only option, for any detailed disclosure of the reforms he intended to introduce during his first six months of office must surely have precipitated a stampede away from his party before any of them had seen the light of day.

Those reforms, taken all together, amounted to a significantly new approach which also involved the taking of some incalculable risks. To allow political protest marches, even in the big centres, while requiring the police to maintain a low profile, while the country was still governed under emergency regulations, was a gamble which worked surprisingly well, especially when contrasted with the amount of unnecessary violence which had erupted in the same centres between police and marchers during the run-up to the elections.

The Cabinet appointed on 16 September still contained the inner core of P. W. Botha's team (Viljoen, 'Pik' Botha, Magnus Malan, Adriaan Vlok and Kobie Coetzee), as well as the first woman ever to hold South African cabinet rank, Mrs Rina Venter (Health). It looked like a cabinet of party reconciliation, but for the fact that on 29 November De Klerk announced a decision to reduce the State Security Council to the level of a cabinet subcommittee and, as he explained, put an end to decisions 'forced down from the top'. At his swearing in as State President on 20 September, De Klerk stressed his intention to tackle discriminating legislation, release security prisoners and end the emergency as soon as possible, and also work out constitutional proposals which would protect all people, includ-ing minorities, by means of constitutional checks and a Bill of Rights. His actions in the immediately succeeding weeks included guarantees to some black communities under threat of removal (like Lawaaikamp, in P. W. Botha's constituency), and the opening of all public beaches to all races on

16 November. In his opening address to Parliament on 2 February 1990 he announced the unbanning of the A.N.C., the P.A.C. (which was showing signs of resurgence owing to the efforts of a revived leadership – van Staden) and the S.A.C.P., and undertook to release large numbers of political prisoners who had not been found guilty of common law offences. He lifted the restrictions on the media, except in unrest situations. He limited emergency detentions to six months, and gave detainees access to legal counsel and their own doctors. He also announced the suspension of all death sentences and the appointment of an investigation into capital punishment itself. The speech made almost no mention of legislation to be repealed, save the Reservation of Separate Amenities Act of 1953 [see p. 336], and left the impression that the Government's political philosophy remained to some extent group-centred. But apart from the spokesmen of the right-wing groups and parties, it received very widespread acclaim both in South Africa and in the outside world. It was followed, on 11 February, by the unconditional release after 27 years in jail of the world's best-known political prisoner, Nelson Rolihlahla Mandela.

18 Salesmanship: *Ethnasia contra Mundum*, 1945–90

> Ethnasia,
> A country which emerges when Ethnosis
> Has been applied a hundred years or two
> And those with similar skin and hair and noses
> Are grouped according to the Race Who's Who.

A. R. Delius, *The Last Division, Canto* II, x.

18.1 SOUTH AFRICA AND THE BIRTH OF THE UNITED NATIONS

As a leader of one of the victorious Allied powers, and an elder statesman in international affairs, Smuts attended the opening conference of the United Nations Organization at San Francisco in April 1945. It was he who drafted the original declaration of aims in the preamble to the United Nations Charter, with its emphasis on fundamental human rights, the value of the human personality, and non-discrimination between the sexes. But as Hancock has shown, he went to the conference in a pessimistic mood. It then looked as if the U.S.A. and the U.S.S.R., though at loggerheads with each other, were nevertheless agreed in their opposition to European-style colonialism. Smuts considered it essential that the Commonwealth (which he regarded as in essence an association of the White Dominions) should act as a third force in the post-war world, especially at a time when western Europe was down and out. He hoped also to gain recognition for the incorporation of South West Africa in the Union, and thus obtain by lawful means what some thought he should have got by simple annexation during the war years. He had conducted an opinion poll among the chiefs of South West Africa and their board members, asking them to state that they supported Union rule and desired incorporation. Most of them did so, but the validity of such a referendum was questionable and the General Assembly rejected it. Smuts could not have foreseen, at this stage, that his critics would not merely forbid incorporation, but insist that South West

446

Africa should be brought under a United Nations trusteeship agreement like all the other territories which had been allocated under a League of Nations mandate.

Forced on to the defensive, Smuts tried, with almost no room to manoeuvre, to alienate as few powers as possible, and therefore agreed to administer South West Africa 'in the spirit of the Mandate', and submit reports to the Trusteeship Committee for information. He also tried from the start to model the U.N. Organization on the pattern of earlier peace-keeping bodies by limiting effective control to the great powers working through the Security Council, and trying to ensure that the General Assembly remained a forum for debate between governments from which private individuals would be rigidly excluded. During his own term of office the Security Council retained such control, and Smuts found solace in the veto which any Permanent Member of that Council could use. But the General Assembly was not precluded by the Charter from listening to criticism of the domestic policies of member states, or from hearing the plaints of representative individuals against their own governments. In December 1946, Mrs Pandit of India made a scorching attack on South Africa's Indian policy at the second session of the General Assembly, while Dr A. B. Xuma of the A.N.C. lobbied Assembly delegates in New York, and Smuts found – as he had found at the Imperial Conference of 1923 – that he was precluded by pressures at home from bending before the gale of criticism. By the time he fell from office pressures had developed at the international level which he could not divert with the argument that these policies were South Africa's private domestic concern.

18.2   THE MALAN–STRIJDOM ERA IN FOREIGN POLICY, 1948–58

Having had time to see the direction in which world opinion was moving, the Malan Government, which took over in 1948, decided to act on the assumption that South Africa's interests would best be served by the vigorous assertion of sovereignty rather than by compromise. It told the United Nations in 1948 that the South West African mandate had lapsed, announced its intention to discontinue sending courtesy reports, and in 1949 it gave South West Africa representation in the Union Parliament. It rejected an advisory opinion of the International Court in 1950 that the Union Government was obliged to submit to U.N. supervision to the extent that it had been obliged to submit to that of the League, and proposed instead that it should negotiate a new agreement with the three remaining Principal Allied Powers (the United States, the United Kingdom and France). The U.N. in turn found this unacceptable, and decided to receive petitions against Union rule in the territory from the Rev. Michael Scott, and – though this would not have been permitted under the Mandate system – listen to the Herero, Nama and Damara chiefs whose case he had presented. In 1954 the Union Native Affairs Department was given direct control of South West African native affairs. In 1955 the Union

Government withdrew from UNESCO on the ground that it had become an anti-South African agitators' forum, and in 1957 it decided to retain only token membership of the U.N.. At a point when South African withdrawal seemed imminent, however, the Government resumed active participation in 1958, asserting that the attitudes of some governments had changed for the better.

Whereas Smuts had taken a cautious line on the influence of Soviet Russia in the post-war world, hoping to limit that influence by bringing the Commonwealth into line with the United States so that they could be *à deux* in a world of three great powers, the Malan and Strijdom Governments saw their greatest security in a posture of unequivocal opposition to the Soviet Union and to communism, first clearly implemented on the home front with the passage of the Suppression of Communism Act in 1950. In February 1956 the Soviet Government was required to close down its Consulate-General in Pretoria, on the ground that it had 'cultivated and maintained contact with subverse elements in the Union' and disseminated Communist propaganda. No person could have presented the Union's anti-communist case at the U.N. more vehemently than E. H. Louw now proceeded to do. The Communist states were in the forefront of the attack on South African domestic policies in the General Assembly. To that extent the Union Government's campaign could be seen as self-explanatory, but it found itself in a predicament when non-communist states like India voted against the same policies for the same reasons. The vehemence of the Government's anti-communism may even have helped to increase the Union's isolation, for other governments distinguished more clearly between those things which were undesirable in Soviet behaviour, and those which were not, while critics could not help noticing that the Union Government's domestic policy was becoming as indifferent to traditional notions of civil liberty as the Russian.

A count of U.N. resolutions directed against South Africa would show those relating to South West Africa to be far more numerous than those directed against South Africa's internal policies. But it was the Union's treatment of her Indian population which first drew international attention to her domestic record, and resolutions on that theme were passed nearly every year after 1946. In 1952 the U.N. extended its concern to cover the policy of apartheid in general. It was not a straightforward matter to bring what appeared to be a purely domestic issue before the international body, but certain clauses in the U.N. Charter were accepted with growing readiness by the bulk of the member states as appropriate for such a purpose, in particular Article 55(*c*), under which the U.N. undertook to 'promote . . . universal respect for, and observance of, human rights and fundamental freedoms for all without distinction as to race, sex, language or religion'. The other heads under which intervention was justified were Article 14, empowering the General Assembly to 'recommend measures for the peaceful adjustment of any situation . . . which it deems likely to impair . . . friendly relations among nations', which was used by India in 1946; and Article 39, requiring the Security Council to 'determine the existence of any threat to peace, breach of the peace, or act of aggression', and to take appropriate steps to avert these things.

It was perhaps an unavoidable weakness of Malan's foreign policy that he followed an uncompromising line without making sure that he remained the close associate of a major power bloc. Like Smuts, he accepted the utility of the Commonwealth association; but like Hertzog, he did so without enthusiasm, supporting Nehru's plea in 1949 to retain Indian membership of the Commonwealth even after becoming a Republic, because he hoped to loosen ties between Great Britain and South Africa in a similar way; revising governmental immigration policy in a manner which reduced the British and increased the Continental element; and destroying the advantages enjoyed by Commonwealth citizens in applying for South African nationality – all quite legitimate actions for which a strong case could be made, yet none of them likely to strengthen South Africa's international position. The support of Britain and of western European states at the U.N. was welcomed by the Union Government during the 1950s, but the price it was prepared to pay for that support was low because there appeared to be little danger of hostile U.N. resolutions being translated into meaningful action. Thus the defence budgets during the early years of Nationalist rule remained at the level of less than £10 million annually, escalating to between £20 and £30 million during the Korean war, in which South Africa participated as an anti-communist gesture.

At the same time, the Government tried, with only mediocre success, to become involved in regional defensive alliances. The North Atlantic Treaty Organization, however, was not designed to operate south of the Tropic of Cancer, though Portugal, a member state, had colonies bordering on South Africa. The treaty between Australia, New Zealand and the United States was designed for the defence of the Pacific rather than the Indian Ocean. The Union Government offered for a short while, and without firm commitments (Berridge and Spence) to join Britain's abortive Middle East Defence Organization, which was abandoned for want of Commonwealth support, but failed to secure an alliance for the defence of Africa at conferences in Nairobi in 1951 and Dakar in 1954, which were attended by the major Colonial Powers in Africa as well as by South Africa, Southern Rhodesia and the United States. Between 1945 and 1953, Malan made reference from time to time to an 'African Charter', the object of which was to be the protection of Africa from Asian domination, the preservation of Africa for the Africans (including the resident white Africans), the development of the Continent along Western and Christian lines, the exclusion of communism, and the demilitarisation of the southern part of the Continent. But this was a project more likely to commend itself to Colonial powers in their heyday than to Colonial powers in the process of decolonising, and it had little outside appeal. Malan's 'roving ambassador' in Africa, Charles te Water, had little diplomatic success. The establishment of the ill-fated Central African Federation in 1953 had the Malan Government's strong endorsement, but this fact in itself helped to widen the gap between the Union Government and black opinion.

The Simonstown Agreement of 1955 was the one breakthrough made by South Africa, and this occurred during Strijdom's premiership after negotiations led by F.C. Erasmus, Minister of Defence, dating from 1949. The South African Navy took over Simonstown, which had been a British base, but the Royal Navy was still allowed to use its facilities, and to maintain a headquarters at the Cape. The South African Navy was to be expanded by the purchase of six frigates, ten minesweepers and four other coastal defence vessels from Britain, as part of a joint plan for the defence of a new maritime strategic zone running from the northern end of South West Africa to a line joining the southern border of Mozambique and the southern tip of Madagascar. South Africa would look after her own internal defence, while Great Britain would take steps to keep the Suez route open from her eastern Mediterranean and Red Sea bases. There was no question before 1964 of military sanctions against South Africa by the western powers, and South Africa's ability to buy military equipment from all the major western states at that time has been illustrated by Austin, who also lays stress on the importance of the Cape sea route in the view of British strategists until the thaw of the Khrushchev era in the mid-1960s.

The Suez crisis of 1956 did much harm both to Commonwealth unity in defence matters and to the understanding which existed in this area between Britain and the Union. South Africa's public disapproval of the Anglo-French attack on the canal zone, following the outbreak of an Arab-Israeli war, was perhaps forced on her by what Barber has called a 'classic example of a breakdown of Commonwealth cooperation'. Sir Percivale Liesching, the British High Commissioner in South Africa, explained on 6 November 1956 that there had been no prior consultation before the seizure of the Canal because it was a decision taken in an emergency; but early the next year E. H. Louw, the South African Minister of External Affairs, insisted that the Egyptian nationalisation of the Canal, which had shortly preceded the Anglo-French action, was a domestic Egyptian issue in which South Africa had no interest as either user or shareholder. It was a significant moment in South Africa's external relations, for the Suez crisis led to the first effective steps by the Soviet Union to extend its influence into Africa, an influence channelled through support for Nasser's Egypt, Nkrumah's Ghana which became independent in 1957, Sékou Touré's Guinea which left the French Community in 1958, and Algeria, which obtained its independence from France in 1962.

18.3   DR VERWOERD AND THE OUTSIDE WORLD

Recognition of the fact of black independent states in Africa required a considerable shift of attitude on the part of the South African Government. It wasted no time in uttering the necessary courtesies once its efforts to prevent the 'blackening' of the Commonwealth had failed, but missed an opportunity to make contact with black Africa by turning down Dr Nkrumah's invitation to the first conference of independent African states in Accra in 1958, on the ground that colonial powers should have been invited as well. The prospects of achieving rapport with the black states were ruled out at this stage by black distaste at Union policies on the one hand and South Africa's reluctance to admit black ambassadors on the other, even though the Reservation of Separate Amenities Act of 1953 had punched a hole in the colour bar for the benefit of black representatives of foreign governments. South Africa tried to gain influence in the new states through participating in the Council for Technical Co-operation in Africa (C.C.T.A.), the Foundation for Mutual Assistance (F.A.M.A.), the Scientific Council for Africa (C.S.A.) and other bodies, thus maintaining contact within a limited sphere of activity; but in the early 1960s she was forced out of these bodies, and out of the Food and Agricultural Organization (F.A.O.) and World Health Organization (W.H.O.) on account of her racial policies.

Soon after taking office in 1958 Dr Verwoerd managed, by a clever shift of emphasis, to end the long wrangle with the Imperial Government over the future of the High Commission Territories, which in due course received self-government under the names of Lesotho and Botswana in 1966, and Swaziland in 1968. On assuming power, Malan had reverted in 1949–51 to the slightly peevish tones of Hertzog, and understandably got nowhere with the British Government, while Strijdom had made a similar demand for their incorporation in the Union in 1955. Verwoerd, however, realising that Britain could not agree to incorporation in view of African opposition in the Territories to such a move, gave support to the British plans for their independence and began to look upon them as African Homelands analogous to those which he began to establish in the Republic under the Promotion of Bantu Self-Government Act of 1959, with independence for the first time as their declared destiny. This was an ingenious rationalisation which made both political and economic sense. The Bantu Homelands, among them Botswana, Lesotho and Swaziland, would – so Verwoerd hoped – become satellites of a southern African Commonwealth, of which the Republic was destined to be the planet.

But in all other respects the spread of decolonisation made the Government's task progressively harder, despite the urbanity of Dr Hilgard Muller, who took over External Affairs in 1964 from the abrasive Louw. By 1960, a large part of northern Africa was decolonised, pressure was developing on the white settler communities of East Africa, and soon afterwards the Belgians suddenly withdrew from the Congo. Decolonisation in turn changed the balance of forces in the General Assembly of the United Nations, where the Afro-Asian element had risen from fifteen out of fifty members in 1946 to seventy-three out of 125 in 1965. The newly independent member-states of the Third World looked increasingly to the Soviet Union for support – and, outside the U.N., to Red China, whose influence in Africa began to be effective from about the time of Chou En-lai's visit to Zanzibar in 1964. The Western powers found themselves under a growing strain, as they were forced into the position of having to support for strategic and economic reasons the surviving colonial regimes of southern Africa, whose policies offended their sensitivities but not their interests.

Harold Macmillan's 'winds of change' speech in February 1960 [see p. 354] offered South Africa continued friendship on the basis of Christian values, racial non-discrimination and the rule of law, and gave an undertaking not to support an economic boycott against her. But his dissociation from South African policies was clear, just as Verwoerd made it clear in his reply that South Africa would abandon accepted values if the survival of the white race in southern Africa seemed to warrant so doing – an undertaking which he fulfilled, after consulting neither Cabinet nor Parliament, by leaving the Commonwealth in 1961.

The era of U.N. resolutions condemning South Africa's policies wholesale, with massive majorities and almost no defending votes, now began. The boycott of South African products was encouraged. In 1962 the General Assembly urged member states to break off diplomatic relations with South Africa, and close their harbours and airports to South African ships and planes. In 1963 the Security Council resolved to ban the sale of arms to South Africa, and the United States and Great Britain were among the first powers to comply. The formation of the Organization of African Unity at Addis Ababa in the same year provided the. decolonisation crusade with a central organisation, if not a high command. In 1964 a large conference in London debated the feasibility of imposing sanctions.

18.4   SOUTH WEST AFRICA, ANGOLA AND THE GROWTH OF CONFRONTATION, 1952–79

An essential part of the background to this intensified international campaign was the growth of confrontation between South Africa and the United Nations over South West Africa. The General Assembly had appointed an *ad hoc* committee to negotiate with the Union Government in 1951. In 1952 it failed in its object, and the Union Government withdrew from the Trusteeship Committee in protest against continued U.N. intervention. It was persuaded to return in 1957 after the General Assembly had set up a Good Offices Committee under Sir Charles Arden-Clarke, which held general discussions with the Union Government on its proposals to partition South West Africa; but such a solution was not acceptable either to the Trusteeship Committee or to the General Assembly. In November 1959 the Assembly noted with grave concern that the Union was administering the territory in a manner contrary to the Mandate, the U.N. Charter, the Universal Declaration of Human Rights, the advisory opinions of the International Court, and earlier resolutions of the Assembly itself. Riots among Africans at Windhoek in December 1959, following government attempts to remove them to a new location, led in turn to the appointment of a one-man judicial commission by the Union Government, which defended the use of force by the police. But it also led the Conference of Independent African States meeting at Addis Ababa in June 1960 to institute proceedings against South Africa in the International Court. Ethiopia and Liberia, the only other independent African states which had been members of the League were the plaintiffs.

19 **'Aw gee, Sheriff, I feel kinda silly being a bastion of the West without no shooting irons.' David Marais captures the mood of the early rounds of the arms embargo against South Africa (Verwoerd and J. F. Kennedy).**

Meanwhile pressure continued at the United Nations. The Trusteeship Committee required South Africa to revoke all apartheid laws which applied in South West Africa, and called on its own South West Africa Committee to visit the territory, if necessary without the cooperation of the Union Government. This proved difficult to do, as Professor Enrique Fabregat, the chairman of that committee, found after arriving in Salisbury in July 1961. Denied access by the British Government even to Bechuanaland, from which it proposed to enter South West Africa, the party returned via Dar-es-Salaam and reported failure. Thereupon the Trusteeship Committee, instead of retreating, proceeded by an impressive majority of 86 votes to one (Portugal's) to appoint a seven-nation committee with instructions to visit South West Africa before 1 May 1962, conduct investigations on the spot, see to the removal of South African control, prepare for democratic elections leading to the establishment of an independent government, arrange U.N. technical assistance, release political prisoners and repeal discriminatory laws. Brazil, Burma, Mexico, Norway, the Philippines, Somalia and Togo accepted membership of this new committee. The South African Government, deeming it wise not to trail its coat, invited the chairman and secretary of this committee, Victorio Carpio of the Philippines and Dr Martinez de Alva of Mexico respectively, to visit South West Africa. They did so, and announced that they had not found evidence of either genocide or any militarisation of South West Africa in violation of the mandate, nor any threat to international peace consequent upon South Africa's administration of the territory. After leaving South Africa, however, the same two men affirmed that apartheid was being rigorously enforced in the territory (as would indeed become clear with the publication of the Odendaal Report in 1964), and that South Africa was administering it in violation of U.N. principles, and had revealed no intention to abandon its policies or prepare the peoples for self-government or independence. They also asserted that the African people desired direct administration by the U.N.. But it was difficult to recommend further action, not only because the initial Carpio – De Alva Report appeared too favourable to South Africa and was later repudiated by Carpio himself, but because the South West African case was all the while *sub judice* at The Hague.

The court decided in 1962 that it had jurisdiction to try the case, and rejected the South African contention that Ethiopia and Liberia had no *locus standi*. From then on, argument at The Hague turned on the South African administrative record, and the case of the plaintiffs was made to rest on the Union Government's restriction of the franchise to whites, its failure to provide adequate educational facilities, its introduction of travel passes, its ban on political party and trade union membership by blacks, its policy of racial segregation, its exclusion of non-white people from certain defined occupations, its exclusion of non-white people from the right to landed property over large areas of the territory, and the forcible deportation of individuals on the orders of the Administrator without any right of appeal. When judgment was given in 1968, however, after a six-year hearing during which one judge had died and a successor with different views had been appointed, the Court by a narrow majority of eight opinions against seven reversed its earlier decision and, without examining the substance of the plaintiffs' case, accepted the South African contention that the plaintiffs had no standing. This narrow decision bought time for South Africa, and put off a situation in which the Security Council might have found itself in the position of having to initiate either sanctions or stronger action against the Republic. It also inflamed the majority in the U.N. General Assembly, which now began to put pressure on the Security Council to compel South African compliance.

The Security Council first took cognisance of the South West African dispute in January 1968, when it demanded the release of thirty-seven South West Africans on trial in Pretoria on political charges. The following year it recognised a resolution of the General Assembly taken in 1966, formally terminating the mandate, and called upon the South African Government to withdraw its administration from the territory. It subsequently called South Africa's refusal to do so 'an aggressive encroachment on the authority of the United Nations'. On 30 July 1970 the Council asked the International Court of Justice for an advisory opinion on the legal implications of South Africa's continued presence in Namibia – as South West Africa was coming to be called – and received the reply that the U.N. resolution of 1966 was valid in law, and that all states, in their

dealings with Namibia, should explicitly indicate that they did not recognise the validity of South African rule there. South Africa's offer of the
same year to hold an all-races plebiscite under joint supervision of the
Republican Government and the International Court, to test the relative
popularity of South African and United Nations administration, was not
accepted by the U.N.

The following year the Security Council asked the Secretary-General,
Dr Kurt Waldheim, to make contact with all parties concerned in order to
establish conditions under which the people of Namibia could exercise
their right to self-determination. Invited by the South African Government, Dr Waldheim arrived in Cape Town in March 1971, and made a
brief tour of South West Africa. He held discussions with Vorster, the
Republican Prime Minister, but they reached deadlock on the question of
whether 'self-determination' could include South Africa's plan for balkan-
isation on the lines of the Odendaal Report. As that report had been partly
implemented, for example by the establishment of representative assemblies for the Ovambo and other groups, since 1967, this point was of
more than academic interest. Those parties in South West Africa which
favoured South Africa's immediate withdrawal and the creation of a
unitary Namibian state, met in convention at Rehoboth in November 1971.
They included the Baster Volksparty, the National Unity Democratic
Action (a Herero movement under Chief Clemens Kapuuo), the South
West African People's Organization (S.W.A.P.O.), and the South West
African National Union (S.W.A.N.U.). Dr Waldheim's personal representative, Dr A. M. Escher of Switzerland, visited southern Africa at the
end of the year and met representatives of this Convention as well as the
Prime Minister. The latter now undertook to form an Advisory Council for
South West Africa. When this Council first met in March 1972, it included
two whites chosen by the Legislative Assembly, two Coloured men chosen
by the Coloured Council (a nominated body then in the process of
becoming partly elective), two representatives each from Ovamboland,
Okavango and East Caprivi, and a single representative (or observer) from
each of the Tswana, Bushman, Herero, Rehoboth Baster, Damara and
Nama groups. It met behind closed doors.

But deadlock between the Security Council and the South African
Government was fully restored in 1973 when the former body resolved
unanimously to call a halt to Dr Waldheim's mediation. Chief Kapuuo of
the Convention, who had been allowed to leave South West Africa by the
Republican authorities, urged upon the Trusteeship Committee the need
for an immediate South African withdrawal. On 17 December 1974, the
Security Council unanimously called on South Africa to transfer power to
the people of Namibia in accordance with the International Court ruling of
1971, and immediately adhere to the Universal Declaration of Human
Rights by releasing political prisoners, ending discriminatory practices and
allowing political exiles to return in safety. A deadline was set at 30 May
1975, whereupon the Council would meet again to consider its next step. It
duly did so, but a proposal to enforce positive economic sanctions by
authorising the seizure of South West African products on the high seas

was vetoed by the combined decisions of Britain, the United States and France.

In the meantime the Portuguese withdrew from their African colonies with very little warning in 1974, and this led to the appearance of a power vacuum to the north of South West Africa as the three rival factions to whom the government of Angola had been entrusted, the Popular Movement for the Liberation of Angola (M.P.L.A.), the National Front for the Liberation of Angola (F.N.L.A.) and the National Union for the Total Independence of Angola (U.N.I.T.A.), became locked in conflict from the beginning of 1975. As the year advanced, it became clear that the M.P.L.A., which had been well supplied with arms by the Soviet Union via Brazzaville, and was also beginning to receive Cuban advisers, was on a winning course.

On 23 October, in response to the threat of a Soviet-backed government taking over Angola, South African troops were sent into the territory. A coastal column, going beyond the normal range of hot pursuit, captured Benguela and Lobito, while another moved north, with U.N.I.T.A. support, up the centre. F.N.L.A. units moved independently against Luanda. But the arrival of three Cuban troopships and of sophisticated Russian rocketry blunted the South African offensive before the end of the year. The South African retreat began in January, by which time the Government had decided that American logistical support, of which it had evidently expected too much, was not likely to be forthcoming. The South African public was informed only in March, when the retreat had ended, of what had evidently been a miscalculation. It was a campaign for which there had been inadequate political preparation either internationally or in consultation between the Departments of Defence and Foreign Affairs, insufficient attention to military logistics, and little concern for public morale. The main effects of South Africa's invasion of Angola on international relations were to legitimise the Russian backing for the M.P.L.A. in the view of members of the Organisation of African Unity, and to make it correspondingly harder for the U.S.A., whose Congress was taking a non-interventionist stance in public, to intervene openly. International recognition of the M.P.L.A. Government followed very quickly and very widely. At the same time, by covering and continuing to give support to Jonas Savimbi, the U.N.I.T.A. leader, the South African Government managed to keep the civil war alive in the south, and thus to make it harder (but by no means impossible) for S.W.A.P.O. to build up its bases with a view to infiltrating into South West Africa.

The Republican Government continued to consult with the Advisory Council in South West Africa, and made public profession of its acceptance of self-determination for the territory. In September 1975 it promoted a conference in the Turnhalle (Gymnasium) at Windhoek, to initiate the drafting of a constitution. The Turnhalle assembly, consisting of nominated representatives of all the ethnic groups in South West Africa, but excluding S.W.A.P.O., reached consensus in April 1977, and submitted a plan for a three-tier system of government under which the territory should proceed to independence by the end of 1978, on terms which guaranteed the rights of 'each of our peoples', whose interests were to be safeguarded at the second level by political bodies created on the ethnic lines already envisaged in the Odendaal Report. This safeguard, however, was soon seen to have stultified the promotion of integrationist reforms carried out at the first-tier level. Thus, although the ten black delegations to the Turnhalle associated politically with the whites under Dirk Mudge, who had done much of the preparatory work for the conference, the latter found himself out of phase with the National Party majority which controlled the white second-tier assembly. He therefore challenged the leadership of A. H. du Plessis at the congress in September 1977, taking his stand on the need to abrogate apartheid laws wholesale for the sake of racial harmony in a future independent Namibia, and resigned from the party after losing the election by 141 votes to 135. His new Republican Party became the core of a new Democratic Turnhalle Alliance (D.T.A.) formed in November, with Chief Kapuuo as its president and Mudge himself as chairman. The D.T.A. dedicated itself – in terms which underplayed its reformist intentions – to working for 'a constitutional dispensation that will enable individuals, language groups and population groups to maintain themselves in the cultural and material sphere and that will eliminate domination'.

The D.T.A. was an innovative attempt by conservative-minded whites to build a bridge across a chasm which was already too wide to receive it, for the invitation to the original Turnhalle conference had alienated the main block of black nationalist parties – S.W.A.P.O.'s internal wing, S.W.A.N.U., and the dominant Rehoboth, Damara and some Nama and Herero groupings – who had met together as a Namibian National Convention (N.N.C.) at Okahandja in 1975 (Du Pisani). It also ran counter to the trend of politics in the United Nations, where the South African Government's refusal to recognise the authority of that body in South West Africa had kept alive the hostility of the General Assembly.

The United States, Britain and France had vetoed a resolution in favour of an arms embargo against South Africa in the Security Council in 1976 in order to give the new South African move a chance; but in terms of its Resolution 435 of September 1978 the Security Council took a stand on U.N.-supervised elections as the only manner in which political change could be brought about. It was in order to bring South Africa to acceptance of this principle that the five western powers represented on the Security Council, namely the U.S.A., Britain, France, West Germany and Canada, had opened contact with the Vorster Government in 1977, and sent a delegation to visit Cape Town and Windhoek in that year.

Taking their stand on Resolution 385 of 30 January 1976, which stressed the illegality of South Africa's presence in Namibia but recognised her rights as a party to a dispute, this Western Contact Group persuaded Vorster to loosen the constitutional bonds linking the Territory to South Africa through legislation which terminated its representation in the Republican Parliament and authorised the President to appoint an Administrator-General over South West Africa, and commission him in any way he chose. Both S.W.A.P.O. and the D.T.A. then accepted that the new Administrator, Judge M. T. Steyn, and the U.N. Commissioner for Namibia, Mr Martti Ahtisaari, should together supervise U.N.-controlled elections once political prisoners had been released and discriminatory laws had been repealed. This plan was presented to the Security Council on 27 July 1978, and adopted without dissent. But when Dr Waldheim reported to the General Assembly on 30 August, his presentation contained new features: it linked the 're-integration' of Walvis Bay and Namibia with the other proposals, though Vorster had explicitly requested its removal from the package, to which S.W.A.P.O. had subsequently agreed; it mentioned a U.N. monitoring force of 7,500 men (no number having been agreed to so far), and it mentioned the appointment of a U.N. police contingent to exercise control during the transfer of power (a role which the South African Government had assumed would be discharged by its own police). It did not prove difficult to make adjustments to these matters. Far harder was it for the U.N. and the Western Contact Group to absorb the shock of a large-scale airborne assault by South African forces on S.W.A.P.O. supply and base camps at Cassinga, 250 kilometres inside Angola, on 4 May, which was carried out, in Du Pisani's view, 'to placate hard-line opposition to the settlement plan inside the South African Cabinet', to induce S.W.A.P.O. to reject the western proposals in the short term so that Pretoria could go ahead with its alternative plan for internal elections in South West Africa, and to 'deny S.W.A.P.O. the opportunity of establishing a close military–political nexus'.

These internal elections, called by Vorster for December 1978, ran directly counter to U.N.-controlled elections planned for April 1979, and might easily have undermined the diplomacy of the Western Contact Group. But during a further round of talks in Pretoria in October 1978 the Western Group managed to hold the negotiations on course, perhaps realising that the December elections would help to defuse white antagonism to the U.N's plan, if they were to lead nowhere. That plan had been enshrined in the Assembly Resolution 435 of 29 September, which endorsed the Waldheim plan. The Western Contact Group had saved much from potential limbo, though it had not by any means solved the Namibian problem, at the same time as it managed to persuade Ian Smith, the Prime Minister of Rhodesia, to accept a conference without preconditions to discuss the transfer of power in his country too.

18.5 SOUTH AFRICA AND RHODESIAN INDEPENDENCE

Rhodesia's Unilateral Declaration of Independence in 1965 increased South Africa's difficulties on the international front, for without wishing to appear to back white supremacy outside her borders, she felt bound to ignore the instruction of the Security Council to impose economic sanctions on the territory, especially as South Africa was itself beginning to feel the chill of an external arms embargo. It was politically impossible to alienate the upstart Government of Rhodesia, to which the white South

African Government felt drawn by ties of common interest. From the outset, therefore, the South African Government treated the dispute between Britain and the Smith regime as a private dispute, and recognised the Smith Government *de facto* but not *de jure*. It also refused to apply sanctions on the ground that it was opposed to such action on principle. The ties between the South African and Rhodesian governments were drawn tighter in 1967 by the dispatch of South African police units to help combat guerrillas on the Zambesi border. South Africans were later discreetly allowed to do their conscript service in the Rhodesian forces (Jaster). Two years later a two-thirds majority in the Security Council voted for the application of sanctions to South Africa and Portugal for the assistance they had given to Rhodesia; but the United States and the United Kingdom vetoed implementation. The situation became more tense with the closure of the Zambian–Rhodesian border in January 1973, which deprived Zambia of the main access route to the outside world for its copper, and tenser still after the success of the Frelimo guerrillas in taking over Mozambique following the overthrow of Dr Caetano's Government in Portugal in April 1974. This left the Republican Government in the difficult position of having to decide whether Rhodesia could be defended indefinitely against guerrilla attacks from the east as well as from the north, or whether it was better to accept the inevitability of black rule north of the Limpopo and strengthen its own bastion further south. Vorster was not to be drawn on this difficult question at first. He withdrew the South African police from Rhodesia, but kept his options open, refusing on the one hand to prescribe policies for a neighbouring state, but applying all the diplomatic pressure at his disposal to bring the Smith Government and Bishop Abel Muzorewa, leader of the African National Council, to the conference table. Such a policy was recommended by the fact that, despite occasional outbursts of mutual hostility, Vorster and the Zambian President, Dr Kenneth Kaunda, had a common desire to avoid a southern African bloodbath, which, as Vorster said in the Senate on 23 November 1974, could produce consequences 'too ghastly to contemplate'. Although little came of their joint attempts to persuade Smith and the rival nationalist groups to negotiate with each other, the convening of a Rhodesian constitutional conference at the Victoria Falls in August 1975 showed that Kaunda and Vorster could at least bring their respective horses to the water, if that was all. Vorster, who supplied the railway carriage for the meetings, saw his role as that of 'creating the climate in which negotiations can take place'. In the same spirit, he acted as host to further meetings between Dr Kissinger, the American Secretary of State, and Smith in Pretoria in September 1976, in another attempt, which proved abortive, to avert a major escalation of conflict north of the Limpopo. It was no different when Vorster met the American Vice-President, Walter Mondale, in Vienna in May 1977. South Africa's role was necessarily marginal to the main developments on account of her lack of international standing. At the same time, by refusing to close her borders with Rhodesia she maintained a consistent attitude of friendship with the Government of Ian Smith, without which he would not have been able to continue the fight, until the moment came, in 1978, when Vorster seems to have decided that a black government north of the Limpopo was unavoidable. His interest, then, with very little leverage on events, was to make it clear to Smith that his assessment had changed, and to hope to be able to deal with a benign Zimbabwean government after the transfer of power.

18.6   VORSTER: DIALOGUE AND DÉTENTE

During Vorster's year of office, South African diplomacy had become, within guarded limits, more flexible. Verwoerd had rejected a request by Sir Abubakar Tafawa Balewa of Nigeria to be allowed to visit South Africa in 1962, and an offer by Dr Kaunda of Zambia in 1964 to establish diplomatic relations with the Republic, in the first instance because he doubted Sir Abubakar's bona fides, and in the second because the offer had been made from a political platform. Kaunda's need to export his copper through East London was, it seems, discounted as a lever which could be used to establish a formal relationship of a kind congenial to the South African Government. Vorster, by contrast, adhered more deliberately, and with far more basic tact, to a policy successively described as 'outward looking', involving 'dialogue', and moving towards 'détente'. He arranged personal meetings with the ruler of Lesotho, Chief Leabua Jonathan, in 1966, with the President of Botswana, Sir Seretse Khama, in 1968, and with Prince Makhosini Dlamini of Swaziland in March 1971, the country's diplomatic relations with black states having become so skewed by ideological compulsions and mistrust that these arrangements were looked upon as a significant breakthrough. Diplomatic relations with Malawi were opened in 1967 (the Malawians appointing a white representative), while Dr Banda paid a state visit to South Africa in 1971. But these were essentially setpiece manoeuvres in which neither side was prepared to give ground, and the distance which still stood between Vorster and the leaders of the black states was shown by his early attempts to score points at the expense of Dr Kaunda, and by his Government's rejection of the Lusaka Manifesto of April 1969. Fourteen East and Central African states were represented on that occasion at a conference which affirmed its disapproval of racialism, but agreed to recognise South Africa as an independent African state like themselves. The governments represented at Lusaka refused to abandon their plan to liberate the blacks in the south, but they affirmed their desire to do this by peaceful means rather than by war. The Lusaka Manifesto, rejected by South Africa, was adopted by the O.A.U. and subsequently by the United Nations. In June 1971, the O.A.U. summit meeting at Addis Ababa decided that South Africa's rejection of the Manifesto justified the abandonment of dialogue with the white regime, and it was left to South Africa to save what she could of the policy by maintaining unpublicised contacts behind the scenes.

The measure of Vorster's achievement in foreign policy, which stands out against the background of a near disastrous record on the domestic front apart from his ability to maintain public order, was the way in which he managed to pull South Africa out of the diplomatic morass which followed his defiance of the Lusaka document. At Nigel in October 1974, he asked for six months in which to be able to surprise the world. The reference appears to have been to impending changes in South Africa's international position, rather than to any directional variation on the home front. By that date he had already entertained the President of Paraguay. He had also paid a secret visit to the Ivory Coast in September, after several years of quiet preparation, and achieved a good rapport via the French Government with President Houphouet-Boigny, though as Johnson observes, this probably had a negative influence on South Africa's relations with Nigeria. In February the following year he visited Liberia, and held conversations with President Tolbert which were reported in *The Times*. In April 1976 he visited a beleaguered country, Israel, which made good diplomatic sense. It would be for his successor to cultivate Taiwan. But it was a measure of the extent of South Africa's isolation that such breakthroughs could be classified as achievements.

18.7 THE THREAT OF ECONOMIC SANCTIONS: EMPLOYMENT CODES, DISINVESTMENT AND TRADE BOYCOTTS

As political confrontation developed between South Africa and the outside world during the premierships of Verwoerd and Vorster, so there grew up a parallel threat of economic confrontation, as part of an international bid to force South Africa to change her policies. The issues were complex, for attempts by South Africa's critics to promote disinvestment (the sale of companies), divestment (the sale of shares) and various forms of sanctions on the one hand, and South Africa's retaliatory flaunting of her globally strategic position and her possession of strategic minerals on the other, had side effects which were not always anticipated. But it was apparent by 1990 that economic pressures were beginning to make the South African state much less resistant to radical political change than had been the case when P. W. Botha took office.

Several attempts were made, by pressure groups in those western countries which traded with South Africa, to make expatriate firms in the Republic take the initiative in the overthrow of apartheid by example. At their best, they were able to lay down codes of employment conduct with sufficient business realism to persuade business organisations to adopt them. The British Department of Trade and Industry recommended such a code in 1974. In 1977 the European Economic Community and the American labour relations expert, Dr Leon Sullivan, proposed other versions, while two South African bodies, the S.A. Council of Churches and the Urban Foundation came out with formulae of their own. These codes had some influence. Sullivan's, in particular, was adopted by a number of American firms over and above the twelve with whom it was originally worked out. But their success was not uniform. Firms often resented the intrusion into their privacy, while hostile labour critics were quick to argue that the real intention of the codes was to forestall more drastic international action rather than to promote real change in the apartheid system. A German church group was particularly sharp in its attack on the German business record under the E.E.C. Code in 1981. African trade unionists in Port Elizabeth attacked the Sullivan Code in 1982 on the ground that it did not get through to the real difficulties of the black worker, while Sullivan himself eventually dissociated himself from his own recommendations. It seems likely, however, that these codes of conduct did help to promote the integration of facilities and the opening up of new employment avenues for blacks in the workplace in a number of instances, and – though this was not always a feature of the codes – in the promotion of black trade unionism.

The codes did not remove apartheid root and branch, and it would have been surprising had they done so. But because of this, another movement started in the countries which had developed stakes in South Africa, to achieve that end result (and incidentally to punish non-cooperative firms) by demanding disinvestment, or at the very least a ban on the expansion of such businesses in South Africa. In its range and its tone, the disinvestment campaign was reminiscent of the nineteenth-century campaign against the slave trade. A large number of American, British and Continental religious, academic and political groups began to mount their attacks in about 1972. In South Africa the Black People's Convention lent its support, as did the black movements in exile. Others though, like Inkatha, echoed the voice of South African business in general, in arguing that disinvestment, by stopping economic growth, was likely to impoverish without necessarily leading to positive change. In 1977–8 several prominent American and British banks terminated their South African business, by which time the Government was showing concern over a net outflow of foreign investment capital after a period of steady growth. In that year the Government could only obtain foreign loans at 2 per cent above the rate available to under-developed countries with poor credit ratings. Its concern had already been revealed in an Act of 1974 which banned the publication of business information abroad without the permission of the Minister of Economic Affairs. The decline in investment was attributed, by Government spokesmen as well as private individuals, to political opposition resulting from the death of Steve Biko and to a decline of confidence in investment prospects during the Soweto crisis and afterwards. In 1979, after the De Kock Commission had devised special concessions for foreign investors with the introduction of the financial rand (which could be traded on a free external market at a rate generally much lower than its controlled commercial counterpart), the volume of investment began to pick up. Foreign investment had risen to R30 billion by 1981, as against R9 billion in 1975. The influence of the Reagan Government in the United States with its policy of 'constructive engagement', and of Margaret Thatcher's Government in Britain with its strong encouragement of free enterprise, more than counterbalanced the negative influence of a new hard line in President Mitterrand's France. The Rockefeller Report on South Africa in 1981 wanted to give business another chance, while Margaret Thatcher's government in Britain not only opposed sanctions with imperturbable consistency, even at risk to Commonwealth unity, but acted ahead of other powers in 1990 to relax the pressures which it had previously applied.

The imposition of trade sanctions grew into a campaign at the United Nations during the 1970s, when the Republic refused to join the boycott of Rhodesia, thus undermining the effectiveness of that campaign. At first the Republic could rely on the vetoing of resolutions demanding sanctions by one or more of its trading partners with permanent seats on the Security Council, namely the United States, Britain and France, the only exception being the arms embargo, which had the endorsement of every other member nation by mid-1987 (Lipton). In 1981 the new socialist government in France began to take a more punitive line. But if a single event can be said to have committed the international community to a general sanctions policy, it was Botha's 'Rubicon' speech of August 1985, for the false expectations which it had aroused after the outbreak of the disturbances of that year, seen against the continuing deadlock in South West Africa and the unstable relationship between South Africa and the Frontline States.

All the Scandinavian countries, which had banned new investment in the Republic in 1979, placed restrictions on trade in 1986-7. The European Community decided on both restrictive and positive measures at Luxemburg in September 1985, and extended these to a ban on new investment and various imports after the failure of Sir Geoffrey Howe's visit to South Africa in 1986, though they found collective punitive sanctions hard to bring together (Holland). The United States Congress went much further by sweeping aside a relatively mild package proposed by President Reagan prior to enacting its Comprehensive Anti-Apartheid Act of 1986. This banned new investment in South Africa, loans to the South African Government, the export of computers and oil, the importation of non-strategic minerals and agricultural products from South Africa, as well as direct air travel between the two countries. Further clauses threatened to deny weapon sales to countries which continued to supply South Africa (which Israel took to heart in 1987 by deciding to cut back on the extent of her scientific cooperation and renouncing new military contracts) and threatened also to slap trade embargoes on countries which took advantage of restrictions imposed on U.S. nationals. (Japan was posing such a threat, as her trade with South Africa rose to $3.6 billion in 1987, reaching near parity with the total volume of American, even though her government had also banned direct investment, bank loans, military sales, computer exports, and the importation of South African iron and steel – Payne).

The Commonwealth was slower to act, but ended with the most decisive package of all. At their meeting in the Bahamas in 1985 most foreign ministers recommended the imposition of various trade and financial restrictions. A committee appointed at their Lusaka meeting in February 1988, consisting of Canadian, Indian and Australian experts, reported in August that the most targetable areas of the South African economy were trade credits, which were commonly converted into medium-term loans. When the Commonwealth leaders met again, at Kuala Lumpur in Malaysia in October 1989, the entire gathering, with the exception of the British representatives, was prepared to adopt a three-wave plan to 'ratchet up' sanctions against South Africa in a manner calculated to make it very difficult indeed for South Africa to reject demands for the effective dismantling of apartheid. The demand for the ending of the Emergency trespassed on an area where no government would normally be expected to surrender its judgment, but this consideration offered no leverage against the threats which followed. The first wave envisaged the ending of all agricultural and manufactured imports from South Africa, and of selected mineral imports excluding high-value or strategic categories such as gold, diamonds, chrome and platinum, and a start to the phasing-out of trade credits. The second phase, should it prove necessary, would tighten oil and arms embargoes and ban the export to South Africa of refined oil products, and computer, electronic and telecommunication equipment, and stop technology transfers, the export of key vehicle parts, all devices which promote automation, and the recruitment of skilled personnel. This phase would also envisage the jailing of sanctions busters (over which South Africa was sensitive on account of recent brushes with the British and French governments), the extension of sanctions to South African-controlled companies anywhere, and retaliation against non-Commonwealth countries which took advantage of sanctions imposed by others. New loans and investments would be precluded, as well as long-term rescheduling of South Africa's debts, double taxation agreements, and air links not through S.A.D.C.C. countries, while consumer and trade union action to promote sanctions would be encouraged. In case a third stage should be necessary, a decision was taken to investigate the possibility of sanctioning South African gold exports and third-country products with significant South African content. These decisions were formidable in their comprehensiveness.

Disinvestment by foreign firms took place, meanwhile, on a considerable scale. One-fifth of the British firms had pulled out by April 1988, and British investment fell from £6 billion to under £3 billion in 1980–6 (*Weekly Mail*, 22 April 1988). In the period January 1984 to April 1989, 184 American companies left South Africa (*Weekly Mail*, 28 April 1988, quoting Alison Cooper for the Investor Responsibility Research Center). Of the 520 companies which had sold all their equity by the middle of 1989, 350 were American (*Race Relations Survey 1988–9*, p. 328). Those disinvesting were driven by the threat of further penalties contemplated by Congress against those which chose to stay – notably the Rangel Amendment of 1988, which chased Mobil out under a threat of double taxation.

Of the 114 American firms which pulled out between January 1986 and April 1988, most sold their assets at bargain prices to South African companies and investors, thus enriching those South Africans (mainly white) who could raise the finance to buy them. Only a handful made continuing provision for their workers' welfare, which led the authors of a report on disinvestment practices by American firms in that period to comment that 'the most noticeable change' was 'a cutback on corporate funding of community programmes and organizations that challenge apartheid policies' (J. Kibbe and D. Hauck report to the I.R.R. Centre, *Weekly Mail*, 21 July 1988). This caused considerable anger among the black trade unions which had agitated for disinvestment. It led in 1989 to a confrontation between Mobil and the Chemical Workers' Industrial Union, which demanded notice of intent to withdraw and a guarantee of employment if the firm were sold to a local buyer. Mobil eventually reached agreement with the C.W.I.U. under which the company would negotiate with its U.S. management for a trust fund to finance community projects in South Africa, and give its employees reasonable separation pay. The union then accepted the sale of Mobil's assets to Gencor, a leading Afrikaner-controlled business house, which then set up Engen, an 'integrated new energy group' combining the search for oil through Soekor, petrol production through Genref and Mossgas (the first payable offshore gas find located by South Africa, off Mossel Bay), and the marketing of motor fuel through three companies, including Mobil under the same name.

The extent to which the Government's willingness to abandon the apartheid citadel can be attributed to sanctions and disinvestment is debatable. Propaganda by some trade unions and church leaders for disinvestment and financial strangulation, on the ground that this was the only available weapon short of massive violence, brought strong moral pressure to bear, even if the size of that constituency was hard to measure. Disinvestment redistributed wealth in the short term, perhaps in a direction not intended, and reduced some job opportunities and welfare projects. Trade embargoes affected the direction of South African commerce, causing a relative but not uniform weakening of American and European links and strengthening ties with the Far East, but without reducing its overall volume. Financial restrictions, imposed by banks, not governments, were chiefly important because of their links with the fall of the rand on the international money market from $1.36 in 1981 to $0.41 in 1989. This resulted in an increase of South Africa's foreign debt to $20 billion by the end of the decade, on which the Government was at one point tempted to renege in response to the economic squeeze. But rescheduling arrangements were made towards the end of 1989, before the Commonwealth Conference, under which South Africa undertook to repay $4.66 billion between 1990 and 1992 (*Economist*, 14–20 October 1989).

The most serious impact of the balance of payments decline was the way the export of capital to service the national debt prevented capital growth, which had averaged 5.8 per cent in the 1960s, 3.3 per cent in the 1970s, and under 2 per cent (with some years of negative growth) in the 1980s, all at a time when a population growth averaging 2.5 per cent necessitated an economic growth rate of 5.5 per cent if living standards were to be prevented from falling. These hard facts, linked to a soaring defence budget of R9 billion in 1989, and the heavy cost of an over-elaborate administrative structure to maintain the controls of the apartheid system, were – it seems – more damaging than contrived economic measures to the national economy. The chief danger of the sanctions campaign was that it drove out of South Africa foreign businesses with important access to overseas markets and technology, which might well divert their interest to the development of other parts of the world rather than return.

One area in which sanctions did bite was in South Africa's inability to expand her trade sufficiently in that part of the world where it ought to have been able to expand rapidly: on the continent of Africa. Guelke and Cooper between them have shown that during the period 1955 to 1978 there was an almost unbroken decline in the African share of South Africa's exports, which were valued at 19.3 per cent of the total in 1956, and fell to 7.38 per cent in 1978, though the actual unadjusted value rose from R128.1 million in 1955 to R537.8 million in 1978. The only upward movement during the period was between 1966 and 1971, when near parity with the early 1950s was reached. This was chiefly as a result of the re-export of goods to Rhodesia while that country was subject to international sanctions. There was an increase in the value of goods exported in 1984–5; but the volume hardly constituted the 'export-led recovery on 1978–1979 lines' hoped for by the *Financial Mail* (9 August). Exports to the Far East and Africa showed the greatest relative increase; but imports from those regions were static.

Other kinds of economic link had developed between South Africa and her northern neighbours. South Africa's agreement to build a new capital for Malawi at Lilongwe, and her investment in the Cabora Bassa dam project in Mozambique, helped here. The mutual dependence of South Africa, Malawi, Zambia and Portuguese East Africa (later Maputo) on the long-standing system of labour migrancy was another such bond. Of 381,000 Africans employed by the Chamber of Mines in 1972, about one third were drawn from north of latitude 22° S., while another third came from Mozambique. The total number of 'tropicals' had risen from 3,000 to 119,000 between 1936 and 1972, but there was a notable cutback in the middle 1970s, particularly from Malawi, when, as a reaction to a plane crash in which a large number of Malawian migrants were killed, the Malawian Government decided to cut down its migrant numbers to the Rand. At the same time it became the policy of the Chamber of Mines to rely more on labour from the South African Homelands than it had done in the past. But in view of existing ties, it was no matter for surprise that the governments of states within South Africa's economic orbit should have contracted out of O.A.U. attempts to promote the economic boycott of the Republic, as Dr Kamuzu Banda of Malawi and Sir Seretse Khama of Botswana did in 1964, and the Government of Zambia did in 1965. The economic predicament of those territories, known after the fall of the Portuguese Empire and Rhodesia as the 'Front-line States' (Zimbabwe, Zambia, Botswana, Tanzania, Swaziland, Lesotho, Mozambique and Angola), is not difficult to appreciate in view of their political pull in one direction and their economic pull in another, but the crisis arising from these tensions would not erupt until 1983.

18.8 THE CAPE ROUTE, STRATEGIC MINERALS AND OIL

The sanctions issue was particularly heavily debated because of South Africa's strategic position as guardian of the Cape route, and on account of her possession of enormous reserves of minerals which were vital to the weapons systems of the West. Western strategists were divided over the importance of the Cape route, not in its own right, but in relation to their fear that to admit dependence on South Africa, a pariah state, was to forgo so much political goodwill in the rest of Africa that this might outweigh the advantages to be gained by using Simonstown as a base. The calculation was hard to make after the Soviet navy had acquired facilities in the Indian Ocean for the first time, at Aden and elsewhere, and at Luanda on the west coast as a result of the Angolan War. South Africa tried from 1968 onwards to build up a system of joint defence for the southern oceans, and opened diplomatic contact with Argentina and Paraguay; but her attempts to use Simonstown as leverage had remarkably little influence, as Coker and Hurrell have shown, and did not deter Britain from terminating the Simonstown Agreement in 1975, even though the French had had to withdraw from Diego Suarez after the Malagasy revolution of 1972. That revolution, in its day, had been largely a reaction to excessive South African zeal in promoting her own image along with extensive aid in the creation of facilities for the island republic. Johnson has even represented it as a 'violent and dramatic defeat for South African expansionism', and it had a ripple effect on developments in Mauritius and the Seychelles, where governments unsympathetic to the west achieved power between 1977 and 1980. The island of Diego Garcia, which Britain placed at the disposal of the United States in 1975, was barely large enough to provide defensible naval repair facilities in the event of conflict, but it was the best base available if political considerations had to be taken into account. An abortive mercenary attempt to topple the new regime of President René in the Seychelles in November 1981, in which a group of specially trained South Africans took part, was a further reminder to the West of the hazards of cooperating with South Africa, even though the coup itself appears to have been plotted by the deposed Mancham Government in exile in Europe.

Under the pressure of these developments, the role of Simonstown for Indian Ocean defence could be seen in a different perspective. It was far from the scene of action, especially when the events of the Iranian revolution of 1979 and the air attacks on tankers during the Gulf War between Iraq and Iran in 1984 underscored the fact that the real defence of the oil route needed to be undertaken, if at all, in the Persian Gulf itself. Nor was the Cape section of the oil route considered particularly vulnerable on account of the absence south of the Mozambique Channel of a maritime choke through which shipping would have to pass. But there can be little doubt that Britain would have retaken the Falkland Islands with greater ease in 1982 if she had had free access to Simonstown, and that the naval intelligence facilities of the South African base would have been of immense value to the west in the event of a major war.

The importance of South Africa as a producer of strategic minerals had led to a controversy similar in character to the debate over the Cape route: that is, it became a question for the western powers of balancing current ease of access to minerals of unquestionable military and economic

468

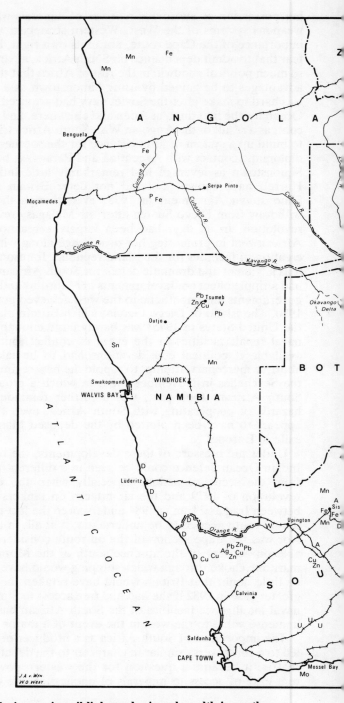

Map 11 Political boundaries, main rail links and mineral wealth in southern Africa, 1990

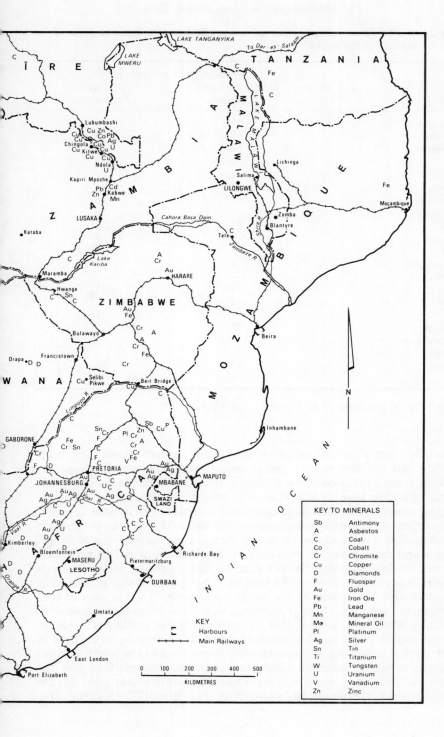

KEY TO MINERALS

Sb	Antimony
A	Asbestos
C	Coal
Co	Cobalt
Cr	Chromite
Cu	Copper
D	Diamonds
F	Fluospar
Au	Gold
Fe	Iron Ore
Pb	Lead
Mn	Manganese
Mo	Mineral Oil
Pl	Platinum
Ag	Silver
Sn	Tin
Ti	Titanium
W	Tungsten
U	Uranium
V	Vanadium
Zn	Zinc

KEY

⊏ Harbours
+⧾+ Main Railways

0 100 200 300 400 500
KILOMETRES

Table 2   South African mineral reserves and production in relation to those of the rest of the world

| | *South Africa's percentage of* | |
| | *Estimated world* | *Total world* |
Mineral	*Reserves*	*Production*
Antimony	5	16
Asbestos	5	5
Chromite	81	36
Coal	6	3
Cobalt	4	–
Copper	2	3
Diamonds	21	18
Fluorspar	35	10
Gold	51	53
Iron ore	3	4
Lead	–	–
Manganese	78	22
Mineral oil	–	–
Platinum	75	51
Silver	4	–
Tin	1	1
Titanium	15	15
Tungsten	–	–
Uranium	–	–
Vanadium	49	45
Zinc	8	–

Source   *Official Year Book of the Republic of South Africa, 1982*

importance, the obtaining of which from other sources would have been possible, but not always easy and probably more expensive, against the need to ensure continued access to South African minerals in the event of a change of regime at some later date. By common agreement, the three key strategic minerals found in large quantities and produced in South Africa, were chrome, manganese and platinum. All had to do with the production of high quality hardened, heat-resistant steel, of special importance for jet engines and the burning of rocket fuels. In 1983 South Africa produced half the world's platinum (90 per cent of that produced in the western world), 36 per cent of the world's chrome (56 per cent of that produced in the west), and 22 per cent of the world's manganese (42 per cent of that produced in the west). These proportions were by any standard impressive, especially when it is realised that 81 per cent of the world's reserves of chrome and 78 per cent of manganese were considered to be located in South Africa. Assessment of the strategic importance of the South African minerals, however, involved various other considerations. One was the extent of stockpiling, to which considerable attention was paid by the United States Government and some of its allies from 1977 onwards. This applied to all strategic minerals, to the point at which the immediate demand for the South African metals had begun to tail off by 1983. Another was the progress made in substitution, which particularly affected the heat-resistant group of metals through the development of ceramics. Another consideration was the availability of undeveloped resources elsewhere, like the reserves of chrome (for which substitution is very difficult) in Turkey and the Philippines, or of manganese in Australia, and vanadium in Australia and China. The value of South Africa lay as much in her technology and her ability to mine and transport the key minerals as in her actual possession of them, and this was particularly the case with cobalt, which was produced in Zambia and Zaire, but exported through East London. This meant, for purposes of practical calculation, that South Africa combined large reserves, skilled technology, good transportation, and an overall ability to produce and market key minerals cheaply, the denial of which to the west would have involved delays and enormous expense in the setting up of equivalent infrastructures elsewhere. But as with the Cape route, the more South Africa traded on her advantages, the more her trading partners resolved to find alternative sources of supply. As Shafer put it, 'leverage is attempted, the lever will bend'.

But if South Africa was in danger of over-playing her hand over the Cape route and strategic minerals, her critics did the same in the matter of armaments and oil. The Security Council ordered an arms embargo against South Africa in 1963. Those countries best placed to supply arms, namely the United States, Britain, France, West Germany and Italy, all complied without much delay, though France imposed only limited restrictions at first. The arms embargo was taken as a challenge. A public armaments manufacturing corporation, Armscor, which had been in existence since the mid-1960s, and spent R30 million in 1966 mainly on imported weaponry, spent R1,600 million in 1980, mainly on weapons manufactured in South Africa. Armscor by then controlled subsidiaries which built military aircraft, firearms and artillery pieces of very high quality, as well as missile-guidance and radar systems, and various types of military vehicle adapted, like the Ratel and its modifications, for conflict under local conditions. A construction yard in Durban was building fast naval patrol boats, and there were plans for building submarines. Arms production was based on a steel industry in which a plentiful supply of all the strategic minerals was married to expert technology, initially imported but subsequently trained on the spot. Only in a few areas, like fast combat aircraft, was the South African arsenal defective. By 1983 South Africa was producing weapons for export. Cooperation with Israel and Taiwan in the design and manufacture of weapons was evidently close. In 1950, South Africa's defence budget had stood at a mere R16 million. It had grown to R230 million by 1966, to R1,350 million by 1976, to R3,092 million by 1984 and to just under R10,000 million by 1989.

Without being able to profit from an offer made by the United States to other countries in 1970 to make uranium enrichment technology available, South Africa announced her own breakthrough in this field in July of that year. When the Rockefeller Report was compiled in 1981, it was generally assumed that once South Africa's first nuclear power station was ready for operation in 1984, it would be dependent on American-supplied nuclear fuel. By May 1981, however, South Africa announced her ability to enrich uranium to the extent required for the production of power. This announcement also implied that she possessed the technology to enrich uranium for military purposes, and drew attention to the possibility that she might already be a nuclear military power, which the American Government had begun to suspect on the evidence of unexplained explosions picked up by satellite observation in the south Atlantic on 25 October 1979. Conflicting pressures, however, enabled the South African Government to guard its secret. One was the determination of member states of the International Atomic Energy Agency to bar South Africa from membership. The other was the desire of the American Government after the accession of President Reagan to power to persuade South Africa to sign the Nuclear Non-Proliferation Treaty which Congress had decided to impose on any state which took delivery of nuclear fuel. In order to safeguard its own nuclear-enrichment secrets, the South African Government held back from signing the treaty, which its independent nuclear technology enabled it to do without risk to its supplies for the Koeberg nuclear reactor near Cape Town which came into production in April 1984, with fuel supplied from France (Jaster).

In the case of oil sanctions, which might have become the Achilles heel of the South African economy, a real crisis threatened, but it was one for which the country had had plenty of time to prepare. Kuwait banned oil exports to South Africa in 1964, with very little effect on the country's supplies. The Organisation of Petroleum Exporting Countries (O.P.E.C.) added its weight to the ban in 1973; but at that time the Republic could still obtain supplies from Iran, and continued to import Iranian oil until the Iranian revolution of 1979 no longer made this possible. But long before then the Government had begun to develop pioneering techniques for the extraction of oil from coal, which South Africa possessed in abundance, at the SASOL plants opened at Vanderbyl Park in 1955, and later at Secunda in the Eastern Transvaal in 1983. A third SASOL plant built at Newcastle in Natal was calculated to bring the country's oil production up to one half of domestic requirements at the 1978 level of consumption. Further research in the 1970s led to successful experimentation with ethanol, derived from vegetable sources, for use as agricultural fuel. Meanwhile the Government had created enormous underground storage facilities and begun to hoard supplies. These precautions, coupled with massive expenditure on another state corporation, Soekor, to prospect for inland and offshore fuel, which made its first economic offshore gas strike at Mossel Bay and the acquisition of substantial supplies of petroleum at exceptionally high premium rates through the diversion of rogue tankers from their normal routes by arrangements not disclosed, enabled the country to live through the early 1980s without needing to impose rationing on the ordinary consumer.

18.9   P. W. BOTHA, THE 'CONSTELLATION' CONCEPT AND THE S.A.D.C.C.: FROM DESTABILISATION TO THE INDEPENDENCE OF NAMIBIA, 1979–90

At the Carlton conference in November 1979, P. W. Botha first described his plan for a 'Constellation' of southern African states to defeat the 'Marxist threat'. It was to be an association of black and white states, supposedly within a framework of separate development, though he evidently hoped to bring in those front-line countries which were involved in the rand monetary area and the Customs Union.

Crisis in Rhodesia, however, blunted his appeal. There the white Government had surrendered power in an internal settlement to Bishop Muzorewa, who was prepared to join Botha's scheme; but the bishop was soon involved in negotiations in London with the victorious Patriotic Front, as a result of which Zimbabwe/Rhodesia returned to nominal British rule on 11 December, and Robert Mugabe took over as prime minister after fresh elections on 14 February.

The fall of the Smith Government was the heaviest defeat for a white regime in settler Africa, and it was hardly surprising in the circumstances that the response to Botha's 'Constellation' offer was limited. South West Africa, Transkei and Bophutatswana joined; but Lesotho and Botswana declined, while Mugabe, on achieving power in Salisbury, (soon to be renamed Harare), immediately began to build up a new relationship with the adjacent black states. He joined a conference at Lusaka in April 1980 to promote and participate in a new economic community formed in 1979 among the 'Front-line' States, including Lesotho, Botswana and Swaziland, with the object of breaking away from dependence on South Africa, and thus further isolating her internationally. The Southern African Development Coordinating Conference (S.A.D.C.C.) needed to attract massive international funding in order to reorientate the entire network of the central African regional transport and communications system if it was to succeed in developing a new regional infrastructure, and it held a succession of meetings in Beira, Maputo, Maseru, and Lusaka again, in 1980–4 with this object in mind.

The moment for such planning could hardly have been less auspicious. The S.A.D.C.C. was hampered by the severe drought of the early 1980s, and by inability to attract sufficient funds in a period of trade depression, as well as by lack of drive from the top. It was also grievously hampered by the political instability of the region. In Mozambique Samora Machel's Government was locked in conflict with a right-wing resistance movement, 'Renamo' (or the M.R.N.) which had first been set up as a Rhodesian-controlled counter-insurgency unit to undermine ties between Z.A.N.U. and F.R.E.L.I.M.O., but had transferred its loyalties to the South African authorities after the end of the Rhodesian war (Flower). Conflict continued in Angola between the M.P.L.A. and Unita, which ran parallel to the fighting between S.W.A.P.O. and the South African Defence Force, taking place largely on Angolan territory. Violence had developed between the forces loyal to the Zimbabwean Government and those in

Matabeleland loyal to Joshua Nkomo; while in Lesotho the Government of Chief Leabua Jonathan was subject to periodic attacks by a Lesotho Liberation Army, which could only enter Lesotho from the Republic of South Africa, as did South African troops in December 1982 in a bid to root out A.N.C. guerrillas who were said to be crossing the other way. It would be unrealistic, on the basis of the substantial body of evidence alluded to by Jenkins and by Price, to assume that the South African Government, which was still keeping sixty of the secret projects of the Rhoodie era going, was an innocent bystander during these months of growing destabilisation, above all in view of the manner in which South African mercenaries broke surface in the Seychelles coup of 1981, using weapons obtained under normal S.A.D.F. indenting procedures. All the signs, indeed, point to the suggestion that the South African Government was beginning to get the measure of the current logistical position, and that after the setback of 1975, when it had pulled out of Angola in the face of the rearming of the M.P.L.A. by the Russians and Cubans, it was taking for granted its ability to fight and beat Soviet surrogate forces even if they possessed superior weapons. By means of a combination of destabilising acts, forward defensive strikes and economic leverage which Price has described, South Africa began to assert effective dominance over the region as a whole, without any more concern for the niceties of inter-state relations than was being shown by their opponents. This new confidence appeared more than ever justified when S.A.D.F. units had a successful encounter in Angola with a force of Russian-built tanks manned by Cubans in January 1984.

This new mood also came to influence South Africa's policy in South West Africa/Namibia, the one area in which her armed forces operated openly in a growing cross-border conflict. There S.W.A.P.O.'s military infiltration was a reality, for its guerrillas had plenty of support among the border Ovambo, and could enter South West Africa with the help of good bush cover during spring and early summer. For the period 1978–83, S.W.A.P.O. guerrillas managed with growing success to mount raids which sometimes reached the white farming areas south of Ovambo; but repeated counter-raids by the S.A.D.F., sometimes deep into Angola, which were justified by the army on the principle of 'hot pursuit', together with the growing success of Savimbi's Unita forces in combating the M.P.L.A. and their Cuban allies further north, prevented the consolidation of S.W.A.P.O. bases on either side of the cutline. In a conflict in which the civilian population of Ovambo and Okavango appear to have suffered considerable distress from abductions and political murders on S.W.A.P.O.'s side, and the notorious attentions of South Africa's counter-insurgency unit, Koevoet, on the other, white rule in South West Africa remained intact.

But from the time of Vorster's final political improvisation in promoting locally-run elections in December 1978 [see p. 458], political developments in that territory went sour. These elections gave the Democratic Turnhalle Alliance a mandate to remove racial discrimination, which it had begun to do. But its failure to gain control of the white second-tier legislature left the Opposition National Party in a position to maintain the *status quo* over large areas of inter-racial contact. The D.T.A. was thus placed in an ambiguous position. It managed to obtain an international platform in January 1981, when the South African Government and S.W.A.P.O. met face to face for talks in Geneva, for on that occasion the South African delegation stood back and allowed the D.T.A. leaders to set the tone of the negotiations, which then broke down. The D.T.A. leadership was in a confident mood, in the knowledge that they had full control over the central legislature, and they appear even to have felt they were a match for S.W.A.P.O. in a straight election fight. It does not seem, however, that the South African Government shared this confidence. At any rate, it did little to promote the D.T.A.'s liberalisation policy, with the result that the D.T.A. itself began to break open at the seams during 1982, when its president, Peter Kalangula, Ovambo's leading political figure, resigned to join forces with the Damara, Coloured and Baster groups in the belief that by doing so he stood a better chance of attracting grassroots support. It was later renamed Christian Democratic Action for Social Justice (C.D.S.). The South African Government decided Mudge was expendable, and turned to these groups, whom a new Administrator-General, Danie Hough, tried to galvanise into an alternative power bloc in September. But this was to discredit the D.T.A. to nobody's advantage, while blocking attempts to promote Resolution 435. Hough's successor, Dr Willie van Niekerk, tried the gesture of nominating a 'state council' consisting of members of all parties in South West Africa, both inside and outside the legislature, in June 1983. The Nationalists and the original D.T.A. parties agreed to come in; but this solution did not commend itself to the parties of the left, least of all to S.W.A.P.O. itself. It was therefore in opposition to van Niekerk's plan that Moses Katjiuonga (S.W.A.N.U., the original Herero party), Andreas Shipanga (a leader of the S.W.A.P.O. Democrats, who had broken with Nujoma in 1978) and Mudge (D.T.A.), decided to set up a Namibian Multi-Party Conference in August. This movement achieved an atmosphere of conciliation, which a visit to South Africa, Namibia and Angola in the same month by Dr Perez de Cuellar, the United Nations Secretary General, managed not to disturb. At its first meeting demands for reform were plentiful, above all for the abolition of the ten ethnic governments which, between them, swallowed up the lion's share of the annual revenue and had managed to amass such massive debts that a commission of inquiry had had to be appointed to look into their affairs. But commentators generally considered that if an election had been called early in 1984, S.W.A.P.O. would still have won.

The war, the needlessly complex political system, and the bleeding of its economy were causing acute distress in South West Africa. The Territory experienced a negative economic growth rate of 7 per cent in 1984, agriculture, fishing and mining (its staple exports) falling from 43 to 34 per cent of the total. Its fishing grounds largely fished out, its farms ruined by drought, its karakul prices right down, and with most of its mineral wealth owned outside the country, and its trade largely subject to external controls. South West Africa needed peace, honest government, a chance to recuperate, and independence at the end of the road. South Africa, for her part, needed relief from the expenditure of over R500 million annually (about half the Territory's budget) to run the country and maintain an army on its border.

Politically, however, the difficulty of reconciling the U.N.'s commitment to Resolution 435 with the South African commitment to a local solution based on the Multi-Party Conference still threatened deadlock. The threat was increased rather than diminished in March 1984 when Pik Botha canvassed for a southern African regional conference to work out a package for both South West Africa and Angola. Such a plan was only feasible if the U.N.'s special commitment to South West Africa, as a territory in which it had international obligations stretching back over thirty years, could be swept under the carpet.

Pik Botha's proposal has to be seen in the context of a major transformation in the southern African diplomatic scene between January and March 1984, the exact nature of which can still be only tentatively explained. A visit by President Samora Machel of Mozambique to western Europe at the end of 1983 built bridges which he would later seek to use. Conversations between South African and Soviet diplomats in New York at the beginning of January – in themselves a rare event – appear to have made the South African Government aware that the deposition of the M.P.L.A. would not be tolerated, but that otherwise the Russians were unlikely to intervene aggressively in the region. Meanwhile the American Assistant Secretary of State for African Affairs, Dr Chester Crocker, visited southern Africa in January and February and regularly thereafter until the end of the Reagan era, patiently displaying his considerable brokerage skills among the rival parties.

In the meantime the South African Government announced that in return for a promise of a cease-fire it was prepared to withdraw its forces from Angola for thirty days from 31 January. P. W. Botha stated in the House of Assembly that South Africa was no longer prepared to carry the burden of South West Africa alone. The cease-fire was accepted by Nujoma on behalf of S.W.A.P.O., provided that talks between South Africa and S.W.A.P.O. were held without delay. But S.W.A.P.O. did not bind itself to refrain from activities inside South West Africa, and tried with indifferent success to exploit a new invasion route through Botswana in early March. Meanwhile, a joint force to monitor disengagement was set up by the Angolan and South African Governments in mid-February, in terms of an agreement reached at a meeting presided over by President Kaunda in Lusaka.

Very soon afterwards the South African Foreign Minister took a strong ministerial team to Maputo and held talks with President Machel, during which the grounds were laid for the signing of a formal non-aggression treaty between South Africa and Mozambique at Komatipoort on 16 March.

The Accord of Nkomati, as the treaty came to be known, was in itself a limited agreement under which both sides undertook to refrain from interference in each other's affairs, to resolve their difficulties peacefully and without recourse to force, sabotage or violation of borders. They would not permit organisations which planned violence or terrorism against the other party to set up bases, training centres, transit facilities or arms depots in their territories. They would also eliminate hostile radio stations on their territories and other propagandist facilities aimed against the other party. The agreement was essentially limited in range, and both sides kept nearly all their political options open. Thus the leaders of the Independent Homelands were absent, out of respect for Machel's refusal to recognise them. Large numbers of South African business leaders, on the other hand, were present, as an indication that developmental aid from the private sector could be expected to follow, whatever the South African Government might itself undertake. In this respect, the two governments presumably had in mind aid which would supplement rather than conflict with the projects undertaken by the S.A.D.C.C., though there can be no doubt at all that South Africa's indirect destabilisation of the S.A.D.C.C., above all through her logistical support for attacks on the Benguela and Beira railway lines, had been an effective lever, along with the drought, for bringing Machel to the negotiating table. To destabilise the S.A.D.C.C. was also to promote the Constellation.

No provision was made for the interests of the liberation movements, and the A.N.C. did not take kindly to being informed by the head of the Mozambican army that it was a civil rights movement not a liberation army, since South Africa was already an independent state. President Mugabe of Zimbabwe was candid when he explained that it was beyond the power of the Front-line States to prevent South African incursions 'should those be mounted against us', and that the A.N.C. would be better advised to channel its activities through the O.A.U.. The Government of Botswana, through whose territory the latest S.W.A.P.O. infiltrators had passed, was critical of the Accord when a delegation under its foreign minister visited Cape Town a week later, but it gave no indication that it would permit any bases to be set up by the guerrilla movements. President Kaunda, whose dedicated brokerage during the negotiations was applauded, though he failed to achieve an agreement between the South African Government, the Multi-Party Conference and S.W.A.P.O. in May, let it be known that he thought that the A.N.C. struggle would and should continue. But there was no obvious place for either the South African liberation movements, or Renamo, or U.N.I.T.A., in the new round of agreements.

In the case of Renamo the situation was particularly complex. Evidence of actual South African involvement with Renamo after the signing of the Nkomati Accord suggests that this took place, not at the level of government, which had its reasons for promoting the economic advantages of the joint South African–Mozambican hydroelectric enterprise at Cabora Bassa, but – as so often in history – in the upper echelons of the Defence Force where some officers operated beyond the call of duty. Of particular moment were well-authenticated press revelations in early October 1985 about contacts between senior S.A.D.F. officers and the Renamo leader, Afonso Dhlakama, in August and September 1984, not long after the Nkomati meeting. Later, in April 1988, a carefully compiled report by

Robert Gersony of the U.S. State Department's Human Rights Bureau reached the conclusion that the Renamo 'nightmare', which had been involved in massive genocide, apparently without the strong anti-communist ideological commitment which had characterised its early years, had been and still was receiving help from South Africa – an accusation which the S.A.D.F. energetically denied. But so much damage was done to the relationship between South Africa and Mozambique through suspicions generated by the alleged Renamo link, supplemented in October 1986 by the mysterious death of President Samora Machel, when the plane in which he was flying crashed over South African territory when about to land at Maputo, that it became necessary for Presidents Botha and Chissano (Machel's successor) to set the Accord on track again in September 1988.

At the beginning of June 1984, P. W. Botha set off with his foreign minister for a placatory assault on the governments of Portugal, Switzerland, Great Britain, West Germany and Italy, in what must be considered the first really significant political journey by a South African head of state since the days of General Smuts. The need for such a mission was great, for South Africa's international stock was low. Botha's journey, however, was not the diplomatic *tour de force* for which the South African Government hoped. His encounters with European heads of state – in particular with Margaret Thatcher of Great Britain – were hardly cordial occasions. Europe first wanted evidence of a real change in South Africa's political direction, and some sign that the diplomatic revolution of Nkomati was more than a case of mere 'thump and talk'. Some of the outer defences of apartheid had gone during his initial period of reform; but the unrest which resulted from the constitutional changes of 1983–4 induced Botha to batten down the hatches, with an unavoidably harmful effect on his reformist image.

Although the Western Contact Group had tried and failed to help resolve the South West African impasse [see p. 457], a further attempt was made in 1986 by a Commonwealth Group of Eminent Persons, appointed at the Heads of State conference in the Bahamas in October 1985, to break the deadlock. This group, jointly chaired by the Prime Minister of Australia, Mr Malcolm Fraser, and General Olusegun Obasanjo, head of the Federal Military Government of Nigeria, toured South Africa, and visited the heads of all the Front-line States between February and May 1986. They reached the conclusion that 'ground existed on the basis of which a negotiated solution to South Africa's problems could be attempted if there was the necessary will among all concerned', and therefore proposed a 'Possible Negotiating Concept' which would involve undertakings by the South African Government and by the 'A.N.C. and others', which elicited a courteous reply from Pik Botha containing a proposal for further discussions, dated 29 May 1986, on the eve of the Group's departure from South Africa. But on the 20th South African planes had raided A.N.C. bases in Lusaka, Harare and Gaborone, at a moment which could only be construed as a rebuff to the Commonwealth visitors, who were left in no doubt that this was intended when the State President rounded on Sir

Geoffrey Howe, the British Foreign Minister, who visited the country at the end of July with the blunt order to 'leave South Africa to the South Africans'. Verwoerd had not handled Macmillan in the same way.

In one area of foreign policy, however – where success seemed least likely, and came from necessity rather than slick management – the Botha Government could claim to have made progress: it contributed to the eventual independence of South West Africa.

To meet an urgent need to establish its international legitimacy, the Multi-Party Conference in South West Africa had engaged S.W.A.P.O. in talks in Lusaka in May 1984, and thereafter visited several francophone African states as well as the American Government and the U.N., but all to little avail (Du Pisani). Thwarted, it then called for a conference of reconciliation between all parties, including S.W.A.P.O., to bring an end to hostilities before the end of the year and set up a transitional government – failing which it would negotiate an independence deal with South Africa. The transitional government of national unity which it proposed was to be headed by a cabinet of eight to be nominated by a national assembly. It would take over the Administrator-General's powers, subject to his veto and to the ultimate control of the State President of South Africa. The assembly of 62 members would consist of representatives of the M.P.C. parties in proportion to their relative strengths.

In default of outside response, the South African Government brought a transitional government on these lines into being on 17 June 1985. This was to confirm a deadlock at the international level, with the South African Government in possession of the field. But in April 1988 P. W. Botha restored the Administrator-General to full authority, in the hope that he would be able to stabilise a situation, which had now been transformed by military considerations, with the backing of the National Party of Namibia.

The Cuban forces, whose removal from Angola had acquired more and more urgency from the South African point of view, had acquired such a measure of air superiority in the border war with the help of new Russian aircraft that they had pinned down the South African troops north of the frontier at Cuito Cuanavale, while advancing columns of Cuban, Angolan and S.W.A.P.O. forces threatened to cut off their line of retreat, thus in effect forcing the South African Government to negotiate. On 4 May South Africa, Angola, Cuba and the United States began discussions in London, while the Angolans and South Africans met in Brazzaville in the presence of Dr Chester Crocker. By the end of August all South African troops were out of Angola, including those investing Cuito Cuanavale. During September Dr de Cuellar returned to Pretoria to renegotiate Resolution 435 with the two Bothas. The State President set off without delay for Zaire to hold discussions with President Mobutu Sese Seko in order to hasten negotiations for an Angolan peace, which were resumed in Brazzaville in December, and a peace protocol signed by South Africa, Angola and Cuba, allowing for the implementation of Resolution 435 on 1 April 1989, the start of an election campaign on 1 July, and elections themselves on 1 November. It also set down procedures for the withdrawal of the Cubans and for handling disputes arising out of the agreement, for the exchange of prisoners. South Africa confirmed that she would stop aiding U.N.I.T.A., and Angola the A.N.C., while S.W.A.P.O. subsequently agreed to abide by the existing ceasefire.

The non-involvement of S.W.A.P.O. and U.N.I.T.A. in the formal negotiations created unforeseen difficulties: with U.N.I.T.A. because no provision was made for the settlement of their longstanding conflict with the M.P.L.A.; with S.W.A.P.O. because of its pressing need to negotiate, if at all possible, from a position of strength gained through the occupation of Namibian territory. Nujoma's stand over the Angolan negotiations had based itself on the substantial fiction that S.W.A.P.O. only had Namibian interests to protect. As soon as Resolution 435 came into force, therefore, S.W.A.P.O. cadres which had slipped south of the 16th parallel in violation of the Angolan–South African agreement crossed the border fully armed, with the intention of setting up bases at a moment when the South African forces were restricted to camp. Heavy fighting consequently broke out again, most of the casualties being among the S.W.A.P.O. infiltrators. The Administrator-General, Louis Pienaar, suspended the timetable for elections. Hasty efforts were made to bring in those contingents of the U.N. peace-keeping force which had not yet arrived, and to persuade the S.W.A.P.O. groups, who were often hard to locate, to surrender or return across the border. But the Administrator and the U.N. Commissioner brought the situation under control, and the former settled down to the removal, by presidential proclamation, of the 46 laws relating to security and race relations which infringed civil rights. Next came provision for the repatriation of refugees from Angola and Zambia, and a further furore over others not accounted for.

Nujoma returned to Namibia on 14 September 1989 after a twenty-nine year exile, soon after the start of the run-up to the elections which were scheduled for 1 November. By comparison with the first Rhodesian independence elections, those in Namibia were restrained. As anticipated, S.W.A.P.O. won, with 41 of the 72 seats in the constituent assembly and 57 per cent of the vote, the D.T.A. 21 seats with 28 per cent, the United Democratic Front 4 seats, and the Afrikaner right-wing grouping, Action Christian National, 3. Without delay, a committee of the Assembly, on which all parties were represented, began to work on the constitution, and reached agreement over the main principles before Christmas. During January and February 1990 the draft was debated publicly in the Assembly, in the presence of neutral legal advisers, and agreed to unanimously in good time for the independence celebrations on 21 March. It was a procedure from which the fathers of the South African constitution of 1909 could have learnt a lot.

Decades of civil conflict had resulted in acceptance of a republican constitution which drew its inspiration from both the American and British systems. A popularly elected executive president was to preside over a cabinet whose other members were to sit in an almost wholly elective National Assembly, whose legislative powers were made subject to review by a smaller, regionally-based elective National Council, and under extreme circumstances to a presidential veto. The presidential powers were as carefully circumscribed as those of the legislature, above all in the matter of discretionary appointments. The judiciary's independence of executive and legislative control, and its power to review legislation and enforce a Bill of Rights, were clearly laid down. The rights protected were extremely wide-ranging, taking in the needs of the exploited as well as of the ordinary citizen, and including safeguards against arbitrary detention and any continuance of the inequalities of the colonial era now ending, if need be by affirmative action. The quality of the document derived not a little from the tested advice of top South African legists, and from the desire of the Namibian people to bury the memories of an unnecessarily long, conflict-torn past.

Section III
The Political Economy of South Africa

19 The Economy and the People of South Africa

South Africa became an economic giant, dominating the southern part of the continent to such an extent that she called the tune in the matter of regional development even though her neighbours found her domestic policies uncongenial in the extreme. In this chapter an attempt is made to focus on the main historical developments in farming, business and communications, in mining and industry. It also draws upon the work of modern writers who have sought to explain the relationship between the State, different kinds of entrepreneur, and the legally differentiated sections of the working population. For all the lip-service paid to the merits of free enterprise, the State has always played a leading role in the South African economy, while the split character of the working class has had an impact on relations of production, on productivity and wage patterns for which it is not easy to find exact parallels elsewhere. In so far as the policy of apartheid can be said to have had an economic dimension, it will be handled here; but the ideological impact of segregation and apartheid, as they affected society as a whole, is left for treatment in the final chapter.

19.1 FROM SUBSISTENCE TO CAPITALIST FARMING

For many decades after its foundation, the settlement of the Cape retained its original character as a staging post, little more, and the encouragement of agricultural enterprise among the free burghers was designed rather to cut losses and allay discontent than to promote viable commerce. Farming for subsistence remained the rule, and – though Neumark attempted to promote a contrary hypothesis by looking for the operation of market forces in trekboer society [see p. 27] – farming as a capitalist enterprise in the subcontinent advanced extremely slowly, though from early times it was not entirely lacking (Ross).

Capitalisation came first under the stimulus of export opportunities. There was a small amount of wine export in the early nineteenth century, and a constant overseas market for products of the hunt; but the first commodity to provide a significant export staple was wool. The merino sheep was introduced from Europe in the 1780s, though exports of wool only picked up from the 1830s, after wool technology had reached the point at which factory production was possible. Then, as Thom has shown, exports increased steadily, both from the Cape (where British settlers played a key role) and from the republics. In due course ostrich feathers, mohair, deciduous and citrus fruit, maize, Transvaal tobacco, Natal sugar, and – in the twentieth century – frozen beef and a growing range of canned foods were added to the list of major exports. It terms of relative value, agricultural exports subsequently maintained a constant position behind mineral exports and ahead of manufacturing, through the twentieth century.

The growth of towns in the late nineteenth century was a further stimulus to the capitalisation of south African farming. But at first white landowners were often slow to respond to the new market opportunities, and much of the food needed in urban areas was obtained from black producers who lived in reserves, or on their own land, or on land rented from white landowners and companies. We must therefore qualify the common assumption that there was a sharp distinction between 'essentially market-oriented farming, as practised by white farmers' and the 'largely subsistence-farming of African peasants' (Hobart Houghton). Such a view derived considerable support from cultural factors, such as the absence of crop rotation in traditional societies where land was plentiful, the ritual significance attached to cattle which often led to numbers being rated above quality, the disruptive influence of superstition which could lead to the burning of crops of successful farmers accused of witchraft, and – at least until the plough transformed the division of labour – the tendency in black society for cultivation to be given over to the women. But research by Bundy and Etherington, based on the evidence of magistrates as well as missionaries, has brought to light the importance of a black peasant farming class in the late nineteenth century. Its existence has been obscured because it was severely hit by the rinderpest in 1896–7, and because, although it staged something of a recovery as a result of new opportunities created by the Anglo-Boer War, it was all but strangled as a consequence of mandatory segregation from 1913 – a fact which is still insufficiently appreciated.

With the late nineteenth-century rise in land values, which awakened a new awareness of commercial possibilities among white farmers, black squatters came under increasing pressure to enter the job market as labour tenants, rather than avoid it as share-croppers. The Natives Land Act of 1913 severely curtailed share-cropping, without stopping an inflow of blacks on to the white farms, even in the Free State (Greenberg). White farmers also preferred to see blacks held in a labour–tenant relationship to the landlord, rather than as migrant workers based on the reserves (Lacey). The Native Service Contract Act of 1932 was a major bid to stabilise that relationship [see p. 267], and Greenberg has stressed (against the argument of Morris) that the full economic rationalisation of South African agricultural labour belongs not to the 1920s (when labour-tenancy was the norm) but to the 1960s and 1970s, when it almost universally gave place to wage labour, so that the landlord could call on all his labourer's working time.

But it was only partial capitalisation even then, for traditional forms of landholding and traditional methods of farming persisted in the reserves as the only forms and methods regarded as suitable by the authorities. Even though individual tenure had been encouraged by the Barry Commission (1883) in the Cape, promoted under the Glen Grey Act (1894), and recommended by the Lagden Commission (1905) wherever it was desired by black communities in preference to the traditional forms, the policy was discouraged by South African governments from the 1920s (Dubow). The explanation is twofold: on the one hand, the abandonment of traditional tenure was seen as bad for the authority of the chief or headman, whose customary role it was to give out and take back land; and on the other, the introduction of mandatory segregation from 1913 so restricted the areas where blacks could legitimately farm, that it became increasingly difficult to allow the establishment of economic farming units in the reserves without reducing their capacity to accommodate the number of blacks whose land rights the authorities wished to restrict to those areas. The introduction of betterment schemes after 1938 afforded some protection to the land, but became increasingly unpopular among Africans, who resented cattle-culling and other controls for understandable political reasons. When the Tomlinson Commission made a strong recommendation for the introduction of freehold tenure in 1955, its proposal was dismissed by the Government out of hand.

The reserves were neither large nor evenly distributed, and it was to the credit of the Beaumont Commission and its successor bodies in 1913–18 that they were able to win public support for the addition of as much land to them as they recommended, in view of the opposition of many farmers to their enlargement. Farmers in general objected to large reserves under traditional forms of government, for they did not find it as easy to draw seasonal labour from such areas as from among squatters living on the land of their neighbours. The mines, on the other hand, with their highly developed recruiting agencies, preferred to draw their contract workers from the reserves. They could not tap the same labour resources as the farmers without friction, for the seasonal labour needs of the farms cut across the continuous contract periods required by the mining houses. That was a main reason why the mines were granted special permission to bring labour in from outside South Africa down to 1922, and again after 1937. Industrialists and commercial employers, by contrast, preferred African workers who were continuously resident in town and had acquired a measure of sophistication to improve their competence at the work bench or behind the counter. Thus the labour needs of the developed part of the economy produced tensions between the major groups, and it is helpful to see the legislative history of the Union as reflecting those tensions in one way or another. [see pp. 503–12].

The tendency to over-promote white economic interests extended to white agriculture, in particular the maize industry which was 'spoonfed to high production levels' (Cross), especially after the Marketing Act of 1937 – perhaps understandably in a country whose climate places so many obstacles in the path of successful farming. But over the years this meant the budgetary starvation of black farming, which suffered from relatively poor support services and poor access to markets, often linked to excessive controls and insufficient concern for the wider social needs of the rural community on the assumption that these were less important than soil conservation. The effects of this approach have been identified in the unpopularity of betterment schemes when linked to stock-culling, state-imposed deliveries at state prices, and the over-emphasis on farming at the expense of other productive activities to increase household incomes and thus promote local cash flow.

An awareness of dispossession also ran deep among blacks, and this has surfaced very clearly as a result of modern research (see Cross, in Cross and Haines, and Keegan, in Beinart, Delius and Trapido). In consequence debate intensified during the 1980s around arguments for a qualified or unqualified repeal of the Land Act, and with reference to the relative merits of traditional, private and collectivised land-holding. Promoters of freehold tenure, who have seen the solution of all problems as lying in increased production, are in tune with changing perspectives on peasant farming in countries like China and Korea, but have not necessarily taken sufficient account of the special problems of South African Homelands, notably the likely increase in landlessness were individual tenure to be promoted without promoting the one-way movement of blacks into areas declared white under the Land Act, at a time when the minimum economic allotment is calculated at 70 hectares (far higher than the Tomlinson calculation). Defenders of traditional forms of tenure, by contrast, have tended increasingly to notice its flexibility: the ease with which informal freehold began to develop even where distribution of land lay in the hands of headmen; the growth of a real (if sometimes tense) relationship between landlord and tenant, but without the burden of tyrannical landlordism which reared itself in some rural economies in the Far East; and above all a concern to preserve the moral economy of the traditional community, with its built-in concern for individual and household security in a rural society long impoverished by land shortages, excessive controls, and consequent demoralisation.

19.2   THE SPREAD OF COMMUNICATIONS, COMMERCE AND BANKING

Agricultural prosperity led to the development of an embryonic road system from the 1840s, when John Montagu was Colonial Secretary at the Cape and Andrew Geddes Bain his energetic and imaginative road engineer. The difficulty of the terrain in mountainous regions, coupled with the ease of transit in roadless areas like the Karoo, must be seen as the main reasons for this slow development. Wool could as easily be transported on pack animals, while slaughter stock could walk long distances to market, so that the demand for wheeled vehicles at first was not great. The development of mining in Kimberley created a need for passenger transport in the form of horse-drawn coaches, which came in to supplement the ox-waggon, the vehicle of that key figure, the transport rider, who did all the bulk carrying before the railway age and did his best to keep the railways out. In the first instance railway building devolved mainly on the state in the Cape (see Purkis), Natal and the Orange Free State, though in the Transvaal, after the abortive attempts of President Burgers and McMurdo in the 1870s and 1880s, it was entrusted to one of Kruger's concession companies but absorbed in Milner's state system from 1903. Not only were the railways indispensible for the expansion of the mining industry and for the transport of perishable carcases and other heavy goods associated with the growth of towns, but their extension became so big a political issue, as in Canada and Australia, that they can be seen as having retarded the unification of South Africa in the first instance, and in the final resort as having brought it into being [see pp. 183–5, 220–2]. Railway construction and the extension of the South African customs union from 1889 onwards cannot be separated from each other. So critical did the issues of railway politics become, that provision was made in the South Africa Act of 1909 for the incorporation of the South African Railways and Harbours as the first of a number of public utilities, whose effect would be steadily to increase the entrepreneurial role of the South African state over the years.

Commerce and banking developed strongly after the start of the mineral revolution, but in point of time preceded it. The growth of chambers of commerce dated back to the Cape Commercial Exchange of 1822, and Immelman has described their proliferation from the 1860s in the towns of the interior. Very often the members of these chambers were immigrants. Business in South Africa, whether in the colonies or the republics, tended to fall into the hands of English-speaking settlers whose shopkeeping activities gradually drove out the itinerant *smous*. Immigrants from continental Europe, Jews and Gentiles, notably Hollanders and Greeks, arrived in increasing numbers from the end of the nineteenth century, at a time when Afrikaner businessmen were relatively scarce. The English language, however, became the dominant language of South African urban life, even in places like Bloemfontein and Pretoria, until the large-scale townward movement of Afrikaners began in the 1920s and 1930s. The rise of Afrikaner business, after various small-scale attempts to organise consortia from the 1870s, reached its peak only in the 1930s and after the Second World War. But from then onwards its growth was spectacular, as has been shown by Du Plessis. Key events were the *Ekonomiese Volkskongres* of 1939 and the founding of the *Afrikaanse Handelsinstituut* in 1942, the movement of Afrikaners into the mining field on a big scale through the founding of *Federale Mynbou* (1953), and into the investment and banking fields through *Volkskas* (1935), *Federale Volksbeleggings* (1939) and the Trust Bank (1955). It was a remarkable case of what Giliomee has called 'ethnic mobilisation' for economic ends, under the blanket of protective political power [see pp. 287–90]. The setting-up of Engen [see p. 465] as a subsidiary of Gencor (the financial house of General Mining) is an indication of the extent to which Afrikaner-controlled business was sustaining its challenge to the dominant English-speaking financial interests in 1990.

There was never any political restriction on white trading rights, but

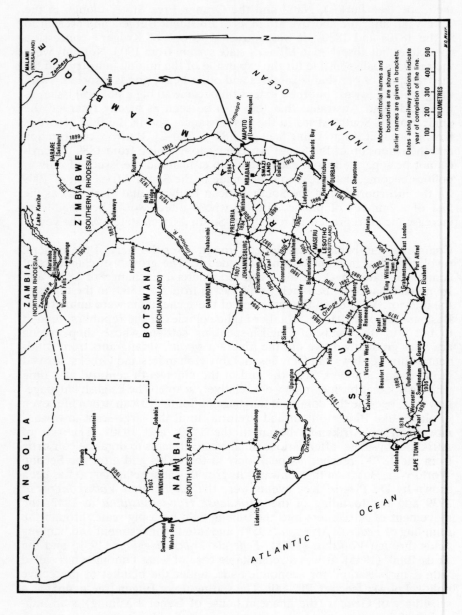

Map 12   The chronological expansion of the southern African railway system

circumstances were very different in the case of Asians and Africans. Historically, this issue first presented itself in relation to the Indian immigrants of the 1880s. Many of these were not indentured workers, but traders who had paid their own passages, and began to arrive in sufficient numbers to alarm white traders in Natal and the Boer Republics. Indians were accordingly excluded from the Orange Free State by stages between 1885 and 1890, largely on the insistence of English-speaking shopkeepers. These years also saw the first attempts in Natal and the South African Republic to restrict their residential and trading rights in the towns, and in Natal to restrict their political influence. In the longer term, fears arising from Indian business success led whites to oppose the introduction of Chinese to the Transvaal after 1903, lest they too should successfully compete. Eventually the Chinese were repatriated, and Indians were placed on the 'wrong' side of the colour bar under the Mines and Works Amendment Act of 1926. A widespread attack on their economic power began with the Transvaal and Natal pegging legislation of the 1930s and 1940s, the Asiatic Land Tenure Act of 1946, which had special reference to Natal, and the Group Areas Act of 1950, which closed the central business districts to Asian and also Coloured businesses in many towns in Natal, the Transvaal and the Cape. In the Age of the Hypermarket, which had not then been foreseen, cheaper prices made possible by lower rates levied on business outside the town enabled Indian businesses to prosper in spite of these restrictions. During the late 1980s, however, relaxation began to take place in two main directions: the century-old ban on Indian residence and businesses in the O.F.S. was repealed; and an amendment to the Group Areas Act in 1984 made it permissible to open central business districts as free trade areas, in consequence of which many local authorities took the initiative and allowed the licensing of businesses owned by people of any race group. The refusal of K.P.-dominated town councils in Boksburg and Carletonville to permit black trading was still strictly legal and resulted in immediate black consumer boycotts – as a result of which, perhaps, this faithful application of apartheid principles did not spread.

African-owned businesses were much slower to develop because, although the Natives (Urban Areas) Act of 1923 enabled local authorities to licence businesses in locations, there was a great deal of resistance to them among urban whites, especially in the Orange Free State (Van Aswegen), and the central government was not prepared to exert pressure to compel their legalisation. By 1945 this resistance had been largely overcome, and in that year black Johannesburg businessmen took a new initiative and set up an Orlando Traders' Association. Hemson records a flourishing black cooperative movement in Natal in 1946. A change of government in 1948, however, ushered in two further decades of uncertainty, as the central authorities promulgated new regulations of a restrictive kind. In 1963 a government circular required local authorities to limit African trading in locations by imposing the rule of one-man–one-shop, prohibiting African trading in all but 'daily essential domestic necessities' (which could not include the sale of petrol, for example), and banning the establishment of African trading partnerships in white areas. An unsuccessful attempt was made by the Government in 1970 to strangle African enterprise in the urban locations altogether [see p. 371].

Trade in the reserves was governed by a different set of laws. A proclamation of 1922 banned the opening of a new trading store within five miles of an existing one. This played into the hands of the white traders already established there, so, to help African traders, the law was changed in 1934 to allow stores within two miles of each other. One of the first acts of the Transkeian legislature after taking power in 1964 was to abolish this kind of geographical restriction, with the result that black-owned stores began to proliferate. Meanwhile the setting up of the Bantu Investment Corporation in 1959, and of subsidiary Homeland development corporations to promote African entrepreneurship, canalised further government and (in due course) white agency capital into the Homelands. This helped to produce a growing number of African commercial trainees, and rather fewer capitalists. It was, however, a step in the direction of African economic emancipation, especially when the development corporations began to buy the stores of white traders. The number of African traders in the African areas continued to grow especially in the larger black towns near white urban centres. There were 1460 in Soweto in 1969, for example.

The growth of black business in the white-dominated cities had to wait until the initial advance had been made in the Homelands, but then it proved too strong for the rules laid down to restrict it. An African Chamber of Commerce was set up in 1964, but was required by the Government to organise itself on ethnic lines. Resentment at this interference, writes Keeble, fired the black businessmen to set up a National African Federated Chamber of Commerce (N.A.F.C.O.C.) in 1969, with its own house journal, *African Business* (1972) and its own African Bank (1975), drawing half its funds from the African public, a rather smaller contribution from the larger white-controlled banks, and some contribution from the Homeland governments. The Soweto troubles of 1976 had an important influence, for they led the central government between 1977 and 1980 to remove nearly all the restrictions which had previously stood in the way of black enterprise. Legitimate trading was extended, by stages, to include such activities as the sale of hardware, electrical equipment, clothes, watches, and liquor for human consumption. The sale of motor fuel was permitted, together with trades such as welding and panel-beating, and eventually all trades so long as they were practised in the black townships, for they were still banned in the central business districts under the Group Areas Act, until the enabling legislation of P.W. Botha in 1984. Administration Board control was removed. Ninety-nine-year leases on, and freehold title to, fixed property were permitted. N.A.F.C.O.C., under the guidance of Sam Motsuenyane and a small leadership cadre, was now in a position to sponsor a commercial revolution in the black South African community, with the promotion of a supermarket, Blackchain, and trusts for the promotion of housing and industrial development. Privately-owned black *kombis* grew into a taxi business on an enormous scale, effectively undercutting municipal bus services in many centres, with the cooperation of leading motor manufacturers, who turned out taxis to the S.A. Black Taxi Association's specifications, and the Shell Company's promotion of a number of African-owned petrol outlets. Perhaps inevitably, differences in strategy led to conflict between N.A.F.C.O.C., which sought to promote black business in its own right, and various other bodies which sought in the early 1980s to link black businesses to equivalent white-controlled firms and Homeland investment corporations sponsored by the South African Government. But these tensions promoted rather than retarded business energies, as African entrepreneurs, set free from restrictions of a kind which had never been imposed on whites, entered into a phase comparable with that entered by the Afrikaners after 1939.

Banking, the chief lubricant of commerce, had started in South Africa during the 1830s, at the local level, but from the 1860s these local banks were gradually swallowed by the larger 'Imperial' banks, like the Standard, which derived their main funds from the London money market. The arrival of the Imperial banks signified the growing importance of South Africa as a market for British products and an investment area for British capital. They stimulated, on the rebound, the founding of Afrikaner 'national' banks in the O.F.S. in 1876, and in the South African Republic in 1890. When these bodies had become incorporated in the business and mining world during the early post-Union years, further politically-inspired banking houses were brought into being, notably *Volkskas* in 1935 and the Trust Bank twenty years later. African banking took a decade to overcome initial obstacles and find its feet, for the African Bank set up in 1975 had first been mooted in 1964; but on its own initiative, combined with the support of all the major white-controlled banks, it had taken root and boasted assets worth over R6 million by 1978.

The greatest structural change in the development of South African commercial history since the establishment of I.S.C.O.R. in 1927 followed from a decision by P. W. Botha's Government in 1985 to promote a policy of privatisation of certain public utilities. A change introduced elsewhere in the world as a way of promoting private initiative and increasing prosperity was attractive to a government which urgently needed to reduce governmental commitments and cut the tax burden in a period of high inflation. A white paper of 1987 laid down, as guidelines, the need to promote efficiency, concentrate economic power and conserve it for developmental purposes. I.S.C.O.R. itself was listed on the Johannesburg Stock Exchange in 1989, and drew a strong public response. The South African Transport Services and the Post Office were placed on the agenda for what could develop into a large-scale movement of government out of a management role. The implications of such a move, at a time when extra-parliamentary political organisations, notably the A.N.C., were campaigning for greater public ownership in the interest of wealth redistribution, gave much food for thought (*Race Relations Survey 1988–9*), pp. 347–52).

The Government also became aware that the promotion of employment required the emancipation of small businesses, especially black-owned businesses. Hence the removal in 1988 of several regulations which interfered with black entrepreneurial activity by making black trading licences hard to acquire, and black multiple businesses illegal, limiting the size or ethnic composition of partnerships, or creating difficulties over the ownership of premises. A Small Business Development Corporation which had come into being at the start of the decade claimed in 1988 to have given advice to over half a million business people and to have created 193,505 employment opportunities at an average cost of R2,400 per job.

19.3 THE RISE OF DIAMOND AND GOLD MINING AND THEIR PECULIAR LABOUR PATTERNS

With the discovery of diamonds in the Orange river valley 1867, the first real revolutionary change in South African society began to take place. Diamond-digging started as a speculative enterprise engaged in for the most part by men of little substance, both immigrant fortune-seekers and local speculators, several of whom were Dutch-speaking, and some were subjects of the Tlhaping chief Mothibi of Dikgatlhong. But Tlhaping involvement, and that of Jantje's Kora chiefdom on the Vaal were soon squeezed out (Shillington). The number of claim-holders diminished nearly tenfold between 1873 and 1879, when a mere 130 of the original 1,200 were left (Worger), the survivors of a game of chance which became all the more costly as the excavations went deeper and the technical difficulties of raising the diamond-bearing gravel increased. The early 1880s saw the formation of prospecting companies on a large scale until by 1888 there were three mining companies left, the French Company of Jules Porges, Barney Barnato's Kimberley Central Mining Company, and De Beers Consolidated, owned by Cecil Rhodes, who bought out the other two in 1888 and 1889 respectively [see p. 95].

At the time of Union, this very important industry accounted for over 98 per cent of the world's total diamond production, and still accounted for more than half at the time of the Great Depression in 1929. The subsequent history of the enterprise is largely covered by the history of De Beers (Gregory), with its movement into the production of both gem and industrial diamonds, its expansion through the Anglo-American Corporation into other parts of Africa (notably the recovery of marine diamonds off South West Africa), its development in the 1960s of artificial diamonds, and its linkage in the early 1980s with a major consortium in Australia, and in the mid-eighties with the very important new diamond discoveries at Arapa and Jwaneng in Botswana, as a result of which the Botswana Government and De Beers entered into a close business association.

The Diamond Fields contributed in a variety of ways to the shaping of South African society. Quite apart from the capital which they unlocked, which would prove beneficially available for the opening of the gold mines twenty years later, they provided a significant bonus for the Cape's export trade after the incorporation of Griqualand West, and also had a decisive influence on the consolidation of labour patterns, promoting the immigration of artisans and helping to reinforce that socio-economic stratification between the races which had already begun to develop into a rigid pattern on the farms.

The politics of the Diamond Fields, both locally and internationally, were turbulent in the early years [see pp. 132, 174], not least on account of the unique system of labour relations which developed there. As the complexity of mining operations grew, it became necessary to attract skilled miners from Britain at rates of up to £8 per week; but the bulk of the labour force continued to consist of Africans hired in the tribal areas through their chiefs on short-term contracts of three to six months, commonly for wages of about 10s per week plus (until 1877) a gun. Arriving at first from nearly all parts of South Africa, the migrant labourers on the diamond fields came increasingly from northern regions chosen by white agents who operated in the tribal areas under the authority of the Griqualand West Government, in succession to the less responsible touts who in the early years had lain in wait for migrants and 'sold' them to individual diggers (Siebörger). The Southey Government did what it could to facilitate the transit of migrant Africans, some of whom had walked 600 miles from their homes; but it proved difficult to arrange satisfactory staging posts in Republican territory, though the Boer Republics insisted on the purchase of transit passes. The confiscation of firearms on the return journey through the Republics, and the theft of wages and clothing, were further hazards. After 1880, when the ownership of the claims had begun to be concentrated in fewer hands, the role of the Government in labour recruitment diminished, and that of the companies increased. But the main areas of recruitment remained unaltered. The Sekhukhune Pedi ('Mahawas'), whom John Edwards had first approached in 1873, provided most of the labourers; Shona workers were first induced to go to Kimberley in 1874; and the recruitment of Ndebele and Tswana labourers followed as a result of A. C. Bailie's expedition of 1876 to Mankurwane, Gaseitswe, Setshele, Kgama, and Lobengula. But wherever they came from, as short-term migrants they were not well placed to acquire the skills or achieve the kind of break with their own traditions which could turn them into the white man's competitors in a strange society which the white men controlled.

The other differential factor which came to matter was the success of the white workers in protecting their privileged position above that of the black labourers. Until the centralisation of control under the large companies, they successfully resisted the indignities of a body-search, whereas the blacks could not. Unlike the blacks, they were able to protect their rights by effective strike action. Unlike the blacks, too, they never had to live in isolated compounds, which became the norm from 1885 onwards, as devices to ensure continuous labour service. These were not the showpieces which Gardner Williams claimed, but, on Turrell's evidence, control centres where dietary, medical and other amenities left much to be desired. Not only did black miners resent the loss of liberty, but Kimberley shopkeepers objected to the loss of business resulting from the trading monopolies held by compound canteens. A movement by De Beers

away from labour migrancy, and from compound to village living conditions for black diamond-miners, started between 1972 and 1977 (Lipton).

As a control device, the lesson of the Kimberley compounds was not
lost. The Durban municipality discovered at the beginning of the twentieth
century that an open compound system could be used for the control of
casual ('togt') labourers. It was a short step from the municipal compound
to the 'native hostel', which became a common feature of municipal
locations in the larger centres under the stimulus of the Urban Areas Act
of 1923. The compound system was also adopted on the gold mines, not to
prevent the theft of gold but to provide a method for maintaining police
control over the much larger number of Africans (and for a short time the
Chinese) who went to the Rand mines on contract. When Commissioner
Buckle conducted an inquiry into the grievances underlying the African
strike at Kleinfontein Mine in 1913, he stressed this feature of the compound system, and with good reason, for the isolation of African strikers in
their compounds later broke the serious African miners' strikes of 1920
and 1946.

Gold-mining, unlike diamond-mining, never became a tight monopoly.
Kubicek helpfully divides the mining houses into four main groups. First,
there was the Corner House Group consisting of Central Mining and Rand
Mines, the latter linked with the London financial firm of Wernher, Beit
and Co., and with Hermann Eckstein's of Johannesburg. Heirs of Porges's
French company, Wernher–Beit had a strong Kimberley connection. They
pioneered deep-level mining, and were able to do so because their enormous investments were well spread across the London and Paris stock
markets. Secondly, there was Consolidated Gold Fields of South Africa, in
which C. D. Rudd rather than C. J. Rhodes played the leading role, with
most of its financial support coming from the London money market. In
the third place, Kubicek lists various 'houses of ill repute' on account of
their reckless stockjobbing and relatively low concern to develop the Rand
– Barnato's company, J. B. Robinson's Randfontein Estates Company and
linked assets, and Sir George Farrar's East Rand Provident Mining.
Finally, he notes the enormous importance of Continental banking houses,
of which the German firm Goerz and Co., and the French Crédit Lyonnais,
were leading examples. In any one year the total of French and German
investments on the Rand roughly equalled that of British.

The setting up of the Chamber of Mines in 1887, the year after the
discovery of the Main Reef outcrop, was an important event for it enabled
the mining houses to work towards and eventually achieve a uniform policy
in the matter of labour recruitment and wages. This was crucial because the
extracting of gold from the reef was a costly business even after the
discovery of the Macarthur–Forrest cyanide process in 1891. This process
was 95 per cent efficient, and transformed investment patterns because it
made deep-level mining possible.

The cost structure of the industry was critical, for the lower the over-
heads, the greater the possibility of mining the less lucrative seams. During
the 1890s, therefore, the Chamber repeatedly attempted to control costs by

stabilising the wages of its African workers. Through a 'group system' under which the mining houses were brought together into nine separate units, the Chamber put pressure on its member companies to keep their wage policies in line; but competition for labour was so keen that a maximum wage agreement of 1890 was soon breached. The war against Mmalaboho (Malaboch) in 1894, however, so seriously interrupted the flow of labour from the northern Transvaal that the Republican Government was itself drawn in to help regulate service contracts. The Chamber had approached the Portuguese, and in response to their requirement that all recruiting in their territory should be conducted by one agency, it had set up a Native Labour Supply Association with monopoly rights, the individual mining companies themselves being the shareholders. A new government pass law now made it possible to apprehend indentured workers who broke their contracts.

The imposition of tighter controls over recruiting made wage reductions – of 20 per cent in 1896 and of a further 30 per cent in 1897 – easier to enforce. Owing to these controls and the deterrent effects of rinderpest in the rural areas, there was no mass exodus from the mines. But if the average monthly unskilled wage rate on the mines had dropped of 48s 7d before the outbreak of the Anglo-Boer war, this hardly bore comparison with the wartime wage itself, which dropped to an average of below 30s in 1901–2, at a time when the Chamber lost something of the order of £24 million in unrealised profits (Levy).

Transfer of conrol from Kruger's Government to Milner's was of direct benefit to the mining houses, because the abandonment of the dynamite monopoly in 1902 substantially offset a simultaneous increase in the gold profits tax from 5 to 10 per cent. Furthermore, Chamberlain's requirement of a £30 million 'war tribute' from the mines for reconstruction purposes was dropped in 1906 (Denoon). Thus, although some political tension developed between the Randlords and Milner's Government, this was not the case on the economic front.

Tension between the capitalists and the white workers, however, increased, as the former came under pressure from Milner to provide the profits out of which the policy of reconstruction was to grow, and the latter began to organise to resist what seemed to them a threat to their own job security. A strike on the Crown Reef Mine in April 1902 over piece-work rates introduced to cut costs led to the formation of the Transvaal Miners' Association, and this artisan body was hardly in existence before it brought out the skilled white workers of Village Main Reef in a protest against an attempt to reduce dependence on black labour through the employment of unskilled whites using rock drills (Katz).

A critical shortage of unskilled labour lay behind these developments. This seems to have been caused, not merely by the collapse of the pre-war recruiting organisation in the African territories, but by the Chamber's decision in 1902 to peg wages well below the pre-war maximum to meet the decline in production (Levy), and at the same time (as Kubicek and Richardson have emphasised) to start the development of lower grade ores from which anticipated profits would be less. The low-wage policy of the mining houses diminished the flow of recruits largely because better-paid work, under more congenial conditions, was available on the railways and in other employment associated with post-war reconstruction. With good insight, Denoon has attributed their stay-away from the mines to an act of protest.

To ensure a good labour supply, Milner had already approached the Portuguese in order to rebuild the arrangements of pre-war days. The latter imposed stiff conditions under a *modus vivendi* of December 1901 requiring – in return for recruiting rights – a royalty of 13s a head plus most-favoured-nation customs duties and competitive railway rates to the advantage of Lourenço Marques over south African ports. To meet their requirements the Chamber of Mines established the Witwatersrand Native Labour Association ('Wenela'), with the task of exercising uniform control over recruiting for both the Transvaal and Southern Rhodesia; but within a year 'Wenela' had discovered that it could not raise sufficient workers to be able to discharge its obligations north of the Limpopo (Levy).

Two rival lines of argument for solving the labour problem now arose. One, named the 'white labour policy', has been associated chiefly with Colonel F. H. P. Creswell, on whose mine (Village Main Reef) the strike of 1902 had occurred. He aimed to replace black by white unskilled labour, on the argument that even unskilled whites using mechanical drills could break more rock than a much larger number of blacks without them. Creswell persuaded his own Johannesburg board that he was right, but he failed to satisfy either his London board or the Chamber, or – as we have noted – his own skilled white miners. Furthermore, as both Richardson and Levy have argued, Village Main Reef was much better suited to the white labour experiment than other mines, for similar experiments conducted on Crown Reef, E.R.P.M., George Goch Mine, and elsewhere had proved much less successful. The white labour policy therefore stood no chance of becoming generally accepted. As Levy has stressed, Creswell ignored such cost factors as rent, housing and welfare, which were bound to tip the scales against white workers with their higher standards of comfort, questions of efficiency quite apart.

The first move in the campaign for Chinese labour, which was the other strategy proposed, came from Sir George Farrar of E.R.P.M. in 1902. Though the Chamber at first needed convincing, the failure of 'Wenela' to raise sufficient recruits in its first year of operation brought it round to Farrar's views. When Milner appointed a Transvaal Labour Commission in 1903, he filled it with men, most of whom already favoured the importation of Asian workers. The Government of India, recalling its unsatisfactory Natal experience, was not prepared to allow recruitment to the mines. But Imperial China agreed to release contract labourers on terms favourable to the Chamber, in the teeth of opposition from Liberals in Britain who denounced it as 'Chinese slavery', from English-speaking miners on the Rand who suspected a plot to make their own labour redundant, from Transvaal Afrikaners who deplored the infusion of yet another racial strain into an already unpalatable Uitlander brew, and from the owners of small businesses who were afraid that the Chinese might find a way of moving out of their indentures to compete with them in the market place.

Richardson has shown that the task of the Chamber's Labour Importation Agency, aided by the British authorities and by British firms based on Hong Kong, Tientsin and elsewhere, was a 'high cost, high risk operation' carried out with considerable skill, and with some ruthlessness in the selection of labourers, but under conditions which laid down rigid standards in relation to health and diet. Profiting from the dislocation of the flow of labour to Manchuria during the Russo-Japanese war of 1904–5, the C.M.L.I.A. brought 63,938 Chinese to South Africa on three-year contracts between 1904 and 1907, though wastage through repatriation, ill health or accidents meant that the maximum number employed at any one time were a thousand fewer. The Chinese were employed increasingly as hand drill operators on the underground stopes, where they recouped the cost of their recruitment (which was necessarily higher than that of African labour) by performing piece-work which was dangerous, skilfully done, and often underpaid. Their efficiency delayed the need for rapid mechanisation. Their presence lowered the turn-over rate among unskilled mineworkers, and brought about a temporary decline in the recruitment of black labour from all parts of southern Africa except Mozambique, though this picked up markedly from 1907. Their availability in sufficient numbers at a crucial time made it possible for the Chamber to maintain its low wage rates for African as well as Chinese workers, and incorporate these rates in the long-term wage structure of the industry. They also helped to save the colour bar on the gold mines, for restrictions imposed on the range of work which the Chinese might do – the first legalised system of job reservation – were subsequently applied to Africans.

The Chinese labourers were systematically returned to China on completion of their contracts, after the accession of Botha's Government to power in the Transvaal in 1907. But, as Levy had demostrated, this was done without a major confrontation between the Republican Government and the Chamber, for the Government also discovered merit in not dislocating the productivity of its major export industry, and took special steps to ensure the continuing efficiency of 'Wenela's' operation in Mozambique (Jeeves). The Chinese were expendable once the machinery for the recruitment of Africans was in working order again. By 1910 there were 183,793 Africans at work on the gold mines, which was double the number employed in 1899, and half the number employed in 1972. Health hazards, notably the vulnerability of African miners to pneumonia, at first discouraged the Governments of Northern Rhodesia and Nyasaland from allowing the Union to recruit mine-workers north of the twenty-second parallel, whereas Southern Rhodesia opposed the migration of its own blacks south of the Limpopo. Between 1912 and 1933 the Union Government barred recruitment beyond its northern borders, but relaxed the embargo for the gold mines when new vaccines had brought the health dangers under control, and when competition from the farms for black labour within South Africa seemed to make the extension of the recruiting area desirable. From 1937 'Wenela' extended its stations beyond the Transvaal and Mozambique to take in Nyasaland, Northern Rhodesia, Bechuanaland and South West Africa (where stations were set up in the Caprivi strip to draw in workers from Angola). A parallel Native Recruiting Corporation concentrated on Basutoland, Swaziland and the African areas of Natal and the eastern Cape. As had been the case with the diamond mines, the main areas of recruitment had moved north. By 1972, nearly four-fifths of the African labour employed by the Chamber of Mines was recruited outside the Republic of South Africa – 25 per cent from Lesotho, Botswana and Swaziland, 21 per cent from Mozambique, and 32 per cent from beyond the northern borders, of whom most came from Malawi (Nyasaland). But disputes between the mining houses and miners from Malawi and Lesotho in 1974, together with growing uncertainty over the long-term prospects of continued recruitment from an independent Mozambique, led the mining houses in 1975 to look for ways of increasing recruitment from the Republic itself. This worked, as can be seen from the Chamber's figures for 1979, when out of 399,123 migrant Africans employed by member companies, 215,577 had been recruited in the Republic and the independent Homelands, excluding the High Commission Territories (Lipton).

Of even greater significance, though, was the changing mood of the Chamber's leadership over the handling of black mine labour, especially in the light of the earlier suppression of strikes in 1920 and 1946. There was unrest in the compounds in 1972–5 arising out of complaints about low wages and bad living conditions at a time of steeply-rising prices. The Chamber was also aware, at a time when mining skills were in very short supply on account of the job colour bar, that the white Mineworkers' union was no longer the force it had been. Sensing that it was time to act in order to forestall a confrontation with black mineworkers which might otherwise have got out of control, the mining directorates, acting in accordance with the Wiehahn Commission's recommendations [see pp. 401–2], now did away with job reservation in principle, removed criminal sanctions from mining contracts, and invested large sums of money in housing senior black staff and even larger on the improvement of compound amenities. They stepped up the wage rates of black mineworkers so that, on average, they rose from one-twentieth of the white man's pay-packet to one-seventh, between 1971 and 1980 (Lipton). They went on, for the first time in history, to recognise an African Mine Workers' Union and this body was able to make some progress in its early attempts at collective bargaining despite the collapse of the gold price in 1983–4.

At least until the Second World War, the gold-mining industry was the strongest pressure group in the South African state, stronger than either the white labour or the Afrikaner nationalist lobbies. Yudelman has presented the era 1902–39 as one in which the Chamber of Mines (in search of profits) and the South African state (in defence of its own legitimacy) made common cause. Things had not always seemed like that. Kubicek's study of the financial operations of the major groups and their respective 'stables' suggested a growing nervousness among directorates after the collapse of the 1903 share boom, and a desire to reduce local commitments in the period down to 1914. Reasons for the industry's moral recovery are helpfully delineated in the recent studies by Richardson and Van Helten. In their investigation of the long-range planning of some of the mining houses, these writers produced evidence of a subtle shift of policy, mainly among groups which had not made significant investments in the first deep-level boom. They included companies like General Mining, and above all the Consolidated Mines Selection Company, which made a successful move into the Far East Rand from 1912 onwards, where the latter's associate, Anglo-American, was soon to become the dominant mining group (Gregory). Speculative investment in mining ventures diminished, as Kubicek had shown; but by dint of increasingly efficient production methods, the ruthless cutting of costs, and successful efforts to generate funds internally which became a continuing strategy, the mining industry built up that position of strength which would enable it to retain its dominance over the economy, in partnership with the state, and at least to hold its own during the years of ascendant Afrikaner nationalism from 1948 onwards.

19.4   SECONDARY INDUSTRY – A LATE DEVELOPMENT

The South African manufacturing industry, which was restricted to small local industries and crafts, such as brick-making and wagon-building, in the years before the age of mechanical transport, enjoyed its first period of expansion during the First World War. Then the real annual value of goods produced increased by one-third on the pre-war figures. These were mainly consumer goods which had become difficult to import. Manufacturing expanded again after the Depression of 1929–32, under the continuing encouragement of a protective tariff policy which had been introduced, first in 1914 on a small scale and mainly for revenue purposes, and much more markedly after 1925, the year in which Hertzog's new tariff policy was designed to fend off outside competition [see above]. Further growth surges took place during the Second World War, and during the 1960s in the aftermath of the Sharpeville crisis, when a fall in share values linked with the imposition of tight controls on the export of currency created bull conditions for bold investors. By 1965, as a result of a 5.6 per cent industrial growth rate over five years, the contribution of manufacturing to the gross domestic product exceeded those of mining and farming together.

Industrial policies of South African governments have been dominated by the consideration that gold, which provided far and away the strongest guarantee against a balance-of-payments problem, is known to be a wasting asset. The discovery of the O.F.S. goldfields at the end of the Second World War gave an unexpected reprieve to the economic planners. But the need remained to work out a policy for the substitution of manufacturing as an alternative. This meant, first, a policy for the substitution of locally made goods and raw materials for imported, and second, the promotion of an export trade in manufactured and other processed goods. The mineral richness of the country ensured that substitution would present few problems other than those arising from the smallness of the local market, and from the shortage of mineral fuels even after the local development of pioneering techniques for extracting oil from coal. But the promotion of the export trade proved far harder to accomplish. In 1975 the manufacturing industry was exporting goods worth R1,771 million whereas imports were worth R5,685 million. What would otherwise have been a deficit in the balance of payments was covered by the export of mining and farm products. But this also meant that the wall of protective tariffs behind which industry had grown up was itself a barrier against mining and agricultural profits on account of the higher price structure which protection promoted.

Industrial development carried important implications for labour policy, but here the emphasis changed noticeably over the years. Manufacturing reached its take-off point in the early twentieth century, at a time when the rapid urbanisation of blacks and rural Afrikaners began, and to some extent because of it. Industrial development, in fact, was one of the strategies promoted by successive governments to counter the unemployment of poor whites who would otherwise have had to compete with blacks for jobs on the farms and mines. The 'civilised labour policy' of the Hertzog era was a product of this conceived need. It involved special provisions under the Customs Tariff Act of 1925 for the withholding of importation rebates from manufacturing firms which could not show the Board of Trade and Industries that they employed a sufficient number of white workers. Its effect on the employment of Africans was damaging, and by the early 1930s Coloured workseekers were feeling the pinch as well.

Relatively little importance was attached by the Native Economic Commission of 1932 to the employment of blacks in industry. Their movement into the industrial economy took place dramatically during the Second World War, when the Board of Trade and Industries noted, in its well-known Report 282 of 1945, that Africans could hold down skilled and semi-skilled jobs with much greater efficiency than they had previously been credited with. This arose from the 'dilution' policy under which unqualified blacks were allowed, under skilled supervision, to do skilled work in a number of trades to help relieve the labour shortage [see pp. 306–7]. It also led to the white political reaction of the post-war years, as fears of job competition came to be reflected in the extension of job reservation in a number of fields of employment, both in manufacturing and the service industries, under the Industrial Conciliation Acts of 1956 and 1959 [see p. 512]. Gradually, however, the emphasis shifted from the protection of whites, as such, to the introduction of blacks into skilled trades when whites proved too few to fill them. This was a product of the manpower shortage caused by the high industrial growth rate during the 1960s.

Considerations of political geography also played their part: on the one hand, the need to decentralise industry in order to conserve water resources, especially in the Vaal Triangle (Pretoria–Witwatersrand–Vereeniging); and on the other, the desire to ensure that the independent Homelands should be provided with an industrial infrastructure to supplement the inadequate agricultural base on which their domestic economies all rested. The Government's establishment of a Permanent Committee for the Location of Industries in 1960 was the first major step towards planned decentralisation. On lines laid down in the Tomlinson Report, it recommended the siting of industries on the white side of the frontier in 'border areas', so that black commuters could work as migrants while living near enough to home to return frequently, and so that the Homelands should not undercut industries in the white heartlands by developing their own 'Hong Kongs'. The Physical Planning Act of 1967 (later renamed the Environmental Planning Act) provided positive incentives in the form of tax holidays, tariff rebates and the prospect of cheaper labour to induce industrialists to move, together with negative constraints such as a ban on the enlargement of black labour forces if they elected to remain in the existing areas of industrial concentration. The policy did not have the success anticipated, partly because the boom of the 1960s gave place to the recession of the 1970s. When, after 1971, white agency capital was allowed into the Homelands (a recommendation of the Tomlinson Commission to this effect having been initially turned down), industrial development did occur in places such as Butterworth in the Transkei; but not even this carrot was sufficient to influence the distribution of industry in a statistically significant way. For both demographic and economic reasons the Government came to realise, on the strength of the Riekert and Wiehahn Reports of 1979, that it could not resolve either the industrial skilled manpower shortage, or the problem of the population explosion, unless it allowed blacks to climb the ladder of industrial employment by entering skilled trades, and unless it gave them much greater freedom not only to seek work in the white industrial areas, but also to bargain more freely over pay and conditions of work [see also pp. 400–3]. Its promotion of small business enterprises [see p. 494] was similarly inspired.

19.5 THE EVOLUTION OF LABOUR MIGRANCY AND THE COLOUR BAR IN A STATE-REGULATED ECONOMIC SYSTEM

We have now noticed the growing importance attached by white farmers, mining magnates and businessmen to bringing the black man into the economic system. They tended to see him as a labour tenant, then as a wage labourer, rather than as a self-sufficient farmer; as a migrant contract worker, living in a compound on the mines and in an industrial world, where the possibility of ownership did no arise; and only very recently, here and there, as a settled villager living with his family. In the world of commerce they saw him as an employee, hedged in by restrictions on property ownership and investment, yet they were encouraging new opportunities for independent initiative by blacks towards the end of the period for which there were relatively few parallels in other walks of life.

The peculiar institutions which determined the position of the black in society, and kept him in it, were the system of migrant labour and the colour bar. But these were not controls which suited all categories of employer. They were devices which reflected the different interests of agriculture, mining, commerce and industry, mediated to some extent by pressure from the white working class, some of whom were unionised skilled or semi-skilled factory workers, some of them displaced casualties of the system who received the special protection of the State.

The growth of labour migrancy during the nineteenth century was gradual. There were some early instances of it. Delius has shown how some Pedi, for example, sought work in the eastern Cape before 1850. It was stimulated by the Xhosa Cattle-killing of 1857 and by the Glen Grey Act of 1894. But there was little systematic recruitment of farm labour until the mid-1960s, when labourers from the Transkei and Ciskei were taken to the sugar farms of Natal and the fruit farms of the western Cape by farmers' cooperative societies on short-term labour contracts (Wilson). The recruitment of migrants received its first big boost from the railway construction programmes of the 1880s onwards; but it was the diamond, and above all the gold mines which placed migrant labour on an organised basis and turned it into a characteristic South African mode of employment. There was a chance during the late 1940s that the Government might have modified the migrant labour policy, on the recommendation of the Fagan Commission, which came out with cautious proposals for the encouragement of a settled mine labour force, the workers being allowed to bring their families to town. The opening of the Orange Free State goldfields also gave the mining houses a chance to reconsider their labour policies, especially as the stabilisation of mine labour had been carried out successfully in the Congo since 1927 and on the Northern Rhodesian copper belt since 1940. Sir Ernest Oppenheimer, opening a new shaft at the Welkom mine in 1952, stated that his company's ultimate aim should be 'to create, within a reasonable time, modern Native villages which will attract Natives from all over the Union, and from which the mines will ultimately draw a large proportion of their Native labour requirements'. The National Party Government, however, opposed this suggestion, fearing the establishment of irremovable 'black spots' far away from the existing reserves if it were adopted, and insisting on the provision of as little married accommodation for African mine workers as possible. Outside the mining industry, a switch to hostel-building also took place in the urban townships, in lieu of earlier schemes developed during the 1950s for single-residential accommodation. Provision was made during the 1960s for the housing of approximately 60,000 migrant workers in 'bachelor' quarters on the Rand, and for the housing of the same number under similar conditions in Alexandra township, Johannesburg, an area previously occupied by Africans in family units.

Cultural and economic arguments have been advanced both for and against the migrant labour system. Support for it was general during the first twenty years of Union, among both white supremacists and liberals. The former feared black numbers, and wanted workers who had completed their stints under white employers to return to the reserves and leave the white areas to the white minority. This attitude was crystallised in what came to be known as the Stallard doctrine, named after the chairman of the 1922 Transvaal Local Government Commission. Liberals felt much as Smuts did when he argued, in the course of his Rhodes Memorial Lectures at Oxford in 1929, that if the black worker returned to his home and his native culture in the reserve, he would not be contaminated by alien ways, and thus remain true to himself. Meanwhile advocates of migrant labour from the economic angle preferred it on the ground that the contract labourer from the reserve was much cheaper to maintain because his family was cared for in the reserve economy, which made it possible to pay him a single man's wage and house him cheaply in a compound. This line of argument formed part of the Chamber of Mines's evidence to the Lansdown Commission as late as 1944.

As black numbers in the urban areas expanded, there was a tendency for Stallardism to gain support among whites, until it grew into the apartheid doctrine of the Sauer Report, and was adopted by the National Party between 1948 and 1976. But the cultural justification of labour migrancy wore thin once it was realised that the impact of the city on traditional African attitudes was strong and irreversible, especially after black homes had begun to appear in the urban areas on a vast scale (Mayer). Similarly, the economic justification for a cheap labour policy began to appear questionable, not merely because the overcrowding of the reserves reduced their capacity to sustain life, but also because increased mechanisation in farming, on the mines, and above all in industry reduced the usefulness of unskilled workers, whose lack of skill at handling complex equipment often made 'cheap' labour expensive. With political arguments pulling in one direction, and cultural and economic in another, the advocates of migrancy were stretched in the 1970s to devise new formulae which could achieve the best of both worlds. Serious references to long-distance high-speed commuter trains between, say, the workplace in Johannesburg and the home base outside Ladysmith, were made at meetings of the Institute of Administrators of Non-European Affairs during the early seventies. Similarly, the 'border industry' policy of the Verwoerd and Vorster governments was in part a bid to gain political security for the white areas while reducing the social dislocation of working black households, by enabling them to live close to their work without being in the white area. The category of commuter thus created or imagined represented a diminution of outright migrancy, real or conceptual, and thus it could be argued a reduction in the social harmfulness of the system. 1,329,000 migrants and 745,500 commuters entered white South Africa from the ten self-governing Homelands in 1981, each figure representing an increase on the previous two years. But the 301,758 Africans entering from foreign countries in Southern Africa in the same year were less than half the number who entered in 1975.

The term 'colour bar' has commonly been taken to mean simply a policy of job reservation under which most lucrative forms of employment were reserved by law for whites, and most poorly-paid, unskilled jobs were left to blacks. White workers were extremely apprehensive at times over the threat of black competition, under what Edna Bonacich (cited by Fredrickson) has called 'split labour market' conditions – conditions, that is, involving 'a three-cornered struggle between capitalists desiring the cheapest possible labour, workers of the dominant ethnic group who resist being undercut or displaced by cheaper labour from a minority or subordinate group, and the alien newcomers who are struggling to find a niche in the economy'.

But instead of being seen as an 'aristocracy of labour', the privileged white workers have been presented by some recent analysts very much as vulnerable participants in a complex economic order – a 'bounded working class' in Greenberg's term, even less able to secure their dominant position in the productive system than skilled workers in countries like Britain. F. A. Johnstone has convincingly placed the 'job colour bar' described above in the context of a wider, more fundamental 'exploitation colour bar', a blanket term to describe all those laws which effectively destroyed the black person's power – that is, the constitutional arrangements which removed his political leverage, the industrial laws which paralysed his ability to bargain for better terms of employment, unequal educational opportunities, and the controls which restricted him as to residence, property rights and movement. These restrictions, Johnstone argues, collectively made it possible to keep his wages down and make him 'ultra-exploitable', and it was precisely because he was ultra-exploitable that he was a threat to the job security of the better-paid white man, who was therefore obliged in self-defence to protect himself in one of two ways: either by insisting on job reservation or, as Hutt has suggested, by operating the apparently equitable 'rate for the job' principle to his own advantage, in anything but an equitable manner. Johnstone's argument is a strong one, provided that allowance is made for the black person's unfamiliarity with the industrial world and the poverty of the reserves which kept his socio-economic status down and his perceived needs relatively low, and would therefore have put him in a good bargaining position even without a contrived exploitation colour bar.

If one attaches importance to the exploitation colour bar, it follows that a study of industrial relations must take into account the actions of the State as well as of capital and labour, for the framework within which the relationships of production develop in this wider sense is supplied by legislation. It therefore becomes necessary to investigate the relationship between the State and the major groups involved in production, if the dynamics of the social order are to be understood. That is why modern social historians have not confined their attention to divisions within the labour force, but also attempted to analyse the various capitalist 'fractions', with a view to seeing if possible how their particular interests were affected by decisions of the legislature.

One approach, adopted by Kaplan, Innes and others, has been to distinguish between different fractions of capital according to the main source of their funds, labelling agricultural and industrial capital as 'national' in the sense that most of their funding came from within South Africa, whereas the funding of mining and commercial interests came mainly from outside, and can therefore be referred to as 'international'. According to this classification, it became customary to regard the era of Botha and Smuts as one in which international capital dominated South African political decision-making, especially when the incorporation of the Unionists in the South African Party in 1920 brought the Government and the representatives of the mining houses under a single political banner. Similarly, Hertzog's period of rule between 1924 and 1933 has been presented as one in which national capital was in the saddle, when tariff policies were developed to protect local industry against overseas competition, and when farming interests were cared for by the grant of financial facilities and export bounties [see pp. 259–60]. This exploratory hypothesis, which has been questioned in detail by other historians within the neo-Marxist school, has also been heavily criticised by outsiders, notably by Yudelman, who doubts whether there was any meaningful combination of agricultural and manufacturing capital during the Pact period, and sees manufacturing capital less as a rival force to mining capital than as its creature. The political fusion of the Hertzog Nationalists and the S. A. Party from 1934 necessitated some kind of alliance of gold and maize from the perspective of the Kaplan school, with the further suggestion that hegemony remained marginally with the 'national' capitalist fraction. Lacey has argued forcefully, from the same premises, that the Fusion Government worked hard to look after the interests of both the farms and the mines. But Yudelman, who rejects the fractionalist argument *in toto*, bases his analysis on two crucial points: he warns against the assumption that greatly increased taxation of the gold mines after 1933 necessarily implied that they were being mulcted to a greater extent than before, in the light of 'profits beyond the dreams of avarice' which the mines had begun to recoup as a result of the doubling of the gold price; and he insists, with good supporting evidence, that the South African State should be viewed not simply as an instrument in the hands of class interests (as Marxist historiography generally implies) but as an independent actor in a triangular relationship involving itself, mining capital, and organised labour, successfully using the industrial conflicts of the period to increase its own legitimacy and its own control over public policy.

Much was done during the Botha–Smuts era, before and after Union, to lay down a legislative colour bar; but it became increasingly evident that the manner in which this was done was more to the advantage of white management than of white labour. The miners' strike of 1907, though it presented an opening for the engagement of jobless Afrikaners and was therefore congenial to Het Volk's leadership also gave Botha's Government reason to fear the power of white labour, and therefore an incentive for legislating in the interest of mining capital to prevent further unrest. Hence the Railway Regulation Act of 1908, which barred railway employees from striking, and the Industrial Disputes Prevention Act of 1909, which excluded blacks from bargaining rights and was attacked by white labour representatives in Parliament on the ground that to deprive the blacks of industrial power was to put them in a position – as the exploited recipients of much lower pay – to challenge white workers for their jobs.

Botha's first Union Government also pursued policies which derived largely from arrangements made with the Chamber of Mines prior to Union, with reference to the supply of mine labour and its control, long before it swallowed the Unionist Party, which had an even closer relationship with the Chamber, in 1920. Thus it placed on the statute book the Mines and Works Act of 1911. Regulations promulgated under this law preserved an existing Transvaal colour bar until they were thrown out by the Supreme Court in the case of *R.* v. *Hildick Smith* in 1923. The South African Party also carried a Native Labour Regulation Act in 1911, which reduced the industrial power of blacks by making strike action by them a criminal offence. The Natives Land Act of 1913 not only helped white landlords to remove black sharecroppers, but held out prospects for the easier recruitment of labour for the mines by proposing to enlarge the recruiting areas, the reserves (Lacey). The Apprenticeship Act of 1922 so adjusted the educational provisions for admission to trades that it gave white trainees real advantages over their coloured rivals (Van der Horst). The Industrial Conciliation Act of 1924, the last major piece of legislation before the Government fell from power, gave the unionised white workers a secure position against undercutting from any quarter, but also helped management by the obstacles it placed in the way of precipitate strike action.

Hertzog's electoral pact with the Labour Party in 1923 has often been taken as *prima facie* evidence that his electoral victory in 1924 brought about a reversal of the industrial power balance to the advantage of organised labour and the disadvantage of mining capital. But Davies, and more recently Yudelman, have convincingly rejected this assumption. White mineworkers may have been on the rampage after their defeat in 1922; but their power had been so broken by their defeat that it never effectively recovered. Furthermore, the interests of skilled white artisans ran counter to those of poor white townsmen who not only faced stiff competition from blacks in the job market, but were also voters whom the prime minister could hardly ignore. The government therefore had three very different interests to satisfy, and its attempts to accommodate all of them, and to soften the impact where their interests clashed, first under economic boom conditions, then in a time of extreme depression, and then once again in an era of industrial expansion provided most of the political drama of the years 1924 to 1939.

The Government's attempt to nurse the industrial sector took the form of high tariffs against imported goods which threatened to compete with local manufactures, together with export bounties for farmers. The Government actually went much further than has commonly been supposed in its support, not only for industrial capital, but of the mining industry, whose needs it simply could not afford to ignore. This was apparent when it declined in 1925 to insist on the fulfilment of a recommendation by Judge Jopie de Villiers, operating under the Industrial Conciliation Act, that wage demands by the white mineworkers should be accepted, and in the same year refrained for technical reasons from taking through Parliament a minimum wage bill for the mines introduced with some gusto by Creswell (Phillips). When, in 1927, F. A. W. Lucas, a member of the newly created Wage Board, made an award which explicitly turned down the mineworkers' claims, the indignation of the Mineworkers' Union was extreme, and Thomas Boydell, who had succeeded Creswell in the Labour Department, had his time cut out to talk the unions out of major strike action.

Yet the Pact Government did back white workers in a number of ways. So far from doing this at the expense of industrial interests, Davies argues, the Government actually helped industry by bringing large numbers of poor whites on to the factory floor at a time when large-scale factory production was just beginning and there was a need for a docile labour force able and willing to perform repetitive work without complaint. It was argued that poor whites would perform as well as black migrants for whom the factory environment was utterly strange. The Labour Party took the point, and decided to press, not for a 'white labour policy' pure and simple, but for the establishment of a free labour market at artificially inflated – or, as governmental jargon put it, 'civilised' – rates of pay.

The outcome was the Wage Act of 1925, a measure complementary to the Industrial Conciliation Act of the previous year. It provided for a Wage Board with authority to make determinations, without any reference to the race of the workers concerned, in those industries where labour was not unionised and technically less well qualified. The 'rate for the job' was the principle on which it operated, a principle which gave the appearance of complete fairness, but which has been described by W. H. Hutt as giving scope for 'the most powerful yet most subtle colour bar that has ever operated'. The body of officials was required, after investigation, to report to the Minister of Labour, either recommending a 'civilised' wage or indicating its inability to do so. In the latter case, the Minister could authorise it to make any award which it thought suitable. The appointment of the Board aroused extreme anxiety in the Chamber of Mines and among industrialists, from a fear that the Government might support the Labour Party's strategy and raise mine wages widely and indiscriminately. But the Wage Board never made a determination for the mining industry; it concentrated mainly on industries which had already developed some degree of mechanisation, significantly promoting not only wages but also profit margins in such firms (Davies), and although it set a precedent for increasing the wages of black unskilled workers when it made a determination for Bloemfontein in 1925, this precedent was not only not followed, but explicitly repudiated after investigations of black wages in Kroonstad in 1932 (Phillips). In due course the Chambers of Mines and Industries came to appreciate what it was doing, above all by the promotion of modern production methods, to stimulate growth in the industrial sector. But as Yudelman has noted, the Pact Government's promotion of the civilised labour policy was financed rather by the public sector and by those industries which were persuaded to absorb poor white labour, than by the mining houses themselves, which were never driven back to the abandoned Status Quo Agreement of 1918 [see p. 254].

While promoting industrial growth, the Government was also able to wean white labour away from industrial action by simultaneously promoting a policy of job reservation in skilled trades. The Mines and Works Amendment (or 'Colour Bar') Act of 1926 was Hertzog's way of disarming the opposition of the skilled white worker. This law simply reserved the grant of certificates of competency in skilled trades to white people and Coloured people, placing Africans and Indians on the wrong side of the fence and giving the force of law to a principle which the Supreme Court had declared invalid. Davies estimates that between 1924 and 1932 Hertzog's Government transferred about 8,000 jobs from black to white hands. Job reservation appeared to favour the Coloured man, as distinct from the African and Indian, but in practice did not do so. The combined pressures of the Cape School Board Act of 1905, which made primary education compulsory for white children but not for others, and of the Apprenticeship Act of 1922, which had for the first time laid down minimal educational and maximum age qualifications for entry into specific trades, had reduced the relative opportunities for Coloured people to qualify as artisans, and their hold over the skilled trades in the Cape actually fell from about half the total in the late nineteenth century to about one-thirteenth of the total by 1961 (Hutt, Lewis). Statistics reveal that between 1924 and 1933 the number of Africans employed by the South African Railways and Harbours as labourers fell from 37,564 to 22,008, and the number of Coloured people (whose jobs were not initially affected under the 1926 Act) from 5,628 to 4,663, while the number of Europeans rose from 4,760 to 17,683. The policy was expensive. It was exceedingly harmful to the economic interests of African workers, for whom the rural betterment proposals of the Holloway Commission of 1932 were relatively cold comfort. It was carried out against the advice of the Economic and Wage Commission of 1925, and it might well have held back industrial growth but for the enormous stimulus created by the freeing of the South African pound at the end of 1932, which released the country from the effects of the Great Depression in a few years, as Smuts and others had argued that it would.

It was as important politically for the Fusion Government as it had been for the Pact to look after the interests of the unskilled, urbanised white man. Openings for his labour needed to be created in the boom years after 1933, because the economy was not expanding fast enough to absorb all the black and white urban immigrants, and because, unlike their black counterparts, who had no political voice, Afrikaner postulants in search of work had the backing of a strident opposition party, the Purified Nationalists of Dr Malan. Government therefore maintained its commitment to the 'civilised' labour policy, enforcing it now through the industrial councils of the 1924 Act, whose powers were redefined in 1937, rather than through the Wage Board machinery, because the mines, and industry, and the unions, all preferred this way of doing things. They did it with such success that the numbers of whites employed on relief works began to drop, and those drafted into permanent employment in the public service rose dramatically, often via a training period in the newly created Special Service Battalion, which was run on military lines and provided openings for careers in such organisations as the police, the prison service and the railways. By these means and with the help of the boom, the Government had as good as eliminated the poor white problem by 1939. It also succeeded in neutralising, or 'bureaucratizing' (Davies) the white trade union movement.

The Fusion Government tried to prevail on private business interests to support the 'civilised labour' policy by promoting 'fair labour' practices, by which was meant accommodating more whites in jobs than was justified in terms of business efficiency. It hoped to induce compliance by threats to cut import quotas, and by other means. Industry did not readily comply; but there was no political break between any of the major branches of industry and the Government because the Fusion Government, like the Pact before it, was careful to promote the labour requirements of both mines and farms. The Native Service Contract Act of 1932, by placing squatters and their families firmly under the farmers' control, looked after one set of needs. The mines, for their part, encountered special labour difficulties after 1928, when the Mozambique Convention made provision for a steady reduction in the recruitment of black mineworkers from that territory; but the Government rectified the position by amending the Native Administration Act of the previous year in 1929, so that all Africans outside the urban areas, whether or not they lived in scheduled native areas as defined under the Land Act, were brought within pass districts for purposes of labour control (Lacey). On top of this, the Native Trust and Land Bill hatched in the Joint Select Committee of 1930–5 reverted to a policy of large reserves (as originally adopted in 1913) which would assist the recruitment of mine labour, while the reopening of recruitment north of the Limpopo in 1933 (effectively from 1937 – Wilson) was a good way of catering for mine labour needs without interfering with the recruiting grounds of the farmers nearer home. It was the urban industrial employers who were most exposed to the labour policies of the Fusion Government. But as owners of businesses which paid relatively high wages, they attracted black workers from the white-owned farms, and were immune even to the effects of influx control, which the Government attempted to enforce under an amendment to the Natives (Urban Areas) Act for the first time in 1937 (Davenport). Indeed, experience was to show that, in face of the greater attractiveness of town work and town wages, and with the ample job opportunities in town during the Second World War, the policy of influx control was largely ineffective.

The war made the job colour bar largely redundant. A Native Farm Labour Committee appointed in 1939 to investigate the number of able-bodied black workers who could be sent back from the towns to the farms reported that there were almost none to find. Expansion of the war industries created such a shortage of skilled labour that the Government was reduced to authorising 'dilution', or in other words allowing unqualified workers to do skilled work under supervision, above all in the engineering industry, but also in textiles, furniture, leatherwork and other fields, in all of which the employment of Coloured and black workers greatly increased. A major concession was made at the end of the war when the Government agreed to the training of African builders to construct houses for Africans in urban locations – a policy which was later endorsed by the Malan Government in its Native Building Workers' Act of 1951.

What needs to be explained, however, is why the job colour bar, which had been effectively breached during the war years, should have been reimposed with such deliberation during the period after 1948. It is helpful, here, to note that the Malanite Nationalists won a critical number of predominantly white working-class seats on the Rand in the 1948 general election, and were thus beholden to an electorate which looked on black competition with extreme fear. Demobilisation of the armed forces had created a fear of redundancy, especially over the presence in the industrial field of a skilled black work force whose competence had drawn the praise of the Board of Trade and Industries, and who could be engaged, it seemed, at cheaper rates than whites.

This fear found expression in the tough action of the Malan Government against black trade unions, and against trade unions in general unless they had grown up under the wing of the National Party [see p. 334], and especially if they manifested left-wing tendencies. It was also reflected in the amendment to the Urban Areas Act of 1952, which reimposed the influx control provisions of the 1937 amendment, but now allowed black workseekers only three days to find employment in town, as against the fortnight of the 1937 law. Strijdom's Government went even further by extending the job reservation provisions of the Colour Bar Act of 1926, through amendments to the Industrial Conciliation Act of 1956 and 1959. Under the former law the Minister of Labour was granted blanket powers to safeguard the economic welfare of employees of any race in any industry or trade by requiring an industrial tribunal to reserve particular kinds of work for particular race groups in particular areas. At first the powers were used for the protection of white people. Skilled work in the clothing industry was reserved for whites in 1957, but the determination was withdrawn when it was declared invalid by the courts, and replaced in 1960 by a new determination designed to stabilise racial percentages as they stood in August 1959. In 1958, the positions of ambulance driver and fireman and most ranks in the traffic police in Cape Town were reserved for whites. In 1959, the operation of lifts in Bloemfontein, Johannesburg and Pretoria, and all kinds of lifts everywhere (unless they were for the conveyance of non-Europeans only, or for goods only) was reserved for whites. A range of other determinations followed.

19.6 THE COLLAPSE OF THE INDUSTRIAL COLOUR BAR AND THE LEGITIMATION OF BLACK COLLECTIVE BARGAINING

It is now known that the high water mark of the industrial colour bar had been reached with the legislation of the 1950s. The policy proved increasingly difficult to implement because of the unexpectedly rapid growth rate of the economy in the years following the Sharpeville shootings, when the value of industrial share prices rose from a mean figure of 65 in March 1960 to about 290 in 1968 on the *Rand Daily Mail* index (see Table 3 p. 514). The ability of the white community to supply the manpower required for the types of work normally reserved for whites steadily receded. This appeared, on the surface, to justify the argument that economic pressures were bound to destroy the apartheid ideology. But the move towards a free labour market in fact had little to do with industrial pressure from those excluded, for black trade unionism had made no inroads into the citadel of industrial power at that date [see pp. 238–9, 309–10, 335–6].

The manner in which the white community could adjust to this changing situation without having to abandon the advantages accruing from the retention of the colour bar can be illustrated from developments in the gold mining industry. In 1964 the owners of twelve gold mines, embarrassed by the white labour shortage, reached an agreement with the unions to allow small inroads by black workers into jobs legally reserved for whites. The experiment resulted in increased productivity and was profitable to all concerned; but when white miners on mines not involved in the experiment objected, the Government, after appointing a commission, decided to block the experiment. The Chamber of Mines subsequently changed its tactics and tried to bargain with the white miners by offering productivity bonuses in return for concessions to black workers; but the radical right-wing miners organised a series of strikes in 1966 in protest against the feared inroads into the colour bar. Eventually, in 1967, a compromise agreement was reached: the white miners agreed that blacks could do some 'white' jobs, such as handling explosives or driving engines slowly: but in return they obtained guarantees against retrenchment and the lion's share of the proceeds from the resultant increase in productivity (Wilson).

Thus blacks were enabled to move upwards in the employment scale, by conferring even greater benefits on whites, under very unequal arrangements which were mutually not disadvantageous. Understandably, the opposition of the white trade union movement to black inroads became less monolithic under arrangements of this kind, and a notable feature of the early 1970s was a tendency for the liberal wing of that movement, represented by the Trades Union Congress of South Africa, to encourage the unionisation of black labour on the supposition that the reason for antagonism between black and white unions was disappearing. The new polarisation of the P. W. Botha era had not yet emerged [see p. 424]. Meanwhile government policy paid increasing attention to methods for improving the efficiency of black labour, setting up labour bureaux in the new administrative 'prescribed areas' under the Bantu Labour Act of 1964, and establishing 'aid centres' to which Africans found guilty of contravening urban influx control regulations could be referred, so that they could be directed to employment in town or country where labour was needed, instead of being punished by short unproductive terms of imprisonment.

The skilled labour shortage which had become manifest during the great era of expansion in the 1960s led to the liberalisation of industrial policy during the 1970s, but not yet to the extent of allowing black collective

514

Table 3 South African industrial share prices, 1911–84

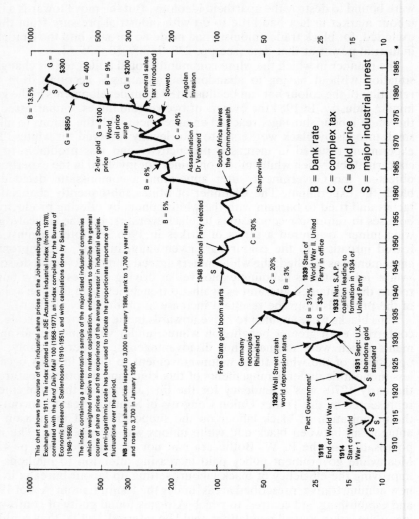

This chart shows the course of the industrial share prices on the Johannesburg Stock Exchange from 1911. The index plotted is the *JSE Actuaries Industrial Index* (from 1978), correlated with the *Rand Daily Mail* 100 (1958-1977), an index compiled by the Bureau of Economic Research, Stellenbosch (1910-1951), and with calculations done by Saniam (1949-1958).

The index, containing a representative sample of the major listed industrial companies which are weighted relative to market capitalisation, endeavours to describe the general course of share prices and the experience of the average investor in industrial equities. A semi-logarithmic scale has been used to indicate the proportionate importance of fluctuations over the period.

NB Industrial share prices leaped to 3,000 in January 1986, sank to 1,700 a year later, and rose to 3,700 in January 1990.

B = 13.5%

G = $300

G = $850

G = $400

B = 9%

2-tier gold   G = $100
price   G = $200

World
oil price
surge

General sales
tax introduced

Soweto

B = 6%

C = 40%

Angolan
invasion

Assassination of
Dr Verwoerd

South Africa leaves
the Commonwealth

B = 5%

1948 National Party elected

Sharpeville

C = 30%

Free State gold boom starts

Germany
reoccupies
Rhineland

1929 Wall Street crash
world depression starts

1931 Sept: U.K.
abandons gold
standard

'Pact Government'

1918
End of World War 1

1914
Start of World
War 1

B = 3½%   1939 Start of
G = $34   World War II. United
           Party in office

C = 20%

B = 3%

1933 Nat. S.A.P.
coalition leading to
formation in 1934 of
United Party

B = bank rate
C = complex tax
G = gold price
S = major industrial unrest

bargaining anything like a free rein. A widespread outbreak of unofficial black strike activity in Durban in 1973 was the signal for change. These strikes, which started in the brick and tile industry and quickly spread to the whole textile complex and to Durban municipal workers, seemed to be leaderless, and were marked by wage demands which went far beyond existing wage levels – for £30 a week, for example, against an existing wage of under £10 in one industry. The workers stood up to the threats of employers, though some dismissals took place. They generally refused to elect negotiating committees, and after resisting initial offers of increased pay they generally settled for an improved offer which fell far short of their initial demands. Although there was a good deal of tension, and some arrests were made, the action of the police was generally very restrained, and drew praise from unexpected quarters. The whole outbreak lasted rather less than two months, though strike activity throughout the country in 1973–4 was widespread. Despite official allegations that the movement had been master-minded by 'agitators', there was widespread sympathy in the press for the strikers' demands, which would soon be given additional force when the world price of oil began to soar and drove the cost of living to unprecedented heights.

The Government decided to set up works and liaison committees in industrial establishments in 1973, but stopped short of allowing blacks to negotiate directly through industrial councils or apply for Wage Board determinations. This concession did not stop the spread of the strike movement, which reached a climax with the massive Soweto stay-at-home in August 1976 [see p. 390]; but 1977 and 1978 were relatively strike-free years, in the course of which a number of large employer companies, notably some in the motor trade, declared their willingness to recognise black unions if they were genuinely representative. The Afrikaanse Handels-Instituut followed suit, and in 1979 the Wiehahn Commission's recommendation that the Industrial Conciliation Act should be amended accordingly was implemented by Parliament [see p. 402]. Black trade unions were recognised for the first time as negotiating bodies, provided they were not racially mixed, and that they excluded homeland citizens. Job reservation on racial lines was in principle abolished, but existing determinations had to be explicitly repealed before they went out of force.

The relaxation of the law facilitated another wave of industrial unrest [see pp. 461–2]. White mineworkers struck in 1979 against the repeal of job reservation but found their employers unyielding. Black workers in the western Cape, the Durban textile workers, and the municipal employees of Johannesburg, went on strike again. There were 342 stoppages in 1981, involving 84,706 black workers, a figure comparable only with 1973–4, but by now reflecting much greater turbulence on the industrial front, as Table on p. 516 shows.

Works and liaison committees, though these had increased respectively from 125 to 327 and from 1,482 to 2,754 between 1973 and 1981, were losing favour among blacks as bargaining instruments; and trade unions registered under the 1979 law were coming to be regarded as less desirable

Table 4   Strike statistics for South Africa 1970–88

Year	No of disputes	No of workers involved	No of working days lost
1970	76	4,168	4,528
1971	69	4,451	3,437
1972	71	9,224	14,167
1973	370	98,378	229,281
1974	384	59,244	98,583
1975	274	23,323	18,709
1976	245	28,013	59,861
1977	90	15,471	15,304
1978	106	14,160	10,558
1979	101	22,803	67,099
1980	207	61,785	174,614
1981	342	92,842	226,550
1982	394	141,571	365,337
1983	336	64,469	124,596
1984	469	181,942	379,712
1985	389	239,816	678,273
1986	793	424,340	1,308,958
1987	1,148	591,421	5,825,231
1988	1,025	161,679	914,388

Source   Department of Manpower and *Surveys of Race Relations*

than unregistered bodies which had begun to force their way into the negotiations. Police action against strikers and against the leaders of black unions was intensified. Many of the striking Johannesburg municipal workers, for example, were sent off to the Homelands, while thirty-two office-bearers of various unions were detained and the majority charged under the Terrorism, Internal Security or other laws during 1981–2. The only white leader to be thus detained, Dr Neil Aggett, met his death in detention under unexplained circumstances on 5 February 1982.

The unsettled mood of the country at the time of the 1983–4 constitutional crisis marked the turning-point at which the new trade union federations began to move strongly into the political arena, which the unions had not really done during the Soweto troubles or during the unrest of 1980. Political issues arising out of the Labour Relations Amendment Act of 1981, which set a premium on proper registration of trade unions and a ban on political affiliation provided a catalyst [see p. 402]. There were some unions which accepted registration, like T.U.C.S.A. (which was on the way down) and C.O.S.A.T.U. (which was very much on the way up), whereas others (like M.A.C.W.U.S.A., which championed the Port Elizabeth motor workers and the General Workers' Union, which had taken up the case of the dockers and railway workers against the State [see pp. 424–6]) preferred unofficial, confrontational action to achieve their ends. The latter, in particular, came in for a good deal of state harassment during 1985–7, when the number of working days lost through strike action easily broke all previous records (see Table 4).

At a time when the leading black political parties still had no right to practise politics, the radical unions needed no excuse for taking on that role, especially when it could be latched onto a strategy of destabilisation. Hence the close association of F.O.S.A.T.U. with the Vaal Triangle rent boycott of September 1984, and the involvement of C.O.S.A.T.U. in the Natal disturbances of 1986–90. Even the N.U.M., in its conflict with Anglo-American, came close to taking a political as distinct from a workerist stance. To counter such a tendency, and check the massive escalation in working days lost in 1985–7, the Government's amendment of the Labour Relations Act in 1987–8 was an over-reaction [see p. 402]. It made far better sense to legalise all political parties, including the A.N.C. and the Communists, in February 1990, for to encourage trade unionism while discouraging political action had been to put the parliamentary system itself at great risk.

20 The Cancer of Apartheid

20.1 SEGREGATION AND APARTHEID

The characteristic international image of the South African system is more commonly summed up by the word *apartheid* (separateness) than by any other single term. This chapter aims to demonstrate what is meant by the term as it has evolved historically, and to illustrate it with reference to some of the more important legislation which has been promulgated in its name, or in the name of 'segregation' (*segregasie*) or of 'separate development' (*aparte ontwikkeling*), with which it is commonly associated.

Unfortunately these terms have not been used consistently to stand for similar or even different concepts. Thus for the nationalist Afrikaner, 'separateness' in the early years of the present century found expression in the isolationist 'two-stream' ideology of General Hertzog, who nevertheless thought by about 1930 that the Afrikaner culture could now merge safely with the English in a common nationhood. Hexham has overstated an interesting case by suggesting that the roots of apartheid are to be seen in the Afrikaner's felt need for such isolation in the early days [see pp. 211–14].

The dominant republican Afrikaner attitude to race relations, built up in the context of frontier communities, held in tension the conflicting notions of territorial separation (as an insurance against numerical swamping) and domination (*baasskap*) to ensure control over labour. Its different emphasis from that more commonly ascribed to English-speaking administrators is particularly well reflected in the published dialogue between President F. W. Reitz and Sir Theophilus Shepstone in 1892 (Webb).

'Segregation' became a key word for early twentieth-century political visionaries who belonged to the liberal, predominantly English-speaking camp which took its inspiration from the Report of the Lagden Commission of 1905 [see p. 207]. This made proposals for the permanent separation of blacks and whites politically and territorially, and suggested the segregation of races in the towns. They wrote during a decade which also saw a hardening of the lines of segregation in the classroom and the job market. By that time, too, the 'Jim Crow' laws had already gathered momentum in the United States (Vann Woodward), and their impact on South African administrative thinking has been convincingly suggested (Cell, Evans).

It has been suggested in the above pages that the most intensive efforts to introduce segregation in South Africa occurred during the premierships of Louis Botha and Jan Smuts between 1910 and 1924 [see pp. 233–6]. The Hertzog era, commonly regarded as the most ideologically segregationist, as is argued by Dubow, may not in fact have deserved quite so much emphasis in this regard [see p. 293]. There was then a distinct movement away from segregationism during the 1940s [see pp. 306–7], but a sharp swing back after 1948 to the most ideological form of separation ever practised, perhaps, anywhere, under the new trade name of *apartheid*.

Early segregation policies came to acquire a theoretical base which commended itself both to humanitarian thinkers and to economic pragmatists, but for different reasons. Just as John Philip had seen the separation of races (but not of cultures, for he preached religious conversion) as a device for the protection of the weak, so early twentieth-century segregationists – often after some sort of flirtation with the then fashionable notion of eugenics (Dubow) – were attracted by the image of cultures as being necessarily separate and self-contained. This line of approach, which was popular among early social anthropologists, encouraged the thought that the diverse cultures of South Africa were different rather than hierarchical, and that intermingling was for cultural (and sometimes biological) reasons undesirable. Theologians might sometimes link this idea with the diversity of divine creation, which man had no business to disturb. Politicians like Smuts, who expounded the idea in his Rhodes Lectures (1929), saw segregation as a justification for labour migrancy, arguing that a temporary sojourn in a mine compound did not destroy a black man's cultural roots, whereas permanent urbanisation would. This came close to the selective cultural 'adaptationism' of G. P. Lestrade, under which blacks could be expected to retain certain of their traditional ways but also absorb certain features of the European culture so as to survive in the modern world. Others, like Alfred Hoernle, Professor of Philosophy at the University of the Witwatersrand between 1923 and 1943, attacked this line of approach. In his Phelps-Stokes Lectures in 1939, Hoernle set out three alternative routes to a just society, via 'total integration', 'parallelism' and 'total separation' respectively. He dismissed the first as unacceptable to whites in general, the second as a covert form of *baasskap*, and approved of the third as the only way to ensure justice for blacks, only to conclude that its achievement was a mere pipe-dream. A similar conclusion that segregation was unacceptable was reached by other liberals in different ways. The economic historian, W. M. Macmillan, never accepted the thesis of the cultural anthropologists because he saw black society as so inexorably interlocked with white on economic grounds that he could not conceive how segregation could be just (H. Macmillan). Edgar Brookes, who had been a devotee of Hertzogian segregation, was converted after listening to counter-arguments by blacks on a visit to Fort Hare. By the 1940s, liberals generally were abandoning segregation and beginning to pay serious attention to the possibility of actually promoting a single non-racial community, and they went a step further by launching the Liberal Party in 1953.

But the high priests of the new Afrikaner nationalism had by this time

latched on to the notion of total separation which Hoernlé was in the
course of discarding. The Broederbond was paying close attention to it by
1935 (Serfontein). The National Party was thinking along these lines in the
1940s (Rhoodie and Venter), and was clarifying its ideas through the
activities of S.A.B.R.A., whose theoretical approach provided a basis for
the Sauer Report [see p. 323] and for the utopian plans of Dr H. F.
Verwoerd during the 1950s [see pp. 336–41], by which time apartheid had
become hypostasised in a quite extraordinary way. In the hands of Verwoerd it became the key to the white man's future in South Africa, a
yardstick by which the validity and the utility of policies were measured
and their morality justified, a test of orthodoxy by which voters could be
asked to choose between candidates at elections.

Disillusionment set in during the closing years of Verwoerd's premiership despite the prosperity of those years, partly as a result of international
pressure, partly from a realisation that the demographic and industrial
calculations of the Tomlinson Report were wrong. A new morality was
sought along the lines of the 'independent Homeland' policy, and by means
of the distinction between 'petty apartheid' (the detailed rules for keeping
the races segregated from each other, and protecting white privilege in a
common area) and 'grand apartheid' (the broad geographical separation of
peoples as a basis for equal rights within their respective Homelands)
which was still prescribed as being fair.

The real crisis for the South African Government came in the 1970s and
1980s, when the morality of grand apartheid, the apartheid of the resettlement policy and the 1983 constitution, also came under strong attack.

20.2 THE TERRITORIAL DIMENSION

Territorially, the ends of segregation were initially served by barriers to the
ownership of property under individual title by blacks, principally in the
northern republics. No law prevented the acquisition of landed property by
blacks in the Cape Colony; but the barriers were all but complete in the
O. F. S., and would have been so in the Transvaal but for the judgement in
Tsewu's Case in 1905 [see p. 165]. But although the Tsewu judgement
legalised African syndicate purchases, white farmers became concerned
over the growth of this new practice, not merely because it seemed to them
to threaten white control over the land, to which they attached high
symbolic value, but also because of the expected chaos resulting from
subdivision of such farms on the deaths of their multiple owners.

The situation of blacks in the matter of property rights became more
restricted after Union than it had been before, despite the recommendations of both the Cape Native Laws Commission (1883) and the Lagden
Commission (1905) that individual tenure should be encouraged (Davenport and Hunt). The introduction of territorial separation with the passage
of the Natives' Land Act of 1913 [see p. 234] hit black land ownership
particularly hard by preventing further purchase in 'white' areas when
purchase was all but impossible in 'black' areas owing to the extent of

overcrowding and the strength of support for communal tenure in the traditional system. These influences together caused the abandonment of individual tenure, as the Government sought to retribalise African life in the rural area from the 1920s (Dubow). Black land ownership thereafter came to be limited to scattered holdings, generally in white areas, which were labelled after 1950 as 'black spots' and scheduled for clearance from the 1960s onwards, often to the accompaniment of considerable social distress [see pp. 372–3, 403–7].

Africans squatting was a far more common phenomenon in all four provinces, as is witnessed by the existence of restrictive squatter legislation on every law book – colour-blind in the Cape, colour-oriented elsewhere. Squatters, black and white, had generally reached an accommodation with the owners of the land, as the evidence before the Beaumont Commission of 1916 and the Transvaal Indigency Commission of 1908 made plain. For the most part, they were either share-croppers, 'sowing on shares' or running stock and paying their landlords a stipulated proportion of the increase; or they were labour tenants, owing their landlord a fixed amount of work each year. The leading complaints of white farmers were that where share-cropping prevailed, it tended to cause a labour shortage and to disturb the traditional master–servant relationship which had become the norm across the colour line. The Beaumont Commission was told in 1916 that 'the half-share system is a pernicious system, because it takes away from your neighbour natives who ought to be servants'. Dr Verwoerd told the House of Assembly in 1958 that if a farmer fed his labourers, cared for them, and housed them separately but did not make them his partners, this would satisfy the norms of apartheid, whether he employed five or fifty, but that partnership between black and white was unthinkable (cols. 3806–7). But share-cropping was coming to be seen by the late 1980s as one of the most effective ways of increasing the number of people with vested interest in the land (Cross and Haines).

One of the paradoxes of the South African land problem was the continued presence of many more Africans in the white farming areas than the white population desired to see there, together with an enduring shortage of farm labourers. Agricultural wages were seldom competitive with industrial, and white farmers accustomed to the system of labour tenancy frequently contented themselves with the employment of very cheap inefficient casual labour of the kind provided by squatters, because it was available on their doorstep, rather than engage more skilled men at competitive rates of pay. In doing this, they were to some extent victims of the policy of separation, for the application of influx control in the towns, and in particular the very strict rules against the urbanisation of African women after 1937, had turned the farms into outdoor relief centres for a growing number of homeless persons – the wives and children of migrant workers for whom there was no room in the Reserves, and who were not allowed in the towns, or refugees driven from the Reserves by shortage of food.

Understandably, therefore, the intensity of white farmers' opposition to squatting grew as the numbers of squatters increased. This was reflected in official policy in the withdrawal of support for labour tenancy, which had been acceptable at the time of the 1913 Land Act. The Native Economic Commission of 1932 poured its wrath on labour tenancy, and started a campaign for the re-establishment of the farm economy on a basis of properly controlled wage labour. This was to increase the pressure on the squatters, and although the anti-squatter provisions of the 1936 legislation were not enforced, after the end of the Second World War the National Party (which had taken a strong line against squatting while in opposition in the 1930s) introduced enabling legislation by its Prevention of Illegal Squatting Act of 1951. This empowered the authorities to remove squatters from public or private land and send them elsewhere at discretion, and gave every local authority the right (or the duty, on ministerial command) to 'establish . . . an emergency camp for the accommodation of homeless persons'. The resettlement policy of the 1960s and 1970s was based mainly on this law, and on a policy statement of December 1967 which outlined three categories of 'Bantu' who could be removed to the Homelands: the elderly, the unfit, and people who did not qualify for residence rights in towns; 'surplus Bantu' on white-owned farms and in 'black spots'; and professional people who were considered to be of more use to their people in the Homelands than in the white areas. The establishment of settlements in the Reserves was necessary if the policy of territorial separation was to have any meaning; but villages of old people and children, with little more than a nucleus of able-bodied men, were an unlikely combination for making a success of virgin settlements, especially as there was little work available in many of the areas selected, so that the residents were largely dependent on very small old age pensions and rations which were frequently insufficient. On this fragile basis, and at indescribable human cost, the Government was to mount one of the biggest human relocation projects ever attempted anywhere, in order to be able to simplify the political map [see pp. 368–74]. Nor was the situation eased, from the point of view of blacks on the land, when the Government of P. W. Botha went over to a new policy of redefining Homeland boundaries so as to exclude black residents of particular villages from South Africa, and thus from South African citizenship rights – a policy which led to widespread protests [see pp. 405].

It may be held to the credit of the Union Parliament that it at least decided to look for land to add to the reserves while it adopted the policy of territorial separation. (This action was a good deal more creditable than the supporting mythology, which often held, in defiance of the evidence, that these addenda would restore to the blacks all the land to which they had any historical claim). Five local committees appointed to look into objections to the Beaumont Commission's recommendations in 1917–18 were able to rescue a surprisingly large proportion of that Commission's proposals, and their implementation was accepted in principle by the Smuts Government before it fell from power (Davenport and Hunt).

When Hertzog took office in 1924, his original land proposals were niggardly beside those of Smuts, whatever the impressions created by his own propaganda; but the legislation of the Fusion Government in 1936 reverted to the earlier policy of enlarging the reserves with the help of government funds, though under a form of tenure – that of the Native Trust – more suited to the requirements of land conservation than to the perceived needs of rural Africans. In accordance with the urgent recommendations of the Native Economic (Holloway) Commission of 1932, the Government tried to ensure that good husbandry would follow transfer. But its institution of trust tenure, which contained little security for the householder, and of betterment schemes, which forced the black farmer to fence, plough, cull and market under state supervision, were improvisations consequent upon the racial separation of land ownership, and for that reason distasteful to people who had not asked for such separation. The adoption of separation had greatly restricted the choice of farming methods open to the African population. The Tomlinson Commission in 1955 felt obliged to recommend a departure from the policy of 1936, and urged the abandonment of the 'one-man–one-lot' principle in the interest of increasing the agricultural productivity of the Reserves to enable them to absorb a large influx of people from the white areas under the apartheid policy of the Nationalist Government. They proposed to absorb this larger population by providing opportunities in the Reserves for businessmen, industrialists and tradesmen, while granting full-time African farmers economic units under freehold title. But the Government refused to allow the amalgamation of farming units because of the effect such a decision might have on the human carrying capacity of the Reserves, which needed for political reasons to be pushed as high as possible.

A further paradox of the land problem was that, at a time when the population of the Reserves was increasing at a steady rate under the twin pressures of natural increase and political repatriation, the white population of the 'white' rural areas was on the decline. There were already clear signs that this was happening in the Karoo at the time of the Drought Investigation Commission in 1923. The Du Toit Commission of 1960, investigating European occupancy of the rural areas, found that many farms had been deserted by Europeans, especially in the south-east Orange Free State – the 'Conquered Territory', as it is commonly called, in memory of the Free State conflict with Moshweshwe – and in north-western Natal. This was partly a result of agricultural consolidation, as successful wool farmers expanded their sheep runs, but partly a natural consequence of the more attractive conditions of town living: better security, higher wages, more amenities. The Commission also found that, where whites had moved out, blacks had moved in – as foremen and bailiffs, taking over from white men, or as squatters in defiance or ignorance of the law. It also drew attention to the emergence of yet another variety of landlord–tenant relationship, the labour farm, where landowners, instead of using the labour of their own squatters, to which they were entitled, had begun to sell that labour to other white farmers in the neighbourhood at considerable profit to themselves.

The destructive impact of segregation on land policy caused growing numbers to question its validity.

20.3   SEGREGATION IN TOWN

Within the broad sweep of segregation policy, the demarcation of separate territorial bases for black and non-black South Africa, it was thought necessary to set aside special residential areas for each group within the territory of the other. In the African Reserves, centres where white magistrates, traders and missions established themselves had often come to acquire the status of autonomous enclaves before 1910. Umtata and the other urban centres of the Transkei were examples of this.

But in the white areas the establishment of 'locations', as the places of African settlement on the edges of towns came to be called, became a matter for explicit legislation. Locations were provided for under some Cape municipal statutes during the nineteenth century, but by no means in all, while in the South African Republic the first locations were designated for the settlement of Asians rather than Africans, the accommodation of African servants being restricted by a regulation of 1899 to rooms in the back yards of white homes. At the beginning of the twentieth century, however, the Cape Parliament carried a Native Reserve Location Act (1902), authorising the Government to set up and control African residential areas outside towns. Natal carried a Locations Act in 1904, empowering local authorities to set them up and control them. The Transvaal Municipal Corporations Ordinance and the Bloemfontein Municipal Ordinance, both of 1903, formed the basis of a new system of urban African administration on segregated lines in the ex-Republics.

Elimination of slums, control of crime, control of disease, and in general the segregation of black from white people, were the main influences behind the decision to establish separate residential areas for Africans, and helped to coordinate the thinking of the Native Affairs Department [see pp. 235–6], which hesitated to introduce a policy of urban segregation before the First World War, at the time of the passage of the Land Act, because it was not yet confident that the principle of segregation had been 'fully accepted by the country'. After the war, however, came the 1918 influenza epidemic and, four years later, the report of Colonel Stallard's Transvaal Local Government Commission, which gained some following for its idea that the urban areas were the white man's creation, and that Africans had a right to be there only in so far as they were ministering to the white man's needs. After false starts in 1918 and 1922, the Department went to considerable trouble to consult both African and white municipal opinion before bringing in the legislation in 1923, which reached the statute book in much amended form as the Natives (Urban Areas) Act. The Act later underwent major amendments in 1930, 1937, 1944, 1952, 1957, 1964 and 1971, as well as consolidation in 1945, and grew into one of the most complex pieces of control legislation ever devised anywhere, prior to its supersession by the Black Local Government and Communities Development Acts of 1983–4.

The Urban Areas Act was a portmanteau law covering a great variety of issues. One objective of the legislators was to clear Africans out of the mixed residential areas which had grown up in some of the larger towns,

'You haven't had 15 years' continuous residence *or* ten years' continuous employment. You aren't qualified to live anywhere at all!' (Section 10 of the Amended Urban Areas Act did make provision for Africans born in an urban area to remain there.)

"I've never figured out which category this falls into — co-operation or development."

20 Sustained criticism of the Government's attempts to control black residence in the urban areas is reflected in these *Cape Times* cartoons by David Marais (1957) and Tony Grogan (1984)

notably Johannesburg, and re-house them in locations. Because these mixed areas were also slums, the policy was not entirely unconventional; but the task of providing homes for blacks in locations proved far more complicated in the long run than the authorities first envisaged. What followed was a saga with many unexpected turns, mainly tragic. To begin with, the authorities found that, instead of moving to locations, Africans evicted from backyards often preferred to move into other backyards. When Orlando Township was built outside Johannesburg in the 1930s, it contained numerous empty houses until as late as 1937 when the pressure of continuing townward migration filled them – too late to enable the Johannesburg Municipality to adjust its sights to the enormous extension of housing demands during the Second World War, when both materials and trained builders to deal with the emergency were lacking. The dramatic Johannesburg squatter movements which resulted from this bottleneck [see p. 308] in turn had an influence on the passage of legislation for the training of African builders, who had been barred by trade union rules, as Africans, from practising their skills even in black locations. An energetic slum clearance programme commenced in the 1950s, as shanties in the larger centres gave place to new, professionally laid out locations like Daveyton outside Benoni, which were provided with communal amenities as well as well-constructed homes. An emergency measure, the 'site-and-service' scheme worked out in the Department of Native Affairs, went a long way towards a solution of the problem. The scheme was based on the provision of water points and sanitary services by the local authority, and a requirement that African residents should build shanties for their immediate use at one end of their plots. Meanwhile the building of more solid homes at the other end of their plots took place under municipal supervision. In Johannesburg's South Western Native Township (Soweto) municipal effort, aided by substantial financial contributions from one of the mining houses, resulted in the proliferation of small but well-built, if architecturally monotonous, 'little boxes' for about three-quarters of a million African residents. Nyanga outside Cape Town and New Brighton outside Port Elizabeth were similar.

But a change of emphasis in government policy during the late 1960s upset the rhythm of this urban development. This was the decision to give priority to the building of homes in the Homelands, as the Reserves had come to be called. Mdantsane near East London, Ga Rankuwa near Pretoria, Kwa Mashu near Durban, and other 'Bantu towns' now consumed the building energies of the Government. There was an enforced cutback on municipal housing. The policy of the Government required a reduction in the number of Africans permanently residing in the urban areas and an increase in the number of workers migrating from the Homelands and living as contract workers in hostels or 'bachelor quarters' (a highly misleading term) while 'temporarily' in the urban area doing the work which – under the Stallard doctrine – legitimised their presence in the town. The parallel policy of re-locating industry in the border regions under the Physical Planning Act of 1967 [see p. 370] also required the building of houses in the Homelands rather than in the existing urban

locations. As a consequence of this redirection of energy, housing shortages in the urban locations again became acute, for African workers
proved less accommodating than the law required them to be, with the
result that slum conditions began to reappear in many urban locations,
large and small. The housing backlog in Johannesburg in 1972 was even
larger than it had been on the eve of Mpanza's squatter movement in 1944.
An exceptional increase in the black birthrate and some irregular influx
from white farms also helped to make the situation critical. Ideological
enthusiasm had recreated the problem which 'site-and-service' had gone a
long way towards solving.

Underlying the policy of urban segregation was a desire to reduce the
power of the black man in the urban areas by making it difficult for him to
acquire a stake in the town or, indeed, in his own location, for – as the
Stallard Commission emphasised – owners of property could hardly be
denied the municipal vote. Thus, although the original Urban Areas Bill of
1923 contained a provision for some Africans to own property in freehold,
this provision was removed, largely on General Hertzog's insistence,
before the Bill became law, and without consultation with the Africans.
During the Second World War, thirty-year leases were made lawful, and
though location plots tended to be small, some African leaseholders built
substantial properties, for example in Dube Township, Soweto. In 1968,
however, local authorities were pressed by the Government to buy in these
leasehold properties on the expiry of their leases. Prime Minister Vorster
relented on this point after an encounter with Homeland leaders in 1974,
and in the course of the following decade, especially after the adoption of
the Riekert recommendations, the Government reverted to the pragmatism of site-and-service days, not merely by allowing owner-built houses
under supervision, but even by clearing the legal obstacles so that black
leaseholders in urban locations could take out building society loans to buy
properties from the municipal housing stocks, and were positively encouraged to do so – provided they had taken out the citizenship of the
appropriate Homeland first, and had rights under the Urban Areas Act to
live in the town. An amendment to the Black Communities Development
Act in 1986 permitted the purchase by blacks of urban properties in
freehold.

A similar history underlay the related issue of African trading rights in
urban locations. The Act of 1923 empowered local authorities to grant
trading licences to African location residents. This was widely done, but
strong resistance developed, especially in the Orange Free State, so that
the Minister of Native Affairs took extra powers under the 1930 amendment to the Act. The Government was reluctant to use these powers, and
did not do so openly; but during the Second World War the principle of
African trading came to be accepted by local authorities in the Orange
Free State as well as elsewhere. It remained Government policy, however,
to prevent the expansion of African businesses in urban locations, in the
hope that these would move to the Homelands – for which reason it was
thought better that blacks should frequent the central business areas for
shopping purposes, where in any case goods bought in chain stores tended

to be cheaper. In 1963, a Government circular required local authorities to limit African trading in the locations by imposing a rule of 'one-man–one-shop', prohibiting African trading in all but 'daily essential domestic necessities' (which could not include the sale of petrol, for example), and banning the establishment of African companies in white areas. But here, too, a subsequent political decision to promote rather than retard the growth of an urban black middle class led to a reversal of the rule. The Stallard doctrine was turned upon its head, but without the removal of influx control.

There were certain residential areas which, though peopled by Africans, did not fall under the scope of the Urban Areas Act, and it became Government policy to regularise these wherever possible. Thus a Natives Resettlement Act was carried in 1954, to enable the Government to remove the African residents of Johannesburg's western suburbs of Sophiatown, Martindale and Newclare, where much property was black-owned, to a new government settlement at Meadowlands. This move, carried out in 1957, was hailed by government officials as a triumph of social engineering, and the new white suburb which arose from the rubble was named Triomf. The action was criticised by many of the residents, by welfare bodies, and notably in Trevor Huddleston's *Naught for your Comfort*, as the break-up of a community, albeit a community in which crime, poverty and disease abounded. The same rationalisation would later be made about Cape Town's District Six.

Another feature of the Urban Areas Act of 1923 was the provision of a system of local government on segregated lines. Under the stimulus of the Act, municipal native affairs departments began to acquire a separate existence, employing as location superintendents – or in the larger centres as managers of native affairs – men who had frequently served in the police or acquired administrative experience elsewhere, and who governed the locations with the aid of partly elected Advisory Boards, usually of six members. Potentially capable of development into either political or responsible executive bodies, the Advisory Boards were prevented from so developing by the ambiguous position of the location as a black enclave in a 'white' area. Some managers, concerned over the developing frustration of Advisory Board members at their own powerlessness, experimented with a policy of downward democratisation, by developing a 'ward' or 'block' system of electoral responsibility within the location itself, but opposition among whites precluded the extension of their powers, though the Native Representative Council frequently asked for this.

In 1961, the Government began to replace Advisory Boards by a new system of Urban Bantu Councils, the chairmen of which were to be Africans. These Councils could also be given various administrative and financial powers by the local authority with the assent of the Minister; but in practice such powers were not extended, and it became clear by the early 1970s that supporters of the Government were less enthusiastic about the Urban Bantu Councils than about the appointment, under the Promotion of Bantu Self-Government Act of 1959, of representatives of the Home-land chiefs in the urban locations. At the end of the Vorster era, the Urban

Bantu Councils were replaced by Community Councils which took over the financial and administrative powers held since 1973 by the Bantu Affairs Administration Boards [see p. 373], and the Boards themselves were in due course turned into developmental bodies without administrative functions. A Black Local Authorities Act of 1982 for the first time gave African residents of urban locations something like autonomy. If they could not have access to Parliament, at least they now had local power. Their sixty-year apprenticeship was over in strict law; but the offer of effective local power at this stage came to be seen as a poor substitute for representation in Parliament, and was widely resented, as violent attacks on the persons of many of the new councillors in 1984–5 made plain [see pp. 438–9].

Municipal control over the urban locations was fundamental to the system established in 1923, though the establishment of a separate Native Revenue Account, which was supposed to be self-balancing, was an important feature of the law. In so far as local authorities had made profits from the running of their locations, this had to come to an end. By the time of the Second World War, more and more local authorities had begun to realise that revenues from 'Kaffir beer' sales (a lucrative source of municipal finance first discovered by Durban at the beginning of the century), and from rents and fines, were not sufficient for the provision of basic amenities in the locations, and they had begun to contribute to the Native Revenue Account from the general rate fund. When the self-balancing principle was revived after the Second World War, therefore, the emphasis of the policy had changed: the intention now was to reduce the dependence of the location on the general rate fund, and to return so far as possible to a policy of economic rents (as opposed to the sub-economic rents subsidised by the central Government during the war years, which had been made available to municipal tenants in all race groups). Where rents were not sufficient, local authorities were encouraged to raise lodgers' fees. By 1971, only twenty-one of over 450 local authorities still contributed funds from general revenue to their Bantu (Native) Revenue Accounts.

Yet another device for regulating the financing of locations was contained in the Native Services Levy Act of 1952. This law amplified a provision in the original 1923 Act that it was the duty of the employer to look after the proper housing of his African employees – a provision which had proved very difficult to enforce. Monthly levies were now imposed on employers of African labour to subsidise location development. But as the emphasis of government policy shifted, so the expenditure permitted from the Native Service Levy Fund came to be restricted to the provision of capital amenities (for example, roads and drainage) in new African townships in the Homelands and for the provision of transport at subsidised rates between the Homelands and the towns from which Africans commuted to work. A law originally intended to encourage employers' involvement in the improvement of the urban townships in which their employees lived was thus recast to serve very different ideological ends. Another regulation which served the same purpose was the obligation imposed on local authorities, after it became lawful for Africans to consume 'European' liquor in 1961, to pay 80 per cent of the profits from municipal liquor outlets (as distinct from beer profits) to the central Government for purposes of Homeland development. To divert funds from black urban revenues for the promotion of Homeland development, however, enormously increased the revenue problems for self-governing African townships in the 'white' area.

This became an important consideration as soon as black local authorities were granted full powers. Even if these local authorities were seen by residents as illegitimate, the Government felt compelled to make it possible for these segregated bodies to fund their own administration and development. The Regional Services Councils Act of 1985 [see p. 401] was the route chosen. It allowed for the demarcation of large administrative regions by each provincial Administrator, each with a council composed of nominees from all local authorities in the region irrespective of race. The R.S.C.'s role was to collect funds from the trading, business and professional community according to their respective turnovers and wage bills, and allocate these for the provision of capital improvements wherever the need was greatest. The voting strength of each local authority represented was determined by the proportion of the total services which it purchased, and controls were built in to prevent large municipalities from obtaining an undue share. This highly complex procedure for achieving a fair allocation of public money at the local level by a non-racial body for expenditure on 'general affairs' was energetically promoted by the Government as a way of achieving a fair distribution of resources without inciting racial friction. Many critics were less sanguine, seeing the Act variously as a way of preventing rather than promoting non-racial local government, or as increasing rather than reducing the cost of services. Inkatha, the *Konserwatiewe* Party, the U.D.F., N.A.F.C.O.C., the Cape Town City Council and other bodies of standing opposed the scheme. Implementation went ahead fastest in the Transvaal, where twelve councils were set up in 1987–8. Control over several of these was won by the K.P. in 1988, and steps taken to restrain the diversion of funds away from white municipalities. None were set up in Natal on account of Inkatha's opposition. Three were established in the Cape (Algoa, Cape Western and Walvis Bay), and one in the O.F.S. But the existence of Regional Services Councils did not stifle the growing demand for elective, non-racial local authorities.

20.4 PASSES AND THE CONTROL OVER BLACK MOVEMENT

The policy of the Urban Areas Act, it was realised from the outset, was likely to stand or fall on the ability of the Government to control the movement of people within the frontiers of the state. Control over people was already a notable feature of the South African legal system for in spite of the celebrated abolition of passes under Ordinance 50 of 1828, all kinds of controls over the movement of Africans, in particular had returned by the time of Union, and some existed in all provinces: travel documents, labour documents, residential documents, curfew documents, the nonproduction of which, when they were asked for by officials, carried penalties of various kinds. The variety of documents which Africans were required to possess was complex to the point of unfairness, even if – within a narrow compass – passes could in some instances serve as a security device. In 1920, following widespread demonstrations against the pass laws in the previous year, an Inter-Departmental Committee of inquiry met to consider their simplification, and recommended that all necessary pass information be coordinated in a single document, made of parchment, to be carried by males from the age of eighteen whenever they were outside the ward of issue, but explicitly not by women on account of the strong feeling against the registration of African women which had been shown by Charlotte Maxeke's demonstration in the Orange Free State in 1913. These proposals were included in a Native Registration and Protection Bill tabled at the same time as the Urban Areas Bill in 1923; but the two measures were amalgamated in Select Committee, the controls retained, and the proposed simplifications ignored – as they would be ignored again when the Holloway (Native Economic) Commission made similar proposals in 1932, following widespread anti-pass demonstrations in 1929–31, and when J. M. Young of the Native Affairs Commission made them again in 1939 after further criticism from the Native Representative Council (Davenport).

The cumulative effect of these repeated attempts to ameliorate the pass laws had a massive influence in undermining African confidence in the good faith of white legislators, especially as the incidence of pass arrests intensified. During the Second World War, so sharply had the number of arrests under the pass laws increased on the Witwatersrand that the Ministers of Justice and of Native Affairs agreed to issue instructions in May 1942 that the police were not to arrest Africans simply for not having their passes on them, unless they suspected that such Africans were engaged in criminal activity. A sharp fall in actual arrests resulted; but unfortunately for this experiment, the Elliott Committee appointed by the same two departments to examine the problem of crime on the Rand came to the conclusion that relaxation of pass controls had resulted in large-scale non-registration at the labour exchanges by Africans entering the towns. Searches were therefore resumed. Within a few months a well-organised Anti-Pass campaign was under way, with the African, Coloured and Indian movements acting together. By endorsing the Fagan proposals of 1948 for softening the impact of pass restrictions [see p. 312], the Smuts Government hoped to turn away black indignation; but by then it had lost political contact with black leaders. Its successors, who were in any case less well disposed towards the emancipation of Africans from existing controls, inherited the problem. Black opposition to the pass laws therefore continued, and found further expression in the Defiance Campaign in 1952, when large numbers courted arrest by deliberately destroying their passes [see p. 335]. The Natives Abolition of Passes and Coordination of Documents Act of the same year belied its title, for it retained control documents and merely renamed them 'reference books'. It did embody the proposals for a simplified system which characterised the suggestions of 1920, 1932 and 1939; but it provided for the extension of reference books to African women, and when this part of the Act was put into operation it led, as in 1913, to racial violence, this time mainly in the western Transvaal [see p. 348]. At the end of the decade, it was anti-pass demonstrations mounted by the new Pan-Africanist Congress and by the A.N.C., that resulted in the shootings at Sharpeville and Langa of March 1960 [see pp. 357–8]. After Sharpeville, the instruction went out again to the police to demand the presentation of passes only when they suspected that a crime was being committed. The figures for pass arrests again diminished; but they gradually returned to previous levels, and by the early 1970s arrests under legislation restricting the movement of Africans had climbed to an annual figure of well over 600,000, after which they fell again, largely on account of the establishment of Dr Koornhof's promotion of non-punitive aid centres, only to pick up in the early 1980s until P. W. Botha's Government abolished formal influx control in 1986 (Savage).

The normal way to maintain social control in towns all over the world is to rely upon the local police to enforce municipal by-laws and deal, as need arises, with vagrants, drunkards and other offenders. Normal social controls, though, were found to be insufficient by the South African legislature because the Urban Areas Act was required to do abnormal things; to make rules for blacks which did not apply to whites; to enforce a segregationist legal system; to restrict the urbanisation of blacks in strict proportion to the availability of work; to expel blacks from town (but not whites) for vagrancy, idleness, disorderliness, failure to pay rent, and other causes. Control over African influx was not an important feature of the original Act, and no special machinery was provided for enforcing it. But the first restrictions on the urbanisation of African women were enacted in 1930, chiefly in an attempt to limit prostitution and illicit brewing, and these were stiffened in 1937. The 1937 amendment [see p. 286] was the first to restrict the number of blacks in town according to the availability of work. Local authorities were required to send to the Minister of Native Affairs regular estimates of local labour requirements in relation to the number of Africans living in the area. The measure also restricted the African immigrant to fourteen days in which to find work in the town, or return to the Reserve – later cut down to 72 hours in the 1952 amendment. Influx control regulations were applied systematically for the first time in 1938, but largely fell into abeyance during the war because of the scarcity of all kinds of labour in the urban areas. In 1952 Parliament enacted the notorious 'Section Ten' provisions, which denied the right to live in an urban area to any African who was not born there, male or female, unless he had either lived there continuously for fifteen years – lawful holidays excepted – or served under the same employer for ten. The law, as enforced, could and did split husbands and wives if only one of them qualified; but it was less effective as a means of excluding blacks from town than the Government hoped, because those who could qualify – and there were by then many of them – now had a statutory as well as a common law right to be in the urban area. Thus, although the rustication clauses grew markedly longer with each new edition of the Act, as the offences which could earn the penalty multiplied, the number of Africans in the towns steadily grew. But the legal status of urban Africans began to change after the passage of the 1964 Bantu Labour Act: the proportion of migrant workers under contract of service grew, and the proportion with rights under the Urban Areas Act diminished. The Komani and Rikhoto judgements of 1980–1, by confirming the right of African wives of lawful urban residents, and of African workers who had broken the continuity of their urban residence by going to their Homelands on leave, to reside in the urban areas, appeared finally to have killed the effectiveness of influx control. But two trump cards played by the Government ensured, even under these trying conditions, that it retained the right to exclude. One was the provision in the various Homeland Independence Acts, assented to by each Homeland Government as it took independence, that the children of Homeland subjects who possessed Section 10 rights would not themselves possess them. The other was a law enacted in 1983, which empowered the local authorities to permit the exercise of Section 10 rights only if housing was available.

As Hindson has argued, the elimination of the pass laws was followed, not by the opening of access to towns without restriction, but by controls which limited access through economic curbs or – from 1984 – diverted it to new development areas under the successive Black Communities Development Acts.

The Black Sash started advice offices in Cape Town, Johannesburg and elsewhere in an attempt to mitigate the social distress caused by the break-up of homes resulting from the strict enforcement of Section Ten. Its monthly reports and records of case histories soon grew into a formidable corpus of evidence for the social historian. The Government followed with experimental aid centres designed to provide Africans who had infringed the influx control laws with employment rather than prison sentences, and in 1975 it announced a plan for rehabilitation camps in the Homelands for the same purpose. These private and public counter-measures, however, left it in no doubt that influx control caused widespread social pain.

20.5 RACIALLY SEGREGATED SCHOOLS AND UNIVERSITIES

The physical separation of the races was powerfully reinforced by a segregated educational system, but this had not always existed. Cape schools in Company days had often catered for the children of slaves as well as their white masters. Mission schools in the nineteenth-century Cape were often mixed. But when government schools were first established they developed into institutions for white children only, and this was true even of the Cape, where Parliament passed a School Boards Act in 1905, limiting attendance to children of 'European parentage and extraction', which was interpreted in *Moller's Case* (1911) to mean white children only.

This advantage enjoyed by white children over pupils of other races became an enduring feature of South African education, the main structural features of which had been established by 1910. Whites acquired a headstart when age-linked educational qualifications were tied to industrial apprenticeship in 1922 [see p. 508]. The advantage enjoyed by white pupils was underpinned by much more lavish budgetary provision, both absolutely and *per caput*. By 1948 white education was subsidised at the rate of £6.85 per head of population, and African at the rate of 4s. In 1982 state investment per white pupil (unadjusted for inflation) had risen to R1021, and per African to R176.2. Significantly, however, state expenditure on African education had risen in 1982 by 205.8 per cent above the 1977 figure, and had risen again by 73.9 per cent to R2,453 million in 1987, of which R1,157.8 had been spent in the white-designated areas at the rate of R41.8 and R476.95 per pupil respectively. By contrast, investment in white education in 1987 stood at 18.98 per cent below the 1982 figure in real terms, with a total expenditure eof R3,320.7 million. Although, by 1989, only R595 per annum was spent on each African child in school, as against the R2,722 spent on each white child, these figures need to be offset against the very rapid increase in the number of African children of school-going age, especially at the costly secondary level, for whom provision had to be made, as is shown in Table 5:

Table 5   Comparative school enrolment figures in the Republic, 1969–89

Enrolment		White	Coloured	Indian	African
1969	total	812,961	515,336	157,891	2,545,755
	secondary	264,519	57,420	37,718	106,945
1979	total	954,426	707,923	214,481	3,247,282
	secondary	349,207	118,661	64,348	443,375
1989	total	897,964	798,507	232,468	6,237,070
	secondary	376,099	202,261	87,319	1,291,125

Source   Annual *Race Relations Surveys*, Malherbe (1977) Appx. 32, and Giliomee and Schlemmer [n. 20.11], p. 106

The burgeoning of African and Coloured secondary-school pupils offset an earlier tendency for children from these backgrounds to leave school in droves before or at the end of their primary training, either from economic necessity or for want of school places or of adequate teaching at the secondary level. But the relative poverty of teacher training outside the white educational system persisted, and was well illustrated in the Report of the De Lange Commission in 1978, which disclosed that, whereas nearly all white teachers had had twelve years' schooling and one-third of them had degrees, only 2.45 per cent of African teachers were degreed, only 16.09 per cent had passed Standard Ten, only 62.9 per cent had passed Standard Eight, and 18.56 per cent had not gone further than Standard Six.

School education was made a provincial matter under the Act of Union, while the administration of Native Affairs was vested in the Governor-General-in-Council. At first, African education was placed under the Provincial education departments, though attempts were made from early days to have it transferred either to the Union Department of Education or to the Department of Native Affairs. The victory of the latter in 1953 was crucial for the direction taken by policy. In 1936 the Native Affairs Commission had urged greater differentiation between black and white schools, and this line of argument was further developed by the Eiselen Commission in 1951, when it came up with the new concept of 'Bantu Education', a special product brought into being by the National Party's Bantu Education Act of 1953 to prepare blacks for their special place in society. This involved a differential syllabus with greater emphasis on practical subjects, the use of vernacular instruction throughout the primary school, and the simultaneous introduction of both English and Afrikaans, not only as subjects but as media of instruction, in the lower secondary school: in other words, education for subordination in the workplace. The Bantu Education Act also made a virtue of African responsibility for the education of their own people through the introduction of African school boards and school committees, and the employment of black teachers (mainly women, to save on the cost of salaries) in the place of whites, especially the white staff of mission schools like Lovedale and Healdtown, which were taken over by the Government because their support for apartheid was thought not to be sufficiently robust.

Bantu Education was also extended to the tertiary level, with the closure of most of the faculties in the open universities to African, Indian and Coloured students in 1959, despite the strong opposition of staff and students in the universities concerned. Separate ethnic institutions of higher education for Xhosa, Coloured, Indian, Zulu and Sotho-Tswana students were set up as agencies of academic apartheid, and their creation did much to alienate black and English-speaking youth from the Government during the 1950s and 1960s.

By then many young blacks had reacted to Government pressure by laying emphasis not on ethnicity, but on colour, by creating the Black Consciousness movement, with its own South African Students' Organization as a counterweight to N.U.S.A.S. They built up resistance to Bantu Education in all its forms, and their anger erupted over the compulsory use of Afrikaans as a medium of instruction in the Soweto disturbances of 1976 [see p. 389].

The Government's response after the turmoil had subsided was to arrange for the appointment of the De Lange Commission to review the whole South African educational system in the light of the political troubles and the country's higher educational needs [see p. 422]. Apart from recommending a greater emphasis on technical education at the tertiary level, De Lange urged the integration of the various ethnic education departments into a single administrative system, and a strategy for the equalisation of amenities and pupil–teacher ratios, which it estimated would cost at least R219 million a year over twenty years for buildings at 1978 prices, and an annual sum of R2,000 million rising to R4,000 million if a pupil–teacher ratio of 31 to one was to be achieved across the board by the year 1990. Even though the educational budget rose spectacularly from R1,550 million in 1979 to R9,390 million in 1989, the achievement of so great a revolution in so short a time was beyond the capacity of the State, great though its efforts were to create more school accommodation while at the same time rebuilding or replacing the 350 schools which were wholly or partially destroyed in 1976–7, and the 294 which suffered a similar fate in 1985–6 in the African residential areas alone.

An issue which the De Lange Commission did not have to face was that of school integration, despite successful private efforts to promote multi-racial boarding schools in neighbouring countries, which seemed – from an elitist perspective at least – to point the way ahead. This lacuna suggests that the inroads of Black Consciousness were already real.

It also made the reluctance of the Government to integrate the educational systems all the more critical, especially as education was about to be classified as an 'own affair' under the new constitution [see p. 434]. This meant that South Africa would be required to keep a proliferation of separate education departments going (four for the Republic, one each for the Homelands) in spite of the administrative chaos and waste of funds as fourteen separate educational budgets ate into the limited resources.

Changes in the structure of the educational system were, of course, not easy to imagine, given the central position accorded to groups in the evolution of Christian National Education since the 1870s, especially in the thinking of the very influential Broederbond [see pp. 93, 212–3, 290]. About one-fifth of the Broederbond's 11,910 members in 1977 were drawn from the teaching profession, including the rectors of all Afrikaans and black universities and all the provincial directors of education (Serfontein). Not surprisingly, the Bloemfontein conference of Afrikaans-speaking educators endorsed the decision of the Government not to amalgamate the educational structures in 1981 [see p. 423].

But the failure to grasp the financial nettle and to make the ideological shift which this would have implied was in no small measure responsible for the outbursts of educational unrest in 1980 and 1984–6 [see pp. 422, 439]. Although the Government was rebuilding schools and rapidly constructing new ones; and even though it had repealed the Bantu Education Act itself (1979), and allowed private schools for the first time to admit black pupils, and relaxed the rules governing the admission of students to universities proclaimed for other race groups, protest remained in the air. A new fascination for 'alternative education', linked to the notion that liberation should come before schooling, ran like wildfire through the age groups whose education had been disrupted, often at the cost of the liberal values which the system was supposed to have cherished.

Meanwhile white pupil enrolments began to decline, and the shortfall in the number and quality of black teachers became critical as pupil numbers pushed the numbers in many black senior-school classes above 60. This pointed to an urgent need to share facilities and human resources (Gaydon). The Government responded in 1990 by introducing an educational budget which far exceeded any of its earlier measures; but its doctrinaire efforts to keep education an 'own affair' still blocked the way to a practical solution.

20.6 THE CHURCHES AND APARTHEID

'Unwritten codes of behaviour', in the view of Rhoodie and Venter, underlay a customary apartheid 'in the field of public transport, entertainment, recreation, and so on'. This summary of what had been substantially true before 1948 over nearly the whole country is picked up, also, in W. Saayman's assertion that 'Christian mission in South Africa tends to conform to societal institutions, such as racialism, rather than to transform society' (Prozesky). The very fact of geographical separation between white-run towns and their locations would have ensured this result, even if there had been no language or cultural barriers between black and white. Congregations in most churches were unilingual and uniracial. The Dutch Reformed Churches were constitutionally structured into separate white and black ('missionary') bodies. The English-speaking Presbyterian Church of South Africa existed side-by-side with a Bantu (later Reformed) Presbyterian Church, though this was a black breakaway body which remained linked to the Church of Scotland, not the result of a white decision to segregate. A number of the African independent churches resulted from similar breakaways, especially from the Methodists [see p. 209], though the Methodist Church was the first to elect a black person as its leader when the Rev. Seth Mokitimi became President of the Methodist Conference in 1964, well before Bishop Desmond Tutu became the first black Anglican Archbishop of Cape Town.

After 1948 the religious isolation of the races from each other became a matter of public policy, though it should be noted that the first unsuccessful attempt to bring this about had occurred under Hertzog in 1937 (Davenport). The second was in 1957 [see p. 344], when renewed public outcries again prevented the Government from enforcing the religious separation now enacted by law. But the relationship between the Government and those Churches which rejected apartheid on religious grounds degenerated into an escalating cultural conflict with growing international ramifications. The State at first took a hard line to cut out the influence of clerical liberalism through the exclusion of the missions from Bantu Education. In 1974 the University of Fort Hare authorities obtained the right to expropriate the Federal Theological Seminary run by a group of English-speaking Churches, to prevent further contact between university students and the members of this liberal institution. The N.G. Kerk had identified itself with the policy of separate development at a People's Conference in Bloemfontein in 1950 (J. Kinghorn, in Prozesky), in accordance with the S.A.B.R.A. philosophy of cultural separatism. In this atmosphere there was a growing preparedness in the World Council of Churches to promote the cause of black political movements in exile and contribute financially to the families of people convicted of political offences, though when the Anglican Archbishop Joost de Blank urged the World Council to expel large sections of the Dutch Reformed Churches in December 1960, it declined to do so.

Affirmations of dissent from the racial policies of the Government were regularly made by church bodies. One such was the declaration by the Anglican bishops in 1957 that if the churches were segregated by law, they would be bound in conscience to disobey that law (Paton). Another was the *Message to the People of South Africa* published by the South African Council of Churches in 1968, which rejected Government race policy as un-Christian. Dutch Reformed clergy gradually became more open in their rejection of apartheid doctrines. Some participated with their English-speaking colleagues in an important consultation at Cottesloe, Johannesburg in December 1960. In June 1982, 123 N.G. clergy published an open letter in the *Kerkbode*, the Church's official organ, protesting against the refusal of the Church authorities to place a document expressing their opposition to apartheid in the Church on the agenda of the general synod.

But it took the emergence of the Black Consciousness movement [see pp. 378–9], and its link with the Christian Institute of South Africa, founded in 1963, to bring anything like a confessional Christian movement into being (De Gruchy). This Institute, under the leadership of the Rev. Beyers Naude, attacked apartheid through its journal, *Pro Veritate*. It also helped to coordinate the activities of already politicised independent churches and was declared an 'affected organization' by Parliament, and thereby barred from receiving funds from abroad, for refusing to testify before the Schlebusch–Le Grange Commission of Inquiry in 1975 [see pp. 426–7]. It was later banned, with the other Black Consciousness organisations, in October 1977.

This banning, however, did not quench religious opposition to state policy, because a new theology of liberation was beginning to emerge, which justified the use of force against a political system which deprived blacks of economic opportunity and political rights, if non-violent protest were ruled out of order. In August 1982 the World Alliance of Reformed Churches pronounced apartheid a heresy, on the motion of Dr Allan Boesak of the N.G. Mission Church, who was subsequently elected President of the Alliance. From this vantage point, he and Archbishop Tutu of Cape Town set in motion a campaign for the imposition of sanctions against the Republic, arguing that this was the only available course of action short of military violence, and their campaign exerted an important influence on world opinion [see pp. 461–6].

20.7   GROUP AREAS

Control over the movement and residential rights of Africans was made relatively simple by the existence of the pass laws. In the case of other non-white race groups it was rather more complicated. Indians could be prevented by existing laws from moving from one province to another, and from residing in particular areas, and were barred from the Orange Free State altogether [see p. 75]. Coloured people were not controlled at all as to their movements, and could live in any province.

As a result of pressure from its own followers, the Smuts Government in 1946 carried an Asiatic Land Tenure Act to restrict Indian residence to particular parts of Natal, as they had already been restricted in the Transvaal since the early 1930s [see p. 318]. To do this, machinery was set up which included the appointment of a Land Tenure Advisory Board with power to screen potential buyers and occupiers and advise on the issuing of permits.

With the introduction of the Group Areas Act in 1950 [see above], the principle of setting aside areas in towns for the ownership or occupation of particular race groups was adopted and machinery thus created for the total ethnic segregation of all South African towns. As the Government went ahead with the implementation of this policy, the Group Areas Act underwent important revisions in 1952, 1956, 1957, 1961, 1962, 1965, 1969, 1975 and 1977, and was consolidated in 1957 and 1966. Its primary purpose was to segregate all race groups, and if need be subgroups (for example, Cape Malay) in urban areas. Africans were hardly affected, for they were already controlled under the Urban Areas Act save in a handful of centres like Alexandra Township, Johannesburg, or the Fingo Village, Grahamstown. The relative incidence of the legislation on particular race groups can be seen from figures for 1972 already quoted in relation to the white, Coloured, Indian and Chinese communities [see p. 380]. These show that in terms of numbers of families moved, the Coloured community had suffered most severely, the Indian very substantially given their smaller population, and the white community hardly at all. By August 1985 there had been a considerable increase in the number of families identified for removal, as against the earlier figure; but in spite of that the target was seen as almost within reach: 83,691 Coloured families had been moved, leaving only 3,790 to resettle; 40,067 Indian families had been moved, leaving 2,366; and only 258 white families remained on the removal list, 2,418 having already been dealt with. No removals statistics were offered by 'own affair' administrations which took over from September 1984, on the ground that subsequent removals had been negligible (*Race Relations Surveys, 1985*, pp. 348–9, 1987–8, p. 502). But alongside the expropriation of property, the Board was given power under a succession of Group Areas Development Acts and Community Development Acts to buy and sell, administer and develop properties on an enormous scale. In 1979 it possessed real estate to the value of R290,237,586. Examples were quoted in Parliament from time to time of cases where the Board had bought cheaply and sold at a large profit, and others in which the Board had sold cheaply and enabled developers who bought properties from it to realise enormous returns on their capital. As a body which had the power to expropriate as well as enter the property market, it was placed in a position to take advantage of rises and falls in property values determined by its own decisions, and the profitability of its own transactions under such conditions gave it the capacity to extend its own activities. As a result, the whole Republic had been covered by the racial zoning plans of the Board and its regional subdivisions by the mid-1970s, and in almost all respects these zoning plans had been finalised.

At about the time when the Act was on the verge of reaching its goal, the first serious official doubts about its desirability began to break surface.

Judge Goldstone's ruling in the Transvaal Supreme Court in November 1982 had shown that the defences of the system could be breached, when he introduced a new flexibility in the law by ordering in *Govender's Case* that the 1966 amendment to the Group Areas Act had made eviction orders by a magistrate permissive where they had once been mandatory, despite numerous precedents where the opposite had been presumed (Festenstein and Pickard-Cambridge). Meanwhile P. W. Botha had already appointed a committee of the President's Council in 1981 to propose changes in the Act without disturbing the principle of residential segregation. The Strydom Committee duly proposed in 1984 that central business districts be opened to all races at the request of local authorities, and that all employees should be freed from Group Area residential restrictions; but it also recommended that the Group Areas and Community Development Acts should only be repealed if racial restrictions were retained in property titles. The State President made it clear during 1985 that he regarded residential segregation as a cornerstone of government policy, despite growing opposition to the principle of Group Areas, even within his own party; but by this time the Govender judgment had effectively removed the threat to offenders against the Act because the movement of blacks into certain areas of the larger cities, like Hillbrow in Johannesburg, had taken place on such a scale that the Act had become virtually unenforceable.

Then, in 1987, the Labour Party in the House of Representatives decided to confront the Government on the issue: it would not agree to a postponement of the next general election for all three houses beyond the 1989 date required under the constitution unless President Botha undertook to repeal the Group Areas, Community Development and Reservation of Separate Amenities Acts *in toto*; nor would it seek a no-confidence vote in the Government, which would enable the President to dissolve the House of Representatives alone, thus enabling him to avoid another conflict with Treurnicht's K.P. on the reform issue in the local elections one year after the 1987 general election.

The confrontation with Labour continued into 1988. The Government sought to undo the effects of the Govender judgment by legislating to raise the penalties for Group Area infringements from R400 to R10,000 in the case of landowners and from R200 to R4,000 in the case of other offenders, while at the same time introducing bills to make possible the setting up of Free Settlement Areas under special forms of local government. When the Labour Party and the entire House of Delegates refused to debate these measures, the Government offered to send all three bills to the Joint Standing Committee of Parliament if they would agree to a joint sitting on 26 September. A breakaway movement within the House of Representatives threatened briefly to undermine Labour's stand; but when the joint sitting was called, Labour and the Delegates refused to participate, thus obliging the Government to drop the measures or refer them to the President's Council, the effect of which would be to leave the Group Areas issue still undecided when the nation-wide municipal elections took place on 25 October. The constitutional affairs committee of the President's

Council in due course found the increased Group Area penalties unacceptable, and the bill was abandoned by the Government in February 1989. A
year later, when F. W. de Klerk had assumed the presidency, Free
Settlement Areas, to be defined by a board set up for the purpose after
approaches from the public, represented the limit to which the Government would at first go to dismantle the Group Areas Act. But the repeal of
the Reservation of Separate Amenities Act during the 1990 session placed
segregated public amenities throughout South Africa beyond the law.

20.8   THE CONFLICT OVER APARTHEID IN ENTERTAINMENT AND SPORT

Group Areas restrictions applied not merely to ownership and occupation
of domestic and business premises, but also to the provision of amenities
for entertainment and access to pleasure resorts like parks and beaches, for
the Strijdom and Verwoerd governments, in particular, were keen to
promote customary separation even in these spheres. To take one example
of many, Cape Town had not previously segregated either its buses or its
city hall for public performances. It was required to segregate both, and to
deny Coloured people access to the latter because it was situated in the
central business district, which had been declared white. But for the
Government this proved to be an untenable line. Great controversy
followed the building of the Nico Malan Theatre in Cape Town, by the
Cape Provincial Administration, as an entertainment centre for whites
only. After considerable public pressure the theatre was made available for
mixed audiences in 1975, though the Government made it clear at the same
time that the principle of segregated audiences for public entertainment in
general was to be maintained, and that special permits would still be
required from Pretoria for every performance before a racially mixed
audience in nearly every theatre in the Republic. But the absurdity of this
bureaucratic strangulation brought its own reaction, in the form of a
growing campaign to eliminate 'petty apartheid'. This was to be seen, for
example, in an agitation to have restaurants and businesses in central
Johannesburg opened to other races during 1977, at a time when – thanks
to the mushrooming of business and shopping complexes closer to the
expanding white suburbs – central Johannesburg was in any case becoming
more and more a black city. Liberalisation occurred without prior amendment of the law. This made it possible, however, for K.P.-dominated
municipalities, a few of which emerged from the local elections of 1988 –
notably Boksburg and Carletonville in the Transvaal – to reimpose petty
apartheid legislation governing access to amenities. A black consumer
boycott ensued, causing some embarrassment to traders. The boycott
flagged, but when the Government repealed the Reservation of Separate
Amenities Act in 1990, exclusion on racial grounds could only be effected
by devious means.

   As in cultural entertainment, so in sport, the ban on inter-racial activity
proved difficult to sustain. Until late in the Vorster era, separate sporting

21 **The early inconsistencies of the new-model apartheid sports policy, as devised by Dr Koornhof, are caught by Kenyon of the *Daily Dispatch***

activities were required by law, and access to sports grounds – both for players and spectators – determined by the group area in which each ground was situated. Mixed sports clubs were not allowed because inter-racial drinking was unlawful outside private homes. Largely as a result of the failure of South African athletes to obtain an invitation to the Olympic Games in Mexico City in 1968, and the violence of the public demonstrations when a South African rugby team visited Britain in 1969, the Government adopted a policy of allowing 'multi-national' (as distinct from multi-racial) sporting activities in 1971, in terms of which teams representing national groups could compete against each other; but inter-racial competition at the club level, and mixed teams, were prohibited. This made little impression on the international sporting world, largely owing to the continuing opposition of the South African Non-Racial Olympic Committee (S.A.N.R.O.C.), and the South African Council on Sport (S.A.C.O.S.), which held the support of world bodies for their policy of isolating the Republic's sporting organisations. By 1976, the South African Government had yielded to the point of allowing selection on merit for members of Springbok teams, which made it possible for Errol Tobias to wear the Springbok rugby jersey, and for Omar Henry to play in a Springbok cricket side. In 1977 the Liquor Act was amended to permit drinking by mixed groups, thus facilitating mixed membership of sporting clubs, whose existence no longer required special permission.

After a controversial Springbok rugby tour of New Zealand in 1981, the application of the apartheid laws to sporting bodies became sufficiently relaxed for two new contradictory trends to appear. On the one hand,

S.A.C.O.S. and the hard-line boycotting organisations, which in due course established political links with the U.D.F. and C.O.S.A.T.U., began to insist that the sports boycott should be maintained until apartheid had ceased to exist in spheres outside the sporting field as well. Enough individual incidents involving racial discrimination in sport took place to give this stand credibility, even if it did involve 'moving the goalposts' in the eyes of some. This, by and large, remained the attitude of the International Olympic and Commonwealth Games Committees, which had to face blackmail tactics by individual national committees which threatened to withdraw their teams from these events if the South African boycott rules were breached by individuals. On the other hand, a growing hawkishness on the part of South African sports administrators, generally backed by business interests, inspired attempts to neutralise the boycott by offering attractive cash benefits to top-ranking sports teams which were prepared to visit South Africa. In this way, teams of cricketers from Britain, Sri Lanka, the West Indies and Australia all toured South Africa between 1982 and 1989. Rebel tours, however, became increasingly problematic on both financial and political grounds, and lost South Africa much of the goodwill which her attempts to integrate sport had already brought her. This was especially the case with cricket, for the S.A. Cricket Union's programme for the training of cricketers in black townships was threatened with closure when English tourists arrived in defiance of the boycott in 1989.

A new National Sports Congress set up in 1989 in an attempt to bridge the racial gap dividing sporting bodies took a firm initiative in the promotion of non-racial sport, by encouraging negotiations which could lead to amalgamation. Its efforts achieved an apparent breakthrough early in 1990, when the white South African Rugby Board agreed in principle to amalgamate with the non-racial South African Rugby Union.

Meanwhile the gradual strengthening of will on the Government's part to open beaches to all races began to have notable success in the 1989–90 summer season, even in Durban, where a number of seemingly contrived interracial incidents were satisfactorily contained.

20.9 APARTHEID AND CIVIL LIBERTY: THE PRESS, THE COURTS AND THE OPERATION OF THE LAW

Underlying the sometimes extraordinary performances of South African governments, especially after 1948, in those intrusions into the private lives of people which their racialist philosophy led them to indulge in, lay a deep fear that if they did not do these things South Africa might sink into a land of chaos rather than continue as the well-ordered utopia which many whites imagined it to be.

Apartheid, seen from this perspective, constituted the necessary rules of the game. The enforcement of those rules involved hard work by the police, and by the courts – especially the lower courts – in the administration of one of the most complex legal systems ever devised by man, and by

22 A symbolic representation, by Kenyon of the *Daily Dispatch*, of Nationalist inroads into the rule of law

the legislature in devising new ways of thwarting the evasions of the alienated.

South Africa was already finding herself, by the middle of the present century, caught in the vortex of a spiralling duel between crime (sometimes strangely defined) and law enforcement, from which it was proving impossible to break out. The Urban Areas Act, passed in order to improve the living standards and control the power of urban blacks, created the African statutory offender – in his hundreds of thousands, every year, queueing up for his two-minute trial in a Commissioner's court on the way to a short-term jail sentence. The serving of such a sentence soon taught him to despise both the law and its administrators. His lack of a means of political redress of necessity turned him into a radical. As a radical, he was as deliberately pursued and chastised – very much more harshly – under another set of laws which began with Riotous Assemblies and ended with Internal Security. Not a year passed between 1961 and 1990 without the holding of one or more major political trials under one or other of the tough security laws. The radical opponent of the regime might also be pursued by other procedures which may have been based on legislation, but came to depend on a minister's or a policeman's will, and on no legal safeguards whatsoever – listings, bannings, deportations, house arrests, periodic detentions with or without trial, detentions without any period attached, detentions without either family or the public knowing where he was, or why, and ultimately – in approximately fifty cases down to 1984 – detentions resulting in the death of the detainee through violence (whether self-inflicted or not it was often impossible to say on account of the absence of impartial witnesses able to testify to the events). The deaths of Steve Biko in 1977, and of Dr Neil Aggett in 1982, were two celebrated episodes in the growing Orwellian nightmare.

Almost incredibly, though, the authorities revealed neither a sufficient sense of shame to force an end to the brutality, nor enough of the swaggering intolerance needed to totally stifle embarrassing information (see Bell and Mackie; Foster, Davis and Sander; Riekert). The press, indeed, came under attack, especially the African press, as exemplified by the banning of *Post* and the detention of its editor, Percy Qoboza, in October 1977 at the time of the onslaught on Black Consciousness, and above all under the extremely harsh controls exercised by the Government during the emergency of 1985–90, which effectively prevented all the media from reporting events related to public violence. The Report of the Steyn Commission in February 1982 opened the way to covert government control over the management of news and ideas by its recommendation that a register of journalists should be compiled, and their enrolment supervised by a council of twelve appointed by the Minister of Internal Affairs. All that emerged in practice, however, was a Media Council, composed mainly of nominees of the National Press Union, on which the Government could lean but to which it could not dictate. Another official body, the Rabie Commission, looked into the operation of the security laws at the same time as the Steyn Commission, and reported in March 1982. Like the Steyn Commission, it justified tough measures by referring to that 'total onslaught' against South Africa which formed a prominent feature of the Government's appeal to the electorate. It made a number of proposals for alleviating the hardship of the security laws, such as the abolition of mandatory minimum five-year sentences in the event of conviction, and of the death penalty for conduct not involving acts of violence, and the removal of a presumption of guilt unless the accused could prove his innocence. But these recommendations, even where they were put into effect, provided no protection for individuals under the emergency regulations of 1985–7 [see pp. 439–41]. On the other hand, it did not explore in depth the regular allegations of police torture made by the defence in political trials, and vividly put together by Foster, or the medical literature on the effects of solitary confinement for long periods and its relationship to the reliability of testimony, or the effectiveness of visits to detainees by district surgeons, which was one of the main points at issue in relation to the death of Steve Biko – the event which provided the occasion for the appointment of the Commission in the first place. Nor did the Rabie Report attempt a comparison between South African security legislation and that of other countries with similar security problems, like Israel and Northern Ireland, where the controls to prevent abuse by the security forces were much more stringent (Mathews). Namibia's constitution of 1990, by contrast, showed how the lessons of foreign experience could be incorporated in a bill of rights [see p. 481].

If the Rabie Report put in a defence of the Republic's security legislation on the plea of reason of state, another commission which reported in March 1984 laid a very heavy hand on the judicial system as a whole. Other commissions had done this from time to time, notably the Lansdown Commission of 1947; but the Hoexter Commission stated in effect that conditions which were bad before 1950 had become infinitely worse since then. It reported the presence of 560,334 persons in South Africa's prisons in June 1983, of whom 267,995 were awaiting trial, which indicated a burden on the courts manifestly beyond their competence to handle, even taking into account the extremely cavalier fashion in which statutory offenders were of necessity handled, without any kind of defence in most cases. Equally serious was the overcrowding of prisons. The Minister of Justice stated in 1983 that South Africa's prisons held a daily average of 105,509 people against a carrying capacity of 74,378, with several prisons containing more than double the number they were authorised to hold. This in turn reflected on prison morale and the discipline of warders, which broke surface with some particularly unsavoury outbursts of fatal violence at the Barberton jail in September 1983, leading to the imposition of heavy sentences on senior prison staff. The Government proposed in 1980 to set up intermediate courts between the magisterial and the Supreme Courts to handle the extra load of judicial business; but this led to a strong protest among the professional lawyers against a further inflow of officials without sufficient legal training on to the bench – a reaction which was strongly endorsed by the Hoexter Commission, which recommended that the Commissioners' courts (whose main burden was the handling of Africans charged with documentary infringements) should be abolished (which they subsequently were), and their business brought within the purview of the ordinary magisterial system. It recommended further that the magistrates (on to whose shoulders most political cases fell in the first instance) should be removed from the public service and freed from all the political constraints which such status implied, given real independence of the State, and required to obtain Bachelor of Laws degrees.

The courts were strained almost to breaking point under a political system weighed down by inequities, and in which the apartheid structures both created new categories of crime and restricted types of criminality to particular groups, notably with regard to the freedom of movement [see pp. 530–3]. The Supreme Court's reputation for impartiality was an important influence for stability under these conditions. That reputation was indeed challenged. Suggestions of political appointments to the Bench, even to the Appellate Division, were made after 1950 and officially denied, that of Chief Justice L. C. Steyn in 1955 being the most controversial because he was promoted above senior judges of appeal. Allegations that the courts were unduly influenced by racial considerations in the sentencing of criminals, above all for crimes of violence such as murder, rape and theft, were not infrequently made, and earned one sharp critic, Dr Barend van Niekerk, a sentence for contempt of court. It would have been surprising if such allegations had not been made, and still more surprising if they had not had substance behind them, above all in a society where the high level of public violence and lawlessness was not unrelated to inter-racial tension arising out of the inequalities of the law. (Criminal statistics for the year ending June 1986 recorded 120,030 crimes of violence against persons, of which 9,665 were murders, 243,335 cases of robbery or house-breaking, 14,975 cases of rape, 59,436 cases of car theft and 22,132 cases of stock theft. Over the period 1983–7 the courts imposed an annual average of 199 death sentences, of which an average of 125 were carried out – *Race Relations Surveys, 1987–8*, p. 509, *1988–9*, p. 532). The image of the police, pressurised as they were to the limit by the nature of the laws which they had to enforce, suffered from an unduly high incidence of criminality within the force (Foster and Luyt). The image of the courts was not helped by the fact that, in many areas and in face of judicial representations, severe statutory penalties had been imposed on political crimes. The Appeal Court acquired a reputation in liberal circles of being sometimes well attuned to the protection of common law rights, and at others of being dominated by the executive (Cameron, Dugard, Forsyth). Certainly the rights of the subject reached a low point when an Appeal bench in a divided judgment in July 1987 reversed three decisions of the Natal Supreme Court granting protection to political detainees against emergency decrees issued by the State President which deprived them of access to lawyers, or of the right to be heard before their detentions were extended.

Whatever the strength of the case against individual judges, however, some of the country's legal custodians were nevertheless able to insist that right be done in the face of executive pressures, in illustration of which a number of key cases may be cited: a very sharp interdict on the use of third degree methods by the security police against a political detainee in *Gosschalk* v. *Rossouw* in March 1966; a ten-year prison sentence imposed on a security policeman for carelessly shooting and killing a detainee whom he was merely attempting to intimidate, in *The State* v. *van As* in 1984; the setting aside of a conviction by the Supreme Court of Bophutatswana under the South African Terrorism Act by the Appeal Court in May 1982, because the Act, though it extended in principle to the Territory, was repugnant to Bophutatswana's Declaration of Fundamental Rights, which placed the onus of proof on the State; a case in 1981, in which the Cape Supreme Court held on appeal that it was unreasonable to expect ordinary readers of books to be aware in every case of whether a book was on the banned list, for, were that so, parliamentarians, artists, theologians, poets, scientists, lawyers, everyone bar the readers of the merely blandly beauti-ful, would be too busy studying *Government Gazettes* to have time for their studies'. Another judgment in the Supreme Court of South West Africa in 1983 laid down that S.W.A.P.O. infiltrators captured while bearing arms were entitled to be tried as prisoners of war.

Justice came under severe stress where the linkage between common law crimes and political action led to the imposition of death sentences by the courts, notably during the late 1980s when a rash of political murders were committed on public officers and private individuals because they were thought to be opponents of 'the struggle'. 'Necklacing', by any standards a barbaric form of deterrence, and reminiscent of the East India Company's efforts to reduce crime by raising the unpleasantness of executions, accounted for between 300 and 400 people between January 1984 and June 1987 (*Race Relations Survey, 1986*, p. 515). The courts understandably reacted. A notable example was the trial of the 'Sharpeville six', who were sentenced to death, on grounds which fell clearly within judicial precedent, for the murder of Dlamini in 1984 [see p. 438], and the sentences were confirmed on appeal. These sentences led to an enormous international outcry, especially after the President had declined to use his prerogative of mercy. They were subsequently commuted to terms of imprisonment in a wider stay of execution granted by the President, which also included four white policemen who had been sentenced to death for the murder of prisoners in their charge. The sentencing of fourteen people to death at Upington in March 1989 for the murder of a policeman, on the ground that there were no extenuating circumstances, led to an appeal over the head of the trial judge to the Appellate Division, which on this occasion upheld the appeal. So widespread had the debate become by the end of 1989 that in February 1990 President de Klerk promised a judicial inquiry into the death penalty and ordered an immediate stay of all executions. (The death penalty was outlawed in Namibia when it obtained its independence in March).

20.10   APARTHEID IN POLITICS

The outstanding characteristic of the apartheid system where civil liberties were concerned was its acceptance of the inequality of people before the law. What was true of civil liberty could hardly fail to be true of political, even though apologists of the system veered round rather sharply during the Verwoerd era from the notion of *baasskap* (white supremacy) to the notion of 'separate freedoms'.

The Act of Union set an important precedent with its restriction of black and Coloured voters to the Cape alone, and the exclusion of blacks everywhere from Parliament. This process of political segregation was taken a step further by the Native Affairs Act of General Smuts, which extended the principles of the Glen Grey Act into wider regions by enabling the Governor-General to appoint local and general councils in the Reserves, from which emerged the United Transkeian Territories General Council in 1931. It also set up a nominated 'Native Conference' which was to meet annually in Pretoria and keep the Union Government informed of African aspirations through another statutory body created under the same Act, the Native Affairs Commission [see pp. 235, 251].

Political segregation received further elaboration through General Hertzog's legislation of 1936, removing Cape Africans from the common to a separate voters' roll, for the return of three white members to the House of Assembly, and three to the Provincial Council, and also making provision for the election of four whites to the Senate by African voters in all provinces. The conversion of Smuts's Native Conference into a predominantly elective Natives' Representative Council with advisory powers completed the 1936 political changes [see pp. 282–3].

The experiment was unhappy, save in so far as the whites elected to Parliament were able to give greater publicity to African needs than had been the case before, and – as Margaret Ballinger explained in her autobiography – extend some marginal benefits such as workmen's compensation and pension rights to Africans during the Second World War. But the Natives' Representative Council reached a deadlock with the Smuts Government in 1946, and was abolished by the Nationalists in 1951. The system of African representation in Parliament by whites was abolished by Verwoerd's Promotion of Bantu Self-Government Act of 1959 [see p. 353]. This law crowned the National Party's Bantu Authorities system which dated from 1951, by defining eight Bantu Homelands and offering, for the first time, the goal of independence. The Government's *bona fides* on this matter was long subject to doubt, above all as most of the Homelands, even if further consolidated, did not seem substantial enough for any meaningful kind of autonomy. But the Transkei took a further step in 1963, when it was given a dyarchical constitution and some of the decorative trappings of autonomy – a flag and an anthem. There was talk among the Homeland leaders of collective action and a refusal to ask for independence until all were ready; but in 1974 the Transkeian Government decided to go the whole way, having reached an agreement with the Republican Government over its boundaries and other issues in preparation for full nominal independence in October 1976. This represented a considerable change of policy from that first put forward by the Nationalists when they took power in 1948.

In the white area it remained Government policy at first to ensure continued white domination. Coloured people, left on the common roll in 1936 by the Hertzog Government, were removed after a bitter parliamentary and legal struggle between 1951 and 1957 [see pp. 329–32, 341–2]. Like the African population, they then enjoyed a brief period of separate representation by whites, until in 1969 their representation in Parliament was abolished, and they were given instead a Coloured Persons' Representative Council to which the Government nominated a minority of the members. This body in turn proved unworkable as soon as the Opposition party obtained a majority of seats in 1975 despite the stacking of nominee seats against it, and the Government found it necessary to remove the leader from office and instal one of his opponents in terms of powers provided in the constitution of the C.P.R.C. against just such an emergency. This third failure in twenty years to provide a satisfactory basis for the representation of Coloured people lay behind the Government's decision to give them a permanent minority status in the new parliamentary system devised in 1983 [see p. 434]; but whether even this was a satisfactory answer remained highly uncertain.

The Indian population had no representation in Parliament at all until, under the Indian Representation Act of 1946, the Smuts Government offered them token representation in both houses of Parliament by whites, and in the Natal Provincial Council by one of their own number; but this legislation was removed from the statute book as soon as the Malan Government took over in 1948, the Indian community having previously decided to ignore the concession. When the Government agreed for the first time to regard Indians as rightful South African citizens, it set up a nominated South African Indian Council in 1964. This body was enlarged from twenty-one to thirty members in 1974, and became half elective, the appointment of its chairman remaining in the discretion of the State President. After Vorster's unsuccessful bid to interest Coloured and Indian leaders in an Inter-Cabinet Council in 1975 [see p. 382], he and his successor turned their attention to meeting Indian demands for a more effective form of representation, and in 1978 the Council was made wholly elective; but opposition to the impotent role of the Council from the revived Natal Indian Congress, and from a new Reform Party which had attracted a majority of council members by 1979, reached a climax in 1981, by which time the Government had found it necessary to postpone elections four times in five years. Very low polls in the 1981 elections showed the Government that a repetition of their failure with the Coloured community was on the cards, and led it to follow Vorster's plan of providing for Indian representation in the central legislature.

At the political level, therefore, there were signs by the early 1980s of a willingness on the Government's part to turn the central legislature into an inter-racial body where the Coloured and Indian communities were concerned; but the exclusion of Africans from the institutions of central government remained total, and the decade ended with a flurry of constitutional improvisations by the Government of P. W. Botha, which failed to convince any of the black or white opposition parties that they contained the germ of a solution. With the accession to power of F. W. de Klerk in 1989, the National Party appeared for the first time to be willing to negotiate a new dispensation with the real black leadership, and both sides began, each with the problem of maverick extremists on its flank, to discuss the ground rules for negotiations.

20.11 THE FORCE AND THE MASS, THE OSTRICH AND THE CRAB

South Africa's isolation arose from social policies which came to offend not only black South Africans but the independent African states, the communist world, and the liberal democratic states of the West. The Government's commitment to these internationally unpopular policies – a commitment endorsed by the plebiscite of nine general elections after 1948 – has elicited various kinds of explanation. These tend to fall into two main groups: explanations which see racism as the chief determinant of white South African attitudes, and explanations which attribute them to a clash of class interests.

Writers who have seen government action as inspired by racial assumptions, the holders of what has come to be referred to as the 'conventional wisdom', included both proponents and critics of racialism. Racial segregationists like Gert Cronje asserted that individual race groups had the moral right to ensure the survival of their separate (divinely ordained) identities, and that separation was the only logical solvent to racial friction. Liberal segregationists like Alfred Hoernlé tended to deny the validity of the first of these propositions, but to accept the second. Both kinds of theorist were not so much innovators as elaborators of a segregationist line of thought which flourished only from the early twentieth century, and enjoyed the support of most of the articulate commentators on South African affairs from the Lagden Commission of 1903–5 onwards, whether their postures were white supremacist or liberal [see pp. 229, 542].

The segregationist position was enthusiastically adopted by the Purified Nationalists in the 1930s. Leading liberal thinkers moved away from segregationist ideas at the same time, but saw no reason to abandon the frame of reference within which the public debate had been placed. Whether segregation was good or bad, they saw racism as the great divisive factor in South African life, the phenomenon which needed to be eliminated above all others if the right public policies were to be prescribed. Hence the significance of works like I. D. MacCrone's *Race Attitudes in South Africa*, which looked for reasons for the evolution of race prejudice and claimed to find them on the Cape frontier in the eighteenth century. Liberals who looked for the origins of racist thinking were seeking to explain a phenomenon of which they disapproved, and it was no accident that they should have been doing this in the decade when Hitler's Germany was in the making. But their grounds of objection to segregation varied. Some saw it simply as economic moonshine, and therefore not viable. Others saw it as politically immoral (whether viable or not) and therefore insufferable. Therefore both the main traditional schools of liberal thinker – the devotees of free enterprise and the guardians of human rights – found reasons for attacking the system.

As Yudelman has stressed, the economic liberals who believed that the pull of the market would crush ideological racism and its supporting structure of pass laws and colour bars all wrote during the period after 1933, which was one of relatively uninterrupted growth for the South African economy. Economic historians in the 1930s, notably William Macmillan and H. M. Robertson, had shown that the degree of integration at the economic level was already so far advanced that racial separation was no longer a serious possibility. Such an argument appeared to be even stronger after the Second World War, as black urbanisation and the movement by blacks into the white economy accelerated, and was watched with approval by the Smuts Government's Social and Economic Planning Council. Indeed, economic pressure was breaking down the barriers of segregation to such an extent that the devotees of apartheid began to insist on a tougher policy of job reservation to keep lucrative urban employment in white hands [see pp. 306–9].

When W. W. Rostow, the American economist, published his *Stages of Economic Growth* in 1953, urging that periods of disequilibrium and labour exploitation necessarily occurred where an industrial society reached 'take-off', and before it had achieved the stage of mass consumption, some South African economists – notably D. Hobart Houghton and M. C. O'Dowd – took his model very seriously. O'Dowd considered in 1964 that large-scale exploitation of labour was probably unavoidable at first, but that the stage of mass consumption would arrive well before the end of the twentieth century. He still adhered to this view in 1974, when he contributed to Schlemmer and Webster's anthology of 1977. Another clear expression of confidence in the ability of the market economy to break apartheid was Ralph Horwitz's *Political Economy of South Africa* (1967), which concluded with the assertion that 'the South African economy is inescapably integrated in the pursuit of productivity. Economic rationality urges the polity forward beyond its ideology.'

The Rostow thesis carried an element of economic determinism, however much the South African economists who made use of it might resist those implications. But not all political economists were prepared to predict the victory of the market over racial ideology as a matter of course. Herbert Blumer's chapter in Guy Hunter's *Industrialization and Race Relations* was important for this reason. Blumer, drawing particularly on the work of the South African economist, Sheila van der Horst, concluded that on the evidence available the demands of industry would not necessarily destroy apartheid, but that industry would rather adapt itself to the political order and content itself with less than optimal profit margins for the sake of preserving industrial peace and maintaining the security of the white ruling group. 'Industry can and does tolerate a wide latitude of inefficient operation and still achieve acceptable production and profit,' he wrote, in spite of very good *a priori* reasons for thinking that industrialisation must 'break through and break up the racial scheme'. He saw industrialisation as neutral in a situation of racial confrontation, 'an incitant to change, without providing the definition of how change is to be met'.

Faith in the power of the market to destroy apartheid thus gave confidence to some critics of segregation but not to all. There were others who judged the South African scene in terms of liberal political values which had evolved in the experience of the Western democracies. Accepting racist aberrations as lying at the root of the disease, they prescribed political reform in the expectation (or perhaps no more than the hope) that the introduction of political liberty and an ending of injustice would sufficiently defuse the situation for peaceful change to be made possible. Their stand has to be seen against a particular background; the steady abandonment of liberal political principles over the years, with a tendency for the already well-advanced process to accelerate after 1948, by means of inroads made into the rule of law over a wide area, the narrowing of the political rights of all black groups, and of the civil liberties of all groups, both black and white, unequal treatment in nearly all situations where separate amenities were laid down for the different races, and the continuing insistence on unequal access to economic opportunity. It was, above all, the proven inequity of the system of segregation that drove leading liberals like Edgar Brookes, W. M. Macmillan, Leo Marquard, Margaret Hodgson (later

Year	Seats	Liberal Party	Progressive Party / Progressive Federal Party / Democratic Party	Federal Party	United Party / New Republic Party	South African Party	National Party	'Herstigte' National Party / Konserwatiewe Party
1953	159	2* ; 1* [unseated]		5	57		**94**	2*
1958	159			0	53		**103**	1*
1961			1		49		**105**	
1966	166		1		39		**126**	4‡
1970	166		1		47		**118**	0
1974	171		7	0	41		**123**	0
1977	165**		17	0	10	3	**134**	0 (1)ˣ
1981			26		8		**131**	
1987			19(+1§)		1		**123** (+10§)	22
1989			33(+1§)				**94**(+9§)	39(+2§)

[Afrikaner Party absorbed by Nationalists]

[S.A.P. absorbed in UNP]

* Elected under the Representation of Natives Act, 1936.
† Mainly Natal Unionists not yet amalgamated with the Unionist Party.
‡ Elected under the Separate Representation of Voters' Act, 1955.
** No elections held in South West Africa.
§ Elected by electoral college/nominated by the State President (all National Party) under the Constitution Act of 1983.
ˣ by-election victory only.
Figures in **bold** indicate that the party participated in the Government.

Bibliographical Notes

The references given in these pages represent a compromise between a conventional bibliography and conventional footnotes. Each section of the references corresponds to the similarly numbered heading in the appropriate chapter. In the case of books, the date given is generally that of the most recent edition, modern reprints of older works generally being preferred to earlier editions. Figures in square brackets refer to a note giving more detail.

The following abbreviations are used in the notes:

AA	*African Affairs*
ACR	*African Contemporary Record*
AHR	*American Historical Review*
AJ	*Acta Juridica*
AJPA	*American Journal of Physical Anthropology*
ANM	*Annals of the Natal Museum*
AP	*African Perspective*
AR	*Africa Report*
AS	*African Studies*
ASR	*African Studies Review*
AYB	*Archives Year Book for South African History*
Benbo	*Buro vir Ekonomiese Navorsing in Sake Bantoe Ontwikkeling*
BS	*Bantu Studies*
BSALR	*Butterworth's South African Law Review*
CAHA	*Central African Historical Association*
CHA	*Cambridge History of Africa*
CHBE	*Cambridge History of the British Empire*
CHR	*Canadian Historical Review*
CSSH	*Comparative Studies in Society and History*
DJ	*De Jure*
DSAB	*Dictionary of South African Bibliography*
E & S	*Economy and Society*
Ec	*Economist*
EcHR	*Economic History Review*
EcJ	*Economic Journal*
EHR	*English Historical Review*
Eth. Pub.	*Ethnological Publications* (Department of Native Affairs)
FAK	*Federasie van Afrikaanse Kultuurvereniginge*
F and TR	*Finance and Trade Review*
FM	*Financial Mail*
H-A	*Hertzog-Annale of the Akademie vir Wetenstep en Kuns*
Hist.	*Historia*
H/A	*History in Africa*

HS	*Historiese Studies*
HSRC	*Human Sciences Research Council*
HT	*History Today*
HW	*History Workshop*
IA	*International Affairs*
IAB	*International Affairs Bulletin of the South African Institute of International Affairs*
ICS	*Institute of Commonwealth Studies Collected Seminar Papers, University of London*
IDASA	*Institute for a Democratic Alternative in South Africa*
IJAHS	*International Journal of African Historical Studies*
ISER	*Institute for Social and Economic Research, Rhodes University*
ISQ	*International Studies Quarterly*
JAAS	*Journal of Asian and African Studies*
JAH	*Journal of African History*
JAS	*Journal of African Studies*
JBS	*Journal of British Studies*
JCAS	*Journal of Contemporary African Studies*
JCCP	*Journal of Commonwealth and Comparative Politics*
JCPS	*Journal of Commonwealth Political Studies*
JDS	*Journal of Development Studies*
JHG	*Journal of Historical Geography*
JICH	*Journal of Imperial and Commonwealth History*
JMAS	*Journal of Modern African Studies*
JNZH	*Journal of Natal and Zululand History*
JP	*Journal of Politics*
JRac.A	*Journal of Racial Affairs*
JRel.A	*Journal of Religion in Africa*
JSAA	*Journal of South African Affairs*
JSAS	*Journal of Southern African Studies*
JThSA	*Journal of Theology for Southern Africa*
KKRS	*Keiskammahoek Rural Survey*
NRS	*Natal Regional Survey*
OHSA	*Oxford History of South Africa*
Opt.	*Optima*
P and P	*Past and Present*
PC	*Problems of Communism*
Pol.	*Politikon*
PSQ	*Political Science Quarterly*
QBSAL	*Quarterly Bulletin of the South African Library*
RAPE	*Review of African Political Economy*
RH	*Rhodesian History*
RP	*Republic [of South Africa] Parliament*
RR	*Race Relations*
RSA 2000	*RSA 2000: Dialogue with the Future, (Human Sciences Research Council, Pretoria)*
SABRA	*South African Bureau of Racial Affairs*
SACC	*South African Council of Churches*
SAGJ	*South African Geographical Journal*
SAHJ	*South African Historical Journal*
SAInt.	*South Africa International*
SAIRR	*South African Institute of Race Relations*
SAJE	*South African Journal of Economics*

SAJHR   *South African Journal of Human Rights*
SALB   *South African Labour Bulletin*
SALDRU   *South African Labour and Development Research Unit University*
             of Cape Town
SALJ   *South African Law Journal*
Sci. Am.   *Scientific American*
SD   *Social Dynamics*
SOAS   *School of Oriental and African Studies, University of London*
SPROCAS   *Study Project on Christianity in Apartheid Society*
SWJA   *South Western Journal of Anthropology*
T-AJH   *Trans-African Journal of History*
THRHR   *Tydskrif vir Hedendagse Romeinse Hollandse Reg*
TRSSA   *Transactions of the Royal Society of South Africa*
UG   *Union Government*
UNISA   *University of South Africa*
VRS   *Van Riebeeck Society*

CHAPTER 1

1.1 The earliest South Africans

Clark, J. D., *The Pre-History of Southern Africa* (1959).
Hall, M., *The Changing Past: Farmers, Kings and Traders in Southern Africa, 200–1860* (1987).
Inskeep, R. R., *The Peopling of Southern Africa* (1978).
Lewis-Williams, J. D., *Believing and Seeing: Symbolic Meanings in Southern San Rock Paintings* (1981), and *The Rock Art of Southern Africa* (1985); in Cameron, T. and Spies, S. B. (eds), *An Illustrated History of South Africa* (1986); and, with Dowson, T., *Images of Power: Understanding Bushman Rock Art* (1989).
Tobias, P. V., *Hominid Evolution – Past, Present and Future* (1985), and in Cameron and Spies (1986) 11–27.

1.2 The Khoisan peoples

Cooke, C. K., 'Evidence of Human Migrations from the Rock Art of Rhodesia', *Africa XXXV* (1965) 263–85.
Ehret, C., 'Cattle-keeping and Milking in Eastern and Southern African History: The Linguistic Evidence', *JAH* (1967) 1–17.
Elphick, R. H., *Khoikhoi and the Founding of White South Africa* (1985), and with Malherbe, V. C., in Elphick and Giliomee, H. (eds) *The Shaping of South African Society* (1989) 3–65.
Harinck, G., 'Interactions between Xhosa and Khoi, 1620–1750', in Thompson, L. M. (ed.) *African Societies in Southern Africa* (1969) 145–69.
Lewis-Williams [n. 1.1].
Marks, S., 'Khoisan Resistance to the Dutch in the 17th and 18th Centuries', *JAH* 13 (1972) 55–80.
Robertshaw, P. T., 'The Origins of Pastoralism in the Cape', *SAHJ* 10 (1978) 117–33.
Schapera, I., *The Khoisan Peoples of South Africa* (1930).
Thomas, E. M., *The Harmless People* (1959).
Westphal, E. O. J., 'The Linguistic Pre-History of South Africa: Bush, Kwadi, Hottentot and Bantu Linguistic Relationships', *Africa* 33, 3 (1963) 237–65.
Wilcox, A. R., *The Rock Art of South Africa* (1963).

Wilson, M., in *OHSA* I (1969) 40–74.
Wright, J. B., *Bushman Raiders of the Drakensberg* (1971).

1.3 The emergence of Bantu-speaking chiefdoms

Beach, D. N., *The Shona and Zimbabwe, 900–1850* (1980).
Evers, T. M. and Vogel, J. C., 'Radiocarbon Dates for Iron Age Sites at Lyden-burg and White River, Eastern Transvaal', *SAJS* 76, 5 (1980) 230–1.
Garlake, P. S., *Great Zimbabwe* (1973).
Hall [n. 1.1].
Hammond-Tooke, W. D. (ed.) *The Bantu-Speaking Peoples of Southern Africa* (1974).
Huffman, T. N. 'African Origins' *SAJS* 75, 5 (1979) 233–7.
Legassick, M., 'The Sotho-Tswana Peoples before 1800', in Thompson (below) 86–125.
Maggs, T. *Iron Age Communities of the Southern Highveld* (1976), and 'The Iron Age Sequence South of the Vaal and Pongola Rivers: Some Historical Implications', *JAH* 21, 1 (1980) 1–15, and in Cameron and Spies [n. 1.1] 37–43.
Marks, S., 'The Traditions of the Natal Nguni: A Second Look at the Work of A. T. Bryant', in Thompson [below] 86–144.
Mason, R., *Pre-History of the Transvaal: A Record of Human Activity* (n.d.).
Oliver, R. and Fagan, B. M., *Africa in the Iron Age, c. 500 BC to AD 1400* (1975).
Phillipson, D. W., *The Later Pre-History of Eastern and Southern Africa (1977)*, and *African Archaeology* (1985).
Schofield, J., *Primitive Pottery* (1948).
Thompson, L. M. (ed.) *African Societies in Southern Africa* (1969).
Van Warmelo, N. J., *A Preliminary Survey of Bantu Tribes in South Africa* (1935), and in Hammond-Tooke [above] 56–84.
Wilson, M., 'The Early History of the Transkei and Ciskei', *African Studies* 18, 4 (1959) 167–79, and in *OHSA* I, 75–186.
Wright, J. B., 'Politics, Ideology and the Invention of the Nguni', in Lodge, T. (ed.) *Ideology and Resistance in Settler Societies* (1986).

1.4 The upheavals of the early nineteenth century

Bonner, P. L., *Kings, Commoners and Concessionaires: The Evolution and Dissolution of the 19th Century Swazi State* (1982).
Cobbing, J. R. D., 'The Mfecane as Alibi: Thoughts on Dithakong and Mbolompo', *JAH* 29 (1988) 487–519.
Daniel, J. B. McI, 'A Geographical Study of Pre-Shakan Zululand', *SAGJ* 55, 1 (1973) 23–31.
Delius, P. N., *The Land Belongs to Us* (1983).
Giliomee [n. 2.5].
Gluckman, M., 'The Rise of the Zulu Empire', *Sci. Am.* CCII, 4 (1960) 157–67, and 'The Kingdom of the Zulu in South Africa' in Fortes, M. and Evans-Pritchard, E. E., *African Political* Systems (1940) 25–55; and 'The Individual in a Social Framework: The Rise of King Shaka of Zululand', *JAS* 1, 2 (1974) 113–44.
Guy, J. J., 'Ecological Factors in the Rise of Shaka and the Zulu Kingdom', in Marks and Atmore (below) 102–19.
Hall [n. 1.1].
Hamilton, C. A., 'An Appetite for the Past: The Re-Creation of Shaka and the Crisis in Popular Historical Consciousness', *SAHJ* 22 (1990) 141–57.
Harries, P., 'Slavery, Social Incorporation and Surplus Extraction: The Nature of Free and Unfree Labour in South-East Africa', *JAH* 22 (1981) 309–30.

Hedges, D. W., *Trade and Politics in Southern Mozambique in the Eighteenth and Nineteenth Centuries* (unpublished thesis, University of London, 1978).

How, M., 'An Alibi for MmaNthatisi', *AS* 13, 2 (1954) 65–76.

Jackson-Haight, M. V., *European Powers and South-East Africa* (1967)

Legassick, M., 'The Northern Frontier to c. 1840: The Rise and Decline of the Griqua People', in Elphick, R. H. and Giliomee, H., *The Shaping of South African Society* (2nd edn 1989) 358–420.

Lye, W. F., 'The Difaqane: The Mfecane in the South Sotho Area', *JAH* 8, 1 (1967) 103–31, and 'The Ndebele Kingdom South of the Limpopo River', *JAH* 10, 1 (1969) 87–109.

Marks, S., and Atmore, A. (eds) *Economy and Society in Pre-Industrial South Africa* (1980).

Newitt, M. D. D., 'Drought in Mozambique, 1823–31', *JSAS* 15, 1 (1988) 15–35.

Newton-King, S., 'The Labour Market in the Cape Colony, 1807–28', in Marks, S. and Atmore, A. (above) 171–207.

Omer-Cooper, J., *The Zulu Aftermath* (1966).

Rasmussen, R. K., *Migrant Kingdom: Mzilikazi's Ndebele in South Africa* (1978).

Sanders, P. B., 'Sekonyela and Moshweshwe: Failure and Success in the Aftermath of the Difaqane', *JAH* 10, 3 (1969) 439–55; and [n. 7.4].

Smith, A., in Thompson [n. 1.3] 171–89.

Thompson, G., *Travels and Adventures in Southern Africa* (VRS, 1967, 1968).

Van der Merwe [n. 2.5].

Webb, C. de B., and Wright, J. B. (eds) *The James Stuart Archive Relating to the History of Zululand and Neighbouring Peoples* (4 vols, 1976–86).

Wright, J. B. and Hamilton, C. A. 'The Phongolo-Mzimkhulu Region in the Late Eighteenth and Early Nineteenth Centuries' in Duminy and Guest [n. 6.4] 49–82.

CHAPTER 2

2.1 The early years of European settlement

(a) Recent works on the Portuguese exploration and early settlement of southern Africa include:

Axelson, E., *The Portuguese in South-East Africa 1600–1700* (1960).

Boxer, C. R., *The Portuguese Seaborne Empire* (1969).

Raven-Hart, R., *Before Van Riebeeck* (1967).

Smith, M. v. W., *Shades of Adamastor* (1988).

(b) For the Dutch Company period, see especially:

Boeseken, A. J., in C. F. J. Muller (ed.) *500 Years: A History of South Africa* (1981 edn) 18–79.

Boxer, C. R., *The Dutch Seaborne Empire* (1965).

Elphick, R. H., and Giliomee, H., *The Shaping of South African Society* (2nd edn 1989).

Katzen M. F., in *OHSA*, I (1969) 187–232.

Moodie, D., *The Record* (1960 edn).

Raven-Hart, R., *The Cape of Good Hope, 1652–1702* (1971).

Spilhaus, M. W., *South Africa in the Making, 1652–1806* (1966).

Thom, H. B. (ed.) *The Journal of Jan van Riebeeck, 1651–62* (1952–8).

(c) On the Huguenots and other immigrants, see:

Botha, C. G., *The French Refugees at the Cape* (1919).

Boucher, M., *French-speakers at the Cape: The European Background* (1981).
De Villiers, C. C., *Geslacht-Register der Oude Kaapsche Familien* (1893–4).
Guelke, L., in Elphick, R. H. and Giliomee, H., [above] 66–108.
Guelke, L. and Shell, R., 'An Early Colonial Landed Gentry: Land and Wealth in the Cape Colony, 1682–1731', *JHG*, 9, 3 (1983) 265–86.
Heese, J. A., *Die Herkoms van die Afrikaner, 1657–1867* (1971).
Hoge, J., *Personalia of the Germans at the Cape, 1652–1806* (*AYB* 1946) and *Bydraes tot die Genealogie van ons Afrikaanse Families (1958).*
Nathan, M., *The Huguenots in South Africa (1939).*
Ross, R., 'The Rise of the Cape Gentry', *JSAS*, 9.2 (1983) 193–217.

2.2 The Khoikhoi and the Dutch

Du Bruyn, J., 'The Oorlams Afrikaners: From Dependence to Dominance, c. 1760–1823' (unpublished typescript, *UNISA*, 1981).
Elphick [n. 1.2.].
Elphick and Malherbe in Elphick and Giliomee [n. 2.1b] 3–65.
Inskeep [n. 1.1].
Leibbrandt, H. C. V., *Précis of the Archives of the Cape of Good Hope: Journal 1651–74, 1676, 1699–1732* (1896–1901).
Marks, [n. 1.2].
Moodie, D. [n. 2.1].

2.3 Cape slavery

Armstrong, J. C., Worden, N., Elphick, R. H. and Shell, R. in Elphick and Giliomee [n. 2.1].
Boeseken, A., *Slaves and Free Blacks at the Cape, 1658–1700* (1977).
Bradlow, F. R. and Cairns, M., *The Early Cape Muslims* (1978).
De Kock, V., *Those in Bondage* (1963).
Edwards, I. E., *Towards Emancipation: A Study in South African Slavery* (1942).
Fredrickson [n. 20.1].
Hattingh, J. L., 'A. J. Boeseken se "Addendum" van Kaapse Slawe-Verkooptransaksies: Foute en Regstellings', in *Kronos* 9 (1984) 3–21.
Marais, J. S., *The Cape Coloured People* (1937).
Reports of De Chavonnes and van Imhoff (*VRS*, I, 1918).
Ross, R., *Cape of Torments: Slavery and Resistance in South Africa* (1983).
Van Zyl, D. J., 'Die Slaaf in die Ekonomiese Lewe van die Westelike Distrikte van die Kaap Kolonie, 1795–1834', *SAHJ*, 10 (1978) 3–25.
Worden, N., *Slavery in Dutch South Africa* (1985).

2.4 The V.O.C. and the Cape station

Katzen, M. and Davenport, T. R. H., in *OHSA* I (1969) 187–232 and 272–333.
Schutte, G., in Elphick and Giliomee, [n. 2.1.] 283–323.
Du Toit, A. and Giliomee, H., *Afrikaner Political Thought* (1983).
Ross, R., 'The rule of law at the Cape of Good Hope in the 18th century', *JICH*, 9, 1 (1980) 5–16, and in Elphick and Giliomee [n. 2.1b].

2.5 The Emergence of the trekboer

Giliomee, H. and Ross, R., in Lamar, H. and Thompson, L. M. (eds) *The Frontier in History: North America and South Africa Compared* (1981) 76–119, 209–33.
Guelke in Elphick and Giliomee [n. 2.1b] 66–108.
Legassick, M., 'The Frontier Tradition in South African Historiography', in

Marks, S. and Atmore, A., *Economy and Society in Pre-industrial South Africa* (1980) 44–79.
Legassick, M. and Giliomee, H., in Elphick and Giliomee [n. 2.1] 358–420.
MacCrone, I. D., *Race Attitudes in South Africa* (1937).
Mandelbrote, H. J., (ed.) *O. F. Mentzel's Description of the Cape of Good Hope VRS* 4, 6, 25, (1921–44).
Neumark, S. D., *The South African Frontier* (1957).
Robertson, H. M., 'Some doubts concerning early land tenure at the Cape', *SAJE*, 3, 2 (1935) 158–72, and '150 years of economic contact between black and white', *SAJE* 2, 4 (1934) 403–25, and 3, 1 (1935) 3–25.
Ross, R. [n. 19.1].
Van der Merwe, P. J., *Die Trekboer in die Geskiedenis van die Kaapkolonie* (1938), and *Die Noordwaarstse Beweging van die Boere voor die Groot Trek, 1772–1842* (1937).
Walker, E. A., *The Frontier Tradition in South Africa* (1930).

2.6 Conflict between the trekboers and the Khoisan, who either accept incorporation or retreat

See works listed in n. 2.2 and Lichtenstein [n. 3.1] and Marais [n. 2.3].

2.7 The creation of a stratified society

Elphick and Giliomee [n. 2.1] 359–90; Guelke and Shell [n. 2.1.]; Ross [n. 2.1].

CHAPTER 3

3.1 The eighteenth century revolution and Cape Colonial 'Calvinism'

(a) For Cape political developments in the V.O.C. period, see:

Badenhorst, J. J., 'H. C. D. Maynier', in *DSAB* II (1972) 456–9.
Beyers, L. C., *Die Kaapse Patriotte, 1779–95* (1967 edn).
Davenport, T. R. H., in *OHSA*, I (1969) 272–80, 298–301.
De Kock, W. J., '*Etienne Barbier*' in *DSAB*, I (1968) 53.
Du Toit and Giliomee [n. 2.4].
Freund, W., in Elphick and Giliomee [n. 2.1b] 324–57.
Giliomee, H., 'Democracy and the Frontier', *SAHJ* 6 (1974) 30–51.
Heese, J. A., *Slagtersnek en sy Mense* (1973).
Idenburg, P. J., *The Cape of Good Hope at the Turn of the Eighteenth Century* (1963).
Lichtenstein, H., *Travels in South Africa* (*VRS* 10, 11, 1928–30).
MacCrone [n. 2.5].
Marais, J. S., *Maynier and the First Boer Republic* (1944).
Muller, C. F. J., *J. F. Kirsten oor die Toestand van die Kaapkolonie in 1795* (1960).
Reyburn, H. A., 'Studies in Cape Frontier History', *The Critic*, October 1934–June 1935.
Ross, R., in Elphick and Giliomee [n. 2.1] 243–80.
Schutte, G. [n. 2.4].
Smuts, J. (ed.) *The Diary of Adam Tas* (*VRS*, 2nd series, I, 1970).
Van der Merwe, P. J., *Die Kafferoorlog van 1793* (1940).

(b) For the debate over Cape Calvinism see:

Adam, H. and Giliomee, H., *The Rise and Crisis of Afrikaner Power* (1979) 16–60.

Booyens, B., *Kerk en Staat, 1795–1843* (*AYB*, 1965).
De Klerk, W. A., *The Puritans in Africa* (1975).
Du Toit and Giliomee [n. 2.4].
Du Toit, A., 'No Chosen People: The Myth of the Calvinist Origins of Afrikaner Nationalism and Racial Ideology', *AHR*, 88, 4 (1983) 920–52, and [n. 6.2.] and [n. 9.7].
Elphick and Giliomee [n. 2.1] 521–58.
Hexham, [n. 9.7] 359–65.
Moodie, [n. 9.7].
Spoelstra, B., *Die Doppers in Suid-Afrika* (1963).

3.2 The first British occupation, 1795

Arkin, M., *John Company at the Cape: a History of the Agency under Pringle, 1794–1815* (*AYB* 1960).
Freund, [n. 3.1].
Giliomee, H., *Die Kaap tydens die Eerste Britse Bewind, 1795–1803* (1975).
Harlow, V. T., in *CHBE*, VIII (1963 edn) 169–98.
Marais, [n. 3.1].
Theal, G. M., *Records of the Cape Colony, 1795–1835* (1897–1905).

3.3 Batavian rule, 1803–6

See works by Freund, Lichtenstein and Theal [nn. 3.1 and 3.2]; and:
Gie, S. F. N. (ed.) *The Memorandum of Commissary de Mist* (*VRS*, 3, 1920).
Van der Merwe, J. P., *Die Kaap onder die Bataafse Republiek, 1803–6* (1926).

3.4 The return of the British, 1806

Arkin [n. 3.2].
Davenport, [n. 3.1a].
Donaldson, M., *The Council of Advice at the Cape of Good Hope, 1825–34* (unpublished thesis, Rhodes University, 1974).
Duly [n. 19.1].
Freund, W. M., in Elphick and Giliomee [n. 2. 1b].
Harlow, V. T. and Macmillan, W. M., in *CHBE* VIII (1963) 169–238, 249–65.
Hunt, K. S., *Sir Lowry Cole* (1974).
Le Cordeur, B. A., *The Politics of Eastern Cape Separatism, 1820–54* (1981).
Leibbrandt, H. C. V., *The Rebellion of 1815 Generally Known as Slachters Nek* (1902).
Millar, A. K., *Plantagenet in South Africa: Lord Charles Somerset* (1965).
Robinson, A. M. L., *None Daring to Make Us Afraid* (1962).
Sturgis, J., *Anglicisation at the Cape in the Early Nineteenth Century', JICH*, XI, 1 (1982) 5–32.
Theal, [n. 3.2].

3.5 The Albany settlement, 1820, and its impact

For the 1820 settlers and their impact on the Cape in the early nineteenth century, see works by Le Cordeur and Robinson [n. 3.4] and:
Butler, F. G. (ed.) *The 1820 Settlers: An Illustrated Commentary* (1974).
Cory, Sir G., *The Rise of South Africa* (1965 reprint).
Edwards, I. E., *The 1820 Settlers in South Africa* (1934).
Hockly, H. E., *The Story of the British Settlers of 1820 in South Africa (1957)*.
Immelman [n. 19.2].

Lewcock, R., *Early Nineteenth Century Architecture in South Africa* (1963).
Morse Jones, E., *The Roll of the British Settlers in South Africa* (1971).
Nash, M. D., *Bailie's Party of 1820 Settlers* (1982).
Peires, J. B., in Elphick and Giliomee [n. 2.1b] 472–520.

3.6 The emancipation of the slaves and the Cape coloured people

Cloete [n. 5.2].
Duly, L. C., 'A revisit with . . . Ordinance 50 of 1828', in Kooy, M. (ed.) *Studies in Economics and Economic History* (1972).
Du Toit [n. 6.2].
Edwards, [n. 2.3].
Gailey, H. A., 'John Philip's Role in Hottentot Emancipation', *JAH*, III, 3 (1962) 419–33.
Galbraith, [n. 7.3].
Kirk, T., 'The Kat River Settlement', *JAH*, XIV, 3 (1973) 411–28.
Macmillan, W. M., *The Cape Colour Question* (1927).
Marais [n. 2.3].
Marincowitz, J., *Rural Production and Labour in the Western Cape, 1838–88, with Special Reference to the Wheat-growing Districts* (unpublished thesis, London University, 1985).
Mellor, G. R., *British Imperial Trusteeship* (1951).
Newton-King, S., 'The Labour Market in the Cape Colony, 1807–28', in Marks, S. and Atmore, A., *Economy and Society in Pre-Industrial South Africa* (1980).
Rayner, M., *Wine and Slaves: The Failure of an Export Economy and the Ending of Slavery in the Cape Colony, South Africa* (unpublished thesis, Duke University, 1986).
Reyburn, [n. 3.1a].
Ross, A., *John Philip, 1775–1851* (1986).
See also works on the missionary factor listed in n. 7.10.

3.7 The start of the Great Trek

Beyers, C., *Die Groot Trek met Betrekking tot ons Nasiegroei* (*AYB*, 1941).
Cloete [n. 5.2.].
Dreyer, A., *Die Kaapse Kerk en die Groot Trek* (1929).
Du Toit and Giliomee [n. 2.4].
Duvenage, G. D. J., 'Hoeveel Kaapse Koloniste het Voortrekkers geword?', *Hist.*, XXI, 1 (1976) 2–14.
Fredrickson [n. 20.1].
Galbraith [n. 7.3].
Giliomee, H., 'Processes in the Development of the Southern African Frontier', in Lamar and Thompson [n. 2.5] 76–119.
Hunt [n. 3.4].
Le Cordeur [n. 3.4].
Liebenberg, B. J., 'Bloedrivier en Gods hand', *SAHJ* (1980) 1–12.
Macmillan [n. 3.6].
Martin, G., 'Two Cheers for Lord Glenelg', *JICH*, 7, 2 (1979).
Muller, C. F. J., *Die Britse Owerheid en die Groot Trek* (1948) and *Die Oorsprong van die Groot Trek* (1974).
Nathan, M., *The Voortrekkers of South Africa* (1937).
Peires, J. B. [n. 3.5].
Preller, G. S., *Voortrekkermense* (4 vols. 1918–25).
Pretorius, H. (ed.) *Voortrekker Argiefstukke 1829–49* (1937).
Reyburn [n. 3.1].

Scholtz, J. du P., *Die Afrikaner en sy Taal 1806–75* (1964).
Theal, G. M., *History of South Africa since 1795* (1908–10).
Thom, H. B., *Die Lewe van Gert Maritz* (1965).
Thompson, L. M., in *OHSA*, I (1969) 405–24.
Van Jaarsveld, F. A., 'A Historical Mirror of Blood River', in König, A. and Keane, H. (eds) *The Meaning of History* (UNISA, 1980).
Walker, E. A., *The Great Trek* (1948).

CHAPTER 4

4.1 Tswana chiefdoms of the Kalahari borderland

Du Bruyn, J., 'Die Tlhaping en die eerste sendelinge', *SAHJ*, 14 (1982) 8–34, and *Die Tlhaping, 1700–1871: Die Opkoms en Verbrokkeling van 'n Suid Tswanastam* (unpublished thesis, UNISA).
Matthews, Z. K., 'The Tshidi-Rolong: A Short History', *Fort Hare Papers* 1, 1 (1945) 9–28.
Pauw, B. A., 'Some Changes in the Social Structure of the Tlhaping', *AS* 19, 2 (1960) 49–76.
Schapera, I., *Handbook of Tswana Law and Custom* (1955).
Shillington [n. 7.8].
Sillery, A., *Founding a Protectorate: A History of Bechuanaland, 1855–95* (1965) and *Sechele: The Story of an African Chief* (1954).

4.2 Chiefdoms of the Eastern Transvaal: Pedi, Lovedu, Venda and Ndzundza

Delius [n. 1.4].
Hunt, D. R., 'An Account of the Bapedi', *BS* (1931) 275–326.
Krige, E. J., 'The Place of the Northern Transvaal Sotho in the Southern Bantu Complex', *Africa*, XI, 3 (1938) 265–93.
Krige, E. J. and J. D., *The Realm of the Rain Queen* [Lovedu] (1943), and 'The Lovedu of the Transvaal' in Forde, D. (ed.) *African Worlds* (1954).
Krige, J. D., 'Traditional Origins and Tribal Relations in the Northern Transvaal', *BS* (1937) 321–56.
Lestrade, G. P., 'Some Notes on the Political Organisation of Venda-speaking Tribes', *Africa* (1930) 306–21.
Mönnig, H., *The Pedi* (1967).
Trumpelmann, G. P. J. (ed.) *Maleo en Secoecoeni van Th. Wangemann* (*VRS*, 38, 1957).
Van Warmelo, N. J., 'Contributions towards Venda History, Religion and Tribal Ritual', *Eth. Pub.*, III (1932) and in Hammond-Tooke (ed.) [n. 1.3].

4.3 The southern Sotho

Ashton, H., *The Basuto* (1952).
Perry, J. and C. (eds) *S. J. Jingoes: A Chief is a Chief by the People* (1975).
Sanders [n. 7.4b].
Saunders, C. C., 'Early Knowledge of the Sotho' *QBSAL* (1966).
Thompson [n. 7.4].
Tylden, G., *The Rise of the Basuto* (1950).

4.4 The southern Nguni Peoples: Xhosa, Thembu, Mpondo

Anderson, E., *A History of the Xhosa of the Northern Cape, 1795–1879* (1987).
Beinart (1982) [n. 7.3].

Cook, P. A. W., *The Bomvana* (n.d.).
De Jager, E. J., 'Geskiedenis van die Ama Xhosa en Ama Thembu', *Hist.*, 9, 3 (1964) 215–27.
Hall [n. 4.6].
Hammond-Tooke [n. 4.8b].
Hunter, M., *Reaction to Conquest* (1961).
Peires, J. B., *The House of Phalo: A History of the Xhosa in the Days of their Independence* (1981) and *Before and After Shaka* (1981) and [n. 7.3].
Soga, J. H., *AmaXhosa Life and Customs* (1931) and *The South-Eastern Bantu* (1930).
Wagenaar, E. J. C., [n. 7.3] and *A History of the Thembu and their Relationship with the Cape, 1850–1900* (unpublished thesis, Rhodes University, 1987).
Wilson, M., 'The Nguni People', in *OHSA*, I (1969) 75–130.

4.5 The Mfengu (Fingo) People

Ayliff, J., and Whiteside, J., *History of the AbaMbo generally known as Fingos* (1912).
Cobbing [n. 1.4].
Hammond-Tooke, W. D., *Bhaca Society* (1962).
Moyer, R., *A History of the Mfengu of the Eastern Cape, 1815–65* (unpublished thesis, University of London, 1976).
Trapido, S., *White Conflict and Non-white Participation in the Politics of The Cape of Good Hope, 1853–1910* (unpublished thesis, University of London, 1970).

4.6 The northern Nguni peoples: Zulu, Gaza, Ngoni and Swazi

Barnes, J. A., *Politics in a Changing Society* [Ngoni] (1924).
Bonner [n. 1.5].
Bryant [n. 1.5].
Gluckman [n. 1.5].
Guy, J. J., *The Destruction of the Zulu Kingdom: The Civil War in Zululand, 1879–84* (1983) and in Peires, J. B. (ed.) *Before and After Shaka* (1981).
Harries, P., 'Slavery amongst the Gaza Nguni', in Peires (ed.) (above, 1981).
Hall, M., 'Ethnography, Environment and the History of the Nguni in the 18th and 19th Centuries', *ICS*, 8 (1977) 11–20.
Kennedy, P. A., 'Mpande and the Zulu kingship', *JNZH*, IV (1981) 21–38.
Krige, E. J., *The Social System of the Zulus* (1950).
Kuper, H., *An African Aristocracy* [Swazi] (1952).
Liesegang, G., 'Aspects of Gaza History', *RH*, 6 (1975) 1–14 and 'Dingane's attack on Lourenço Marques, 1833', *JAH*, X, 4 (1969) 565–79 and in Peires (ed.) *Before and After Shaka* [n. 4.4, above].
Marks, S., 'Traditions of the Natal Nguni', in Thompson [n. 1.3].
Matsebula, J. S. M., *A History of Swaziland* (1972).
Okoye, F. N., 'Dingane . . . a reappraisal', *JAH*, X, 2 (1969) 221–35.
Vail, L., in J. B. Peires (ed.) (1981) [n. 4.4].
Webb, C. de B., and Wright, J. B. (eds) [n. 1.5].
Wright, J. B. and Manson, A., *The Hlubi Chiefdom in Zululand–Natal: A History* (1983).

4.7 The Khumalo Ndebele

Cobbing J. R. D., *The Ndebele under Khumalo Kings* (unpublished thesis, University of Lancaster, 1976).
Rasmussen [n. 1.6].

4.8 The bonds of African society in the nineteenth century

(a) For general and cosmological aspects, see n. 7.10 and the following:

Hammond-Tooke (ed.) [n. 1.3].
Hodgson, J., *The God of the Xhosa* (1982).
Peires, J. B., 'Nxele and Ntsikana and the Origins of the Xhosa Religious Reaction', *JAH*, 20, I (1979) 51–61.
Setiloane, G. M., *The Image of God among the Sotho-Tswana* (1976).

(b) For governmental aspects, see:

Fortes, M. and Evans-Pritchard, E. E., *African Political Systems* (1940).
Hammond-Tooke, W. D., 'Segmentation and Fission in Cape Nguni Politics', *Africa* XXXV, 2 (1965) 143–67; and 'Descent Groups, Chiefdoms and South African Historiography', *JSAS*, 11, 2 (1985) 305–19.
Peires, J. B., 'The Rise of the "Right-Hand House" in the History and Historiography of the Xhosa', *HIA* (1975) 113–25.
Sansom, B., in Hammond-Tooke (ed.) [n. 1.3] 246–83.
Schapera, I., *Government and Politics in Tribal Societies* (1956).
Vansina, J., 'A Comparison of African Kingdoms', *Africa*, XXXII 4 (1962) 324–35.
Van Warmelo [n. 1.3].

4.9 New concentrations of power after the Mfecane

Legassick, M., *The Griquas, the Sotho-Tswana and the Missionaries, 1780–1840: The Politics of a Frontier Zone* (unpublished thesis, University of California, Los Angeles, 1970).
Lye, W. F. and Murray, C., *Transformations on the Highveld: The Tswana and Southern Sotho* (1980).
Omer-Cooper [n. 1.4].
Peires, J. B. (ed.) *Before and After Shaka: Papers in Nguni History* (*ISER*, 1981).
Saunders, C. C., 'Political Processes in the Southern African Frontier Zones' in Lamar and Thompson [n. 2.5] 149–71.
Thompson, L. M., 'Cooperation and Conflict: The Zulu Kingdom and Natal', in *OHSA* I (1969) 334–446.

CHAPTER 5

5.1 Voortrekker tribulations

(a) For the interpretation of the events of the Great Trek, see works by Beyers, Dreyer, Liebenberg, Muller, Preller, Pretorius, Van Jaarsveld and Walker [n. 3.7].
(b) On Afrikaner republicanism as an ideology, see nn. 13.2, 15.6, 17.6, and:
Coetzee, J. A., Meyer, P. J. and Diederichs, N., *Ons Republiek* (1941).
Du Toit and Giliomee [n. 2.4].
Gey van Pittius, E. F. W., *Staatsopvattinge van die Voortrekkers en die Boere* (1941).
Malan, D. F., *Afrikaner Volkseenheid en my Ervarings op die Pad daarheen (1959)*.
Marais [n. 3.1].
Scholtz, G. D., *Die Ontwikkeling van die Politieke Denke van die Afrikaner* (4 vols, 1967–77).
Van Jaarsveld, F. A. and Scholtz, G. D., *Die Republiek in Suid Afrika: Agtergrond, Ontstaan en Toekoms* (1966).

Van Schoor, M. C. E. and van Rooyen, J. J., *Republieke en Republiekeine* (1960).
Wieringa, P. A. C., *De Oudste Boeren Republieken in Zuid Afrika* (1921).
Wypkema, A., 'Die Volkstemidee in Suid Afrika', *HS*, I (1939).

(c) The history of Voortrekker constitutionalism can be consulted in the following works:

Du Plessis, J. S., *Die . . . Amp van Staat-President in die Z A Republiek* (*AYB* 1955).
Du Toit and Giliomee [n. 2.4].
Mandelbrote, H. J., 'Constitutional Development, 1834–58' in *CHBE*, VIII (1963), 367–97.
Preller, G. S. (ed.) *Voortrekker-Wetgewing* (1924).
Scholtz, G. D., *Die Konstitusie en die Staatsinstellinge van die Oranje-Vrystaat, 1854–1902* (1937).
Thompson, L. M., 'Constitutionalism in the Boer Republics', *BSALR* (1954) 49–72.
Van den Bergh, G. N., 'Die Drie-en-Dertig Artikels: Grondwet of Regsprekende Handleiding?', *SAHJ*, I (1969) 5–14.
Van Heerden, J. J., *Die Kommandant-Generaal in die Geskiedenis van die Z A Republiek* (*AYB* 1964).
Van Jaarsveld, F. A., *Die Veldkornet . . . in die Opbou van die Z A Republiek tot 1870* (*AYB* 1950).

5.2 The Republic Natalia

Bird, J., *Annals of Natal* (1965 reprint).
Brookes, E. H. and Webb, C. de B., *A History of Natal* (1965).
Cloete, H., *A History of the Great Boer Trek* (1900 reprint).
Du Plessis, A. J., *Die Republiek Natalia* (*AYB* 1942).
Liebenberg, B. J., *Andries Pretorius in Natal* (1977).
Pretorius [n. 3.7].
Van Jaarsveld, F. A., *Die Eenheidstrewe van die Republikeinse Afrikaners*, I, *1836–64* (1951).

5.3 Potgieter and Pretorius on the highveld

In addition to the works cited in n. 3.7, see:

Du Plessis [n. 5.1c];
Potgieter, F. J., *Die Vestiging van Blanke in Transvaal 1837–86* (*AYB* 1958).
Preller, G. S., *Andries Pretorius* (1938) and (ed.) *Voortrekkermense* [n. 3.7].
Van Heerden [n. 5.1c].
Van Jaarsveld [n. 5.1c].
Wichmann, F. A. F., *Die Wordingsgeskiedenis van die Z. A. Republiek, 1836–60* (*AYB* 1941).

5.4 The Orange Free State Republic

Collin, W. W., *Free Statia, or Reminiscences . . . 1852 to 1875* (1907).
Fraser, Sir J. G., *Episodes in My Life* (1922).
Gerdener, G. B. A., *Ons Kerk in die Trans-Gariep* (1934).
Malan, J. H., *Die Opkoms van 'n Republiek . . . tot 1863* (1929).
Orpen, J. M., *Reminiscences of a Life in South Africa from 1846 to the Present Day* (1964 edn).
Scholtz, G. D., *President J. H. Brand, 1823–88* (1957).

Van Schoor, M. C. E., *Politieke Groepering in die Transgariep* (*AYB* 1950) and *Nasionale en Politieke Bewuswording van die Afrikaner in Transgariep tot 1854* (*AYB* 1963) and in Muller, C. F. J., (ed.) *500 Years* (1969) 203–20.

Thompson, L. M., 'Cooperation and Conflict: The Highveld', in *OHSA*, I (1969).

5.5 The South African Republic, the civil war, and the rise of Paul Kruger

Agar-Hamilton [n. 7.5].

Cornwell, R., 'Land and Politics in the Transvaal in the 1880s', *ICS*, 4 (1974) 29–40.

du Plessis [n. 5.1c].

Kleynhans, W. A., *Volksregering in die Z. A. Republiek: die Rol van Memories* (1966).

Kruger, D. W., *Paul Kruger* (2 vols. 1961–3).

Marais, J. S., *The Fall of Kruger's Republic* (1961).

Mouton, J. A., *Generaal Piet Joubert in die Transvaalse Geskiedenis* (*AYB* 1957).

Smit, F. P., *Die Staatsopvattinge van Paul Kruger* (1951).

Trapido, S., 'The S. A. Republic: Class Formation and the State, 1850–1900', *ICS* 3 (1973) 57–65 and 'Landlord and Tenant in a Colonial Economy: The Transvaal 1880–1910', *JSAS*, 5, 1 (1978) 26–58, and 'Aspects in the Transition from Slavery to Serfdom: The South African Republic 1842–1902', and 'Reflections on Land, Office and Wealth in the S. A. Republic, 1850–1900', in Marks, S. and Atmore, A., *Economy and Society in Pre-industrial South Africa* (1980) 24–31 and 350–68 respectively.

Van Heerden [n. 5.1c].

Van Jaarsveld [n. 5.1c].

Wichmann [n. 5.3].

5.6 Ideological rifts under Pretorius and Burgers

Appelgryn, M. S., *T. F. Burgers, Staatspresident 1872–7* (1979).

Cachet, F. L., *De Worstelstryd der Transvalers* (1882).

De Kiewiet, C. W., *The Imperial Factor in South Africa* (1937).

Engelbrecht, S. P., *President T. F. Burgers* (1946) and *Geskiedenis van die Nederduits Hervormde Kerk van Afrika* (1953).

Hanekom, T. N., *Die Liberale Rigting in Suid-Afrika: 'n Kerk-Historiese Studie* (1957).

Spoelstra [n. 3.1c].

Uys, C. J., *In the Era of Shepstone 1842–77* (1933).

See also n. 3.1.

5.7 Kruger's Republic and the Uitlander challenge

For the domestic divisions in the South African Republic during Kruger's presidency, see the following, and for international aspects see n. 8.9.

Blainey, G., 'Lost Causes of the Jameson Raid', *EcHR* (2nd series) XVIII (1964–5) 350–66.

Denoon, D. J. N., 'Capital and Capitalists in the Transvaal in the 1890s and 1900s', *HJ*, 23, 1 (1980) 111–32.

Dormer, F. J., *Vengeance as a Policy in Afrikanderland* (1901).

Duminy, A. H. and Guest, W. R., *Interfering in Politics: A Biography of Sir P. FitzPatrick* (1987), and (eds) FitzPatrick: Selected Papers 1888–1906 (1976).

FitzPatrick [n. 8.9].

Gordon, C. T., *The Growth of Boer Opposition to Kruger* (1970).

Hobson, J. A., *The War in South Africa* (1900).
Jeeves, A. H., *Migrant Labour and South Africa's Mining Economy: The Struggle for the Gold Mines' Labour Supply, 1890–1920* (1985).
Jeppe, C., *The Kaleidoscopic Transvaal* (1906).
Kubicek, R. V., 'Randlords in 1895: A Reassessment', *JBS*, XI, 2 (1972) 84–103, and *Economic Imperialism in Theory and Practice: The Case of South African Gold-mining Finance, 1886–1914* (1979).
Le Roux and Van Zyl [n. 8.9].
Marais [n. 5.5].
Mendelsohn, R., 'Blainey and the Jameson Raid: The Debate Renewed', *JSAS*, 6, 2 (1980) 157–70.
Scholtz, G. D., *Die Geskiedenis van die Nederduits Hervormde of Gereformeerde Kerk van Suid-Afrika* (1959–60).
Spoelstra [n. 3.1b].
Trapido [n. 5.5].
Vander Poel [n. 8.8].
Van Helten, J. J., 'German Capital, the Netherlands Railway Company and the Political Economy of the Transvaal, 1886–1900', *JAH*, 19, 1 (1978) 369–90, and (with P. Richardson) 'The Gold-Mining Industry in the Transvaal, 1886–99', in Warwick, P. (ed.) *The South African War* (1880) 18–36; and 'The Development of the South Africa Gold-mining industry, 1895–1918', *EcHR*, 2nd Series XXXVII, 3 (1984) 319–40.

CHAPTER 6

6.1 Cape political and constitutional growth, 1820–72

Davenport, T. R. H., 'The Consolidation of a New Society: The Cape Colony' in *OHSA* I (1969) 311–33.
Donaldson [n. 3.4].
Duminy, A. H., *The Role of Sir A. Stockenstrom in Cape Politics, 1825–54* (*AYB* 1960).
Edgecombe, D. R., 'The Non-racial Franchise in Cape Politics, 1853–1910', *Kleio*, X, 1, 2 (1978) 2–37.
Fryer, A. K., 'The Government of the Cape of Good Hope, 1825–54' (*AYB* 1964).
Hattersley, A. F., *The Convict Crisis and the Growth of Unity* (1965).
Kilpin, R., *The Romance of a Colonial Parliament* (1938).
Le Cordeur, B. A., *Robert Godlonton as Architect of Frontier Opinion* (*AYB* 1959); and *A History of Eastern Cape Separatism 1820–54* (1981).
Mandelbrote, H. J., [n. 5.1].
McCracken, J. L., *The Cape Parliament* (1967).
Rutherford, J., *Sir George Grey 1812–98: A Study in Colonial Government* (1961).
Scholtz [n. 3.7].
Smith, K. W., *From Frontier to Midlands: A History of the Graaff–Reinet District, 1786–1910* (1976).
Sole, D. B., *The Separation Movement and the Demand for Resident Government in the Eastern Province, 1828–78* (unpublished thesis, Rhodes University 1939).
Stead, J. L., *The Development and Failure of the Eastern Cape Separatist Movement* (*AYB*, 1982).
Taylor, N. H., *The Separation Movement during the Period of Representative Government at the Cape, 1854–72* (unpublished thesis, University of Cape Town, 1938).

Trapido, S., 'The Origins of the Cape Franchise Qualifications of 1853', *JAH*, V, 1 (1964) 37–54.
Van Jaarsveld, F. A., *The Awakening of Afrikaner Nationalism, 1868–81* (1961).
Vanstone, J. P., *Sir G. Sprigg: a Political Biography* (unpublished thesis, Queen's University, Canada, 1974).
Zeeman, M. J., *The Making of Representative Government at the Cape under Sir P. Wodehouse, 1862–70* (unpublished thesis, University of Cape Town, 1940).

6.2 The Afrikaner revival and the Rhodes–Hofmeyr alliance

The development of Cape political life during the last quarter of the nineteenth century can be approached through the following works:

Bitensky, M. F., *The South African League* (unpublished thesis, Witwatersrand University, 1951).
Christopher, A. J., 'Growth of Landed Wealth in the Cape Colony, 1860–1910', *Hist.*, XXII, 1 (1977) 53–61.
Davenport, T. R. H., *The Afrikaner Bond* (1966).
Davidson, A. B., *Cecil Rhodes and his Time* (1988).
Du Toit, A., 'Puritans in Africa? Afrikaner "Calvinism" and Kuyperian Neo-Calvinism in Late Nineteenth-Century South Africa', *CSSH* 27, 2 (1985) 209–40.
Du Toit, S. J., *Die Geskiedenis van Ons Land in die Taal van Ons Volk* (1876).
Edgecombe D. R. [n. 6.1] and 'The Glen Grey Act', in Benyon, J. *et al.* (eds) *Studies in Local History* (1976).
First, R. and Scott, A., *Olive Schreiner* (1980).
Flint, J., *Cecil Rhodes* (1976).
Giliomee, H., 'Western Cape Farmers and the Beginning of Afrikaner Nationalism', *JSAS* 14, 1 (1987) 38–63.
Hofmeyr, J. H., *Life of J. H. Hofmeyr (Onze Jan)* (1913).
Lewsen (1982) [n. 6.8].
Lockhart, J. G. and Woodhouse, C. M., *Rhodes* (1963).
McCracken [n. 6.1].
Newbury, C. W., 'Out of the Pit: The Capital Accumulation of Cecil Rhodes', *JICH* 10, 1 (1981) 25–49 and [n. 19.3].
Ranger, T., 'The last word on Cecil Rhodes?', *P and P* 28 (1964) 116–27.
Roberts, B., *Cecil Rhodes: Flawed Colossus* (1987).
Rotberg, R. I., *The Founder: Cecil Rhodes and the Pursuit of Power* (1988).
Shepperson, G., 'C. J. Rhodes: Some Biographical Problems', *SAHJ*, 15 (1983) 53–67.
Turrell, R., 'Rhodes, De Beers and Monopoly', *JICH*, X, 3 (1982) 311–43 and 'The 1875 Black Flag Revolt in the Kimberley Diamond Fields', *JSAS*, 7, 2 (1981) 194–235, and *Capital and Labour in the Kimberley Diamond Fields* (1987).
Van Jaarsveld [n. 6.1].
Walker, E. A., *W. P. Schreiner: A South African* (1937).
Williams, B., *Cecil Rhodes* (1938).
Worger, W., *South Africa's City of Diamonds: Mine Workers and Monopoly Capitalism in Kimberley, 1867–95* (1987).
Wright, H. M., *Sir James Rose Innes: Selected Correspondence 1884–1902* (*VRS*, II, 3, 1972).

6.3 Black politics in the nineteenth-century Cape Colony

Karis, T. and Carter, G. M., *From Protest to Challenge: Documents of African Politics in South Africa, 1882–1964*, I (1972) (ed. S. Johns III).
McCracken [n. 6.1].

Odendaal, A., *Vukani Bantu! The Beginnings of Black Protest Politics in South Africa to 1912* (1984), and *African Political Mobilisation in Eastern Cape, 1880–1990* (unpublished thesis, Cambridge University, 1983).

Saunders [n. 7.10].

Trapido, S. [n. 6.1] and 'African Divisional Politics in the Cape Colony, 1884–1910', *JAH*, IX, 1 (1968) 69–98, and 'The Origin and Development of the APO', *ICS*, 1 (1970) 89–111.

Williams, D., 'African Nationalism in South Africa: Origins and Problems', *JAH*, XI, 3 (1970) 371–83.

6.4 The founding and settlement of colonial Natal

Bird, J., *Annals of Natal* (1965 reprint).

Bryant, A. T., *Olden Times in Zululand and Natal* (1929).

Brookes, E. H. and Webb, C. de B. [n. 5.2].

Duminy, A. and Guest, W. R. (eds) *Natal and Zululand from Earliest Times to 1910* (1989).

Hattersley, A. F., *The British Settlement of Natal* (1950), *More Annals of Natal* (1936), *Latter Annals of Natal* (1938) and *The Natalians* (1940).

Holden, W. C., *History of the Colony of Natal* (1855).

Isaacs, N., *Travels and Adventures in Eastern Africa* (VRS, 16, 17, 1936–7).

Kotze, D. J., *Letters of the American Missionaries 1835–8* (VRS, 31, 1950).

Richardson, P., 'The Natal Sugar Industry, 1849–1905: An interpretative Essay', *ICS*, 12 (1981) 33–43.

Slater, H., 'Land, Labour and Capital in Natal: The Natal Land and Colonisation Company, 1860–1948', *JAH*, 16, 2 (1975) 257–84.

Stuart, J. and Malcolm, D. McK., *The Diary of H. F. Fynn* (1950).

Van Zyl, M. C., *Luitenant-Goewerneur M. West en die Natalse Voortrekkers, 1845–9* (AYB, 1955).

Trapido, S., 'Natal's Non-racial Franchise, 1856', *AS*, 22, 1 (1963) 22–3.

6.5 Shepstone and African administration in Natal

Ballard, C. C., 'Migrant Labour in Natal, 1860–79, with Special Reference to Zululand and Delagoa Bay', *JNZH*, I (1978) 25–42, and 'A Reapproach to Civilisation: John Dunn and the Missionaries', *SAHJ*, 11 (1979) 36–55.

Brookes, E. H., *White Rule in South Africa* (1974).

Edgecombe, D. R., 'Sir Marshall Clarke and the Abortive Attempt to "Basutolandise" Zululand, 1893–7', *JNZH*, I (1978) 43–53.

Etherington, N., 'Why Langalibalele Ran Away', *JNZH*, I (1978) and 'Labour Supply and the Genesis of South African Confederation in the 1870s', *ICS*, 10 (1981) 13–30.

Geyser, O., *Die Bantoe-beleid van Theophilus Shepstone* (AYB 1968).

Guy, J. J., *The Heretic: A Study of the Life of J. W. Colenso* (1983).

Kennedy, P., 'Mpande and the Zulu Kingship', *JNZH*, IV (1981) 21–38.

Marks, S., *Reluctant Rebellion* (1970).

Webb, C. de B. (ed.) 'Native Policy: The Reitz-Shepstone Correspondence of 1891–2', *Natalia*, 2 (1972) 7–20.

6.6 Political developments in Natal to responsible government, 1893

Davenport, T. R. H., 'The Responsible Government Issue in Natal, 1880–2', *BSALR* (1957) 84–133.

Lambert, J., 'Sir J. Robinson, 1839–1903', *JNZH*, III (1980) 45–56, and *Sir*

J. Robinson and Responsible Government, 1863–97 (unpublished thesis, University of Natal, 1975).

Lehmann, J. H., *All Sir Garnet: A Life of Field Marshal Lord Wolseley* (1964).

Preston, A. (ed.) *Sir Garnet Wolseley's South African Diaries, Natal, 1875* (1971).

Talbot, C. J., *Harry Escombe and the Politics of Responsible Government in Natal, 1879–85 (unpublished thesis, University of Natal, 1974)*.

6.7 The arrival of Natal's Indians

On the early story of Indians in Natal and South Africa generally, see:

Bhana, S., 'M. H. Nazaar, Gandhi and the Indian Opinion', *Hist.* 23, 1 (1978) 56–62; and (with B. Pachai) (eds) *A Documentary History of Indian South Africans* (1984).

Bradlow, E., 'Indentured Indians in Natal and the £3 tax', *SAHJ*, 2 (1970) 38–53.

Calpin, G. H., *Indians in South Africa* (1940).

Doke, J. J., *M. K. Gandhi* (1909).

Gandhi, M. K., *Satyagraha in South Africa* (1954).

Hancock, W. K., *Smuts*, I (1965) 309–47, II (1968) 128–49; and *Four Studies in War and Peace in this Century* (1961).

Huttenback, R. A., *Gandhi in South Africa* (1971).

Joshi, P. S., *The Tyranny of Colour* (1942).

Meer, Y. S. *et al.*, *Documents of Indentured Labour: Natal 1851–1917* (1980).

Pachai, B., *International Aspects of the S. A. Indian Question, 1860–1971* (1971).

Palmer, M., *History of the Indians in Natal* (*NRS* 10, 1957).

Swan [n. 9.6].

Swanson, M. W., 'The Asiatic Menace: Creating Segregation in Durban, 1870–1900', *IJAHS*, 16, 3 (1983) 401–21.

Thompson, L. M., *Indian Immigration into Natal, 1860–72* (*AYB*, 1952).

See also references in n. 9.6.

6.8 The Cape, Natal, and the debate about liberalism

Davenport, T. R. H., in *OHSA* I (1969) 297–311, and in Butler, J. Elphick, R. H. and Welsh D. (eds) *Democratic Liberalism in South Africa* (1987) 21–34.

Du Toit, A., 'The Cape Afrikaner's Failed Liberal Moment', in Butler, Elphick and Welsh (above) 35–63.

Hanekom [n. 5.6].

Le Cordeur, B. A., *The Relations between the Cape and Natal 1846–79* (AYB, 1965).

Legassick, M., 'The Rise of Modern South African Liberalism: Its Social Base' (unpublished typescript, *ICS*, 1972).

Lewsen, P., 'The Cape Liberal Tradition, Myth or Reality?', *Race*, XIII, 1 (1971) 65–80, and *John X. Merriman* (1982).

Macmillan, W. M., *Bantu, Boer and Briton* (1963) [on Dr. J. Philip].

Marquard, L., *Liberalism in South Africa* (*SAIRR*, 1965).

McCracken, J. L., 'The Hon. William Porter, an Irish Liberal at the Cape of Good Hope', (unpublished typescript).

Peires, J. B., 'Sir George Grey *versus* the Kaffir Relief Committee', *JSAS*, 10, 2 (1984) 145–69.

Rich, P., *White Power and the Liberal Conscience* (1984).

Rose Innes, J., *Autobiography* (1944).

Ross [n. 2.4].

Rutherford [n. 6.1].

Solomon, W. E. G., *Life of Saul Solomon* (1948).
Trapido, S., 'The Friends of the Natives: Merchants, Peasants and the Political and Ideological Structure of Liberalism in the Cape, 1884–1910', in Marks, S. and Atmore, A., *Economy and Society in Pre-industrial South Africa* (1980).
Welsh [n. 11.3].

CHAPTER 7

7.1 The territorial confrontation: preliminary observations

For the debate on the significance of the frontier, see n. 2.5.

7.2 Conflicts on the San frontiers during the eighteenth and nineteenth centuries

Burchell, W. J., *Travels in the Interior of South Africa* (2 vols., 1822).
Collins, R., in Theal G. M. (ed.) *Records of the Cape Colony* (1897–1905) VII, 98–139.
Marais [n. 2.3].
Moodie [n. 2.2].
Ross, R., 'The Kora Wars on the Orange River, 1830–1880', *JAH*, 16, 4 (1975) 561–76.
Strauss, T., *War along the Orange* (1979).
Thompson, G., [n. 1.4].
Wright [n. 1.2].

7.3 The eastern frontier of the Cape Colony

Beinart, W. J., 'European Traders and the Mpondo Paramountcy', *JAH*, 20 (1979) 471–86', 'Conflict in Qumbu: Rural Consciousness, Ethnicity and Violence in the Colonial Transkei, 1880–1913', *JSAS*, 8, 1 (1981) 94–122, and *The Political Economy of Pondoland, 1860–1930* (1982).
Campbell, W. B., *The South African Frontier, 1865–85: A Study in Expansion* (*AYB* 1959).
Cragg [n. 7.10].
Crankshaw, G. B., *The Diary of C. L. Stretch* (unpublished thesis, Rhodes University 1960).
Derricourt, R. and Saunders, C. C. (eds) *Beyond the Cape Frontier* (1973).
Du Toit, A. E., *The Cape-Frontier: A Study of Native Policy with Special Reference to the Years 1847–1866* (*AYB* 1954).
Freund, W., 'The Eastern Frontier of the Cape Colony during the Batavian Period', *JAH*, XIII, 4 (1972) 631–45.
Galbraith, J. S., *Reluctant Empire* (1963).
Hunter [n. 4.4].
Lancaster, J. C. S., *Sir Benjamin D'Urban* (unpublished thesis, Rhodes University, 1981).
Le Cordeur, B. A. (ed.), *The Journal of C. L. Stretch* (1988).
Lewsen (1982) [n. 6.8].
Maclennan, B., *A Proper Degree of Terror: John Graham and the Cape's Eastern Frontier* (1986).
Macmillan [n. 6.8].
MacQuarrie, J. W., *The Reminiscences of Sir Walter Stanford, 1850–1929* (*VRS*, 39, 43, 1958–62).
Milton, J. R. L., *The Edges of War: a History of the Frontier Wars, 1702–1878* (1983).

Peires [n. 4.4]; and *The Dead will Arise: Nongawuse and the Great Xhosa Cattle-killing Movement of 1856–7* (1989).

Pretorius, J. G., *The British Humanitarians and the Cape Eastern Frontier, 1834–6* (unpublished thesis, Witwatersrand University, 1970).

Saunders, C. C., *The Annexation of the Transkeian Territories, 1872–95* (*AYB*, 1976) and 'The Transkeian Rebellion of 1880–1', *JAH*, 8 (1976) 32–9.

Spicer, M. W., *The War of Ngcayecibi, 1877–8* (unpublished thesis, Rhodes University, 1977).

Visagie, J. C., *Die Katriviernedersetting, 1829–39* (unpublished thesis, *UNISA*, 1978).

Wagenaar, E. J. C. *A Forgotten Frontier Zone–Settlements and Reactions in the Stormberg Area between 1820 and 1860* (*AYB*, 1984) and [n. 4.4].

Welsh [n. 11.3].

Wilson, M., 'Cooperation and Conflict: The Eastern Cape frontier', in *OHSA* I (1969) 233–71.

7.4 The conflicts on the Griqua and Orange Free State frontiers

(a) On the Griqua frontiers, see Collins, Marais, Ross, and Strauss [n. 7.2], and:

Agar-Hamilton [n. 7.5].

Beinárt, W., 'Settler Accumulation in East Griqualand', in Beinart, W., Delius P, and Trapido, S., *Putting a Plough to the Ground: Accumulation and Dispossession in Rural South Africa, 1850–1930* (1986).

De Kiewiet, C. W., *British Colonial Policy and the South African Republics, 1848–72* (1929).

Edgar, R. C. and Saunders, C. C., 'A. A. S. le Fleur and the Griqua Trek of 1917: Segregation, Self-help and Ethnic Identity', *IJAHS*, 15, 2 (1982) 201–20.

Halford, S. J., *The Griquas of Griqualand* (1949).

Kurtz, J. M., *The Albania Settlement of Griqualand West, 1866–78* (unpublished thesis, Rhodes University, 1987).

Macmillan [n. 3.6].

Marais [n. 2.3].

Morrell, W. P., *British Colonial Policy in the Age of Peel and Russell (1930)* and *British Colonial Policy in the mid-Victorian Age* (1969).

Ross [n. 7.2].

Shillington [n. 7.8].

Strauss [n. 7.2].

Van Aswegen, H. J., *Die Verhouding tussen Blank en Nie-Blank in die Oranje-Vrystaat, 1854–1902* (*AYB*, 1971).

Worger, W. [n. 6.2].

(b) On the frontier between the South Sotho, the Rolong of Thaba 'Nchu and the Orange Free State, see:

Benyon, J. A., *Basutoland and the High Commission, 1868–84* (unpublished thesis, Oxford University, 1968).

Burman, S. B., *Chiefdom Politics and Alien Law: Basutoland under Cape Rule, 1871–84* (1982).

Murray, C., 'The "Land of the Barolong": Annexation and Alienation, 1884–1900', *ICS*, 13 (1984) 24–35.

Sanders, P. B., *Moshoeshoe, Chief of the Sotho* (1975).

Theal, G. M. (ed.) *Basutoland Records* (1964 reprint).

Thompson, L. M., *Survival in Two Worlds: Moshoeshoe of Lesotho, 1786–1870* (1975).

Tylden [n. 4.3].
Van der Poel, J., *Basutoland as a Factor in South African Politics, 1852–70* (*AYB*, 1941).
Wales, J., *The Relationship between the O.F.S. and the Rolong of Thaba 'Nchu during the Presidency of J. H. Brand, 1864–88*, (unpublished thesis, Rhodes University, 1979).
Watson, R. L., 'The Subjugation of a South African State: Thaba 'Nchu 1880–84', *JAH*, 21 (1980) 357–73.

7.5 Conflict on the eastern and northern frontiers of the Transvaal

On the South African Republic's frontier with the Pedi, Lovedu, Venda, and Transvaal Ndebele, see:

Agar Hamilton, J. A. I., *The Native Policy of the Voortrekkers* (1928) and *The Road to the North* (1937).
Delius [n. 1.5], and 'Abel Erasmus: Power and Profit in the Eastern Transvaal', in Beinart, Delius and Trapido [n. 7.4] 176–217.
De Vaal, J. B., *Die Rol van Joào Albasini in die Geskiedenis van die Transvaal* (*AYB*, 1955).
Hunt [n. 4.2].
Ncube, A. M., 'The Venda and the Mphephu war of 1898' (unpublished typescript *CAHA*, 1972).
Preston, A. (ed.) *Sir Garnet Wolseley's South African Journal, 1978–80* (1973).
Rademeyer, J. I., '*Die Oorlog teen Magato*', *HS*, 2 (1944) 79–122.
Siebörger [n. 19.3].
Smith, K. W., *The Campaigns against the Bapedi of Sekhukhune, 1877–9* (*AYB*, 1967) and 'The Fall of the Bapedi of the North-eastern Transvaal', *JAH*, X, 2 (1969) 237–52.
Trumpelmann [n. 4.2].
Uys [n. 5.6].
Van der Merwe, D. W., 'Johannes Dinkwanyane, 1842–76', *SAHJ*, 8 (1976) 15–31.
Van Jaarsveld, A., *Die Verhouding tussen die Ndzundza en die Blankes, 1845–83* (unpublished thesis, Rhodes University, 1985).
Van Rooyen, T. S., *Die Verhoudinge tussen die Boere, Engelse en Naturelle in die Geskiedenis van die Oos-Transvaal tot 1882* (*AYB*, 1951).
Van Warmelo, N. J., *Transvaal Ndebele Texts*, (*Eth. Pub.* I 1930).
Wagner, R., 'Zoutpansberg: The Dynamics of a Hunting Frontier', in Marks, S. and Atmore, A. (eds) *Economy and Society in Pre-industrial South Africa* (1980).

7.6 The Swazi and their 'documents'

On the Swazi frontier with the Transvaal, see:

Bonner, [n. 1.5].
Garson, N. G. *Swaziland and a Road to the Sea, 1887–1895* (*AYB*, 1957).
Hyam, R., *Elgin and Churchill at the Colonial Office* (1968).
Kuper, H., *An African Aristocracy* (1947) and *Sobhuza II, Ngwenyama and King of Swaziland* (1978).

7.7 The survival and overthrow of the Zulu monarchy, 1838–1906

On the Natal–Zululand frontier, see:

Ballard, C., 'A Reproach to Civilisation: John Dunn and the Missionaries,

1879–84', *SAHJ*, II (1979) 36–55, and 'The Political Transformation of a Trans-frontiersman: The Career of John Dunn of Zululand, 1856–79', *JICH*, 7, 3 (1979) 248–73, and 'John Dunn and Cetshwayo: The Material Foundations of Political Power in the Zulu Kingdom 1857–78', *JAH*, 21 (1980) 75–91.
Brookes and Webb [n. 5.2].
Clarke, S., *Invasion of Zululand, 1879* (1979).
De Kiewiet [n. 8.6].
Duminy, A. and Ballard, C. (eds.) *The Anglo-Zulu War: New Perspectives* (1981).
Edgecombe, D. R. [n. 7.8].
Etherington N. A., 'Why Langalibalele Ran Away', *JNZH* (1978).
Guy [n. 4.6].
Marks, S., *Reluctant Rebellion* (1970).
Morris, D. R., *The Washing of the Spears* (1964).
Van Zyl, M. C., *Die Uitbreiding van Britse Gesag oor die Natalse Noordgrensge-beid* (*AYB*, 1966).

7.8 The frontier conflicts of the Tswana on the 'Road to the North'

On the Transvaal–Tswana border, see:

Agar-Hamilton (1937) [n. 7.5].
Davenport and Hunt [n. 19.1].
Edgecombe, D. R., 'Sir Alfred Milner and the Bechuana Rebellion: A Case-study in Imperial–Colonial Relations, 1897–8', *SAHJ*, 11 (1979) 56–73.
Maylam, P., *Rhodes, the Tswana and the British* (1980).
Mouton, J. A., *General Piet Joubert in die Transvaalse Geskiedenis* (*AYB* 1957).
Saker, H. and Aldridge, J., 'Origins of the Langeberg Rebellion, 1896', *JAH*, 12, 2 (1971) 299–317.
Shillington, K., *The Colonisation of the Southern Tswana, 1870–1900* (1985).
Sillery, A., *Founding a Protectorate* (1965), and *Sechele: The Story of an African Chief* (1954).

7.9 The Khumalo Ndebele and the British South Africa Company

Beach, D., 'Ndebele raiders and Shona power', *JAH*, 15, 4 (1974) 633–52; and 'Chimurenga: the Shona rising of 1896–7', *JAH*, 20, 3 (1979) 395–420; and *The Shona and Zimbabwe, 900–1850: An Outline of Shona History* (1980).
Bhebe, N. M. B., 'Ndebele Trade in the 19th Century', *JAS*, 1, 1 (1974) 87–100.
Chanaiwa, D., 'The Army and Politics in Pre-industrial Africa: The Ndebele Nation, 1822–93', *ASR*, 19, 2 (1976) 49–68.
Cobbing, J. R. D., 'Lobengula, Jameson and the Occupation of Mashonaland', *RH*, 4 (1973) 39–56, and 'The Evolution of the Ndebele *Amabutho*' *JAH*, 15, 4 (1974) 607–32, and 'The Absent Priesthood', *JAH*, 18, 1 (1977) 61–84.
Dorey, A., 'The Victoria Incident and the Outbreak of the Ndebele War', (Occasional paper, *CAHA*, 1972).
Fripp, C. E. and Hiller, V. W., *Gold and the Gospel in Mashonaland* (1949) 219–20 (text of Rudd concession).
Galbraith, J. S., *Crown and Charter* (1974).
Glass, S., *The Matabele War* (1968).
Hiller, V. W., *Guide to the Public Records of Southern Rhodesia* (1956).
Lye, W. F., 'The Ndebele Kingdom South of the Limpopo', *JAH*, X (1969) 87–103.
Mason, P., *The Birth of a Dilemma* (1958).
Mutunhu, T., 'The Matabele Nation: The Dynamic Socio-political Developments of an African State, 1840–93', *JAS*, 3, 2 (1976) 165–82.

Ranger, T., *Revolt in Southern Rhodesia* (1967) and 'The Role of the Ndebele and Shona Religious Authorities in the Rebellions of 1896 and 1897', in Stokes, E. and Brown, R. (eds) *The Zambesian past* (1965).
Rasmussen [n. 1.6].
Samkange, S., *The Origins of Rhodesia* (1968).
Stigger, P. 'Volunteers and the Profit Motive in the Anglo-Ndebele War of 1893', *RH*, 2 (1971) 11–23.
Tsomondo, M., 'Shona Reaction and Resistance to European Colonisation of Zimbabwe, 1890–8: A Case against Colonial and Revisionist Historiography', *JSAS*, 2, 1 (1977) 11–32.

7.10 The role of the missionaries

Ashley, M. J., 'Universes in Collision: Xhosa Missionaries and Education in 19th Century South Africa', *JThSA*, 32 (1980) 28–38.
Brock, S., *James Stewart of Lovedale: A Reappraisal of Missionary Attitudes in Eastern Cape, South Africa, 1870–1905* (unpublished thesis, Edinburgh University, 1974).
Cragg, D. G. S., *Relations of the Amampondo and the Colonial Authorities, 1830–86, With Special Reference to the Role of the Wesleyan Missionaries* (unpublished thesis, Oxford University, 1959).
Dachs, A. J., 'Missionary Imperialism: The Case of Bechuanaland', *JAH*, XIII, 4 (1972) 647–58; and *Christianity South of the Zambesi* (1973).
Du Bruyn, J., 'Die Tlhaping en die Eerste Sendelinge', *SAHJ*, 14 (1982) 8–34.
Du Plessis, J., *History of Christian Missions in South Africa* (1911).
Elphick, R. H., 'Africans and the Christian Campaign in Southern Africa', in Lamar and Thompson [n. 2.5.].
Etherington, N., *Preachers, Peasants and Politics in South-East Africa, 1835–80: African Christian Communities in Natal, Pondoland and Zululand* (1979).
Flournoy, B. M., 'The Relationship of the American Methodist Church to its South African Members', *JAS*, 2, 4 (1975) 529–45.
Galbraith [n. 7.3].
Goedhals, M. M., *Anglican Missionary Policy in the Diocese of Grahamstown, 1853–71* (unpublished thesis, Rhodes University, 1979).
Hodgson [n. 4.8].
Horton, R., 'African Traditional Thought and Western Science', *Africa*, 37 (1967) 50–71; 'African Conversion', *Africa*, 41, 2 (1971) 85–108, and 'On the Rationality of Conversion', *Africa*, 45, 3 (1975) 219–35.
Jarrett Kerr, M., *Patterns of Christian Acceptance: A Study of the Missionary Impact, 1550–1950* (1972).
Kruger, B., *The Pear Tree Blossoms: The History of the Moravian Church in South Africa, 1737–1869* (1966).
'Majeke, N.' (Taylor, D.), *The Role of the Missionaries in Conquest* (1952).
Marks [n. 6.5].
Mills, W. G., 'The Taylor Revival of 1866, and Roots of African Nationalism in the Cape Colony', *JRel. A.*, 8, 2 (1976) 105–22; 'The Fork in the Road: Religious Separatism and African Nationalism in the Cape Colony, 1890–1910', *JRel. A.*, 9, 1 (1978) 50–9, and (with C. C. Saunders) 189–210.
Pauw, B. A., *Christianity and Xhosa Tradition* (1975).
Peires [n. 7.3].
Ross [n. 3.6].
Sales, J., *Mission Stations and Coloured Communities of the E. Cape, 1800–52* (1975).
Schutte, A. G., 'Mwali in Venda: Some Observations on the Significance of the High God in Venda History', *JRel. A*, 9, 2 (1978) 109–22.

Saunders, C. C., 'James Read: Towards a Reassessment', *ICS*, 7 (1977), and 'Nehemiah Tile and the Thembu Church', *JAH*, 11, 4 (1970) and 'The New African Elites in the Eastern Cape: Some Late Nineteenth-century Origins of African Nationalism', *ICS*, 1 (1970) 44–55.

Schapera, I., *Apprenticeship in Kuruman . . . Journals and Letters of Robert and Mary Moffat* (1951), and *David Livingstone: South African Papers, 1849–53* (*VRS*, II, 5, 1974).

Setiloane [n. 4.8].

Seton, B. E., *Wesleyan Missionaries and the Sixth Frontier War* (unpublished thesis, University of Cape Town, 1962).

Strayer, R., 'Mission History in Africa: New Perspectives in an Encounter', *ASR*, XIX (1976) 1–15.

Sundkler, B. G. M., *Bantu Prophets in South Africa* (1961).

Switzer, L. E., *An African Mission in a White-dominated Multi-racial Society: The American Zulu Mission in South Africa, 1885–1910* (unpublished thesis, University of Natal, 1971).

Thomas, K., *Religion and the Decline of Magic* (1971).

Whisson, M. G. and West, M. (eds) *Religion and Social Change in Southern Africa* (1975).

Williams, D., *The Missionaries on the Eastern Frontier of the Cape Colony, 1799–1853* (unpublished thesis, University of the Witwatersrand, 1959) and *Umfundisi: A Biography of Tiyo Soga* (1979).

Wilson, M., *Religion and the Transformation of Society: A Study of Social Change in Africa* (1971).

7.11 The changing ownership of the land

Ally, R. T., *The Development of the System of Individual Tenure for Africans, with special reference to the Glen Grey Act, c. 1894–1922*, (unpublished thesis, Rhodes University, 1985).

Arrighi and Saul (eds) [n. 19.1].

Ballard, C., 'The Dunn Reserve, 1895–1948: A Case of Segregation and Underdevelopment in a Reserved Land Category', *JSAS*, 3, 4 (1978) 521–36.

Bundy [n. 19.1].

Burton [n. 9.4].

Clark, D. G., 'Land Inequality and Income Distribution in Rhodesia', *ASR*, 18, 1 (1975) 1–8.

Davenport and Hunt (eds) [n. 19.1].

Elton Mills, M. E. and Wilson, M. [n. 19.1].

Keegan, T., 'The Restructuring of Agrarian Class Relations in a Colonial Economy: The Orange River Colony, 1902–10', *JSAS*, 5, 2 (1979) 234–54.

Palmer, R. H., *Aspects of Rhodesian Land Policy, 1890–1936* (1968).

Palmer, R. H. and Parsons, Q. N., *The Roots of Rural Poverty in Central and Southern Africa* (1977).

Van Onselen, C., 'Reactions to Rinderpest in Southern Africa, 1896–7', *JAH*, 13, 3 (1972) 473–88.

Whitehead, R., 'The Aborigines Protection Society and White Settlers in Rhodesia', *ICS*, 3 (1973) 96–109.

Wickins [n. 10.2].

Willan, B., 'The Anti-slavery and Aborigines Protection Societies and the South African Natives Land Act of 1913', *JAH*, 20, 1 (1979) 83–102.

Wilson, F., 'Farming, 1866–1966', *OHSA*, II (1971) 104–71.

7.12 The role of trade in colonial expansion

Ballard, C., 'Trade, Tribute and Migrant Labour: Zulu and Colonial Exploitation of the Delogoa Bay Hinterland', in Peires, J. B. (ed.) *Before and After Shaka* (1981).

Beinart, W. J., 'European Traders and the Mpondo Paramountcy, 1878–86', *JAH*, 20 (1979) 471–86.

Campbell [n. 7.3].

Gray, R. and Birmingham, D., *Pre-Colonial African Trade* (1970).

Harinck, G., 'Interaction between Xhosa and Khoi: Emphasis on the Period 1620–1750', in Thompson (ed.) [n. 1.3] 145–70. Legassick, M., 'The Sotho-Tswana Peoples before 1800', in Thompson [n. 1.3] 86–125.

Neumark [n. 2.5].

Parsons, Q. N., 'The Economic History of Khama's Country in Botswana, 1844–1930', in Palmer and Parsons [n. 7.11].

Peires [n. 4.4].

Pretorius [n. 3.7].

Robertson [n. 2.5].

Smith, A., 'The Trade of Delogoa Bay as a Factor in Nguni Politics' in Thompson [n. 1.3] 171–89, and in Gray and Birmingham (above) 265–89.

Wagner [n. 7.5].

CHAPTER 8

8.1 Formal and informal Empire

Atmore A. and Marks, S., 'The Imperial Factor in South Africa in the 19th Century: Towards a Reassessment', *JICH* (1969) 105–39.

Benyon, J. A., *Proconsul and Paramountcy in South Africa: The High Commission, British Supremacy and the Sub-continent, 1806–1910* (1980).

De Cecco, M., *Money and Empire: The International Gold Standard, 1890–1914* (1974).

Etherington, N. A., 'Theories of Imperialism in Southern Africa Revisited', *AA*, 81, 323 (1982) 385–407 and *Theories of Imperialism: War, Conquest and Capital* (1984).

Fieldhouse, D. K., *Economics and Empire, 1830–1914* (1973).

Hobson, J. A., *Imperialism: A Study* (1902).

Galbraith [n. 7.3].

Gallagher, J. and Robinson, R. E., 'The Imperialism of Free Trade', *EcHR*, 2nd series, VI, 1 (1953) 1–15.

Kubicek [n. 5.7].

Lenin, V. I., *Imperialism: The Highest Stage of Capitalism* (1916).

Macdonagh, O., 'The Anti-imperialism of Free Trade', *EcHR*, 2nd series, XIV, 3 (1962) 489–501.

Macmillan [n. 6.8].

Robinson, R. E. and Gallagher, J., *Africa and the Victorians* (1981 edn).

Schreuder [n. 8.6].

Stokes, E. T., 'Late Nineteenth-century Colonial Expansion and the Attack on the Theory of Economic Imperialism: A Case of Mistaken Identity?', *HJ*, XII, 2 (1969) 285–301.

8.2 The pursuit of the Voortrekkers

Agar-Hamilton (1937) [n. 7.5].

Benyon [n. 8.1].
De Kiewiet, C. W., *British Colonial Policy and the South African Republics 1848–72* (1929).
Harington, A. L., *Sir Harry Smith: Bungling Hero* (1980).
Midgley, J. F., *The Orange River Sovereignty, 1848–54 (AYB,* 1949).
Muller (1948) [n. 3.7].
Morrell (1930) [n. 7.4a].
Thompson L. M., 'The Great Trek, 1836–54' in *OHSA,* I (1969) 405–24.
Van Jaarsveld [n. 5.2].

8.3 Republican independence: the Sand River and Bloemfontein Conventions

Benyon [n. 8.1].
De Kiewiet [n. 8.2].
Eybers, G. W., *Select Constitutional Documents Illustrating South African History* (1918).
Morrell (1969) [n. 7.4a].
Orpen [n. 5.4].
Van Schoor [n. 5.4].

8.4 The High Commissionerships of Sir George Grey (1854–61) and Sir Philip Wodehouse (1862–70)

Benyon [n. 8.1].
du Toit [n. 7.3].
Rutherford [n. 6.1].

8.5 Sir Henry Barkly and the diamond fields, 1870–7

Agar-Hamilton (1937) [n. 7.5].
Jackson-Haight, M. V., *European Powers and South-East Africa* (1967).
Kallaway, P., 'Labour in the Kimberley Diamond Fields', *SALB,* 1, 7 (1974) 52–61.
Lockhart and Woodhouse [n. 6.2].
Macmillan, M., *Sir Henry Barkly* (1969).
Matthews, J. W., *Incwadi Yami* (1887).
Oberholster, J. J., *Die Anneksasie van Griekwaland-Wes (AYB* 1945).
Robertson, M., *Diamond Fever: South African Diamond History, 1866–9* (1974).
Sauer, H., *Ex Africa* (1937).
Shillington [n. 7.8].
Simons, P. B. (ed.) *John Blades Currey, 1850 to 1900* (1986).
Smith, K. W., *Alfred Aylward: The Tireless Agitator* (1983).
Turrell, R. [n. 6.2], and 'Kimberley: Labour and Compounds, 1871–88', in Marks, S. and Rathbone, R. (eds) *Industrialisation and Social Change in South Africa 1870–1930* (1982) 45–76 and 'Kimberley's Model Compounds', *JAH,* 25, 1 (1984) 59–75.
Van Jaarsveld, F. A., *Vaalrivier, Omstrede Grenslyn* (1974).
Williams [n. 6.2].
Worger [n. 19.3].

8.6 Federal strategies, 1874–80: Carnarvon, Frere, Shepstone and the annexation of the Transvaal

Appelgryn [n. 5.6].

Atmore and Marks [n. 8.1].
Brookes, E. H., *White Rule in South Africa* (1974).
Cope, R. L., 'Shepstone, the Zulus and the Annexation of the Transvaal', *SAHJ*, 4 (1972) 45–63.
De Kiewiet, C. W., *The Imperial Factor in South Africa* (1937).
Dunn, W. H., *James Anthony Froude* (1961).
Engelbrecht (1946) [n. 5.6].
Etherington, N. A., 'Labour Supply and the Generation of South African Confederation in the 1870s', *JAH*, 20, (1979) 235–53.
Goodfellow, C. F., *Great Britain and South African Confederation* (1966).
Macmillan [n. 8.5].
Schreuder, D. M., *The Scramble for Southern Africa, 1877–95* (1980).
Solomon, W. E. G., *Saul Solomon* (1948).

8.7 Republican independence again, 1881–4: the Pretoria and London Conventions; conflict over Basutoland and the 'Road to the North' 1880–5

Agar-Hamilton (1937) [n. 7.5].
Dachs [n. 7.10].
Davenport [n. 6.2].
Hall, K. O., *Imperial Proconsul: Sir Hercules Robinson and South Africa, 1881–9* (1980).
Schreuder, D. M., *Gladstone and Kruger* (1969) and [n. 8.6].
Shillington [n. 7.8].
Sillery, A., *John Mackenzie of Bechuanaland* (1971).
Van Jaarsveld, F. A. *et al.* (eds.) *Die Eerste Vryheidsoorlog, 1880–1* (1980).

8.8 The scramble for southern Africa: gold, railways and rival imperialisms 1880–95

Axelson, E., *Portugal and the Scramble for Africa* (1962).
Butler, J., 'The German Factor in Anglo-Transvaal Relations', in Gifford, P. and Louis, W. R. (eds.) *Britain and Germany in Africa* (1967) 179–214.
Galbraith [n. 7.9].
Kubicek (1979) [n. 5.7].
Marais [n. 5.5].
Marks, S., 'Scrambling for Southern Africa', *JAH*, 23, (1982) 97–113.
Maylam [n. 7.8].
Mendelsohn [n. 5.7].
Phimister, I. R., 'Rhodes, Rhodesia and the Rand', *JSAS*, 1, 1 (1974) 74–90.
Purkis [n. 19.2].
Schreuder, [n. 8.6].
Van der Poel, J., *Railway and Customs Policies in South Africa, 1885–1910* (1933).
Van Winter, P. J., *Onder Krugers Hollanders* (1937).
Van Helten [n. 5.7].
Warhurst, P. R., *Anglo-Portuguese Relations in South-Central Africa, 1890–1900* (1962).
Wilburn [n. 19.2].

8.9 Chamberlain, Rhodes, Milner and the confrontation with Kruger, 1895–9

Benyon [n. 8.1].
Blainey [n. 5.7].
Butler, J., *The Liberal Party and the Jameson Raid* (1968).

Davenport [n. 6.2].
De Cecco [n. 8.1].
Duminy [n. 5.7].
Duminy and Guest (eds) [n. 5.7].
Fitzpatrick, J. P., *The Transvaal from Within* (1896) and *Further South African Memories* (ed. D. Lavin) (1979).
Hancock, W. K., *Smuts I: the Sanguine Years* (1962).
Kubicek (1972) [n. 5.7].
Le May, G. H. L., *British Supremacy in South Africa* (1965).
Le Roux, F. J., and Van Zyl, D. J. (eds) *Een Eeuw van Ohreg* (1985).
Lewsen (1982) [n. 6.8].
Marais [n. 5.5].
Mendelsohn [n. 5.7].
Ovendale, R., 'Profit and Patriotism: Natal, the Transvaal and the Coming of the Second Anglo-Boer War', *JICH*, 8, 3 (1980) 209–34.
Pakenham, E., *Jameson's Raid* (1960).
Porter, A. N., *The Origins of the South African War: Joseph Chamberlain and the Diplomacy of Imperialism, 1895–9* (1980).
Rotberg [n. 6.2].
Smith, I. R., 'The Origins of the South African War (1899–1902): a Reappraisal', *SAHJ* 22 (1990) 24–60.
Spies, S. B., *The Origins of the Anglo-Boer War* (1972).
Van der Poel, J., *The Jameson Raid* (1951).
Van Helten [n. 5.7] and 'Empire and High Finance: South Africa and the International Gold Standard, 1890–1914', *JAH*, 23, 4 (1982) 529–48.
Wylde, R. H., *Joseph Chamberlain and the South African Republic, 1895–9* (*AYB*, 1956).

8.10 The Anglo-Boer War of 1899–1902

Bailes, H. L., 'Military Aspects of the War', in Warwick, P. (1980, below) 65–102.
Belfield, E., *The Boer War* (1975).
Blanch, M. D., in Warwick, P. (1980, below) 210–38.
Breytenbach, J. J., *Die Geskiedenis van die Tweede Vryheidsoorlog in Suid-Afrika, 1899–1920* (4 vols 1969–77).
Brits, J. P. (ed.) *The Diary of a National Scout, P. J. du Toit* (1974).
Davenport [n. 6.2].
Davey, A. M., *The British Pro-Boers 1877–1902* (1978), and (ed.) *Lawrence Richardson's Selected Correspondence, 1901–3* (*VRS*, II, 8, 1977) and *Breaker Morant and the Bushveldt Carbineers* (VRS, II, 18, 1987).
Denoon, D. J. N., 'Participation in the "Boer War": People's War, People's Non-war, or Non-people's War?', in Ogot, B. A., *War and Society in Africa* (1972) 109–22.
De Wet, C. R., *Three Years War* (1902).
Fuller, J. F. C., *The Last of the Gentlemen's Wars* (1937).
Foxcroft, E., *Russia and the Anglo-Boer War* (1981).
Grundlingh, A., 'Collaborators in Boer Society', in Warwick, P., *The South African War*, 258–78.
Hancock, [n. 8.9].
Hobhouse, E., *The Brunt of the War and Where it Fell* (1902).
Holt, E., *The Boer War* (1958).
Jordaan, G., *Hoe Zij Stierven* (1915).
Judd, D., *The Boer War* (1977).

Kipling, R., *The Science of Rebellion* (1900) and *The Five Nations* (1917).
Koss, S., *The Anatomy of an Anti-war Movement: The Pro-Boers* (1973).
Le May [n. 8.9].
Lewsen, P., (1982) [n. 6.8], and *Selections from the Correspondence of John X. Merriman* (*VRS*, 47, 1966).
Magnus, P., *Kitchener: Portrait of an Imperialist* (1958).
Marquard, L. (ed.) *Letters from a Boer Parsonage* (1967).
Morton, R. F., 'Linchwe I and the Kgatla Campaign in the S.A. War, 1899–1902', *JAH* 26, 2 (1985) 169–92.
Nasson, W. R., 'Doing down their Masters: Africans, Boers and Treason in the Cape Colony during the South African War of 1899–1902', *JICH*, XII, 1(1983) 29–53, and 'Moving Lord Kitchener: Black Military Transport and Supply Work in the S.A. War, 1899–1902, with Particular Reference to the Cape Colony', *JSAS* 11, 1 (1984) 25–51.
Pakenham, T., *The Boer War* (1979).
Plaatje, S. T., *Boer War Diary* (ed. J. Comaroff) (1973).
Porter, B., 'The Pro-Boers in Britain', in Warwick (1980) below 239–57.
Preller, G. (ed.) *Scheepers se Dagboek* (1938).
Price, R., *An Imperial War and the British Working Class* (1972).
Reitz, D., *Commando* (1931).
Schulenburg, C. A. R., 'Die Bushveldt Carbineers: n Groep uit die Anglo–Boere Oorlog', *Hist.* 26, 1 (1981).
Smuts, J. C., 'Memoir of the Boer War', in Hancock, W. K. and van der Poel, J. (eds) *Selections from the Smuts Papers*, I (1966) 537–663.
Snyman, J. H., *Rebelle Verhoor in Kaapland 1899–1902* (*AYB* 1962).
Spies, S. B., *Methods of Barbarism? Roberts and Kitchener and Civilians in the Boer Republics, 1900–2* (1977).
Strydom, C. J. S., *Kaapland in die Tweede Vryheidsoorlog* (1937).
Travers, T. H. E., 'Technology, Tactics and Morale; Jean de Bloch, the Boer War and British Military Theory', *JMH*, 51, 2 (1979) 264–86.
Van Reenen, R. (ed.) *Emily Hobhouse: Boer War Letters* (1984).
Van Wyk Smith, M., *Drummer Hodge: the Poetry of the Anglo-Boer War 1899–1902*, (1978).
Viljoen, B., *My Reminiscences of the Anglo-Boer War* (1903).
Warwick, P., *Black People in the Anglo-Boer War* (1984) and (ed.) *The South African War* (1980).
Wrigley, W. D., 'The Fabian Society and the S. A. War', *SAHJ*, 10, (1978) 65–78.
Wright, H. M. (ed.) *Sir James Rose Innes Selected Correspondence, 1884–1902* (*VRS*, II, 3, 1972).

CHAPTER 9

9.1 The Treaty of Vereeniging, 1902

De Wet, C. R. *Three Years War* (1902).
Halperin, V., *Lord Milner and the Empire* (1952).
Hancock, W. K., *Four Studies in War and Peace in this Century* (1961) and *Smuts: The Sanguine Years* (1962), and (with J. van der Poel) *The Smuts Papers*, I (1966) 511–36.
Headlam, C., *The Milner Papers*, II (1933) 324–66.
Kestell, J. D. and Van Velden, D. E., *The Peace Negotiations between Boer and Briton* (1912).

Le May [n. 8.9].

Magnus [n. 8.10].

Marais [n. 2.3].

Worsfold, W. B., *Lord Milner's Work in South Africa* (1906).

9.2 The Cape and Natal in the post-war era

Brookes and Webb [n. 5.2].

Cuthbert, P., *The Administration of Dr Jameson as Prime Minister of the Cape Colony, 1904–8* (unpublished thesis, University of Cape Town, 1950).

Davenport [n. 6.2].

Dhupelia, U., 'African Labour in Natal: Attempts at Coercion and Control, 1893–1903', *JNZH*, V (1982) 36–48.

Lewsen P. (1982) [n. 6.8], and *Selections from the Correspondence of John X. Merriman* (*VRS*, 47, 50, 1966–9) and 'John X. Merriman as Prime Minister of the Cape Colony', *SAHJ*, 7 (1975) 62–87.

Marks [n. 6.5].

Siepman, M. R., *An Analytical Survey of the Political Career of L. S. Jameson, 1900–12* (unpublished thesis, University of Natal, 1979).

Thompson, L. M., 'The Colony of Natal and the Closer Union Movement', *BSALR*, (1957) 81–106.

9.3 Milner and reconstruction

Benyon [n. 8.1].

Denoon, D. J. N., *A Grand Illusion: the Failure of Imperial Policy in the Transvaal Colony during the Period of Reconstruction, 1900–5* (1973); 'The Transvaal Labour Crisis, 1901–6', *JAH*, VII, 3 (1967) 481–94; 'Capitalist Influence and the Transvaal Government during the Crown Colony Period', *HJ*, XI, 2 (1968) 301–31, and 'Capital and Capitalists in the Transvaal in the 1890s and 1900s', *HJ*, 23, 1 (1980) 111–32.

Duminy [n. 5.7], and (with Guest) [n. 5.7].

Gollin, A. M., *Proconsul in Politics: A Study of Lord Milner in Opposition and in Power* (1964).

Halperin, V., *Lord Milner and the Empire* (1952).

Hancock [n. 8.9].

Headlam, C., *The Milner Papers*, II (1933).

Jeeves, A. H., 'The Control of Migratory Labour in the South African Gold Mines in the Era of Kruger and Milner', *JSAS*, 2, 1 (1975) 3–39, and [n. 5.7].

Katz, E., *A Trade Union Aristocracy* (1976).

Katzenellenbogen, S. E., 'Reconstruction in the Transvaal', in Warwick, P. (ed.) *The South African War* 341–61.

Kubicek [n. 5.7].

Levy, N., *Foundations of the South African Cheap Labour System* (1982).

Mawby [n. 9.8].

Marks, S. and Trapido, S., 'Lord Milner and the South African State', *HW*, 8 (1979) 50–80.

Newton, A. P., *Select Documents on the Unification of South Africa* (2 vols, 1924).

Nimocks, W., *Milner's Young Men: The 'Kindergarten' in Edwardian Imperial Affairs* (1970).

Richardson, P., *Chinese Mine Labour in the Transvaal* (1982) and (with Van Helten, J. J.) [nn. 5.7, 19.3].

Stokes [n. 8.1].

Streak, M., *Lord Milner's Immigration Policy for the Transvaal, 1897–1905* (1969).
Synge, B., *The Story of the World* (5 vols, 1903).
Van Onselen, C., *Studies in the Social and Economic History of the Witwatersrand 1886–1914* (2 vols, 1982).
Warwick [n. 8.10].

9.4 The Milner regime and South African blacks: the Lagden Commission, segregation and the Zulu rebellion of 1906

Beinart, W. and Bundy, C. J., *Hidden Struggles in Rural South Africa: Politics and Popular Movements in the Transkei and Eastern Cape, 1890–1930* (1987).
Burton, D., *Sir Godfrey Lagden: Colonial Administrator* (unpublished thesis, Rhodes University, 1989).
Cell [n. 20.1]
Davenport, T. R. H., *The Beginnings of Urban Segregation in South Africa* (ISER, 1971) and (with Hunt, K. S.) [n. 19.1].
Jeeves [n. 9.3].
Karis and Carter, I (1972) [n. 6.3].
Keegan, T. J., *Rural Transformations in Industrializing South Africa: The Southern Highveld to 1914* (1986).
Marks [n. 6.5].
Maylam, P., *A History of the African People of South Africa: From the Early Iron Age to the 1970s* (1986).
Odendaal [n. 6.3].
Pyrah [n. 9.9].
Stuart, J., *A History of the Zulu Rebellion, and Dinuzulu's Arrest, Trial and Expatriation* (1913).
Welsh, D., *The Roots of Segregation* (1971).

9.5 Independent churches and the growth of African and Coloured political movements

See references listed in n. 7.10, and:

Karis and Carter, I (1972) [n. 9.4].
Lewis, G. L. M., *Between the Wire and the Wall: A History of South African 'Coloured' Politics* (1987).
Marais [n. 2.3].
Maylam [n. 9.4].
Odendaal [n. 6.3].

9.6 Gandhi

See references in n. 6.7 and:

Bhana, S., 'The Tolstoy Farm: Gandhi's Experiment in "Co-operative Commonwealth"', *SAHJ*, 7 (1975) 88–100; and with Mesthrie, U. S. 'Passive Resistance among Indian South Africans: A Historiographical Survey', *SAHJ*, 16 (1984) 118–31.
Ginwala, F., *Class Consciousness and Control: Indian South Africans, 1860–1946* (unpublished thesis, Oxford University, 1974).
Hancock [n. 8.9].
Joshi, P. S., *The Tyranny of Colour: A Study of the Indian Problem in South Africa* (1942).

Keiser, R. D., 'The South African Indians' Challenge to the Union and Imperial Governments, 1910–19', *SAHJ*, 13 (1981) 78–95.
Nanda, B. R., *Mahatma Gandhi* (1958).
Pachai, B. (ed.) *South Africa's Indians: The Evolution of a Minority* (1979) and *The History of the Indian Opinion* (*AYB*, 1961).
Pillay, B., *British Indians in the Transvaal: Trade, Politics and Imperial Relations, 1885–1906* (1976).
Potgieter, A. J., 'Die Johannesburgse Stadsraad en die Indiers en Andere Gekleurdes van die Goudstad, 1900–10', *SAHJ*, 12 (1980) 29–47.
Power, P. F., 'Gandhi in South Africa', *JMAS*, 7, 3 (1969) 441–56.
Swan, M., *Gandhi: The South African Experience* (1985).

9.7 The revival of Afrikanerdom

Antonissen, R., *Die Afrikaanse Letterkunde* (1960).
Davenport [n. 6.2].
Dekker, G., *Afrikaanse Literatuurgeskiedenis* (1963).
Du Toit, A., 'Captive to the Nationalist Paradigm: F. A. van Jaarsveld and the Historical Evidence for the Afrikaner's Ideas on his Calling and Mission', *SAHJ* 16 (1984) 49–80, and [n. 6.2].
Engelenburg, F. V., *General Louis Botha* (1929).
Garson, N. G., '*Het Volk*: The Botha–Smuts Party in the Transvaal, 1904–11', *HJ*, IX, 1 (1966) 101–32.
Giliomee, H., 'Constructing Afrikaner Nationalism', *JAAS*, XVIII, 1–2 (1983) 83–98.
Hancock [n. 8.9].
Hexham, I., *The Irony of Apartheid* (1981).
Kirstein, J., *Some Foundations of Afrikaner Nationalism* (unpublished thesis, University of Cape Town, 1956).
'Knop' (G. S. Preller), *Agt Jaar s'n Politiek: skoon Geskiedenis van die Suid Afrikaanse Nationale Party, 1902–10* (1910).
Moodie, T. D., *The Rise of Afrikanerdom: Power, Apartheid and the Afrikaner Civil Religion* (1975).
Pienaar, E. C., *Die Triomf van Afrikaans* (1943).
Scholtz, G. D., *Generaal C. F. Beyers* (1941).
Trollip, A. E. G., *The First Phase of Hertzogism* (unpublished thesis, Witwatersrand University, 1947).
Van den Heever, C. M., *General J. B. M. Hertzog* (1946).
Van Jaarsveld, F. A., *The Afrikaner's Interpretation of South African History* (1964)
Van Onselen [n. 9.3].
Yudelman, D., 'Afrikaner Scabs and the 1907 Strike: A State–Capital Daguerrotype', *AA*, 81, 323 (1982).

9.8 The Transvaal British

Denoon [n. 9.3].
Duminy and Guest [n. 5.7].
Fraser, M. and Jeeves, A. H., *All that Glittered: Selected Correspondence of Lionel Phillips, 1890–1924* (1977).
Katz [n. 9.3].
Kubicek [n. 8.9].
Marks and Trapido [n. 9.3].
Mawby, A. A., *The Political Behaviour of the British Population of the Transvaal*

1902–7 (unpublished thesis, Witwatersrand University, 1969) and 'Capital Government and Politics in the Transvaal, 1990–7', *HJ*, XVII, 2 (1974) 387–415.
Yudelman [n. 19.3].

9.9 The move towards responsible government in the Transvaal and the Orange River Colony

Bennett, A. E., *The West Ridgeway Committee, 1905–7* (unpublished thesis, Oxford University, 1984).
Duminy [n. 5.7].
Hancock [n. 8.9].
Hyam, R., *Elgin and Churchill at the Colonial Office* (1968) and (with G. Martin) *Reappraisals in British Imperial History* (1975).
Le May [n. 8.9].
Mansergh, N., *South Africa 1906–61: the Price of Magnanimity* (1962).
Newton, A. P., *The Unification of South Africa* (2 vols, 1924).
Pyrah, G. B., *Imperial Policy and South Africa, 1902–10* (1955).

9.10 The formation of the Union of South Africa 1908–10

Booth, A. R., 'Lord Selborne and the British Protectorates, 1902–10', *JAH*, X, 1 (1969) 133–48.
Brand, R. H., *The Union of South Africa* (1909).
Briand-Kyrik, F., *The Delimitation of Constituencies for the House of Assembly under the South African Act* (unpublished thesis, University of Cape Town, 1953).
Friedman, B., *Smuts: A Reappraisal* (1975).
Hyam, R., 'African Interests in the South Africa Act, 1908–10', *HJ*, XIII, 1 (1970) 85–105.
Hancock [n. 8.9].
Hancock and van der Poel (eds) (1966) [n. 9.1].
Malan, F. S., *Konvensie-Dagboek* (*VRS*, 32, 1951).
Newton [n. 9.9].
Odendaal (1984) [n. 6.3].
Thompson, L. M., *The Unification of South Africa* (1960).
Union of South Africa, *Minutes of Proceedings of the South African National Convention* (ed. G. R. Hofmeyr) (1911).
Van der Poel, [n. 8.8].
Walker [n. 6.2].
Walton, E. H., *The Inner History of the National Convention* (1912).

9.11 The unacknowledged protest of the blacks

Hyam [9.10].
Lewis [n. 9.5].
Maylam [n. 9.4].
Odendaal [n. 6.3].
Thompson [9.10].
Walker [n. 6.2].

CHAPTER 10

10.1 Botha's accession to power and quarrel with Hertzog

Davenport [n. 6.2].
Engelenburg [n. 9.7].

Garson, N. G., *Louis Botha or John X. Merriman: The choice of South Africa's First Prime Minister* (1969).
Hancock [n. 8.9], and *Smuts II: The Fields of Force* (1968);
Hancock, W. K. and van der Poel, J. (eds) (1966) III, IV [n. 9.1].
Kruger, D. W., *South African Parties and Policies, 1910–60* (1960).
Lewsen P. (1982) [n. 6.8], and *Selections from the Correspondence of John X. Merriman* (*VRS*, 50, 1969).
Malan, M. P. A., *Die Nasionale Party van Suid-Afrika, 1914–64* (1964).
Marais, A. H. (ed.) *Politieke Briewe 1909–12* (1971–3).
Spies, F. du T., Kruger, D. W. and Oberholster, J. J. (eds) *Hertzog Toesprake* (6 vols., 1977).
Thompson [n. 9.10].
Van den Heever [n. 9.7].

10.2 The segregationist policies of the Botha–Smuts regime

Davenport [n. 9.4].
Grobler, J. C. H., *Politieke Leier of Meeloper? Die Lewe van Piet Grobler, 1873–1942* (1988).
Kallaway, P., 'F. S. Malan, the Cape Liberal Tradition, and South African Politics, 1908–24', *JAH*, XV, 1 (1974) 113–29.
Lacey, M. J., *Working for Boroko: The Origins of a Coercive Labour System in South Africa* (1981).
Legassick, M., 'The Making of South African "Native Policy", 1903–23: The Origins of "Segregation"' (unpublished typescript, 1972).
Plaatje, S. T., *Native Life in South Africa* (1915).
Rich [n. 6.8].
Smuts, J. C., *Africa and Some World Problems* (1929).
Swanson, M. W., 'The Sanitation Syndrome: Bubonic Plague and Urban Native Policy in the Cape Colony, 1900–9, *JAH, XVIII, 3* (1977) 387–410.
Tatz, C. M., *Shadow and Substance in South Africa* (1962).
Wickins, P. L., 'The Natives Land Act of 1913: A Cautionary Essay on Simple Explanations of Complex Change', *SAJE*, 49, 2 (1981) 105–29.
Willan [n. 10.3].

10.3 The growth of African political opposition: the S.A.N.N.C. and the I.C.U.

Baines, G., *The Port Elizabeth Disturbances of October 1920* (unpublished thesis, Rhodes University, 1988).
Beinart and Bundy [n. 15.1].
Benson, M., *The Struggle for a Birthright* (1966).
Bonner, P., 'The 1920 Black Mineworkers' Strike: A Preliminary Account', in Bozzoli, B. (ed.) *Labour, Township and Protest* (1979) 273–97.
Bradford, H., 'Mass Movements and the Petty Bourgeoisie: The Social Origins of ICU Leadership', *JAH*, 25, 3 (1984) 295–320.
Bundy, C., 'A Voice in the Big House: The Career of Headman Enoch Mamba', *JAH*, 22, (1981) 531–50.
Kadalie, C., *My Life and the ICU* (ed. S. Trapido) (1970).
Karis and Carter, I (1972) [n. 6.3].
Lacey, [n. 10.2].
Maylam [n. 9.4].
Odendaal (1984) [n. 6.3].
Plaatje [n. 10.2].
Reed, A., 'The Journalism of S. T. Plaatje' (unpublished typescript).
Roux, E., *Time Longer than Rope* (1964).

600 *Bibliographical Notes*

Simons, H. J. and R. E., *Class and Colour in South Africa* (1969).
Walshe, P., *The Rise of African Nationalism in South Africa, 1912–52* (1970).
Whitehead, R., 'The Aborigines Protection Society and White Settlers in Rhodesia', *ICS*, 3 (1973) 96–109.
Wickins, P. L., *The Industrial and Commercial Workers' Union* (1978).
Willan, B., 'The Anti-Slavery and Aborigines Protection Societies and the South African Natives Land Act of 1913', *JAH*, 20, 1 (1979) 83–102.

10.4 Indian affairs: the climax of the Gandhi–Smuts encounter, and the defiance of Sapru

Bhana and Pachai [n. 6.7].
Bradlow, E. [n. 6.8] and *Immigration into the Union 1910–48: Policies and Attitudes* (unpublished thesis, University of Cape Town, 1978), Part I.
Hancock (1961) [n. 9.1].
See also the works listed in n. 9.6.

10.5 White worker resistance, 1913–14

Christie, R., 'Slim Jannie and the Forces of Production: South African Industrialisation, 1915–25', *ICS*, 8 (1977) 94–144.
Davies [n. 19.3].
Doxey [n. 19.5].
Hancock [n. 8.9].
Hutt [n. 19.5].
Johnstone, F. A., [n. 19.3], and 'The Labour History of the Witwatersrand in the Context of South African Studies, with Reflections on the New School', *SD*, 4, 2 (1978) 101–8.
Katz [n. 9.3].
Moroney, S., 'Mine Worker Protest on the Witwatersrand 1901–12' in Webster, E. (ed.) (below).
Simons [n. 10.3].
Ticktin, D., *The Origin and Development of the South African Labour Party* (unpublished thesis, University of Cape Town, 1973).
Webster, E. (ed.) *Essays in Southern African Labour History* (1978).
Yudelman [n. 19.3].

10.6 The invasion of German South West Africa and the Afrikaner rebellion

Davenport, T. R. H., 'The South African Rebellion of 1914', *EHR*, LXXVII, 306 (1963) 73–94.
Garson, N. G., 'The Boer rebellion of 1914', *HT*, XII (1962) 132–9.
Grobler [n. 10.2].
Hancock [n. 8.9].
Kemp, J. C. G., *Die Pad van die Veroweraar* (1946).
Malan, D. F., *Glo in U Volk* (1964) 90–5.
Maritz, S. G., *My Lewe en Strewe* (1939).
Naude, J. D., *Generaal Hertzog en die Ontstaan van die Nasionale Party, 1913–4* (1970).
Scholtz, G. D., *Generaal C. F. Beyers* (1941) and *Die Rebellie* (1942).
Stadler, A. W., 'The Afrikaner in Opposition, 1910–48', *JCPS*, VII, 3 (1969) 204–15.
Spies, S. B., *The Rebellion in South Africa, 1914–15* (unpublished thesis, Witwatersrand University, 1963).
Steinmeyer, J., *Spykers met Koppe* (1946).

10.7 South Africa in the Great War

Buchan, J., *The South African Forces in France* (1920).
Garson, N. G., 'South Africa and World War I', *JICH*, 8, 1 (1979) 68–85.
Grundlingh, A. M., *Black Men in a White Man's War: South African Blacks and the First World War* (1986).
Hancock [n. 8.9].
Spies, S. B., 'The Outbreak of the First World War and the Botha Government', *SAHJ*, I (1969) 47–57.
Ticktin, D., 'The War and the Collapse of the South African Labour party', *SAHJ*, I (1969) 59–80.
The Union of South Africa and the Great War, 1914–18 (1924);
Willan, B. P., 'The South African Native Labour Contingent, 1916–18', *JAH*, 19, 1 (1978) 61–86.

10.8 Party Realignments, 1915–21

Bouch, R. J., 'Farming and Politics in the Karroo and Eastern Cape, 1910–24', *SAHJ*, 12 (1980).
Hancock [n. 8.9] and (1968) [n. 10.1].
Lewsen, P. (ed.) *Selections from the Correspondence of John X. Merriman* (*VRS* 50, 1969).
Marais, A. H. (ed.) [n. 10.1] and 'Aspekte van die 1915 Verkiesing', *SAHJ*, 5 (1973) 61–93.
Reid, B., 'The General Elections of 1920 and 1921 in Natal: Labour in Triumph and Defeat', *JNZH*, II (1979) 37–48.
Spies, F. du T. *et al.* (eds) (1977) [n. 10.1].
Ticktin [n. 10.5].
Van der Schyff, P. F. *Die Unioniste Party en die Suid-Afrikaanse Politiek, 1910–21* (unpublished thesis, Potchefestroom University, 1964).

10.9 Smuts at Versailles, the South West African mandate and the bid to incorporate Southern Rhodesia and the Protectorates

Chanock, M., *Britain, Rhodesia and South Africa, 1900–45: The unconsummated Union* (1977).
Curry, G., 'Woodrow Wilson, Jan Smuts and the Versailles Settlement', *AHR*, LXVI, 4 (1961) 963–86.
Hailey, Lord, *The Republic of South Africa and the High Commission Territories* (1963).
Hancock [n. 8.9], [n. 10.1], and (1961) [n. 9.1], and *Survey of British Commonwealth Affairs* I (1937).
Hummel, H. C., *Sir Charles Coghlan* (unpublished thesis, London University, 1975).
Hyam, R., *The Failure of South African Expansion 1908–48* (1972).
Lee, M. E., 'The Origins of the Rhodesian Responsible Government Movement', *RH* 6 (1975) 33–52, and 'An Analysis of the Rhodesian Referendum, 1922', *RH* 8 (1977) 71–98.
Long, B. K., *Drummond Chaplin* (1941).
Lowry, D. W., *The Life and Times of Ethel Tawse-Jollie: A Case Study of the Transference and Adaptation of British Social and Political Ideas of the Edwardian Era in a Colonial Society* (unpublished thesis, Rhodes University, 1989).
Mackenzie, J. M., 'Southern Rhodesia and Responsible Government', *RH* 9 (1978) 23–40.
Palley, C., *The Constitutional History and Law of Southern Rhodesia* (1966).

Smuts, J. C., *The League of Nations, a Practical Suggestion* (1917) and *Africa and Some World Problems* (1929).
Van der Poel, J. (ed.) *Selections from the Smuts Papers*, V (1973).
Wallis, J. P. R., *One Man's Hand: the Life of Sir Charles Coghlan* (1950).
Warhurst, P. R., 'Rhodesian–South African Relations, 1900–23', *SAHJ*, 3 (1971) 92–107, and 'Smuts and Africa: A Study in Sub-imperialism', *SAHJ*, 16 (1984) 82–100.

10.10 Shadows over the Smuts regime, 1921–2: Bondelswarts, Bulhoek and the Rand Rebellion

Bonner [n. 10.3].
Davey, A. M., *The Bondelswarts Affair* (*UNISA*, 1961).
Davies [n. 19.3].
Edgar, R. C., *The Fifth Seal: Enock Mgijima, the Israelites and the Bulhoek Massacre* (unpublished thesis, University of California, 1977);
Freislich, R., *The Last Tribal War* (1964).
Hancock (1968) [n. 10.1].
Herd, N., *1922: the Revolt on the Rand* (1966).
Hunter [n. 4.4].
Johnstone [n. 19.3].
Lewis, G. L. M., *The Bondelswarts Rebellion of 1922* (unpublished thesis, Rhodes University, 1977).
Roux [n. 10.3].
Simons [n. 10.3.]
Sundkler (1961) (n. 7.10).
Walker, I. L. and Weinbren, B., *2,000 Casualties* (1961).
Yudelman [n. 19.3].

10.11 The Nationalist–Labour Pact and the 1924 general election

Creswell, M., *An Epoch in the History of South Africa: The Life of F. H. P. Creswell* (1956).
Hancock (1968) [n. 10.1].
Kruger [n. 10.1].
Lewis [n. 9.5].
O'Dowd, C. E. M., 'The General Election of 1924', *SAHJ*, 2 (1970) 54–76.
Spies *et al.* (eds) (1977) [n. 10.1].
Van den Heever [n. 9.7].
Yudelman [n. 19.3].

CHAPTER 11

11.1 1924–a turning point?

Bradford [n. 11.5].
Davies, R. [n. 19.3] and (with D. Kaplan, M. Morris and D. O'Meara) 'Class Struggle and a Periodisation of the South African State', *RAPE* 7 (1976).
Kaplan, D., 'The Politics of Protection in South Africa', *JSAS*, 3, 1 (1976) 70–91, and 'An Analysis of the South African State in the "Fusion" Period, 1932–39', *ICS*, 7 (1977) 149–59.
Lacey [n. 10.2].
Macmillan, W. M., *Complex South Africa* (1930)

Report of the Carnegie Commission on Poor Whiteism (5 vols. 1932).
Salomon, L., 'The Economic Background to Afrikaner Nationalism', in Butler, J. (ed.) *Boston University Papers on African History*, I (1964) 217–43.
Spies *et al.* (eds) (1977) [n. 10.1].
Terblanche, H. O., 'Die trek van die Afrikaner na Port Elizabeth', *Hist.* 22, 2 (1977) 90–107.
Yudelman [n. 19.3].

11.2 Dominion status, the flag crisis, and the protectorates

Blackwell, L., *African Occasions* (1938).
Davenport, T. R. H., 'Nationalism and Conciliation: The Bourassa–Hertzog Posture', *H–A*, X, 16 (1963) 72–87, and *CHR*, XLIV, 3 (1963) 193–212.
Dawson, R. M., *The Development of Dominion Status, 1900–36* (1937).
Hailey, Lord [n. 10.9].
Hancock (1968) [n. 10.1], and (1937) [n. 10.9].
Hyam [n. 10.9].
Kruger, D. W., *The Making of a Nation* (1969).
Long, B. K., *In Smuts's Camp* (1945).
Malan, D. F., *Afrikaner Volkseenheid en my Ervarings op die Pad daarheen* (1959).
Mansergh, N., *Survey of Commonwealth Affairs, 1931–59: Problems of External Policy* (1952) and *Documents and Speeches on Commonwealth Affairs, 1931–52* (1953).
Marais, G., 'The Value of the Ottawa Agreement Reconsidered', *F and TR*, III, 19 (1958) 143–58.
Paton, A., *Hofmeyr* (1964).
Pienaar, S., *South Africa and International Relations between the Two World Wars: The League of Nations Dimension* (1987).
Pirow, O., *J. B. M. Hertzog* (1957).
Reitz, D., *Trekking on* (1933).
Reitz, H., *The Conversion of a South African Nationalist* (1946).
Report of the Native Economic Commission (*UG* 22 of 1932).
Saker, H., *The South African Flag Controversy 1925–8* (1980).
Scholtz, G. D., *Hertzog, Smuts en die Britse Ryk* (1975).
Smuts, J. C., *Africa and Some World Problems* (1929).
Spies *et al.* (eds) (1977), IV, V [n. 10.1].
Thom, H. B., *D. F. Malan* (1980).
Turrell, A. D., *The South African Party, 1932–4: the Movement towards Fusion* (unpublished thesis, University of Natal, 1977) and 'General Smuts and the General Election of 1933 in Natal', *JNZH* (1980).
Van den Heever, (1946) [n. 9.7].
Wheare, K. C., *The Constitutional Structure of the Commonwealth* (1960), and *The Statute of Westminster* (5th edn, 1953).

11.3 Hertzog's policies for Asians and Africans

Beinart, W. J. and Bundy, C., 'The Union, the Nation and the Talking Crow: The Language and Tactics of the Independent ICU in East London', *ICS*, 12 (1981) 69–76.
Bhana and Pachai [n. 6.7].
Bradford [n. 11.5].
Calpin [n. 6.7].
Hancock (1968) [n. 10.1].

Jabavu, D. D. T., *The Segregation Fallacy, and other Papers* (1928).
Joshi [n. 6.7].
Karis and Carter, I (1972) [n. 6.3].
Lacey [n. 10.2].
Lewis [n. 9.5].
Maylam [n. 9.4].
Pachai [n. 6.7].
Pahad, E., *The Development of Indian Political Movements in South Africa, 1924–46* (unpublished thesis, University of Sussex, 1972).
Palmer, M., *History of the Indians in Natal* (1957).
Roux [n. 10.3].
Simons [n. 10.3].
Tatz [n. 10.2].
Van der Poel [n. 10.9] V 305–24, 368–77.
Walshe, [n. 10.3].
Welsh, D., 'The State President's Powers under the Bantu Administration Act', *AJ* (1968) 81–100.
Wickins [n. 10.3].

11.4 The general election of 1929

Briand-Kyrik [n. 9.10].
Hancock (1968) [n. 10.1].
O'Dowd, C. E. M., 'The General Election of 1929' (unpublished typescript, n.d.).
Pirow [n. 11.2].
Roux [n. 10.3].
Smuts (1929) [n. 10.9].
Spies *et al.* (eds) (1977) V [n. 10.1].
Van den Heever [n. 9.7].

11.5 The I.C.U. and the A.N.C. in the 1920s

Bradford, H., *A Taste of Freedom: the ICU in rural South Africa, 1924–30* (1987).
Hill, R. A. and Pirio, G. A., 'Africa for the Africans: The Garvey Movement in South Africa, 1920–40', in Marks, S. and Trapido, S., *The Politics of Race, Class and Nationalism in Twentieth Century South Africa* (1987) 209–53.
Kadalie [n. 10.3].
Karis and Carter (1972) I [n. 6.3].
Lacey [n. 10.2].
Lewis [n. 9.5].
Mahabane, Z. R., *The Good Fight* (unpublished typescript, North Western University, n.d.).
Maylam [n. 9.4].
Roux E., *S. P. Bunting: A Political Biography, 1873–1936* (1944), and [n. 10.3].
Simons [n. 10.3].
Swanson, M. W., *The Views of Mahlathi: Writings of A. W. G. Champion, A Black South African* (1983).
Tatz [n. 10.2].
Walshe [n. 10.3].
Wickins [n. 10.3].

11.6 The Great Depression and the politics of coalition and fusion

Basson [n. 12.3].

Brits J. P., *Tielman Roos: sy Rol in die Suid-Afrikaanse Politiek, 1907–35* (1979).
Frankel, S. H., 'South Africa's Monetary Policy', *SAJE*, 1, 1 (1933) 79–87.
Hancock (1968) [n. 10.1].
Hobart Houghton, D., *The South African Economy* (4th edn, 1976) and (with J. Dagut) *Source Material on the South African Economy, 1860–1970* (3 vols, 1972).
Long [n. 11.2].
Malan [n. 11.2].
Nicholls, G. H., *South Africa in my Time* (1961).
O'Meara [n. 12.3].
Paton [n. 11.2].
Pirow [n. 11.2].
Richards, C. S., 'Economic Revival in South Africa', *EcJ*, XLIV (1934) 616–30.
Roberts and Trollip [n. 12.3].
Sadie, J. L., *Die Ekonomiese Ontwikkeling van Suid-Afrika* (c. 1956).
Schumann C. G. W., [n. 19.2] and *The World Depression: South Africa and the Gold Standard* (n.d.).
Spies *et al.* (eds) [n. 10.1].
Thom [n. 11.2].
Turrell [n. 11.2].

CHAPTER 12

12.1 The Fusion Government and the 'native bills'

Ballinger, M., *From Union to Apartheid* (1969).
Davenport, T. R. H., 'The Triumph of Colonel Stallard', *SAHJ*, 2 (1970) 77–96.
Dubow [n. 20.1].
Nicholls [n. 11.6].
Karis, T., and Carter, G. M., *From Protest to Challenge*, II (1973).
Lacey [n. 10.2].
Molteno, D. B., 'The Betrayal of Native Representation' (*SAIRR*, 1959).
Paton [n. 11.2].
Report of the Cape Coloured Commission (*UG* 54 of 1937) [Wilcocks Report].
Reports of the Joint Select Committee on the Native Bills (1930–4 and 1935).
Report of the Native Affairs Commission (*UG* 48 of 1937) [Fagan Report].
Rich, P., 'African Politics and the Cape African Franchise, 1926–36', *ICS*, 9 (1978) 127–36.
Roux [n. 10.3].
Simons [n. 10.3].
Tatz, [n. 10.2].
Turrell [n. 11.2].
Union of South Africa, *Joint Sitting Debates* (1936).
Walshe [n. 10.3].

12.2 The black reaction to Hertzog's 1936 legislation

Ballinger [n. 12.1].
Benson, M., *South Africa: The Struggle for a Birthright* (1966).
Davenport [n. 12.1].
Gerhart, G. M., *Black Power in South Africa* (1979).
Karis and Carter (1973) II [n. 12.1].

Matthews, Z. K., *Freedom for my People* (ed. M. Wilson, 1983).
Maylam [n. 9.4].
Mouton, F. A., *Die Politieke Loopbaan van Margaret Ballinger* (unp. thesis, Pretoria University, 1990).
Roux [n. 10.3].
Simons [n. 10.3].
Swanson [n. 11.5].
Tatz [n. 10.2].
Walshe [n. 10.3].

12.3 The party split of 1934 and the rise of 'purified' Afrikaner nationalism

Adam, H. and Giliomee, H., *The Rise and Crisis of Afrikaner Power* (1979).
Basson, J. A., *J. G. Strijdom: Sy Politieke Loopbaan van 1929 tot 1948* (1980).
Cilliers, A. C., *Quo Vadis?* (1939).
Coetzee, J. A., *Nasieskap en Politieke Groepering in Suid-Afrika, 1652–1968* (1969).
Diederichs, N., *Nasionalisme as Lewensbeskouing* (1936).
De Klerk [n. 3.1].
Du Plessis, E. P., *'n Volk Staan Op: Die Ekonomiese Volkskongres en Daarna* (1964).
Giliomee [n. 9.7].
Malan (1959) [n. 11.2] and (1964) [n. 10.6].
Meyer, P. J., *Die Stryd van die Afrikaner Werker* (1944) and *Die Afrikaner* (1940).
Moodie [n. 9.7].
Paterson, S., *The Last Trek* (1957).
O'Meara, D., *Volkskapitalisme: Class, Capital and Ideology in the Development of Afrikaner Nationalism, 1934–48* (1983) and 'White Trade Unionism, Political Power and Afrikaner Nationalism', in Webster, E. (ed.) *Essays in Southern African Labour History* (1978) 164–80, and 'The Afrikaner Broederbond, 1927–48: Class Vanguard of Afrikaner Nationalism', *JSAS*, 3, 2 (1977) 156–86.
Pelzer, A. N., *Die Afrikaner Broederbond* (1978).
Pirow [n. 11.2].
Roberts, M. and Trollip, A. E. G., *The South African Opposition, 1939–45* (1947).
Serfontein, J. H. P., *Brotherhood of Power* (1978).
Sharp, J., 'Roots and Development of Volkekunde in South Africa', *JSAS*, 8, 1 (1981) 16–36.
Stadler [n. 10.6].
Stultz, N. M., *The Nationalist in Opposition, 1934–48* (1974).
Thom [n. 11.2].
Van Onselen [n. 9.7] 111–70.
Vatcher, W. H., *White Laager: The Rise of Afrikaner Nationalism* (1965).
Wilkins, I. and Strydom, H., *The Super-Afrikaners* (1978).

12.4 The foreign policy of the Fusion era

Basson [n. 12.3] 248–64.
Hahlo, H. R., and Kahn, E., *The Union of South Africa: The Development of its Laws and Constitution* (1960) 174.
Hailey, Lord [n. 10.9].
Hancock (1937) [n. 10.9], and (1968) [n. 10.1].
Hyam, R., *The Failure of South African Expansion* (1972).
Kienzle, W., 'German–South African Trade in the Nazi Era', *African Affairs*, 78, 310 (1979) 81–90.

Long, [n. 11.2].
Mansergh, [n. 11.2].
Oothuizen, W. S., *Die Suid Afrikaanse Parlementêre Krisis van 1939* (unpublished thesis, Pretoria University, 1970).
Pienaar [n. 11.2].
Spies *et al.* (1977) VI 265–306 [n. 10.1].
Van den Heever [n. 9.7].
Van der Poel (ed.) (1973) VI 187–91 [n. 10.9].
Walker, E. A., *A History of Southern Africa* (1957).

CHAPTER 13

13.1 South Africa enters the Second World War

Agar-Hamilton, J. A. I. and Turner, L. C. F., *Crisis in the Desert* (1952) and *The Sidi Rezegh Battles* (1957).
Brown, J. A., *Eagles Strike* (1974).
Hancock (1968) [n. 10.1].
Mansergh, N., *Survey of Commonwealth Affairs, 1939–52: Problems of Wartime Co-operation and Post-War Change* (1958) and *Documents and Speeches on Commonwealth Affairs, 1931–52* (1953).
Orpen, N., *The East African and Abyssinian Campaigns* (1968) and *War in the Desert* (1971).
Turner, L. C. F., *War in the Southern Oceans* (1961).

13.2 The Afrikaner Opposition, 1939–43

Basson [n. 12.3] (1980).
Blackwell, L., *Farewell to Parliament* (1946).
D'Oliviera [n. 16.1].
Hancock (1968) [n. 10.1].
Heard, K., *General Elections in South Africa, 1943–70* (1974).
Malan [n. 11.2].
O'Meara (1983) [n. 12.3].
Paton [n. 11.2].
Pirow [n. 11.2].
Roberts and Trollip [n. 12.3].
Spies *et al.* (1977) VI 307–33 [n. 10.1].
Stultz [n. 12.3].
Van Rensburg, J. F. J., *Their Paths Crossed Mine* (1956).
Thom [n. 11.2].
Van den Heever [n. 9.7].
Van der Poel (ed.) (1973) VI [n. 10.9].
Vatcher [n. 12.3].

13.3 Liberal reform initiatives and a polarised response, 1942–3

Ballinger [n. 12.1].
Davenport, T. R. H., 'The Smuts Government and the Africans, 1939–48', *ICS* 5 (1974) 80–91.
Hancock (1968) [n. 10.1].
Hellmann, E. (ed.) *Handbook on Race Relations* (1949).
Johns, S., 'The Birth of Non-white Trade Unionism in South Africa', *Race*, IX (1967) 173–92.

Karis and Carter II (1973) [n. 12.1].
Lewsen, P., in Butler, Elphick and Welsh [n. 6.8] 98–115.
Lewis [n. 9.5].
Maylam [n. 9.4].
Nuttall, T. A., *Principle and Pragmatism: Dr E. H. Brookes and the Natives Representative Council Crisis, 1946–9* (unpublished thesis, University of Natal 1981).
Roux [n. 10.3].
Simons [n. 10.3].
Stadler, A. W., 'Birds in the Cornfield: Squatter Movements in Johannesburg, 1944–7', *JSAS*, 6, 1 (1979) 93–123.
Tatz [n. 10.2].
Walshe [n. 10.3].

13.4 The mineworkers' strike of 1946 and the Fagan Report

See works by Ballinger, Davenport, Karis and Carter, Nuttall, Roux, Simons and Walshe in n. 13.3, and:

Diamond, C. R., *African Labour Problems on the South African Gold Mines, with Special Reference to the Strike of 1946* (unpublished thesis, University of Cape Town, 1969).
Hemson, D., 'Dock Workers, Labour Circulation and Class Struggles in Durban, 1940–59', *JSAS* 4, 1 (1977) 88–124.
Hirson, B., 'The Reorganisation of African Trade Unions in Johannesburg, 1936–42', *ICS*, 7 (1976) 182–94.
Lodge, T., *Black Politics in South Africa since 1945* (1983).
O'Meara, D., 'The 1946 African Mineworkers' Strike and the Political Economy of South Africa', *JCCP*, 13, 2 (1975) 146–73.
Report of the Native Laws Commission, (*UG* 28 of 1948) [Fagan Report].

13.5 Xuma's A.N.C. and the rise of the Youth League

See works by Gerhart, Karis and Carter, Matthews [n. 12.2], Walshe [n. 10.3], Lodge [n. 13.4], and:
Benson, M. [n. 12.2] and *Nelson Mandela* (1980).
Maylam [n. 9.4].
Meer, F. *Higher than Hope: Rolihlahla* [Nelson Mandela] *we love you* (1988).
Ralston, R. D. 'American Episodes in the Making of an African Leader: A Case Study of Alfred B. Xuma', *IJAHS*, 6, 1 (1973) 72–93.

13.6 'C.A.D.', anti-C.A.D. and the Non-European Unity Movement

Bunting, B., *Moses Kotane, South African Revolutionary* (1975).
Lewis [n. 9.5].
Lodge [n. 13.4].
Roux [n. 10.3].
Simons [n. 10.3].

13.7 Durban's Indians and the 'Pegging' and 'Ghetto' Acts

Bagwandeen, D. R., *The Questions of 'Indian Penetration' in the Durban Area and Indian Politics: 1940–6* (unpublished thesis, University of Natal, 1983).
Bhana and Pachai (eds) [n. 6.7].
Calpin [n. 6.7].

Ginwala [n. 9.6].
Hancock (1968) [n. 10.1].
Nicholls [n. 11.6].
Nuttall, T., '"It seems Peace but it can be War": The Durban "Riots" of 1949 and the Struggle for the City' (unpublished typescript, 1989).
Pahad [n. 11.3].
Paton [n. 11.2].
Swan, M., 'Ideology in Organized Indian Politics, 1891–1948', in Marks and Trapido [n. 11.5] 182–208.
Webb, M. and Kirkwood, K., 'The Durban Riots and After' (*SAIRR*, 1949).
Webb, M. and Keppel Jones, A., in Hellmann, E. (ed.) [n. 13.3] 206–28.

13.8 The Nationalist victory in 1948

Basson [n. 12.3].
Bradlow [n. 10.4].
Briand-Kyrik [n. 9.10].
D'Oliviera [n. 16.1].
Hancock (1968) [n. 10.1].
Heard [n. 13.1].
Legassick, M., 'Legislation, Ideology and Economy in post-1948 South Africa', *JSAS*, 1, 1 (1974) 5–35.
Malan [n. 11.2].
O'Dowd, C. E. M., 'The General Election of 1948' (unpublished typescript).
Paton [n. 11.2].
Serfontein [n. 12.3].
Stultz [n. 12.3].
Rhoodie [n. 20.1].
Thom [n. 11.2].
Tiryakian, E. A., 'Apartheid and Politics in South Africa', *JP*, 22, 4 (1960) 682–97.
Verslag van die Kleurvraagstuk-Kommissie van die Herenigde Nasionale Party (unpublished typescript, 1948) [Sauer Report].

CHAPTER 14

14.1 The first purely Afrikaner government

Ballinger [n. 12.1].
Blackwell, L., *Blackwell Remembers* (1971).
Bradlow [n. 110.4].
Carter, G. M., *The Politics of Inequality* (1959).
Heard [n. 13.2].
Horrell, M. *et al.* (ed.) *Survey of Race Relations* (*SAIRR* annual volumes).
Malan (1959) [n. 11.2] and (1964) [n. 10.6].
Malan [n. 10.1].
Robertson, J., *Liberalism in South Africa 1949–63* (1971).
Schoeman, B. M., *Van Malan tot Verwoerd* (1973).
Thom [n. 11.2].
Watson [n. 16.4].

14.2 The Coloured vote issue and the Torch Commando

Beinart, B., 'Sovereignty and the Law', *THRHR*, 15 (1952) 101–34.

Carter [n. 14.1].
Cowen, D. V., 'Parliamentary Sovereignty and the Entrenched Clauses of South Africa Act' (1951).
Hahlo and Kahn [n. 12.4].
Irvine, D., in Butler, Elphick and Welsh [n. 6.8] 116–33.
Lewis [n. 9.5].
May, H. J., *The South African Constitution* (1955).
Sher, D. M., *The Disfranchisement of the Coloured Voters, 1948–56* (unpublished thesis, *UNISA*, 1984).
Thompson, L. M., *The Cape Coloured Franchise* (*SAIRR*, 1949).

14.3 The politics of the Defiance Campaign

Benson [n. 12.2].
Carter, C., 'The Defiance Campaign – a Comparative Analysis of the Organis-ation, Leadership and Participation in the Eastern Cape and Transvaal', *ICS*, 2 (1971) 76–97.
Feit, E., *South Africa: The Dynamics of the African National Congress* (1962).
Gerhart [n. 12.2].
Karis, Carter and Johns, II (1973) [n. 12.1].
Kuper, L., *Passive Resistance in South Africa* (1957).
Lodge [n. 13.4].
Luthuli, A., *Let my People go* (1963).
Maylam [n. 9.4].
Ngubane, J. K., *An African Explains Apartheid* (1963).
Raboroko, P. N. and Nokwe, D., 'Congress and the Africanists', *AS*, 4, 3 (1960) 24–38.
Walshe [n. 10.3].

14.4 Tomlinson, Verwoerd and the ideology of apartheid

Ballinger [n. 12.1].
Hepple, A., *Verwoerd* (1967).
Hirson [n. 16.8].
Kenney, H. F., *Architect of Apartheid: H. F. Verwoerd – an Appraisal* (1980).
Pelzer, A. N., *Verwoerd Speaks* (1966).
Scholtz, G. D., *Dr H. F. Verwoerd* (1974).
Schoeman [n. 14.1].
Summary of the Report of the Commission for the Socio-Economic Development of the Bantu Areas (*UG* 61 of 1955) [Tomlinson Report].
Tatz [n. 10.2].
Verwoerd, H. F., in *Senate Debates* (1951) cols 2203–35, (1952) cols 3587–614, (1954) cols 2595–620, (1955) cols 4527–46, (1956) cols 3861–908 (policy motions.)
See also Chapter 20 for references on apartheid.

14.5 The Strijdom interlude

Carter [n. 14.1].
Malan [n. 14.1].
Schoeman [n. 14.1].

14.6 The defeat of the Coloured parliamentary struggle

Ballinger [n. 12.1].
Carter [n. 14.1].

Dlamini, C. R. M., 'The Senate Case revisited', *SALJ* 105 (1988) 470–8.
Hahlo and Kahn [n. 12.4] 146–63.
Lewis [n. 9.5].
Mansergh, N., *Documents and Speeches on Commonwealth Affairs, 1952–62* (1963) 306–32.
Miller [n. 15.6].
Robertson [n. 19.2].
Schoeman [n. 14.1].
Sher [n. 14.2].
Van der Ross, R. E., *The Rise and Decline of Apartheid: A Study of Political Movements among the Coloured People of South Africa 1880–1965* (1986).
Wiechers, M., 'The Fundamental Laws behind our Constitution', in Kahn, E. (ed.) *Fiat Justitia*: *Essays in Memory of O. D. Schreiner* (1983).

14.7 Residential and cultural apartheid

Brookes [n. 20.1].
Cronje [n. 20.1].
Eiselen [n. 20.1].
Hoernlé [n. 20.1].
Horrell, M. (ed.) [n. 14.1]; and *The Group Areas Act: Its Effect on Human Beings* (*SAIRR*, 1956) and *Group Areas: The Emerging Pattern* (1966).
Marquard [n. 20.1].
Pinnock, D., *The Brotherhoods: Street Gangs and State Control in Cape Town* (1984).
Rhoodie and Venter [n. 20.1].
Rive [n. 20.7].
Thompson [n. 20.1].
Van Biljon [n. 20.1].
Welsh [n. 20.6].

CHAPTER 15

15.1 Rural resistance to the apartheid regime

Beinart, W. J. and Bundy, C., 'State Intervention and Rural Resistance: The Transkei, 1900–65', in Klein, M. (ed.) *Peasants in Africa* (1980).
Benson [n. 12.2].
Bradford [n. 11.5].
Bundy, C., 'Land and Liberation: Popular Rural Protest and the National Liberation Movements in South Africa, 1920–60', in Marks and Trapido [n. 11.5] 254–85.
Gerhart [n. 12.2].
Hirson, B., 'Rural Revolt in South Africa, 1937–51', *ICS*, 8 (1977) 115–32
Hooper, C., *Brief Authority* (1960).
Horrell, M. (ed.) *Survey of Race Relations* (1956–7) 66–72, (1957–8) 48–76 (1958–9) 122–46, (1959–60) 39–68, (1961) 42–61, (1962) 11–25, (1963) 11–21, (1964) 25–33.
Lodge [n. 13.4].
Luthuli [n. 14.3].
Maylam [n. 9.4].
Mbeki, G., *South Africa: The Peasants Revolt* (1964).
Moroney, S., 'The 1950 Witsieshoek Rebellion', *AP*, 3 (1976).

Report of the Departmental Committee of Inquiry into Unrest in Eastern Pondoland (1960) [Van Heerden Report].

15.2 The Congress of the People and the Freedom Charter, 1955

Ballinger [n. 12.1].
Feit, [n. 14.3].
Gerhart [n. 12.2].
Karis, T., Carter, G. M., and Gerhart, G., *From Protest to Challenge*, III (1977).
Lodge, [n. 13.4].
Luthuli [n. 14.3].
Maylam [n. 9.4].
Robertson [n. 14.1].
Suttner and Cronin [n. 17.7].

15.3 The first of the treason trials

Feit [n. 14.3].
Froman, L. and Sachs, E. S., *The South African Treason Trial* (1957).
Horrell, M. (ed.) *Survey of Race Relations* (1956–7) 41–5, (1957–8) 34–7, (1958–9) 44–7, (1959–60) 37–9, (1961) 62–3.
Joseph, H., *If This be Treason* (1963).
Karis, T., 'The South African Treason Trial', *PSQ*, LXXVI, 2 (1961) 217–39, and *The Treason Trial in South Africa: A Guide to the Microfilm Record* (1965).
Matthews [n. 12.2].
Sampson, A., *The Treason Cage* (1958).
Stultz, N. M., 'The Politics of Security: South Africa under Verwoerd', *JMAS*, VII (1969) 3–20.

15.4 Verwoerd's 'new vision' and Macmillan's 'winds of change'

Buthelezi, M. G., 'White and Black Nationalism, Ethnicity and the Future of the Homelands' (*SAIRR*, 1974).
Eiselen, W. W. M., 'Harmonious Multi-community Development', *Opt*. (Mar 1959) 1–15.
Hepple [n. 14.4].
Kenney [n. 14.4].
Lipton, M., 'Independent Bantustans?', *IA*, 48, 1 (1972) 1–19.
Macmillan, H., *Pointing the Way* (1972).
Mansergh [n. 14.6].
Rhoodie, N. J., *South African Dialogue* (1972) 113–210.
Schoeman [n. 14.1].
Scholtz [n. 14.4].
Verwoerd, H. F., in *House of Assembly Debates* (1959) cols 6214–27.

15.5 The A.N.C., the P.A.C. and Sharpeville, 1960

Ballinger [n. 12.1].
Benson [n. 12.2].
Driver, C. J., *Patrick Duncan: South African and Pan-African* (1980).
Gerhart [n. 12.2].
Horrell, M. (ed.) *Survey of Race Relations* (1958–9) 44–7, (1959–60) 37–9, (1961) 62–3.
Karis, Carter and Gerhart [n. 15.2].

Lodge [n. 13.4].
Luthuli [n. 14.3].
Maylam [n. 9.4].
Ngubane [n. 14.3].
Pogrund, B., *Sobukwe and Apartheid* (1990).
Robertson [n. 14.1].
Reeves, J. A., *Shooting at Sharpeville* (1960).
Van Staden [n. 17.8].
The official report on the Sharpeville shootings (An. 25 of 1961) was not published.

15.6 The first republican referendum, October 1960

Carpenter, G., *Introduction to South African Constitutional Law* (1987).
Delius, A. R., *The Last Division* (1959).
Harnetty, P., 'Canada, South Africa and the Commonwealth', *JCPS II*, 1 (1963) 33–44.
Heard [n. 13.2].
Kahn, E., *The New Constitution* (1962).
Kenney [n. 14.4].
Macmillan, H., *Pointing the Way* (1972).
Mansergh, N., *Documents and Speeches on Commonwealth Affairs, 1952–62* (1963) 306–400.
Menzies, R. G., *Afternoon Light: Some Memories of Men and Events* (1967).
Miller, J. D. B., *Survey of Commonwealth Affairs, 1953–69* (1974) 126–66, and 'South Africa's Departure', *JCPS* I, 1 (1961) 56–74.
Robinson, K. and Madden, A. F. (eds) *Essays in Imperial Government presented to Margery Perham* (1963).
Rhoodie [n. 15.4].
Scholtz [n. 14.4].
Wessels, F. J., *Die Republikeinse Grondwet* (1962).
Worrall, D., *South African Government and Politics* (1971).
Wheare (1960) [n. 11.2].

15.7 Post-Sharpeville resistance: B. J. Vorster and the political underground

Barrell, H., in Johnson [n. 17.1].
Benson, M., *Nelson Mandela* (2nd edn, 1989). and 'The Poqo Insurrection' in Lodge T., *Resistance and Ideology in Settler Societies* (1986) 179–222.
De Villiers, H. H. W., *Rivonia: Operation Mayibuye* (1964).
Driver [n. 15.5].
Feit, E., *Urban Revolt in South Africa, 1960–4* (1971).
Gerhart [n. 12.2].
Karis, Carter and Gerhart [n. 15.2].
Lodge [n. 13.4].
Mandela, N., *No Easy Walk to Freedom* (1965).
Maylam [n. 9.4].
Mbeki, G., *South Africa: The Peasant's Revolt* (1964).
Meer [n. 13.5].
Report of the Commission appointed to Inquire into the Events on the 20th to 22nd November 1962 at Paarl (RP 51 of 1963) [Snyman Report].
Schoeman [n. 14.1].
Van Staden [n. 17.8].

15.8 The murder of Dr Verwoerd

Hepple [n. 14.4].

Kenney [n. 14.4].
Scholtz [n. 14.4].

CHAPTER 16

16.1 Living with the Tomlinson Report: industrial licensing and rural resettlement

Adam [n. 20.1].
Baldwin [n. 17.2].
Bekker, S. and Humphries, R., *From Control to Confusion: The Changing Role of Administration Boards in South Africa, 1971–83* (1985).
Bell, R. T., *Industrial Decentralisation in South Africa* (1973).
Desmond, C., *The Discarded People* (1970).
Lötter, J. M., 'The South African Population, its Growth and Expected Trends', *RSA 2000* 3, 2 (1981) 1–19.
D'Oliviera, J., *Vorster: the Man* (1978).
Leftwich (ed.) [n. 20.11].
Leistner, G. M. E., *Economic and Social Forces affecting the Urbanisation of the Bantu Population of South Africa* (1972).
Rhoodie [n. 15.4].
Sadie, J. L., *Projections of the South African Populations, 1970–2020* (n.d., based on the 1970 census).
Thompson, L. M. and Butler, J. (eds) *Change in Contemporary South Africa* (1975).

16.2 The extension of Homeland self-government and the first reactions of Homeland leaders and liberal whites

Buthelezi [n. 15.4].
Carter, G. M., Karis, T. and Stultz, N. M., *South Africa's Transkei: The Politics of Domestic Colonialism* (1967).
Hill, C. R., *Bantustans: The Fragmentation of South Africa* (1964).
Kotze, D. A., *African Politics in South Africa, 1964–74* (1975).
Laurence, P., *The Transkei: South Africa's Politics of Partition* (1976).
Lodge [n. 13.4].
Maré, G. and Hamilton, G., *An Appetite for Power: Buthelezi's Inkatha and the Politics of 'Loyal Resistance'* (1987).
Matanzima, K. D., *Independence my Way* (1976).
Molteno, F., 'The Bantustan Strategy', *SD*, 3, 2 (1977) 15–33.
'Mzala', *Gatsha Buthelezi: Chief with a Double Agenda* (1988).
Reports of the Study Project on Christianity in Apartheid Society (1971–3) [*SPRO-CAS* Reports].
Southall, R. J., *South Africa's Transkei: The Political Economy of an Independent Bantustan* (1982).
Streek, B. and Wicksteed, R., *Render unto Kaiser: A Transkei Dossier* (1981).
Stultz, N. M., *Transkei's Half-Loaf* (1979).
Sutcliff, M. and Wellings, P., 'Inkatha versus the Rest: Black Opposition to Inkatha in Durban's African Townships', *AA* 87, 348 (1988) 325–60.
Temkin, B., *Gatsha Buthelezi: Zulu Statesman* (1976).
Van der Merwe, H. W., Charton, N. C. J., Kotze, D. A. and Magnusson, A., *African Perspectives on South Africa: A Collection of Speeches, Articles and Documents* (1978).

16.3 Black Consciousness

Adam, H., 'The Rise of Black Consciousness in South Africa', *Race*, 15, 2 (1973) 149–65.
Brewer, J. D., 'The Modern Janus: Inkatha's Role in Black Liberation', *ICS*, 12 (1981) 100–7.
Gerhart [n. 12.2].
Hirson [n. 16.8].
Horrell, M. (ed.) *Survey of Race Relations in South Africa* (annual vols 1976–83).
Karis, Carter and Gerhart [n. 15.2].
Kotze [n. 16.2].
Lodge [n. 13.4].
Moore, B., *Black Theology: The South African Voice* (1973).
Stubbs, A. (ed.) *Steve Biko: I Write what I Like* (1979).
Van der Merwe H. W. *et al*. [n. 16.2], and, with Welsh, D. (eds) *Student Perspectives on South Africa* (1978).

16.4 The end of indirect representation for Coloured people and the failure of the Coloured Representative Council

Botha, D. P., *Die Opkoms van ons Derde Stand* (1960).
Hirson [n. 16.8].
Horrell, M. (ed.) *Survey of Race Relations* (annual vols, 1974–81).
Hugo, P., *Quislings or Realists? A Documentary Study of 'Coloured' Politics in South Africa* (1978).
Simons, M., 'Organized Coloured Political Movements', in Van der Merwe, H. W. *et al.*, *Occupational and Social Change among Coloured People in South Africa* (1976).
Unterhalter, B., 'Changing attitudes to "Passing for White" in an Urban Coloured community', *SD*, 1, 1 (1975) 53–62.
Watson, G., *Passing for White* (1970).
Whisson, M. G., 'The Coloured People', in Randall, P. (ed.) *South Africa's Minorities* (1971).

16.5 The Erika Theron Report and Vorster's constitutional reform proposals, 1976–7

Report of the Commission of Enquiry into Matters relating to the Coloured Population Group (*RP* 38 of 1976) [Theron Report].
Van der Horst, S. T., *The Theron Commission: A Summary* (*SAIRR*, 1976).

16.6 Vorster and the Opposition: the extrusion of the Hertzogites and the harrying of the Liberals

Barnard, S. L., *Politieke Orientasie in die Suid–Afrikaanse Opposisie sedert 1958* (unpublished thesis, University of the Orange Free State, 1979).
D'Oliviera [n. 16.1].
Carlson, J., *No Neutral Ground* (1973).
Potter, E., *The Press as Opposition* (1975).
Schoeman, B. M., *Vorster se 1000 Dae* (1974).
Serfontein, J. H. P., *Die Verkrampte Aanslag* (1970).
State v. the Dean of Johannesburg (*SAIRR*, 1972).
Strangwayes-Boothe, J., *A Cricket in the Thornbush: Helen Suzman and the Progressive Party* (1976).
Uys, S., 'The White Opposition Splits', *AS* (1960) 12–19.

16.7 Black movements in exile and the start of the terrorist campaign

Davidson, B., Slovo, J. and Wilkinson, A., *Southern Africa: The New Politics of Revolution* (1976).
Davis, S. M., *Apartheid's Rebels: Inside South Africa's Hidden War* (1988).
Driver [n. 15.5].
Grundy, K. W., *The Guerilla Struggle in Africa: Analysis and Preview* (1971).
Johns, S., III, 'Obstacles to Guerilla War: A South African Case Study', *JMAS*, XI, 2 (1973) 267–303.
Johnson [n. 18.6].
Kane-Berman [n. 16.8].
Lodge [n. 13.4].
Marcum, J., 'The Exile Condition and Revolutionary Effectiveness: Southern African Liberation Movements', in Potholm, C., and Dale, R. (eds) *Southern Africa in Perspective* (1979).
Morris, M., *South African Terrorism* (1971).

16.8 The Soweto disturbances of 1976–7

Anon, *South Africa in Travail: The Disturbances of 1976–7 (SAIRR*, 1978).
Brooks, A. and Brickhill, J., *Whirlwind before the Storm* (1980).
Frankel, P., 'Municipal Transformation in Soweto: Politics and Mal-administration in Black Johannesburg', *ASR*, 22, 2 (1979) 49–64.
Hirson, B., *Year of Fire, Year of Ash: The Soweto Revolt: Roots of a Revolution?* (1979).
Kane-Berman, J., *Soweto: Black Revolt, White Reaction* (1978).
Lodge [n. 13.4].
Molteno, F., 'The Uprising of 16 June', *SD*, 5, 1 (1979) 54–76.
Report of the Commission of Inquiry into the Riots at Soweto and Elsewhere from the 16th June 1976 to the 28th February 1977 (*RP* 55 of 1980) [Cillié Report].

16.9 The information scandal and the fall of Vorster

Geldenhuys [n. 18.1].
Pottinger [n. 17.1]
Report of the Commission of Inquiry into Alleged Irregularities in the Former Department of Information (*RP* 113 of 1978) [Erasmus Report].
Rees, M., and Day, C., *Muldergate: The Story of the Information Scandal* (1980).
Rhoodie, E., *The Real Information Scandal* (1983).

CHAPTER 17

17.1 P. W. Botha's political style and aims

Barber, J., 'Boss in Britain', *AA*, 82, 328 (1983) 311–28.
Cock, J. and Nathan, L. (eds) *War and Society: The Militarisation of South Africa* (1989).
Economic Review of South Africa, FM (Apr., June, Oct., Dec. 1982).
Frankel, P., *Pretoria's Praetorians: Civil-Military Relations in South Africa (1984)*.
Geldenhuys, D., *The Diplomacy of Isolation: South Africa's Foreign Policy Making* (1984); and, with Kotze H., 'Aspects of Political Decision-making in South Africa', *Pol.* 10, 1 (1983) 33–45.
Grundy, K. W., *The Militarisation of South African Politics* (1988 edn), and 'The

Rise of the South African Security Establishment: An Essay on the Changing Locus of State Power' (*S.A. Int.*, 1983).
Jaster [n. 18.6].
Johnson, S. (ed.) *South Africa: No Turning Back* (1988).
McCarthy, C. L., 'Industrial Decentralisation–Reflections on the New Initiatives', *SAJE* 50, 3 (1982) 238–52.
Mining Surveys, FM (Oct. 1982, Sept. 1983).
Posel, D., 'Language, Legitimation and Control: The South African State after '78', *ICS* 13, (1984) 139–51.
Pottinger, B., *The Imperial Presidency: P. W. Botha – the First Ten Years* (1988).
Report of the Commission of Inquiry into Legislation affecting the Utilisation of Manpower (*RP* 32 of 1979) [Riekert Report].
Report of the Commission of Inquiry into Labour Legislation (*RP* 47 of 1979) [Wiehahn Report].
Report of the Committee on Legislation concerning Black Community Development (1981) [Grosskopf Report].
Savage [n. 20.4].
Schlemmer, L., 'South Africa's National Party Government', in Berger, P. L. and Godsell, B., *A Future for South Africa: Visions, Strategies and Realities* (1988).
Seegers, A., 'The Military in South Africa – a Comparison and Critique', *SAI* 16, 4 (1986).
Spence, J., 'The Military in South African Politics' in Johnson (above) 240–57.

17.2 The climax of population resettlement

Baldwin, A., 'Mass Removals and Separate Development', *JSAS*, 1, 2 (1975) 215–27.
Cole, J., *Crossroads: The Politics of Reform and Repression* (1987).
Davenport and Hunt [n. 19.1].
Desmond [n. 16.1].
Maré, G., *African Population Relocation in South Africa* (*SAIRR*, 1980).
Nash, M., *Black Uprooting from 'White' South Africa* (*SACC*, 1980).
Platsky, L. and Walker, C., *The Surplus People: Forced Removals in South Africa* (1985).
Rive [n. 20.5].
Surplus People Project (ed.) *Forced Removals in South Africa* (5 vols 1983).
Walt, E. and Waite, B., *South Africa: A Land Divided* (1977).

17.3 The conspiracy of gold and maize

Agriculture: A Survey (*FM*, 17 September 1982).
Hugo, P., 'Frontier Farmers in South Africa', *AA* 8, 34 (1988) 537–52.
Wickins, P. L., 'Agriculture', in Coleman, F. L. (ed.) *Economic History of South Africa* (1983).
Wilson and Ramphele [n. 19.1].

17.4 Signs of a white backlash

Adam, H., 'The Ultra-Right in South Africa', *Opt.* 35, 1 (1987).
Bekker, S. and Grobbelaar, J., 'The White Right-Wing Movement in South Africa: Before and After the May 1987 Election', in Van Vuuren, D. J. *et al.*, *South African Election 1987: Context, Process and Prospect* (1987) 65–80.
Charney, C., 'Class Conflict and the National Party Split', *JSAS*, 10, 2 (1984) 269–82.
Frankel, P., 'Race and Counter-revolution: South Africa's "Total Strategy"', *JCCP*, 18, 3 (1980).

Giliomee, H., *The Parting of the Ways: South African Politics 1976–82* (1982). Hugo [n. 17.3].

Ries, A. and Dommisse, E., *Broedertwis: Die Verhaal van die 1982 Skeuring in die Nasionale Party* (1982).

Van Vuuren, D. J., Wiehahn, N. E., Lombard, J. A. and Rhoodie, N. J. (eds) *Change in South Africa* (1983).

Zille, H., 'The Right Wing in South African Politics', in Berger and Godsell [n. 17.1] 55–94.

17.5 Reactions to denationalisation in the Homelands

Alternatives to the Consolidation of Kwa Zulu (Bureau for Economic Policy and Analysis, University of Pretoria, 1982) [JA Lombard Report].

Brewer, J. D., *After Soweto* (1986).

Cooper, C. *et al.*, *Survey of Race Relations* (annual vols, 1977–89).

Gordon, L., Cooper, C. *et al.*, *Survey of Race Relations* (annual vols 1977–89).

Kane-Berman, J., 'Inkatha, the Paradox of South African Politics', *Opt..* 30, 2 (1982) 144–77.

Mare and Hamilton [n. 16.2].

McCaul, C., 'The Wild Card: Inkatha and Contemporary Black Politics', in Frankel, P., Pines, N. and Swilling, M., *State, Resistance and Change in South Africa* (1988) 146–73; and *Satellite in Revolt: KwaNdebele – an Economic and Political Profile* (1987).

Report of the Commission of the Kwa Zulu Government: The Requirements for Stability and Development in Kwa Zulu and Natal (1982) [Buthelezi Report].

Report of the Ciskei Commission (1980) [Quail Report].

Report of the Human Sciences Research Council Investigation into Education in the Republic of South Africa (1982) [De Lange Report].

Rich, P., 'Inkatha – Truth in Diversity', *IAB* 12, 2 (1988) 67–70.

Southall, R. J., *South Africa's Transkei* (1982) and [n. 17.7].

Streek and Wicksteed [n. 16.2].

White Paper on the Provision of Education in the Republic of South Africa (1983).

17.6 Resistance to denationalisation in the common area: school boycotts, resurgent trade unionism, and the revival of Black Consciousness and A.N.C.-related activities

Adam, H., 'Exile and Resistance: The A.N.C., the S.A.C.P. and the P.A.C.', in Berger and Godsell [n. 17.1] 95–124.

Barrell, H., 'The Outlawed South African Resistance Movements', in Johnson [n. 17.1] 52–93.

Brookes and Brickhill [n. 16.8].

Cooper, C. *et al.*, *Survey of Race Relations, 1983* (1984).

Davenport, T. R. H., 'Unrest, Reform and the Challenges to Law, 1976–87', *AJ* (1987) 1–33.

Lodge [n. 16.8].

Van Niekerk, P., 'The Trade Union Movement in the Politics of Resistance in South Africa', in Johnson [n. 17.1] 153–71.

Zulu, P., 'The Politics of Internal Resistance Groupings', in Berger and Godsell [n. 17.1] 125–63.

17.7 Confrontation about consensus: the constitutional debate, 1978–90

African National Congress (ed.) *Constitutional Guidelines, SAJHR* (1989) 129–32.

Archer, S., in Butler, Elphick and Welsh [n. 6.8] 335–52.
Benyon, J. A. (ed.) *Constitutional Change in South Africa* (1978).
Boulle, L. J., *South Africa and the Consociational Option* (1984).
Buthelezi Report (1982) [n. 17.5].
Constitutional Committee of the President's Council, *First Report* (1982) (Chairman D. Worrall) *Second Report* (1982) (Chairman S. W. van der Merwe).
Cooper *et al.* [n. 17.6] 71–98.
Dugard [n. 20.9].
Hanf, T. *et al.*, *South Africa: The Prospects of Peaceful Change* (1981).
Huntington, S. P., 'Reform and Stability in a Modernising Multi-ethnic Society', *Pol.* 8, 2 (1981) 8–26.
Lemon, A., 'The Indian and Coloured Elections: Co-optation Rejected?', *SA Int.* 18, 2 (1984) 84–107.
Lijphart, A., *Democracy in Plural Societies* (1977).
Polley, J. A., *The Freedom Charter and the Future* (IDASA conference, Cape Town, 1988).
Report of the Commission on Constitutional Change (*RP* 68 of 1980) [Schlebusch].
Sachs, A., 'Towards the Reconstruction of South Africa', *JSAS* 12, 1 (1985) 49–59, and 'Towards a Bill of Rights in a Democratic South Africa' (unpublished draft, 1988). South African Law Commission, *Working Paper 25: Group and Human Rights* (1989).
Slabbert, F. van Z. and Welsh, D., *South Africa's Options: Strategies for Sharing Power* (1979).
Slabbert, F. van Z. and Opland, J. (eds) *South Africa: Dilemmas of Evolutionary Change* (1980).
Southall, R. J., 'Consociationalism in South Africa: The Buthelezi Commission and Beyond', *JMAS*, 21, 1 (1983) 77–112, and 'Buthelezi, Inkatha and the Politics of Compromise', *AA* 80, 321 (1981) 453–81.
SPROCAS (ed.) *South Africa's Political Alternatives* (1973).
Suttner, R. and Cronin, J., *30 Years of the Freedom Charter* (1985).
Van der Vyver, J. D., 'Judicial Review under the New Constitution', *SALJ* (1986) 236–58; and 'Comments on the Constitutional Guidelines of the A.N.C.', *SAJHR* (1989) 133–53.
Welsh, D., 'Constitutional Changes in South Africa', *AA*, 83, 331, (1984) 147–62.
Worrall D., [n. 15.6] and in de Villiers, A. (ed.) *English-speaking South Africa Today* (1976) 193–216.

17.8 The emergency of 1985–90, the rise of F. W. de Klerk and the release of Nelson Mandela

Cooper, C. *et al.*, *Race Relations Surveys* (1985) 455–63, (1986) 830–45, (1987–8) 582–95, (1988–9) 559–69.
Davenport [n. 17.6].
Hall, M., 'Resistance and Rebellion in Greater Cape Town, 1985' (unpublished typescript, University of Cape Town, 1986).
Pottinger [n. 17.1].
Rhoodie, E., *P. W. Botha; The Last Betrayal* (1989).
Slabbert, F. van Z., *The Last White Parliament* (1986).
Thornton, R. J., 'The Shooting at Uitenhage, 1985: The Context and Interpretation of Violence' (unpublished typescript, University of Cape town, 1989).
Van Niekerk, G. J. [n. 20.9].
Van Niekerk, P. [n. 17.6].
Van Staden, G., 'Return of the Prodigal Son: Prospects for a Revival of the Pan-Africanist Congress', *IAB* 12, 3 (1988) 35–64.

CHAPTER 18

18.1 South Africa and the birth of the United Nations

Austin, D., *Britain and South Africa* (1966).
Barber, J., *South Africa's Foreign Policy, 1945–70* (1973), and *The Uneasy Relationship* (1983), and with Barratt, J., *South Africa's Foreign Policy: The Search for Status and Security, 1945–8*, (1990).
Geldenhuys, D., *The Diplomacy of Isolation: South African Foreign Policy Making* (1984).
Hancock, W. K., (1968) [n. 10.1] and *Smuts and the Shift of World Power* (*SOAS*, 1964).
Hyam [n. 10.9].
Mansergh (1953) [n. 13.1].
Nicholas, H. G., *The United Nations as a Political Institution* (1971).
Spence, J. E., 'South Africa and the Modern World', in *OHSA*, II (1971) 477–528.
Van der Poel (1973) VI, VII [n. 10.9].

18.2 The Malan–Strijdom era in foreign policy, 1948–58

See works by Austin, Barber, Geldenhuys, Mansergh, Spence [n. 18.1], and:
Berridge, G., *Economic Power in Anglo-South African Diplomacy: Simonstown, Sharpeville and After* (1981); and, with J. E. Spence, 'South Africa and the Simonstown Agreements', in Young, J. W. (ed.) *The Foreign Policy of Churchill's Peacetime Administration* (1988).
Dugard, C. J. R. and Lawrie, G. G., 'The Simonstown Agreement', *SALJ*, LXXXV, 1 (1968) 142–77.
Geldenhuys [n. 18.1].
Grundy, K. W., *Confrontation and Accommodation in Southern Africa: The Limits of Independence* (1973).
Louw, E. H., *The Case for South Africa* (1963).
Nolutshungu, S. C., *South Africa: A Study of Ideology and Foreign Policy* (1975).
Seiler, J., 'South African Perspectives and Responses to External Pressures', *JMAS*, 13, 3 (1975) 447–68.
Spence, J. E., *Republic under Pressure* (1965).
Vandenbosch, A., *South Africa and the World* (1970).

18.3 Dr Verwoerd and the outside world, 1958–66

See works by Austin, Barber, Geldenhuys, Spence [n. 18.1], and Berridge, Grundy, Nolutshungu Seiler, Spence, Vandenbosch [n. 18.2], and Hepple, Kenney, Pelzer, Scholtz, [n. 14.4].

18.4 South West Africa, Angola and the growth of confrontation, 1952–79

Ballinger, R. B., *South-west Africa: The Case against the Union* (*SAIRR*, 1961).
D'Amato, A. A., 'The Bantustan Proposals for South-west Africa', *JMAS*, 4, 2 (1966) 177–92.
Dugard, C. J. R., *The South West Africa (Namibia) Dispute* (1973).
Du Pisani, A., *SWA/Namibia: The Politics of Continuity and Change* (1986).
First, R., *South West Africa* (1963).
Geldenhuys [n. 18.1].
Goldblatt, I., *History of South West Africa from the Beginning of the Nineteenth*

Century (1971) and *The Mandated Territory of South West Africa in Relation to the United Nations* (1961).

Green, R. H., Kiljunen, K. and M. L., *Namibia: The Last Colony* (1981).

Hallett, R., 'The South African Intervention in Angola, 1975–6', *AA*, 77, 308 (1978) 347–86.

Heunis, J. C., *United Nations versus South Africa: A Legal Assessment of United Nations . . . Activities in Respect of South Africa* (1986).

Imishue, R. W., *South West Africa* (1966).

Jaster [n. 18.6].

Legum, C. and Hodges, T., *After Angola: The War over Southern Africa* (1976).

Moorsom, R., *Walvis Bay: Namibia's Port* (1984).

Namibia. A Survey (FM 22 July 1983).

Seiler, J., 'South Africa in Namibia: Persistence, Misperception and Ultimate Failure', *JMAS*, 20, 4 (1982) 689–712, and (ed.) *South Africa since the Portuguese Coup* (1980).

South Africa: Time Running Out [n. 18.7].

18.5 South Africa and Rhodesian independence

Barber, J., *Rhodesia: The Road to Rebellion* (1967) and 'Supping with the Devil: Zimbabwe–South African relations', *IAB* (1982) 4–16.

Blake, R., *A History of Rhodesia* (1977).

Flower [n. 18.9].

Jaster [n. 18.6].

Mason, P., *Year of Decision: Rhodesia and Nyasaland, 1960* (1960).

Palley [n. 10.9].

Windrich, E., *The Rhodesian Problem: A Documentary Record, 1923–73* (1975).

18.6 Vorster: 'dialogue' and *détente*

See works by Austin, Barber, Geldenhuys [n. 18.1], Grundy, Nolutshungu, Seiler, Vanderbosch [n. 18.2] and:

Baffoe, F., 'Some Aspects of the Political Economy of Economic Co-operation and Integration in Southern Africa: The Case of South Africa and the BLS Countries', *JSAA*, 3, 3 (1978) 327–42.

Barratt, J., 'South Africa's Outward Policy: From Isolation to Dialogue', in Rhoodie, N. (ed.) (1972) [n. 15.4].

Bowman, L., 'The Subordinate State System of Southern Africa', *ISQ*, 12, 3 (1968) 231–61.

Chambati, A. M., 'Detente–an external view' (unpublished typescript, *SAIRR*, 1976).

Cowen, D., 'Towards a Common Market in Southern Africa', *Opt.* 17, 2 (1967) 43–51.

Cockram, G., *Vorster's Foreign Policy* (1970).

Crush, J. S., 'Parameters of dependence in South Africa: Swaziland', *JSAA*, IV, 1 (1979) 55–66.

Geldenhuys [n. 18.1].

Guelke, A., 'Africa as a Market for South African Goods', *JMAS*, 12, 1 (1974) 69–88.

Hirschmann, D., 'Southern Africa: Détente?', *JMAS*, 14, 1 (1976) 107–26.

Jaster, R. S., *The Defence of White Power: South African Foreign Policy under Pressure* (1988).

Johnson, R. W., *How Long will South Africa Survive?* (1977).

Legum, C., 'The Secret Diplomacy of Détente', *ACR* 7 (1974–5) A3–15.

Molteno, R., *Africa and South Africa: The Implications of South Africa's 'Outward-Looking' Policy* (1971).

Organisation of African Unity, 'The Dar-es-Salaam Declaration on Southern Africa, 10 April 1975', *JAS* 3, 1 (1976) 125–32.

Setai, B., Prospects for a Southern African Common Market', *JAS* 1, 3 (1974) 310–34.

Shaw, T. M., 'Southern Africa: Cooperation and Conflict in an International Sub-system', *JMAS* 12, 4 (1974) 633–55; and with Mugomba A. T., 'The Political Economy of Regional Détente: Zambia and Southern Africa', *JAS* 4, 4 (1977) 392–413.

Venter D., 'South Africa as an African power: The Need for a Purposeful Détente Policy in Southern Africa', *IAB* 8, 2 (1976) 7–12.

Worrall D., 'The Republic of South Africa and Détente', (*CAHA*, 1976).

18.7 The threat of economic sanctions: employment codes, disinvestment and trade boycotts

Adam, H., 'Outside Influence on South Africa: Afrikanerdom in Disarray', *JMAS*, 21, 2 (1983) 235–51.

Albrecht, V. and Sohn, W., *The Dilemma of Code Three* (*SACC*, 1981).

Barber, J. and Spicer, M. W., 'Sanctions against South Africa–Options for the West', *AA*, 55, 3 (1979) 385–401.

Berridge [n. 18.2].

Budlender, D., *Assessing U.S. Corporate Disinvestment. The C.A.S.E. Report for the Equal Opportunity Foundation* (1989).

Cooper, J. H., 'Economic Sanctions and the South African Economy', *IAB*, 7, 2 (1983) 25–47.

First, R., Steele, J. and Gurney, C., *The South African Connection: Western Investment in Apartheid* (1972).

Guelke [n. 18.6].

Hanlon, J. and Omond, R., *The Sanctions Handbook* (1987)

Henderson R. d'A., 'The Food Weapon in Southern Africa', *IAB*, 7, 3 (1983) 38–52.

Holland, M., 'Disinvestment, Sanctions and the European Community's Code of Conduct in South Africa', *AA* 88, 353 (1989) 529–47.

Lipton, M., *Sanctions and South Africa: The Dynamics of Economic Isolation* (*Economist* Intelligence Unit, 1988).

Matthews, J., 'South Africa's Trade Relations: Foreign and Regional Interdependence', *IAB*, 4, 2 (1980) 3–18.

Payne, R. J., 'Japan's South African Policy: Political Rhetoric and Economic Realities', *AA* 86, 343 (1987) 167–78.

Sampson, A., *The Money Lenders* (1981).

South Africa and Sanctions: Genesis and Prospects–a Symposium (*SAIRR*, 1979).

South Africa: Time Running Out (1981) [Rockfeller Report].

Sullivan, L., *The Role of Multinational Corporations in South Africa* (*SAIRR*, 1980).

Whisson, M. G., Roux, M. C. and Manona, C. W., *The Sullivan Principles at Ford* (*SAIRR*, 1979).

18.8 The Cape route, strategic minerals and oil

Anderson, E. W. and Blake, G. H., 'The Republic of South Africa as a Supplier of Strategic Minerals: An Assessment', (S.A. Institute of International Affairs, typescript, 1984).

Baker, P., 'South Africa's Strategic Vulnerabilities: The Citadel Assumption Reconsidered', *ASR*, 20, 2 (1977) 89–99.

Coker, C., 'The Western Alliance and Africa, 1949–81', *AA*, 81, 324 (1982) 319–35.

Feustel, S., 'African Minerals and American Policy', *AR*, 22, 5 (1978) 12–17.

Foltz, W. J., 'United States Policy towards Southern Africa: Economic and Strategic Constraints', *PSQ*, 92 (1977) 47–64.

Hurrell, A., 'The Politics of South Atlantic Security: A Survey of Proposals for A South Atlantic Treaty Organisation', *IA*, 59, 2 (1983) 179–93.

Jaster [n. 18.6].

Millar, T. B., 'The Indian Ocean in International Strategy', *IAB*, 1, 1 (1977) 22–32.

Price, R. M., *U.S. Foreign Policy and Sub-Saharan Africa: National Interest and Global Strategy* (1978).

Roux, A. J. A., 'South Africa in a Nuclear World', *SA Int.* 4, 3 (1974) 149–67.

Shafer, M., 'No Crisis: The Implications of U.S. Dependence on Southern African Strategic Minerals', (*SAIIA* typescript, 1983).

Vale, P. C. J., 'The Atlantic Nations and South Africa: Economic Constraints and Community Fracture', (unpublished thesis, University of Leicester, 1980).

Von Maltitz, A. A., 'South African Minerals and their Importance to World Industry', *SA Int.* 1, 4 (1971) 221–8.

18.9 P. W. Botha, the 'constellation' concept and the S.A.D.C.C.: through destabilisation to the independence of Namibia, 1979–90

Brand, S. S., 'Economic linkages', *IAB*, 8, 1 (1984) 41–9.

Crush, J. and Wellings, P., 'Southern African Pleasure Periphery', *JMAS*, 21, 4 (1983) 673–98.

Du Pisani, A., 'South Africa and Namibia: Variations on a Theme', *IAB* 10, 3 (1986) 6–18.

Flower, K., *Serving Secretly: Rhodesia's C10 Chief on Record* (1987).

Geldenhuys, D., 'South Africa and the West', in Schrire R. (ed.) *South Africa: Public Policy Perspectives*' (1982) 299–339, and (with D. Venter) 'A Constellation of States: Regional Co-operation in Southern Africa', *IAB*, 3, 3 (1979) 36–72.

Henderson [n. 18.7].

Hill, C. R., 'Regional Co-operation in Southern Africa', *AA*, 82, 327 (1983) 215–40.

Isaacman, A. and B., 'South Africa's Hidden War', *AR*, 27, 6 (1982) 4–8.

Jaster [n. 18.6].

Jenkins, S., 'The Great Evasion. South Africa: A Survey', (*Ec.* 21 June 1980); 'The Survival Ethic' (*Ec.* 19 September 1981) and 'Destabilisation in Southern Africa', (*Ec.* 16 July 1983).

Leistner, G. M. E., 'Towards a Regional Development Strategy for Southern Africa', *SAJE*, 50, 4 (1982) 349–64.

Maasdorp, G., 'Squaring up to Economic Dominance: An Analysis of SADCC' (unpublished typescript *SAIIA*, 1948) and *SADCC: a Post-Nkomati Evaluation* (*SAIIA*, 1984).

MacFarlane, S. N., 'The Soviet Union and Southern African Security', *PC* 38 (1989) 71–89.

Mission to South Africa: The Commonwealth Report (1986)

Olivier, G. C., 'Co-operation or National Security? Choices and Options for White and Black Africa', *IAB*, 4, 3 (1980) 26–31, and 'South Africa's Relations with Africa', in Schrire, R. (ed.) *South Africa's Public Policy Perspectives* (1982) 269–98.

Price, R. M., '*Pretoria's Southern African Strategy*', *AA*, 83, 330 (1984) 11–32.
Shaw, J. A., 'The South African Development Co-ordination Conference (*SADCC*) and the South African Response', *IAB*, 5, 3 (1981) 15–21.
Thomas, W. H., 'A Southern African Constellation of States: Challenge or Myth?', *SAInt*. 10, 3 (1980) 113–28.

CHAPTER 19

19.1 From subsistence to capitalist farming

Antrobus, G. G., 'Farm Labour in the Eastern Cape, 1950–73', (*SALDRU*, 1976).
Arrighi, G. and Saul, J. S., *Essays on the Political Economy of Africa* (1973).
Beinart, W. J., 'Soil Erosion, Conservationism and Ideas about Development: A Southern African Exploration', *JSAS* 11, 1 (1984) 52–83; and, with Delius, P. and Trapido, S. (eds) *Putting a Plough to the Ground: Accumulation and Dispossession in Rural South Africa, 1850–1930* (1986).
Bisschop, J. H. R. and Tomlinson, F. R., 'South Africa: Two agricultures?'*SD*, 6, 1 (1980) 49–52.
Bundy, C., *The Rise and Fall of the South African Peasantry* (2 edn. 1988).
Cooper, F., 'Peasants, Capitalists and Historians', *JSAS*, 7, 2 (1981) 284–314.
Cross, C. and Haines, R. J. (eds) *Towards Freehold? Options for Land and Development in South Africa's Black Rural Areas* (1988).
Davenport, T. R. H., 'Some Reflections on the History of Land Tenure in South Africa, Seen in the Light of Attempts by the State to Impose Political and Economic Control', *AJ* (1985) 53–76.
De Wet, C. J., 'Betterment Planning in South Africa: Some Thoughts on its History, Feasibility and Wider Policy Implications', *JCAS* 6 (1987) 85–122; and with McAllister, P. A. and Hart, T. (eds) *Development South Africa* 4, 3 (1987) 371–592.
Dubow [n. 20.1].
Duly, L. C., *British Land Policy at the Cape, 1795–1844* (1968).
Elton Mills, M. and Wilson, M., *Land Tenure* (*KKRS*, IV, 1952).
Greenberg, S. B., *Race and State in Capitalist Development* (1980).
Hobart Houghton, D. (1976) [n. 11.6] and (with E. M. Walton) *The Economy of a Native Reserve*, (*KKRS*, II, 1952).
Keegan [n. 7.11] and *Rural Transformations in Industrialising South Africa: The Southern Highveld to 1914* (1986), and *Facing the Storm: Portraits of Black Lives in Rural South Africa* (1988), and 'Crisis and Catharsis in the Development of Capitalism in South African Agriculture', *AA* 84, 336 (1985) 371–98.
Lacey [n. 10.2].
Lipton, M., 'White Farming in South Africa', *JCCP*, 12, 1 (1974) 42–61, and 'Some Realities of African Agriculture', *SD*, 5, 2 (1979) 31–5.
Morris, M., 'Development of Capitalism in South African Agriculture: Class Struggle in the Countryside', *E and S*, 5, 3 (1976) 292–343.
Neumark [n. 2.5].
Palmer, R. H., (1968) and (with Q. N. Parsons) (1977) [n. 7.11].
Ross, R., 'The Rise of the Cape Gentry', *JSAS* 2 (1983) and in Beinart, Delius and Trapido [n. 7.4] 56–100.
Simkins, C., 'Agricultural Production in the South African Reserves', *JSAS*, 7, 2 (1981) 256–83.
Slater [n. 6.4].
Thom, H. B., *Die Geskiedenis van Skaapboerdery in Suid-Afrika* (1936).

Van der Horst, S. T., *Native Labour in South Africa* (1942).
Van der Merwe [n. 2.5].
Waters, A. R., 'Understanding African Agriculture and its Potential for Change', *JMAS*, 12, 1 (1974) 45–56.
Wilson, F., 'Farming, 1866–1960', in *OHSA*, II (1970) 104–71, and with Kooy, A. and Hendrie, D. (eds) *Farm Labour in South Africa* (*SALDRU*, 1977), and with Ramphele, M., *Uprooting Poverty: The South African Challenge. Report of the Second Inquiry into Poverty and Development in Southern Africa* (1989).
Yawitch, J., *Betterment: The Myth of Homeland Agriculture* (1981).

19.2 The spread of communications, commerce and banking

Arndt, E. H. D., *Banking and Currency Development in South Africa*, 1652–1927 (1928).
Bozzoli, B., *The Political Nature of a Ruling Class: Capital and Ideology in South Africa, 1890–1933* (1982).
Du Plessis [n. 12.3].
Frankel, S. H., *Capital Investment in Africa* (1938).
Franklin, N. N., *Economics in South Africa* (1954).
Greenberg [19.1].
Hart, G., *Some Socio-Economic Aspects of African Entrepreneurship* (*ISER*, 1971).
Henry, J. A., *The First Hundred Years of the Standard Bank* (1963).
Hobart Houghton [n. 11.6].
Hofmeyr, J. H., 'The Problem of Cooperation, 1886–95: Railways, Customs and the Non-European Question', *CHBE*, VIII (1963 edn) 551–64.
Horwitz [n. 20.11].
Immelman, R. F. M., *Men of Good Hope: The Cape Town Chamber of Commerce, 1804–1954* (1955).
Keeble, S. M. S., *The Expansion of Black Business into the South African Economy, with Special Reference to the Initiatives of the National African Federated Chamber of Commerce in the 1970s* (unpublished thesis, Witwatersrand University, 1981).
Natrass, J., *The South African Economy* (1981).
Nedbank Group (ed.) *South Africa: an Appraisal* (1983).
Purkis, A., *The Politics, Capital and Labour of Railway Building in the Cape Colony, 1870–85* (unpublished thesis, Oxford University, 1978).
Robertson, H. M., *South Africa: Political and Economic Aspects* (1957).
Savage, R. B., *A Study of Bantu Retail Trades in Certain Areas of the Eastern Cape* (*ISER*, 1956).
Schumann, C. G. W., *Structural Changes and Business Cycles in South Africa 1806–1936* (1938).
Southall, R., 'African Capitalism in Contemporary South Africa', *JSAS*, (1982).
Van Winter, P. J., *Onder Krugers Hollanders* (2 vols, 1937).
Wilburn, K., *The Climax of Railway Competition in South Africa, 1886–99* (unpublished thesis, Oxford University, 1982).

19.3 The rise of diamond and gold mining and their peculiar labour patterns

Blainey [n. 5.7].
Cartwright, A. P., *The Corner House* (1965) and *Gold Paved the Way* (1967).
Davies, R. H., *Capital, State and White Labour in South Africa, 1910–60* (1979) and 'Mining Capital, the State and Unskilled White Workers, 1910–13', *JSAS*, 3, 1 (1976) 41–69.

Denoon [n. 9.3].
Duminy and Guest (eds) [n. 5.7].
Fraser and Jeeves [n. 9.8].
Greenberg [n. 19.1].
Gregory, Sir T., *Ernest Oppenheimer and the Economic Development of Southern Africa* (1962).
Hatch, F. H. and Chalmers, J. A., *The Gold Mines of the Rand* (1895).
Innes, D., *Anglo-American and the Rise of Modern South Africa* (1982).
Jeeves [n. 9.3].
Johnstone, F. A., *Class, Race and Gold* (1976).
Kallaway [n. 8.5].
Katz [n. 9.3].
Katzenellenbogen, S. E., *South Africa and Southern Mozambique: Labour, Railways and Trade in the Making of a Relationship* (1982).
Kubicek [n. 5.7].
Lacey [n. 10.2].
Levy [n. 9.3].
Lipton [n. 19.5].
Morrell, W. P., *The Gold Rushes* (1940).
Newbury [n. 6.2], and *The Diamond Ring: Business, Politics and Precious Stones in South Africa, 1867–1945* (1989).
Richardson P. [n. 9.3] and (with J. J. van Helten) [n. 5.7], and 'Labour in the South African Gold-mining Industry, 1886–1914', in Marks, S. and Rathbone, R. (eds) *Industrialisation and Social Change in South Africa* (1982).
Robertson [n. 8.5].
Siebörger, R. F., *The Recruitment and Organisation of African Labour for the Kimberley Diamond Mines, 1871–88* (unpublished thesis, Rhodes University, 1976).
Smalberger, J., 'IDB and the Mining Compound System in the 1880s', *SAJE*, (1974) 398–414.
Turrell [n. 8.5].
Van der Horst [n. 19.1].
Williams, G. F., *The Diamond Mines of South Africa* (1902).
Wilson, F., *Labour in the South African Gold Mines, 1911–69* (1972).
Worger [n. 8.5].
Yudelman, D., *The Emergence of the Modern South Africa: State, Capital and the Incorporation of Organised Labour on the South African Gold Fields, 1902–39* (1983).

19.4 Secondary industry, a late development

Bell [n. 16.1].
Bozzoli [n. 19.2].
du Plessis [n. 12.3].
Greenberg [n. 19.1].
Hobart Houghton [nn. 11.6 and 19.1].
Horwitz [n. 20.11].
Natrass [n. 19.2].
Riekert Report [n. 17.1].
Trapido, S., 'South Africa in a Comparative Study of Industrialisation', *JDS*, 8, (1971) 309–20.
Van der Horst [n. 20.11].
Wiehahn Report [n. 17.1].

19.5 The evolution of labour migrancy and the colour bar in a state-regulated economic system

Board of Trade and Industries, *Report 282* (1945).
Davenport [n. 12.1].
Delius [n. 1.4].
Denoon [n. 9.3].
Doxey, G. V., *The Industrial Colour Bar in South Africa* (1961).
Fredrickson [n. 20.1].
Hutt, W. H., *The Economics of the Colour Bar* (1964).
Johnstone [n. 19.3.].
Kallaway [n. 8.5].
Levy [n. 9.3].
Lewis [n. 9.5].
Lipton, M., 'Men of Two Worlds: Migrant Labour in South Africa', *Opt.* 29, 2/3 (1980) 72–201.
Mayer, P. (ed.) *Black Villagers in an Industrial Society* (1980).
Phillips, I. M., *The Civilised Labour Policy and the Private Sector: the Operation of the South African Wage Act, 1925–37* (unpublished thesis, Rhodes University, 1984).
Richardson, [n. 19.3].
Schlemmer, L. and Webster E. (eds) *Change, Reform and Economic Growth in South Africa* (1978).
Siebörger [n. 19.3].
Smalberger [n. 19.3].
Turrell [n. 8.5].
Van der Horst [n. 19.1].
Wilson, F., *Labour in the South African Gold Mines, 1911–69* (1972) and *Migrant Labour in South Africa* (1972), and with Ramphele [n. 17.3].
Yudelman [n. 19.3].

19.6 The collapse of the industrial colour bar and the legitimation of black collective bargaining

Bonner, P., 'Black Trade Unions in South Africa Since World War II', in Price, R. and Rosberg, C. (eds) *The Apartheid Regime* (1980), and [10.3].
Cooper, C. and Ensor L., *PEBCO: A Black Mass Movement* (*SAIRR*, 1981).
Davenport, T. R. H., 'Unrest, Reform and the Challenges to Law, 1976–87', *AJ* (1987) 1–33.
Davies [n. 19.3].
Du Plessis [n. 12.3].
Friedman, S., *Building Tomorrow Today: African Workers in Trade Unions, 1970–84* (1987).
Greenberg [n. 19.1].
Hepple, A., *Trade Unions in Travail* (1954).
Hirson [n. 16.8].
Katz [n. 9.3].
Lewis, J., *Industrialisation and Trade Union Organisation in South Africa 1924–55: The Rise and Fall of the S.A.T.L.C.* (1985).
Luckhart, K. and Wall, B., *Organise or Starve: A History of the S.A.C.T.U.* (1980).
Maré, G., *The Durban Strikes, 1973* (1974).
Miller, S., *South African Trade Unions – Directory and Statistics* (*SALDRU*, 1982).
Moodie [n. 9.7].

Ncube, D., *The Influence of Apartheid and Capitalism in the Development of Black Trade Unions in South Africa* (1985).
O'Meara (1983) [n. 12.3] and [13.4].
Passmore, J., 'FOSATU: Perspective on a Non-racial Trade Union', *Reality* (September 1981).
Roux, M., 'Labour in Port Elizabeth and Uitenhage', *Reality* (November 1980).
Thomas, W. H. (ed.) *Labour Perspectives on South Africa* (1974).
Van Niekerk, P., in Johnson [n. 17.1] 153–71.
Walker and Weinbren [n. 10.10].
Webster, E. (ed.) *Essays in Southern African Labour History* (1978).
Wilson [n. 19.5].

CHAPTER 20

20.1 Segregation and apartheid

Adam, H., *Modernising Racial Domination* (1971), and (with H. Giliomee) *Ethnic Power Mobilised* (1979).
Brookes, E. H., *Apartheid: A Documentary Study of Modern South Africa* (1968).
Butler, Elphick and Welsh [n. 6.8].
Cell, J. W., *The Highest Stage of White Supremacy: The Origins of Segregation in South Africa and the American South* (1982).
Cronje, G., *'n Tuiste vir die Nageslag* (1945) and (*Regverdige Rasse–apartheid* (1947).
Cross and Haines [n. 19.1].
Dubow, S., *Racial Segregation and the Origins of Apartheid in South Africa, 1919–36* (1989); and 'Race, Civilisation and Culture: The Elaboration of Segregationist Discourse in the Inter-war years', in Marks and Trapido (below) (1987).
Dvorin, E. P., *Racial Separation in South Africa: An Analysis of the Apartheid Theory* (1952).
Eiselen, W. W. M., 'The Meaning of Apartheid', *RR* (1948) 69–86.
Evans, M. S., *Black and White in South East Africa: A Study in Sociology* (1911).
Fredrickson, G. M., *White Supremacy: A Comparative Study in American and South African History* (1981).
Hexham [n. 9.7].
Hoernlé, R. F. A., *South African Native Policy and the Liberal Spirit* (1939) and *Race and Reason* (1945).
Integration and Separate Development (*SABRA* 1952).
Legassick, M., 'The Making of South African "Native Policy", 1903–23: The Origins of Segregation' (unpublished typescript, London University, 1972).
MacCrone [n. 2.5].
Macmillan, H., '"Paralysed Conservatives": W. M. Macmillan, the Social Scientists, and the "Common Society", in Macmillan, H., and Marks, S. (eds) *Africa and Empire: W. M. Macmillan, Historian and Social Critic* (1989) 72–90.
Macmillan, W. M., *My South African Years* (1975).
Marks, S. and Trapido, S. (eds), *The Politics of Race, Class and Nationalism in 20th Century South Africa* (1987).
Marquard, L., *The Peoples and Policies of South Africa* (1962).
Meer, Y. S. and Mlaba, M. D., *Apartheid – our Picture* (1983).
Rhoodie, N. J. (ed.) [n. 15.4], and (with H. J. Venter) *Apartheid* (1959).
Rich, P., *White Power and the Liberal Conscience: Racial Segregation and South African Liberalism* (1984).

Serfontein [n. 12.3].
Tatz [n. 10.2].
Thompson, L. M., *The Political Mythology of Apartheid* (1985).
Van Biljon, P., *Grensbakens tussen Blank en Swart in Suid-Afrika* (c1947).
Vann Woodward, C., *The Strange Career of Jim Crow* (1974).
Webb, C. de B. (ed.) 'The Reitz–Shepstone Correspondence of 1891–2', *Natalia* 2 (1972) 7–20.

20.2 The territorial dimension

Baldwin [n. 17.2].
Burton [n. 9.4].
Davenport and Hunt [n. 19.1].
Desmond [n. 16.1].
Dubow [n. 20.1].
Maasdorp, G., in Giliomee, H. and Schlemmer L., *Up against the Fences: Poverty, Passes and Privilege in South Africa* (1985) 219–33.
Plaatje [n. 10.2].
Report of the Commission of Inquiry into European Occupancy of Rural Areas (RP, 1959–60) [Du Toit Report].
Roux, E., 'Land and agriculture in the Native Reserves', and with Keppel Jones, A. M., 'Land and Agriculture Outside the Reserves', in Hellmann, E. (ed.) *Handbook on Race Relations in South Africa* (1949) 171–205.
Surplus People Project (ed.) [n. 17.2].
Tatz [n. 10.2].
Summary of the Report of the Commission for the Socio-Economic Development of the Bantu Areas . . . (UG 61 of 1955) [Tomlinson Report].
White Paper 'F' of 1956 [on the Tomlinson Report].

20.3 Segregation in town

Bekker and Humphries [n. 16.1].
Davenport, T. R. H., 'African Townsmen?', *AA*, 68, 271 (1969) 95–109; and [n. 9.4] and [n. 12.1].
Davis, G., Melunsky, L. and du Rand, F., *Urban Native Law* (1959).
Hellmann, E., 'Urban Areas', in Hellmann, E. (ed.) *Handbook on Race Relations* (1949) 229–74.
Huddleston, T., *Naught for your Comfort* (1956) [Sophiatown removals].
Mathewson, J. E., *The Establishment of an Urban Bantu Township* (1957).
Maylam, P., 'The Rise and Decline of Urban Apartheid in South Africa', *AA* 89, 354 (1990) 57–84.
Report of the Native Laws Commission (UG 28 of 1948) [Fagan Report].
SAIRR (ed.) *Councils and Controversy: South Africa's New Regional Services Councils* (1987).
Saunders, C. C., 'The Creation of Ndabeni: Urban Segregation, Social Control and African Resistance', and 'From Ndabeni to Langa, 1919–35' in Saunders C. C. (ed.) *Studies in the History of Cape Town* I (1979).
Stadler [n. 13.3].
Steward, A., *You are Wrong, Father Huddleston* (1956).
Swanson [n. 10.2].
Welsh, A. S., *Natives in Urban Areas* (1946).
Welsh, D., 'The Growth of Towns', *OHSA*, II (1971) 172–244.
Western Areas – Mass Removal (SAIRR, 1953).

20.4 Passes and the control over black movement

Davenport [n. 20.3].
Hindson, D., *Pass Controls and the Urban African Proletariat* (1987).
Horrell, M., *The Pass Laws* (*SAIRR*, typescript, 1960).
Kahn, E., 'The Pass Laws', in Hellmann [n. 20.3] 275–91.
Report of the Native Laws Commission [n. 20.3].
Report of the Inter-Departmental Committee on the Social, Health and Economic Conditions of Urban Natives (1942) [Smit Report].
Savage, M. 'The Imposition of Pass Laws on the African Population in South Africa', *AA* 85 (1986) 181–205.
Wilson and Ramphele [n. 17.3].

20.5 Racially segregated schools and universities

Bantu Education: Oppression or Opportunity? (*SABRA*, 1955).
Cook, P. A. W., 'Non-European Education', in Hellmann, [n. 20.3] 348–86.
Christelike Nasionale Onderwys Beleid (*FAK*, 1948).
Gaydon, V., *Race against the Ratios* (SAIRR, 1987).
Giliomee and Schlemmer [n. 20.11].
Hoernle, (1939) 123–45 [n. 20.1].
Hunt Davis, R., 'C. T. Loram and an American Model for African Education in South Africa', *ASR*, 19, 2 (1976) 87–100, and 'The Black American Component in African Responses to Colonialism in South Africa, c. 1890–1914', *JSAA*, 3, 1 (1978) 65–84.
Jones, T. J. (ed.) *Report of the Phelps Stokes Commission on Native Education* (1922).
Kallaway, P. (ed.) *Apartheid and Education* (1984).
Lewis [n. 9.5].
Loram, C. T., *The Education of the South African Native* (1917).
Malherbe, E. G., *History of Education in South Africa* (2 vols, 1925, 1977); *Education and the Poor White* (1932); *The Bilingual School* (1946) and *Bantu Manpower and Education* (*SAIRR*, 1969).
Open Universities in South Africa (Universities of Cape Town and the Witwatersrand, 1957).
Report of the Commission on Native Education (*UG* 53 of 1951) [Eiselen Report].
Report of the Inter-Departmental Committee on Native Education (*UG* 29 of 1936).
Report of the Native Affairs Commission, 1936 (*UG* 48 of 1937).
Ross, B., and Tunmer, R. (eds) *Documents in South African Education* (1975).
Shingler, J., *Educational Policies and Political Order in South Africa 1902–61* (unpublished thesis, Yale University, 1973).
Van der Merwe, H. W. and Welsh, D. (eds) *Student Perspectives on South Africa* (1972).

20.6 The churches and apartheid

Apartheid and the Church (*SPROCAS*, 1972).
Boesak, A. A., *Farewell to Innocence* (1978).
Clarke, R. G., *For God or Caesar? An Historical Study of Christian Resistance to Apartheid by the Church of the Province of South Africa, 1946–57* (unpublished thesis, University of Natal, 1983).
Cochrane, J., *Servants of Power: The Role of the English-speaking Churches in South Africa, 1903–30* (1987).
Davenport [n. 12.1].
De Gruchy, J. W., *The Church Struggle in South Africa* (1979).

Elphick, R., in Butler, Elphick and Welsh [n. 6.8] 64–80.
Geyser, A. S. and Marais, B. J., *Delayed Action* (1961).
Keet, B. B., *Whither South Africa?*(1956).
Kinghorn, J. (ed.) *Die N. G. Kerk en Apartheid* (1986).
Landman, W. A., *A Plea for Understanding* (1968).
Mofokeng, T., 'Black Theology in South Africa: Achievements, Problems and Prospects', in Prozesky (below) (1990).
Moodie [n. 9.7].
Paton, A., *Apartheid and the Archbishop: The Life and Times of Geoffrey Clayton* (1973).
Prozesky, M. (ed.) *Christianity in South Africa* (1990).
Rhoodie and Venter [n. 20.1].
Villa-Vicencio, C. (ed.) *Theology and Violence: the South African Debate* (1987), and in Prozesky (above) 193–207.
Welsh, D., 'The Cultural Dimension of Apartheid', *AA*, 71, 282 (1972) 35–53.

20.7 Group areas

Festenstein, M., and Pickard-Cambridge, C., *Land and Race: South Africa's Group Areas and Land Acts* (*SAIRR*) (1987).
Horrell, M. *et al.*, *The Group Areas Act: Its Effect on Human Beings* (*SAIRR*, 1956); *Group Areas: the Emerging Pattern* (1966); and (ed.) *Survey of Race Relations* (1967) 191–213, (1968) 190–209, (1969) 162–80, (1970) 186–201, (1971) 155–71, (1972) 128–51, (1973) 11–26, (1974) 156–64, (1975) 66–80, (1976) 152–80, (1977) 428–60, (1978) 377–98, (1979) 459–84, (1980) 345–66, (1981) 216–30, (1982) 335–51, (1983) 228–45, (1984) 468–90, (1985) 348–62, (1986) 218–30, (1987–8) 478–508, (1988–9) 217–34.

20.8 The conflict over apartheid in entertainment and sport

Archer, A. and Bouillon, A., *The South African Game: Sport and Racism* (1980).
Davis, J., 'Politics, Sport and Education in South Africa', *AA* 85, 340 (1986) 351–64.
Horrell, M. *et al.* (eds) *Survey of Race Relations* 1955–6 to 1983 (entries for all years).

20.9 Apartheid and civil liberty: the press, the courts and the operation of the law

Beinart, B., 'The Rule of Law', *AJ* (1962) 99–138.
Bell, A. N. and Mackie, R. D. A., *Detention and Security Legislation* in South Africa (University of Natal Conference Proceedings, 1982).
Brookes, E. H. and Macaulay, J. B., *Civil Liberty in South Africa* (1958).
Cameron, E., 'Legal Chauvinism, Executive-mindedness and Justice – L. C. Steyn's Impact on South African Law', *SALJ* 99 (1982) 38–75.
Cowen, D. V., *The Foundations of Freedom* (1961).
Davenport, T. R. H., 'Civil Rights in South Africa, 1910–60', *AJ* (1960) 11–28.
Dugard, C. J. R., *Human Rights and the South African Legal Order* (1978), and (ed.) *Report on the Rabie Report: An Examination of Security Legislation in South Africa* (Centre for Applied Legal Studies, Witwatersrand University, 1982).
Forsyth, C., 'The Judges and Judicial Choice: Some Thoughts on the Appellate Division of the Supreme Court of South Africa since 1950', *JSAS* 12 (1985) 102–14.
Foster, D. *et al.*, *Detention and Torture in South Africa: Psychological, Legal and*

Historical Studies (1987); and, with C. Luyt, 'The Blue Man's Burden: Policing the Police in South Africa', *SAJHR* 2 (1986) 297–311.

Grogan, J., 'News Control by Decree', *SALJ* 103 (1986) 118–35.

Mathews, A. S., *Law, Order and Liberty in South Africa* (1971) and *The Darker Reaches of Government* (1978).

Potter [n. 16.6].

Randall, P., *The Taste of Power* (*SPROCAS*, 1973).

Report on the Commission of Inquiry into Alleged Irregularities in the Former Department of Information (*RP* 113 of 1978) [Erasmus Report].

Report of the Commission of Inquiry into Security Legislation (*RP* 90 of 1981) [Rabie Report].

Riekert, J., 'The Silent Scream; Detention without Trial, Solitary Confinement and Evidence in South Africa's Security Law Trials', *THRHR* (1985) 245–50, and in Bell and Mackie (above) 121–47.

Sachs, A., *Justice in South Africa* (1973).

State v. the Dean of Johannesburg (*SAIRR*, 1972).

Taitz, J., 'The Administration of Justice and Due Process', in Schrire, R. (ed.) *South Africa's Public Policy Perspectives* (1982) 1–53.

Tyson, H., *Conflict and the Press* (1989).

Van Niekerk, G. J., 'People's Courts and People's Justice in South Africa', *DJ* (1987) 270–84.

20.10 Apartheid in politics

See works by Tatz [n. 10.2], Ballinger [n. 12.1], Kenney [n. 14.4], Buthelezi, Eiselen, Lipton [n. 15.4] Adam, Brookes, Eiselen, Rhoodie and Venter, and Thompson [n. 20.1].

20.11 The force and the mass, the ostrich and the crab

Adam [n. 20.1].

Bozzoli [n. 19.2].

Cronje [n. 20.1].

Dugard [n. 20.10].

Elphick, R. H., 'Methodology in South African Historiography: A Defence of Idealism and Empiricism', *SD*, 9, 1 (1983) 1–17.

Giliomee, H. and Schlemmer, L., *From Apartheid to Nation-Building* (1989).

Hobart Houghton [n. 11.6].

Hoernlé [n. 20.1].

Horwitz, R., *The Political Economy of South Africa* (1967).

Hunter, G. (ed.) *Industrialisation and Race Relations* (1965).

Johnstone, F. A., 'White Prosperity and White Supremacy in South Africa Today', *AA*, LXIX, 274 (1970) 124–40 and '"Most painful to our hearts": South African History Through the Eyes of the Marxist School', (unpublished typescript, Yale University, 1979).

Kuper, L., *Race, Class and Power* (1974).

Leftwich, A. (ed.) *Economic Growth and Political Change* (1974).

Legassick, M., 'South Africa: Capital Accumulation and Violence', *E and S*, 3, 3 (1974) 253–91, and [n. 13.8].

MacCrone [n. 2.5].

Natrass [n. 19.2].

O'Dowd, M. C., 'South Africa in the Light of the Stages of Economic Growth', in Leftwich, A. (ed.) *Economic Growth and Political Change* (1974) 29–43, and 'The Stages of Economic Growth and the Future of South Africa' in Schlemmer,

L. and Webster, E. (eds) *Change, Reform and Economic Growth in South Africa* (1977).

Robertson [n. 2.5].

Van den Berghe, P. L., *South Africa: A Study in Conflict* (1965).

Van der Horst, S. T., 'The Effect of Industrialisation and Race Relations in South Africa', in Hunter G. (ed.) *Industrialisation and Race Relations* (1965).

Wolpe, H., 'Capitalism and Cheap Labour Power in South Africa: From Segregation to Apartheid', *E and S*, 1, 4 (1972).

Wright, H. M., *The Burden of the Present* (1977).

Yudelman, D., 'Industrialisation, Race Relations and Change in South Africa', *AA*, 74, 294 (1975) 82–96 and [n. 19.3].

Index